Classic Plays from the Negro Ensemble Company

Classic Plays
from the
Negro Ensemble
Company

PAUL CARTER HARRISON

&

GUS EDWARDS, Editors

UNIVERSITY OF PITTSBURGH PRESS   *Pittsburgh & London*

Published by the University of Pittsburgh Press, Pittsburgh, Pa. 15260
Foreword copyright © 1995, University of Pittsburgh Press
Afterword copyright © 1995, Paul Carter Harrison and Gus Edwards
Manufactured in the United States of America
Printed on acid-free paper

Library of Congress Cataloging-in-Publication Data
Classic plays from the Negro Ensemble Company / Gus Edwards and Paul Carter Harrison, editors.
   p.   cm.
   ISBN 0-8229-3882-0 — ISBN 0-8229-5560-1 (pbk.: alk. paper)
   1. American drama—Afro-American authors. 2. American drama—20th century. 3.
Afro-Americans—Drama. 4. Negro Ensemble Company.
I. Edwards, Gus. II. Harrison, Paul Carter, 1936–
PS628.N4C57 1995
812'.5408089673—dc20   95-3825
            CIP
A CIP catalogue record for this book is available from the British Library.
Eurospan, London

Dedicated to the memory of

BERT ANDREWS

the principal photographer of NEC

and

MOSES GUNN

a principal actor for the NEC

BERT
DEAR FRIEND
AND FAITHFUL CURATOR OF THE BLACK THEATRE EXPERIENCE
YOU HAVE LONG BEEN A RELIABLE AND UNTIRING BEACON
STALKING THE SHADOWS OF THE GREAT WHITE WAY
WITH YOUR PERSONAL CORONA
TO ILLUMINATE THE INCANDESCENCE
OF THE BLACK PRESENCE ON THE AMERICAN STAGE
THANK YOU FOR TAKING THE TIME TO CRADLE THE EXPERIENCE
THANK YOU FOR THE COURAGE OF YOUR UNFAILING COMMITMENT
THANK YOU FOR THE OPPORTUNITY TO BEAR WITNESS TO A LEGACY
WHICH WILL ALWAYS ALLOW US TO ACCESS YOUR SHINING SPIRIT,
A TESTAMENT OF YOUR MOST WELCOMED LUMINOSITY
IN OUR LIVES
THANK YOU, BERT!

Paul Carter Harrison
16 February 1993

ELEGY FOR MOSES GUNN
On the Occasion of His Great Ascent to Kingdom Come

We are gathered to praise Moses
        Not to bury him
And he would like that
        this honest man
        of noble gesture
        fixed in our minds
        permanently
        and living heroically
        in our hearts
Yet to praise Moses
        this father
        son and lover
is to engulf his spirit
        with an avalanche
        of precious words

And he would like that too
        this lover of language
        his spirit consumed
        in volumes of words
        that engage us deep
        into the night
        probing new issues
        to illuminate
the course of persuasion altered
        by verbal invention
        that calls into question
the subtleties of the obvious
        agreement hopelessly
        out of reach
since the purpose of it all
        is a passionate exercise
        of personal inquiry
        for the lover
And we discover in the tempest
        of contested words
how easy it is to trust
        the passion
        of an honest man
        who renews our bond
        with genuine affection
The same generosity of affection
        revealed in his role as
        father
        who would dare be
        a loving/caring/reliable
        father
        an uncompromising
        father
who dared to love his family
        more than Hollywood
        more than public adulation
        more than professional peerage
however compelling
        the transformative
        magic of the stage
which he loved
        this son

who had the courage
    to lift the veil of
    dark early beginnings
    to pursue a dream
that transformed him into
    a beacon of hope
    for a new generation
    of aspiring black actors
to bear the torch of excellence
    of the father/son/lover
    who faithfully shared
    his bright light
    with all of us
who offer thanks and enduring praise
    to the father/son/lover
    whom we know as Moses
    our loving brother

Paul Carter Harrison
Chicago 1994

CONTENTS

FOREWORD

DOUGLAS TURNER WARD
Artistic Director of the Negro Ensemble Company

Eclectic is a word I was always offhandedly familiar with. From the mid-1960s on, it would define my life in theater. The term certainly describes the cross section of plays in this volume. As the artistic director of the Negro Ensemble Company, I selected and produced them all.

This opportunity arose as a result of a 1965 Off-Broadway production of two one-act plays of mine, *Happy Ending* and *Day of Absence*. During the run I wrote a front-page cultural section article for the Sunday *New York Times* titled "American Theater . . . for Whites Only . . . ?" In the article I assessed the position of blacks in theater and articulated the need for an independent African-American theater institution. Although I hoped that my suggestion would lead to positive results, it was never my intention to head the project. During earlier attempts I had always been content to serve as a behind-the-scenes participant. Now the reins were suddenly placed in my hands.

The *New York Times* article gained the attention of McNeil Lowry, cultural chief of the Ford Foundation, who initiated discussions with me and my production associates, Robert Hooks and Gerald Krone. The meetings ended with him inviting us to draw up a proposal for the theater institution we had in mind. He then asked who would be in charge full-time. Robert had a thriving acting career, and Gerald had the most successful managing company Off-Broadway. I was selected for the position.

This prospect didn't thrill me. Besides diverting me from my own writing and acting careers, I was leery about being the final decision maker. More than ten years earlier, while functioning as a political activist, I had opted out of this role, deciding instead to concentrate exclusively on becoming an artist. Ever since, the results of my thinking were my private property. My likes, dislikes, tastes, biases, and judgments were nobody's business but my own. Being head of the Negro Ensemble Company would change this.

What other drawbacks?

Would my own playwriting credentials be a handicap? Would my choices incline toward a mirror image of my own writings?

The task would be made no easier with the proposal we drew up. Our plan called for a unique combination of a professional producing unit offering a season of plays performed by a resident ensemble; a playwrights' workshop; a tuition-free training program for advanced and beginning actors; and formal and on-the-job instructions in every phase of theater, including backstage and front-of-the-house vocations. A formidable challenge under any circumstances.

But the most immediate difficulty would arise from the rash promise we had made to begin our first season within a year upon receiving the grant. (I suspect we didn't have patience for a long-term blueprint.) Even worse, I had exacerbated the problem by insisting on not producing any of my own plays or the works of friends and also ruled out doing well-known plays that had gone long unproduced for lack of sponsorship. I was determined that the new company should start with fresh material.

This was all well and good in theory, but in April 1967 when the Ford grant was approved, these restrictions didn't leave me with much room to maneuver. I didn't have many candidates. There wasn't enough time to seek unknown plays, and there was even less time for submissions of new works by unknowns. Despite my assertion that black writing would flower in diversity, I had to organize too fast to gain sight of first buddings. The pressure of start-up time left me with little more than a firm desire to display artistic variety, coupled with a desperate need to come up with the right play to launch the company with a provocative impact.

Life sometimes takes pity on audacious fools.

One morning while scanning the *New York Times* I zeroed in on a description of a new play which had premiered recently at the Swedish National Theater in Stockholm: *Song of the Lusitanian Bogey* by Peter Weiss, the world-renowned author of *Marat Sade*. As I read vivid details of the production, I quickened with excitement. Peter and I had met when he and his wife/set designer, Gunilla, attended a performance of my Off-Broadway double bill. Stimulated by shared political and artistic interests, we became friends. During our time together, Peter mentioned his intent to write a play about the imperialist colonialist conflict in the then-Portuguese territories: Angola, Mozambique, and Guinea. The *New York Times* feature described the completed results. Immediately, I called Stockholm and requested a script from Peter. He told me it only existed in the Swedish production version and a published German text. I asked him to send me a tape of the production and the German publication.

Upon receipt I sat listening to the tape while looking at the text spread before me. I couldn't read or understand either language. Aided by my memory of the feature's description of the subject matter, I was hoping that some form of osmosis would seep in and enlighten me more. To the ear, the jazz-based musical score was undoubtedly compelling. The acid bite and intonations of the actors communicated the interpretive approach. And, lo and behold, the German text through linguistic elements, occasional recognizable terms and phrases, and typographical/lithographic configurations, began to contribute sense. By the time I finished, I knew I had indeed found the perfect vehicle to start the season and launch the company.

It was a gift.

A new play about a current topic of universal political and human importance—supremely theatrical, utilizing a form and style combining music, dance, and drama—a prototypical ensemble work enlisting flexible numbers of performers to portray a multiplicity of characters, types, situations, and versatile shifts of points of view. This play was ideally suited to introduce the new company to the world and alert the public as to who we were, what we were about, and what we intended to do at our most stimulating best.

I optioned the play quickly, an acquisition which Peter Weiss kindly helped to accomplish.

When the decision about *Song of the Lusitanian Bogey* was announced I knew I would get flack for Peter not being black. But no matter. The fact, in this instance, was that authorship had no significance. The play was "authored" by the real historical situation itself. Peter was merely a conduit. More significantly, the material was going to be authored by an all-black creative team, giving it life.

Now all I had to do was find the team.

Michael Schultz surfaced not long out of college—and with an even shorter résumé—but with the good fortune to have a directing assignment that I was able to monitor. Coleridge-Taylor Perkinson was recommended by an actress, Rosalind Cash, who later became a member of the ensemble herself. Louis Johnson was choreographer of his own highly regarded Dance Company. Edward Burbridge had designed sets for a recent Broadway drama. Bernard Johnson, a former dancer, was making a name as a fashion designer. Marshall Williams was one of the rare black lighting designers in professional theater. They were all unknown to me before *Bogey*.

Once assembled, their collective input changed production plans considerably, dictating an entire new outlook. For a start, I had to rewrite the commissioned translation by Lee Baxandall into a more idiomatic spoken text, which would enable Coleridge-Taylor Perkinson to compose a completely new score instead of transposing the wonderful but inapplicable Swedish music. In the end, the whole production emerged uniquely original in every aspect. On January 2, 1968, it proved to be one of the most impressive births in the history of American theater—a major landmark in the development of black theater and its declaration of independence and autonomy.

Bogey became the hub around which so much of the Negro Ensemble Company's (NEC) shape revolved: from the versatile composition of the acting ensemble to the type of companion pieces required to round out the first season.

Summer of the Seventeenth Doll was the second play scheduled. I had seen it with an original Australian cast and was struck by its pertinence to black life. Besides its relevance, I chose it because it also provided roles for NEC actors who had not appeared in *Bogey*. I changed the setting of the play to the American South—New Orleans, to be precise—and adapted it accordingly. Nominally, it was by a white writer, but the treatment was mine, albeit I took no credit. The play's robust, earthy portrayal of black migrant laborers and other working-class blacks was a poignant, bittersweet, realistic counterpoint to the Brecht-like, expressionistic canvas of *Bogey*.

Kongi's Harvest followed next in line. I had become acquainted with Wole Soyinka's work in the early 1960s and soon regarded him as one of the greatest playwrights in the English language. With the NEC a reality, I thought automatically of producing him. *The Trials of Brother Jero,* whose title role I had performed in a low-budget public TV broadcast, and another play of his, *The Swamp Dwellers,* were already tied up for Off-Broadway production. Fortunately, Wole visited New York around this time. We met and he recommended that I look at a more recent work of his, *Kongi's Harvest.*

With its lush but trenchant verse, sweeping pageant-laden scope, steeped in indigenous African Yoruba-source ethos, yet possesing a classical modern feel—and its scathing dissection of contemporary, postcolonial African politics—*Kongi* was a perfect complement to the first two selections.

However, before the production opened, real life drama overwhelmed make-believe. The Nigerian-Biafrica conflict exploded and Wole Soyinka's personal fate was at stake. A neutral voice for reconciliation, he had been imprisoned by Federal authorities.

Producing his play took on greater urgency. The public visibility of the production and the media attention surrounding it were enlisted to prevent further victimization of Soyinka by his jailors. Ironically, *Kongi's* plot-specifics paralleled Wole's circumstances. Thankfully, real life climaxed happily. After months of difficult incarceration, Wole was finally released. Whether our modest efforts contributed or not, Wole Soyinka survived his ordeal and, as the world knows, went on to more distinguished achievements, including winning the 1987 Nobel Prize for Literature.

Daddy Goodness, last of the season's quartet, fell into my lap unexpectedly—literally from a closet shelf. While visiting Robert Hooks, my friend and NEC cofounder, he casually mentioned that he had a closet shelf of plays submitted to him after producing *Happy Ending* and *Day of Absence*—among them a play by Richard Wright.

"A play by Richard Wright?" I replied with astonishment. "I never heard of Richard Wright writing a play. You've got to be kidding."

We searched the closet shelf and finally came across a hard brown cover. The inside title page of the script said *Daddy Goodness* and disclosed that Wright had adapted the play from a French work, *Papa Mon Dieu* by Louis Sapin. I knew immediately that the script was authentic since its typewritten text still contained misspellings and other errata. It was obviously a personal draft that Wright had left uncorrected before he died.

An unknown play by one of America's greatest writers. It was a bonus beyond my wildest expectations. Reading, I found it rough around the edges, unpolished in spots, and awkward in minor transitions, but it was sufficiently completed and eminently producible. A play like this was *exactly* what the NEC had been created to do. Also, in style it added the final piece to the season's puzzle—a light, racy, tart-tongued comedy, brimming with folk humor and pointed observations about black folks' enduring travails with spiritual faith and belief.

Daddy Goodness also necessitated my debut as stage director. When the play was scheduled, there was enough time to find a director. The search proved unsuccessful, and I was faced with either canceling the production or directing it myself. I was learning fast that my faith in the viability of a play was not always going to be shared honestly by others. This forced me to embark upon a new career that I was more than eager to leave to someone else.

With *Daddy Goodness* ending the first season successfully, we at NEC could finally breathe sighs of relief. The company and the entire project was off and running. The pilot season, as I had calculated, was a model barometer of future artistic explorations. Yet it was still premature to gauge whether my optimistic contentions about reaping a bountiful crop of new plays from black African-American writers would bear fruit.

One positive early indication was forthcoming when I was fortunate to open the second season with a wild, wicked, wackily original, yet curiously elegant, satire, *God is Guess What . . . ?*, a play that had arrived in the mail written by Ray McIver, an Atlanta schoolteacher principal.

The stage was now appropriately set for *Ceremonies in Dark Old Men,* the first-produced of works appearing in this volume. *Ceremonies* by Lonne Elder III was the main play excluded from production at the beginning because of a conflict of interest. Prior to the NEC I had been associated with the play repeatedly as an actor and workshop stager. The play had earned important playwriting awards and came close to being produced on numerous occasions. Despite its quality reputation, I judged it would be better to postpone it until the fanfare of NEC creation had abated. The strategy worked since this delay defused all incipient objections upon its debut.

If the wait wasn't the cause for silence, the impact of the production certainly was. *Ceremonies* was greeted with thunderous acclaim and presented the NEC with its first decision-making dilemma. Potentially it was a bonafide commercial hit.

After its opening, Robert, Jerry, and I had to debate whether to transfer it to Broadway, extend it for a long stay Off-Broadway, or close it on schedule. I argued that it was too early in our existence to gain positive advantages from the first two options. Only into our second year, not enough time had passed for our institutional aims and purposes to solidify and gain credibility. Also, we couldn't tie up our actors in a long-run engagement because they were already assigned to the next two plays. In a cynical climate, we were vulnerable to being attacked as having desired commercial success all along.

Regretting that we couldn't satisfy the numerous ticket-seekers who wished to see our production, we decided to extend *Ceremonies* for a brief four-week period at our home theater, The St. Mark's Playhouse, then we ceded the rights back to the author. Lonne immediately acquired an independent producer who reopened the play with an entirely new cast for a substantial run Off-Broadway.

The three one-act bill that followed *Ceremonies* included a short play, *Malcochon,* by Derek Walcott, which paved the way to *Dream on Monkey Mountain* included in this collection.

Like *Daddy Goodness* sitting in Robert's closet, *Malcochon* was even closer to home—upon *my* family bookshelf. My wife had inherited it from an earlier friendship. It was included in *The Hasty Papers—A One Time Review,* a multiartform avant-garde collection published and edited by my wife's friend. Derek had permitted the play's inclusion just before undergoing a vicious physical assault on the streets of Little Italy in New York City—an attack which caused him to disavow the grant that had brought him to American shores and sent him home to the Carribbean, never to return for many years.

The NEC presented his towering, poetic-drama masterpiece, *Dream on Monkey Mountain,* during its 1971 season, and performed it later at the 1972 Olympics in Munich, Germany. This soaring verse epic dramatized wrenchingly the agony and contradictions of divided identity and the grandeur of authentic transcendent reconciliation. It was given extraordinary performances by a cast led by Roscoe Lee Brown, Antonio Fargas, Esther Rolle, and Ron O'Neal.

Derek Walcott, in 1971, gave the NEC the enviable status of having produced on stage two living winners of the Nobel Prize for Literature.

Daughters of the Mock by Judi Ann Mason, rode in on the back of her play *Livin' Fat.* Like a host of plays, *Livin' Fat* came through the mail. I liked it and contacted the author. She was not only talented but, I discovered, also young. In fact she was still in college. I reached her on a communal phone in her dorm. Whoever answered called her. After a short wait she appeared on the line. I announced who I was, told her I liked her play and wanted to produce it. For what seemed like millennia there was complete silence. I went on to indicate that I was not talking about a reading or workshop project but a mainstage production that I would produce and direct with her cooperation. Eventually, I heard a weak, trembly voiced assent to my offer—something like "of—of course. . . ." I learned later that Judi Ann Mason had thought someone was playing a practical joke on her, and that when she indeed became convinced it wasn't a prank, the truth did little to improve her composure since the enormity of her good fortune was equally threatening to her equilibrium. Nevertheless, she survived the shock and *Livin' Fat* was produced in 1975.

However, her buoyant, farcical, roguish comedy was little preparation for the mature, starkly severe, womanist savagery of *Daughters of the Mock* with its fierce Greek-drama passions and intensities. The absoluteness and uncompromising rejectionist gender stance was unsettling to many in 1979, but over the years the play has achieved almost cult status.

Judi Ann Mason, along with a poet-dramatist like Alexis DeVeaux, author of the complex psychological phantasmagorical *A Season to Unravel,* provided the NEC with unique female perspectives and additional stylistic diversity.

Charles Fuller's plays have been performed regularly by the NEC. The relation began modestly enough with *In the Deepest Part of Sleep,* his four-character domestic drama. This intense, small-scale work was a deceptive introduction to the succession of larger size, often historical plays that followed. Due to their factual content and provocative themes about justice, social responsibility, and moral accountability, these plays made headlines on many occasions going beyond their theatrical reception. *The Brownsville Raid* cast the spotlight on surviving relatives of actual soldiers unjustly court-martialed by the U.S. Army at the turn of the century. Zooman, the title character portrayed so malevolently and menacingly by Gian Carlo Esposito, frightened some reviewers so much when they failed to separate their dread of real street violence from their reaction to the fictional play.

Interestingly, it was *Zooman and the Sign* that caused me to doubt whether the productive relationship between Charles and the NEC would last. After I accepted the first draft of *Zooman,* Charles rewrote the play. I developed strong reservations about the result, and I feared that my negative opinions would alienate him. In order to soften my criticisms, I lured Charles to the idyllic setting of Martha's Vineyard where I was vacationing with my family. After a breathtaking tour of the island's bucolic environs, I fed him a sumptuous lunch, and only when the peaceful, colorful, panoramic view out the Gay Head living-room window had created the most beatific ambience did I start discussing the play. I would like to suppose that this tactic won the day for me, but I'm more convinced that it was Charles's seasoned professionalism which enabled him to listen with aplomb, then accept my suggestions positively.

Conversely, *A Soldier's Play* was as problem free as *Zooman* had been problematical. Whatever minimal script revisions (I knew at once), would evolve out of rehearsals. By then I was immune to speculating about the commercial potential of a dramatic property, but I was confident about ascertaining what made for a powerful evening of theater. I was never so certain than about *A Soldier's Play.*

Most of the casting was ready-made since a majority of the actors already had appeared at the NEC. Others I remembered from auditions. I slated the play to open the 1981–82 season and was poised to begin preproduction activity when Charles threw me a bombshell. He had jumped the gun and promised the role of Sergeant Walters to an actor friend of ours who was not the actor I had in mind. My producer's rights empowered me to countermand the promise, but, with reluctance, I deferred to Charles's commitment. Fortunately, the actor was unavailable and, with alacrity, I moved to hire the performer I had targeted for the role in the first place—Adolph Caesar.

Fortune smiled again when Larry Riley, then unknown to me, showed up with his guitar. It beamed even stronger when Denzel Washington, only slightly more familiar, managed to show up barely under the wire just as I was about to close auditions. This trio completed a hockey hat-trick score of perfect casting.

Once underway, *A Soldier's Play* rehearsals progressed ridiculously smooth until the performers had to "waste time" in order for the set, lighting, and costume designers to "catch up." *A Soldier's Play* opened in November 1981 to unanimous praise. Little more needs be said since the play's fortunes, beginning with the Pulitzer Prize, have been well-recorded.

Gus Edwards is also often produced at the NEC. *The Offering* printed here marked his initial appearance. I discovered it through Reverand Harold Eads, a mutual friend of Gus and mine. Harold, at a house party in his East Harlem apartment, where he was pastor of a ghetto congregation, introduced me to a mild-mannered young man, saying he was a writer I should check out. I was conditioned to reading anybody, but my experiences didn't prepare me for the discrepancy between Gus Edwards the person and the shocking amoral universe of his characters along with the plot details of *The Offering*. It promised to stretch boundaries even wider.

Like *Daddy Goodness,* I was faced with the necessity of directing the play myself. Even my own staff, although they never voiced it out loud, seemed puzzled by my enthusiasm for the play. The four characters (and ultimately the actors' interpretations) had no redeeming social qualities. They orbited in their low-life ambience of alienated behavior and asocial values without apology or justification. Just as striking was the play's cryptic, matter-of-fact, understated style. The drama's surface elements were transparent enough—recognizable, specific, concrete (there was no attempt to mystify or obfuscate)—but what was not explicated carried equal weight or even more.

The impact of the production was provocative in the best ways. The chilling narratives, casual verbal violence, self-contained nonconventional conduct, and engulfing sexuality were so riveting that the deeper implications of the text were not consciously acknowledged. The audience was left disturbed, divided, fractured. One segment was so anxious to pacify or seek solace from its conflicting, possibly contradictory responses, that it appealed to have discussions afterward. I rejected the importunings, firmly believing that the audiences' spontaneous reactions and feelings should remain intact and not be dissipated by postattendance intellectual discourse. Despite controversies, *The Offering* was as gripping as its ingredients were sensational.

Paul Carter Harrison, like Gus Edwards, exhibited a striking dichotomy between his person and his work. I met him soon after he had ended a long stay in Europe. On first encounter he was articulate, suave, almost debonair. His work then surprised by being as nitty-gritty as his demeanor was sophisticated.

The Great MacDaddy was supremely representative. Inspired by Amos Tutuola's *The Palm-Wine Drinkard*, it is a superlative synthesis of African and African-American motifs drawing upon myth, folklore, fantastic forces, spirits-beliefs, superstitions, and hyperbolic tales (sacred and profane) from both cultures—merging them into a seamless formal and stylistic unity of drama, music, and dance. It was innovative in form, content, and production method. Its message was simple, but the telling was complex.

A prominent reviewer hailed *The Great MacDaddy* as the "birth of the new black musical." Its powerful scintillating realization buttressed the reputations of its talented creative team: Diane McIntrye and Coleridge-Taylor Perkinson, et al. Two separate NEC productions were the sites of a who's who roster of stellar performers: Adolph Caesar, Hattie Winston, Phylicia Allen Rashad, Cleavon Little, Lynn Whitfield, Charles Brown, Barbara Montgomery, Charles Weldon, Al Freeman, Jr., Carl Gordon, Frankie Faison, BeBe Drake Hooks, Majorie Barnes, Victor Willis, Graham Brown, Martha Short-Golsen, Dyane Harvey, Freda Vanderpool, Carol Maillard, Joella Breedlove, David Downing, among others.

Home, while light-years different from *The Great MacDaddy*, belongs to the same family of stylistic innovation. It was the prideful culmination of an in-house talent. Samm-Art Williams arrived at the NEC shortly after relocating from Philadelphia where he had once waylaid me at the door of my hotel while I was performing in *Ceremonies in Dark Old Men*. Samm-Art was as prepossessing in physical appearance as Gus had been unassuming. In size he looked like the heavyweight prizefighter whose profession he was strenuously attempting to escape. I recall him badgering me more about acting than writing; it was as an actor that he first became involved at the NEC. While engaged he also attended the Playwrights' Workshop which eventually staged a duo of his plays. His writing efforts culminated in the script for *Home*.

Unquestionably drawn from felt experience, and sympathetically expressed through earthy lyricism and sly, piquant humor, the three-character *Home* created a shimmering world of rural provenance and black providence. Its stylistic masterstroke was employing two female performers to depict a whole tapestry of people, settings, moods, and incidents surrounding the intrepid odyssey of Cephus Miles, the protagonist. With the barest of props, costumes, and set places, *Home* enlisted audience support and made them actual accomplices in the act of creation. The partnership of author, actors, and production resulted in the magic of achievement. Having Charles Brown, Michele Shay, and L. Scott Caldwell on board didn't hurt.

Compared to the fate of *The Great MacDaddy*, whose influence on subsequent attempts was short-circuited by lack of followup resources, *Home* did stimulate similar undertakings. Unfortunately, some imitations have equated simplicity of means with simplemindedness of effort. The simplicity of *Home* was grounded in a genuine sensibility and a depth of presentation.

I have saved the remaining plays of this volume for final commentary. Along with the earlier-mentioned *Ceremonies*, they comprise the great rhythmic-realist dramas that made up a significant component of the NEC's roster. These plays attracted large audience support and commercial visibility with appearances on Broadway and in other media.

The River Niger was the third Joseph Walker play to be performed at the NEC. *Ododo* and *The Harangues*, Joe's previous works, were so different in form, I was taken aback momentarily on receiving Niger. But it didn't take long to recognize that *Niger* was a more deeply personal work and perfectly matched its brawny "lion hearted" creator. This was a "big," raucous, passionate, roaring play—generous and tender in sensibility, yet deliciously vulgar-spoken—crackling with acerbic wit, fearless in demolishing hypocrisies and pretensions, emotionally raw and vulnerable, bravely critical, and ultimately redemptive. The play dramatized pointedly the pressing social, political, and humane concerns of its time with an incisive grasp of worldwide forces and issues. It was peopled with more than a dozen fully developed characters and tracked generational relations spanning three eras, revealing all continuities and dissonances.

When *Niger* premiered in December 1972 it was obvious that the 150-seat St. Marks Playhouse could not accommodate the public clamoring for tickets. The Brooks Atkinson Broadway Theater became available, and we moved there after completing our scheduled run. We had come full circle—this time making an opposite decision from *Ceremonies*.

But our circumstances were different. Over six years and some fifteen productions, we had proven commitment to our original goals and purposes; our dedication and integrity were documented and could not be questioned. Moreover, our material fortunes had changed. To our sorrow and regret we had not been able to sustain the resident acting company. But this also freed us from ensuing conflicts about seasonal obligations. *Niger* actors had no other assignments, therefore were available for a long-run engagement. Most important to our consideration, we had built an audience of our targeted black constituency that would remain the backbone of our support. In fact, size of the Broadway house would allow us to offer a large section of even cheaper seats. Assuredly, we were not "moving to Broadway" for the age-old reasons of commercial gain and status, despite the byproduct of being rewarded with a modicum of both.

The Broadway move in March 1973 led to the pioneering achievement of a play lasting on the "Great White Way" for almost a year solely because of an 80 percent black audience—a record still unmatched. For a time, Broadway became the "Great Black Way." Before concluding its stay, *Niger* won the 1974 Tony Award for Best Play.

Like *Niger* before and *Home* after, *The First Breeze of Summer* was also transferred to Broadway, and it too, like them, became a candidate for the Tony Award in 1975.

First Breeze shared many of *Niger*'s features—large in scope, passionate in emotions, fully drawn characters, and equally acute in measuring tensions across generational fault lines. Leslie Lee, affable and modest in person, offered triumphant homage to the indomitable spirit and tenacious survival of Gremmar, an archetypal black woman, lovingly created with compassion, but without a trace of concession to sentimentality.

In plays like *First Breeze* and *Niger*, the black audience was able to recognize, identify, relate, criticize, and grapple directly with the particularities of its own ethos and history. It was privy to being the subject of its own narratives presented from within the culture.

Thankfully, *First Breeze* received a first-rate TV production that recorded the work of its original cast headed by Frances Foster, Janet League, Moses Gunn, Ethel Ayler, Charles Brown, Reyno, Barbara Montgomery, Lou Myers, BeBe Drake Hooks, Petronia, and others—unlike *Niger* which suffered a less sanguine fate in its appearance as a feature movie.

Sty of the Blind Pig, in contrast to *First Breeze* and *Niger*, has only four characters. But the play resonates with the sounds and echoes of an entire world, quivering with the everwidening ripples of a vanishing way of life. Phillip Hayes Dean, as combative in person as his work is sensitive, succeeds in delivering a threnody to a regional Southern past, while pointing the way to emerging upheavals in American social life and human relationships. It is an elegiac play whose repercussions continue to haunt long after experiencing it. The quartet of actors who brought it to incandescent life was one of NEC's finest, all of whom went on to earn distinguished recognition in American theater and performing media: Adolph Caesar, Moses Gunn, Frances Foster, and Clarice Taylor.

Sty of the Blind Pig was paired with *Dream on Monkey Mountain* at the 1972 Munich Olympics.

My emphasis all along has been on the enormous variety contained in this volume and how the term eclectic became embedded in consciousness as my predominant determining concept and orienting practice. However, the quality shared by all works here is that I judged them good plays.

Accepting decision-making responsibility required that I expand my taste and open myself to broader inclusion. I was guided tremendously in advance by my belief that the black experience is a diverse and inexhaustible fecund source. The musical arena had proven this already. I was determined to induce a similar development in theater. While ideas of "good" and "bad" are inevitable subjective constructs and premises, fortunately in theater, some objective verification is attainable within the crucible of performance practice and audience reception. My empirical involvement sharpened my critical, evaluative, and judgmental faculties, resulting in standards and norms, firmly held, yet flexibly defined, and never codified. Eclecticism may have been the guiding principle but not for its own sake. Each individual work had to withstand scrutiny on its own terms, according to applicable criteria.

The plays in this volume are all "text" plays—that is scripted by individual authors and "completed" before submission for production—different from theater pieces developed through improvisitory exercises or experimented into theater-form from other artistic modes. My own background as a text playwright made this orientation natural. But it also emanated from my desire to produce a body of work that could more readily be reproduced independently by others—contrasted to signature "performance-type" pieces hard to duplicate.

As stated earlier, when the Negro Ensemble Company began I speculated that a cornucopia of plays would flow in. Yet I wasn't sure I would be right. So I staked out alternate paths. These bailout routes proved unnecessary as the NEC was inundated almost instantly with new plays by writers, an overwhelming majority African Americans. The best of these submissions were of such superior quality until the need to seek alternative sources was obviated.

The ten plays in this volume amount to merely 10 percent of the NEC's total mainstage productions over thirty years. Altogether this output offers a comprehensive view of the magnitude and importance of black theater accomplishments throughout this last quarter century.

Incredible as it seems, black theater remains misperceived and underval-ued. What is usually seen of its horizon is only the tip of the iceberg. The sole peaks being a handful of market- and media-validated successes. Yet these summit sights are merely visible appearances attached to an expand-ing monolith below—hidden from view but sustained by the nurturing sea surrounding it.

These ten plays access to a true measurement of significance, multi-plicity, munificence, and magnificence. They destroy the myth of singular representation. No one black writer, no matter how worthy his or her indi-vidual talent may be, can serve as the measure of group adequacy. Only several can add up to a sufficiency.

Much of the ignorance of the breadth of the representative black canon can be attributed to an unholy negative trinity: the paucity of professional reproductions, academia's failure to disseminate, and sparse publication.

The resulting ignorance fallout insures a distorted perception of black theater and a myopic pigeonholing of the entire output into a narrow slot of sameness. What this volume confirms is that there is no one black spokesperson, no one point of view, no one form or style of expression. Black writers are as diverse as their experience is complex. They differ as much as they share in common. History has bequeathed a legacy of com-monality, but history, time, space, and geography have assured divergences and particularities. All this is reflected here.

Undoubtedly, I have been uniquely involved with these plays. As men-tioned, I selected and produced every one of them. I script-edited some. I directed more than half and performed in almost as many. This almost unprecedented participation gave me an unusual vantage point. Conven-tional wisdom suggests that such closeness can be blinding to objectivity. However, any impairment supposedly inflicted by blinders was more than offset by evidences absorbed and lessons learned by being in almost daily attendance as these plays impacted on their public.

Also, in my multiple capacities I was privileged to be constantly on hand to witness the African-American audiences themselves developing in their encounter with their own theater—accepting the manifold diversity, verisimilitude, and, yes, eclecticisms of their own representations. How-ever much they may have embraced or quarrelled with the results, they accepted the plurality of reflections as the natural truths of their lives as expressed through the medium of drama. The only outcome that was not acceptable was inferior productions.

A Soldier's Play

CHARLES FULLER

Left to right: Denzel Washington as PRIVATE FIRST CLASS MELVIN
PETERSON, *Adolph Ceasar as* TECH/SERGEANT VERNON C. WATERS,
Samuel L. Jackson as PRIVATE LOUIS HENSON, *and Larry Riley as* PRIVATE
C. J. MEMPHIS *in a scene from* A Soldier's Play. *Photograph copyright © 1981
by Bert Andrews. Reprinted by permission of Marsha Hudson, the Estate of
Bert Andrews.*

Charles Fuller, a native of Philadelphia, studied at Villanova University. He is a prominent contributor to the repertory of the NEC, who, in addition to producing his 1982 Pulitzer Prizewinning *A Soldier's Play,* also performed his *Brownsville Raid, Zooman and the Sign,* an early epic cycle, *In My Many Names and Days,* and the recent epic cycle, *We.* He is the recipient of a Guggenheim Award and a National Endowment of the Arts Fellowship for playwriting. He has taught playwriting on the faculty of Temple University and is currently engaged in writing for the screen.

A Soldier's Play was produced in New York by the NEC at Theatre Four, opening on November 10, 1981, with the following cast:

Tech/Sergeant Vernon C. Waters	Adolph Ceasar
Captain Charles Taylor	Peter Friedman
Corporal Bernard Cobb	Eugene Lee
Private First Class Melvin Peterson	Denzel Washington
Corporal Ellis	James Pickens, Jr.
Private Louis Henson	Samuel L. Jackson
Private James Wilkie	Steven A. Jones
Private Tony Smalls	Brent Jenings
Captain Richard Davenport	Charles Brown
Private C. J. Memphis	Larry Riley
Lieutenant Byrd	Cotter Smith
Captain Wilcox	Stephen Zettler

Directed by Douglas Turner Ward; scenery by Felix E. Cochren; lighting by Allen Lee Hughes; costumes by Judy Dearing; sound by Regge Life; production stage managed by Wayne Elbert.

A Soldier's Play

For LARRY NEAL *whom I will miss for the rest of my life*

CHARACTERS

in order of appearance

TECH/SERGEANT VERNON C. WATERS

CAPTAIN CHARLES TAYLOR

CORPORAL BERNARD COBB

PRIVATE FIRST CLASS MELVIN PETERSON

CORPORAL ELLIS

PRIVATE LOUIS HENSON

PRIVATE JAMES WILKIE

PRIVATE TONY SMALLS

CAPTAIN RICHARD DAVENPORT

PRIVATE C. J. MEMPHIS

LIEUTENANT BYRD

CAPTAIN WILCOX

ACT ONE

TIME

1944

PLACE

Fort Neal, Louisiana

SCENE

The inner shell of the stage is black. On the stage, in a horseshoe-like half circle, are several platforms at varying levels.

On the left side of this horseshoe is a military office arrangement with a small desk (a nameplate on the desk reads: CAPTAIN CHARLES TAYLOR*), two office-type chairs, one straight-backed, a regimental, and an American flag. A picture of F.D.R. is on the wall.*

On the right side of the horseshoe, and curved toward the rear, is a barracks arrangement, with three bunk beds and footlockers set in typical military fashion. The exit to this barracks is a freestanding doorway on the far right. (This barracks should be changeable—these bunks with little movement can look like a different place.) On the edge of this barracks is a poster, semi-blownup, of Joe Louis in an army uniform, helmet, rifle, and bayonet. It reads: PVT. JOE LOUIS SAYS, "WE'RE GOING TO DO OUR PART—AND WE'LL WIN BECAUSE WE'RE ON GOD'S SIDE."

On the rear of the horseshoe, upstage center, is a bare platform, raised several feet above everything else. It can be anything we want it to be—a limbo if you will.

The entire set should resemble a courtroom. The sets, barracks, and office, will both be elevated, so that from anywhere on the horseshoe one may look down onto a space at center stage that is on the stage floor. The levels should have easy access by either stairs or ramps, and the entire set should be raked ever so slightly so that one does not perceive much difference between floor and set, and the bottom edges of the horseshoe. There must also be enough area on both sides of the horseshoe to see exits and entrances.

Lighting will play an integral part in the realization of the play. It should therefore be sharp, so that areas are clearly defined, with as little spill into other areas as possible. Lights must also be capable of suggesting mood, time, and place.

As the play opens, the stage is black. In the background, rising in volume, we hear the song "Don't Sit Under the Apple Tree," sung by the Andrews Sisters. Quite suddenly, in a sharp, though narrow, beam of light, in limbo, TECH/SERGEANT VERNON C. WATERS, *a well-built, light-brown-skinned man in a World War II, winter army uniform, is seen down on all fours. He is stinking drunk, trying to stand and mumbling to himself.*

WATERS (*repeating*): They'll still hate you! They still hate you . . . They still hate you!

(WATERS *is laughing as suddenly someone steps into the light. [We never see this person.] He is holding a .45 caliber pistol. He lifts it swiftly and ominously toward* WATERS's *head and fires.* WATERS *is knocked over backward. He is dead. The music has stopped, and there is a strong silence onstage.*)

VOICE: Le's go!

(*The man with the gun takes a step, then stops. He points the gun at* WATERS *again and fires a second time. There is another silence as limbo is plunged into darkness, and the barracks is just as quickly lit. We are in the barracks of Company B, 221st Chemical Smoke Generating Company, at Fort Neal. Five black enlisted men stand at "parade rest" with their hands above their heads and submit to a search. They are:* CORPORAL BERNARD

COBB, *a man in his mid to late twenties, dressed in a T-shirt, dog tags, fatigues, and slippers.* PRIVATE JAMES WILKIE, *a man in his early forties, a career soldier, is dressed in fatigues from which the stripes have been removed, with a baseball cap on, and smoking a cigar.* PRIVATE LOUIS HENSON, *thin, in his late twenties or early thirties, is wearing a baseball T-shirt that reads "Fort Neal" on the front and "#4" on the back, with fatigues and boots on.* PFC MELVIN PETERSON, *a man in his late twenties, wearing glasses, looks angelic. His shirt is open but he does not look sloppy; of all the men, his stripe is the most visible, his boots the most highly polished.* PRIVATE TONY SMALLS, *a man in his late thirties, a career man, is as small as his name feels. All five men are being searched by* CORPORAL ELLIS, *a soldier who is simply always "spit and polish."* ELLIS *is also black, and moves from man to man, patting them down in a policelike search.* CAPTAIN CHARLES TAYLOR, *a young white man in his mid to late thirties, looks on, a bit disturbed. All the men's uniforms are from World War II.*)

TAYLOR: I'm afraid this kind of thing can't be helped, men—you can put your arms down when Ellis finishes. (*Several men drop their arms.* ELLIS *is searching* PVT. HENSON.) We don't want anyone from Fort Neal going into Tynin looking for rednecks.

COBB: May I speak, sir? (TAYLOR *nods.*) Why do this, Captain? They got M.P.'s surrounding us, and hell, the Colonel must know nobody colored killed the man!

TAYLOR: This is a precaution, Cobb. We can't have revenge killings, so we search for weapons.

PETERSON: Where'd they find the Sarge, sir?

TAYLOR: In the woods out by the Junction—and so we don't have any rumors, Sergeant Waters was shot twice—we don't know that he was lynched! (*Pause.*) Twice. Once in the chest, and a bullet in the head. (ELLIS *finishes with the last man.*) You finished the footlockers?

ELLIS: Yes, sir! There aren't any weapons.

TAYLOR (*relaxing*): I didn't think there would be. At ease, men! (*The men relax.*) Tech/Sergeant Waters, in my opinion, served the 221st and this platoon, in particular, with distinction, and I for one shall miss the man. (*Slight pause.*) But no matter what we think of the Sergeant's death, we will not allow this incident to make us forget our responsibility to this uniform. We are soldiers, and our war is with the Nazis and Japs, not the civilians in Tynin. Any enlisted man found with unauthorized weapons will be immediately subject to summary court-martial. (*Softens*) Sergeant Waters's replacement won't be assigned for several weeks. Until that time, you will all report to

Sergeant Dorsey of C Company. Corporal Cobb will be barracks N.C.O.—any questions?

PETERSON: Who do they think did it, sir?

TAYLOR: At this time there are no suspects.

HENSON: You know the Klan did it, sir.

TAYLOR: Were you an eyewitness, soldier?

HENSON: Who else goes around killin' Negroes in the South?—They lynched Jefferson the week I got here, sir! And that Signal Corps guy, Daniels, two months later!

TAYLOR: Henson, unless you saw it, keep your opinions to yourself! Is that clear? (HENSON *nods*.) And that's an order! It also applies to everybody else!

ALL (*almost simultaneously*): Yes, sir!

TAYLOR: You men who have details this afternoon, report to the orderly room for your assignments. The rest of you are assigned to the Colonel's quarters—cleanup detail. Cobb, I want to see you in my office at 1350 hours.

COBB: Yes, sir.

TAYLOR: As of 0600 hours this morning, the town of Tynin was placed off-limits to all military personnel. (*Slight groan from the men*) The Friday night dance has also been canceled—(*All the men moan.* TAYLOR *is sympathetic.*) OK, OK! Some of the officers are going to the Colonel—I can't promise anything. Right now, it's canceled.

ELLIS: Tenn-hut!

(*The men snap to. The* CAPTAIN *salutes. Only* COBB *salutes him back. The* CAPTAIN *starts out.*)

TAYLOR: As you were!

(*The* CAPTAIN *and* ELLIS *exit the barracks. The men move to their bunks or footlockers.* WILKIE *goes to the rear of the bunks and looks out.*)

COBB: They still out there, Wilkie?

WILKIE: Yeah. Got the whole place surrounded.

HENSON: I don't know what the hell they thought we'd go into that town with—mops and dishrags?

WILKIE: Y'all recruits know what Colonel's cleanup detail is, don't you? Shovelin' horseshit in his stables-

COBB: Ain't no different from what we been doin'. (*He lies down and begins scratching around his groin area.*)

PETERSON (*to* COBB): Made you the barracks Commander-in-Chief, huh? (COBB *nods.*) Don't git like ole Stone-ass—What are you doin'?

COBB: Scratchin'!

HENSON (*overlapping*): Taylor knows the Klan did it—I hope y'all know that!

SMALLS (*sudden*): Then why are the M.P.'s outside with rifles? Why hold us prisoner?

PETERSON: They scared we may kill a couple peckerwoods, Smalls. Calm down, man!

WILKIE (*quickly*): Smalls, you wanna play some coon-can?

(SMALLS *shakes his head no. He is quiet, staring.*)

COBB (*examining himself*): Peterson, you know I think Eva gave me the crabs.

HENSON: Cobb, the kinda women you find, it's a wonda your nuts ain't fell off—crabs? You probably got lice, ticks, bedbugs, fleas— tapeworms—

COBB: Shut up, Henson! Pete—I ain't foolin', man! (*He starts to open his pants.*)

PETERSON: Get some powder from the PX.

WILKIE (*almost simultaneously*): Which one of y'all feels like playin' me some cards? (*He looks at* HENSON.)

HENSON: Me and Peterson's goin' down the mess hall—you still goin', Pete?

PETERSON (*nods*): Wilkie? I thought all you could do was play gofer?

HENSON (*slyly*): Yeah, Wilkie—whose ass can you kiss, now that your number-one ass is dead?

COBB (*laughing*): That sounds like something C. J. would sing! (*Looks at himself again*) Ain't this a bitch? (*Picks at himself*)

WILKIE (*overlapping, to* HENSON): You know what you can do for me, Henson—you too, Peterson!

PETERSON: Naughty, naughty!

WILKIE (*moves to his bunk, justifying*): I'm the one lost three stripes—and I'm the only man in here with kids, so when the man said jump, I jumped!

HENSON (*derisively*): Don't put your wife and kids between you and Waters's ass, man!

WILKIE: I wanted my stripes back!

COBB: I'm goin' to sick call after chow.

WILKIE (*continuing*): Y'all ain't neva' had nothin', that's why you can't understand a man like me! There was a time I was a sergeant major, you know!

HENSON (*waves disdainfully at* WILKIE, *turning his attention to* COBB): Ole V-girl slipped Cobb the crabs! How you gonna explain that to the girl back home, Corporal? How will that fine, big-thighed Momma feel, when the only ribbon you bring home from this war is the Purple Heart for crab bites? (HENSON *laughs as* SMALLS *stands suddenly.*)

SMALLS: Don't any of you guys give a damn?

PETERSON: What's the matta', Smalls?

SMALLS: The man's dead! We saw him alive last night!

COBB (*quickly*): I saw him, too. At least I know he died good and drunk!

SMALLS (*loud*): What's the matter with y'all?

HENSON: The man got hisself lynched! We're in the South, and we can't do a goddamn thing about it—you heard the Captain! But don't start actin' like we guilty of somethin'. (*Softens*) I just hope we get lucky enough to get shipped outta this hellhole to the war! (*To himself*) Besides, whoever did it, didn't kill much anyway.

SMALLS: He deserved better than that!

COBB: Look, everybody feels rotten, Smalls. But it won't bring the man back, so let's forget about it!

PETERSON (*moving to pat* SMALLS *on the back*): Why don't you walk it off, man?

(SMALLS *moves away to his bunk.* PETERSON *shrugs.*)

HENSON: Yeah—or go turn on a smoke machine, let the fog make you think you in London!

(SMALLS *sits down on his bunk and looks at them for a moment, then lays down, his face in the pillow.*)

WILKIE (*overlapping*): Let Cobb bring his Eva over, she'll take his mind off Waters plus give him a bonus of crabs!

(*The men laugh, but* SMALLS *doesn't move as the lights begin slowly to fade out.*)

HENSON (*counting*): —an' blue-balls. Clap. Syphilis. Pimples! (COBB *throws a pillow at* HENSON.) Piles! Fever blisters. Cockeyes. Cooties!

(*The men are laughing as the lights go out. As they do, a rather wiry black officer wearing glasses,* CAPTAIN RICHARD DAVENPORT, *walks across the stage from the wings, dressed sharply in an M.P. uniform, his hat cocked to the side and strapped down, the way airmen wear theirs. He is carrying a briefcase, and we are aware of a man who is very confident and self-assured. He is smiling as he faces the audience, cleaning his glasses as he begins to speak.*)

DAVENPORT: Call me Davenport—Captain, United States Army, attached to the 343rd Military Police Corps Unit, Fort Neal,

Louisiana. I'm a lawyer the segregated Armed Services couldn't find a place for. My job in this war? Policing colored troops. (*Slight pause.*) One morning, during mid-April 1944, a colored tech/sergeant, Vernon C. Waters, assigned to the 221st Chemical Smoke Generating Company, stationed here before transfer to Europe, was brutally shot to death in a wooded section off the New Post Road and the junction of Highway 51—just two hundred yards from the colored N.C.O. club—by a person or persons unknown. (*Pauses a little*) Naturally, the unofficial consensus was the local Ku Klux Klan, and for that reason, I was told at the time, Colonel Barton Nivens ordered the Military Police to surround the enlisted men's quarters—then instructed all his company commanders to initiate a thorough search of all personal property for unauthorized knives, guns—weapons of any kind. (*Slight pause.*) You see, 90 percent of the Colonel's command—all of the enlisted men stationed here are Negroes, and the Colonel felt—and I suppose justly—that once word of the Sergeant's death spread among his troops, there might be some retaliation against the white citizens of Tynin. (*Shrugs*) What he did worked—there was no retaliation, and no racial incidents. (*Pause.*) The week after the killing took place, several correspondents from the Negro press wrote lead articles about it. But the headlines faded—(*Smiles*) The NAACP got me involved in this. Rumor has it, Thurgood Marshall ordered an immediate investigation of the killing, and the army, pressured by Secretary of War Stimson, rather randomly ordered Colonel Nivens to initiate a preliminary inquiry into the Sergeant's death. Now, the Colonel didn't want to rehash the murder, but he complied with the army's order by instructing the Provost Marshal, my C.O., Major Hines, to conduct a few question-and-answer sessions among the men of Sergeant Waters's platoon and file a report. The matter was to be given the lowest priority. (*Pause.*) The case was mine, five minutes later. It was four to five weeks after his death—the month of May. (*He pauses as the light builds in* CAPTAIN TAYLOR'*s office.* TAYLOR *is facing* DAVENPORT, *expressionless.* DAVENPORT *is a bit puzzled.*) Captain?

TAYLOR: Forgive me for occasionally staring, Davenport, you're the first colored officer I've ever met. I'd heard you had arrived a month ago, and you're a bit startling. (*Quickly*) I mean you no offense. (*Starts back to his desk and sits on the edge of it, as* DAVENPORT *starts into the office a bit cautiously*) We'll be getting some of you as replacements, but we don't expect them until next month. Sit down, Davenport. (DAVENPORT *sits.*) You came out of Fort Benning in '43?

DAVENPORT: Yes.

TAYLOR: And they assigned a lawyer to the Military Police? I'm Infantry and I've been with the Engineers, Field Artillery, and Signal Corps—this is some army. Where'd you graduate law school?

DAVENPORT: Howard University.

TAYLOR: Your daddy a rich minister or something? (DAVENPORT *shakes his head no.*) I graduated the Point—(*Pause.*) We didn't have any Negroes at the Point. I never saw a Negro until I was twelve or thirteen. (*Pause.*) You like the army, I suppose, huh?

DAVENPORT: Captain, did you see my orders?

TAYLOR (*bristling slightly*): I saw them right after Colonel Nivens sent them to Major Hines. I sent my orderly to the barracks and told him to have the men waiting for you.

DAVENPORT: Thank you.

TAYLOR: I didn't know at the time that Major Hines was assigning a Negro, Davenport. (DAVENPORT *stiffens.*) My preparations were made in the belief that you'd be a white man. I think it only fair to tell you that had I known what Hines intended I would have requested the immediate suspension of the investigation—May I speak freely?

DAVENPORT: You haven't stopped yet, Captain.

TAYLOR: Look—how far could you get even if you succeed? These local people aren't going to charge a white man in this parish on the strength of an investigation conducted by a Negro!—and Nivens and Hines know that! The Colonel doesn't give a damn about finding the men responsible for this thing! And they're making a fool of you—can't you see that?—and—take off those sunglasses!

DAVENPORT: I intend to carry out my orders—and I like these glasses—they're like MacArthur's.

TAYLOR: You go near that sheriff's office in Tynin in your uniform—carrying a briefcase, looking and sounding white, and charging local people—and you'll be found just as dead as Sergeant Waters! People around here don't respect the colored!

DAVENPORT: I know that.

TAYLOR (*annoyed*): You know how many times I've asked Nivens to look into this killing? Every day, since it happened, Davenport. Major Hines didn't tell you that!

DAVENPORT: Do you suspect someone, Captain?

TAYLOR: Don't play cat and mouse with me, soldier!

DAVENPORT (*calmly*): Captain, like it or not, I'm all you've got. I've been ordered to look into Sergeant Waters's death, and I intend to do exactly that.

(*There is a long pause.*)

TAYLOR: Can I tell you a little story? (DAVENPORT *nods.*) Before you were assigned here? Nivens got us together after dinner one night, and all we did was discuss Negroes in the officer ranks. We all commanded Negro troops, but nobody had ever come face to face with colored officers—there were a lot of questions that night—for example, your quarters—had to be equal to ours, but we had none—no mess hall for you! (*Slight pause.*) Anyway, Jed Harris was the only officer who defended it—my own feelings were mixed. The only Negroes I've ever known were subordinates—My father hired the first Negro I ever saw—man named Colfax—to help him fix the shed one summer. Nice man—worked hard—did a good job, too. (*Remembering; smiles thoughtfully*) But I never met a Negro with any education until I graduated the Point—hardly an officer of equal rank. So I frankly wasn't sure how I'd feel—until right now—and—(*struggles*) I don't want to offend you, but I just cannot get used to it—the bars, the uniform—being in charge just doesn't look right on Negroes!

DAVENPORT (*rising*): Captain, are you through?

TAYLOR: You could ask Hines for another assignment—this case is not for you! By the time you overcome the obstacles to your race, this case would be dead!

DAVENPORT (*sharply*): I got it. And I *am* in charge! All your orders instruct you to do is cooperate!

(*There is a moment of silence.*)

TAYLOR: I won't be made a fool of, Davenport. (*Straightens*) Ellis! You're right, there's no need to discuss this any further.

ELLIS (*appears on the edge of the office*): Yes, sir!

TAYLOR: Captain Davenport will need assistance with the men—I can't prevent that, Davenport, but I intend to do all I can to have this so-called investigation stopped.

DAVENPORT: Do what you like. If there's nothing else, you'll excuse me, won't you, Captain?

TAYLOR (*sardonically*): Glad I met you, Captain.

(DAVENPORT *salutes and* TAYLOR *returns salute. For an instant the two men trade cold stares, then* DAVENPORT *gestures to* ELLIS, *and the two of them start out of the office by way of the stage.* DAVENPORT *follows* ELLIS *out. Behind them,* TAYLOR *stares after them as the lights in his office fade out.* DAVENPORT *removes his glasses.*)

ELLIS: We heard it was you, sir—you know how the grapevine is. Sad thing—what happened to the Sarge.

DAVENPORT: What's on the grapevine about the killing?

(The two men stop as slowly, almost imperceptibly, on the right the barracks area is lit. In it, a small table and two chairs have been set up. ELLIS *shrugs.)*

ELLIS: We figure the Klan. They ain't crazy about us tan Yanks in this part of the country.

DAVENPORT: Is there anything on the grapevine about trouble in the town before Sergeant Waters was killed?

ELLIS: None that I know of before—after, there were rumors around the post—couple our guys from the Tank Corps wanted to drive them Shermans into Tynin—then I guess you heard that somebody said two officers did it—I figure that's why the Colonel surrounded our barracks.

DAVENPORT: Was the rumor confirmed—I didn't hear that! Did anything ever come of it?

ELLIS: Not that I know of, sir.

DAVENPORT: Thanks, Ellis—I'd better start seeing the men. *(They start into the barracks from the stage floor.)* Did you set *that* up? (ELLIS *nods.*) Good—*(He sets his briefcase on the table.)* Are they ready?

ELLIS: The Captain instructed everybody in the Sarge's platoon to be here, sir. He told them you'd be starting this morning.

DAVENPORT *(smiles, then to himself)*: Before he found out, huh?

ELLIS *(puzzled)*: Sir?

DAVENPORT: Nothing. Call the first man in, Corporal—and stay loose, I might need you.

ELLIS: Yes, sir! Sir, may I say something? (DAVENPORT *nods.*) It sure is good to see one of us wearin' them Captain's bars, sir.

DAVENPORT: Thank you.

*(*ELLIS *salutes, does a sharp about-face, and starts out.)*

ELLIS *(loud)*: Private Wilkie!

WILKIE *(offstage)*: Yes, sir! *(Almost immediately,* WILKIE *appears in the doorway. He is dressed in proper uniform of fatigues, boots, and cap.)*

ELLIS: Cap'n wants to see you!

WILKIE: Yes indeed! *(Moves quickly to the table, where he comes to attention and salutes)* Private James Wilkie reporting as ordered, sir.

DAVENPORT: At ease, Private. Have a seat. *(To* ELLIS *as* WILKIE *sits)* That will be all, Corporal.

ELLIS: Yes, sir. *(He salutes and exits.)*

*(*DAVENPORT *waits until* ELLIS *leaves before speaking.)*

DAVENPORT: Private Wilkie, I am Captain Davenport—

WILKIE (*interjecting*): Everybody knows that, sir. You all we got down here. (*Smiles broadly*) I was on that first detail got your quarters togetha', sir.

(DAVENPORT *nods.*)

DAVENPORT (*coldly*): I'm conducting an investigation into the events surrounding Sergeant Waters's death. Everything you say to me will go in my report, but that report is confidential.

WILKIE: I understand, sir.

(DAVENPORT *removes pad and pencil from the briefcase.*)

DAVENPORT: How long did you know Sergeant Waters?

WILKIE: 'Bout a year, sir. I met him last March—March 5th—I remember the date, I had been a staff sergeant exactly two years the day after he was assigned. This company was basically a baseball team then, sir. See, most of the boys had played for the Negro League, so naturally the army put us all together. (*Chuckles at the memory*) We'd be assigned to different companies—Motor Pool—Dump Truck all week long—made us do the dirty work on the post—garbage, cleanup—but on Saturdays we were whippin' the hell out of 'em on the baseball diamond! I was hittin' .352 myself! And we had a boy, C. J. Memphis? He coulda hit a ball from Fort Neal to Berlin, Germany—or Tokyo—if he was battin' right-handed. (*Pauses, catches* DAVENPORT'*s impatience*) Well, the army sent Waters to manage the team. He had been in Field Artillery—Gunnery Sergeant. Had a Croix de Guerre from the First War, too.

DAVENPORT: What kind of man was he?

WILKIE: All spit and polish, sir.

(*At that moment, in limbo, a spotlight hits* SERGEANT WATERS. *He is dressed in a well-creased uniform, wearing a helmet liner, and standing at parade-rest, facing the audience. The light around him, however, is strange—it is blue gray like the past. The light around* DAVENPORT *and* WILKIE *abates somewhat. Dialogue is continuous.*)

DAVENPORT: Tell me about him.

WILKIE: He took my stripes! (*Smiles*) But I was in the wrong, sir!

(WATERS *stands at ease. His voice is crisp and sharp, his movements minimal. He is the typical hard-nosed N.C.O.—strict, soldierly.*)

WATERS: Sergeant Wilkie! You are a noncommissioned officer in the army of a country at war—the penalty for being drunk on duty is severe in peacetime, so don't bring me no po'colored-folks-can't-do-nothin'-unless-they-drunk shit as an excuse! You are supposed to be an example to your men—so, I'm gonna send you to jail for ten days *and* take them goddamn stripes. Teach you a lesson—You in the army! (*Derisively*) Colored folks always runnin' off at the mouth 'bout what y'all gonna do if the white man gives you a chance—and you get it, and what do you do with it? You wind up drunk on guard duty—I don't blame the white man—why the hell should he put colored and white together in this war? You can't even be trusted to guard your own quarters—no wonder they treat us like dogs—Get outta' my sight, *Private!*

(*Light fades at once on* WATERS.)

DAVENPORT: What about the other men?

WILKIE: Sometimes the Southern guys caught a little hell—Sarge always said he was from up North somewhere. He was a good soldier, sir. I'm from Detroit myself—born and raised there. Joe Louis started in Detroit—did you know that, sir?

DAVENPORT: What about the Southerners?

WILKIE: Sarge wasn't exactly crazy 'bout 'em—'cept for C. J. Now C. J. was from the South, but with him Sarge was different—probably because C. J. was the best ball player we had. He could sing too! (*Slight pause.*) Sarge never got too close to nobody—maybe me—but he didn' mess with C. J., you know what I mean? Not like he did with everybody else.

(*In limbo the spotlight illuminates* C. J. MEMPHIS, *a young, handsome black man. He is in a soldier's uniform, cap on the side. He is strumming a guitar.* WATERS *is watching him, smiling. Their light is the strange light of the past.* C. J. *begins to sing, his voice deep, melodious, and bluesy.*)

C. J.: It's a low / it's a low, low / lowdown dirty shame! Yeah, it's a low / it's a low, low / lowdown dirty shame!

WILKIE (*before* C. J. *finishes*): Big Mississippi boy!

C. J. AND WILKIE (*simultaneously sing*): They say we fightin' Hitler! But they won't let us in the game!

(C. J. *strums and hums as* WATERS *looks on.*)

WILKIE: Worked harder and faster than everybody—wasn' a man on the team didn't like him. Sarge took to him the first time he saw him. "Wilkie," he says.

WILKIE AND WATERS (*simultaneously*): What have we got here?

WATERS: A guitar-playin' man! Boy, you eva' heard of Blind Willie Reynolds? Son House? Henry Sims?

(C. J. *nods to everything.*)

C. J.: You heard them play, Sarge?

WATERS: Every one of 'em. I was stationed in Mississippi couple years ago—you from down that way, ain't you?

C. J.: Yes, sah!

WATERS: Well, they use ta play over at the Bandana Club outside Camp J. J. Reilly.

C. J.: I played there once!

WATERS (*smiling*): Ain't that somethin'? I'd go over there from time to time—people use ta come from everywhere! (*To* WILKIE) Place was always dark, Wilkie—smoky. Folks would be dancin'—sweatin'— guitar pickers be strummin', shoutin'—it would be wild in there sometimes. Reminded me of a place I use ta go in France durin' the First War—the women, the whiskey—place called the Café Napoleon.

C. J.: You really like the blues, huh?

WATERS: No other kind of music—where'd you learn to play so good? I came by here yesterday and heard this pickin'—one of the men tol' me it was you.

C. J.: My daddy taught me, Sarge.

WATERS: You play pretty good, boy. Wilkie, wasn' that good?

WILKIE: Yes indeed, Sarge.

WILKIE (*to* DAVENPORT): I mostly agreed with the Sarge, sir. He was a good man. Good to his men. Talked about his wife and kids all the time—(WATERS *starts down from the limbo area, as the lights around* C. J. *fade out.* WATERS *pulls a pipe from his pocket, lights it as he moves to the edge of the* CAPTAIN's *office, and sits on the edge of the platform supporting it. He puffs a few times.* WILKIE's *talk is continuous.*) Use ta write home every day. I don't see why nobody would want to kill the Sarge, sir.

WATERS (*smiling*): Wilkie? (WILKIE *rises and walks into the blue-gray light and the scene with* WATERS. DAVENPORT *will watch.*) You know what I'ma get that boy of mine for his birthday? One of them Schwinn bikes. He'll be twelve—time flies, don't it? Let me show you something?

WILKIE (*to* DAVENPORT): He was always pullin' out snapshots, sir.

(WATERS *hands* WILKIE *a snapshot.*)

WATERS: My wife let a neighbor take this a couple weeks ago—ain't he growin' fast?

WILKIE: He's over your wife's shoulder! (*Hands it back*—WATERS *looks at the photo.*)

WATERS: I hope this kid never has to be a soldier.

WILKIE: It was good enough for you.

WATERS: I couldn't do any better—and this army was the closest I figured the white man would let me get to any kind of authority. No, the army ain't for this boy. When this war's over, things are going to change, Wilkie—and I want him to be ready for it—my daughter, too! I'm sendin' bot' of 'em to some big white college—let 'em rub elbows with the whites, learn the white man's language—how he does things. Otherwise, we'll be left behind—you can see it in the army. White man runnin' rings around us.

WILKIE: A lot of us didn't get the chance or the schoolin' the white folks got.

WATERS: That ain't no excuse, Wilkie. Most niggahs just don't care—tomorrow don't mean nothin' to 'em. My daddy shoveled coal from the back of a wagon all his life. He couldn't read or write, but he saw to it we did! Not havin' ain't no excuse for not gettin'.

WILKIE: Can't get pee from a rock, Sarge.

WATERS (*rising abruptly*): You just like the rest of 'em, Wilkie—I thought bustin' you would teach you something—we got to challenge this man in his arena—use his weapons, don't you know that? We need lawyers, doctors—generals—senators! Stop thinkin' like a niggah!

WILKIE: All I said—

WATERS: Is the equipment ready for tomorrow's game?

WILKIE: Yeah.

WATERS: Good. You can go now, Wilkie. (WILKIE *is stunned.*) That's an order!

(WILKIE *turns toward* DAVENPORT. *In the background, the humming of* C. J. *rises a bit as the light around* WATERS *fades out.*)

WILKIE: He could be two people sometimes, sir. Warm one minute—ice the next.

DAVENPORT: How did you feel about him?

WILKIE: Overall—I guess he was all right. You could always borrow a ten-spot off him if you needed it.

DAVENPORT: Did you see the Sergeant any time immediately preceding his death?

WILKIE: I don't know how much before it was, but a couple of us had been over the N.C.O. club that night and Sarge had been juicin' pretty heavy.

DAVENPORT: Did Waters drink a lot?

WILKIE: No more than most—(*Pause.*) Could I ask you a question, sir? (DAVENPORT *nods.*) Is it true, when they found Sarge all his stripes and insignia were still on his uniform?

DAVENPORT: I don't recall it being mentioned in my preliminary report. Why?

WILKIE: If that's the way they found him, something's wrong, ain't it, sir? Them Klan boys don't like to see us in these uniforms. They usually take the stripes and stuff off, before they lynch us.

(DAVENPORT *is quiet, thoughtful for a moment.*)

DAVENPORT: Thank you, Private—I might want to call you again, but for now you're excused.

(WILKIE *rises.*)

WILKIE: Yes, sir! (*Sudden mood swing, hesitant*) Sir?

DAVENPORT: Yes?

WILKIE: Can you do anything about allotment checks? My wife didn' get hers last month.

DAVENPORT: There's nothing I can do directly—did you see the finance officer? (WILKIE *nods.*) Well—I'll—I'll mention it to Captain Taylor.

WILKIE: Thank you, sir. You want me to send the next man in?

(DAVENPORT *nods.* WILKIE *salutes, does an about-face, and exits.* DAVENPORT *returns the salute, then leans back in his chair thoughtfully. In the background, the humming of* C. J. *rises again as the next man,* PFC MELVIN PETERSON, *enters. Dressed in fatigues, he is the model soldier. He walks quickly to the table, stands at attention, and salutes. The humming fades out as* DAVENPORT *returns the salute.*)

PETERSON: Private First Class Melvin Peterson reporting as ordered, sir!

DAVENPORT: Sit down, Private. (PETERSON *sits.*) Do you know why I'm here?

PETERSON: Yes, sir.

DAVENPORT: Fine. Now, everything you tell me is confidential, so I want you to speak as freely as possible. (PETERSON *nods.*) Where are you from?

PETERSON: Hollywood, California—by way of Alabama, sir. I enlisted in '42—thought we'd get a chance to fight.

DAVENPORT (*ignoring the comment*): Did you know Sergeant Waters well?

PETERSON: No, sir. He was already with the company when I got assigned here. And us common G.I.'s don't mix well with N.C.O.'s.

DAVENPORT: Were you on the baseball team?

PETERSON: Yes, sir—I played shortstop.

DAVENPORT: Did you like the Sergeant?

PETERSON: No, sir.

(*Before* DAVENPORT *can speak,* ELLIS *enters.*)

ELLIS: Beg your pardon, sir. Captain Taylor would like to see you in his office at once.

DAVENPORT: Did he say why?

ELLIS: No, sir—just that you should report to him immediately.

DAVENPORT (*annoyed*): Tell the men to stick around. When I finish with the Captain, I'll be back.

ELLIS: Yes, sir! (*He exits.*)

DAVENPORT (*to* PETERSON): Feel like walking, Private? We can continue this on the way. (*Begins to put his things in his briefcase*) Why didn't you like the Sergeant?

(DAVENPORT *and* PETERSON *start out as the light begins to fade in the barracks. They go through doorway, exit, and reenter the stage in full view.*)

PETERSON: It goes back to the team, sir. I got here in—baseball season had started, so it had to be June—June of last year. The team had won maybe nine—ten games in a row, there was a rumor that they would even get a chance to play the Yankees in exhibition. So when I got assigned to a team like that, sir—I mean, I felt good. Anyway, ole Stone-ass—

DAVENPORT: Stone-ass?

PETERSON: I'm the only one called him that—Sergeant Waters, sir.

(*As the two of them pass in front of the barracks area, the light begins to rise very slowly, but it is the blue-gray light of the past. The chairs and table are gone, and the room looks different.*)

DAVENPORT: Respect his rank, with me, Private.

PETERSON: I didn't mean no offense, sir. (*Slight pause.*) Well, the Sergeant and that brownnosin' Wilkie? They ran the team—and like it was a chain gang, sir. A chain gang!

(*The two men exit the stage. As they do,* C. J. MEMPHIS, HENSON, COBB, *and* SMALLS *enter in their baseball uniforms. T-shirts with "Fort Neal" stamped on the fronts, and numbers on the back, and baseball caps.*)

They are carrying equipment—bats, gloves. c. j. *is carrying his guitar.* smalls *enters tossing a baseball into the air and catching it. They almost all enter at once, with the exuberance of young men. Their talk is locker-room loud, and filled with bursts of laughter.*)

HENSON: You see the look on that umpire's face when C. J. hit that home run? I thought he was gonna die on the spot, he turned so pale!

(*They move to their respective bunks.*)

SMALLS: Serves the fat bastard right! Some of them pitches he called strikes were well ova' my head!

(c. j. *strums his guitar.* COBB *begins to brush off his boots.*)

COBB: C. J.? Who was that fine, river-hip thing you was talkin' to, homey?

(c. j. *shrugs and smiles.*)

HENSON: Speakin' of women, I got to write my Lady a letter. (*He begins to dig for his writing things.*)
COBB: She looked mighty good to me, C. J.
SMALLS (*overlapping*): Y'all hear Henson? Henson, you ain't had a woman since a woman had you!

(HENSON *makes an obscene gesture.*)

c. j. (*overlapping* SMALLS): Now, all she did was ask me for my autograph.
COBB: Look like she was askin' you fo' mor'n that. (*To* SMALLS) You see him, Smalls? Leanin' against the fence, all in the woman's face, breathin' heavy—
HENSON: If Smalls couldn't see enough to catch a ground ball right in his glove, how the hell could he see C. J. ova' by the fence?
SMALLS: That ball got caught in the sun!
HENSON: On the ground?
COBB (*at once*): We beat 'em nine to one! Y'all be quiet, I'm askin' this man 'bout a woman he was with had tits like two helmets!
c. j.: If I had'a give that gal what she asked fo'—she'da give me somethin' I didn' want! Them V-gals git you a bad case a' clap. 'Sides, she wasn' but sixteen.
SMALLS: You shoulda introduced her to Henson—sixteen's about his speed.

(HENSON *makes a farting sound in retaliation.*)

c. j.: Aroun' home? There's a fella folks use ta call, Lil' Jimmy One Leg—on account of his thing was so big? Two years ago—ole young pretty thing laid clap on Jimmy so bad, he los' the one good leg he had! Now folks jes' call him Little!

(*Laughter.*)

c. j.: That young thing talkin' to me ain' look so clean.

HENSON: Dirty or clean, she had them white boys lookin'.

COBB: Eyes popin' out they sockets, wasn' they? Remind me of that pitcher las' week! The one from 35th Ordnance? The one everybody claimed was so good? Afta' twelve straight hits, he looked the same way!

(PETERSON *enters, carrying two baseball bats.*)

SMALLS: It might be funny ta ya'll, but when me and Pete had duty in the Ordnance mess hall, that same white pitcher was the first one started the name-callin'—

HENSON: Forget them dudes in Ordnance—lissen to this! (HENSON *begins to read from a short letter.*) "Dear, Louis"—y'all hear that? The name is Louis—

COBB: Read the damn letter!

HENSON (*makes obscene gesture*): "Dear, Louis. You and the boys keep up the good work. All of us here at home are praying for you and inspired in this great cause by you. We know the Nazis and the Japs can't be stopped unless we all work together, so tell your buddies to press forward and win this war. All our hopes for the future go with you, Louis. Love Mattie." I think I'm in love with the sepia Winston Churchill—what kinda' letter do you write a nut like this?

COBB: Send her a round of ammunition and a bayonet, *Louis!*

(HENSON *waves disdainfully.*)

PETERSON: Y'all oughta listen to what Smalls said. Every time we beat them at baseball, they get back at us every way they can.

COBB: It's worth it to me just to wipe those superior smiles off they faces.

PETERSON: I don't know—seems like it makes it that much harder for us.

c. j.: They tell me, coupla them big-time Negroes is on the verge a' gittin' all of us togetha'—colored and white—say they want one army.

PETERSON: Forget that, C. J.! White folks'll neva' integrate no army!

c. j. (*strums*): If they do—I'ma be ready for 'em! (*Sings*) Well, I got me a bright red zoot suit / And a pair a' patent-leatha' shoes / And my woman she sittin' waitin' / Fo' the day we hea' the news! Lawd, lawd, lawd, lawd, / Lawd, lawd, lawd, lawd!

(SERGEANT WATERS, *followed by* WILKIE, *enters, immediately crossing to the center of the barracks, his strident voice abruptly cutting off* C. J.'s *singing and playing.*)

WATERS: Listen up! (*To* C. J.) We don't need that guitar playin'-sittin'-round-the-shack music today, C. J.! (*Smiles*) I want all you men out of those baseball uniforms and into work clothes! You will all report to me at 1300 hours in front of the Officers Club. We've got a work detail. We're painting the lobby of the club.

(*Collective groan.*)

SMALLS: The officers can't paint their own club?

COBB: Hell no, Smalls! Let the great-colored-cleanup company do it! Our motto is: Anything you don't want to do, the colored troops will do for you!

HENSON (*like a cheer*): Anything you don't want to do, the colored troops will do for you! (*He starts to lead the others.*)

OTHERS: Anything you don't—

WATERS: That's enough!

(*The men are instantly silent.*)

HENSON: When do we get a rest? We just played nine innings of baseball, Sarge!

SMALLS: We can't go in the place, why the hell should we paint it?

COBB: Amen, brother!

(*There is a moment of quiet before* WATERS *speaks.*)

WATERS: Let me tell you fancy-assed ball-playin' Negroes somethin'! The *reasons* for any orders given by a superior officer is none of y'all's business! You obey them! This country is at war, and you niggahs are soldiers—nothin' else! So baseball teams—win or lose—get no special privileges! They need to work some of you niggahs till your legs fall off! (*Intense*) And something else—from now on, when I tell you to do something, I want it done—is that clear? (*The men are quiet.*) Now, Wilkie's gonna' take all them funky shirts you got on over to the laundry. I could smell you suckers before I hit the field!

PETERSON: What kinda colored man are you?

WATERS: I'm a soldier, Peterson! First, last, and always! I'm the kinda colored man that don't like lazy, shiftless Negroes!

PETERSON: You ain't got to come in here and call us names!

WATERS: The Nazis call you *schvatza!* You gonna tell them they hurt your little feelings?

C. J.: Don't look like to me we could do too much to them Nazis wit' paint brushes, Sarge.

(*The men laugh. The moment is gone, and though* WATERS *is angry, his tone becomes overly solicitous, smiling.*)

WATERS: You tryin' to mock me, C. J.?

C. J.: No, sah, Sarge.

WATERS: Good, because whatever an ignorant, low-class geechy like you has to say isn't worth paying attention to, is it? (*Pause.*) Is it?

C. J.: I reckon not, Sarge.

PETERSON: You' a creep, Waters!

WATERS: Boy, you are something—ain't been in the company a month, Wilkie, and already everybody's champion!

C. J. (*interjecting*): Sarge was just jokin', Pete—he don't mean no harm!

PETERSON: He does! We take enough from the white boys!

WATERS: Yes, you do—and if it wasn' for you Southern niggahs, yessahin', bowin' and scrapin', scratchin' your heads, white folks wouldn' think we were all fools!

PETERSON: Where you from, England?

(*Men snicker.*)

HENSON (*at once*): Peterson!

WATERS (*immediately*): You got somethin' to say, Henson?

HENSON: Nothin', Sarge.

(HENSON *shakes his head as* WATERS *turns back to* PETERSON.)

WATERS: Peterson, you got a real comic streak in you. Wilkie, looks like we got us a wiseass Alabama boy here! (*He moves toward* PETERSON.) Yes, sir—(*He snatches* PETERSON *in the collar.*) Don't get smart, niggah!

PETERSON (*yanks away*): Get your fuckin' hands off me!

WATERS (*smiles, leans forward*): You wanna hit ole Sergeant Waters, boy? (*Whispers*) Come on! Please! Come on, niggah!

(CAPTAIN TAYLOR *enters the barracks quite suddenly, unaware of what is going on.*)

HENSON: Tenn-hut!

(*All the men snap to.*)

TAYLOR: At ease! (*He moves toward* WATERS, *feeling the tension.*) What's going on here, Sergeant?

WATERS: Nothin', sir—I was going over the *Manual of Arms*. Is there something in particular you wanted, sir? Something I can do?

TAYLOR (*relaxing somewhat*): Nothing—(*To the men*) Men, I congratulate you on the game you won today. We've only got seven more to play, and if we win them, we'll be the first team in Fort Neal history to play the Yanks in exhibition. Everyone in the regiment is counting on you. In times like these, morale is important—and winning can help a lot of things. (*Pause.*) Sergeant, as far as I'm concerned, they've got the rest of the day off.

(*The men are pleased.*)

WATERS: Begging your pardon, sir, but these men need all the work they can get. They don't need time off—our fellas aren't getting time off in North Africa—besides, we've got orders to report to the Officers Club for a paint detail at 1300 hours.

TAYLOR: Who issued that order?

WATERS: Major Harris, sir.

TAYLOR: I'll speak to the Major.

WATERS: Sir, I don't think it's such a good idea to get a colored N.C.O. mixed up in the middle of you officers, sir.

TAYLOR: I said, I'd speak to him, Sergeant.

WATERS: Yes, sir!

TAYLOR: I respect the men's duty to service, but they need time off.

WATERS: Yes, sir.

(*Pause.*)

TAYLOR: You men played a great game of baseball out there today—that catch you made in center field, Memphis—how the hell'd you get up so high?

C. J. (*shrugs, smiles*): They say I got "Bird" in mah blood, sir.

(TAYLOR *is startled by the statement, his smile is an uncomfortable one.* WATERS *is standing on "eggs."*)

TAYLOR: American eagle, I hope. (*Laughs a little*)

C. J.: No, sah, crow—(WATERS *starts to move, but* C. J. *stops him by continuing. Several of the men are beginning to get uncomfortable.*) Man tol' my daddy the day I was born, the shadow of a crow's wings—

TAYLOR (*cutting him off*): Fine—men, I'll say it again—you played superbly. (*Turns to* WATERS) Sergeant. (*He starts out abruptly.*)

WATERS: Tenn-hut!

(WATERS *salutes as the men snap to.*)

TAYLOR (*exiting*): As you were.

(TAYLOR *salutes as he goes. There is an instant of quiet. The men relax a little, but their focus is* C. J.)

WATERS (*laughing*): Ain't these geechies somethin'? How long a story was you gonna tell the man, C. J.? My God! (*The men join him, but as he turns toward* PETERSON, *he stiffens.*) Peterson! Oh, I didn't forget you, boy. (*The room quiets.*) It's time to teach you a lesson!
PETERSON: Why don't you drop dead, Sarge?
WATERS: Nooo! I'ma drop you, boy! Out behind the barracks—Wilkie, you go out and make sure it's all set up.
WILKIE: You want all the N.C.O.'s?

(WATERS *nods.* WILKIE *goes out smiling.*)

WATERS: I'm going outside and wait for you, geechy! And when you come out, I'm gonna whip your black Southern ass—let the whole company watch it, too! (*Points*) You need to learn respect, boy—how to talk to your betters. (*Starts toward the door*) Fight hard, hea'? I'ma try to bust your fuckin' head open—the rest of you get those goddamn shirts off like I said! (*He exits.*)

(*The barracks is quiet for a moment.*)

COBB: You gonna fight him?
HENSON (*overlapping*): I tried to warn you!
PETERSON: You ain't do nothin'!
SMALLS: He'll fight you dirty, Pete—don't do it!

(PETERSON *goes to his bunk and throws his cap off angrily.*)

COBB: You don't want to do it?
PETERSON: You wanna fight in my place, Cobb? (*He sits.*) Shit!

(*Slight pause.* HENSON *pulls off his shirt.*)

C. J.: I got some Farmers Dust—jes' a pinch'll make you strong as a bull—they say it comes from the city of Zar. (*Removes a pouch from his neck*) I seen a man use this stuff and pull a mule outta a sinkhole by hisself!
PETERSON: Get the hell outta here with that backwater crap—can't you speak up for yourself—let that bastard treat you like a dog!

C. J.: 'Long as his han's ain't on me—he ain't done me no harm, Pete. Callin' names ain't nothin', I know what I is. (*Softens*) Sarge ain't so bad—been good to me.

PETERSON: The man despises you!

C. J.: Sarge? You wrong, Pete—plus I feel kinda sorry for him myself. Any man ain't sure where he belongs must be in a whole lotta pain.

PETERSON: Don't y'all care?

HENSON: Don't nobody like it, Pete—but when you here a little longer—I mean, what can you do? This hea's the army and Sarge got all the stripes.

(PETERSON *rises, disgusted, and starts out.* SMALLS *moves at once.*)

SMALLS: Peterson, look, if you want me to, I'll get the Captain. You don't have to go out there and get your head beat in!

PETERSON: Somebody's got to fight him. (*He exits.*)

(*There is quiet as* SMALLS *walks back to his bunk.*)

C. J. (*singing*): It's a low / it's a low, low / lowdown dirty shame! It's a low / it's a low, low / lowdown dirty shame! Been playin' in this hea' army / an ain't even learned the game! Lawd, lawd, lawd, lawd—

(C. J. *begins to hum as the lights slowly fade out over the barracks. As they do, the lights come up simultaneously in the* CAPTAIN's *office. It is empty.* PETERSON *[in proper uniform] and* DAVENPORT *enter from offstage. They stop outside the* CAPTAIN's *office.*)

PETERSON: He beat me pretty bad that day, sir. The man was crazy!

DAVENPORT: Was the incident ever reported?

PETERSON: I never reported it, sir—I know I should have, but he left me alone after that. (*Shrugs*) I just played ball.

DAVENPORT: Did you see Waters the night he died?

PETERSON: No, sir—me and Smalls had guard duty.

DAVENPORT: Thank you, Private. That'll be all for now. (PETERSON *comes to attention.*) By the way, did the team ever get to play the Yankees?

PETERSON: No, sir. We lost the last game to a Sanitation Company.

(PETERSON *salutes.* DAVENPORT *returns salute.* PETERSON *does a crisp aboutface and exits. Slowly* DAVENPORT *starts into the* CAPTAIN's *office, surprised that no one is about.*)

DAVENPORT: Captain? (*There is no response. For a moment or two,* DAVENPORT *looks around. He is somewhat annoyed.*) Captain?

(DAVENPORT *starts out.* TAYLOR *enters. He crosses the room to his desk, where he sits.*)

TAYLOR: I asked you back here because I wanted you to see the request I've sent to Colonel Nivens to have your investigation terminated. (*He picks up several sheets of paper on his desk and hands them to* DAVENPORT, *who ignores them.*)

DAVENPORT: What?

TAYLOR: I wanted you to see that my reasons have nothing to do with you personally—my request will not hurt your army record in any way! (*Pause.*) There are other things to consider in this case!

DAVENPORT: Only the color of my skin, Captain.

TAYLOR (*sharply*): I want the people responsible for killing one of my men found and jailed, Davenport!

DAVENPORT: So do I!

TAYLOR: Then give this up! (*Rises*) Whites down here won't see their duty—or justice. They'll see *you!* And once they do, the law—due process—it all goes! And what is the point of continuing an investigation that can't possibly get at the truth?

DAVENPORT: Captain, my orders are very specific, so unless you want charges brought against you for interfering in a criminal investigation, stay the hell out of my way and leave me and my investigation alone!

TAYLOR (*almost sneering*): Don't take yourself too seriously, Davenport. You couldn't find an officer within five hundred miles who would convey charges to a court-martial board against me for something like that, and you know it!

DAVENPORT: Maybe not, but I'd—I'd see to it that your name, rank, and duty station got into the Negro press! Yeah, let a few colored newspapers call you a Negro-hater! Make you an embarrassment to the United States Army, Captain—like Major Albright at Fort Jefferson, and you'd never command troops again—or wear more than those captain's bars on that uniform, Mr. West Point!

TAYLOR: I'll never be more than a captain, Davenport, because I won't let them get away with dismissing things like Waters's death. I've been the commanding officer of three outfits! I raised hell in all of them, so threatening me won't change my request. Let the Negro press print that I don't like being made a fool of with phony investigations!

DAVENPORT (*studying* TAYLOR *for a moment*): There are two white officers involved in this, Captain—aren't there?

TAYLOR: I want them in jail—out of the army! And there is no way *you* can get them charged, or court-martialed, or put away! The white officers on this post won't let you—they won't let me!

DAVENPORT: Why wasn't there any mention of them in your preliminary report? I checked my own summary on the way over here, Captain—nothing! You think I'ma let you get away with this? (*There is a long silence.* TAYLOR *walks back to his desk as* DAVENPORT *watches him.* TAYLOR *sits.*) Why?

TAYLOR: I couldn't prove the men in question had anything to do with it.

DAVENPORT: Why didn't you report it?

TAYLOR: I was ordered not to. (*Pause.*) Nivens and Hines. The doctors took two .45 caliber bullets out of Waters—army issue. But remember what it was like that morning? If these men had thought a white officer killed Waters, there would have been a slaughter! (*Pause.*) Cobb reported the incident innocently the night before—then suddenly it was all over the Fort.

DAVENPORT: Who were they, Captain? I want their names!

TAYLOR: Byrd and Wilcox. Byrd's in Ordnance—Wilcox's with the 12th Hospital Group. I was Captain of the Guard the night Waters was killed. About 2100 hours, Cobb came into my office and told me he'd just seen Waters and two white officers fighting outside the colored N.C.O. club. I called *your* office, and when I couldn't get two M.P.'s, I started over myself to break it up. When I got there—no Waters, no officers. I checked the officers' billet and found Byrd and Wilcox in bed. Several officers verified they'd come in around 2130. I then told Cobb to go back to the barracks and forget it.

DAVENPORT: What made you do that?

TAYLOR: At the time there was no reason to believe anything was wrong! Waters wasn't found until the following morning. I told the Colonel what had happened the previous night, and about the doctor's report, and I was told, since the situation at the Fort was potentially dangerous, to keep my mouth shut until it blew over. He agreed to let me question Byrd and Wilcox, but I've asked him for a follow-up investigation every day since it happened. (*Slight pause.*) When I saw you, I exploded—it was like he was laughing at me.

DAVENPORT: Then you never believed the Klan was involved?

TAYLOR: No. Now, can you see why this thing needs—someone else?

DAVENPORT: What did they tell you, Captain? Byrd and Wilcox?

TAYLOR: They're not going to let you charge those two men!

DAVENPORT (*snaps*): Tell me what they told you!

(TAYLOR *is quiet for a moment. At this time, on center stage in limbo,* SERGEANT WATERS *is staggering. He is dressed as we first saw him. Behind him a blinking light reads: 221st N.C.O. Club. As he staggers toward the stairs leading to center stage, two white officers,* LIEUTENANT BYRD, *a spit-and-polish soldier in his twenties, and* CAPTAIN WILCOX, *a medical officer, walk onstage. Both are in full combat gear—rifles, pistol belts, packs—and both are tired.* TAYLOR *looks out as if he can see them.*)

TAYLOR: They were coming off bivouac.

(*The two men see* WATERS. *In the background is the faint hum of* C. J.*'s music.*)

TAYLOR: They saw him outside the club.

(*He rises, as* WATERS *sees* BYRD *and* WILCOX, *and smiles.*)

WATERS: Well, if it ain't the white boys!

(WATERS *straightens and begins to march in a mock circle and then down in their direction. He is mumbling, barely audibly: One, two, three, four! Hup, hup, three, four! Hup, hup, three, four!"* BYRD*'s speech overlaps* WATER*'s.*)

BYRD: And it wasn't like we were looking for trouble, Captain—were we, Wilcox?

(WILCOX *shakes his head no, but he is astonished by* WATER*'s behavior and stares at him, disbelieving.*)

WATERS: White boys! All starched and stiff! Wanted everybody to learn all that symphony shit! That's what you were saying in France—and you know, I listened to you? Am I all right now? Am I?

BYRD: Boy, you'd better straighten up and salute when you see an officer, or you'll find yourself without those stripes! (*To* WILCOX *as* WATERS *nears them, smiling the "coon" smile and doing a juba*) Will you look at this niggah? (*Loud*) Come to attention, Sergeant! That's an order!

WATERS: No, sah! I ain't straightenin' up for y'all no more! I ain't doin' nothin' white folks say do, no more! (*Sudden change of mood, smiles, sings*) No more, no more / no more, no more, noooo! No more, no more / no more, no more, noooooo!

(BYRD *faces* TAYLOR *as* WATERS *continues to sing.*)

BYRD (*overlapping*): Sir, I thought the man was crazy!
TAYLOR: And what did you think, Wilcox?

(BYRD *moves toward* WATERS, *and* WATERS, *still singing low, drunk and staggering, moves back and begins to circle* BYRD, *stalk him, shaking his head no as he sings.* WILCOX *watches apprehensively.*)

WILCOX (*at once*): He did appear to be intoxicated, sir—out of his mind almost! (*He turns to* BYRD.) Byrd, listen—

(BYRD *ignores him.*)

DAVENPORT (*suddenly*): Did they see anyone else in the area?

TAYLOR: No. (*To* BYRD) I asked them what they did next.

BYRD: I told that niggah to shut up!

WATERS (*sharply*): No! (*Change of mood.*) Followin' behind y'all? Look what it's done to me!—I hate myself!

BYRD: Don't blame us, boy! God made you black, not me!

WATERS (*smiles*): My daddy use ta say—

WILCOX: Sergeant, get hold of yourself!

WATERS (*points*): Listen!

(BYRD *steps toward him and shoves him in the face.*)

BYRD: I gave you an order, niggah!

(WILCOX *grabs* BYRD, *and stops him from advancing, as* WATERS *begins to cry.*)

WATERS: My daddy said, "Don't talk like dis'—talk like that!" "Don't live hea'—live there!" (*To them*) I've killed for you! (*To himself; incredulous*) And nothin' changed!

(BYRD *pulls free of* WILCOX *and charges* WATERS.)

BYRD: He needs to be taught a lesson!

(*He shoves* WATERS *onto the ground, where he begins to beat and kick the man, until he is forcibly restrained by* WILCOX. WATERS *moans.*)

WILCOX: Let him be! You'll kill the man! He's sick—leave him alone!

(BYRD *pulls away; he is flush.* WATERS *tries to get up.*)

WATERS: Nothin' changed—see? And I've tried everything! Everything!

BYRD: I'm gonna bust his black ass to buck private!—I should blow his coward's head off! (*Shouts*) There are good men killing for you, niggah! Gettin' their guts all blown to hell for you!

(WILCOX *pulls him away. He pulls* BYRD *offstage as the light around* WATERS *and that section of the stage begins to fade out. As it does, a trace of* C. J.'s *music is left on the air.* WATERS *is on his knees, groveling, as the lights go out around him.*)

DAVENPORT: Did they shove Waters again?

TAYLOR: No. But Byrd's got a history of scrapes with Negroes. They told me they left Waters at 2110—and everyone in the officers' billet verifies they were both in by 2130. And neither man left—Byrd had duty the next morning, and Wilcox was scheduled at the hospital at 0500 hours—both men reported for duty.

DAVENPORT: I don't believe it.

TAYLOR: I couldn't shake their stories—

DAVENPORT: That's nothing more than officers lying to protect two of their own and you know it! I'm going to arrest and charge both of them, Captain—and you may consider yourself confined to your quarters pending my charges against *you!*

TAYLOR: What charges?

DAVENPORT: It was *your* duty to go over Nivens's head if you had to!

TAYLOR: Will you arrest Colonel Nivens too, Davenport? Because he's part of their alibi—he was there when they came in—played poker—from 2100 to 0300 hours the following morning, the Colonel—your Major Hines, "Shack" Callahan—Major Callahan, and Jed Harris—and Jed wouldn't lie for either of them!

DAVENPORT: They're all lying!

TAYLOR: Prove it, hotshot—I told you all I know, now you go out and prove it!

DAVENPORT: I will, Captain! You can bet your sweet ass on that! I will!

(DAVENPORT *starts out as the lights begin to fade, and* TAYLOR *looks after him and shakes his head. In the background, the sound of "Don't Sit Under the Apple Tree" comes up again and continues to play as the lights fade to black.*)

ACT TWO

SCENE

As before.

Light rises slowly over limbo. We hear a snippet of "Don't Sit Under the Apple Tree" as DAVENPORT, *seated on the edge of a bunk, finishes dressing. He is putting on a shirt, tie, bars, etc., and addresses the audience as he does so.*

DAVENPORT: During May of '44, the Allies were making final preparations for the invasion of Europe. Invasion! Even the sound of it made Negroes think we'd be in it—be swept into Europe in the waves of men and equipment—I know I felt it. (*Thoughtfully*) We hadn't seen a lot of action except in North Africa—or Sicily. But the rumor in orderly rooms that spring was, pretty soon most of us would be in combat—somebody said Ike wanted to find out if the colored boys could fight—shiiit, we'd been fighting all along—right here, in these small Southern towns—(*Intense*) I don't have the authority to arrest a white *private* without a white officer present! (*Slight pause.*) Then I get a case like this? There was no way I wouldn't see this through to its end. (*Smiles*) And after my first twenty-four hours, I wasn't doing too badly. I had two prime suspects—a motive, and opportunity! (*Pause.*) I went to Colonel Nivens and convinced him that word of Byrd's and Wilcox's involvement couldn't be kept secret any longer. However, before anyone in the press could accuse him of complicity—I would silence all suspicions by pursuing the investigation openly—on his orders—(*Mimics himself*) "Yes, sir, Colonel, you can even send along a white officer—not Captain Taylor, though—I think he's a little too close to the case, sir." Colonel Nivens gave me permission to question Byrd and Wilcox, and having succeeded *sooo* easily, I decided to spend some time finding out more about Waters and Memphis. Somehow the real drama seemed to be there, and my curiosity wouldn't allow me to ignore it.

(DAVENPORT *is dressed and ready to go as a spotlight in the barracks area opens on* PRIVATE HENSON. *He is seated on a footlocker. He rises as* DAVENPORT *descends to the stage. He will not enter the barracks, but will almost handle this like a courtroom interrogation. He returns* HENSON'S *salute.*)

DAVENPORT: Sit down, Private. Your name is Louis Henson, is that right?
HENSON: Yes, sir.

(HENSON *sits, as* DAVENPORT *paces.*)

DAVENPORT: Tell me what you know about Sergeant Waters and C. J. Memphis. (HENSON *looks at him strangely.*) Is there something wrong?
HENSON: No, sir—I was just surprised you knew about it.
DAVENPORT: Why?
HENSON: You're an officer.
DAVENPORT (*quickly*): And?
HENSON (*hesitantly*): Well—officers are up here, sir—and us enlisted

men—down here. (*Slight pause.*) C. J. and Waters—that was just between enlisted men, sir. But I guess ain't nothin' a secret around colored folks—not that it was a secret. (*Shrugs*) There ain't that much to tell—sir. Sarge ain't like C. J. When I got to the company in May of las' year, the first person I saw Sarge chew out was C. J.! (*He is quiet.*)

DAVENPORT: Go on.

(HENSON's *expression is pained.*)

HENSON: Is that an order, sir?

DAVENPORT: Does it have to be?

HENSON: I don't like tattletalin', sir—an' I don't mean no offense, but I ain't crazy 'bout talkin' to officers—colored or white.

DAVENPORT: It's an order, Henson!

HENSON (*nods*): C. J. wasn' movin' fast enough for *him*. Said C. J. didn' have enough *fire-under-his-behind* out on the field.

DAVENPORT: You were on the team?

HENSON: Pitcher. (*Pause.* DAVENPORT *urges with a look.*) He jus' *stayed* on C. J. all the time—every little thing, it seemed like to me—then the shootin' went down, and C. J. caught all the hell.

DAVENPORT: What shooting?

HENSON: The shootin' at Williams's Golden Palace, sir—here, las' year!—way before you got here. Toward the end of baseball season. (DAVENPORT *nods his recognition.*) The night it happened, a whole lotta gunshots went off near the barracks. I had gotten drunk over at the enlisted men's club, so when I got to the barracks I just sat down in a stupor!

(*Suddenly shots are heard in the distance and grow ever closer as the eerie blue-gray light rises in the barracks over the sleeping figures of men in their bunks.* HENSON *is seated, staring at the ground. He looks up once as the gunshots go off, and as he does, someone—we cannot be sure who—sneaks into the barracks as the men begin to shift and awaken. This person puts something under* C. J.'s *bed and rushes out.* HENSON *watches—surprised at first, rising, then disbelieving. He shakes his head, then sits back down as several men wake up.* DAVENPORT *recedes to one side of the barracks, watching.*)

COBB: What the hell's goin' on? Don't they know a man needs his sleep? (*He is quickly back to sleep.*)

SMALLS (*simultaneously*): Huh? Who is it? (*Looks around, then falls back to sleep*)

DAVENPORT: Are you sure you saw someone?

HENSON: Well—I saw something, sir.

DAVENPORT: What did you do?

(*The shooting suddenly stops and the men settle down.*)

HENSON: I sat, sir—I was juiced—(*Shrugs*) The gunshots weren't any of my business—plus I wasn't sure what I had seen in the first place, then out of nowhere Sergeant Waters, he came in.

(WATERS *enters the barracks suddenly, followed by* WILKIE. HENSON *stands immediately, staggering a bit.*)

WATERS: All right, all right! Everybody up! Wake them. Wilkie!

WILKIE (*moving around the bunks, shaking the men*): Let's go! Up! Let's go, you guys!

(COBB *shoves* WILKIE's *hand aside angrily as the others awaken slowly.*)

WATERS: Un-ass them bunks! Tenn-hut! (*Most of the men snap to.* SMALLS *is the last one, and* WATERS *moves menacingly toward him.*) There's been a shooting! One of ours bucked the line at Williams's pay phone and three soldiers are dead! Two colored and one white M.P. (*Pauses*) Now, the man who bucked the line, he killed the M.P., and the white boys started shootin' everybody—that's how our two got shot. And this lowdown niggah we lookin' for got chased down here—and was almost caught, 'til somebody in these barracks started shootin' at the men chasin' him. So, we got us a vicious, murderin' piece of black trash in here somewhere—and a few people who helped him. If any of you are in this, I want you to step forward. (*No one moves.*) All you baseball niggahs are innocent, huh? Wilkie, make the search. (PETERSON *turns around as* WILKIE *begins.*) Eyes front!

PETERSON: I don't want that creep in my stuff!

WATERS: You don't talk at attention!

(WILKIE *will search three bunks, top and bottom, along with footlockers. Under* C. J.'s *bed he will find what he is looking for.*)

WATERS: I almost hope it is some of you geechies—get rid of you Southern niggahs! (*To* WILKIE) Anything yet?

WILKIE: Nawwww!

WATERS: Memphis, are you in this?

C. J.: No, sah, Sarge.

WATERS: How many of you were out tonight?

SMALLS: I was over at Williams's around seven—got me some Lucky Strikes—I didn't try to call home, though.

COBB: I was there, this mornin'!

WATERS: Didn't I say *tonight*—uncle?

WILKIE: Got somethin'!

> (WILKIE *is holding up a .45 caliber automatic pistol, army issue. Everyone's attention focuses on it. The men are surprised, puzzled.*)

WATERS: Where'd you find it?

> (WILKIE *points to* C. J., *who recoils at the idea.*)

C. J.: Naaaawww, man!

WATERS: C. J.? This yours?

C. J.: You know it ain't mine, Sarge!

WATERS: It's still warm—how come it's under your bunk?

C. J.: Anybody coulda' put it thea', Sarge!

WATERS: Who? Or maybe this .45 crawled in through an open window—looked around the whole room—passed Cobb's bunk, and decided to snuggle up under yours? Must be voodoo, right, boy? Or some of that Farmers Dust round that neck of yours, huh?

C. J.: That pistol ain't mine!

WATERS: Liar!

C. J.: No, Sarge—I hate guns! Make me feel bad jes' to see a gun!

WATERS: You're under arrest—Wilkie, escort this man to the stockade!

PETERSON (*stepping forward*): C. J. couldn't hurt a fly, Waters, you know that!

WATERS: I found a gun, soldier—now get out of the way!

PETERSON: Goddammit, Waters, you know it ain't him!

WATERS: How do I know?

HENSON: Right before you came in, I thought I saw somebody sneak in.

WATERS: You were drunk when you left the club—I saw you myself!

WILKIE: Besides, how you know it wasn't C. J.?

COBB: I was here all night. C. J. didn't go out.

> (WATERS *looks at them, intense.*)

WATERS: We got the right man. (*Points at* C. J., *impassioned*) You think he's innocent, don't you? C. J. Memphis, playin' cotton-picker singin' the blues, bowin' and scrapin'—smilin' in everybody's face—this man undermined us! You and me! The description of the man who did the shooting fits C. J.! (*To* HENSON) You saw C. J. sneak in here! (*Points*) Don't be fooled—that yassah boss is hidin' something—niggahs ain't like that today! This is 1913—he shot that white boy!

> (C. J. *is stunned, then suddenly the enormity of his predicament hits him, and he breaks free of* WILKIE *and hits* WATERS *in the chest. The blow*

knocks WATERS *down, and* C. J. *is immediately grabbed by the other men in the barracks.* COBB *goes to* WATERS *and helps him up slowly. The blow hurt* WATERS, *but he forces a smile at* C. J., *who has suddenly gone immobile, surprised by what he has done.*)

WATERS: What did you go and do now, boy? Hit a noncommissioned officer.
COBB: Sarge, he didn't mean it!
WATERS: Shut up! (*Straightens*) Take him out, Wilkie.

(WILKIE *grabs* C. J. *by the arm and leads him out.* C. J. *goes calmly, almost passively.* WATERS *looks at all the men quietly for a moment, then walks out without saying a word. There is a momentary silence in the barracks.*)

SMALLS: Niggah like that can't have a mother.
HENSON: I know I saw something!
PETERSON: C. J. was sleepin' when I came in! It's Waters—can't y'all see that? I've seen him before—we had 'em in Alabama! White man gives them a little ass job as a servant—close to the big house, and when the boss ain't lookin', old copycat niggahs act like they the new owner! They take to soundin' like the boss—shoutin', orderin' people aroun'—and when it comes to you and me—they sell us to continue favor. They think the high-jailers like that. Arrestin' C. J.—that'll get Waters another stripe! Next it'll be you—or you. He can't look good unless he's standin' on you! Cobb tol' him C. J. was in all evening—Waters didn't even listen! Turning somebody in (*mimics*) "Look what I done, Captain Boss!" They let him in the army 'cause they know he'll do anything they tell him to—I've seen his kind of fool before. Someone's going to kill him.
SMALLS: I heard they killed a sergeant at Fort Robinson—recruit did it—
COBB: It'll just be our luck, Sarge'll come through the whole war without a scratch.
PETERSON: Maybe—but I'm goin' over to the stockade—tell the M.P.'s what I know—C. J. was here all evening. (*He starts dressing.*)
SMALLS: I'll go with you!
COBB: Me too, I guess.

(*They all begin to dress as the light fades slowly in the barracks area.* HENSON *rises and starts toward* DAVENPORT. *In the background,* C. J.'s *music comes up a bit.*)

DAVENPORT: Could the person you thought you saw have stayed in the barracks—did you actually see someone go out?

HENSON: Yes, sir!

DAVENPORT: Was Wilkie the only man out of his bunk that night?

HENSON: Guess so—he came in with Sarge.

DAVENPORT: And Peterson—he did most of the talking?

HENSON: As I recall. It's been a while ago—an' I was juiced!

DAVENPORT (*rising*): Ellis!

ELLIS (*appearing at the door*): Sir!

DAVENPORT: I want Private Wilkie and Pfc Peterson to report to me at once.

ELLIS: They're probably on work detail, sir.

DAVENPORT: Find them.

ELLIS: Yes, sir!

(ELLIS *exits quickly, and* DAVENPORT *lapses into a quiet thoughtfulness.*)

HENSON: Is there anything else?—Sir?

DAVENPORT (*vexed*): No! That'll be all—send in the next man.

(HENSON *comes to attention and salutes.* DAVENPORT *returns salute as* HENSON *exits through the barracks.* C. J.'s *music plays in background. There is a silence.* DAVENPORT *rises, mumbling something to himself.* COBB *appears suddenly at the doorway. He watches* DAVENPORT *for a moment.*)

COBB: Sir? (DAVENPORT *faces him*) Corporal Cobb reporting as ordered, sir. (*He salutes.*)

DAVENPORT: Have a seat, Corporal (COBB *crosses the room and sits.*) And let's get something straight from the beginning—I don't care whether you like officers or not—is that clear?

COBB (*looking at him strangely*): Sir?

(*Pause.* DAVENPORT *calms down somewhat.*)

DAVENPORT: I'm sorry—Did you know Sergeant Waters well?

COBB: As well as the next man, sir—I was already with the team when he took over. Me and C. J., we made the team the same time.

DAVENPORT: Were you close to C. J.?

COBB: Me and him were "homeys," sir! Both came from Mississippi. C. J. from Carmella—me, I'm from up 'roun' Jutlerville, what they call snake county. Plus, we both played for the Negro League before the war.

DAVENPORT: How did you feel about his arrest?

COBB: Terrible—C. J. didn't kill nobody, sir.

DAVENPORT: He struck Sergeant Waters—

COBB: Waters made him, sir! He called that boy things he had never heard of before—C. J. he was so confused he didn't know what else to do—(*Pause.*) An' when they put him in the stockade, he jus' seemed to go to pieces. (*Lowly in the background,* C. J.*'s music comes up.*) See, we both lived on farms—and even though C. J.'s daddy played music, C. J., he liked the wide-open spaces. (*Shakes his head*) That cell? It started closin' in on him right away. (*Blue-gray light rises in limbo, where* C. J. *is sitting on the edge of a bunk. A shadow of bars cuts across the space. His guitar is on the bunk beside him.*) I went to see him, the second day he was in there. He looked pale and ashy, sir—like something dead.

(C. J. *faces* COBB.)

C. J.: It's hard to breathe in these little spaces, Cobb—man wasn' made for this hea'—nothin' was! I don't think I'll eva' see a' animal in a cage agin' and not feel sorry for it. (*To himself*) I'd rather be on the chain gang.

(COBB *looks up at him.*)

COBB: Come on, homey! (*He rises, moves toward* C. J.)

C. J.: I don't think I'm comin' outta here, Cobb—feels like I'm goin' crazy. Can't walk in hea'—can't see the sun! I tried singin', Cobb, but nothin' won't come out. I sure don't wanna die in this jail!

COBB (*moving closer*): Ain't nobody gonna die, C. J.!

C. J.: Yesterday I broke a guitar string—lost my Dust! I got no protection—nothin' to keep the dog from tearin' at my bones!

COBB: Stop talkin' crazy!

(C. J. *is quiet for a moment. He starts forward. Slowly, in center stage,* WATERS *emerges. He faces the audience.*)

C. J.: You know, he come up hea' las' night? Sergeant Waters?

(WATERS *smiles, pulls out his pipe, lights it.*)

WATERS (*calmly*): You should learn never to hit sergeants, boy—man can get in a lot of trouble doin' that kinda thing durin' wartime—they talkin' 'bout givin' you five years—they call what you did mutiny in the navy. Mutiny, boy.

C. J.: That gun ain't mine!

WATERS: Oh, we know that, C. J.! (C. J. *is surprised.*) That gun belonged to the niggah did the shootin' over at Williams's place—me and Wilkie caught him hidin' in the Motor Pool, and he confessed his head off. You're in here for striking a superior officer, boy. And I got a whole barracks full of your friends to prove it! (*Smiles broadly, as* C. J. *shakes his head*)

DAVENPORT (*to* COBB, *at once*): Memphis wasn't charged with the shooting?

COBB: No, sir—

WATERS: Don't feel too bad, boy. It's not your fault entirely—it has to be this way. The First War, it didn't change much for us, boy—but this one—it's gonna change a lot of things. Them Nazis ain't all crazy—a whole lot of people just can't fit into where things seem to be goin'—like you, C. J. The black race can't afford you no more. There use ta be a time when we'd see somebody like you, singin', clownin'—yas-sah-bossin'—and we wouldn't do anything. (*Smiles*) Folks liked that—you were good—homey kinda' niggah—they needed somebody to mistreat—call a name, they paraded you, reminded them of the old days—corn bread bakin', greens and ham cookin'—Daddy out pickin' cotton, Grandmammy sit on the front porch smokin' a pipe. (*Slight pause.*) Not no more. The day of the geechy is gone, boy—the only thing that can move the race is power. It's all the white respects—and people like you just make us seem like fools. And we can't let nobody go on believin' we all like you! You bring us down—make people think the whole race is unfit! (*Quietly pleased*) I waited a long time for you, boy, but I gotcha! And I try to git rid of you wherever I go. I put two geechies in jail at Fort Campbell, Kentucky—three at Fort Huachuca. Now I got you—one less fool for the race to be ashamed of! (*Points*) And I'ma git that ole boy Cobb next! (*Light begins to fade around* WATERS.)

DAVENPORT (*at once*): You?

COBB: Yes, sir. (*Slight pause.*)

DAVENPORT: Go on.

C. J.: You imagin' anybody sayin' that? I know I'm not gittin' outta' hea', Cobb! (*Quiets*) You remember I tol' you 'bout a place I use ta go outside Carmella? When I was a little ole tiny thing? Place out behind O'Connell's Farm? Place would be stinkin' of plums, Cobb. Shaded—that ripe smell be weavin' through the cotton fields and clear on in ta town on a warm day. First time I had Evelyn? I had her unda' them plum trees. I wrote a song for her—(*Talks, sings*) My ginger-colored Momma—she had thighs the size of hams! (*Chuckles*) And when you spread them, Mommaaaa! / (*Talks*) You let me have my jelly roll and jam! (*Pause, mood swing.*) O'Connell, he had a dog—meanes' dog I eva' did see! An' the only way you could enjoy them plum trees was to outsmart that dog. Waters is like that ole dog, Cobb—you gotta run circles roun' ole Windy—that was his name. They say he tore a man's arm off once, and got to likin' it. So, you had to cheat that dog outta' bitin' you every time. Every time. (*Slowly the light begins to fade around* C. J.)

COBB: He didn't make sense, sir. I tried talkin' about the team—the war—ain't nothin' work—seem like he jes' got worse.

DAVENPORT: What happened to him?

COBB (*looking at him incredulously*): The next day—afta' the day I saw him? C. J., he hung hisself, sir! Suicide—jes' couldn't stand it. M.P.'s found him hung from the bars.

DAVENPORT (*after pause*): What happened after that?

COBB: We lost our last game—we jes' threw it—we did it for C. J.— Captain, he was mad 'cause we ain't git ta play the Yankees. Peterson was right on that one—somebody needed to protest that man!

DAVENPORT: What did Waters do?

COBB: Well, afta' we lost, the commanding officer, he broke up the team, and we all got reassigned to this Smoke Company. Waters, he started actin' funny, sir—stayed drunk—talked to hisself all the time.

DAVENPORT: Did you think you were next?

COBB: I ain't sure I eva' believed Waters said that, sir—C. J. had to be outta' his head or he wouldna' killed hisself—Sarge, he neva' came near me afta' C. J. died.

DAVENPORT: What time did you get back the night Waters was killed?

COBB: I'd say between 2120 and 9:30.

DAVENPORT: And you didn't go out again?

COBB: No, sir—me and Henson sat and listened to the radio till Abbott and Lou Costello went off, then I played checkers with Wilkie for 'notha' hour, then everybody went to bed. What C. J. said about Waters? It ain't botha' me, sir.

(DAVENPORT *is silent.*)

DAVENPORT: Who were the last ones in that night?

COBB: Smalls and Peterson—they had guard duty.

(TAYLOR *enters the barracks area and stops just inside the door when he sees* DAVENPORT *isn't quite finished.*)

DAVENPORT: Thank you, Corporal.

(COBB *rises at attention and salutes.* DAVENPORT *returns salute and* COBB *starts out. He nods to* TAYLOR, *who advances toward* DAVENPORT.)

TAYLOR (*smiling*): You surprise me, Davenport—I just left Colonel

Nivens. He's given you permission to question Byrd and Wilcox? (DAVENPORT *nods.*) How'd you manage that? You threatened him with an article in the *Chicago Defender,* I suppose.

DAVENPORT: I convinced the Colonel it was in his best interests to allow it.

TAYLOR: Really? Did he tell you I would assist you?

DAVENPORT: I told him I especially didn't want you.

TAYLOR: That's precisely why he sent me—he didn't want you to think you could get your way entirely—not with him. Then neither Byrd or Wilcox would submit to it without a white officer present. That's how it is. (*There is a rather long silence.*) But there's something else, Davenport. The Colonel began talking about the affidavits he and the others signed—and the discrepancies in their statements that night. (*Mimics*) He wants me with you because he doesn't want Byrd and Wilcox giving you the wrong impression—he never elaborated on what he meant by the wrong impression. I want to be there!

DAVENPORT: So you're not on *that* side anymore—you're on *my* side now, right?

TAYLOR (*bristling*): I want whoever killed my sergeant, Davenport!

DAVENPORT: Bullshit! Yesterday you were daring me to try! And today we're allies? Besides, you don't give that much of a damn about your men! I've been around you a full day and you haven't uttered a word that would tell me you had any more than a minor acquaintance with Waters! He managed your baseball team—was an N.C.O. in your company, and you haven't offered *any* opinion of the man as a soldier—sergeant—platoon leader! Who the hell was he?

TAYLOR: He was one of my men! On my roster—a man these bars make me responsible for! And no, I don't know a helluva lot about him—or a lot of their names or where they come from, but I'm still their commanding officer, and in a little while I may have to trust them with my life! And I want them to know they can trust me with theirs—here and now! (*Pause.*) I have Byrd and Wilcox in my office. (DAVENPORT *stares at him for a long moment, then rises and starts out toward center stage.*) Why didn't you tell Nivens that you'd placed me under arrest?

(DAVENPORT *stops.*)

DAVENPORT: I didn't find it necessary.

(*They stare at one another.* TAYLOR *is noticeably strained.*)

DAVENPORT (*starts away*): What do you know about C. J. Memphis?

(TAYLOR *follows*.)

TAYLOR (*shrugs*): He was a big man as I recall—more a boy than a man, though. Played the guitar sometimes at the Officers Club—there was something embarrassing about him. Committed suicide in the stockade. Pretty good center fielder—

(DAVENPORT *stops*.)

DAVENPORT: Did you investigate his arrest—the charges against him?

TAYLOR: He was charged with assaulting a noncommissioned officer—I questioned him—he didn't say much. He admitted he struck Waters—I started questioning several of the men in the platoon and he killed himself before I could finish—open-and-shut case.

DAVENPORT: I think Waters tricked C. J. into assaulting him.

TAYLOR: Waters wasn't that kind of a man! He admitted he might have provoked the boy—he accused him of that Golden Palace shooting—

(*Behind them, the* CAPTAIN's *office is lit. In two chairs facing* TAYLOR's *desk are* LIEUTENANT BYRD *and* CAPTAIN WILCOX, *both in dress uniform*.)

TAYLOR: Listen, Waters didn't have a fifth-grade education—he wasn't a schemer! And colored soldiers aren't devious like that.

DAVENPORT: What do you mean we aren't devious?

TAYLOR (*sharply*): You're not as devious—! (DAVENPORT *stares as* TAYLOR *waves disdainfully and starts into the office*.) Anyway, what has that to do with this? (*He is distracted by* BYRD *and* WILCOX *before* DAVENPORT *can answer.* TAYLOR *speaks as he moves to his desk*.) This is *Captain* Davenport—you've both been briefed by Colonel Nivens to give the Captain your full cooperation.

(DAVENPORT *puts on his glasses.* TAYLOR *notices and almost smiles*.)

BYRD (*to* DAVENPORT): They tell me you a lawyer, huh?

DAVENPORT: I am not here to answer your questions, Lieutenant. And I am Captain Davenport, is that clear?

BYRD (*to* TAYLOR): Captain, is he crazy?

TAYLOR: You got your orders.

BYRD: Sir, I vigorously protest as an officer—

TAYLOR (*cutting him off*): You answer him the way he wants you to, Byrd, or I'll have your ass in a sling so tight you won't be able to pee, soldier!

(BYRD *backs off slightly*.)

DAVENPORT: When did you last see Sergeant Waters?

BYRD: The night he was killed, but I didn' kill him—I should have blown his head off, the way he spoke to me and Captain Wilcox here.

DAVENPORT: How did he speak to you, Captain?

WILCOX: Well, he was very drunk—and he said a lot of things he shouldn't have. I told the Lieutenant here not to make the situation worse and he agreed, and we left the Sergeant on his knees, wallowing in self-pity. (*Shrugs*)

DAVENPORT: What exactly did he say?

WILCOX: Some pretty stupid things about us—I mean white people, sir.

(BYRD *reacts to the term* "*sir.*")

DAVENPORT: What kind of things?

BYRD (*annoyed*): He said he wasn't going to obey no white man's orders! And that me and Wilcox here were to blame for him being black, and not able to sleep or keep his food down! And I didn't even know the man! Never even spoke to him before that night!

DAVENPORT: Anything else?

WILCOX: Well—he said he'd killed somebody.

DAVENPORT: Did he call a name—or say who?

WILCOX: Not that I recall, sir.

(DAVENPORT *looks at* BYRD.)

BYRD: No—(*Sudden and sharp*) Look—the goddamn Negro was disrespectful! He wouldn't salute! Wouldn't come to attention! And where I come from, colored don't talk the way he spoke to us—not to white people they don't!

DAVENPORT: Is that the reason you killed him?

BYRD: I killed nobody! I said "where I come from," didn't I? You'd be dead yourself, where I come from! But I didn't kill the—the *Negro!*

DAVENPORT: But you hit him, didn't you?

BYRD: I knocked him down!

DAVENPORT (*quickening pace*): And when you went to look at him, he was dead, wasn't he?

BYRD: He was alive when we left!

DAVENPORT: You're a liar! You beat Waters up—you went back and you shot him!

BYRD: No! (*Rises*) But you better get outta my face before I kill you!

DAVENPORT (*standing firm*): Like you killed Waters?

BYRD: No! (*He almost raises a hand to* DAVENPORT.)

TAYLOR (*at once*): Soldier!

BYRD: He's trying to put it on me!

TAYLOR: Answer his questions, Lieutenant.

DAVENPORT: You were both coming off bivouac, right?

WILCOX: Yes.

DAVENPORT: So you both had weapons?

BYRD: So what? We didn't fire them!

DAVENPORT: Were the weapons turned in immediately?

WILCOX: Yes, sir—Colonel Nivens took our .45's to Major Hines. It was all kept quiet because the Colonel didn't want the colored boys to know that anyone white from the Fort was involved in any way—ballistics cleared them.

DAVENPORT: We can check.

BYRD: Go ahead.

TAYLOR: I don't believe it—why wasn't I told?

WILCOX: The weapons had cleared—and the Colonel felt if he involved you further, you'd take the matter to Washington and there'd be a scandal about colored and white soldiers—as it turned out, he thinks you went to Washington anyway. (*To* DAVENPORT) I'd like to say, Captain, that neither Lieutenant Byrd or myself had anything whatsoever to do with Sergeant Waters's death—I swear that as an officer and a gentleman. He was on the ground when we left him, but very much alive.

TAYLOR: Consider yourselves under arrest, *gentlemen!*

BYRD: On what charge?

TAYLOR: Murder! You think I believe that crap—

DAVENPORT: Let them go, Captain.

TAYLOR: You've got motive—a witness to their being at the scene—

DAVENPORT: Let them go! This is still my investigation—you two are dismissed!

(BYRD *rises quickly.* WILCOX *follows his lead.*)

WILCOX: Are we being charged, sir?

DAVENPORT: Not by me.

WILCOX: Thank you.

(WILCOX *comes to attention, joined by a reluctant* BYRD. *They both salute.* DAVENPORT *returns salute.*)

BYRD (to TAYLOR): I expected more from a white man, Captain.

TAYLOR: Get out of here, before I have you cashiered out of the army, Byrd!

(*Both men exit quietly, and for a moment* TAYLOR *and* DAVENPORT *are quiet.*)

TAYLOR: What the hell is the matter with you? You could have charged both of them—Byrd for insubordination—Wilcox, tampering with evidence.

DAVENPORT: Neither charge is murder—you think Wilcox would tell a story like that if he didn't have Hines and Nivens to back it up? (*Slightly tired*) They've got a report.

TAYLOR: So what do you do now?

DAVENPORT: Finish the investigation.

TAYLOR: They're lying, dammit! So is the Colonel! You were ordered to investigate and charge the people responsible—charge them! I'll back you up!

DAVENPORT: I'm not satisfied yet, Captain.

TAYLOR: I am! Dammit!—I wish they'd sent somebody else! I do— you—you're afraid! You thought you'd accuse the Klan, didn't you?— and that would be the end of it, right? Another story of midnight riders for your Negro press! And now it's officers—white men in the army. It's too much for you—what will happen when Captain Davenport comes up for promotion to major if he accuses white officers, right?

DAVENPORT: I'm not afraid of white men, Captain.

TAYLOR: Then why the hell won't you arrest them?

DAVENPORT: Because I do what the facts tell me, Captain—not you!

TAYLOR: You don't know what a fact is, Davenport!

ELLIS (*entering suddenly and saluting*): Begging your pardon, sir.

TAYLOR: What is it, Corporal?

ELLIS: Ah—it's for Captain Davenport— (*To* DAVENPORT) We found Private Wilkie, sir. We haven't located Pfc Peterson yet. Seems him and Private Smalls went out on detail together, and neither one of 'em showed up—but I got a few men from the company lookin' for 'em around the N.C.O. club and in the PX, sir.

DAVENPORT: Where's Wilkie?

ELLIS: He's waiting for you in the barracks, Captain.

(DAVENPORT *nods, and* ELLIS *goes out after saluting. The lights come up around* WILKIE, *who is seated in a chair in the barracks reading a Negro newspaper.* DAVENPORT *is thoughtful for a moment.*)

TAYLOR: Didn't you question Wilkie and Peterson yesterday? (DAVENPORT *starts out.*) Davenport? (DAVENPORT *does not answer.*) Don't you ignore me!

DAVENPORT: Get off my back! What I do—how I do it—who I interrogate is my business, Captain! This investigation is mine! (*Holds out the back of his hand, showing* TAYLOR *the color of his skin*) Mine!

TAYLOR: Don't treat me with that kind of contempt—I'm not some redneck cracker!

DAVENPORT: And I'm not your yessirin' colored boy either!

TAYLOR: I asked you a question!

DAVENPORT: I don't have to answer it!

(*There is a long silence. The two men glare at one another*—TAYLOR *in another time, disturbed.*)

TAYLOR: Indeed you don't—*Captain.*

(*Pause.*)

DAVENPORT: Now, *Captain*—what if Byrd and Wilcox are telling the truth?

TAYLOR: Neither one of us believes that.

DAVENPORT: What if they are?

TAYLOR: Then who killed the goddamn man?

DAVENPORT: I don't know yet. (*Slight pause.*) Is there anything else?

(TAYLOR *shakes his head no as* DAVENPORT *starts toward center stage, headed toward* WILKIE.)

TAYLOR: No, hotshot. Nothing.

(DAVENPORT *enters the barracks area.* WILKIE *quickly puts his paper aside and snaps to attention and salutes.* DAVENPORT *returns salute but remains silent, going right to the desk and removing his pad and pencil. The light around the office fades out.*)

DAVENPORT (*snapping at* WILKIE): When did you lose your stripes? (*He is standing over* WILKIE.)

WILKIE: Couple months before they broke up the team—right after Sergeant Waters got assigned to us, sir.

DAVENPORT: Nervous, Wilkie?

WILKIE (*smiles haltingly*): I couldn't figure out why you called me back, sir? (*Laughs nervously*)

DAVENPORT: You lost your stripes for being drunk on duty, is that correct?

WILKIE: Yes, sir.

DAVENPORT: You said Waters busted you, didn't you?

WILKIE: He got me busted—he's the one reported me to the Captain.

DAVENPORT: How did you feel? Must have been awful—(DAVENPORT *paces.*) Weren't you and the Sergeant good friends? Didn't you tell me he was all right? A nice guy?

WILKIE: Yes, sir.

DAVENPORT: Would a nice guy have gotten a friend busted?

WILKIE: No, sir.

DAVENPORT: So you lied when you said he was a nice guy, right?

WILKIE: No, sir—I mean—

DAVENPORT: Speak up! Speak up! Was the Sergeant a nice guy or not?

WILKIE: No, sir.

DAVENPORT: Why not? Answer me!

WILKIE: Well, you wouldn't turn somebody in over something like that!

DAVENPORT: Not a good friend, right?

WILKIE: Right, sir—I mean, a friend would give you extra duty—I would have—or even call you a whole buncha' names—you'd expect that, sir—but damn! Three stripes? They took ten years to get in this army, sir! Ten years! I started out with the 24th Infantry—I—

DAVENPORT: Made you mad, didn't it?

WILKIE: Yeah, it made me mad—all the things I did for him!

DAVENPORT (*quickly*): That's right! You were his assistant, weren't you? Took care of the team—(WILKIE *nods*.) Ran all his errands, looked at his family snapshots (WILKIE *nods again*.), policed his quarters, put the gun under C. J.'s bed—

WILKIE (*looking up suddenly*): No!

DAVENPORT (*quickly*): It was you Henson saw, wasn't it, Wilkie?

WILKIE: No, sir!

DAVENPORT: Liar! You lied about Waters, and you're lying now! You were the only person out of the barracks that night, and the only one who knew the layout well enough to go straight to C. J.'s bunk! Not even Waters knew the place that well! Henson didn't see who it was, but he saw what the person did—he was positive about that—only you knew the barracks in the dark!

WILKIE (*pleadingly*): It was the Sarge, Captain—he ordered me to do it—he said I'd get my stripes back—he wanted to scare that boy C. J.! Let him stew in jail! Then C. J. hit him—and he had the boy right where he wanted him—(*Confused*) But it backfired—C. J. killed hisself—Sarge didn't figure on that.

DAVENPORT: Why did he pick Memphis?

WILKIE: He despised him, Captain—he'd hide it, 'cause everybody in the company liked that boy so much. But underneath—it was a crazy hate, sir—he'd go cold when he talked about C. J. You could feel it.

(*In limbo, the blue-gray light rises on* C. J. *and* WATERS. C. J. *is humming a blues song and* WATERS *is standing smiling, smoking a pipe as he was in Act One.* WATERS *turns away from* C. J. *His speech takes place over* C. J.*'s humming.*)

WATERS: He's the kinda boy seems innocent, Wilkie. Got everybody around the post thinking he's a strong, black buck! Hits home runs— white boys envy his strength—his speed, the power in his swing. Then this colored champion lets those same white boys call him Shine—or Sambo at the Officers Club. They laugh at his blues songs, and he just smiles—can't talk, barely read or write his own name—and don't care! He'll tell you they like him—or that colored folks ain't supposed to have but so much sense. (*Intense*) Do you know the damage one ignorant *Negro* can do? (*Remembering*) We were in France during the First War, Wilkie. We had won decorations, but the white boys had told all the French gals we had tails. And they found this ignorant colored soldier. Paid him to tie a tail to his ass and parade around naked making monkey sounds. (*Shakes his head*) They sat him on a big, round table in the Café Napoleon, put a reed in his hand, a crown on his head, a blanket on his shoulders, and made him eat bananas in front of them Frenchies. And ohhh, the white boys danced that night—passed out leaflets with that boy's picture on them—called him Moonshine, King of the Monkeys. And when we slit his throat, you know that fool asked us what he had done wrong? (*Pause*) My daddy told me, we got to turn our backs on his kind, Wilkie. Close our ranks to the chittlin's, the collard greens—the corn-bread style. We are men—soldiers, and I don't intend to have our race cheated out of its place of honor and respect in *this* war because of fools like C. J.! You watch everything he does—*everything!*

(*Light fades slowly around* WATERS *and* C. J., *and as it does,* C. J. *stops humming.*)

WILKIE: And I watched him, sir—but Waters—he couldn't wait! He wouldn't talk about nothin' else—it was C. J. this—C. J. all the time!
DAVENPORT (*troubled*): Why didn't he pick Peterson—they fought—
WILKIE: They fought all the time, sir—but the Sarge, he likes Peterson. (*Nods*) Peterson fought back, and Waters admired that. He promoted Pete! Imagine that—he thought Peterson would make a fine soldier!
DAVENPORT: What was Peterson's reaction—when C. J. died?
WILKIE: Like everybody else, he was sad—he put together that protest that broke up the team, but afta' that he didn' say much. And he usually runs off at the mouth. Kept to himself—or with Smalls.

(*Slight pause.*)

DAVENPORT: The night Waters was killed, what time did you get in?
WILKIE: Around nine forty-five—couple of us came from the club and listened to the radio awhile—I played some checkers, then I went to

bed. Sir? I didn't mean to do what I did—it wasn't my fault—he promised me my stripes!

(*Suddenly, out of nowhere, in the near distance, is the sound of gunfire, a bugle blaring, something like a cannon going off. The noise is continuous through scene.* DAVENPORT *rises, startled.*)

DAVENPORT: I'm placing you under arrest, Private!

ELLIS (*bursting into the room*): Did you hear, sir? (DAVENPORT, *surprised, shakes his head no.*) Our orders! They came down from Washington, Captain! We're shippin' out! They finally gonna let us Negroes fight!

(DAVENPORT *is immediately elated, and almost forgets* WILKIE *as he shakes* ELLIS's *hand.*)

DAVENPORT: Axis ain't got a chance!

ELLIS: Surrre—we'll win this mother in six months now! Afta' what Jesse Owens did to them people? Joe Louis?

HENSON (*bursting in*): Did y'all hear it? Forty-eight-hour standby alert? We goin' into combat! (*Loud*) Look out, Hitler, the niggahs is comin' to git your ass through the fog!

ELLIS: With real rifles—it's really OK, you know?

HENSON: They tell me them girls in England—woooow!

(DAVENPORT *faces* WILKIE *as* COBB *enters, yelling.*)

COBB: They gonna let us git in it! We may lay so much smoke the Germans may never get to see what a colored soldier looks like 'til the war's over! (*To* HENSON) I wrote my woman jes' the otha' day that we'd be goin' soon!

ELLIS: Go on!

HENSON (*overlapping*): Man, you ain't nothin'!

(DAVENPORT *begins to move* WILKIE *toward* ELLIS.)

HENSON: If the army said we was all discharged, you'd claim you did it! (*He quiets, watching* DAVENPORT.)

COBB (*quickly*): You hea' this fool, sir?

HENSON: Shhhhh!

DAVENPORT (*to* ELLIS): Corporal, escort Private Wilkie to the stockade.

ELLIS (*surprised*): Yes, sir!

(ELLIS *starts* WILKIE *out, even though he is bewildered by it. They exit.*)

HENSON: Wilkie's under arrest, sir? (DAVENPORT *nods.*) How come? I apologize, sir—I didn't mean that.

DAVENPORT: Do either of you know where Smalls and Peterson can be located?

(HENSON *shrugs*.)

COBB: Your men got Smalls in the stockade, sir!
DAVENPORT: When?
COBB: I saw two colored M.P.'s takin' him through the main gate. Jes' a while ago—I was on my way ova' hea'!

(DAVENPORT *goes to the desk and picks up his things and starts out*.)

COBB: Tenn-hut.

(DAVENPORT *stops and salutes*.)

DAVENPORT: As you were. By the way—congratulations!

(DAVENPORT *exits the barracks through the doorway*.)

HENSON: Look out, Hitler!
COBB: The niggahs is coming to get yo' ass.
HENSON and COBB: Through the fog.

(*The lights in the barracks go down at once. Simultaneously, they rise in limbo, where* SMALLS *is pacing back and forth. He is smoking a cigarette. There is a bunk, and the shadow of a screen over his cell. In the background, the sounds of celebration continue.* DAVENPORT *emerges from the right, and begins to speak immediately as the noises of celebration fade*.)

DAVENPORT: Why'd you go AWOL, soldier?

(SMALLS *faces him, unable to see* DAVENPORT *at first. When he sees him, he snaps to attention and salutes*.)

SMALLS: Private Anthony Smalls, sir!
DAVENPORT: At ease—answer my question!
SMALLS: I didn't go AWOL, sir—I—I got drunk in Tynin and fell asleep in the bus depot—it was the only public place I could find to sleep it off.
DAVENPORT: Where'd you get drunk? Where in Tynin?
SMALLS: Jake's—Jake's and Lilly's Golden Slipper—on Melville Street—
DAVENPORT: Weren't you and Peterson supposed to be on detail?
(SMALLS *nods*.) Where was Peterson? Speak up!
SMALLS: I don't know, sir!
DAVENPORT: You're lying! You just walked off your detail and Peterson did nothing?

SMALLS: No, sir—he warned me, sir—"Listen, Smalls!" he said—

DAVENPORT (*cutting him off*): You trying to make a fool of me, Smalls? Huh? (*Loud*) Are you?

SMALLS: No, sir!

DAVENPORT: The two of you went A-W-O-L together, didn't you? (SMALLS *is quiet.*) Answer me!

SMALLS: Yes!

DAVENPORT: You left together because Peterson knew I would find out the two of you killed Waters, didn' you? (SMALLS *suddenly bursts into quiet tears, shaking his head.*) What? I can't hear you! (SMALLS *is sobbing.*) You killed Waters, didn't you? I want an answer!

SMALLS: I can't sleep—I can't sleep!

DAVENPORT: Did you kill Sergeant Waters?

SMALLS: It was Peterson, sir! (*As if he can see it*) I watched! It wasn't me!

(*The blue-gray light builds in center stage. As it does,* SERGEANT WATERS *staggers forward and falls on his knees. He can't get up, he is so drunk. He has been beaten, and looks the way we saw him in the opening of Act One.*)

SMALLS: We were changing the guard.

WATERS: Can't be trusted—no matter what we do, there are no guarantees—and your mind won't let you forget it. (*Shakes his head repeatedly*) No, no, no!

SMALLS (*overlapping*): On our way back to the Captain's office—and Sarge, he was on the road. We just walked into him! He was ranting, and acting crazy, sir!

(PETERSON *emerges from the right. He is dressed in a long coat, pistol belt and pistol, rifle, helmet, his pants bloused over his boots. He sees* WATERS *and smiles.* WATERS *continues to babble.*)

PETERSON: Smalls, look who's drunk on his ass, boy! (*He begins to circle* WATERS.)

SMALLS (*to* DAVENPORT): I told him to forget Waters!

PETERSON: Noooo! I'm gonna' enjoy this, Smalls—big, bad Sergeant Waters down on his knees? No, sah—I'm gonna' love this! (*Leans over* WATERS) Hey, Sarge—need some help? (WATERS *looks up; almost smiles. He reaches for* PETERSON, *who pushes him back down.*) That's the kinda help I'll give yah, boy! Let me help you again—all right? (*Kicks* WATERS) Like that, Sarge? Huh? Like that, dog?

SMALLS (*shouts*): Peterson!

PETERSON: No! (*Almost pleading*) Smalls—some people, man—If this

was a German, would you kill it? If it was Hitler—or that fuckin'
Tojo? Would you kill him? (*Kicks* WATERS *again*)

WATERS (*mumbling throughout*): There's a trick to it, Peterson—it's the
only way you can win—C. J. could never make it—he was a clown!
(*Grabs at* PETERSON) A clown in blackface! A niggah!

(PETERSON *steps out of reach. He is suddenly expressionless as he easily
removes his pistol from his holster.*)

WATERS: You got to be like them! And I was! I was—but the rules are
fixed. (*Whispers*) Shhh! Listen. It's C. J.—(*Laughs*) I made him do it,
but it doesn't make any difference! They still hate you! (*Looks at*
PETERSON, *who has moved closer to him*) They still hate you! (WATERS
laughs.)

PETERSON (*to* SMALLS): Justice, Smalls. (*He raises the pistol.*)

DAVENPORT (*suddenly, harshly*): That isn't justice!

(SMALLS *almost recoils.*)

PETERSON (*simultaneously, continuing*): For C. J.! Everybody!

(PETERSON *fires the gun at* WATERS's *chest, and the shot stops everything.
The celebration noise stops. Even* DAVENPORT *in his way seems to hear it.*
PETERSON *fires again. There is a moment of quiet on stage.* DAVENPORT
is angered and troubled.)

DAVENPORT: You call that justice?

SMALLS: No, sir.

DAVENPORT (*enraged*): Then why the fuck didn't you do something?

SMALLS: I'm scared of Peterson—just scared of him!

(PETERSON *has been looking at* WATERS's *body throughout. He now
begins to lift* WATERS *as best he can, and pull him offstage. It is done with
some difficulty.*)

SMALLS: I tried to get him to go, sir, but he wanted to drag the
Sergeant's body back into the woods—

(*Light fades quickly around* PETERSON, *as* DAVENPORT *paces.*)

SMALLS: Said everybody would think white people did it.

DAVENPORT (*somewhat drained*): Then what happened?

SMALLS: I got sick, sir—and Peterson, when he got done, he helped me
back to the barracks and told me to keep quiet. (*Slight pause.*) I'm
sorry, sir.

(*There is a long pause, during which* DAVENPORT *stares at* SMALLS *with disgust, then abruptly starts out without saluting. He almost flees.* SMALLS *rises quickly.*)

SMALLS: Sir?

(DAVENPORT *turns around.* SMALLS *comes to attention and salutes.* DAVENPORT *returns salute and starts out of the cell and down toward center stage. He is thoughtful as the light fades around* SMALLS. DAVENPORT *removes his glasses and begins to clean them as he speaks.*)

DAVENPORT: Peterson was apprehended a week later in Alabama. Colonel Nivens called it "just another black mess of cuttin', slashin', and shootin'!" He was delighted there were no white officers mixed up in it, and his report to Washington characterized the events surrounding Waters's murder as "the usual, common violence any commander faces in Negro Military units." It was the kind of "mess" that turns up on page 3 in the colored papers—the Cain and Abel story of the week—the headline we Negroes can't quite read in comfort. (*Shakes head and paces*) For me? Two colored soldiers are dead—two on their way to prison. Four less men to fight with—and none of their reasons—nothing anyone *said,* or *did,* would have been worth a life to men with larger hearts—men less split by the madness of race in America. (*Pause.*) The case got little attention. The details were filed in my report and I was quickly and rather unceremoniously ordered back to my M.P. unit. (*Smiles*) A style of guitar pickin' and a dance called the C. J. caught on for a while in Tynin saloons during 1945. (*Slight pause.*) In northern New Jersey, through a military foul-up, Sergeant Waters's family was informed that he had been killed in action. The Sergeant was, therefore, thought and unofficially rumored to have been the first colored casualty of the war from that county and under the circumstances was declared a hero. Nothing could be done officially, but his picture was hung on a Wall of Honor in the Dorie Miller VFW Post #978. (*Pause.*) The men of the 221st Chemical Smoke Generating Company? The entire outfit—officers and enlisted men—was wiped out in the Ruhr Valley during a German advance. (*He turns toward* TAYLOR, *who enters quietly.*) Captain?

TAYLOR: Davenport—I see you got your man.

DAVENPORT: I got him—what is it, Captain?

TAYLOR: Will you accept my saying, you did a splendid job?

DAVENPORT: I'll take the praise—but how did I manage it?

TAYLOR: Dammit, Davenport—I didn't come here to be made fun of—
(*Slight pause.*) The men—the regiment—we all ship out for Europe

tomorrow, and (*hesitates*) I was wrong, Davenport—about the bars—
the uniform—about Negroes being in charge. (*Slight pause.*) I guess
I'll *have* to get used to it.

DAVENPORT: Oh, you'll get used to it—you can bet your ass on that.
Captain—you will get used to it.

(*Lights begin to fade slowly as the music "Don't Sit Under the Apple Tree"
rises in the background, and the house goes to black.*)

Ceremonies in Dark Old Men

LONNE ELDER III

Left to right: Arthur French as MR. WILLIAM JENKINS, *David Downing as* BOBBY PARKER, *William Jay as* THEOPOLIS PARKER, *and Douglas Turner Ward as* MR. RUSSELL B. PARKER *in a scene from* Ceremonies in Dark Old Men. *Photograph copyright © 1968 by Bert Andrews. Reprinted by permission of Marsha Hudson, the Estate of Bert Andrews.*

Lonne Elder III, a native of Georgia, spent most of his life in New York and New Jersey where he had worked as a professional political activist, dock worker, time study and motion man, waiter, numbers runner, and professional gambler. His initial experience with writing came in the form of poetry and short stories. However, upon reading a play by Douglas Turner Ward, whom he had encountered in the Harlem community of New York City, he committed himself exclusively to writing for the theater. Soon after the unanimous acclaim he received for his first professionally produced play, *Ceremonies in Dark Old Men,* he moved to Los Angeles to write for the screen, scripting the Academy-nominated screenplay for the film *Sounder.* He is currently a Hollywood screenwriter.

Ceremonies in Dark Old Men was produced in New York by the NEC at the St. Marks Playhouse, and opened on February 4, 1969, with the following cast:

Mr. Russell B. Parker	Douglas Turner Ward
Mr. William Jenkins	Arthur French
Theopolis Parker	William Jay
Bobby Parker	David Downing
Adele Eloise Parker	Rosalind Cash
Blue Haven	Samual Blue, Jr.
Young Girl	Judyann Elder

Directed by Edmund Cambridge; scenery by Whitney Le Blanc; costumes by Gertha Brock; lighting by Shirley Prendegast.

Ceremonies in Dark Old Men

CHARACTERS
in order of appearance

MR. RUSSELL B. PARKER

MR. WILLIAM JENKINS

THEOPOLIS PARKER

BOBBY PARKER

ADELE ELOISE PARKER

BLUE HAVEN

YOUNG GIRL

TIME
Late spring, about 4:30 in the afternoon, this current time

PLACE
A small poverty stricken barbershop on 126th Street between Seventh and Lenox avenues, Harlem, USA.

Downstage on a lower level is the outer barbershop area. At far stage left is the street entrance to the shop, and near the entrance is a single barber's throne. Behind the throne is an enclosure for the barber's paraphernalia—over the enclosure is a mirror, and to both sides of the mirror are old worn photos of vaudeville and sports stars; Bill Bojangles Robinson, Joe Louis, etc . . .

At the farthest point downstage center is a bench. Moving farther to stage right and downstage in the outer area is an old card table, and just behind the table are two old chairs, flush against a two foot divider. Upstage from the table is a set of two steps leading to an upper level, which is the back room to the shop. Just inside the back room, near the entrance from the shop, is an old bed—to stage left of the bed is a sink, and farther stage left is an old painted refrigerator—to the left of the refrigerator is a group of stairs leading upward toward an unseen apartment—left of the stairs, at center, in a semi cubbyhole area, rests an old beat-up dining room table.

The entire action of the play takes place in these two areas.

ACT ONE : Scene One

As the curtain rises, MR. RUSSELL B. PARKER *is seated in the single barber's throne, reading a* Daily News. *He is a man in his early or middle fifties. He rises nervously, moves to the window and peers outward with his right hand over the brows of his eyes. He returns to the chair and continues to read his book. He checks his watch, rises once again and moves to the window for another look-see. It appears that he finally recognizes the party he has been waiting for, nearing him. He moves to the door and opens it. A man enters.* MR. WILLIAM JENKINS: *In his early fifties, dressed well in a complete suit of clothes, and carrying a newspaper under his arm.*

MR. PARKER (*moving away from his friend*): Where have you been?

MR. JENKINS: Watcha mean? You know where I was . . .

MR. PARKER: You want to play the game or not?

MR. JENKINS: That's what I came here for . . .

MR. PARKER (*bending down by the counter and opening up one of the sliding panels*): I wanted to get in at least three games before Adele got home, but this way we'll be lucky if we get in one . . .

MR. JENKINS: Stop complaining and get the board out—I'll beat you, and that will be that.

MR. PARKER: I can do without your bragging. . . . (*Pulls out a checkerboard and a small can. . . . He moves quickly and places the items on the table. . . . He shakes up the can.*) Close your eyes and take a man . . .

MR. JENKINS (*closing his eyes*): You never learn. . . . (*reaches into the can and pulls out a checker*) It's red. . . .

MR. PARKER: All right, I get the black. . . . (*Sits at the table and rushes to place his men in their respective spots*) Get your men down, Jenkins!

MR. JENKINS (*sitting at the table*): Aw man, take it easy, the checkers ain't gon' run away! (*Setting his men up*) If you could play the game I wouldn't mind it—but you can't play! (*His men are in order now.*) Your move . . .

MR. PARKER: I'll start here—I just don't want Adele to catch us here playing checkers—She gave me and the boys a notice last week that we had to get jobs or get out of the house.

MR. JENKINS: Don't you think it's about time you got a job? In the five years I've been knowing you, I can count the heads of hair you done cut in this shop on one hand . . .

MR. PARKER: This shop is gon' work yet—I know it can—just give me one more year and you'll see. . . . Going out to get a job ain't gone solve nothing—all it's gon' do is create a lot of bad feelings with everybody. I can't work! I don't know how to! (*Moves checker*)

MR. JENKINS: I bet if all your children were living far from you like mine. You'd know how to—That's one thing I don't understand about you, Parker. How long do you expect your daughter to go on supporting you and those two boys?

MR. PARKER: I don't expect that!—I just want some time until I can straighten things out. My dear Doris understood that—She understood me like a book. . . . (*Makes another move*)

MR. JENKINS: You mean to tell me your wife enjoyed working for you?

MR. PARKER: Of course she didn't—but she never worried me. You been married, Jenkins—you know what happens to a man when a woman worries him all the time, and that's what Adele been doing, worrying my head off! (*Makes another move*)

MR. JENKINS: Whatcha gon' do about it?

MR. PARKER: I'm gon' get tough evil and bad—that's the only sign a woman gets from a man— (*Makes move*)

(THEOPOLIS PARKER *enters briskly from the outside—in his twenties, of medium height, and a lean solid physique. He is followed by his younger brother,* BOBBY, *carrying a huge paper bag with heavy and fragile contents.*)

THEO: That's the way I like to hear you talk, Pop, but she's gon' be walking through that door soon, and I wants see how tough you gon' be—

MR. PARKER: Leave me alone, boy—

THEO: Pop, we got six more days, you got to do something!

MR. PARKER: I'll do it when the time comes—

THEO: Pop, the time is *now*. . . .

MR. PARKER: And right now I am playing a game of checkers with Mr. Jenkins, so leave me alone!

THEO: All right—don't say I didn't warn you when she locks us out of the house!

(THEO *and* BOBBY *rush through the back room with* BOBBY *placing the brown bag into an old refrigerator as they dart up the stairs leading to the apartment.* PARKER *makes another move.*)

MR. PARKER: You're trapped, Jenkins! (*Pause.*)

MR. JENKINS (*pondering*): Hmmm . . . It looks that way, don't it?

MR. PARKER (*moving to the door*): While you're moaning over the board, I'll just make a little check to see if Adele is coming—don't cheat now! (*He moves backwards toward the window to make certain that his adversary does not cheat on him. He gets to the window and quickly takes a look out.*) Uh uh! It's Adele! She's in the middle of the block, talking to Miss Thomas! (*Rushes to the shelf, takes a towel out, returns to the table, and spreads it over the checkerboard*) Come on, man! (*Grabbing* JENKINS *by the arm and forcibly leading him toward the back room*)

MR. JENKINS: WHAT ARE YOU DOING, PARKER!

MR. PARKER: You gon' have to hide out in the back room, cause if Adele comes in here and sees you, she'll think that we been playing checkers all day!

MR. JENKINS: I don't care about that!

MR. PARKER: You want to finish the game, don't you?

MR. JENKINS: Yeah, but—

MR. PARKER: —All, you have to do, Jenks, is lay low for a minute, that's all—she'll stop in and ask me something about getting a job, I'll tell her I got a good line on one, and then she'll go on upstairs. There won't be nobody left here but you and me. . . . whatcha say, Jenks?

MR. JENKINS (*pausing*): All right, I'll do it. . . . I don't like it, but I'll do it, and you better not mention this to nobody, you hear!

MR. PARKER: Not a single soul in this world will know but you and me.

MR. JENKINS (*moving just inside the room and standing*): This is the most ridiculous thing I ever heard of . . . hiding in somebody's back room just to finish up a checker game . . .

MR. PARKER: Stop fighting it, man!

MR. JENKINS: All right!

MR. PARKER: Not there!

MR. JENKINS: What in the hell is it now!

MR. PARKER: *You've got to get under the bed!*

MR. JENKINS: No, I'm not gettin' under nobody's bed!

MR. PARKER: Now look . . . Adele never goes through the front way. She comes through the shop and the back room, up the basement stairs to the apartment. . . . now you want her to catch you hiding in there, looking like a fool?

MR. JENKINS: No, I can take myself out of here and go home!

MR. PARKER (*pushing his friend over to the table and lifting the towel from the checkerboard*): Look at this! Now you just take a good look at this board! (*Releases him*)

MR. JENKINS: I'm looking, so what?

MR. PARKER: So what!? I got you and you know it! There ain't no way in the world you'll ever get out of that little trap I got you in. *And it's your move.* How many years we been playing against each other?

MR. JENKINS: Three . . .

MR. PARKER: —Never won a game from you in all that time, have I?

MR. JENKINS: That ain't the half of it—you ain't gon win one either.

MR. PARKER: Now that I finally got you, that's easy talk comin' from running man. . . . All right, go on—run. . . . (*Moves away from him*)

MR. JENKINS: Go on hell! All I gotta do is put my king here, give you this jump here, move this man over there, and you're dead!

MR. PARKER (*turning to him*): Try me then—try me or are you scared at last I'm gon' beat you!

MR. JENKINS: I can't do it now, there ain't enough time!

MR. PARKER (*moving away from him, strutting like a sport*): Run rabbit, run. . . .

MR. JENKINS: All right! I'll get under the bed, but I swear, Parker, I'm gon' beat you silly!

(*They move into the back room.*)

MR. PARKER: Hurry it up then—we ain't got much time . . .

(*As* PARKER *struggles to help his friend to get under the bed in the back room—* ADELE *is entering the shop from the street entrance. She is in her late twenties, well dressed in the conventional New York female office worker's attire. She is carrying a smart looking handbag, and a brown office envelope in her right hand. She stops near the table where the checkerboard is covered with the towel, as* PARKER *enters from the back room.*)

MR. PARKER: Hi, honey . . .

(ADELE *does not respond to his greeting. She busies herself putting minor things in order.*)

ADELE: You looked for work today?

MR. PARKER: All morning—(*Pause.*)

ADELE: No luck in the morning and so you played checkers all afternoon.

MR. PARKER: No, I've been working on a few ideas of mine—my birthday comes up the tenth of the month, and I plan to celebrate it with an idea to shake up this whole neighborhood, and then I'm gon' really go to the country!

ADELE: Don't go to the country—go to work, huh? (*Moves as if to enter back room*) Oh God, I'm tired!

MR. PARKER (*rushing to get her away from bed*): Come on and let me take you upstairs—I know you must've had yourself a real tough day at the office. . . . —and you can forget about cooking supper and all of that stuff . . .

ADELE (*breaking away from him and moving back into shop toward counter*): Thank you, but I've already given myself the privilege of not cooking your supper tonight . . .

MR. PARKER: You did?

ADELE: The way I figure it, you should have my dinner waiting for me.

MR. PARKER: But I don't know how to cook. . . .

ADELE (*turning sharply*): You can learn. . . .

MR. PARKER: Now look, Adele, if you got something on your mind, say it, cause you know damn well I ain't doin' no cooking . . .

ADELE (*pausing*): All right, I will—A thought came to me today as it does every day, and I'm damn tired of thinking about it—

MR. PARKER: What—

ADELE: —And that is, I've been down at that motor license bureau so long, sometimes I forget the reasons I ever took the job in the first place.

MR. PARKER: Now look, everybody knows you quit college and came home to help your mama out—everybody knows it! What you want me to do? Write some prayers to you!?

(BOBBY *and* THEO *enter the back room from upstairs.*)

ADELE: I just want you to get a job!

(*The boys step into shop and stand apart from each other.*)

BOBBY: Hey, Adele!

ADELE: Well! From what cave did you fellows crawl out of? I didn't know you hung around barbershops—want a haircut, boys?

THEO: For your information, this is the first time we been in this barbershop today—we been upstairs, thinking . . .

ADELE: With what?

THEO: With our *minds,* baby!

ADELE: If the two of you found that house upstairs so attractive, to keep you in it all day, then I can think of only three things: the telephone, the bed, and the kitchen.

BOBBY: The kitchen, that's it—we been washing dishes all day!

ADELE: I don't like that, Bobby!

THEO: And I don't like your attitude!

ADELE: Do you like it when I go out of here every morning to work!?

THEO: There you go again with that same old tired talk; work! Mama understood about us—I don't know why you gotta give everybody a hard time . . .

ADELE: That was one of Mama's troubles: understanding everybody.

THEO: Now don't start that shit with me!

ADELE: I have got to start that, Mr. Theopolis Parker!

MR. PARKER: Hold on now, there's no need for all this—Can't we settle this later on, Adele . . .

ADELE: We settle it now—you got six days left so you gotta do something and quick—I got a man coming here tomorrow to change the locks on the door—so for the little time you have left you'll have to come by me to enter this house.

THEO: Who gives you the right to do that?

ADELE: Me, Adele Eloise Parker, black, over twenty-one, and the only working person in this house! (*Pause.*) I am not going to let the three of you drive me into the grave the way you did Mama—And if you really want to know how I feel about that, I'll tell you: Mama killed herself because there was no kind of order in this house—there was nothing but her old-fashion love for a bum like you, Theo—and this one. . . . (*Points to* BOBBY) —Who's got nothing better to do with his time but to shoplift every time he walks into a department store. And you, Daddy, you and those fanciful stories you're always ready to tell, and all the talk of the good old days when you were the big vaudeville star, of hitting the numbers, big. How? How, Daddy? . . . The money you spent on the numbers you got from Mama—In a way, you let Mama make a bum out of you—you let her kill herself!

MR. PARKER: That's a terrible thing to say, Adele, and I'm not going to let you put that off on me!

ADELE: But the fact remains, that in the seven years you've been in this barbershop, you haven't earned enough money to buy two hot dogs! Most of your time is spent playing checkers with that damn Mr. Jenkins.

THEO: Why don't you get married or something. We don't need you— Pop is here, it's *his house!*

ADELE: You're lucky I don't get married and—

THEO: Nobody wants you, baby!

(THEO's *remark stabs and stops* ADELE *for a moment. She resettles herself.*)

ADELE: All right—you just let someone ask me, and I'll leave you with *Pop,* to starve with Pop—Or there's another way—Why don't the three of you just leave right now, and try making it on your own? Why don't we try that!

MR. PARKER: What about my shop!?

ADELE: Since I'm the one that has to pay the extra forty dollars a month for you to keep this place, there's going to be no more shop . . . It was a bad investment and the whole of Harlem knows it!

MR. PARKER (*grabbing her by the arm in desperation*): I'm fifty-four years old.

ADELE (*pulling away from him*): Don't touch me!

MR. PARKER: You go ahead and do what you want, but I'm not leaving this shop! (*Crosses away from her*)

ADELE: Can't you understand, Father! I can't go on forever supporting three grown men! THAT AIN'T RIGHT!

(*Long pause.*)

MR. PARKER (*shaken by her remarks*): No, it's not right—it's not right at all . . .

ADELE: —It's going to be *you* or *me*.

BOBBY (*after a pause*): I'll do what I can, Adele . . .

ADELE: You'll do more than you can . . .

BOBBY: I'll do more than I can . . .

ADELE: Is that all right by you, Mr. Theopolis?

THEO: Yes.

ADELE (*pausing*): That's fine . . . Out of this house tomorrow morning—before I leave here or with me—suit your choice. And don't look so mournful. . . . (*Gathers up her belongings at the shelf*). . . . Smile, you're going to be happier than you think, earning a living for a change. . . . (*Moves briskly through the back room and up the stairs*)

BOBBY: You do look pretty bad, Theo—A job might be just the thing for you. . . .

(JENKINS *comes rushing from the bed into the shop.*)

MR. PARKER: Jenkins! I plumb forgot—

MR. JENKINS: I let you make a fool out of me, Parker!

MR. PARKER: We can still play!

MR. JENKINS (*gathering his apparel at coatrack*): We can't play nothing, I'm going home where I belong!

MR. PARKER: Okay okay, I'll come over to your place tonight . . .

MR. JENKINS: That's the only way—I ain't gon' have my feelings hurt by that daughter of yours. . . .

MR. PARKER: I'll see you tonight—about eight . . .

MR. JENKINS (*at the door*): And Parker, tell me something?

MR. PARKER: Yeah, what Jenks?

MR. JENKINS: Are you positively sure Adele is your daughter?

MR. PARKER: Get out of here!

(JENKINS *rushes out.*)

Now what made him ask a silly question like that?

THEO: I think he was trying to tell you that you ain't supposed to be taking all that stuff from Adele.

BOBBY: Yeah, Pop, he's right. . . .

(PARKER *starts putting his checker set together.*)

THEO: I don't know what you talking about—you had your chance a few
minutes ago, but all you did was poke your eyes at me, and nod your
head like a fool.

BOBBY: I don't see why you gotta make such a big thing out of her
taking charge—somebody's gotta do it—I think she's right!

THEO: I know what she's up to. . . . She wants us to get jobs so she can
fix up the house like she always wanted it, and then it's gon'
happen. . . .

BOBBY: What's that?

THEO: She gon' get married to some konkhead out on the avenue, and
then she gon' throw us out the door. . . .

BOBBY: She wouldn't do that. . . .

THEO: She wouldn't, huh? Put yourself in her place . . . She's busting
thirty wide open. . . . *Thirty years old*—that's a lot of years for a broad
that's not married.

BOBBY: I never thought of it that way . . .

THEO (*in half-confidence*): And you know something else, Pop? I sneaked
and peeped her bankbook, and you know what she got saved?

MR. PARKER and BOBBY (*both turning their heads simultaneously*):
How much!?

THEO: Two thousand, two hundred, and sixty-five dollars!

BOBBY: What!!!

MR. PARKER: I don't believe it!

THEO: You better—and don't let her hand you that stuff about how she
been sacrificing all these years for the house. . . . The only way she
could've saved up that kind of money, was by staying right here!

MR. PARKER: Well, I'll be damn—two thousand dollars!

THEO: She better watch out is all I gotta say, cause I know some guys out
there on that avenue who don't do nothing but sit around all day,
figuring out ways to beat working girls out of their savings.

MR. PARKER: You oughta know, cause you're one of them yourself—the
way I figure it, Theo—anybody that can handle you the way she did a
few minutes ago, can very well take care of themselves. (*He occupies
himself, putting checkers and board away and cleaning up, etc.*)

THEO: That's mighty big talk coming from you, after the way she
treated you.

MR. PARKER: Lay off me, boy. . . .

THEO: You going out to look for a job?

MR. PARKER: I'm giving it some serious thought. . . .

THEO: Well, I'm not. . . . I ain't wasting myself on no low dirty dead-end job. I got my paintings to think about.

BOBBY: Do you really think you're some kind of painter or something?

THEO: You've seen them.

BOBBY: Yeah, but how would I know.

THEO (*rushing into the back room and taking a painting from behind the refrigerator and moving toward his brother*): All right, look at 'em.

BOBBY: Don't bring that stuff in here to me—show it to Pop!

(THEO *holds up two ghastly inept paintings before his brother.* PARKER *pays them no attention and is sweeping the floor.*)

THEO: Look at it! Now tell me what you see. . . .

BOBBY: Nothing. . . .

THEO: You've got to see something—even an idiot has impressions.

BOBBY: I ain't no idiot. . . .

THEO: All right, fool then. . . .

BOBBY: Now look, you better stop throwing them words, "fool" and "idiot" at me anytime you feel like it. I'm gon' be one more fool, and then my fist is gonna land right upside your head!

THEO: Take it easy now—I tell you what: try to see something . . .

BOBBY: Try?

THEO: Yeah, close your eyes and really try . . .

BOBBY (*closes his eyes*): Okay, I'm trying but I don't know how I'm gon' see anything with my eyes closed!

THEO: Well, open them!

BOBBY: They opened . . .

THEO: Now tell me what you see . . .

BOBBY: I see paint. . . .

THEO: I know you see paint, stupid.

BOBBY (*slapping him ferociously across the face*): Now I told you about that! Every time you call me out of my name, you get hit!

THEO: You'll never understand!

BOBBY: All I know is that a picture is supposed to be pretty, but I'm sorry, that mess you got there is downright ugly!

THEO: You're hopeless—You understand this, don't you, Pop? (*Holding the painting for him to see*)

MR. PARKER (*not looking at the painting*): Don't ask me—I don't know nothing about no painting.

THEO: You were an artist once. . . .

MR. PARKER: That was a different kind . . .

THEO: Didn't you ever go out on the stage with a new thing inside of you? One of them nights when you just didn't want to do that ol' soft-shoe routine. You knew you had to do it—after all, it was your job—but when you did it, you gave it a little bite here, a little acid there, and still with all that, they laughed at you anyway. Didn't that ever happen to you?

MR. PARKER: More than once. . . . But you're B.S.n', boy and you know it. . . . You been something new every year since you quit school—First you was going to be a racing car driver, then a airplane pilot, then a office big shot, and now it's a painter. As smart a boy as you is, you should've stayed in school, but who do you think you're fooling with them pictures—It all boils down to one thing; you don't want to work. But I'll tell you something, Theo—time done run out on you—Adele's not playing, so you might as well put all that junk and paint away.

THEO: Who the hell is Adele—You're my father, you're the man of the house. . . .

MR. PARKER: True, and that's what I intend to be, but until I get a job, I'm gon' play it cool. . . .

THEO: You're going to let her push you out into the streets to hussle up a job. You're an old man—you ain't used to working—it might kill you. . . .

MR. PARKER: Yeah, but what kind of leg do I have to stand on if she puts me out in the street?

THEO: She's bluffing!

MR. PARKER: A buddy of mine who was in this same kind of fix, told me exactly what you just said—Well, the last time I saw him, he was standing on the corner of Eighth Avenue and 125th Street, at four o'clock in the morning, twenty degree weather, in nothing but his drawers, mumbling to himself, "I could've sworn she was bluffing!"

THEO: Hey, Pop! Let me put it to you this way: If none of us come up with anything in that two-week deadline she gave us—none of us, you hear me?

MR. PARKER: I hear you and that's just about all . . .

THEO: Don't you get the point? That's three of us—you, me, and Bobby. What she gon' do? Throw the three of us out in the street? I tell you, she ain't gon' do that!

MR. PARKER: If you want to take that chance, that's your business, but don't try to make me take it with you. Anyway, it ain't right that she has to work for three grown men—It just ain't right. . . .

THEO: Mama did it for you. . . .

MR. PARKER (*sharply*): That was different—She was my wife—She knew things about me you will never know. We oughtn' talk about her at all. . . .

THEO: I'm sorry, Pop, but ever since Mama's funeral I've been thinking. Mama was the hardest working person I ever knew, and it killed her! Is that what I'm supposed to do? No, that's not it—I knew it's not . . . You know what I've been doing? I've been talking to some people, to a very important person right here in Harlem, and I told him about this big idea of mine—

MR. PARKER: You're loaded with ideas, boy—*bad ideas!* (*Putting broom away in corner near counter*)

THEO: Why don't you listen to what I have to say!

MR. PARKER: Listen to you for what—another con game you got up your sleeve because your sister's got fed up with you lying around this house all day while she's knocking herself out. You're pulling the same damn thing on me you did with those ugly paintings of yours a few minutes ago. . . .

THEO: Okay, I can't paint—so I was jiving, but now I got something I really want to do . . . something I got to do!

MR. PARKER: If you're making a point Theo, you've gotta be smarter than you're doing to get it through to me.

(THEO *moves into the back room, opens the refrigerator and takes out the brown paper bag, and moves back into the shop.*)

THEO: Pop, I got something here to show how smart I really am—(*Lifts an old jug out of the bag*) Check this out, Pop! Check it out!

MR. PARKER: What is it?

THEO: Whiskey—corn whiskey—you want some?

MR. PARKER (*moving to table*): Well, I'll try a little bit of it out, but we better not let Adele see us. . . .

THEO: That girl sure puts a scare in you, Pop, and I remember when you wouldn't take no stuff off Mama, Adele, or nobody. . . .

MR. PARKER: God is the only person I fear. . . .

THEO (*unscrewing the bottle*): God! Damn, you're all alike!

MR. PARKER: What are you talking about, boy?

THEO: You, the way Mama was—Ask you any question you can't answer, and you throw that Bible stuff at us. . . .

MR. PARKER: I don't get you. . . .

THEO: For instance, let me ask you about the black man's oppressions; and you'll tell me about some small nation in the East rising one day to rule the world. . . . Ask you about pain and dying, and you say, "God wills it." . . . Fear?—and you'll tell me about Daniel, and how Daniel wasn't scared of them lions—Am I right or wrong?

MR. PARKER: It's all in the book and you can't dispute it. . . .

THEO: You wanta bet? If that nation in the East ever do rose, how can I be sure they won't be worse than the jokers we got running things now—Nobody but nobody wills me to pain and dying—not if I can do something about it. That goes for John, Peter, Mary, JC, the whole bunch of 'em! And as for ol' Daniel—Sure, Daniel didn't care nothing about them lions—*but them lions didn't give a damn about him either! They tore him into a million pieces!*

MR. PARKER: That's a lie! That's an un-Godly, unholy lie! (*Takes his Bible from the shelf*) And I'll prove it!

THEO: What lie?

MR. PARKER (*moving from the counter, thumbing through the pages of the Bible*): You and those bastard ideas of yours. . . . Here, here it is! (*Reading from the Bible:*)

And when he came near unto the den to Daniel, he cried with a pained voice; The King spoke and said to Daniel: "O Daniel, servant of the living God, is thy God, whom thou servest continually, able to deliver thee from the lions?" Then said Daniel unto the King: "O King, live forever! My God hath sent his angel, and hath shut the lions' mouths, and they have not hurt me; for as much as before him innocence was found in me, and also before thee, O King, have I done no hurt." Then was the King exceedingly glad, and commanded that they should take Daniel up out of the den. So Daniel was taken up out of the den, and no manner of hurt was found upon him, BECAUSE HE TRUSTED IN HIS GOD!!! (*Slams the book closed, triumphantly*)

THEO: Hollywood, Pop, Hollywood!

MR. PARKER: Damn you! How I ever brought something like you into this world, I'll never know! You're no damn good! Sin! That's who your belief is! Sin and corruption! With you, it's nothing but women! Whiskey! Women! Whiskey!

(*While PARKER is carrying on in this ranting fashion, THEO pours out a glass of his corn, and puts it in his father's hand.*)

Women! Whiskey! (*Takes a taste*). . . . Whisk — . . . Where did you get this from? (*Sits on throne*)

THEO (*slapping BOBBY's hand*): I knew you'd get the message, Pop—I just knew it!

MR. PARKER: Why boy, this is the greatest corn I ever tasted!

BOBBY: And Theo puts that stuff together like he was born to be a whiskey maker!

MR. PARKER: Where did you learn to make corn like this?

THEO: Don't you remember—you taught me.

MR. PARKER: By George, I did—Why you weren't no moren' nine years old—

THEO: Eight—let's have another one. . . . (*He pours another for* PARKER.) Drink up. . . . Here's to ol' Daniel. . . . You got to admit one thing— he had a whole lot of heart!

MR. PARKER (*drinks up, putting his hand out again*): Another one, please . . .

THEO (*pouring*): Anything you say, Pop! *You're the boss of this house!*

MR. PARKER: Now that's the truth if you ever spoke it. . . . (*Drinks up*) Whew! This is good! (*Putting his glass out again and getting slightly tipsy*)

THEO: About this idea of mine, Pop—Well, it's got something to do with this corn. . . .

MR. PARKER (*still drinking*): Wow! Boy, people oughta pay you to make this stuff. . . .

THEO: Well, that's what I kinda had in mind—I tested some of it out the other day, and I was told this corn liquor could start a revolution— that is, if I wanted to start one—I let a preacher taste some, and he asked me to make him a whole keg for him.

MR. PARKER (*pausing in a sudden change of mood*): God! Dammit!

BOBBY: What's wrong, Pop?

MR. PARKER: I miss her, boy, I tell you, I miss her! Was it really God's will?

THEO: Don't you believe that—*don't you ever believe that!*

MR. PARKER: But I think, boy—I think hard!

THEO: That's all right. . . . We think hard too. We got it from you, ain't that right, Bobby?

BOBBY: Yeah . . .

MR. PARKER (*pausing*): You know something? That woman was the first woman I ever got close to. . . . Your mama . . .

BOBBY: *How old were you?*

MR. PARKER: Twenty. . . .

BOBBY: Aw come on, Pop!

MR. PARKER: May God wipe me away from this earth. . . .

THEO: Twenty years old and you had never touched a woman? You must've been in bad shape.

MR. PARKER: I'll tell you about it. . . .

THEO: Here he goes with another one of his famous stories!

MR. PARKER: I can always go on upstairs, you know. . . .

THEO: No Pop, we want a hear it . . .

MR. PARKER: Well, I was working in this circus in Tampa, Florida— your mother's hometown. You remember Bob Shepard—well, we had this little dance routine of ours we used to do a sample of outside the tent. One day, we was out there doing one of our numbers, when right in the middle of the number, I spied this fine, foxy-looking thing, blinking her eyes at me. Course o' Bob kept saying it was him she was looking at, but I knew it was *me*—cause if there was one thing that was my specialty, it was a fine-looking woman.

THEO: You live twenty years of you life not getting anywhere near a woman, and all of a sudden they become *your specialty?*

MR. PARKER: Yeah, being that—

THEO: Being that you had never had a woman for all them terrible years, naturally it was on your mind all the time. . . .

MR. PARKER: That's right. . . .

THEO: —and it being on your mind so much, you sorta became a specialist on women?

MR. PARKER: Right again. . . .

THEO (*laughing*): I don't know, but Pop, I guess you got a point there! (*Continues to laugh*)

MR. PARKER: You want to hear this or not!?

BOBBY: Yeah, go on, Pop. . . . *I'm* listening.

MR. PARKER: Well, while I was standing on the back of the platform, I motions to her with my hand to kinda move around to the side of the stand, so I could talk to 'er. She strolled round to the side, stood there for awhile, and you know what? Ol' Bob wouldn't let me get a word in edgewise. But you know what she told him; she said, mister, you talk like a fool!

(They all laugh.)

BOBBY: That was Mama, all right.

MR. PARKER: So, I asked her if she would like to meet me after the circus closed down. When I got off that night, sure enough, she was waiting for me. We walked up to the main section of town, off to the side of the road, cause we had a hard rain that day, and the road was full of muddy little ponds. I got to talking to her and telling her funny stories, and she would laugh—boy, I'm telling you that woman could laugh!

THEO: That was your technique, huh? Keep 'em laughing!

MR. PARKER: Believe it or not, it worked—cause she let me kiss her. I kissed her under this big ol' pecan tree. She could kiss too. When that woman kissed me, somethin' grabbed me so hard, and shook me so, I fell flat on my back into a big puddle of water! *And that woman killed herself laughing!* (*Pause.*) I married her two weeks later. . . .

THEO: And then you started making up for lost time. I'm glad you did, Pop—cause if you hadn't, I wouldn't be here today.

MR. PARKER: If I know you, you'd have made some kind of arrangement.

BOBBY: What happened after that?

MR. PARKER: We just lived and had fun—and children too, that part you know about. We lived bad and we lived good—and then my legs got wobbly, and my feet got heavy, I lost my feeling, and everything just stayed as it was. (*Pause.*) I only wish I had been as good a haircutter as I was a dancer. Maybe she wouldn't have had to work so hard. She might be living today.

THEO: Forget it, Pop—it's all in the gone by. . . . Come on, you need another drink. . . . (*Pouring*)

MR. PARKER: Get me talking about them old days—it hurts, I tell you, it—

THEO: —Pop, you have got to stop thinking about those things. We've got work to do!

MR. PARKER: You said you had an idea. . . .

THEO: Yes—you see, Pop, this idea has to do with Harlem. It has to do with the preservation of Harlem. That's what it's all about. So, I went to see this leader, and I spoke to him about it. He thought it was great and said he would pay me to use it!

MR. PARKER: Who wants to preserve this dump! Tear it down is what I say!

THEO: But this is a different kind of preserving—Preserve it for black men—preserve it for men like you, me, and Bobby—that's what it's all about.

MR. PARKER: That sounds good. . . .

THEO: Of course now, after I told this leader, I couldn't promise to do anything until I had spoken to my father—I said, after straightening everything out with you, I would make arrangements for the two of you to meet.

MR. PARKER: Meet him for what?

THEO: For making money! For business! *This man knows how to put people in business!*

MR. PARKER: All right, I'll meet him, what's his name—

THEO: —But first you gotta have a showdown with Adele, and put her in her place, once and for all. . . .

MR. PARKER: Now wait just a minute—You didn't say Adele would have anything to do with this. . . .

THEO: Pop, this man can't be dealing with men who let women rule them. Pop, you've got to tell that girl off or we can't call ourselves men!

MR. PARKER (*pausing*): All right, if she don't like it, that's too bad—Whatever you have in mind for us to do with this leader of yours, we'll do it. . . .

THEO: Now that's the way I like to hear my old man talk! Take a drink, Pop! (*Starts popping his fingers and moving dancingly about the room*)
WE'RE GONNA SHOW 'EM NOW
WE'RE GONNA SHOW 'EM NOW
ALL OVER
THIS OL' HARLEM TOWN!

(THEO *and* BOBBY *start making rhythmic scat sounds with their lips as they move about dancing on the floor.*)

Come on, Pop, show us how you used to cut one of them things!

BOBBY (*trying his hand at the dance*): This is how he did it!

THEO: Nawwww, that's not it—he did it like this! (*Makes an attempt*)

MR. PARKER (*rising*): No, no! Neither one of you got it! Speed up that riff a little bit. . . .

(*The* TWO BOYS *speed up the riff, singing, stomping their feet, and clapping their hands.* PARKER *is humped over, looking down on the floor with pointed concentration*)

Faster!

(*They speed it up more.*)

THEO: Come on now, Pop—let 'er loose!

MR. PARKER: Give me time. . . .

BOBBY: *Let that man have some time!*

(PARKER *breaks into his dance.*)

THEO: Come on, Pop, take it with you!

BOBBY: Work, Pop!

THEO: Downtown!

(PARKER *does a coasting "camel walk."*)

BOBBY: Now bring it on back uptown!

(PARKER *really breaks loose into a rapid series of complicated dance steps.*)

THEO: Yeahhhhhhh!

BOBBY: That's what I'm talkin' about!

(ADELE *enters and stops at the entrance to the shop, observes the scene bemusedly.* PARKER *glimpsing her, first abruptly ceases dance, and in one motion reaches for his broom.* BOBBY *looks for an object to grab.* THEO *merely stares at them all.*)

ADELE: Supper's ready fellows!

(*Curtain*)

ACT ONE : Scene Two

Six days later . . . late afternoon.

BOBBY *is seated in the barber's throne, eating away on a sandwich.* THEO *enters from the front of the shop.*

THEO: Did Pop get back yet?

(BOBBY *shrugs shoulders.*)

You eating again? Damn. (*Calling upstairs*) Pop!. . . . (*No answer.*)

(THEO *checks his watch . . . looks back into shop . . . through window . . . then crosses to* BOBBY *and snatches the sandwich out of his mouth.*)

You eat too damn much!
BOBBY: What the fuck you do that for?
THEO (*handing the sandwich back to him*): —cause you always got a mouth full of peanut butter and jelly!
BOBBY: I'm hungry! And let me tell you something—don't you *ever* snatch any food from my mouth again.
THEO: You'll hit me—You don't care nothing about your brother. . . . One of these days, I'm gon hit back.
BOBBY: Nigger! the day you swing your hand at me, you'll draw back a nub.
THEO: You see! That's exactly what I mean. Now when Blue gets here tonight I don't want you talking like that or else you gon blow the whole deal.
BOBBY: I know how to act—I don't need no lessons from you.
THEO: Good—I got a job for you.
BOBBY: A job? Shit!

THEO: Don't get knocked out now—it ain't no real job. I just want you to jump over to Smith's on 125th Street, and pick me up a portable typewriter.

BOBBY: Typewriter—for what?

THEO: Don't ask questions, just go and get it. . . .

BOBBY: Them typewriters cost a lotta money. . . .

THEO: You ain't go use money. . . .

BOBBY: You mean—

THEO: —I mean you walk in there and take one. . . .

BOBBY: Naw, you don't mean I walk into nowhere and take nothing!

THEO: Now, Bobby.

BOBBY: No!

THEO: Aw, come on Bobby, you the one been bragging about how good you are, how you can walk into any store and get anything you wanted, provided it was not too heavy to carry out.

BOBBY: I ain't gon do it!

THEO: You know what day it is?

BOBBY: Thursday. . . .

THEO: That's right, Thursday, May 10th. . . .

BOBBY: What's that suppose to mean; thieves convention on 125th Street?

THEO: It's Pop's birthday!

BOBBY: I didn't know he was still having them. . . .

THEO: Well, let me tell you something—Adele remembered it and she's planning on busting into this shop tonight with a birthday cake to surprise him—

BOBBY: She suppose to be throwing us out today—that don't make no sense with her buying him a birthday cake. . . .

THEO: He's been looking for work, I guess, she changed her mind about him—maybe it's gon be just me and you that goes. . . .

BOBBY (*pausing*): What's he gon type?

THEO: Them lies he's always telling—like the one about how he met Mama. Pop can tell some of the greatest lies you ever heard of, and you know how he's always talking about writing them down.

BOBBY: Pop don't know nothing bout writing—specially no typewriting!

THEO (*taking out his father's notebook*): Oh! No, take a look at this. . . . (*Hands the book to his brother*) All he has to do is put it down on paper the way he tells it. Who knows, somebody might get interested in it for television or movies, and we can make ourselves some money, and besides, I kinda think he would get a real charge out of you thinking about him that way—don't you?

BOBBY (*pausing*): Well, ain't no use in lettin' you go over there, gettin' yourself in jail with them old clumsy fingers of yours.

THEO: Good boy, Bobby!

(PARKER *enters the shop.*)

Hey Pop! Did you get that thing straightened out with Adele, yet?

MR. PARKER: What?

THEO: *Adele?*

MR. PARKER: Oh yeah, I'm gon take care of that right away. . . . (*Moves* BOBBY *out of* THRONE *and sits*)

THEO: Where you been all day?

(BOBBY *moves into back room.*)

MR. PARKER: Downtown, seeing about some jobs. . . .

THEO: You sure don't care much about yourself . . .

MR. PARKER: I can agree with you on that because lookin' for a job can really hurt a man. . . . I was interviewed five times today, and I could've shot every last one of them interviewers—the white ones and the colored ones too. I don't know if I can take any more of this.

THEO: Yeah, looking for a job can be very low grading to a man, and it gets worse after you get the job. Anyway, I'm glad you got back here on time or you would've missed your appointment. Now don't tell me you don't remember! The man, the man that's suppose to come here and tell you how life in Harlem can be profitable.

MR. PARKER (*stepping out of* THRONE *on his way to back room*): Oh, that. . . .

THEO (*following him*): Oh that my foot! Today is the day we're suppose to come up with those jobs, and you ain't said one word to Adele about it—not one single word! All you do is waste your time looking for work! Now that don't make no sense at all Pop, and you know it. . . .

MR. PARKER: Look, son—Let me go upstairs now and tell her about all the disappointments I suffered today, soften her up a bit, and then I'll come on back down here to meet your man. I promise, you won't have to worry about me going downtown anymore—not after what I went through today, and I certainly ain't giving up my shop for nobody! (*Exits upstairs.*)

THEO (*turning to* BOBBY, *who's at the mirror*): Now that's the way I like to hear my old man talk! Hey, baby don't forget that thing, it's late, we ain't got much time.

BOBBY: All right!

(*A jet-black complexioned young man, dressed in all blue, wearing sunglasses, and holding a gold-top cane in his right hand, enters. He is also carrying a large salesman's valise in his left hand. He stops just inside the door.*)

THEO: Blue, baby!

BLUE: Am I late . . . ?

THEO: No, my father just walked in the door—he's upstairs now, but he'll be right back down in a few minutes. . . . Let me take your things. . . . (*Relieves* BLUE *of his cane and valise*) Sit down man while I fix you a drink. . . .

(THEO *places* BLUE's *things on the table and moves into back room.* BOBBY *enters shop.*)

BLUE: Hey, Bobby . . . how's the stores been treating you?

BOBBY: I'm planning on retiring next year. . . . (*Laughs*)

(THEO *returns with his jug and two glasses. Moves to the table and starts pouring*)

THEO: I was thinking, Blue—We can't let my old man know about our Piano Brigade. I know he ain't going for that, but we can fix it where he will never know a thing. . . .

BLUE: You know your father better than I do. . . . (*Takes a drink*)

BOBBY: What's the Piano Brigade?

THEO: Blue here has the best thieves and store burglars in this part of town, and we plan to work on those businesses over on 125th Street until they run the insurance companies out of business. . . .

BOBBY: You mean breaking into people's stores at night, and taking their stuff?

THEO: That's right, but not the way you do it. We'll be organized, we'll be revolutionary.

BOBBY: If the police catch you, he ain't gon care what you is, and if Pop ever finds out, the police gon seem like church girls! (*Moves hurriedly out of the front door*)

THEO: You just remember that the only crime you'll ever commit is the one you get caught at! (*Pause.*) Which reminds me, Blue—I don't want Bobby to be a part of that Piano Brigade.

BLUE: If that's the way you want it—that's the way it shall be, Theo— How's your sister?

THEO: You mean, Adele?

BLUE: You got a sister named Mary or something?

THEO: What's this with Adele?

BLUE: I want to know how you are going to get along with her, selling bootleg whiskey in this place?

THEO: This is not her place—it's my father's, and once he puts his okay on the deal, that's it. . . . What kind of house do you think we're living in, where we gon let some woman tell us what to do. . . . Come here, let me show you something. . . . (*Moves into the back room as* BLUE *follows*) How you like it—ain't it something?

BLUE (*standing in the doorway*): It's a back room . . .

THEO: Yeah I know, but I have some great plans for reshaping it by knocking down this wall, and putting—

BLUE: Like I said, it's a back room—All I wanta know is will it do the job. . . . It's a good room. . . . You'll do great with that good-tasting corn of yours. You're going to be so busy here, you're going to grow to hate this place—You might not have any time for your love life, Theopolis!

THEO (*laughing*): Don't you worry about that—I can manage my sex life!

BLUE: Sex! Who's talking about sex? You surprise me, Theo. . . . Everyone's been telling me about how you got so much heart, how you so deep—I sit and talk to you about life, and you don't know the difference between sex and love.

THEO: Is it that important?

BLUE: Yes it is ol' buddy if you want to hang out with me, and you do want to hang out with me, don't you?

THEO: That depends. . . .

BLUE: It depends upon you knowing that sex's got nothing to do with anything but you and some woman laying up in some funky bed, pumping and sweating your life away all for one glad moment—you hear that, *one moment!*

THEO: I'll take that moment!

BLUE: With every woman you've had?

THEO: One out of a hundred!

BLUE (*laughing, and moving back into shop*): One out of a hundred! All that sweat! All that pumping and grinding for the sake of one little dead minute out of a hundred hours!

(PARKER *descends the stairs, moves through the back room, and enters the shop.*)

THEO (*stopping* PARKER): Pop, you know who this is?

MR. PARKER: I can't see him. . . .

THEO: This is Blue!

MR. PARKER: Blue, who?

THEO: The man I was telling you about. . . . *Mr. Blue Haven.*

MR. PARKER (*extending his hand for a shake*): Please to make your acquaintance, Mr. Haven . . .

BLUE (*shaking* PARKER'S *hand*): Same to you, Mr. Parker. . . .

THEO: You sure you don't know who Blue Haven is, Pop?

MR. PARKER: I'm sorry, but I truly don't know you, Mr. Haven. . . . If you're a celebrity, you must accept my apology. You see, since I got out of the business, I don't read the *Variety* anymore.

THEO: I'm not talking about a celebrity. . . .

MR. PARKER: Oh, no?

THEO: He's the leader!

MR. PARKER: Ohhhhh!

THEO: Right here in Harlem . . .

MR. PARKER: Where else he gon be but in Harlem—we got more leaders within ten square blocks of this barbershop than they got liars down in City Hall—That's why you dressed up that way, huh boy? So people can pick you out of a crowded room!

THEO: Pop, this is serious!

MR. PARKER: All right, go on don't get carried away—there are some things I don't catch on to right away, Mr. Blue—

THEO: Well, get to this—I got to thinking the other day when Adele busted in here shoving everybody around—I was thinking about this barbershop, and I said to myself: Pop's gon lose this shop if he don't start making himself some money.

MR. PARKER: Now tell me something I don't know. . . . (*Sits on* THRONE)

THEO: Here, I go. . . . What would you say, if I were to tell you, that Blue here can make it possible for you to have a thriving business going on, right here in this shop, for twenty-four hours a day?

MR. PARKER: What is he? Some kind of hair grower!

THEO: Even if you don't cut but one head of hair a week!

MR. PARKER: Do I look like a fool to you?

THEO (*holding up his jug*): Selling this!

MR. PARKER (*pausing.*): Well, well, well. I knew it was something like that—I didn't exactly know what it was, but I knew it was something, and I don't want to hear it!

THEO: Pop, you've always been a man to listen—even when you didn't agree, even when I was wrong, you listened! That's the kind of man you are! You—

MR. PARKER: OK, OK, I'm listening . . . !

(*Pause.*)

THEO: Tell him who you are, Blue. . . .

BLUE: I am the Prime Minister of the Harlem De-Colonization Association.

(*Pause.*)

MR. PARKER: Some kind of organization?

BLUE: Yes. . . .

MR. PARKER (*as an aside—almost under his breath*): They got all kinds of committees in Harlem. What was that name again, "De"?

THEO: De-colo-ni-zation! Which means that Harlem is owned and operated by "Mr. You Know Who." Let me get this stuff—we gon show you something. . . . (*Moves to the table to fetch* BLUE's *materials*)

BLUE: We're dead serious about this project, Mr. Parker. . . . I'd like you to look at this chart.

THEO: And you see we're not fooling. . . . (THEO *hurriedly pins the charts up on the wall out in the shop.*)

MR. PARKER (*reading from the center chart*): The Harlem De-Colonization Association, with future perspective for Bedford Stuyvesant. (*Turns to* BLUE) All right, so you got an organization. What do you do? I've never heard of you.

BLUE: The only reason you've never heard of us is because we don't believe in picketing, demonstrating, rioting and all that stuff. We always look like we're doing something that we ain't doing, but we are doing something—and in that way, nobody gets hurt. . . . Now you may think we're passive—to the contrary, we believe in direct action. We are doers, enterprisers, thinkers, and most of all, we're business men! Our aim is to drive "Mr. You Know Who" out of Harlem.

MR. PARKER: Who's this "Mr. You Know Who?"

THEO: Dam, Pop! The white man!

MR. PARKER: Oh, himmm!

BLUE: We like to use that name for our members in order to get away from the bad feelings we have whenever we use the word "white." We want our members to always be objective, and in this way, we shall move forward. Before we get through, there won't be a single "Mr. You Know Who" left in this part of town. We're going to capture the imagination of the people of Harlem. And that's never been done before, you know.

MR. PARKER: Now tell me how?

BLUE (*standing before the charts with his cane pointed on the wall*): You see this here. . . . This is what we call a Brigade. And you see this yellow circle?

MR. PARKER: What's that for?

BLUE: My new and entertaining system for playing the numbers. . . . You do play the numbers, Mr. Parker?

MR. PARKER: I do . . .

BLUE: You see, I have a lot of colors in this system, and these colors are mixed up with a whole lot of numbers, and the idea is to catch the right number with the right color. The right number can be anything from one to a hundred, but in order to win, the color must always be black. . . . the name of this game is called black heaven. . . . it's the color part that gives everybody all the fun in playing this game of mine.

MR. PARKER: Anybody ever catch it?

BLUE: Sure, but not until every number and every color has paid itself off. The one thing you'll find out about my whole operation: You can't lose. . . .

MR. PARKER: Keep talking. . . .

BLUE: Now over here is the Red Square Circle Brigade, and this thing here is at the heart of my dream to create here in Harlem a symbolic life-force in the heart of the people.

MR. PARKER: You don't say. . . .

BLUE: Put up that target, Theo. . . .

(THEO *hurriedly pins a large sheet of paper on the wall. It is a dart target with the face of a beefy-faced southern looking white man right in the bull's-eye area of the target.*)

MR. PARKER: Why that's that ol' dirty sheriff from that little town in Mississippi!

BLUE (*taking one of the darts from* THEO): That's right—we got a face on a target for every need. We got governors, mayors, backwoods crackers, city crackers, southern crackers, and northern crackers. We got all kinds of faces on these targets that any good Harlemite would be willing to buy for the sake of slinging one of these darts in that bastard's throat! (*Throws the dart and it punctures the face on the board*)

MR. PARKER: Let me try it one time. . . . (*Rising, he takes a dart from* BLUE *and slings it into the face on the target*) Got him! (*A big laugh*)

BLUE: It's like I said, Mr. Parker, the idea is to capture the imagination of the people!

MR. PARKER: You got more? Let me see more!

BLUE: Now this is our Green Circle—that's Theo and his corn liquor— for retail purposes will be called: "black lightning." This whiskey of Theo's can make an everlasting contribution to this life-force I've been telling you about. . . . I've tested this whiskey out in every neighborhood in Harlem, and everybody claimed it was the best they ever tasted this side of Washington, D.C. You see, we plan to supply every after-hours joint in this area, and this will run "Mr. You Know Who" and his bonded product out of Harlem.

THEO: You see, Pop, this all depends on the barbershop being opened night and day so the people can come and go as they please, to pick up their play for the day, to get a bottle of corn, and to take one of them targets home to the kiddies. They can walk in just as if they were getting a haircut. In fact, I told Blue, that we can give a haircut as a bonus for anyone who buys two quarts.

MR. PARKER: What am I suppose to say now?

THEO: You're suppose to be daring. You're suppose to wake up to the times, Pop. . . . These are urgent days—a man has to stand up and be counted!

MR. PARKER: The police might have some counting of their own to do. . . .

THEO: Do you think I would bring you into something that was going to get us in trouble? Blue has an organization! Just like "Mr. You Know Who." He's got members on the police force! In the city government, the state government.

BLUE: Mr. Parker, if you have any reservations concerning the operation of my association, I'd be only too happy to have you come to my summer home, and I'll let you in on everything—especially our protective system against being caught doing this thing.

THEO: Did you hear him, Pop, *he's got a summer home!*

MR. PARKER: Aw shut up boy! Let me think! (*Turns to* BLUE) So you want to use my place as a headquarters for Theo's corn, the colored numbers, and them targets?

BLUE: Servicing the area of 125th to 145th, between the East and West rivers.

MR. PARKER (*pausing*): I'm sorry fellows, but I can't do it. . . . (*Moves into back room*)

THEO (*following* PARKER): Why . . . ?

MR. PARKER: It's not right. . . .

THEO: Not right! What are you talking about? Is it right, that all that's out there for us is to go downtown and push one of them carts? I have done that, and I ain't gon do it no more!

MR. PARKER: That still don't make it right . . .

THEO: I don't buy it! I'm going into this thing with Blue, with or without you!

MR. PARKER: Go on, I don't care! You quit school, I couldn't stop you! I asked you to get a job, you wouldn't work! You have never paid any attention to any of my advice, and I don't expect you to start heeding me now!

THEO: Remember what you said to me about them paintings, and being what I am—well this is me! At last I've find what I can do, and it'll work—I know it will, please, Pop, just—

MR. PARKER: Stop begging, Theo. (*Crosses back into shop, looks at* BLUE) Why?

BLUE: I don't get you. . . .

MR. PARKER: What kind of boy are you, that you went through so much pain to dream up this cockeyed, ridiculous plan of yours?

BLUE: Mr. Parker, I was born about six blocks from here, and before I was ten, I had the feeling I had been living for a hundred years. I got so old and tired, I didn't know how to cry. Now you just think about that—But now I own a piece of this neighborhood—I don't have to worry about some bastard landlord or those credit crooks on 125th Street—beautiful, black Blue, they have to worry about me! (*Reaches into his pocket and pulls out a stack of bills and places them in* PARKER'*s hands*) Can't you see man—I'm here to put you in business!

(PARKER *runs his fingers through the money.*)

Money, Mr. Parker—brand new money . . .

(*After concentrated attention* PARKER *drops money upon table and moves into back room.* THEO *hurriedly follows.* PARKER *sits on bed in deep thought.*)

THEO: That's just to get us started—And if we can make a dent into "Mr. You Know Who's" goings-on in Harlem, nobody's going to think of us as crooks. We'll be heroes from 110th Street to Sugar Hill. And just think, Pop, you won't have to worry about jobs and all that. You'll have so much time for you and Mr. Jenkins to play checkers, your arms will drop off. You'll be able to sit as long as you want, and tell enough stories and lies to fit between the cover of a 500-page book. That's right! Remember you said you wanted to write all them stories down! Now you'll have time for it! You can dress up the way you used to—and the girls—remember how you used to be so tough with the girls before you got married? All that can come back to you, and some of that you never had. It's so easy! All you have to do is call Adele down those stairs and let her know that you're going into business, and if she don't like it, she can pack up and move out, because you're not going to let her drive you down.

MR. PARKER: All right! (*Moves back into shop, where* BLUE *is putting away his chart, etc.*) I'll do it! (*Pause.*) I'll do it under one condition. . . .

BLUE: And that is . . . ?

MR. PARKER: If my buddy Jenkins wants to buy into this deal, you'll let him. . . .

BLUE: Theo . . . ?

THEO: It's all right. . . .

MR. PARKER (*extending his hand to* BLUE): Then you got yourself some partners, Mr. Haven!

BLUE: Welcome into the association, Mr. Parker. . . .

MR. PARKER: Welcome into my barbershop!

THEO (*jubilantly*): Yeahhhhhhhhhh!

(BLUE *checks his watch.* ADELE *moves down into back room.*)

BLUE: Well, I have to check out now, but I'll stop over tomorrow, and we will set the whole thing up just as you want it, Mr. Parker. . . . See you later, Theo.

MR. PARKER (*to* BLUE *as he is moving out of the front door*): You should stick around awhile and watch my polish!

THEO: Pop, don't you think it would be better if you would let me give the word to Adele?

MR. PARKER: No—If I'm going to run a crooked house, *I'm* going to run it, and that goes for you as well as her.

THEO: But Pop, sometimes she kinda gets by you . . .

MR. PARKER: Boy, I have never done anything like this in my life, but since I've made up my mind to it, you have nothing to say—not a word—you have been moaning about me never making it so you can have a chance. Well, this time you can say I'm with you—but let me tell you something—I don't want no more lies from you, and no more conning me about painting, airplane piloting, or nothing. If being a crook is what you want to be, you're going to be the best crook in the world—even if you have to drink mud to prove it.

THEO (*pausing*): Okay, Pop . . .

MR. PARKER (*moving toward the back room*): Well, here goes nothing—Adele!

(*Just as he calls,* ADELE *steps out of the back room, stopping him in his tracks.*)

ADELE: Yes, Father. . . .

MR. PARKER: Oh, you're here already—Well, I want to talk to—well I er—

ADELE: What is it?

MR. PARKER (*pausing*): Nothing, I'll talk to you later. . . . (*He spots* BOBBY *entering from the outside with a package wrapped in newspapers.*) —what you got there?

BOBBY: Uh, uh—fish!

MR. PARKER: Well, you better get them in the refrigerator before they stink on you . . .

THEO (*going over to* BOBBY *and taking the package from him*): No, no now Bobby, I promised Pop we would never lie to him again—It ain't fish, Pop, we've got something for you. . . . (*puts the package down on the table and starts unwrapping it.*)

(*The two boys are standing over the table as* THEO *unwraps the package. It is open, the typewriter is revealed, and they both turn to him simultaneously.*)

THEO and BOBBY: Happy Birthday!

MR. PARKER: Birthday? Birthday?

THEO and BOBBY: Yes, Happy Birthday!

MR. PARKER: Now hold on just a minute!

BOBBY: What are we holding on for, Pop?

MR. PARKER (*pausing*): That's a good question, son—we're—we're holding on for a celebration! (*Laughs loudly*) Thanks, fellows! But what am I going to do with a typewriter! I don't know nothing about no typing!

ADELE: I would like to know where they got the money to buy one!

THEO (*ignoring her*): You know what you told me about writing down your stories—Now you can write them down three times as fast!

MR. PARKER: But I don't know how to type!

THEO: With the money we're gonna be having, I can hire somebody to teach you!

ADELE: What money you're going to have?

THEO: We're going into business, baby—right here in this barbershop!

MR. PARKER: Theo. . . .

THEO (*paying no attention to his father*): We're going to sell bootleg whiskey, numbers, and—

ADELE: You're what!?

MR. PARKER: Theo. . . .

THEO: You heard me, and if you don't like it, you can pack your bags and leave!

ADELE: Leave? I pay the rent here!

THEO: No more! I pay it now!

MR. PARKER: Shut up, Theo!

THEO: We're going to show you something, girl—you think—

MR. PARKER: I SAID SHUT UP!

ADELE: Is he telling the truth?

MR. PARKER: Yes, he is telling the truth. . . .

ADELE: You mean to tell me, you're going to turn this shop into a bootleg joint?

MR. PARKER: I'll turn it into anything I want to!

ADELE: Not while I'm still here!

MR. PARKER: The lease on this house has my signature, not yours!

ADELE: I'm not going to let you do this!

MR. PARKER: You got no choice, Adele,—You don't have a damn thing to say!

ADELE (*turning sharply to* THEO): You put him up to this!

MR. PARKER: Nobody puts me up to anything I don't want to do! These two boys have made it up in their minds, they're not going to work for nobody but themselves, and the thought in my mind is *why should they!* I did like you said, I went downtown, and it's been a long time since I did that, but you're down there every day, and you oughta know by now that I am too old a man to ever dream I . . . could overcome the dirt and filth they got waiting for me down there. I'm surprised at you, that you would have so little care in you to shove me into the middle of that mob.

ADELE: You can talk about caring? What about Mama? She *died* working for you! Did you ever stop to think about that! In fact, DID YOU EVER LOVE HER! NO!!!

MR. PARKER: That's a lie!

ADELE: I hope that one day you'll be able to do one good thing to drive that doubt out of my mind. . . . *But this is not it!* You've let this hoodlum sell you his twisted ideas of making a shortcut through life— But let me tell you something—this bastard is going to ruin you!

THEO (*into her face*): Start packing, baby!

ADELE (*striking him across the face*): DON'T YOU TALK TO ME LIKE THAT!

(THEO *raises his hand to strike her back.*)

MR. PARKER: Drop your hand, boy!

(THEO *does not respond to his father's order.*)

I said, DROP YOUR GOD DAMN HAND!

THEO: She hit me!

MR. PARKER: I don't care if she had broken your jaw—if you ever draw your hand back to hit this girl again—*as long as you* live!—You better not be in my hand reach when you do, cause *I'll split your back in two!* (*To* ADELE) We're going into business, Adele. I have come to that, and I have come to it on my own. I am going to stop worrying once and for all whether I live naked in the cold or whether I die like an animal, unless I can live the best way I know how to. I am getting old and I oughta have some fun. I'm going to get me some money, and I'm going to spend it! I'm going to get drunk! I'm going to dance some more! I'M GETTING OLD! I'M GOING TO FALL IN LOVE ONE MORE TIME BEFORE I DIE! So get to that, girl, and if it's too much for you to bear, I wouldn't hold it against you if you walked away from here this very minute. . . .

(ADELE *opens the door to the back room for him to see the birthday surprise she had in store for him.*)

ADELE: Happy Birthday!

PARKER (*moving into the room and standing over the table where the birthday cake is*): I guess I fooled all of you—today is not my birthday. It never was. (*Moves up the stairs*)

ADELE: It's not going to work! You're going to cut your throat! You hear me! You're going to rip yourself into little pieces! (*Turns to* THEO) It's not going to be the way you want it—because I know Mr. Blue Haven—and he is not a person to put your trust in—

(THEO *turns his back on her and heads for the entrance to the counter.*)

I AM TALKING TO YOU!

THEO (*stopping and turning*): Why don't you leave us alone—you're the one who said we had to go out and do something—well, we did, but we're doing it our way—me and Bobby, we're men—if we lived the way you wanted us to, we wouldn't have nothing but big fat veins popping out of our heads.

ADELE: I'll see what kind of men you are every time a cop walks through that door, every time a stranger steps into this back room, and you can't be too sure about him, and the day they drag your own father off and throw him into a jail cell.

THEO: But tell me, what else is there left for us to do—you tell me, and I'll do it—you show me where I can go to spin the world around before it gets too late for somebody like Mama living fifty years just to die on a 126th Street! YOU TELL ME OF A PLACE WHERE THERE ARE NO OLD CRIPPLED VAUDEVILLE MEN!

ADELE: THERE IS NO SUCH PLACE! (*Pause.*) But you don't get

so hung up about it you have to plunge a knife into your own body—
you don't bury yourself here in this place—YOU CLIMB UP OUT
OF IT! Now that's something for you to wonder about, boy—

THEO: I wonder all the time—how you have lived here all your whole
life on this street, and you haven't seen, heard, learned or felt a thing
in all those years—I Wonder how you ever got to be such a damn fool!

(*End of Act One*)

ACT TWO : Scene One

Two months later. . . . It is about 9:00 P.M. in the evening.

As the curtain rises, the lights come up on the back room. BOBBY *is discovered in back room listening to a record of James Brown's "Money Won't Change You, But Time Will Take You On." As he is dancing out into the shop,* THEO *appears from the cellar, which has been created by taking out a panel in the lower section of the wall. The cellar houses the whiskey-making operation.* THEO *brings on two boxes filled with the corn whiskey and places them under the bed.*

BOBBY *descends the stairs and moves right past* THEO *out into the shop, carrying a target rolled up in his hand, and two darts. He is wearing a fancy sport shirt, new trousers, new keen-toed shoes, and a stingy diddy bop hat. He pins the target up on the wall of the shop. The face at the very center of the target is that of a well-known American racist. . . .* BOBBY *moves away from the target, aims the dart, and throws it hard force.*

BOBBY: That's for Pop! Huh! (*Throws another dart*) And this is for me!
Huh! (*He moves to the target to pull the darts out.*)

(THEO *cuts record off abruptly. There's a knock at the door.*)

THEO (*calling out to* BOBBY *from the back room*): Lock that door!
BOBBY: Lock it yourself!

(THEO *with definite, hurried steps moves out into the shop for the front door.*)

THEO: I'm not selling another bottle, target, or anything till I get some
help! (*Locks the door to the persistence of the knocking*). . . . We're closed!
BOBBY: I don't think Blue is gon like you turning customers away. . . .
(*Sits in the barber's chair, lighting up a cigar*)

THEO: You can tell Blue, I don't like standing over that stove all day, that I don't like him promising me helpers that don't show up. There are a lot of things I don't go for, like Pop taking off and not showing up for two days. I make this whiskey, I sell it, I keep books, I peddle numbers and those damn targets. AND I DON'T LIKE YOU STANDING AROUND HERE ALL DAY NOT LIFTING A FINGER TO HELP ME!

BOBBY (*taking a big puff on his cigar*): I don't hear you. . . .

THEO: Look at you—all decked out in your new togs—look at me, I haven't been out of these dungarees since we opened this place up.

BOBBY (*jumping down out of the chair*): I don't wanta hear nothing! You do what you wanta do, and leave me alone!

THEO: What am I supposed to be, a work mule or something?

BOBBY: You're the one that's so smart, you can't answer your own stupid questions?

THEO: You done let Blue turn you against me, huh?

BOBBY: You ask the questions, and you gon answer them—but for now, stop blowing your breath in my face!

THEO: You make me sick . . . (*Moves into the back room . . . sits on bed*)

(ADELE *enters from upstairs, dressed in a smart Saks Fifth Avenue outfit.*)

ADELE: Getting tired already, Theo?

THEO: No, just once in awhile I'd like to have some time to see one of my women!

ADELE: You being the big industrialist and all that, I thought you had put girls off for a year or two!

THEO: Get away from me. . . . (*Crosses to desk and sits*)

ADELE: I must say, however—it is sure a good sight to see you so wrapped up in work. I never thought I'd live to see the day, but—

THEO: Don't you ever have anything good to say!?

ADELE: I say what I think and feel—I'm honest. . . .

THEO: Honest? You're just hot because Pop decided to do something my way for a change. . . .

ADELE: That's a joke when you haven't seen him for two whole days— Or do you know where he has gone to practically every night since you opened up this little store.

THEO: He's out having a little sport for himself. What's wrong with that? He hasn't had any fun in a long time.

ADELE: Is fun all you can think of? When *my* father doesn't show up for two days, I worry.

THEO: You're not worried about nobody but yourself—I'm on to your game. . . . You'd give anything in the world to go back just the way we were because you liked the idea of us being dependent on you—Well, that's all done with, baby, we're on our own—So, don't worry yourself about Pop—when Blue gets here tonight with our money, he'll be here!

ADELE: If my eyes and ears are clear, then I would say that Father isn't having the kind of money troubles these days that he must rush home for your payday.

THEO: What do you mean by that?

ADELE: I mean that he has been dipping his hands into that little drawer of yours at least two or three times a week.

THEO: You ain't telling nothing I don't know. . . .

ADELE: What about your friend, Blue . . . ?

THEO: I can handle him. . . .

ADELE: I hope so, since it is a known fact that he can be pretty evil when he thinks someone has done him wrong—and it happened once, in a bar uptown, he actually killed a man.

THEO: You're lying . . . . (*He quickly moves to entrance into shop.*) Bobby, have you heard anything about Blue killing a man?

(BOBBY *looks to him and then turns his face with no response.* THEO *reenters in back room.*)

ADELE: Asking him about it is not going to help you. Ask yourself a few questions and you will know that you are no better than Blue—because it is you two who are the leaders of those mysterious store raids on 125th Street, and your ace boy on those robberies is no one other than your brother, Bobby Parker!

THEO: Bobby!

ADELE: I don't know why that should surprise you, since he is known as the swiftest and coolest young thief in Harlem . . .

THEO: I didn't know about Bobby—*who told you!*

ADELE: As you well know by now, I've been getting around lately, and I meet people, and people like to have something to talk about, and you know something: this place is becoming the talk along every corner and bar on the avenue!

THEO: You're just trying to scare me. . . .

ADELE: I wish to God I was. . . . (*Starts out*)

THEO: Where are you going?

ADELE (*stopping and turning abruptly*): Out, do you mind!?

THEO: That's all you ever do!

ADELE: Yes, you're right. . . .

THEO: They tell me you're going with Wilmer Robinson?

ADELE: Yes, that's true. . . . (*Moving through shop toward door*)

THEO (*following behind her*): He's a snake . . .

ADELE: No better or worse than someone like you or Blue . . .

THEO: He'll bleed you for every dime you've got!

ADELE: So what—He treats me like a woman, and that's more than I can say for any man in this house!

THEO: He'll treat you like a woman until he's gotten everything he wants, and then he's gon split your ass wide open!

ADELE (*turning sharply at door*): THEOOOOOOOOOOOO! (*Pause.*) You talk like that to me because you don't know how to care for the fact that I am your sister. . . .

THEO: But why are you trying to break us up? Why!?

ADELE: I don't have to waste that kind of good time—I can wait for you to bust it up yourself—good-night! (*Slams the door and exits abruptly*)

(THEO *stands with a long deep look in his eyes, then goes to back room and exits in cellar.* PARKER *steps into the shop, all dapper, dressed up to fair-thee-well, holding a gold-top cane in one hand, and a book in the other.* BOBBY *is staring at him with bewildered eyes.*)

BOBBY: What's that you got on?

MR. PARKER: What does it look like?

BOBBY: Nothing. . . .

MR. PARKER: You call this nothing!

BOBBY: Nothing—I mean, I didn't mean nothing when I asked you that question . . .

MR. PARKER: Where's Theo?

BOBBY: In the back, working. . . .

MR. PARKER: Good! Shows he's got his mind stretched out for good and great things. . . . (*Hangs up hat and rids self of cane*)

BOBBY: He's been stretching his mind out to find out where you been.

MR. PARKER: Where I been is none of his business—Blue is the man to think about—it's payday, and I wanta know where the hell is he! (*Checks his watch, taps* BOBBY, *indicating that he should step down from the chair*)

BOBBY (*hopping down from the chair as* PARKER *sits*): Whatcha reading?

MR. PARKER: A book I picked up yesterday. I figured since I'm in business, I might as well read a businessman's book.

BOBBY: Let me see it. . . . (*Takes the book in his hand*) The Thief's Journal by Jean Gin-net. . . (*Fingering through the pages*) Is it a good story?

MR. PARKER: So far. . . .

BOBBY (*handing it back to him*): What's it all about?

MR. PARKER: A Frenchman who was a thief. . . .

BOBBY: Steal things?

MR. PARKER: Uh huh. . . .

BOBBY: Where did he get all that time to write a book?

MR. PARKER: Oh, he had the time all right, cause he spent most of it in jail. . . .

BOBBY: Some thief!

MR. PARKER: —the trouble with this bird, is that he became a thief, and then he became a thinker.

BOBBY: No shucking!?

MR. PARKER: No shucking—but it is my logicalism—that you've got to become a thinker, and then you become a crook! Or else, why is it when you read up on some of these politicians' backgrounds, you find they all went to one of them big law colleges—that's where you get your start!

BOBBY: Well, I be damn!

MR. PARKER (*jumping down out of the chair and moving briskly for the door*): Now where is Blue! He said he would be here nine-thirty on the nose! (*Opens the door and* JENKINS *enters*) Hey, Jenkins! What's up!

MR. JENKINS: That Blue fellow show up yet?

MR. PARKER: No, he didn't, and I'm gon call him down about that too—

MR. JENKINS: It don't matter—I just want whatever money I got coming, and then I'm getting out of this racket . . .

MR. PARKER: Don't call it that, it's a committee!

MR. JENKINS: This committee ain't no committee—it ain't nothing but a racket, and I'm getting out of it!

MR. PARKER: You put your money into this thing, man—it ain't good business to walk out on an investment like that . . .

MR. JENKINS: I can and that's what I'm doing before I find myself in jail! Man, this thing you got going here is the talk in every bar in this neighborhood.

MR. PARKER: There ain't nothing for you to be scared of, Jenkins—Blue guaranteed me against ever being caught by the police. Now that's all right by me, but I've got some plans of my own. When he gets here tonight, I'm gon force him to make me one of the leaders in this group, and if he don't watch out, I just might take the whole operation over from him—I'll make you my right-hand man, and not only will you be getting more money, and I won't just guarantee you against getting caught, but I'll guarantee you against being scared!

MR. JENKINS: There's nothing you can say to make me change my mind. I shouldn't've let you talk me into this mess, in the first place. I'm getting out, and that's it! (*Starts for the door*) And if he gets back before I do, you hold my money for me! (*Starts to exit*)

MR. PARKER (*pursuing him to door*): Suit yourself, but you're cutting your own throat—this little setup is the biggest thing to hit this neighborhood since the day I started dancing! (*Slams door*) Fool. . . . (*Takes off coat, hangs it up—goes to mirror to primp*)

BOBBY: Going somewhere again?

MR. PARKER: Got myself a little date to get to if Blue ever gets here with our money—*and he better get here with our money!*

BOBBY: You been dating a lot lately—nighttime dates, and day ones too, and Theo's not happy about it. He says you don't stay here long enough to cut Yul Brynner's head . . .

MR. PARKER: He can complain all he wants to—I'm the boss here, and he better not forget it. . . . He's the one that's got some explaining to do—don't talk to nobody no more—don't go nowhere, looking like he's mad all the time. . . . I've also noticed that he don't get along with you anymore . . .

BOBBY: Well, Pop, that's another story. . . .

MR. PARKER: Come on, boy, there's something on his mind, and you know what it is. . . .

BOBBY (*moving away*): Nothing, except he wants to tell me what to do all the time—but I've got some ideas of my own. I ain't no dumbbell—I just don't talk as much as he do—If I did, the people I talk to would know just as much as I do—I just want him to go his way, and I'll go mine.

MR. PARKER: There's more to it than that, and I wanta know what it is.

BOBBY: There's nothing. . . .

MR. PARKER: Come on now, boy. . . .

BOBBY: That's all, Pop!

MR. PARKER (*grabbing him*): It's not and you better say something!

BOBBY: He—I don't know what to tell you, Pop—He just don't like the way things are going—with you, me—Adele. He got in a fight with her today and she told him about Blue killing a man . . .

MR. PARKER: Is it true?

BOBBY: Yeah—Blue killed this man one time for saying something about his woman, and this woman got a child by Blue, but Blue never married her, and so this man started signifying about it—Blue hit him, the man reached for a gun in his pocket, Blue took the gun from him, and the—man started running, but by that time, Blue had fire in his eyes, and he shot the man three times.

MR. PARKER: Well. . . .

BOBBY: Blue got only two years for it!

MR. PARKER: Two years, huh? That's another thing I'm gon throw in his face tonight if he tries to get smart with me. Ain't that something.

Going around bumping people off, and getting away with it too! What do he think he is, white or something!

(THEO *reenters and sits at desk.*)

(PARKER *checks his watch.*) I'm getting tired of this! (*Moves into back room*) Where's that friend of yours!? I don't have to wait around this barbershop all night for him. It's been two months now, and I want my money! When I say be here at nine-thirty, I mean be here!

THEO (*rising from the chair at the desk*): Where have you been, Pop?

MR. PARKER: That's none of your business! Now where is that man with my money!?

THEO: Money is not your problem—you've been spending it all over town! And you've been taking it out of this desk!

MR. PARKER: So? I borrowed a little. . . .

THEO: You call four hundred dollars a little! Now I've tried to fix these books so it don't show too big, and you better hope Blue don't notice it when he starts fingering through these pages tonight.

MR. PARKER: To hell with Blue! It's been two months now, and he ain't shown us a dime!

THEO: What are you doing with all that money, Pop?

MR. PARKER: I don't have to answer to you! I'm the boss here. And another thing, there's a lot about Blue and this association I want to know about! I want a position! I don't have to sit around here every month or so, waiting for somebody to bring me *my* money.

THEO: Money! Money! That's all you can think about!

MR. PARKER: Well, look who's talking—You forget, this was all your idea. . . . Remember what I told you about starting something and sticking with it—What is it now, boy? The next thing you'll tell me is that you've decided to become a priest, or something—What's the new plan, Theo?

THEO: No new plans, Pop—I just don't want us to mess up. . . . Don't you understand—things must be done right or else we're going to get ourselves in jail—We have to be careful, we have to think about each other all the time—I didn't go into this business just for myself—I wasn't out to prove how wrong Adele was—I just thought the time had come for us to do something about all them years we laid around here letting Mama kill herself!

MR. PARKER: I have told you, a thousand times I don't wanta hear any talk about your Mama—She's dead, dammit! So let it stay that way! (*Moves toward shop*)

THEO: All right, let's talk about Adele, then. . . .

MR. PARKER (*stopping at steps*): What about her?

THEO: She's out of this house every night. . . .

MR. PARKER: Boy, you surprise me—what do you think she should do—Work like a dog all day and then come to this house and bite her fingernails all night. . . .

THEO: She's got herself a boyfriend too, and—

MR. PARKER (*crossing to counter*): Good! I got myself a girlfriend, now that makes two of us!

THEO (*following him*): But he's—Aw, what's the use—But I wish you'd stay in the shop more!

MR. PARKER: That's too bad—I have things to do. I don't worry about where you're going when you leave here . . .

THEO: I don't go anywhere and you know it—If I did, we wouldn't do an hour's business. *But we have been doing great business!* And you wanta know why? They love it! *Everybody* loves the way ol' Theo brews corn! Every after-hours joint is burning with it! And for us to do that kind of business, I've had to sweat myself down in this hole for something like sixteen hours a day for two whole months!

MR. PARKER: What do you want from me?

THEO: —I just want you here in the shop with me, so at least we can pretend that this is a barbershop. A cop walked through that door today while I had three customers in here, and I had to put one of them in that chair and cut his hair!

MR. PARKER: How did you make out?

THEO: Pop, I don't need your jokes!

MR. PARKER: All right, don't get carried away. (*Goes to his son and places his arm around the boy's shoulders*) I'll make it my business to stay here in the shop with you more. . . .

THEO: And make Blue guarantee me some help.

MR. PARKER: You'll get that too—But you've got to admit one thing, though—you've always been a lazy boy. I didn't expect you to jump and all of a sudden, act like John Henry!

THEO: I have never been lazy—I just didn't wanta break my back for the man!

MR. PARKER: Well, I can't blame you for that. I know because I did it. I did it when they didn' pay me a single dime!

BOBBY: When was that?

MR. PARKER: When I was on the chain gang!

BOBBY: Now you know you ain't never been on no chain gang!

MR. PARKER (*holds up two fingers*): Two months, that's all it was—just two months . . .

BOBBY: Two months my foot!

MR. PARKER: I swear to heaven I was—It was in 19-something, I was living in Jersey City, New Jersey . . . . (*Crosses to throne and sits*)

BOBBY: Here we go with another story!

MR. PARKER: That was just before I started working as a vaudeville man and there was this ol' cousin of mine we used to call "Dub," and he had this job driving a trailer truck from Jersey City to Jacksonville, Florida. One day he asked me to come along with him for company— I weren't doing nothing at the time, and—

BOBBY: As usual. . . .

MR. PARKER: I didn't say that!—Anyway, we drove along—everything was fine 'til we hit Macon, Georgia. We weren't doing a thing, but before we knew it, this cracker police stopped us, claiming we'd ran through a red light. He was yelling and hollering, and boyyy did I get mad—I was ready to get a hold of that cracker, and work on his head, until . . .

BOBBY: Until what. . . . ?

MR. PARKER: Until, they put us on the chain gang, and the chain gang they put us on was a chain gang and a half! I busted some rocks, John Wayne couldn't've busted! I was a rock-busting fool! (*Rises and demonstrates how he swung the hammer*) I would do it like this! I would hit the rock, and the hammer would bounce—bounce so hard, it would take my hand up in the air with it, but I'd grab it with my left hand, and bring it down like this; Hunh! (*He gets carried away by the rhythm of his story and he starts twisting his body to the swing of it.*) It would get so good to me, I'd say: Hunh! Yeah! Hunh! I'd say, Ooooooooooooweeeee! I'm wide open now! (*Swinging and twisting*) Yeah baby, I say Hunh! Sooner or later, that rock would crack! Old Dub ran into a rock one day that was hard as Theo's head. He couldn't bust that rock for nothing. He pumped and swung, but that rock would not move. So, finally he said to the captain: "I'm sorry, Cap, but a elephant couldn't break this rock. Cap didn't wanna hear nothing—he said: "Well, Dub, I wanna tell you something—your lunch and your supper is in the middle of that rock." On the next swing of the hammer, Dub busted that rock into a thousand pieces! (*Laughs*) I'm telling you, them crackers is mean—don't let nobody tell you about no communists, Chinese, or anything—there ain't nothing on this earth meaner and dirtier than an American-born cracker!— We used to sleep in them long squad tents on the ground, and we was all hooked up to this one big long chain—the guards had orders to shoot at random in the dark if ever one of them chains would rattle. You couldn't even turn over in your sleep! (*Sits on throne*)

BOBBY: A man can't help but turn over in his sleep!

MR. PARKER: Not on this chain gang you didn't. You turn over on this chain gang in your sleep, and your behind was shot! But if you had to, you would have to wake up, announce that you was turning over, and then you go back to sleep!

BOBBY: What!

MR. PARKER: Just like this: (*Illustrating physically*) Number four turning over! But that made all the chains on the other convicts rattle, so they had to turn over too and shout: Number five turning over! Number six turning over! Number seven!

THEO: Why don't you stop it!

MR. PARKER: I ain't lying!

BOBBY: Is that all?

MR. PARKER: Yeah, and I'm gon get Adele to type that up on my typewriter! (*Goes to the window*) Now where the hell is that Blue Haven!

MR. JENKINS (*rushing in*): Did he show up yet?

MR. PARKER: Naw, and when he does, I'm—

MR. JENKINS: I told you I didn't trust that boy—who knows where he is! Well, I'm going out there and get him! (*Starts back out*)

MR. PARKER (*grabbing him by the arm*): Now don't go out there messing with Blue, Jenkins!—IF there's anybody got a reason for being mad with him, it's me—now take it easy—when he gets here, we'll all straighten him out—come on, sit down and let me beat you a game one time—(*Rushes to take the board out*)

BOBBY: Tear him up, Pop!

MR. JENKINS (*pausing*): Okay, you're on— (*Moves toward* PARKER *and the table*) It's hopeless—I been playing your father for three solid years, and he has yet to beat me one game!

MR. PARKER: Yeah! But his luck done come to past!

MR. JENKINS: My luck ain't come to pass, cause my luck is skill—(*Spells the word out*) S-K-I-L-L . . .

MR. PARKER (*shaking up the can*): Come on now, Jenkins, let's play the game—Take one . . . (JENKINS *pulls out a checker.*) —You see there, you get the first move. . . .

MR. JENKINS: You take me for a fool, Parker, and just for that, I ain't gon let you get a king. . . .

MR. PARKER: Put your money where your lips is—I say, I'm gon win this game!

MR. JENKINS: I don't want your money, I'm just gon beat you!

MR. PARKER: I got twenty dollars here to make a liar out of you! (*Slams down a twenty dollar bill on the table*) Now you doing all the bragging about how I never beat you, but I'm valiant enough to say that from here on in, you can't win air, and I got twenty dollars up on the table to back it up.

MR. JENKINS: Oh well, he ain't satisfied with me beating him all the time for sport—he wants me to take his money too. . . .

MR. PARKER: But that's the difference. . . .

MR. JENKINS: What kind of difference?

MR. PARKER: We're playing for money, and I don't think you can play under that kind of pressure. You do have twenty dollars, don't you?

MR. JENKINS: I don't know what you're laughing about, I always keep some money on me. (*Pulls out little change pouch and puts twenty dollars on the table*) You get a little money in your pocket, and you get carried away . . .

MR. PARKER: It's your move. . . .

MR. JENKINS: Start you off over here in this corner . . .

MR. PARKER: Give you that little ol' fellow there . . .

MR. JENKINS: I'll take him. . . .

MR. PARKER: I'll take this one.

MR. JENKINS: I'll give you this man here.

MR. PARKER: I'll jump him—so that you can have this one.

MR. JENKINS: I'll take him.

MR. PARKER: Give you this man here.

MR. JENKINS: All right. (*He moves.*)

MR. PARKER: I'll take this one. (*There are a series of grunts and groans as they exchange men.*) And I'll take these three—Boom! Boom! Boom! (*Jumping JENKINS' men and laughing loud*)

(*The game is now in definite favor of PARKER. JENKINS is pondering over his situation. PARKER is relishing JENKINS' predicament*)

—Study long, you study wrong. . . . I'm afraid that's you, ol' buddy. . . . I knew it, I knew it all the time—I used to ask myself! I wonder how ol' Jenks would play if he really had some pressure on him? You remember how the Dodgers used to raise hell every year until they met the Yankees in the World Series, and how under all that pressure, they would crack up? (*Laughs*) That pressure got him!

MR. JENKINS: Hush up, man, I'm trying to think!

MR. PARKER: I don't know what you could be thinking about, cause the rooster done came and wrote, skiddy biddy!

MR. JENKINS (*finally making a move*): There!

MR. PARKER (*in singsong*): That's all—That's all. . . . (*Makes another jump*) Boom! Just like you say, Bobby, "tear him up!" (*Rears his head back in ecstatic laughter*)

MR. JENKINS (*making a move*): It's your move. . . .

(PARKER *brings his head back down, but the laughing trails off sickly upon the realization that the game is now in his opponent's favor*)

PARKER: Well, I see—I guess that kinda changes the color of the game. . . . Let me see, now . . .

MR. JENKINS (*getting revenge*): Why don't you laugh some more—I like the way you laugh, Parker . . .

MR. PARKER: Shut up, Jenkins, I'm thinking!

MR. JENKINS: Thinking? Thinking for what? The game is over! (*Now he is laughing heavily.*)

(PARKER *sorrily makes his move.*)

—Uh uh! Lights out! (*Still laughing and making his move*) Game time and you know it! Take your jump!

(PARKER *is forced to take his jump.*)

(*Taking* PARKER's *last three men*) I told you about laughing and bragging in my game! Boom! Boom! Boom!

MR. PARKER (*rising abruptly from the table and dashing to coatrack*): Dammit!!!

MR. JENKINS: Where you going—ain't we gon play some more!?

MR. PARKER (*putting on coat*): I don't wanta play you no more—you too damn lucky!

MR. JENKINS: Aw come on, Parker—I don't want your money, I just want to play!

MR. PARKER: You won it, you keep it—I can *afford* it! But one of these days you're going to leave that voodoo root of yours home, and that's gonna be the day—you hear me, you sonofabitch!

BOBBY: Pop!

MR. PARKER: I don't want to hear nothing from you!

MR. JENKINS (*realizing that his friend is honestly upset over the affair*): It's only a game—and it don't have nothing to do with luck. . . . But you keep trying, Parker, and one of these days you're going to beat me—and when you do, it won't have nothing to do with luck—it just might be the unluckiest and worst day of your life. You'll be champion checker player of the world. Meanwhile, I'm the champ, *and you're gonna have to live with it.*

MR. PARKER (*smiling, begrudgingly moving out toward him with his hand extended*): All right, Jenkins! You win this time but I'm gon beat you yet—I'm gon whip your behind until it turns white!

BOBBY: That's gon be some strong whipping!

(*There's a tap at the door.*)

That must be Blue. . . . (*Quickly rushes to the door and opens it*)

MR. PARKER: About time. . . .

(BLUE *enters.*)

Hey boy, where have you been?

BLUE (*moving in carrying an attaché case*): I got stuck with an emergency council meeting. . . .

MR. PARKER: What kind of council?

BLUE: The Council of the Association—I see you're sporting some new clothes there, Mr. P.—You must be rolling in extra dough these days.

MR. PARKER: Just a little something I picked up the other day. . . . All right, where is the money, Blue?

BLUE: You'll get your money, but first I want to see those books. (*Moves to the desk in the back room and immediately starts going over the books*)

(*In the shop an uneasy silence prevails.* JENKINS, *out of nervousness resets the checkers on the board for another game.*)

I see. . . . (*Takes out his pencil and pad and starts scribbling on a sheet of paper*) Uh huh—uh huh. . . . (*Reenters shop*)

MR. PARKER: Well?

BLUE: Everything seems to be okay. . . .

MR. PARKER: Of course everything is all right—What did you expect? (*Angrily impatient*) Now come on and give me my money.

BLUE: Take it easy, Mr. Parker! (*He takes a white envelop from his case and passes it on to him.*) Here's your money. . . .

MR. PARKER: Now this is what I like to see!

BLUE (*passing a group of bills on to* JENKINS): And you, Mr. Jenkins. . . .

MR. JENKINS: Thank you, young man, but from here on in, you can count me out of your operation. . . .

BLUE: What's the trouble?

MR. JENKINS: No trouble at all—I just want to be out of it . . .

BLUE: People and headaches—that's all I ever get from all the Mr. Jenkinses in this world!

MR. JENKINS: Why don't you be quiet sometime, boy. . . .

MR. PARKER: I'm afraid he's telling you right, Blue. . . .

BLUE: HE'S TELLING ME THAT HE IS A DAMN IDIOT, WHO CAN GET HIMSELF HURT!

THEO: Who's going to hurt him?

(*They all stare at* BLUE.)

BLUE (*calming himself*): I'm sorry—I guess I'm working too hard these days. . . . I got a call today from one of them "black committees" here in Harlem. . . .

THEO: What did they want?

BLUE: They wanted to know what we did—they said they had heard of us, but they never see us—meaning, they never see us picketing, demonstrating, and demanding something all the time. . . .

MR. PARKER: So . . . ?

BLUE: They want us to demonstrate with them next Saturday, and I have decided to set up a demonstrating committee, with you in charge, Mr. Parker . . .

MR. PARKER: You what!?

BLUE: You'd be looking good!

MR. PARKER: You hear that! (*Cynical laughter*) *I'd be looking good!* Count me out! When I demonstrate, it's for real!

BLUE: You demonstrate in front of any store out there on that street, and you'll have a good sound reason for being there!

MR. PARKER: I thought you said we was suppose to be different, and we was to drive out that "Mr. You Know Somebody"—well ain't that what we doing? Two stores already done put up going out of business signs. . . .

BLUE: That's what we started this whole thing for, and that's what we're doing.

MR. PARKER: I got some questions about that too—I don't see nothing that we're doing that would cause a liquor store, a clothing store, and a radio store to just all of a sudden close down like that, unless we've been raiding and looting them at night or something like that . . .

(BOBBY *quickly moves out of the shop into the back room and exits upstairs.*)

BLUE: It's the psychological thing that's doing it, man!

MR. PARKER: Psychological!? Boy, you ain't telling me everything, and anyway, I wanta know who made this decision about picketing.

BLUE: The council!

MR. PARKER: Who is on this council?

BLUE: You know we don't throw names around like that!

MR. PARKER: I don't get all the mystery, Blue. This is my house, and you know everything about it from top to bottom. I got my whole family in this racket!

BLUE: You're getting a good share of the money—ain't that enough?

MR. PARKER: Not when I'm dealing with you in the dark . . .

BLUE: You're asking for something, so stop beating around corners and tell me what it is you want!

MR. PARKER: All right! You been promising my boy some help for two months now, and he's still waiting—Now I want you to give him that help starting tomorrow, and I want you to put somebody in this shop who can cut hair to relieve me when I'm not here. And from here on in, I want to know everything that's to be known about this "decolonization committee"—how it works, who's in it, who's running it, *and I want to be on that council you was talking about!*

BLUE: No!

MR. PARKER: Then I can't cooperate with you anymore!

BLUE: What does that mean?

MR. PARKER: It means we can call our little deal off, and you can take your junk out of here!

BLUE: Just like that?

MR. PARKER: Just any ol' way you want it—I take too many risks in this place, not to know where I stand . . .

BLUE: Mr. Parker. . . .

MR. PARKER: All right, let me hear it and let me hear it quick!

BLUE: There is an opening on our council—it's a—

MR. PARKER: Just tell me what position is it!

BLUE: President. . . .

MR. PARKER: President?

BLUE: The highest office on our council. . . .

MR. PARKER: Boy, you're gonna have to get up real early to get by an old fox like me. A few minutes ago you offered me nothing, and now you say I can be president—that should even sound strange to *you!*

BLUE: There's nothing strange—a few minutes ago you weren't ready to throw me out of your place, but now *I've got no other choice!*

MR. PARKER (*pointing his finger at him and laughing*): That's true! You don't!. . . . All right, I'll give you a break—I accept! Just let me know when the next meeting is. (*Checks watch and grabs his hat*) Come on Jenkins, let's get out of here! (*Starts out with* MR. JENKINS)

THEO: Hey Pop—you're going out there with all that money in your pocket . . .

MR. PARKER: Don't worry about it—I'm a grown man, I can take care of myself. . . .

THEO: But what about our part of it. . . .

MR. PARKER: Look, son, he held me up, I'm late already—you'll get yours when I get back. . . .

THEO: But Pop—

MR. PARKER: Good-night, Theo! (*He bolts out of the door with* JENKINS *following.*)

THEO (*rushing to the door*): Pop, you better be careful! I'll be waiting for you! I don't care if it's 'til dawn!

BLUE: You're becoming a worrier, Theo! (*Pause.*) But that's the nature of all things. . . . I'm forever soothing and pacifying someone— sometimes I have to pacify myself. You don't think that president stuff is going to mean anything, do you? He had me uptight, so what I did was to bring him closer to me so I would be definitely sure of letting him know less, and having more control over him—And over you too. . . .

THEO: What do you mean by that?

BLUE: It didn't take me more than one glance into those books to know that he's been spending money out of the box—and to think—you didn't bother to tell me about it.

THEO: Why should I? I trust your intelligence. . . .

BLUE: Please don't let him do it anymore. . . .

THEO: Why don't you hire your own cashier and bookkeeper? (*He goes into back room.*)

BLUE (*following him*): That's an idea! What about Adele! Now that was a thought in the back of my mind, but I'm putting that away real quick—Seems this sweet, nice-girl sister of yours has took to partying with the good-time set, and keeping company with a simple ass clown like Wilmer Robinson—No, that wouldn't work, would it? I'd have more trouble with her than I'm having with you. When a girl as intelligent as your sister, who all of a sudden gets into things, and hooked up to people who just don't go with her personality, that could mean trouble.—To be honest with you, I didn't think this thing was going to work, but *it is working,* Theo! I've got three places just like this one, and another on the way. A man has to care about what he does. Don't you want to get out of this place!?

THEO: Yes, but lately, I've been getting the feeling that I'm gonna have to hurt someone.

BLUE: I see. . . .

THEO: —you think the old man was asking you those questions about stores closing down as a joke or something?

BLUE: He asks because he thinks, but he is still in the dark!

THEO: He was playing with you! And when my father holds something inside of him and plays with a man, he's getting meaner and more dangerous by the minute.

BLUE: I don't care what he was doing—he is messing with my work! He has gotten himself into a "thing" with one of the rottenest bitches on the Avenue, who happens to be tight with a nigger who is trying to fuck up my business. Now that's something you had better get straight—it's your turn to soothe and pacify!

THEO: Why should I do anything for you when you lied to me and sent my brother out with that band of thieves of yours?

BLUE: —He said he needed the money and I couldn't stop him.

THEO: But I told you I didn't want that!

BLUE: Let's face it, baby! Bobby's the greatest thief in the world! He's been prancing around stores and stealing all of his life!—And I think that's something to bow down to—because he's black and in trouble, just like you and me. So, don't ride so hard, Theo! (*Crosses back into shop, picks up attaché case preparing to leave*)

THEO: Blue! Now, I don't care what kind of protection you got, but I say those store raids are dangerous, and I don't want my brother on them, and I mean it!

BLUE: When we first made our plans, you went along with it—you knew somebody had to do it—What makes you and your brother so special!?

THEO: Well, you better. . . .

BLUE: TO HELL WITH YOU, THEO! I could take this hand and make you dead! You are nothing, but what I make you be!

THEO (*pausing*): That just might be—but what if tomorrow this whole operation were to bust wide open in your face because of some goof up by my father or sister—something that would be just too much for you to clean up—What would you do? Kill them?

BLUE (*pausing—then speaking calmly and deliberately*): The other day, I went up on the hill to see my little boy. . . . I took him out for a ride, and as we were moving along the streets, he asked me where all the people were coming from. I said: from work, going home, going to the store, and coming back from the store. . . . Then we went out to watch the river, and then he asked me about the water, the ships, the weeds—everything—that kid threw so many questions at me, I got dizzy—I wanted to hit him once to shut him up. . . . He was just a little dark boy discovering for the first time, that there are things in the world like stones and trees. . . . It got late and dark—so I took him home and watched him fall asleep. Then I took his mother into my arms and put her into bed—I just laid there for awhile, listening to her call me all kinds of dirty motherfuckers. . . . After she got that out of her system, I put my hands on her, and before long, our arms were locked at each other's shoulders, and then my thighs moved slowly down between her thighs, and then we started that sweet rolling until the both of us were screaming as if the last piece of love was dying forever. After that, we just laid there, talking soft up into the air—I would tell her she was the loveliest bitch that ever lived, and all of a sudden, she was no longer calling me a dirty motherfucker, she was calling me a sweet motherfucker. It got quiet. I sat up on the edge of the bed, with my head hanging long and deep, trying to push myself out of the room, and back into it at one and the same time. She looked up at me, and I got that same question all over again. Will you marry me and be the father of your son! I tried to move away from her, but she dug her fingernails into my shoulders—I struck her once, twice, and again and again—with this hand!—And her face was a bloody mess! And I felt real bad about that, I said: I'll marry you, YES! YES! YES! (*Pause.*) I put my clothes on and I walked out into the streets, trembling with the knowledge that now I have a little boy who I must walk through the park with every Sunday, who one day just may blow my head off—and an abiding wife who on a given evening may get herself caught in the bed of some other man, and I could be sealed in a dungeon until dead! I was found lying in a well of blood on the day I was born! But I have been kind! I have kissed babies for the simple reason they were babies! I'm going to get married to some bitch and that gets me to shaking all over! (*He moves toward and stands close to* THEO.) The last time I trembled this way, I KILLED A MAN!

(*Quickly and rhythmically he takes out a long shiny switchblade knife—it pops open just at* THEO's *neck.* BLUE *holds it there for a moment then withdraws and closes it, puts it away, collects his belongings then calmly addresses* THEO.) Things are tight and cool on my end, Theo, and that's how you should keep it here—if not, everything gets messy, and I find myself acting like a policeman, keeping order—I don't have the time for that kind of trick. (BLUE *exits.*)

(*After a moment of silent thought* THEO *moves decisively to the back room stairs.*)

THEO: Bobby!

(BOBBY *comes downstairs.*)

I want you to stay away from those store raids, Bobby.

BOBBY: Not as long as I can get myself some extra money. . . . (*Moving close to him*) You didn't say nothing to me before, when I was stealing every other day, and giving you half of everything I stole—you didn't think nothing that day you sent me for that typewriter!

THEO: I don't know what you're going to do from here on in because I'm calling the whole affair off with Blue. . . .

BOBBY: That won't stop me and you know it!

THEO: What is it, Bobby—we used to be so close! Bobby, don't get too far away from me!

BOBBY (*heatedly*): What do you want me to do? Stick around you all the time? Hell, I'm tired of you! I stick by you and I don't know what to do! I steal and that puts clothes on my back and money in my pockets! That's something to do! But I sit here with you all day just thinking about the next word I'm going to say—I'm not stupid! I sit here all day thinking about what I'm going to say to you. I stuck by you and I hoped for you because whatever you became, I was gonna become. . . . I thought about that, and that ain't shit! (*He exits thru shop door.*)

(THEO *is alone with his troubled thoughts. Suddenly he rushes into back room gets hat and shirt, puts them on, exits thru shop and into street.*)

MR. PARKER (*stepping down into the back room from the apartment upstairs*): Come on, girl!

(*A very attractive well-dressed young girl in her early twenties, steps down into the room behind him.* PARKER *continues into shop,* YOUNG GIRL *following.*)

MR. PARKER: You wanted to see it, well here it is . . .

YOUNG GIRL (*looking about the place and stepping out into the shop*): So, this is where you do your business . . . like I keep asking you Russell, what kind of business is it for you to make all that money you got?

(PARKER *heads back into rear room and goes to the refrigerator.*)

MR. PARKER: Come on in here sweetheart, I'll fix us a drink!

YOUNG GIRL (*moving briskly into the room*): I asked you a question, Russell—

(*Still ignoring her question,* PARKER *takes jug out of refrigerator and grabs two glasses.*)

MR. PARKER: I'm going to make you a special drink, made from my own hands—it's called, Black Lightning.

YOUNG GIRL (*surveying the room as* PARKER *pours drink*): That should be exciting . . .

MR. PARKER: Here you go— (*Hands her the drink*) *Toujours l'amour!*

YOUNG GIRL (*gasping from the drink*): What the fuck is this! What is this Russell . . .

MR. PARKER (*patting her on the back*): Knocks the tail off of you, don't it! But it gets smoother after the second swallow. . . . Go on, drink up!

YOUNG GIRL: Okay—(*Tries it again—frowningly . . . moves away from him as he sits on bed*)

MR. PARKER: Now, did you think about what I asked you last night?

YOUNG GIRL: About getting married?

MR. PARKER: Yes. . . .

YOUNG GIRL: Why do you want to marry me, Russell?

MR. PARKER: Because I love you, and I think you could make me happy.

YOUNG GIRL: Well I don't believe you—when I asked you a question about your business, you deliberately ignored me—it was like you didn't trust me, and I thought that love and trust went together.

MR. PARKER: I'm not so sure about that—my son, Theo, I'm wild about him, but I wouldn't trust him no farther 'n I could throw a building.

YOUNG GIRL: I'm not your son!

MR. PARKER: What is it you wanta know?

YOUNG GIRL: Where you gettin' all that money from?

MR. PARKER: Oh, that—that's not for a girl to know—baby-doll.

YOUNG GIRL: Then it's time for me to go—I'm not gettin' myself hooked up with no mystery man! (*Moves as if to exit*)

(PARKER *stops, then pauses for a moment.*)

MR. PARKER: All right, I'll tell you—I'm partners in a big business, which I'm the president of.

YOUNG GIRL: Partners with who, Russell.

MR. PARKER: That's not important, baby. . . .

YOUNG GIRL: Partners with who, Russell.

MR. PARKER: Mr. Blue Haven.

YOUNG GIRL: Blue Haven! Then it's crooked business.

MR. PARKER: Oh, no baby, it's nothing like that. . . . It's real straight.

YOUNG GIRL: What does that mean?

MR. PARKER: That what we're doing is right!

YOUNG GIRL: Tell me about it, then—

MR. PARKER: I've said enough, now let's leave it at that! (*Tries to embrace her*)

YOUNG GIRL (*warding him off, sitting on bed*): All you take me for is something to play with.

MR. PARKER: That's not true, I wanna marry you. (*Sits beside her*)

YOUNG GIRL: You say you want to marry me, but how do you expect me to think about marrying somebody who won't confide in me about what they're doing. How do I know I'm not letting myself in for trouble.

MR. PARKER (*thinking for a moment then rising*): All right, I'll tell you! We peddle a variety of products to the community and we sell things, to people at a price they can't get nowhere else in this city—Yes, according to the law it's illegal but we help our people, our own people. We take care of business, and at the same time we make everybody happy. We take care of our people. Just like I been taking care of you.

YOUNG GIRL: You take care of me? How? You've never given me more than ten dollars in cash since I've known you.

MR. PARKER: Well, I've got a big present for you coming right out of this pocket and I'm gon take you downtown tomorrow and let you spend till the store runs out.

YOUNG GIRL: Taking me to a store and giving me spending change, makes me feel like a child and I don't like it, and I'm not gonna stand for it anymore.

MR. PARKER: Then take this, and you do whatever you want with it.

YOUNG GIRL (*taking the money and putting it away*): Now, don't get the idea I'm just in love with your money.

MR. PARKER: Now, I want you to stop talking to me about money. I've got *plenty* of it! You've got to understand—I'm the most different man you ever met—I've been around this world, I danced before the king and queen of England—I've seen and heard many a thing in my lifetime—and you know what—I'm putting it all down on paper— my story!

YOUNG GIRL: Your story!

(MR. PARKER *moves into shop—gets notebook from behind one of the sliding panels. During his absence* YOUNG GIRL *checks out what's under the bed.*)

MR. PARKER (*reentering back room*): Here it is, right here. . . . (*Sits back down next to her on the bed, giving her the notebook*)

YOUNG GIRL (*thumbing through the pages*): You write things too!?

MR. PARKER: I certainly do . . . and I've been thinking about writing a poem about you . . .

YOUNG GIRL: A poem about me!

MR. PARKER (*taking book from her, dropping it on floor*): I'm gon do it tonight before I go to sleep . . . (*He kisses her neck and reaches for the tip of her dress.*)

YOUNG GIRL (*breaking out of his embrace*): No, Russell, not here!

MR. PARKER: Why not?

YOUNG GIRL: Just because there's a bed wherever we go don't mean that we have to jump into it. You don't understand, Russell! You've got to start treating me the same as if I was your wife.

MR. PARKER: THAT'S EXACTLY WHAT I'M TRYING TO DO!

YOUNG GIRL (*rising*): Don't yell at me!

MR. PARKER: All right. . . . I tell you what: I'm kinda tired, let's just lie down for awhile and talk—I ain't gon try nothing.

YOUNG GIRL: Russell. . . .

MR. PARKER: May the Lord smack me down this minute into hell—I swear I won't do nothing . . .

YOUNG GIRL: What are the three biggest lies men tell to women, Russell?

MR. PARKER: I ain't just any man—I'm the man you gon spend your life with. . . .

YOUNG GIRL: Okay, Russell, we'll lie down but you've got to keep your word. If I'm the girl you want to marry, you've got to learn to keep your word.

(*They lay on bed. To her surprise* PARKER *is motionless, seemingly drifting off to sleep. After a moment she takes the initiative and begins to arouse him with lovemaking. He responds, and once his passion has reached an aggressive peak she discontinues abruptly.*)

Where do you get these things you sell to people?

MR. PARKER: What are you talking about?

YOUNG GIRL: You know what I'm saying—I overheard you tell Mr. Jenkins you suspected your son was robbing stores.

MR. PARKER: You heard no such thing!

YOUNG GIRL (*desperately*): Where do they keep the stuff?

MR. PARKER: Now, baby you've got to relax and stop worrying about things like that! (*Pulls her by the shoulders, receiving no resistance*) Come here . . . (*He pulls her down to the bed, takes her into his arms and kisses her, and immediately starts reaching for the tip of her dress.*)

YOUNG GIRL (*struggling, but weakening to his ardor*): Russell, you said you wouldn't do nothing!

MR. PARKER: I ain't! I just want to get a little closer to you!

YOUNG GIRL: Russell, not here!

MR. PARKER: Just let me feel it a little bit!

YOUNG GIRL: You swore to God, Russell!

(THEO *enters from barbershop heading toward back room.*)

MR. PARKER: I ain't gon do nothing!

YOUNG GIRL (*hears* THEO): Russell! Russell! Somebody is out there!

(PARKER *jumps up quickly as* THEO *stands before him.*)

MR. PARKER: What are you doing here?

THEO: The question is: *what are you doing!*

MR. PARKER: I have been having a private talk with a good friend of mine, now get out of here!

(*The* GIRL *jumps up, moving by* MR. PARKER.)

MR. PARKER (*stopping her*): Where are you going?

YOUNG GIRL: Home!

MR. PARKER: Hold it now, honey!

YOUNG GIRL: —I never should have come here in the first place!

MR. PARKER: No, you're not going anywhere—This is my place and you don't have to run off because of this Peeping Tom!

THEO: Pop, it's time to give us our money. . . .

MR. PARKER: You'll get your share tomorrow and not before!

THEO: I want it now before you give it all to that girl—Pop, cut that broad loose!

MR. PARKER: What was that?

THEO: I SAID, CUT HER LOOSE! SHE DON'T NEED AN OLD MAN LIKE YOU, SHE'S JUST PUMPING YOU FOR INFORMATION, THAT BITCH IS A HUSTLER!

MR. PARKER (*striking him across the face with the back of his hand*): BITE YOUR TONGUE!

YOUNG GIRL: I think I better go, Russell. . . . (*Crossing into shop heading toward door*)

MR. PARKER (*following her*): Okay, but I'll be right with you as soon as I get things straight here—you will be waiting for me, won't you?

YOUNG GIRL: Sure!

MR. PARKER: You run along now and I'll be right over there. . . . (*The* YOUNG GIRL *exits.* PARKER *whirls back into shop.*) What do you think you're doing, boy?

THEO: Just be careful, Pop—please be careful. . . .

MR. PARKER: If there's anybody I got to be careful of, it's you! You lying selfish sonofabitch! You think I don't know about you and Blue running that gang of thieves—about you sending your own brother out there with them?

THEO: I didn't do that!

MR. PARKER: If Bobby gets hurt out on them streets, I'm gonna kill you, boy! I'm gonna kill you. . . . (*Rushes to collect hat and coat*)

THEO: You're not worried about Bobby! All you can think of is the money you're rolling in! The clothes! And that stupid outfit you've got on!

(ADELE *enters shop from outside obviously distraught.*)

MR. PARKER: What's wrong with you—Are you drunk?

(*Moves to* ADELE—*she does not respond. . . . moves away from her*)

THEO: Of course she's drunk. What did you expect—Did you think everything would stop and stand still while you were being reborn again!

MR. PARKER: What do you want from me? Call this whole thing off? It was your idea, not mine! But now that I've got myself something— I'm not going to throw it away for nobody!

THEO: But can't you see what's happening here!?

MR. PARKER: If she wants to be a drunken wench, let her! I'm not going to take the blame—And as for you . . . (*goes in side coat pocket*) If you want this money, you can take it from me—I can throw every dollar of it into the ocean if I want to! You can call me a fool too, but I'm a *burning fool!* I'm going to marry that little girl. She is not a whore! She is a woman! And I'm going to marry her! And if the two of you don't like it, you can kiss my ass! (*Bolts out of the door and into the streets*)

THEO: You're not drunk—what happened?

ADELE (*crossing toward back room*): What does it look like. . . . Wilmer hit me.

THEO (*following her*): Why?

ADELE (*sitting on bed*): He caught me in Morgan's with a friend of his, after I had lied about going bowling with the girls—he just walked in and started hitting me, over and over again. His friend just stood there, pleading with him not to hit me, but he never did anything to stop him—I guess he figured: "Why should I risk getting myself killed over just another piece of ass"—I thought he was going to kill me, but then Blue came in with some of his friends, and they just grabbed him by the arms and took him away.

THEO: Was Bobby with them?

ADELE: I couldn't tell—

THEO: Dammit! Everything gets fucked up!

ADELE: It had to because you don't think—if you're going to be a crook, you don't read a comic book for research—you don't recruit an old black man that's about to die!

THEO: —No matter what you do, he's gon die anyway—this whole place was built for him to die in—so, you bite, you scratch, you kick—you do anything to stay alive!

ADELE: Yes, you bite! You scratch, you steal, you kick, and you GET KILLED ANYWAY! Just as I was doing, coming back here to help Momma—

THEO: Adele, I'm sick and tired of your talk about sacrifices—you were here because you had no other place to go—you just got scared too young and too soon.

ADELE: You're right—all I was doing was waiting for her to die so I could get on with what I thought I wanted to do with myself—but God, SHE TOOK SO LONG TO DIE!—but then I found myself doing the same things she had done, taking care of three men, trying to shield them from the danger beyond that door, BUT WHO THE HELL EVER TOLD EVERY BLACK WOMAN SHE WAS SOME KIND OF GOD DAMN SAVIOR! Sure, this place was built for us to die in, but if we aren't very careful, Theo—that can actually happen—good-night. (*She heads for the stairs.*)

THEO: Adele . . .

(ADELE *stops in her tracks and turns*)

I've decided that there's going to be no more of Blue's business here—it's over, we're getting out.

ADELE (*after a long pause*): Theo, do you really mean it?

(THEO *nods yes.*)

What about Daddy?

THEO: He will have to live with it—this setup can't move without me.

ADELE: And, Bobby?

THEO: I'll take care of him. . . .

ADELE: That's fine, Theo—we'll throw the old things into the river—and we'll try something new—I won't push and you won't call me a bitch! (ADELE *exits up the stairs.*)

(THEO *picks up pop's notebook off the floor from beside the bed.* JENKINS *knocks at door.*)

THEO: We're closed!

(*Knock continues.*)

WE'RE CLOSED!

(*The banging persists with a voice calling out to* THEO. *He rushes to the door and opens it.*)

I SAID WE'RE CLOSED! (Pause.) Oh, I'm sorry, Mr. Jenkins, I

didn't know that was you—what are you doing here this time of night?

MR. JENKINS: I want to speak to Parker. . . .

THEO: You know him—he's been keeping late hours lately. . . .

MR. JENKINS: I'll wait for him. . . .

THEO: Suit yourself, but don't you have to work tomorrow?

MR. JENKINS: I have something to tell him, and I'll wait if it takes all night. . . .

THEO: In that case, you can tell me about it. . . .

(ADELE *descends stairs, through the back room, stops on steps leading to shop, looks about confusingly. . . . She has a deadly, almost blank look on her face.*)

What's wrong with you?

ADELE (*pausing*): Some . . . somebody just called me. . . .

THEO: What did they call you about?

(*She does not answer him.* JENKINS *rises and seats her on bed.*)

Didn't you hear me—what about?

(*She still does not respond to him.*)

WHAT IS IT, ADELE!!!

MR. JENKINS: THEO!!!

(THEO *turns to* JENKINS.)

I think she probably just heard that your brother Bobby has been killed in a robbery by a night watchman—

THEO: Uh uh, nawww, nawww, that's not true—

MR. JENKINS: Yes it is, son. . . .

ADELE: Yes. . . .

THEO: No. . . .

MR. JENKINS: Yes! (*Moves out into shop toward the door*)

THEO: I DON'T BELIEVE YOU!

MR. JENKINS: I saw him boy, I saw him.

(*Dead silence as* JENKINS *slowly moves for the street exit*)

THEO: You should've seen this dude I caught the other day on 32nd Street—He had on a bright purple suit, gray shirt, yellow tie, and his hair was processed with bright purple color—what a sight he was— but I have to say one thing for him—he was clean—

(*The lights are slowly coming down.*)

—used to be a time when a dude like that came in numbers, but you don't see too many of them nowadays—I have to say one thing for him—he was clean—you don't see too many like—he was clean—he was—he was clean—

(*Blackout*)

ACT TWO : Scene Two

About two hours later, in the shop.

PARKER *and* JENKINS *enter the front part of the shop.* PARKER *is drunk, and his friend is assisting him to move on his feet. He finally seats him on the barber's throne.*

MR. PARKER: Thank-you, Jenkins—you are the greatest friend a man can have. They don't make 'em like you anymore. You are one of the last of the great friends, Jenkins—Pardon me, Mr. Jenkins. No more will I ever call you Jenks or Jenkins. From now on, it's Mr. Jenkins!

MR. JENKINS: Thank-you, but when I ran into Theo and Adele tonight, they said they had something important to say to you, and I think you oughta see them. . . .

MR. PARKER: I know what they want—They want to tell me what an old fool I am. . . .

MR. JENKINS: I don't think that's it, and you should go on upstairs and—

MR. PARKER: Never! Upstairs is for the people upstairs!

MR. JENKINS: Russell, I—

MR. PARKER: I am downstairs people! You ever hear of downstairs people?

MR. JENKINS (*pausing*): No. . . .

MR. PARKER: Well, they're the people to watch in this world. . . .

MR. JENKINS: If you say so. . . .

MR. PARKER: *Put your money on 'em!*

MR. JENKINS: Come on, Mr. Parker—Why don't you lie down in the back room, and—

MR. PARKER: Oh! no—You don't think I'd have you come all the way over here just for me to go to bed, do you? I wouldn't do a thing like that to you, Jenkins—I'm busy—"Mr. Jenkins." Just stay with me for a little while. . . .

MR. PARKER: Why did that girl lock me out? She said she would be waiting for me, but she locked me out. Why did she do a thing like that? I give her everything—money, clothes, pay her rent—I even love her!

MR. JENKINS: Russell. . . .

MR. PARKER (*rising precariously*): Tell me something, Mr. Jenkins—since you are my friend—why do you think she locked me out?

MR. JENKINS (*steadying him*): I don't know. . . .

MR. PARKER: I'll tell you why—I'm an old man, and all I've got is a few dollars in my pocket—ain't that it?

MR. JENKINS: I don't know. . . . Good-night, Parker. . . . (*Starts out*)

MR. PARKER (*grabbing him*): You think a man was in that room with my girl?

MR. JENKINS: YES!

MR. PARKER: GOD DAMMIT! GOD DAMMIT!

MR. JENKINS: Russell—

MR. PARKER: I don't believe it! When I love 'em, they stay loved!

MR. JENKINS: NOBODY'S GOT THAT MUCH LOVE, MAN!

MR. PARKER (*pausing*): No, no—you're wrong—my wife—my dear Doris had more love in her than life should've allowed—a hundred men couldn't have taken all that love . . .

MR. JENKINS: We ain't talking about Doris, Russell—

MR. PARKER: Aw, forget it! (*Crossing toward table*) GOD DAMMIT! You stumble around like an old black cow and you never get up again. . . .

I HAVE HAD MY FUN!
IF I DON'T GET WELL NO MORE!
I HAVE HAD MY FUN!

IF I— (PARKER *falls down.*) Get up, old bastard! Get up! (*Rises to his feet aided by* JENKINS) Get up and fall back down again—come on, Mr. Jenkins, let's play ourselves a game of checkers. . . .

MR. JENKINS: I don't want to play no damn checkers. . . .

MR. PARKER: Why do you curse my home, Mr. Jenkins?

MR. JENKINS (*pausing*): I apologize for that. . . .

MR. PARKER: Come on, have a game of checkers with your good friend. (*Sits at table*)

MR. JENKINS (*moving to the table*): All right, one game and then I'm going home. . . .

MR. PARKER: One game. . . .

MR. PARKER (*pausing while* JENKINS *sits*): I said a lot of dirty things to my children tonight—the kind of things you have to live a long time to overcome.

MR. JENKINS: I know exactly what you mean. . . . (JENKINS *sets up jumps for* PARKER. *He is unaware of it. The game proceeds briefly.* PARKER *stops.*)

MR. PARKER: . . . Theo is a good boy, and a smart one too, but he lets people push him around. That's because he's always trying to con somebody out of something—you know the kind; can't see for looking—And Bobby?—He wouldn't hurt a flea—A lot of people think that boy is dumb, but just let somebody try to trick or fool him if they dare! (*Recommences a series of checker jumps. Pause.*) Got a story for you . . .

MR. JENKINS: No stories tonight, Parker . . .

MR. PARKER: "Mr. Parker." (*The last move is made, the game is over and* PARKER *is at long last the victor after the slow realization of his conquest.* PARKER *rises from the table.*) Call me champ!

(THEO *and* ADELE *enter into the shop from the outside and stand just inside the door.*)

You're beat! I beat you! I beat you! (*Laughing,* PARKER *throws his arm around* JENKINS's *waist and holds him from behind.*) You fall down and you never get up! (*Still laughing*) Fall down, old man! Fall down! (*He releases his friend upon seeing* ADELE *and* THEO.) You hear that, children, I beat him! I beat him! (*His laughter subsides as he realizes they are not responding to him. Guilt ridden, he approaches* THEO, *looks at him intently, then reaches into his inside coat pocket and pulls out the money.*)

Here, Theo—here's the money—here's all of it. . . . Take it, it's yours—go out and try to get happy, boy. . . .

(THEO *does not move, nor does he take the money from his father's outstretched hand. He turns to* ADELE *only to see that her face is almost a blank.*)

WHY DON'T SOMEBODY SAY SOMETHING!

(ADELE *attempts to speak but* PARKER *cuts her off.*)

I know, you have some trouble with me. . . . (*He spies the notebook in the phone seat, takes it into his hand and approaches* ADELE.) You have a woman, you love her, you stop loving her, and sooner or later, she ups and dies, and you sit around behaving like you was a killer. I didn't have no more in me. I just didn't have no more in me! (*Pause.*) I know

you don't believe I ever loved your mother, but it's here in this book—
read it. . . .

(ADELE *does not respond.*)

You wanta read something, boy!

(THEO turns away. PARKER slowly crosses, hands the book to
JENKINS, and addresses his remarks to him.)

I got sour the day my legs got so trembly and sore on the stage of the
Strand Theatre—I couldn't even walk out to take a proper bow. It was
then I knew nobody would ever hire me to dance again—I just
couldn't run downtown to meet the man the way she did—not after
all those years of shuffling around like I was a dumb clown, with my
feet hurting and aching the way they did, having my head patted as if
I was some little pet animal—back of the bus, front of the train,
grinning when I was bleeding to death! . . . After all of that I was
going to ask for more by throwing myself into the low drags of some
dusty old factory in Brooklyn. All I could do was stay here in this shop
with you, my good friend. And we acted out the ceremony of a game.
And you boy—(*turns to* THEO) You and Blue with your ideas of
overcoming the evil of the white man—to an old man like me, it was
nothing more than an ounce of time to end my dragging about this
shop. All it did was to send me out into those streets to live a time—
and I did live myself a time for awhile. I did it amongst a bunch of
murderers—all kinds of 'em—where at times it gets so bad, 'til it
seems that the only thing that's left is for you to go out there and kill
somebody before they kill you. That's all . . . that's out there! (*Goes to*
ADELE) Adele, as for that girl that was here tonight, she's probably no
good, but if at my age, I was stupid enough to think that I could have
stepped out of here, and won that little girl, loved her, and moved
through the rest of my days without killing anybody, THAT WAS A
VICTORY! (*Moves to the center of the floor, stands silently for awhile,
and then does a little dance*) Be a dancer—any kind of dancer you wanta
be—but dance it! (*Tries out a difficult step, but can't quite make it*) Uh
uhhh! Can't make that one no more. . . . (*Continues to dance*) Be a
singer—Sing any song you wanta sing, but sing! (*Stops in his tracks*)
AND YOU'VE GOT ENOUGH TROUBLE TO TAKE
YOU TO THE GRAVEYARD! (*Pause.*) But think of all that life
you had before they buried you. (PARKER *breaks into a frantic dance
attempting steps that are crossing him up. He stumbles about until he falls.
Everyone in the room rushes to pick him up from the floor.*) . . . I'm okay,
I'm okay . . . (*He rises from the floor slowly.*) I'm tired, I'm going to bed,

and by time tomorrow comes around, let's see if we can't all throw it into the river. (*moves into the back room, singing*)
HAVE HAD MY FUN!
IF I DON'T GET WELL NO MORE
I HAVE HAD MY FUN
IF I DON'T GET WELL NO MORE
(*A thought strikes him. He turns and moves back to where* JENKINS *is standing . . . step entrance of back room*) Jenkins, you said that the day I beat you playing checkers, you said it could be the unluckiest day of my life—But after all that's happened today—I'm straight—I feel just great! (*Moves to the stairs leading up, he suddenly stops, turns and briskly moves back to the doorway leading to the shop*) Say, where's Bobby?

(*Curtain*)

Home

SAMM-ART WILLIAMS

Left to right: Michelle Shay as WOMAN TWO, *Charles Brown as* CEPHUS MILES, *and L. Scott Caldwell as* WOMAN ONE *in a scene from* Home. *Photograph copyright © 1982 by Bert Andrews. Reprinted by permission of Marsha Hudson, the Estate of Bert Andrews.*

Samm-Art Williams, a native of Burgaw, North Carolina, received a B.A. from Morgan State University in Baltimore, then settled in Philadelphia, Pennsylvania, to study acting at the Freedom Theater's Acting Workshop. He later joined the Negro Ensemble Company as an actor in 1973, making formidable appearances in such plays as *First Breeze of Summer, Brownsville Raid,* and Steve Carter's *Eden and Nevis Mountain Dew.* As a playwright, NEC produced his *A Love Play, Welcome to Black River, Eyes of the American,* and the award-winning *Home* which played on Broadway and received a Tony nomination for Best Play, the Outer Critics Circle Award, and the Drama Desk Award. He currently lives in Los Angeles where he writes and produces for television.

Home was produced in New York by the NEC at the St. Marks Playhouse in December 1979, and was subsequently transferred to the Cort Theatre on Broadway with the original cast:
  Cephus Miles Charles Brown
  Woman One L. Scott Caldwell
  Woman Two Michele Shay
Directed by Douglas Turner Ward; scenery by Felix E. Cochren; lighting by Martin Aronstein; costumes by Alvin B. Perry; production stage managed by Horacena J. Taylor.
The Broadway presentation at the Cort Theatre was produced by Elizabeth I. McCann, Nelle Nugent, Gerald S. Krone, and Ray Larson. Associate Producer, Tommy DeMaio.

Home

This play is dedicated to my mother, Mrs. Valdosia J. Williams, and all of the folks in Burgaw, North Carolina. I love you all.

CHARACTERS
in order of appearance

CEPHUS MILES, *young Southern farmer who moves to the North. Character is portrayed as a teenager, in his early twenties, age thirty-five, and age forty.*

WOMAN ONE, *young Southern woman who is the girlfriend of* CEPHUS MILES. WOMAN ONE, *in addition to portraying* PATTIE MAE WELLS, *portrays several male and female characters with an age range from the teens to forty.*

WOMAN TWO, *portrays several male and female characters ranging in age from the teens to forty.*

TIME
Late 1950s to the present

PLACES
Cross Roads, North Carolina. A prison in Raleigh, North Carolina. And a very, very large American city.

SET
In the original Negro Ensemble Company production, the set consisted of four joined platforms of varying levels. A series of wooden beams, columns, and porch posts, along with metal pipes, ran along the offstage edge of the platforms suggesting a mixture of rural and urban environments. The tallest platform, Up Center (UC), had a set of escape stairs Up Right (UR) and Up Left (UL). Upstage of the platform, on a bench between the two escape stairs, were preset a minister's stole, a long red satin stole trimmed with orange boa feathers, and a prison guard's cap. Two identical flowered print shawls, an army helmet, and an army "cunt" cap were preset on the floor to the right of the UR escape stairs. Center on the UC platform was an old rocking chair with a blue, long sleeve shirt hanging on the back. Two breakaway porch posts were Down Right (DR) and Down Left (DL) on this platform.

Stage right, adjacent to the UC platform was a smaller platform with a two-step stair unit leading down to the stage floor. A bannister constructed from pipe ran along the offstage edge of these stairs. Perpendicularly attached to the bannister rail were three short pieces of pipe on which were preset a boy's corduroy cap; an old, worn hat and scarf; a blue sweater; an orange sweater with a sweater guard; a pair of oval, plastic frame eyeglasses; and a third flowered shawl identical to those preset UC.

Center stage (C) was a large low platform with breakaway bases of two porch posts stage right (R) and stage left (L). UC on this platform was a hollow wooden bench with a hinged top allowing for storage within the bench. Two small wooden boxes, on which the actors stood and sat, were in the UR and UL corners of the platform, respectively.

Stage left, a single step unit lead up to the fourth platform, which was adjacent to the UC and CS platforms. A single stair, upstage on the stage left platform joined it to the platform UC. A pipe bannister similar to the one stage right, ran along the offstage edge of the downstage stair unit. A bus driver's cap was preset at this bannister. Center on the stage left platform was a second hollow, wooden bench with a hinged top. Preset inside this bench were a madras jacket and a "dress" straw hat.

Preset offstage left were a wide brim hat with feather, a matching silk scarf, a black handbag, and a black, ladies' dress hat with feather.

The entire set was surrounded by black/velour drapes with entrances stage left, UC, and stage right. There was sufficient room between the set and these curtains to allow the actors a complete "cross-over" along the offstage edge of the set.

AUTHOR'S NOTE

This play is written with dialogue and poetry which might seem to lend itself to music. Any music or rhythms used should not be provided with instruments, but instead, by the actors only. The poetry and dialogue should be acted and presented in a realistic manner as the actors act and inter-act with each other. In many instances, the dialogue may be presentational, that is, spoken directly to the audience as opposed to another actor. It is of the utmost importance that this play be directed very simply and free of excessive choreography and movement, but not to the point of being static.

In darkness, WOMAN ONE *and* WOMAN TWO *enter DR and DL, respectively, singing "Great Gitt'n Up Morning." As the song concludes, two pools of light fade up isolating* WOMAN ONE *CR and* WOMAN TWO *CL on the C platform.*

WOMAN TWO: If there was ever a woman or man, who has everlasting grace in the eyes of God, it's the farmer woman . . . and man. (*Enter* CEPHUS *UC. He crosses to the edge of the UC platform and looks out over the R platform as if it is farmland and he is contemplating and preparing for the day's work.*)

WOMAN ONE: Tenders to the soil. Children of the land.

WOMAN TWO: Babies of the soil.

WOMAN ONE: Everlasting grace in the eyes of God.

WOMAN TWO: Working and sweating, and moving and moaning, and hurting and praying. Just to get the next load of cabbage to market.

(CEPHUS *steps down onto the R platform and mimes picking up a hoe.*)

Two bushels of squash, twenty quarts of strawberries. Four bushels of corn. Three baskets of snap beans.

(*Lights up on the R platform as* WOMAN ONE *and* CEPHUS *synchronously mime hoeing and making furrows in the soil*)

WOMAN ONE: Chop that row . . . hut, hut, hut . . .
Chop that row . . . hut, hut, hut . . .

WOMAN TWO: Sweating, sweating, sweating.

WOMAN ONE: Chop, chop, chop.

WOMAN TWO: Sweat, sweat, sweat.

WOMAN ONE: Hut, hut, hut.

WOMAN TWO: Hurting, hurting, hurting.

WOMAN ONE: Chop, hut, chop, hut, chop, hut.

WOMAN TWO (*crossing L on the platform*):
Blisters, blisters, blisters.
Hands bleed, hands bleed,
Head hurts, head hurts, (*crosses back CL slightly bent with a hand on her hip in an attitude of weary pain*)
Aching, aching, aching.

WOMAN ONE: Burning sun, chop, hut.

(WOMAN ONE *and* CEPHUS *throw down their imaginary hoes.* CEPHUS *momentarily surveys the land, then slowly, wearily, crosses to the rocking chair on the UC platform.* WOMAN ONE *crosses to the bench on the C platform and sits.*)

WOMAN TWO: So that someone, somewhere, can eat steak. Double cuts. Tossed salad with Russian. Champagne. While he eats black-eyed peas and fatback. Grits and red-eye gravy. (*Points and takes a few steps U toward* CEPHUS) That one Cephus Miles, had a girl, that he loved.

(CEPHUS *sits in rocker.*)

WOMAN ONE: Too bad he can't afford all of the things, that he's working to buy. But he has everlasting grace.

WOMAN TWO: Shit. Big deal. (*Crosses to* WOMAN ONE, *L of the bench on the C platform*) He can think about grace, while he's chopping wood this winter to go in that "pop belly" stove that he cooks on. Or when he has to pack mud in the cracks of his house to keep the wind out, or when he has to use newspaper to wipe his "behind," because toilet paper is just not in his budget.

WOMAN ONE (*rising*): Don't be cold.

WOMAN TWO: Sorry.

WOMAN ONE (*crossing D of the L platform*): Maybe they'll all leave.

WOMAN TWO (*crossing L on the C platform*): Most of them have. He left. But he came back. Fool.

WOMAN ONE (*crossing up on the L platform, right of the downstage end of the bench. Faces onstage*): Gone.

WOMAN TWO (*crossing up on the L platform, U and beside* WOMAN ONE): You see them every day in the city. With sad, displaced faces. Pastel green shirt and a shoestring necktie. Hat cocked to one side. Black gabardine pants that are pegged at the ankles, with large pink stripes down the sides to accent his white knob-toed shoes. The ones with the sad, displaced faces.

WOMAN ONE: And the blisters and calluses in their hands. Shouting and screaming, at Cornerstone Baptist Church every Sunday morning. "Lord Have Mercy on My Soul."

WOMAN TWO: That's them. Shouting and screaming for a ticket back home. Back to the land. The land waits. And it ask . . .

WOMAN ONE (*focusing out to the audience*):
Where have they all gone?
What has happened to the days?
Where have they all gone?
Time rushes by.

(WOMAN TWO *crosses U and around* CEPHUS *observing him in the rocking chair on the UC platform. She then crosses C on the R platform.*)

So fast it rushes by.
Children of the land. Babies of the soil.
Where have they all gone?
With the good teachings. The spiritual souls of their mother's and dad's.
To cities and places far to the North.
Changed and rearranged by life and circumstance.
That's where they've all gone.

WOMAN TWO (*extending arms, reaching out to the audience*):
Come home.
Come home.

The land sadly cries.
Come home from where you've all gone.
Children of the land. Babies of the soil.

CEPHUS (*rising and crossing DL of rocking chair*): I once rode a swift, strong horse. Hooves of sterling. Coat of white.

WOMAN ONE: Until you met the daylight. It set you right.

(WOMAN ONE *crosses down to the stage floor L of the platform. She removes a white bow from her skirt pocket and puts it in her hair.* WOMAN TWO *crosses down to the R pipe bannister, picks up a corduroy boy's cap and puts it on. They become young children.* ONE *is a young girl.* TWO *is a young boy named* JOHNNY MACK.)

CEPHUS: I have no regrets. No bitterness. I'm thankful. And I pray from time to time.

(CEPHUS *slowly crosses D of the rocking chair, halting momentarily at the sound of the women's voices.* WOMAN ONE *and* TWO *slowly creep, sneak up on* CEPHUS, *crossing D of the L and R platforms, respectively. During the following beat,* CEPHUS *does not relate directly to the children. Their's are voices he hears within.*)

WOMAN ONE/YOUNGSTER: Cephus Miles. The stories say. Disappeared some ten years ago.

WOMAN TWO/JOHNNY MACK: Burning in hell and deservedly so. The thing inside is only a ghost.

CEPHUS: No! (*Sits in rocking chair*) I'm here and alive. Flesh, blood and bone.

(WOMAN ONE *and* TWO *run to the boxes UL and UR, respectively, on the C platform.*)

WOMAN ONE/YOUNGSTER: But the spirit's turned to stone.

(WOMAN ONE *and* TWO *climb atop the wooden boxes. They taunt* CEPHUS.)

YOUNGSTERS (*in unison*): Cephus Miles. Dead in the grave. Old Cephus Miles can't be saved. Too late Cephus, you can't be saved. Too late Cephus. You can't be saved. (WOMAN ONE *and* TWO *crouch down on the boxes hiding from* CEPHUS.)

CEPHUS: Children casting stones at my door. Crashing and thrashing at the windowpane. Children in their folly. Lovely, beautiful children. Learning and living the fantasies of their parents. Fostering the myths and the lies. Cephus lives! I live! The town of Cross Roads, North Carolina. Place of my birth. I live.

WOMAN TWO/JOHNNY MACK: The voice of a ghost. A thing without form. (WOMAN TWO *straightens up into a standing position on top of the wooden box, followed by* WOMAN ONE.) A joke. Yes a joke. And he used to be a fine young man, so they say.

YOUNGSTERS (*in unison*): Scarry Cephus, dead in the grave. Mean old Cephus, can't be saved. (WOMAN ONE *and* TWO *run and hide behind the L and R breakaway porch post bases, respectively, on the C platform. They peep out at* CEPHUS, *who rises and takes a few steps L.*)

CEPHUS: Each board. Each shutter that is nailed tight. Was done so with love and passion and purpose. They like to believe that it's haunted. Let them. I'm a ghost! I'm a ghost! They make it all up in their sweet, brattish minds just as they do the boogey man and witches and the tooth fairy. (*Directly to the audience*) Take some time with me please. I had my day in the warm, I have felt God's hot rays. Take a minute with me . . . please. (*Lost in thought,* CEPHUS *crosses L on the UC platform.*)

(WOMAN ONE *runs UL on the C platform taunting* CEPHUS.)

WOMAN ONE/YOUNGSTER: You felt the devil's hot rays.

WOMAN TWO/JOHNNY MACK (*running UR on the platform*): They say you believed in witchcraft.

WOMAN ONE/YOUNGSTER: Conjure.

WOMAN TWO/JOHNNY MACK: Voodoo.

CEPHUS (*crossing back to his rocking chair*): I believed in God!

(WOMAN ONE *and* TWO *crouch, hide D of the UL and UR wooden boxes, respectively.*)

I gave him my life, my soul, my breathing, my sight, my speech. All of me I gave to him. I believed in him totally until he took a vacation to the sun-soaked, cool beaches of Miami, while I needed his help and love in the hot sticky tobacco fields of North Carolina. In a prison in Raleigh, North Carolina. A child. (CEPHUS *crosses L on the UC platform.*)

YOUNGSTERS (*in unison*): Blasphemy! You sold your soul to Lucifer. That's why you went to prison.

WOMAN TWO/JOHNNY MACK (*rising*): Infidel. (*Crouches*) He once spat on the flag. He waits for a girl who will never return.

CEPHUS (*crossing DC on the UC platform*): I didn't spit on the flag. I just wanted to be proud of it. I can't be proud if I'm fighting. Pride takes time and effort and . . . peace.

(WOMAN ONE *and* TWO *run and hide behind the L and R breakaway porch bases respectively.*)

YOUNGSTERS (*in unison*): Voodoo Man! Voodoo Man!

CEPHUS: Been a Christian all my born days. Never turned my back on the cross. They tried to make me. Lots of times. But I wouldn't. When bad luck set on me and took my Gramps and my uncle. Black Sarah the conjure woman tried to give me a potion. Told me it would take the bad spell off me. They say Black Sarah could raise the dead. Or bring back your loved ones and let you sit and talk with them, and hold their hand. Her conjure was known and respected throughout five or six countys. Old Man Clifton Jones seen his wife, dead for seven years, through the works of that conjure woman. Turned his hair as white as snow. The second time she come to me I struck her down. (*Crosses R of the rocking chair*) You devil! I believe in God!

WOMAN TWO/JOHNNY MACK: They said he was violent.

WOMAN ONE/YOUNGSTER: He is. Look at those scary old eyes.

CEPHUS: God. I want to speak with God. No . . . no I don't have the wrong number. I know his number. This is Cephus Miles. Cephus . . . he knows me. We're friends. Miami . . . on vacation? I need him now Miss. No! Don't hang up! My Uncle Lewis just had a sunstroke. We were working in the tobacco fields. (*Points to the R platform*) It's hot. 102 degrees. We can't afford to pay help. (*Crosses to the edge of the platform, seeing, recreating the scene of Uncle Lewis's stroke on the R platform.*) Uncle Lewis has a bad heart. He shouldn't even be out here. Where is God? Don't die please.

YOUNGSTERS (*in unison*): Stop screaming.

CEPHUS (*slowly crossing to the rocking chair*): The same place he was when my Gramps and my horse Polly died. The same place he was when my dog Brownie got run over by Reverend Jim Parker's horse and buggy. The same place he was when my Uncle Lewis died in my arms in the middle of that tobacco field. In Miami on vacation. (*Sits in the rocking chair*)

WOMAN ONE/YOUNGSTER: The man needs a rest. He's got more to do than to wait on you hand and foot.

WOMAN TWO/JOHNNY MACK: Who do you think you are? The president?

WOMAN ONE/YOUNGSTER: You got another horse. You got another dog. The uncle, and the grandfather, well . . .

WOMAN TWO/JOHNNY MACK: But, you had aunts. Lots of aunts.

CEPHUS: Grown-up kids. Turned loose, on the world. Having so much compassion for Cephus Miles. And they wonder why I have the shutters nailed?

WOMAN ONE/YOUNGSTER: You're a kook. Ready for the laughing farm.

WOMAN TWO/JOHNNY MACK: The twinkie wagon. The butterfly net.

CEPHUS: Ready for God.

YOUNGSTERS (*in unison*): He's not back.

WOMAN ONE/YOUNGSTER (*running R to* WOMAN TWO, *who rises*): Leave the man alone.

WOMAN TWO/JOHNNY MACK: Don't you call God. He'll call you.

WOMAN ONE/YOUNGSTER: Ten minutes. Person to person. For eighty-five cents.

WOMAN TWO/JOHNNY MACK: You're taller than a sparrow. You weigh more. You're bigger. Surely his eye is on you.

(*Giggling,* WOMAN ONE *crosses R and around the set returning the white hair bow to her pocket.* WOMAN TWO *follows replacing the corduroy cap on the R pipe bannister.*)

CEPHUS: I can't really be bitter. I was very fortunate. In many ways. I had my family.

(CEPHUS *rises and picks up the shirt on the back of the rocking chair. He crosses down in the "cul de sac" between the R stairs and the C platform putting on the shirt as* WOMAN ONE *crosses up the UR escape stairs D of the rocking chair on the UC platform.* WOMAN TWO *crosses to the top UR escape stairs, sits.*)

My beginnings.

WOMAN ONE:
The land of sand flies and lightning bugs.
Back to his beginning.
Young boy runs the fields, with Brownie by his side.
Back to the beginning.
Molasses bread and strong black coffee.
The burning of fodder fills the air and sky.
Back to his beginnings.
Sssh! Sssh! It's a quiet peaceful land.
The land of his beginning.
Roll, roll. No subway rolls.
It's almost paradise.
The earth smells sweet. Nature sings.
The land of his beginning.

(WOMAN ONE *sits in the rocking chair.* WOMAN TWO *crosses UL of the chair and gently rocks it as* CEPHUS *crosses C on the C platform.*)

CEPHUS: I love the land, the soft beautiful black sod crushing beneath my feet. A fertile pungent soil. A soil to raise strong children on. I love the rain. That feeds the earth. It's especially nice in May. The warm sparkling drops, cover your face and the ground with its sweet blanket of pure wet. I love the land. I love touching the crops. And gently holding each plant in my hand. And feeling the love and care that Grand-Daddy, Uncle, and me put into its cultivation. When you hold a plant, you can feel the heartbeat of God. I love the land. "Dust the crops," "chop and pull the weeds," "It's your day to plow Cephus," my Grandfather's voice would sound. Right away Gramps. Give me a hand Uncle Lewis. "You're on your own boy." I've got the South Twenty to plow. I love the land. "I love it Gramps. I'll never leave it Uncle Lewis. I want to be a farmer like you and Gramps." A lawyer or schoolteacher you'll be. No. (CEPHUS *claps his hands and kneels. He mimes being licked on the face by a dog.*) Brownie and me won't never leave. All right whatever you say. "Go to the well and wash up." "Time for supper." We won't never leave. I love the land.

(WOMAN ONE *rises and crosses L of* WOMAN TWO. *They clap their hands as they sing. During the following beat,* CEPHUS *keeps his focus out, not relating to the women. They are merely voices he hears within.*)

WOMAN ONE and TWO (*singing in unison*):
In the great gitt'n up morning fare you well.
Fare you well. In that great gitt'n up morning fare you well. Fare you well.
I'm gonna tell you about the Coming of Judgment.
Fare you well. Fare you well.
I'm gonna tell you about the Coming of Jesus.
Fare you well. Fare you well. (WOMAN ONE *and* TWO *fold their arms.*)
WOMAN ONE: Sunday school time. Put on your Sunday go to meetings and that new straw hat.
CEPHUS: I hate that hat.
WOMAN TWO: Your Uncle Lewis bought it for you down at the hardware store. So you'd better wear it.
CEPHUS (*rising, taking a few steps DC*): I swear it's nothing like wearing a straw hat that you hate. They're going to make fun of me. I just know it.

(WOMAN ONE *crosses to the bench on the L platform, sits. She mimes shaking a pair of dice in her hand.* WOMAN TWO *crosses to the R edge of the UC platform, sits.*)

It's bad enough that I got to wear those wool knickers and this stupid bow tie, in the middle of August. Damn! Scuse me Lord. I didn't mean to use no cuss words on your holy day. Please forgive and don't strike me blind.

WOMAN ONE: Don't forget the Sunday morning crap game in the graveyard.

CEPHUS (*playing C on the C platform*): Now you didn't have to remind me of that. See you got to understand that the graveyard was where we went to gamble. The roads were all dirt because the county couldn't afford to have hard-surface highways. The land was black dirt and sand. And in order to get a good roll on the dice, you needed a hard surface. What better place than the cement vaults in the graveyard. The graveyard was still segregated at that time. You had the colored folks section, which was on the back side, naturally. Our crap shooting was done in the white folks section because that's where all the nice cement vaults were. Colored folks couldn't afford nothing but a regular casket. There weren't no streetlights. So at night we'd take a lantern with us so we could see. But don't get caught by our one policeman. He'd lock you up for trespassing. We all had lucky vaults. My lucky vault belonged to Mr. Hezekiah Simmons. Born July 7, 1877, died July 7, 1957. All those sevens made it lucky. I heard that he was a mean white man when he was living. But in death, Mr. Simmons was definitely my friend. I won six or seven dollars every time I gambled on his vault. Though I didn't do too bad on Mrs. Liza Mae Bullocks's vault either, God rest her soul.

WOMAN TWO (*rising, crossing DL on the R platform*): You wearing those brogan shoes to church? Why don't you buy yourself a good pair of shoes? Well at least shine the things.

(WOMAN TWO *crosses and sits on the top UR escape step, her back to the audience.*)

WOMAN ONE (*crossing to the R edge of the platform*): Pssst!

CEPHUS: What?

WOMAN ONE: Come here.

CEPHUS: What?

WOMAN ONE: Don't go to church. You know how hot it's going to be in there. All of your buddies, Tommy, Pete, and Joe-Boy are in the graveyard.

CEPHUS: I lost all of my church money last Sunday. (*Takes a few steps R away from* WOMAN ONE) I don't think I'll go this Sunday.

WOMAN ONE: Take that seventy-five cents that you . . .

CEPHUS: How do you know how much money I've got?

WOMAN ONE: Don't worry about that. Take that money and go join the dice game.

CEPHUS (*moving farther away from* WOMAN ONE, *crossing DR on platform*): Ain't proper to shoot dice on Sunday. Anyway this is my Sunday school and church money.

WOMAN ONE: Ain't God rich enough? He don't need your seventy-five cents. Cephus.

CEPHUS (*crossing C on the platform*): You've got a point. My Grand-Daddy will beat me to death if he finds out I been sinning on the Sabbath. He almost caught me last week.

WOMAN ONE: Be brave. He won't know. (WOMAN ONE *crosses R on the UC platform, her back to the audience. She removes a pair of wire frame eyeglasses from her pocket and puts them on.*)

CEPHUS: The worse whipping I ever got. That man beat me for a solid hour damn near. Made me go out in the backyard and cut my own switch. That's the ultimate insult. And he didn't whip me right away. No, no. He waited until I got in the bed and drifted soundly off to sleep. The covers were suddenly snatched from my body. And my Gramps and that switch went to work. So much for shooting craps, on the Sabbath. By the way, while all of this was going on, Brownie, my old "sooner," was hiding under the bed with his ears covering his eyes. Pretending that he was sick.

(WOMAN ONE *crosses to the D edge of the UC platform, steps down onto the UL wooden box on the C platform, puts her hands on her hips, and bends slightly toward* CEPHUS.)

WOMAN ONE/MRS. HATTIE SMITH: Repeat after me, Cephus Junior.

(CEPHUS *straightens up, stands very erect.*)

Thou shall not steal.

CEPHUS: Thou shall not steal.

WOMAN ONE/MRS. HATTIE SMITH: Thou shall not kill.

CEPHUS: Thou shall not kill.

WOMAN ONE/MRS. HATTIE SMITH: Love thy neighbor as thy self.

CEPHUS: Love thy neighbor as thy self.

WOMAN ONE/MRS. HATTIE SMITH: That's a very important one Cephus. (WOMAN ONE *steps back up on the UC platform, crosses to the top UR escape stair and sits by* WOMAN TWO. *She removes the eyeglasses putting them in her pocket, puts on the pink hair bow, picks up one of the flowered shawls C of the escape stairs and puts it on.*)

CEPHUS (*playing the C area on the C platform*): Mrs. Hattie Smith, my Sunday School teacher. She should have been a Baptist preacher. She was righteous. And nobody seemed to mind that her husband, John, was the biggest bootlegger in the county. John was a man after my own heart. For one dollar and fifty cents, John would sell you one of the best bottles of 'moonshine' that you have ever tasted. Sometimes he'd put food coloring in it and tell folks it was scotch. He'd then sell the pint bottles for two fifty. Back there in those woods, none of us knew the difference. The nearest "wet county" where alcohol was legal, was twenty-five miles away. Too far to walk. So John and I had a corner on the market. I say John and I because at age fifteen I went to work for John making bootleg whiskey. I'd work at "the still" for three nights a week and John would pay me twenty whole dollars. A good batch of moonshine should be allowed to cook two or three days. Cook it right, and you got yourself a drink as smooth as silk. Sometimes a possum or a racoon would fall over in the barrel while the whiskey was cooking but that just added to the taste. I told Gramps and Uncle Lewis that I was working for Mr. Farlow up near the creek, catching chickens. But they found out that I was helping John make whiskey and they made me go out in the backyard and cut that damn switch again. Only this time it was a full-fledged stick.

(WOMAN ONE *rises and crosses around the side of the set, R of the R pipe bannister.*)

WOMAN ONE/PATTIE MAE WELLS: Cephus. Cephus. Can you come out?
CEPHUS: Yeah, I reckon. Wait a minute.

(WOMAN ONE *crosses R on the C platform.* CEPHUS *crosses to greet her.*)

Howdy Pattie Mae. What you doing this far up the road?
WOMAN ONE/PATTIE MAE: Come to see you. Mama said I could.

(CEPHUS *takes* WOMAN ONE'*s hand and begins to lead her L.*)

Cept she said for me not to let you git me in the hayloft.

(CEPHUS *begins to suggest another place to take* WOMAN ONE, *but is stopped by her line.*)

Or under the house. And to stay outta the cornfield. And be home before dark.

(CEPHUS *strokes* WOMAN ONE's *hand.*)

Been pullin "dog tongue" all day, so my hands are a little rough.

CEPHUS: I'm glad we courting Pattie Mae.

WOMAN ONE/PATTIE MAE: Me too.

(CEPHUS *leads her to the bench UC on the platform. They sit.*)

My family's already got plans to get us hitched up. At least my daddy has. Mama ain't too set on us get'n married. Wants me to be a schoolteacher.

CEPHUS: We can get hitched next year. I can work the farm in the spring and summer and work at the sawmill in the winter.

WOMAN ONE/PATTIE MAE: I reckon.

CEPHUS: You look awful pretty Pattie Mae.

WOMAN ONE/PATTIE MAE: Thanks. I got religion last night at revival meeting. I jumped up and was shouting and everything. That didn't sit well with Miss Lula. She don't like for nobody to start shouting before her. You know what she did?

CEPHUS: What?

WOMAN ONE/PATTIE MAE: She took them three hundred and fifty pounds of hers and rose out of that seat. She started speaking in tongue. So naturally everybody started paying attention to her. Miss Lizzie was beating the drum and Mr. Edward was framing his guitar. All of a sudden Miss Lula turned her old red eyes toward me. I'm still shouting. She started coming toward me just a flinging her old big fat arms, foaming at the mouth and hollering, "You done me wrong." Joe-Boy with his devilish old self whispered in my ear. "She's gonna whip your ass." "You'd better run." I got scared. I stopped shouting and run out of the church. They all thought I had the holy ghost.

CEPHUS: I'm glad you got saved.

WOMAN ONE/PATTIE MAE: Now you got to get saved. If we gonna go together, we got to be pure in the eyes of God. And you got to stop drinking that liquor like you do.

CEPHUS: I want to kiss you Pattie Mae.

WOMAN ONE/PATTIE MAE: Well I reckon one is all right.

CEPHUS: I love you so much, sometimes I feel like I'm gonna bust.

WOMAN ONE/PATTIE MAE: Me too.

(CEPHUS *leans in to kiss* WOMAN ONE, *putting one arm around her waist and lifting her dress with the other hand.* WOMAN ONE *slaps his hand.*)

No. Now you can't git under my dress Cephus. You ain't saved. You got to be baptized.

CEPHUS: What's that got to do with anything?
WOMAN ONE/PATTIE MAE: A lot.
CEPHUS: Then I won't never git under your dress. Cause I won't be saved! And I won't be baptized!

(WOMAN TWO *crosses DL on the UC platform wearing the minister's stole preset on the bench U of the UC platform.*)

WOMAN TWO/REV. DORIS: We open the doors of the church this morning. To receive you!
CEPHUS: Shucks Pattie Mae. You know I don't wanna do this.
WOMAN TWO/REV. DORIS: If there is one among you. Let him raise his hand. (*Singing.*) Steal Away. Steal Away.

(CEPHUS *buries his head in his hands.*)

Steal Away to Jesus.
WOMAN ONE/PATTIE MAE (*nudging* CEPHUS *with her elbow*): Put your hand up, Cephus.
WOMAN TWO/REV. DORIS (*singing*): Steal Away. Steal Away Home.

(CEPHUS, *thinking the song has ended, attempts to raise his hand several times. Each time,* WOMAN TWO *continues to sing with increased volume and vigor.*)

I ain't got long to stay here.
CEPHUS (*finally succeeding in raising his hand*): I . . . I'm ready Reverend Doris. I think.
WOMAN TWO/REV. DORIS: Then kneel sinner!
CEPHUS: Sinner? I ain't no sinner, Pattie Mae.
WOMAN ONE/PATTIE MAE: Just kneel . . . sinner.

(WOMAN ONE *pushes* CEPHUS *to the floor. He kneels, hands clasped in prayer.* WOMAN TWO *extends her hand to bless* CEPHUS.)

WOMAN TWO/REV. DORIS: The Father, the Son, the blessed Holy Ghost. Keep your eyes on this one, honey. He ain't a whole Christian yet. (WOMAN TWO *crosses to the top UR escape stair, sits, removes the stole, and returns it to the bench, UC.*)
WOMAN ONE/PATTIE MAE: I will Reverend Doris.
CEPHUS (*rising, then sitting, straddling the bench, putting one arm around* WOMAN ONE's *waist*): It's done Pattie Mae.
WOMAN ONE/PATTIE MAE: Cephus, suppose I get in a family way? Mama checks me close, every month.
CEPHUS (*reaching into his pocket and pulling out an imaginary packet*): I

got some of them things from the drug store. See. Uncle Lewis told me about them.

WOMAN ONE/PATTIE MAE: I wish we were somewhere else besides this hayloft.

CEPHUS (*putting packet back in his pocket*): We could get in the back seat of Uncle Lewis's car. But we might get caught.

WOMAN ONE/PATTIE MAE: Let's stay here then.

CEPHUS: My doggone heart is beating so fast Pattie.

WOMAN ONE/PATTIE MAE: Mine too.

CEPHUS: You . . . you're the first girl for me. I never done it before.

WOMAN ONE/PATTIE MAE: Me either. I'm scared Cephus. Will it hurt?

CEPHUS: I don't know. I love you and I'll never love no one else.

WOMAN ONE/PATTIE MAE: Me and you forever.

(WOMAN ONE *turns R on the bench, her back to* CEPHUS, *who moves in closer to her putting his arms around her waist.* WOMAN ONE *is now sitting between* CEPHUS'S *legs as he straddles the bench. They begin to rhythmically rock back and forth.*)

CEPHUS: I'm getting so worked up Pattie Mae.

WOMAN ONE/PATTIE MAE: Me too. Me too.

WOMAN TWO/REV. DORIS: Keep your eyes on this one, honey.

(*They stop rocking motion.*)

WOMAN ONE/PATTIE MAE: Holy Jesus!?

CEPHUS: What!?

WOMAN ONE/PATTIE MAE (*rising*): Did you hear that?!

WOMAN TWO/REV. DORIS: He ain't a whole Christian yet.

WOMAN ONE/PATTIE MAE (*taking a few steps DC looking around*): There! There it goes again!

CEPHUS: I don't hear nothing.

WOMAN ONE/PATTIE MAE: It was Reverend Doris's voice.

CEPHUS: You feeling all right Pattie?

WOMAN ONE/PATTIE MAE (*backing UR of the bench, shaking her head "no"*): Cephus, we can't do it. Uh, uh. No sir buddy. It ain't right.

CEPHUS (*grabbing* WOMAN ONE's *hands*): What ain't right? What are you talking about?

WOMAN ONE/PATTIE MAE: Us. Up here in this hayloft. We gonna have to wait until we're married before we do it.

CEPHUS: Oh Lord have mercy, Pattie Mae! Don't do me like this! I'm so worked up, that I'm about to bust myself out of my breeches! Look honey it's all right with the Good Lord. He won't mind. I swear he won't. Come on.

WOMAN ONE/PATTIE MAE (*pulling away from* CEPHUS): No, Cephus, I want to. But not until we're married. I love you.

CEPHUS: I love you.

WOMAN ONE/PATTIE MAE (*turning R freeing one hand*): Let's go pick some plums.

CEPHUS (*grabbing* WOMAN ONE's *hand, pulling her to him*): Pick plums? At a time like this? Lord have mercy. I don't even like plums.

WOMAN ONE/PATTIE MAE: We can gather up some "rabbit tobacco," too. Pa wants some for his cold.

CEPHUS: Girl this ain't no time to be gathering up no rabbit tobacco. Patricia please. Listen to . . .

(WOMAN TWO *runs around the R side of the set to right of the R pipe bannister. At the sound of his name,* CEPHUS *rises quickly, straightens his clothes, etc., while* WOMAN ONE *runs off the set and stands in front of the L entrance.*)

WOMAN TWO: Cephus! Cephus! Come quick! Your Gramp is dead. He had Polly hitched up to the buggy and was riding across Mason's bridge on the way to the feed store. The ole bridge broke in half and they fell into the river. Him and Polly are both dead.

CEPHUS (*running U of the rocking chair on the UC platform and grips its back*): No. Gramps! Gramps!

(*Pause. The lights change to denote a passage of time.* CEPHUS *takes a few steps L looking around him.* WOMAN TWO *sits on the offstage side of the top R stair.*)

Me and this big house. I can't take care of no house. I'll quit school. I'll call Aunt Hannah over in Raleigh. She always wanted me to stay with her. (CEPHUS *crosses back to the rocking chair, grips its back.*) Gramps, Uncle Lewis. The greatest two men God ever made. I'll do you proud.

WOMAN ONE/PATTIE MAE (*crossing L of the bench on the L platform. Facing* CEPHUS): Cephus, I'm going off to college.

CEPHUS: But we're supposed to be married. The old folks done matched us up.

WOMAN ONE/PATTIE MAE: Mama wants me to go to this college in Virginia. I'll write you every day. And I'll be home every chance I get. We'll live on your grand-daddy's land.

CEPHUS: I'll never love another girl. Not in my whole life.

(WOMAN ONE *sits on the D end of the bench facing the audience.* CEPHUS *crosses DR on the C platform.*)

The gayly colored leaves float and dance, on a soft summer day. Kissed for a moment by the wind, then slowly drift away. The cool night is around me. Alone I stop to pray. God. Bring her closer to me. She's my soft summer day.

WOMAN ONE/PATTIE MAE: I've got to get an education. A man can always

(CEPHUS *slowly crosses UR on the C platform bearing this voice from the past within himself.*)

get a job. But a woman needs her education, Cephus. We have children to raise. They can't all go around cussing like you. I hope that you

(CEPHUS *turns his head D,* WOMAN ONE *rises.*)

don't cuss like you used to. (WOMAN ONE *crosses D and around the L side of the L platform. She removes the pink bow from her hair and puts it back in her pocket, takes off the shawl and hangs it on the L pipe bannister, then sits on the offstage side of the L platform observing* CEPHUS)

(CEPHUS turns and takes a few steps D keeping his focus out to the audience.)

CEPHUS: Cussing runs in my family.

WOMAN TWO: He got it from his mother.

CEPHUS (*crossing C on the platform*): Grandfather. Gramps took a lot of pride in his cussing abilities. To call a man a good old-fashion son of a bitch took training and concentration and pride. You see the lips have to be very relaxed. You let the words roll off the tongue. You don't push them. Like this. You son of a . . .

WOMAN TWO: Just like his mother.

CEPHUS: My grand-daddy.

WOMAN TWO: The family cuss box.

CEPHUS: If you cuss and do it right, it won't sound nasty. Think of each cuss word as a note on a guitar. I used to practice cussing while a buddy of mine, "One Arm Ike," played his guitar. That's why my cuss words don't sound nasty.

WOMAN TWO: Wash your mouth out with lye soap.

CEPHUS (*playing the C area on the platform*): Ike lost his arm while trying to steal Sydney Joe Murphy's hogs. Ike was a big hog thief. One night he busted into Sydney's hog pen. He'd already stole three of the hogs when he got greedy. And went back to steal Sydney Joe's prize-winning sow. It was pitch black dark and Sydney's house was about a half a mile from the hog pen, so Ike felt safe knowing that Sydney couldn't see his pick-up truck. Well it just so happens that Sydney had been back up in the woods making whiskey that night and he was walking back to his house on a path near the pig pen. Ike was leading the sow out of the pen and he spotted old Sydney. Scared Ike damn near to death. He turned the sow loose and she went off just a squealing, into the woods. Sydney heard this and he knew something was up. Old Sydney started peeping around in the dark. Real sly like. This way. Then that a way. Sydney reached in his pocket and pulled his .38 special out. She was glistening in the moonlight. Ike seen that gun and he peed on himself, but he didn't make a sound. Just stood there. Motionless. Sydney fired three shots into the air. Ka-pow! Ka-pow! Ka-pow! Ike dived into the bushes. Sydney just knowed somebody was close by so he squatted down. Like a Indian, and began to wait. Old Ike was scared to death. He could see that gun in Sydney's hands just a shining. "I'll find you." "You goddamn hog thief," Sydney shouted. Now Ike had landed on his back when he dived into the bushes. His right arm was caught between the ground and his body and he was laying on it. He couldn't move or else Sydney Joe would hear him. One hour passed. Then two. Ike felt his arm go to sleep on him. Then it started to hurt. Four hours passed. Old Sydney still squatting like an Indian. Finally after six hours, Sydney gave up and walked toward his house. By now Ike was crying. As black as Ike was, his arm had turned blue. No blood circulating. Well they had to cut his arm off after that. Right at the elbow joint. So now he just sits around strumming his guitar with (CEPHUS *holds up a bent right arm to illustrate* IKE's *stump.*) that stump, what used to be a arm. I tried to lift his spirits by telling him I needed music to practice my cussing by. (CEPHUS *begins to mime strumming a guitar with his bent arm/stump.*)

(WOMAN ONE *rises and crosses D on the L platform.* WOMAN TWO *rises and crosses to the top R platform stair. They halt and fix* CEPHUS *with reproachful glances.*)

WOMAN TWO: Don't start up.
WOMAN ONE: It's late at night. And sound travels.
CEPHUS: Ike would hit a 'G' and I'd say, "Son"! He'd hit a 'E' and I'd say, "of"! 'D,' I'd say, "a." 'E' again and I'd say . . .
WOMAN ONE: Stop!
CEPHUS: While I was waiting for Pattie,

(*Disgusted,* WOMAN ONE *crosses to the UL step on the L platform, while* WOMAN TWO *crosses U on the R platform.*)

I took up with my second cousin. Pearlene Costin.

WOMAN TWO: He ain't a whole Christian yet.

CEPHUS (*sitting on the bench UC on the platform*): All my other relatives got mad as a wet hen.

(WOMAN ONE *and* TWO *cross DLC on the UC platform. They stand with their backs slightly to each other, hands on hips.*)

WOMAN ONE/COUSIN: He never asked me for no date.

WOMAN TWO/COUSIN: Me either. I'm his first cousin. I think he should have chosen me first.

WOMAN ONE/COUSIN: I'm a first cousin too. But I'm the oldest. So it should have been me.

WOMAN TWO/COUSIN: Pearlene has short hair.

WOMAN ONE/COUSIN: She doesn't like to cook.

WOMAN TWO/COUSIN: She's a little on the dark side.

WOMAN ONE/COUSIN: She won't work.

CEPHUS: I don't care. I had to have somebody. Cousins I hadn't seen in years started to show up. Telling me how sinful it was for me to take up with Pearlene.

WOMAN TWO/COUSIN: God don't like ugly Cephus Junior.

WOMAN ONE/COUSIN: Sinful.

WOMAN TWO/COUSIN: A shame.

WOMAN ONE/COUSIN: A disgrace.

WOMAN TWO/COUSIN: A black mark on the family name.

WOMAN ONE and TWO/COUSINS: We're jealous!

CEPHUS: Go home.

(WOMAN ONE *and* TWO *begin to cross R on the platform.*)

Irma.

(WOMAN ONE *and* TWO *stop.*)

Tell Aunt Hannah I said hello.

WOMAN TWO/COUSIN: Tell her yourself, Judas.

(WOMAN ONE *and* TWO *cross and sit on the UR escape stairs.* WOMAN ONE *picks up and puts on the second flowered shawl and the pink hair bow.*)

CEPHUS: I figured us being cousins would make us understand each other better. People told us our young ones would be deformed. Pearlene didn't believe that. She was born with a veil over her face and she could foresee the future. Things other people couldn't see. Pearlene, though second cousin she was, was one of the evilest young women in the county. But she was pretty. Short and pretty. She had big "sway" hips. Which was good for having babies. She said that she learned to fight so well by watching her pet rooster, whose name was Lee Roy, whip on Lester, her father's old hound dog. Now it ain't natural for a rooster to be able to whip a hound dog. Especially when Lee Roy, the chicken, only weighed about eight pounds, and old Lester the hound, weighed about eighty. I never seen a dog so scared of a chicken in all my life. If you called Lee Roy's name around Lester, that hound would faint. I swear, he'd fall right out from fear. Anyway, Pearlene thought that this was a sign from God, which gave little, short people the right to whip larger people. See that logic. Pearlene and me stayed together for two months, and then she took up with a Marine Corps fellow from over at Camp LeJeune. She needed somebody who was trained in fighting. Maybe that Marine could even teach Lee Roy a few new tricks. I never loved her. Only as a cousin.

(WOMAN ONE *and* TWO *cross D of the R stairs.*)

WOMAN TWO/PATTIE'S MOTHER: Cephus Junior is a wild boy Patricia. And that crowd!

WOMAN ONE/PATTIE MAE: He's fine Mama. Papa says he just got to find himself.

WOMAN TWO/PATTIE'S MOTHER: He does go to church, every now and then. I guess he's all right. . . .

WOMAN ONE/PATTIE MAE (*hugging* WOMAN TWO): Thanks Mama.

(WOMAN TWO *crosses and sits on the top UR escape stair.* WOMAN ONE *steps up on the C platform and crosses L of the bench.* CEPHUS *stands.*)

Mama said she doesn't know why you hang out with that no-good crowd like you do. Joe-Boy and Tommy ain't no good for nobody Mama said. Joe-Boy got Calie Sue pregnant.

CEPHUS: He married her.

WOMAN ONE/PATTIE MAE: No decent girl would stay at that fish fry past twelve o'clock.

CEPHUS: I don't like for you to come to the fish fry. That's not your kind of crowd.

WOMAN ONE/PATTIE MAE: But I'm with you, so it's all right. Papa said it's all right for you to sow your wild oats, and get all of that devilment out of you. Cause if you get it all out now, you'll make me a better husband later on. Papa said he sowed a lot of wild oats when he was your age. Mama got so mad. (WOMAN ONE *begins to cross L on the platform.*)

CEPHUS: I'll see you after church on Sunday. We'll go to the beach. Uncle Lewis will let me drive his car.

WOMAN ONE/PATTIE MAE (*her voice trailing off as if in a memory*): We'll go swimming. (WOMAN ONE *crosses beside the L entrance. She removes the pink bow and puts on the neck scarf which is in her pocket.*)

CEPHUS (*following a long, solitary beat*): Crickets, crickets. Singing. A crystal clear sky. Billions of stars and a moon. (*Sits on the bench UC.*) And I sit alone. She's away in a school in Virginia. Look at that dirt road. Walk for miles and not see another house. (*Mimes petting a dog.*) Just me and you Brownie. Plenty of rain this year. Good corn crop. I'm turning out to be a good farmer Gramps. Just like you Uncle Lewis. I got fifteen cows now. Gonna plant an extra acre of tobacco this year. I love the land. She didn't come home for Christmas like she said she would. Went to Baltimore with a classmate. I'll wait. She'll be proud of this place.

(WOMAN ONE *crosses to and sits on the L platform bench. She faces the audience and during the following beat, she and* CEPHUS *do not relate to each other, but keep their focus out to the audience.*)

I'll be the farmer and she'll be the schoolteacher.

WOMAN TWO (*crossing R of the rocking chair on the UC platform*): Forget it Cephus. You're wasting your time. She graduated last month. Married a lawyer fellow from Baltimore. Living in Richmond. Happy as a lark. So she says.

WOMAN ONE/PATTIE MAE: I have outgrown the Cross Roads, Cephus. It was too small. Your world was too small. The socioeconomic conditions are not to my standards anymore. I have outgrown the land. I have outgrown . . . you. I see more in a day, than you've seen in your whole life. But I'll always love you. And who knows, one of these days when we drive down, maybe I'll see you. It was just not on my level. Too small. Good luck with the farm. You're a natural with the land.

WOMAN TWO (*crossing down to the R platform facing* CEPHUS): Roll, roll. The subway rolls. Take it to the city. Bright lights and party lights. (*Crosses into the "cul de sac" between the R stairs and C platform*) The subway rolls. Escape. Run to the city. Black gabardine pants, pegged at the ankles. White knob-toed shoes. Strut. Strut. The Avenue Strut. Take it to the city.

CEPHUS: No. I'll wait.

WOMAN TWO: Jack-ass.

WOMAN ONE/PATTIE MAE: My husband's clients are absolutely ecstatic about his office. I did the decorating myself. He's a Boston fellow you

know. Reared in Baltimore. The best of two cultures. South
and North.

(WOMAN TWO *crosses L on C platform. She relates to* CEPHUS *and*
WOMAN ONE *without their relating directly to her or each other, yet
responding as if they did.*)

WOMAN TWO: Those calloused hands, got to be too much for you, huh?
Or not enough.
WOMAN ONE/PATTIE MAE: I prefer the softer touch . . . I think. I'm
different now.
WOMAN TWO: Your Papa has calloused hands.
CEPHUS: Yeah. Like mine.
WOMAN TWO: Made from the same hoe and shovel, that digs the
pungent black earth.
CEPHUS: The same soil. Like mine.
WOMAN TWO: So that you could eat. And grow smart. And go off to a
college in Virginia. And turn your back . . . on your own.
WOMAN ONE/PATTIE MAE: A person has to better herself. I still love
you all, but . . .
WOMAN TWO: You're different.
CEPHUS (*rising*): I'll change. Look I don't have to dig the dirt. I'll go to
school. I'll be a big shot. Be what you want.
WOMAN ONE/PATTIE MAE: I can't grow old and fat and slow. Burdened
with babies, in a dusty old farmhouse. Looking like ninety by the time
I'm thirty. With arthritis, high blood, and a touch of sugar.
WOMAN TWO: You were born in a dusty old farmhouse.
WOMAN ONE/PATTIE MAE (*rising*): But I've since learned to clean.
(WOMAN ONE *exits L. She removes her scarf and shawl.*)
WOMAN TWO: Smart ass ain't she? Split Cephus. Get on the next thing
smoking and ride to the concrete baby. (*Crosses L of* CEPHUS.)
Everybody's going North man. The city. Move fast. Step out. Good
God! Do it! Do it! It will change you. You will be what they call,
"somebody else."
CEPHUS: She's gone. The subway?
WOMAN TWO: A train. Uptown. Make you forget these cornfields and
hog pens.
CEPHUS: How do I make it out. What's it like? (CEPHUS *crosses to the
bench UC on the platform and sits, continuing to respond to* WOMAN
TWO, *throughout, without making eye contact with her as she
badgers him.*)

(WOMAN TWO *crosses UL of* CEPHUS *on the bench.*)

WOMAN TWO:
Fast girls, party girls.
Sweet perfume and satin dresses.
The subway rolls.
Take it to the city.
Get a factory job you farmer boy.
And listen to blues and jazz in the middle of the night.
The subway rolls.
Live the fast life farmer boy,
Smoke it, coke it, and love it.
You can take it, make it, and love it.
The subway rolls.
Take it to the city. Take it to the city.
Hot, wet, and sticky in the fields.
One hundred and one degrees in the shade.
Ain't fit for a mule, freeman, or slave.
Take it to the mighty, mighty.
The mighty city.
The subway rolls.
A train, E train, D train, B train.
The fast life. Hayseed. The fast life.
Moving so fast that your soul will burst.
The subway rolls, and rolls and rolls and rolls.
Well water's no good for you.
Stop drinking out of Parson's creek.
City water baby. City water's the best.
They've chloride it, fluoride it, and
Notarized it.
Take it to the city.
Nobody here for you to see after.
No reason for you to stay.
Lord knows you can forget Pattie Mae.
Catfish stew, corn fritters, potato pone,
Fresh cold buttermilk, red-eye gravy.
Ain't fit for a hog.
Steak it. Double cuts. Scotch it, champagne it,
Tossed salad with Russian.
Take it to the city.
The subway rolls.

CEPHUS (*rising, crossing DRC on the platform*): Too noisy. Too many
people. God didn't intend for man to travel that fast under the
ground. Nothing for me up there.

WOMAN TWO (*crossing L of* CEPHUS): Nothing for you here either. Joe-Boy and Tommy both got spanking brand new houses. The city's been good to them.

CEPHUS (*crossing DC on the platform*):

(WOMAN TWO *counter-crosses R of* CEPHUS.)

How are they doing? Haven't seen them since Christmas before last.

WOMAN TWO: They both got drafted. Green Berets. Special forces. Fort Dix, New Jersey.

CEPHUS: Well I'll be doggone. Joe-Boy and Tommy always did like that John Wayne stuff. (*Leaping at the opportunity to change the subject and evade her pressuring.*) Which reminds me. Did I ever tell you how I learned to speak Indian?

(*In frustration,* WOMAN TWO *angrily crosses and sits on the UR edge of the platform leaning against the UR column.*)

Well there was this light-skinned colored man in Cross Roads. Told everybody that he was a Cherokee Indian and didn't speak no English. He was a drifter, but everybody knew he was colored. Cept him. Use to wear buckskins and everything. Smoked a peace pipe. Couldn't speak no English. Till he wanted something. He took up with Lottie Bell McKoy from over in the Hollow. Pete McKoy's sister. How they ever got together, only the Lord knows. (*Crosses to the bench, sits*) One night we were down in the Bay, which was a Piccolo Joint about five miles from Cross Roads. We were dancing, eating fried chicken, and having a ball, when Ole Chief, that's what we called the colored Indian. Ole Chief come up to me and said in plain English, "Loan me two dollars. I want to buy me and Lottie Bell a chicken sandwich and a beer." I gave him the money but I told him I needed it back by Wednesday. He said, ugh! And started being an Indian again. I should have known something was wrong. Everybody was laughing at me and calling me a fool. Saying Old Chief wasn't gonna never pay me my two dollars. I waited one week. No money. I waited two weeks. No money. Every time I'd ask him about it, he'd start speaking Indian. "Erosh me Toh. Kowa wa'ee." No understand. Well, finally I got tired. (*Rises, plays C area*) I caught Old Chief asleep in front of the hardware store one day. Tommy and Joe-Boy was laughing their heads off. "You know you don't speak Indian." I woke Old Chief up and I spoke very slow and soft. "Chief I want my fucking money. Now I know that you don't speak English, so what I'm saying won't mean nothing. But I'm gonna walk in back of this store and find me a brick. When I come back, if my two dollars is not laying on this bench, I'm going to bust that brick into a thousand pieces across your head. Then I'm going to whip your lying ass all the way into your happy hunting ground." When I come back, there was my two dollars sitting on the bench. And Old Chief pretending to be asleep. I held it up and showed it to the fellows. They stopped laughing. And that's how I learned to speak Indian. (*Crosses back to the bench, sits*) Oh yeah. I called him a son of a bitch, too.

WOMAN TWO (*leaning in toward* CEPHUS): You're just going to sit there spinning tales, and acting like an old man, huh? So quiet at night down here that you can hear your own heartbeat. That is if the crickets singing all night don't drive you batty. Mosquitoes as big as turkeys. Sound like airplanes when they land on you.

CEPHUS (*taking refuge in yet another tale to avoid making a decision, sharply retorts*): The children love for me to spin my tales. Every Saturday we "pull the Seine." Put a net across the white stocking river and catch fish. Cook up the fish and have a big time. Everybody (*stepping*) out in their Saturday night finery for the big fish fry. (*Rises, plays C area*) My job was skinning the catfish. Ever skin a catfish? It takes talent. You use wire pliers. Catfish don't have scales. A tough skin. And watch out for his mouth. He's sharp around the mouth. You can get a gash cut in your arm that will rival the best laid razor scar you ever saw. Joe-Boy met Calie Sue, his wife, at a fish fry. As a matter of fact, Henry, their oldest boy is the result of some passionate lovemaking on the banks of the White Stocking River. I guess that's why that boy can swim so good. He likes catfish too. (CEPHUS *crosses to the bench, sits.*)

(WOMAN ONE *enters UC crosses R of the UR escape stairs, hands on hips.*)

One Saturday night old "Hard Headed Herbert" came to the fish fry. Man had a head harder than steel. And would fall asleep anywhere. We were all dancing and having a good time, so we didn't notice Herbert being missing. Well, there was this large fourteen wheel truck loaded with logs, standing in the road a little ways from the river. The truck stood there for four hours straight. After a while I walked up the road to take a leak. I heard all this cussing and hollering coming from beneath the truck. I took a look. Low and behold, Hard Headed Herbert's head was caught under the back tires of the truck. And his head had been buried in the mud with this truck sitting on top of it for four hours. (*He rises.*)

(WOMAN ONE *and* TWO *pick up the army "cunt" cap and helmet respectively, from the floor R of the stairs.*)

"Git this big mother fucker off my head," he screamed. "Ain't safe to go to sleep nowhere around here." (*Crosses to bench, sits*) Well we got the truck off his head. But his head had burst two of the tires on the truck and he didn't have a scratch. That's the truth. Bubba Junior hit him in the head with a pitchfork one day and bent the fork in half. Didn't even crack the skin on Herbert's head.

WOMAN TWO (*commandingly*): Man, do something.

(WOMAN ONE *crosses L of the rocking chair on the UC platform with the army cap in her hand.* WOMAN TWO *puts on the army helmet and crosses to the top of the UR escape stairs.*)

WOMAN ONE (*forcefully*): Move. Move.
(WOMAN TWO *begins to sing "America the Beautiful," under the following dialogue.*):
Sitting and rocking, swatting flies
While the whole world cries.
There's a war going on. (WOMAN TWO *marches in place in time with her singing.*)
He's quite content, but hardly alive.
He seems a hundred, though he's only twenty-five.
War going on.
He's well-respected by neighbors.
And friends,
Trying to live up to his Grand Pa's legend.
War going on. (WOMAN TWO *marches down to the "cul de sac" L of the R stairs. She then marches in place.*)
WOMAN ONE (*quickly changing character*): Thou shall not kill Cephus.
CEPHUS: I know Gramps.
WOMAN ONE: Love thy neighbor boy.
CEPHUS: I try hard Uncle Lewis.
WOMAN ONE (*resuming narration*): Rice paddies. Jungle. The living be damned. The land that we fight in. Is called Viet Nam. (WOMAN ONE *puts on the army cap.*) War going on.

(WOMAN ONE *and* TWO *salute. Song, "America the Beautiful," ends.*)

War going on. Greetings Cephus Miles. This is your rich Uncle, Sam. You have been inducted into the Armed Forces of the United States.
CEPHUS: No.
WOMAN ONE: What!
CEPHUS (*rising*): No. Love thy neighbor. Thou shall not kill.

(CEPHUS *crosses to the rocking chair on the UC platform, sits.* WOMAN ONE *crosses to the R platform, stands "at ease" facing L.* WOMAN TWO *crosses U of the bench on the C platform, crouching and ducking as if on a battlefield. She kneels, resting her arms on the bench.* WOMAN ONE *hums "American the Beautiful" under the following monologue.*)

WOMAN TWO: Nightfall. A jungle in Viet Nam. Dear Cephus Junior, the only fool that could ever drink more corn whiskey than me. How goes everything? There's a war going on old buddy. I miss home something awful, man. How's Pattie? You all married yet? This Viet Nam is rough. Hot. Muddy. Blood and bodies everywhere. I'm scared man. Scared to death. Done killed a few. Had to. Joe-Boy is doing fine. We're in the same company. He has a lot of bad dreams these days. Wakes up crying a lot. Last night I held him in my arms and we rocked each other to sleep. The jungle is quiet, and death is everywhere. Sssssh. Sssssh. Hush now Joe-Boy I'm here. I'm here old buddy. I won't let nothing hurt you. Won't be long before we're back in Cross Roads, North Carolina. Won't be long. Frying fish on the banks of the White Stocking.

(WOMAN ONE *stops humming.*)

The shooting has stopped. Well, you be good old dude. Be glad you aren't over here. Take care and pray for me and Joe. You son of a bitch. Your main partner. Tommy. P.S. Joe-Boy says that Old Chief, the colored Indian, owes him a dollar. Since you speak Indian so well, he would like you to collect it and give it to his sister, Loraine. (*Ducking and dodging* WOMAN TWO *crosses UL on the UC platform. She hangs her helmet on the UL column and faces U.*)

WOMAN ONE (*saluting*): Cephus Miles you are to report for your induction physical. On June 23, 1966. Raleigh, North Carolina. Congratulations.

CEPHUS (*rising, crosses L of rocking chair*): No. Thou shall not kill. Love thy neighbor.

WOMAN ONE: Shit! Lock this fool up till doomsday. (WOMAN ONE *stands "at ease."*)

(WOMAN TWO *turns, facing D.*)

WOMAN TWO (*intoning*): A jury of your peers having found you guilty. Having found you guilty. Having found you guilty.

CEPHUS (*putting hands behind his back as if handcuffed*): I never even heard of Viet Nam. I got ten acres of corn, fifteen cows, and seventy-three chickens to worry about. What do I care about Viet Nam? I don't want to go to prison. I want to be free. Not in a cage. But I won't fight. (CEPHUS *stumbles onto the L platform as if thrown. He sits, facing R on the bench.*)

(WOMAN TWO *crosses to the top UL escape stairs, sits. She puts on the prison guard's cap.* WOMAN ONE *removes the army cap and continues to stand "at ease" while resuming the narrative.*)

WOMAN ONE:
Clanging, clanging, clanging, the huge, cold steel gates of the prison.
Taking the freedom from one more Bird of Reason.
Chopping off the wings and Burning the Feathers. No more
To Fly on land. Earth bound
In a pit of steel and concrete.
A cubicle to sleep in. Freedom a bastard.
Just because, "Thou shall not kill."
Love thy neighbor as thyself. (WOMAN ONE *crosses UR on the UC platform, drops the army cap on the floor U of the set, puts on the wire frame glasses, then crosses to the rocking chair and sits.*)

WOMAN TWO (*rising and reassuming the jailer's stance and sarcastic attitude*): A letter for Cephus Miles.

CEPHUS: Here. (CEPHUS *extends his hand directly in front of him as if reaching for the letter. He keeps his focus out.*)

(WOMAN TWO *crosses L on the UC platform briefly reassuming the city siren identity.*)

WOMAN TWO: Somebody finally done writ you Benedict Arnold. You show tore your ass old patriot.
The boys talking about painting you red, white, and blue. (WOMAN TWO *turns and faces U.*)

(CEPHUS *mimes grabbing and reading the letter.*)

WOMAN ONE/AUNT HANNAH: Dear Cephus. We've been praying for you every day. You've got only two more years. God provides. We would have wrote sooner, but we were afraid. Folks don't like your stand. Say you're a communist.

WOMAN TWO: Love thy neighbor!

WOMAN ONE/AUNT HANNAH: We had to sell your Grand Pa's place. Couldn't keep up the taxes. But you can live with me when you get out. Joe-Boy and Tommy are dead. Killed in Viet Nam. They shipped their bodies home and they were buried with full military honors.

WOMAN TWO (*crossing R on the R platform, kneeling and taking off the guard's cap*): Isn't that great Cephus. They're heroes. Look at you.

WOMAN ONE/AUNT HANNAH: Then again. Maybe you'd better not come here. We don't want no trouble. But we love you. Aunt Hannah.

WOMAN TWO (*rising, crossing C on the platform*): The subway rolls. Listen to blues and jazz in the middle of the night. Perfume. Satin dresses. Smoke it, coke it, love it. Nobody will know you there. Take it to the city. (WOMAN TWO *jumps on the floor R of the platform, picks up and puts on the guard's cap, then crosses U of the set. She paces back and forth as if on guard duty.*)

CEPHUS: The subway rolls.

WOMAN ONE/AUNT HANNAH: Dear Cephus. Some folks from up North came by today. Two Negro girls and a white fellow. From the People's Party they called themselves. Said they wanted to take up your fight.

CEPHUS: I don't have no fight. That's why I'm here cause I don't have no fight.

WOMAN ONE/AUNT HANNAH: You still playing your basketball. You used to be awfully good at it. Maybe you can make something out of that. They're paying Negroes a lot of money to play basketball, these days. (WOMAN ONE *crosses, in character, R of the R stairs. She removes the wire frame glasses, picks up the flowered shawl from the bannister and puts it on.*)

CEPHUS: They haven't let me see the sun in six months. How can I play basketball. The subway rolls. I can see her, I can see that Big City Babe, just as plain as day. Red satin dress. Soft skin. Blues and jazz in the middle of the night. I'm coming. You just wait. I'll be there baby. You just wait for Cephus. Damn the land! Take it to the city! (CEPHUS *clasps his hands in prayer.*)

WOMAN TWO (*crossing L on the UC platform*): Head count. One, two, three, four, five, six . . . Look at Old Benedict Arnold. Who you praying to, General Hershey?

CEPHUS: I'm calling Miami.

WOMAN TWO: Miami? This damn fool done finally snapped. Bet (*turns head U, as if talking to another guard*) this blackjack of mine could beat some sense into you. Whop! Whop! Right cross your big nappy (*mimes striking palm with a blackjack*) head. Thou shall not kill. You got your nerve.

CEPHUS (*ceasing prayer*): Guess he's not back. He's been gone a long time jailer. A long time.

WOMAN TWO: You gonna be gone a long time too, you simple ass. (*Crosses to the top UL escape stair*) Lights out on this tier. Lights out. (*Turns to* CEPHUS) Sleep tight old patriot. (WOMAN TWO *sits on the stair.*)

(CEPHUS *lays down on the bench.* WOMAN ONE *crosses C on the C platform. Lights go down as a special comes up on* CEPHUS *and* WOMAN ONE. WOMAN ONE *dances, as* CEPHUS *dreams.* WOMAN ONE *is* PATTIE MAE *in dream sequence.*)

WOMAN ONE/PATTIE MAE: I've seen your face. Far from this dungeon you now call home. You've heard my voice. And gently touched my hand. You've laid your troubled head many a night on my breast, and softly, very softly. You kissed them. Remember?

CEPHUS: I remember, Pattie Mae. I remember.

WOMAN ONE/PATTIE MAE: Hot. Hot in the summer. We lay in your Grandfather's hay loft. Wet with love and perspiration. We had a blanket. (*Holds up a shawl*) It was damp and sticky from our lovemaking. Remember?

CEPHUS: Yes.

WOMAN ONE/PATTIE MAE (*dancing R of the bench UC on the platform*): Dancing. Dancing in your head. Trapped. Trapped. Poor trapped bird. I wish that I could help you fly. But I am far away.

CEPHUS: Come home.

WOMAN ONE/PATTIE MAE: I've held you close during our moments of passion. And the softness of my womanhood, would make you cry out and be electrified with pleasure. Moving together. Touching. Kissing. Bodies wet. Dripping. Sliding against each other. (*Straddles the bench, facing* CEPHUS, *she begins the undulating, grinding motions of sexual intercourse*) Hot. Good! Good! Good! No don't scream. Someone will hear. That's it. Easy. Easy. Remember?

CEPHUS: I remember.

WOMAN ONE/PATTIE MAE: Restless with passion. The dungeon dances. See it dance. See it. My naked body everywhere. That's it. Come on! Come on! Come on!

CEPHUS (*bolting upright on the bench*): Aaaaaaaaaaah! Aaaaaaaah! Oh God. Please come back.

(WOMAN ONE *crosses UR on the UC platform, drops the shawl U of the set, and remains stationary with her back to the audience. Simultaneous with the above,* WOMAN TWO *crosses L on the UC platform holding the guard's cap in her hand. Lights restore to normal as dream sequence ends.*)

WOMAN TWO: Clanging, clanging, clanging. The huge, cold steel gates of the prison. Sets to freedom a harder and older and colder bird of reason. Five years of his youth, left behind in the pit of steel and concrete. The soft, innocent, downy feathers of the young bird. Turned to hardened rock. (*Puts on guard's cap.*) Time for you to leave old patriot. I'd advise you to run long and far. Some folks might not feel that five years is long enough. Spit'n on the flag like you did.

(CEPHUS *takes madras jacket and hat from within the bench and slowly crosses down the stairs to the stage floor. He crosses along the D edge of the set to DC on the stage floor.* WOMAN TWO *crosses down the UL escape stairs, puts the guard's cap on the bench U of the set.* WOMAN ONE *crosses DR on the UC platform.*)

WOMAN ONE: Blues. Blues down that lonesome highway. Running fast and far. Trying to outrun the sun. Moving on up. Into the promised land. Suitcase in his hand.

WOMAN TWO (*crossing DL on the UC platform*):
Clickity clack. Clickity clack.
Midnight Special and the Shoefly.
Take this country boy to the promised land.
Rock and sock his soul with new found life-styles.
Blues. Blues down the lonesome highway.

(WOMAN ONE *and* TWO *do a stylized side-stepping, swaying motion in rhythm with the lines.*)

Train whistle blows. Smoke from the stack.
Cold and wet. Clickity clack. Clickity clack.
Moving on up. Into the promised land.
WOMAN ONE and TWO (*in unison*): The Promised Land. The Promised Land. Clickity clack. Clickity clack.

(WOMAN TWO *crosses and sits on the top UL escape stair. She puts on the red satin stole trimmed with boa feathers.*)

CEPHUS (*focusing out*): Yes sir. The twelfth grade. I graduated. I can read and write just as good as anybody. I . . . I sho need this job Mister Marshall. I'm a good worker. Strong back. See I used to work and plow the land, so hard work ain't no stranger. No sir I'm not trying to be funny. Reference. Well no . . . no sir. Well I can't rightly do that sir. You see my mama died in forty-four. My father was in World War Two. But he wasn't one of the lucky ones. Oh, thank you sir. Thank you. You won't be sorry. I'll load them trucks like they was my very own.

WOMAN ONE (*stepping down onto the UR wooden box, then crossing down L on the C platform*): Handle it slick. You in the city now. Deal with the fast track. Show them who's boss.

CEPHUS (*putting on madras jacket, looking about him*): Strange place to be in. A monster is what it is.

WOMAN ONE (*crossing DR on the platform*): No man no. This is it. You are tasting success baby. This is nine-teen seventy-one. Progress. People are moving and grooving. And freaking out.

CEPHUS (*putting on the hat, brim turned up*): Yeah. How do I look?

WOMAN ONE: Slick baby. You look slick. (WOMAN ONE *crosses to the bench UC on the platform. She swings the R end of the bench D slightly so that the bench is on a diagonal. She then moves one wooden box UL of the bench and the other DR of the bench. The bench and boxes now become a table and chairs in a lounge.*) Move on out. Spend some of that factory money. Calluses and blisters on your hands money.

(CEPHUS *crosses into the "cul de sac" R of the R stairs.* WOMAN ONE *crosses to the top UR escape step and sits.* WOMAN TWO *crosses down to the L wooden box making a sensuous, percussive, whispering "chi-choop-powww" sound. She sits and crosses her legs.*)

Flash baby. Flash. But don't be no square.

WOMAN TWO/MYRNA: Hey killer. Buy a girl a drink? You looking spiffy. Here in the promised land.

CEPHUS (*crossing to the R wooden box on the C platform*): I feel spiffy. What's your pleasure. And don't play me cheap. The subway rolls and Cephus Miles is on board. (*Sits*) Am I smooth enough?

WOMAN TWO/MYRNA: Smooth as glass. No rough edges. And handsome to boot. I think I love you daddy. Where you from Sweet Cephus?

CEPHUS: Ah . . . ah . . . Philly.

WOMAN TWO/MYRNA: All right! A Philadelphia smoothie. Myrna done caught herself a Philly man. (*She extends her hand.*)

CEPHUS (*rising, shaking her hand*): Don't rile me mama. My game's tight and I don't want it to snap. (*Slaps bench*) Bartender. Two drinks for me and my peach. Jack Daniels. (*Sits*) Black Label.

WOMAN TWO/MYRNA: All right! What kind of work you do?

CEPHUS: Load trucks. Shirt factory. One twenty-five a week. Dig it? Got a pocket full of money and nowhere to spend it.

WOMAN TWO/MYRNA: Shit, I want to move in with you. I think I'm in love. One twenty-five a week makes Myrna fall hard.

CEPHUS: I can dig it. Hop to it.

WOMAN TWO/MYRNA: A Philadelphia smoothie.

WOMAN ONE (*interjecting while observing the action from her seated position UR on escape stairs*): Thou shall not covet. Pattie Mae is over in Richmond Town.

WOMAN TWO/MYRNA: You like to drink "smoothie"?

CEPHUS: I've made plenty of it in my day. Could always hold my own.

Never drunk. Although I did go to jail two or three times for gitt'n drunk and disturbing the peace. The third time I got arrested for public exposure. I got drunk and forgot myself. The Sheriff caught me taking a piss on the courthouse lawn. I told him I was watering the flowers. Fifty dollars fine, and three days in jail. That was a long three days.

WOMAN TWO/MYRNA: In Philly?

CEPHUS: Oh . . . no . . . I was visiting some relatives down South. I was just visiting some . . .

WOMAN TWO/MYRNA: It's all right.

CEPHUS (*rising*): I'm gonna be so mean. I'm gonna blow out every neon light in every bar in this city. I'm gonna blow. I'm gonna blow. I'm gonna walk and strut. (*Crosses L on platform.*) Just a mean "motor scooter." That's what they gonna say when I strut by. (*Turns the brim down on his hat and crosses R of the R wooden box*) Carolina . . . I mean Philadelphia Cephus is my name from now on.

WOMAN TWO/MYRNA: I like that daddy. But no guns. I don't like men who carry guns.

CEPHUS: Believe me Myrna. I hate guns. Neon. Neon. Get me some fake diamond rings. One on each finger. (*Puts foot on wooden box*) Play the numbers every day. Run the bar when I win. A little something for everybody "Bar Keep."

WOMAN TWO/MYRNA: Strut baby, strut.

(CEPHUS *"struts" DL of* WOMAN TWO.)

CEPHUS: I am so cool. (*Crosses L of* WOMAN TWO *leans in toward her and whispers*) Whoopee! (*Takes a few steps D*) I love the monster. Should have been here years ago. (*Crosses back L of* WOMAN TWO *leans in toward her and whispers again*) Whoopee! (*Crosses R of the R wooden box*) And I'll forget that calico dress, and that smile, and that voice, and those clear country nights if it's the last thing that I do.

WOMAN TWO/MYRNA: What country daddy?

CEPHUS: South America.

WOMAN TWO/MYRNA: A world traveler. Well stop! Speak something in South American.

CEPHUS: I just did. (*Sits*) This bar done got quiet. I don't like silence. Too much, ain't good for you.

WOMAN TWO/MYRNA: Helps you to think, between the lies.

CEPHUS: What?

WOMAN TWO/MYRNA: I should be a proper lady. Got the background for it. I been lied to so many times. No truth left in the world. No honor. Yeah, Cephus, they are here tonight, and gone in the morning.

I deserve better. But I ain't no better, so I guess I don't. In and out. In and out. My behind feels like Grand Central Station at rush hour. (*She mimes pulling out a tiny box from her pocket and opening it. She offers the imaginary box to* CEPHUS.) Here. Coke it.

CEPHUS: What?

WOMAN TWO/MYRNA: Snow blow. Your nose. Like this. (*She mimes snorting the cocaine.*)

CEPHUS: Oh, I see.

WOMAN ONE (*interjecting*): Remember Gethsemane. Paul the Apostle.

CEPHUS (*answering without relating to* WOMAN ONE): A time far removed.

WOMAN ONE: Thou shall not bow down thyself to them or serve them.

(WOMAN TWO *mimes dipping up some cocaine on her fingernail. She offers it to* CEPHUS.)

CEPHUS: Did not mean me. (CEPHUS *sniffs the cocaine.*)

WOMAN TWO/MYRNA: You like hanging out with me Cephus? (*She mimes closing the box and putting it back in her pocket.*)

CEPHUS: I love hanging out with you. I'm a mean, bad Lobo Wolf and this is my time to howl. (*He makes a howling sound and begins to slowly rise.*) See what I been missing?

WOMAN TWO/MYRNA: Let's go up to your room at the hotel (*She begins to rise, synchronizing the completion of her rise with that of* CEPHUS.) and listen to some blues or jazz. (*Rushes into* CEPHUS's *arms—The impact swings them around a few times and they begin to dance.*) I'm moving in with you daddy. You wanna take care of Myrna.

CEPHUS: I can handle it. I can dig it. Ain't nothing but some sport.

WOMAN TWO/MYRNA: Oh yes.

(*They spin and turn in big circles as they dance.* WOMAN ONE *crosses DR on the UC platform.*)

Swing me. Sway me. Take me smoothie. Sway me.

WOMAN ONE: Fly bird! Fly! If you're smart you'll fly away. You'll fly South.

CEPHUS (*crossing DR on the platform*):

(WOMAN TWO *dances alone L on the platform.*)

There's nothing there. Only a few graves of those I love. My land taken for taxes. (*Extends his hand to* WOMAN TWO, *who crosses to him, takes his hand and circling around him, spins and turns him*) Anyway, I dig the monster. See how slick. See my city ways coming through. See me fight the monster. See me fight. Watch him fall.

WOMAN ONE: Whistle blows sharp and clear.

(WOMAN TWO *stops circling* CEPHUS *and spins him in place at an ever-increasing rate.*)

Screech. Screeeeech! Screeeeeeeeeeeech! Eight o'clock shift. Make it to the factory, farmer boy.

(CEPHUS *crosses off the platform, DC on the stage floor. He takes off his hat.* WOMAN TWO *crosses D of the L platform stairs.* WOMAN ONE *crosses L of the rocking chair.*)

CEPHUS: Morning boss. You wanted to see me.

WOMAN ONE: We got to let you go Cephus. Your records came today. We don't hire ex-cons. Communist who spit on the flag. You shirked your duty. Pick up your pay. And leave the premises.

CEPHUS: Thou shall not kill. What about the teachings?

WOMAN ONE: What about them? You tell me.

CEPHUS: I need this job. I can't do much else.

WOMAN ONE: Tell it to the lord in prayer. I can't help you.

CEPHUS: He's in Miami, on vacation.

WOMAN ONE: That's where I'm going next week. If I see him. I'll tell him that you're looking for him. (WOMAN ONE *crosses to the UL escape stair. She stands watching the action, her profile to the audience.*)

CEPHUS: Yeah. Tell him to call me. Collect if he has to. (CEPHUS *crosses DL of the L stairs. He hangs his hat on the pipe bannister.*)

(WOMAN TWO *crosses up to the L platform, walks around the bench appraising her environment.*)

WOMAN TWO/MYRNA: A roof over my head when the cold wind blows. Food in my belly. A drink. A nice red satin dress. One twenty-five a week. (*Sits and leans back on the bench making herself comfortable.*) If you tell me this ain't heaven, I say you're lying.

CEPHUS: I lost my job today.

WOMAN TWO/MYRNA (*rising instantly—beginning to speak even as she crosses down and holds at the bottom of the L stairs.*): Well time for me to split. Done overstayed my time. Take care of old smoothie. There is a TV dinner in the oven. Bye. (WOMAN TWO *begins to cross R on the floor along the D edge of the set.*)

CEPHUS (*taking a few steps toward her*): Wait. I'll find another job.

WOMAN TWO/MYRNA (*halting, turning to Cephus*): Where there's no money. There can be no love. I think the Bible says that. Yeah. John three, sixteen. (*She continues her cross R.*)

CEPHUS: Wrong.

WOMAN TWO/MYRNA (*halting, turning toward* CEPHUS): Well it ought to say it. (*Continues cross*) Too bad you ain't really from Philly.

CEPHUS: How'd you know?

WOMAN TWO/MYRNA (*halting, turning to* CEPHUS): Looked at your feet while you were sleeping. Saw all those corns and calluses. You got some ugly feet old smoothie. Anybody with that many corns on their toes has stepped between many a cotton row. Tobacco fields too. (*Takes a few steps R*) Well, see you at the judgment. I'm going to pay my fare and ride the train. Find me a man who can afford to listen to blues and jazz in the middle of the night. See you old smoothie. And don't call me no son of a bitch after I leave. (WOMAN TWO *crosses R of the R pipe bannister. She removes the red satin shawl and puts on the orange sweater, along with the pair of oval, plastic frame eyeglasses.*)

(WOMAN ONE *crosses R of the bench on the L platform.* CEPHUS *slowly begins to cross R on the stage floor along the D edge of the set.*)

WOMAN ONE: You start to wander. Look over there. No job. Over there. The same. They've heard about your kind. Follows you where ever you go. The welfare rolls to replace the subway roll. (WOMAN ONE *exits L. She puts on the wide brim hat and matching silk scarf.*)

WOMAN TWO (*crossing to the R wooden box on the C platform, sitting*): Is this all of the information sir?

CEPHUS (*crossing to the L wooden box on the C platform, sitting*): Yes.

WOMAN TWO (*irked, but matter-of-fact in delivery throughout*): Why do you people come here ill prepared? No education. Just to get on welfare. You embarrass the race. It's people like myself who have to uphold it. You people put a lot of pressure on the black middle class.

CEPHUS: If I could do better I would. I don't like begging.

WOMAN TWO: One hundred and twenty-five dollars a month.

CEPHUS: Hardly enough to live on.

WOMAN TWO: Take it or leave it.

CEPHUS: I'll take it.

WOMAN TWO: Of course you will.

CEPHUS: Can't even pay rent with this.

WOMAN TWO: The agency will find you a nice little room somewhere for ten dollars a week or less. Now if there's no heat or hot water in the winter, don't you fret. Spring is just around the corner. Whenever you see the thermometer drop below five degrees, just repeat to yourself, "Spring is just around the corner." There is a Salvation Army Mission Church just a short train ride from here. You can . . .

CEPHUS: Uptown. Downtown. The Mission Church.

WOMAN TWO: Right. The Mission Church. There's clothing there. I would advise lots of large coats. You're young and strong. You should live a few years, at least.

CEPHUS: You must be from Miami.

WOMAN TWO: Jacksonville.

CEPHUS: How the hell do you expect me to live on this?

WOMAN TWO: We don't.

CEPHUS (*rising*): But I will.

WOMAN TWO: What will? You've got no will. Not for long.

CEPHUS (*crossing L on the platform*): I'll fight. Fight!

WOMAN TWO: Die trying. Who cares?

CEPHUS: Are you going to be my regular caseworker?

WOMAN TWO: You're the case. I'm the worker. Yes. I'm assigned to . . . help you. If I can. If I can't, well, 'dem's de brakes."

CEPHUS (*crossing UL of* WOMAN TWO, *raises fist*): I never hit a woman in my life. You're putting that record in danger.

WOMAN TWO: Hit me and that one twenty-five a month goes bye-bye.

(CEPHUS *lowers his fist.*)

That's right, put your fist back in your pocket! (WOMAN TWO *crosses R of the R pipe bannister. She removes the sweater and glasses and puts on the old, worn hat and scarf.*)

(WOMAN ONE *enters L, crosses along the D edge of the set, DLC on the stage floor. She beckons* CEPHUS. CEPHUS *turns up the collar on his jacket, as if against the cold and crosses DLC on the C platform. They are now on the street.*)

WOMAN ONE: Psst! Pssst! (*Holds open her scarf and points inside as if it were a jacket—She maintains an urgent, hip, secretive attitude throughout.*) Sell ten of these a day and five of these and you can drive one of these. (*With her hand, indicates a long, imaginary car*) Bright and shiny four-door sedan. Velvet seats. Mink steering wheel cover, AM/FM stereo. Plays blues and jazz twenty-four hours a day.

CEPHUS: What's that?

WOMAN ONE (*pointing to imaginary items inside her scarf*): This is coke-a-cola and this is Mary Jane. For those who like their nightmares in color. (*Mimes kicking at a dog who is biting at her heels.*) Down boy. Down.

CEPHUS: Who are you talking to?

WOMAN ONE: Dingles, the invisible dog.

CEPHUS: I don't see no dog.

WOMAN ONE (*offering an imaginary needle to* CEPHUS): Shoot up with some of this "Hero-wine," and you will. Here. Take the "spike."

CEPHUS (*taking a few steps R, away from* WOMAN ONE): Not my style. Been surrounded by enough steel.

WOMAN ONE (*taking a few steps R, following* CEPHUS): I got pills too. You'd be a good pill salesman. (*Mimes pulling bottles from her scarf.*) I got these for folks over sixty. To ease arthritis pain. And these for the twenty-five-to-thirty group, just for fun. And these, chocolate-coated quaaludes. For kids under six. Children hate taking medicine.

WOMAN TWO (*crossing DC on the stage floor as a wino*): Leave that scene alone, hayseed. I've got your beat.

WOMAN ONE (*beginning to exit L, walking backward*): If you change your mind. My names the "Dream Donator." Me and Dingles are on this corner every day, 9 to 5. (*Turns around, exits L*) Down Dingles, down.

WOMAN TWO (*offering* CEPHUS *an imaginary bottle*): Take a swig of this choo-choo. Let's ride to the moon.

CEPHUS (*accepting bottle, reading the label*): Night Train? (*Mimes unscrewing the cap off the bottle.*)

WOMAN TWO: Night train. Wine is made from grapes. That come from the rich, black soil.

CEPHUS: You don't use drugs do you?

WOMAN TWO: Hell no man. I'm an alcoholic. Can't supply but one habit at a time.

(CEPHUS *mimes drinking the wine. He and* WOMAN TWO *sit on the DRC edge of the C platform. He offers the imaginary bottle to* WOMAN TWO, *who refuses it.*)

I got two more. Steals them from a friend of mine. My name's Birmingham, what's yours?

CEPHUS: Cross Roads.

(*They shake hands.*)

WOMAN TWO: That's pretty hip. This steam pipe comes from the dry cleaners. Keep real close and you'll stay warm.

(CEPHUS *mimes drinking the remainder of the wine and throwing the bottle into the street. He and* WOMAN TWO *huddle closer trying to stay warm. Enter* WOMAN ONE, *L wearing the black, pillbox hat and carrying a handbag. She crosses along the D edge of the set, DC on the stage floor. She dryly mimes selling papers.*)

WOMAN ONE: *Watch Tower! Watch Tower!* Read the word. The holy word.

WOMAN TWO (*rising, crossing R of* WOMAN ONE): Praise Jesus holy name! I love the Lord!

(*Offended by the odor,* WOMAN ONE *takes a few steps L away from* WOMAN TWO.)

Could you spare a quarter Miss? For a bowl of soup?

WOMAN ONE (*crossing DRC on the stage floor away from* WOMAN TWO): Come to Jesus and be filled, Brother.

WOMAN TWO (*following* WOMAN ONE): I will, I will. But right now, could you spare a quarter?

WOMAN ONE: You are bringing down the race.

CEPHUS: Do you have a daughter?

WOMAN ONE: Yes. She's a caseworker at the welfare office.

(CEPHUS *rises in disgust.* WOMAN ONE *begins to cross R.*)

Read the word.

CEPHUS: You two make a good couple.

(WOMAN ONE *halts, looks over her shoulder.*)

WOMAN TWO: Wanna get married baby.

(*Offended,* WOMAN ONE *crosses, hurriedly, R of the R pipe bannister. She takes off the hat and hangs the handbag on the bannister.*)

WOMAN ONE: *Watch Tower! Watch Tower!*

(WOMAN TWO *crosses to* CEPHUS, *mimes giving him a bottle of wine. She then hands him her hat and scarf.*)

WOMAN TWO: Here, take one of these. Some heat in your belly when the cold wind blows. (WOMAN TWO *crosses to the bench on the C platform. She swings the R end U, restoring it to its original playing position. She then stacks the two wooden boxes, side by side, on top of the bench. She is a bartender cleaning up the bar.*)

(CEPHUS *crosses into the "cul de sac" L of the R stairs. He mimes drinking from a wine bottle.*)

CEPHUS: Yeah. Choo-choo.

WOMAN ONE (*crossing DL on the R platform, leaning in toward* CEPHUS, *whispering to him as the objective narrator*): Sounds begin to have smells. Sight and dreams begin to smell. Night Train, and sleeping on park benches, and cement floors, your head swimming in urine and vomit, in the subway toilet, as you struggle to sleep, undisturbed. But you never smell the promised land. Only frost from your mouth.

(WOMAN ONE *crosses R of the rocking chair on the UC platform.* CEPHUS *mimes finishing the bottle of wine and throwing the empty bottle into the street. He then crosses R of the bench on the C platform.* WOMAN TWO *is UL of the bench.*)

CEPHUS: How you doing bartender? Need the floor swept today?
WOMAN TWO: Yeah. (*Points R*) Broom's over there.
CEPHUS: How much do you . . .
WOMAN TWO: I'll give you a dollar and a shot of wine. If I catch you stealing, I'll break both your hands and stick them in your ears. Clean off the tables too.
CEPHUS (*crossing R, mimes picking up and beginning to sweep with a push broom*): Thank you sir.
WOMAN TWO: And hurry. I want you out of here before the customers come. You smell a little ripe.
CEPHUS (*pausing*): I'm sorry. I didn't know.
WOMAN TWO: Well I'm telling you. And make sure that you sweep in the corners.
CEPHUS: I will sir.

(WOMAN TWO *crosses L of the rocking chair on the UC platform.* CEPHUS's *sweeping motions blend into a weary walk. He crosses to the DL breakaway porch post base, sits and leans against it.*)

WOMAN ONE: Survive. Got to survive, smells. It's moving fast now.
WOMAN TWO (*singing—Song should have a "lowdown, lonesome, blues beat*): Lordy, Lordy, Lordy. Why do I have to hurt so bad? Oh, Lordy. Lordy. Why do I have to hurt so bad? Life just passed me by. Took everything I ever had.
WOMAN ONE: Blues playing on my radio. Hey, you! Get up! You can't afford to listen to blues and jazz. Wake up!

(*Hearing, but not relating directly to the women,* CEPHUS *crosses DL on the stage floor, D of the platform.*)

CEPHUS: OK, OK, Guess I'll go out and shine a few.
WOMAN ONE: Yeah. Shoeshine boy. Trying to be a shoeshine man! You won't never grow into a shoeshine man!
WOMAN TWO: Shine them shoes. Pop. Pop. You looking weak.
CEPHUS (*crossing DR on the stage floor talking to imaginary customers*): Shine mister? Only a quarter. Pretty shoeshine mister? Only a quarter. Shine them up for you buddy? No, no. Don't you worry about that. My hands shake like this all the time. But I give a good shine. No . . . come back . . . honest I do. I give a good shine.
WOMAN ONE: Shoeshine boy! You won't never grow into a shoeshine

man. Better go back to sweeping barroom floors. It's a better profession.

(CEPHUS *crosses in the "cul de sac" L of the R stairs. He mimes arguing with an employee of a health clinic as* WOMAN ONE *and* TWO *intensify and increase the momentum of their delivery.*)

WOMAN TWO: Faded pastel green shirt. Black, ragged gabardine pants, that are torn at the ankles. Dirty, white knob-toed shoes, that have holes in the soles and turned-over heels.

WOMAN ONE: From walking up too many flights of stairs. And sleeping on too many lice-infested cots. Bedbug bites on the face and arms. On the displaced face and arms.

(CEPHUS *crosses to the bench UC on the C platform. He takes the wooden boxes off the bench, looking underneath each one and putting them R and L of the bench, respectively. He is searching for his medical card.*)

CEPHUS: Goddamn clinic won't treat nobody less they got they card. I lost mine somewhere. I need medicine! Medicine!

WOMAN TWO: The bites will heal.

CEPHUS (*crossing C on the platform*): They aren't bites. They are sores, goddamnit! Sores! And they hurt. I need a card! A new card to get medicine. You won't listen!

WOMAN TWO: Go ahead.

CEPHUS: Aaaaaah! Aaaaaaah!

WOMAN TWO: That's it, scream. Nobody's listening.

CEPHUS, WOMAN ONE, and WOMAN TWO (*in unison*): Aaaaaaah!

WOMAN ONE: Feel better? (WOMAN ONE *exits UC.*)

(CEPHUS *crosses to the bench UC on the platform, sits.*)

WOMAN TWO: Enough to hear the latest news? People are talking about amnesty and how wrong the war in Viet Nam was.

CEPHUS: Too late for me. Everywhere I go. It follows. I can't work. I can't breathe. It has to change.

(WOMAN TWO *slowly crosses to* CEPHUS *freely moving as she addresses him—Though he is affected,* CEPHUS *never relates directly to* WOMAN TWO *during this beat.*)

WOMAN TWO: Smells never change. The seasons change and change. Winter to spring to summer to fall. But the smells never change. The smell of the rooms. The gravelike smell of the rooms that house the displaced faces. Smelling of Sloan's Liniment or alcohol or witch hazel, or urine, or Youth Dew or Chanel Number Five, or minks, or diamonds, or vomit and cuss words, or heat or cold, or longing. The smoky, dry, white hot summer of the urban genre has once again turned to winter. Bundle up, bird. Bundle up tight. Not much heat this year. Even less than last. Smelling of radiators, rust and steam. Pipes clanging and banging. The animal smells of vice and the low-life. As you watch from your window, in your cubicle of a room. Smells of the legit life. Add to the smells of your loneliness. But the dead promises of the wonderland have no smells. Steak, champagne, tossed salad with Russian have no smells. But frost from your mouth smells. "Far from natural space and place old smoothie," has a very pungent smell. Garbage and neon lights smell. But blues and jazz in the middle of the night and the good life, have no smells. Dead promises of the wonderland. But frost from your mouth smells. Freezing smells. (WOMAN TWO *crosses around to the off R side of the R platform. She holds there watching the action.*)

(*Enter* WOMAN ONE *L wearing a flowered shawl and neck scarf. She crosses D of the bench on the L platform facing R. She is* PATTIE MAE *in her early forties in Richmond, although the dialogue may suggest she and* CEPHUS *are together.* CEPHUS *does not relate to* WOMAN ONE, *but keeps his focus out.*)

WOMAN ONE/PATTIE MAE: I've tried to find you. But your Aunt Hannah won't let anybody know. She says that you don't want to be bothered. I've had two miscarriages. Not built for having children I guess. He leaves me alone a lot. Not that we were ever that much together. I was back in Cross Roads for the Fourth of July. Things are changing there.

CEPHUS: My thoughts are of you.

WOMAN ONE/PATTIE MAE: Dancing in my head. My soft summer day. (WOMAN ONE *exits L and removes the shawl and scarf.*)

(WOMAN TWO *crosses R of the rocking chair on the UC platform.*)

WOMAN TWO: You look twice your age. Why don't you rise up? Rebel. Fly to the sunshine.

CEPHUS: What does it matter? They can ship me back in my case of pine. A borrowed suit or one of little cost. A bright, shiny Cadillac. It doesn't matter what the year. Lay my body on the banks of the White Stocking River. So that I can oversee the Saturday night fish fry. I won't miss a one then. All my folks can say, "He weren't much in life, but he sure loved a good Saturday night fish fry."

(WOMAN TWO *sits in the rocking chair, removes the wire frame eyeglasses from her pocket and puts them on. As she addresses him,* CEPHUS *listens while remaining focused outward.*)

WOMAN TWO: Dear Cephus. You never come home like you said you would. I hope you still living in the same place and that this letter will somehow find you. The man that owned your old homestead died. A Mr. P. Harper has bought up all of your Granddaddy's land and has put the deed in your name. I don't know this Mr. P. Harper, but they says the land is rightfully yours whenever you want it. I hope that you will come back home. Things is way different now for colored folks. We well off now. Love, Aunt Hannah. (WOMAN TWO *crosses R on the platform putting the glasses back in her pocket.*)

CEPHUS (*rising, taking a few steps DC*): This is the deed to my land. Somebody . . . somehow. Who could have . . .

(WOMAN TWO *crosses down onto the R platform. She challenges* CEPHUS *with her lines, who, for the first time, relates directly to one of the omnipotent voices, characters.*)

WOMAN TWO: Forget it. What about that lowdown lonesome . . .

CEPHUS: Blues and jazz has choked and gagged me with my own spit. The notes are so ugly that the devil, hisself, won't listen.

WOMAN TWO (*crossing down to the bottom R platform stair*): The promised land?

CEPHUS: A dry, ugly, hot, mean place. Wasn't intended for a man of the soil.

WOMAN TWO (*crossing to floor D of R platform*): The myth of perfumed nights. Sweet in the air.

CEPHUS: Poison fills the air. The cheap, red satin dress ran like blood as my tears soaked it from top to bottom, as I lay my head in her lap. Crying from pain. The red satin can never replace the soft calico that Pattie wore.

WOMAN TWO (*crossing to the R pipe bannister and picks up the blue sweater—She then crosses R of* CEPHUS *on the C platform.*) That's right. When are you leaving?

CEPHUS (*crossing R of* WOMAN TWO): I don't know. I'm in bad shape. Fight. I'll try. Dry out. I'll . . . try. I need help. (*Begins to cross stage right.*) I need a drink.

WOMAN TWO: No, man, no.

(CEPHUS *halts.*)

Don't give up.

CEPHUS: I won't sink. I won't.

(WOMAN TWO *puts the blue sweater across one shoulder and extends her arms beseechingly to* CEPHUS.)

I'll feel the warm again. I'll feel the hot rays. I'll get back.

(CEPHUS *takes off his hat, jacket, and scarf and hands them to* WOMAN TWO, *who puts them on the bench. She picks up the blue sweater, helps* CEPHUS *put it on, then places his jacket, hat, and scarf inside the bench.* WOMAN ONE *enters UC, crosses DL on the UC platform.*)

WOMAN ONE: May I have your attention please. Greyhound now leaving Port Authority for Dover, Delaware, Salisbury, Maryland, Norfolk, Virginia, and points South. Making one local stop at Cross Roads.

(CEPHUS *crosses DC on the platform and mimes buying a bus ticket.*)

WOMAN TWO: Move on out. That's right! Bust on out! Strut baby strut! The Cross Roads strut.

CEPHUS (*crossing L of* WOMAN TWO): Ticket cost thirty-nine dollars. Last one I bought cost nineteen. (*He mimes putting the ticket in his pocket.*)

WOMAN TWO: It's been a while.

(WOMAN ONE *crosses U of the bench on the L platform.*)

How do I look?

WOMAN TWO: Alive.

CEPHUS: Like I been living?

WOMAN TWO: Just alive.

CEPHUS: Going home from up the road you got to look prosperous. The North is suppose to be good for you. I don't want to damage the myth.

WOMAN TWO: Don't worry about how you look. Get on board.

CEPHUS (*taking a few steps DR on the platform*): Suppose this Mr. P. Harper has changed his mind?

WOMAN TWO: You've got the deed in your hand. The land is yours. He gave it to you.

CEPHUS: I'm scared. I want to go to the bathroom.

(CEPHUS *crosses off the platform, DR on the stage floor.* WOMAN TWO *crosses R of* CEPHUS *and chases him DLC on the stage floor.* WOMAN ONE *crosses down to the C platform, sets one of the wooden boxes DC and the other RC on the platform. She then sits on the R end of the bench. This seating arrangement forms the bus.*)

WOMAN TWO: Get on the bus man. In fifteen hours you'll be home. Safe and sound. It'll be a welcome sight after thirteen years. God will look out for you. (WOMAN TWO *begins to cross L.*)

(CEPHUS *grabs her arm and stops her.*)

CEPHUS: If you want to keep on being my friend, don't mention his name.

(WOMAN TWO *turns and takes a step toward* CEPHUS *with an exasperated, no-nonsense look.* CEPHUS *crosses D of the wooden box RC on the C platform.* WOMAN TWO *crosses to the L pipe bannister, puts on the bus driver's cap and crosses to the wooden box DC on the C platform. She sits.*)

I'm going. Could have picked a better day than Christmas Eve. Every Negro God ever made is going South for Christmas. Why don't some of yall buy cars or ride the train or fly? (CEPHUS *sits on the box.*)

(WOMAN TWO *mimes driving the bus. She sways and rocks gently from side to side duplicating the motion of the bus.* WOMAN ONE *and* CEPHUS *sway in unison with her. The lights change to indicate a bus ride at night.*)

Guess not. The Greyhound bus is a national Negro institution. Like a shoebox full of chicken. Grease spots soaking through. (*Looks to his left*) Hey stop that baby from crying. Folks want to sleep. (CEPHUS *leans back as if to sleep, then quickly turns and looks over his right shoulder.*) Man will you put your shoes back on. No I don't drink gin and beer.

(WOMAN ONE *sings "Silent Night" softly in the background under the dialogue.*)

Merry Christmas Gramps. Uncle Lewis. Merry Christmas Pattie Mae Wells. Merry Christmas Aunt Hannah. Oh. No. I was just talking out loud. Excuse me.

WOMAN TWO: Christmastime and we're all going home. Packed aboard trains, planes, cars, and buses. We're riding to the warm. Heading South to see the folks. Babies and packages and suitcases filling the hands and arms of the prodigal children. Dresses for Grandma, a new hat for Papa, an imitation gold necklace for Mother. Presents from the child who fled North. To the promised land.

WOMAN ONE: Through the night we ride. The air is getting warmer.

CEPHUS: And so is my heart and soul. Far away from the subway roll.

WOMAN TWO: It's hot, sweaty, and sticky on old Greyhound. Every seat taken. Some standing.

(WOMAN TWO *hums "Silent Night." CEPHUS drifts off to sleep.*)

WOMAN ONE: We're packed on this slave ship from all over you know. Henry Lee now lives in Buffalo. Going to see the folks in Tupelo. Mary Lou Spencer and Alice Brown make their stop in Charleston Town. There's Willie Batson. They call him the "Baltimore Gambler with nothing to lose." Heading on down to Baton Rouge. There's Sadie, Larry, Bill, and Carrie. Cousins living in Boston. It's been six years since they've been back in Austin. But it's Christmastime and we're all going home.

WOMAN TWO: We'll tell tall tales of how well we're doing. Man everything is fine. Nothing but steak. The finest wine. They'll never ask about bleak tenements and projects and slums stacked up to the sky row by row. It's Christmas and they don't need to know.

WOMAN ONE (*mimes wiping and looking out a window to her right*): Rain pounding down as we cross into Virginia.

WOMAN TWO/BUS DRIVER: Next stop. Cross Roads, North Carolina. (*Mimes stopping bus. Looks over her shoulder at* CEPHUS.) You wanted Cross Roads buddy? Hey! Wake up back there! You wanted Cross Roads?

(WOMAN ONE *hits* CEPHUS *on his shoulder.*)

CEPHUS: Yeah. Thanks. (*Rises*) How long they had colored bus drivers?

WOMAN TWO/BUS DRIVER: A long time. Where have you been? Asleep?

CEPHUS: Dead.

WOMAN TWO/BUS DRIVER: Yeah. You look a little worn and beat. But, chin up, buddy. It's nice down here. You can stretch out and be free. Healthy air and soil.

CEPHUS: Where are you headed?

WOMAN TWO/BUS DRIVER: Miami Beach.

CEPHUS: If you see . . . Forget it.

WOMAN TWO/BUS DRIVER: If I do. I will. Take care.

CEPHUS: You too. Tell him it's my last chance!

(*Lights restore to normal.* WOMAN ONE *exits L.* WOMAN TWO *kneels L of the wooden box on which she was sitting. She takes off the bus driver's cap and places it U of the box. Then, she puts on the plastic hair brace which was in her pocket. She lays her head and arms on the wooden box, asleep.* CEPHUS *crosses DRC on the stage floor, takes a deep breath, looks around, then crosses to the R edge of the L platform. He is in the bus station.*)

Well I'll be damned. A new bus station. Bus used to stop at a gasoline station out on the bypass. White folks and colored folks in the same waiting room? Don't even see no colored rest room. Maybe they stop letting them go to the rest room. (CEPHUS *crosses to* WOMAN TWO *shakes and awakens her.*) Hey, you. Where is the colored rest room? (CEPHUS *crosses DR on the platform looking around.*)

WOMAN TWO/YOUNGSTER (*looking up at* CEPHUS): Colored rest room? What are you talking about?

CEPHUS: Guess you're too young to know what I mean.

WOMAN TWO/YOUNGSTER: Everybody use the same toilet. What's wrong with that?

CEPHUS: Nothing. I was just a bit . . .

WOMAN TWO/YOUNGSTER: What you got to do? Number one or number two?

CEPHUS: Curious. Guess I forgot. Things started to change before I left.

WOMAN TWO/YOUNGSTER: Hey ain't you that man they put in jail for not going to the army? Left here bout thirteen years ago. Yeah. Yeah! It's you! I seen your pictures. You older, but it's still you. Folks think that you dead. Hey. You ain't no ghost is you? (*Crosses to* CEPHUS, *pokes him in the stomach, repeatedly, with her finger.*) No. My hand won't go all the way through your body so I guess you ain't no hant.

CEPHUS: Who are your people?

WOMAN TWO/YOUNGSTER: Joe-Boy Smith was my daddy. I'm his youngest daughter, Hazel.

CEPHUS (*reaching to touch her*): Joe-Boy's daughter?

WOMAN TWO/YOUNGSTER (*backing away from* CEPHUS): Hey don't touch me, man. Don't want you trying none of that weird stuff.

CEPHUS: Joe-Boy was my buddy. My friend. Him and Tommy Hankins.

WOMAN TWO/YOUNGSTER (*crossing L on the platform—angry and near tears.*): My daddy was a war hero. He wouldn't have been friends with no coward. People ain't gonna want you back around here.

CEPHUS: The Government said it's all right.

WOMAN TWO/YOUNGSTER: The Government don't live in Cross Roads, North Carolina. I'm gonna tell everybody that you're back. (WOMAN TWO *exits L, removes hair brace.*)

CEPHUS: Yeah. You do that, little Joe-Boy's daughter. You do that. Must have taken her looks from her momma. Cause, Joe-Boy ain't never won no beauty contest. (*Crosses DRC on the stage floor.*) Bet she was a "fish fry baby" like her brother. (*Crosses to the R platform*) The old homestead. Got a lot of work to do here. Trash and weeds everywhere. (*Crosses to the rocking chair on the UC platform—He removes his sweater and hangs it on the back of the chair.*) Got to get to it. A new coat of paint. The barn is still in good condition. Some new tools. Shovels, hoes, rakes, and bush hooks. (*Steps down onto the R platform*) I'll work it into shape. Cause it's mine. Would be nice to know who bought it back and give me the deed. I know that it wasn't you old "sun-bather." You just clean forgot about me, ain't you? Well not totally. I know. I know. (*Crosses back to the rocking chair. Sits.*) You helped me get my farm back. Kept me from dying when I was up North. Thanks. I appreciate it. You ain't a bad guy. You just don't stay in your office too much.

(WOMAN TWO *enters R, crosses to the R pipe bannister, puts on the boy's corduroy cap, and crosses U on the R platform, taunting* CEPHUS. CEPHUS *observes her actions through half-closed eyes.*)

WOMAN TWO/JOHNNY MACK: Cephus Miles dead in the grave. Mean old Cephus. Can't be saved. (*Looks C on the platform*) Them some good-looking tomatoes ghost man. Seen you chopping in your garden yesterday. He must be asleep. Think I'll swipe me a tomato. Lord please don't let him catch me. He'll eat me alive for sure. Well here goes.

(WOMAN ONE *kneels*, CEPHUS *rises, crosses to the R edge of the UC platform.*)

CEPHUS: Get out of here!
WOMAN TWO/JOHNNY MACK (*falling down on hands and knees*): Oh shit! I'm dead!
CEPHUS: Go home child. If you want a tomato or a head of cabbage, ask me the next time.
WOMAN TWO/JOHNNY MACK: Yes sir. Yes sir. Don't eat me alive, please. (CEPHUS *crosses to* WOMAN TWO, *grabs her by the arm, pulls her up to a standing position.*)
CEPHUS: I wouldn't think of eating you alive . . . this time! Now git!
(CEPHUS *shoves* WOMAN TWO *down to the bottom step.*)
WOMAN TWO/JOHNNY MACK: You . . . you ain't no ghost. You're flesh and blood and bone. Your hand is warm.
CEPHUS: Warm enough to whip your behind if I catch you stealing again. You understand me boy?
WOMAN TWO/JOHNNY MACK: Yes . . . yes. Bye. (WOMAN TWO *runs U of the bench on the C platform. She hides behind it kneeling on her hands and knees.*)
CEPHUS: Stealing my tomatoes and cabbage. Children got no manners.

No respect for grown people. Time was when you could tan the hide of a child for smart-mouthing you like that. And their parents would thank you. Do it now and you'll go to jail. (*Slowly crosses DC on the stage floor*) All the roads are hard-surfaced, industry moving in. Hard to find a good farmer anymore. Everything integrated. The schools, the churches. No more back door for colored folks. Weren't really much to integrate. White folks and colored folks lived right together anyway. Guess they had to make it official. Can't even buy a good mule anymore. That mule I bought. He's fifty years old, if he's a day. Old and lazy. A bad combination. Man I bought him from said that the mule was one of the finest animals in the county. Course though he was a little, short colored fellow, with a harelip. The nervous type. Hands always moving. I ain't never trusted a man who used his hands a lot, when he talked. They hiding something. Mark my words. Devilish mule will plow two rows and he wants to rest. Head right for a shade tree every time. And don't let it thunder. He'll run right out of the field. Dragging the plow behind him. Knocking down corn stalks and screaming at the top of his voice. Yeah. I got beat on that deal. Every once in a while somebody will drive past and throw up their hand. I wave back. Too bad they can't give me back that five years that I spent in prison, for something that they was gonna forgive me for anyway. (*Crosses to the bench on the C platform.*) Losing my land. Driving me North. But I'm thankful. I seen some that's worse off than me. (*Sits*) Went to a nice wedding last week. Hard-headed Herbert married Black Sarah, the conjure woman. He calls his black magic sweetie pie, she calls him her hard-headed sugar dumpling. Their children are bound to be strange.

WOMAN TWO/JOHNNY MACK (*rising to a kneeling position*): Cuse me . . . Sir.

CEPHUS: You back? Whatchu want?

WOMAN TWO/JOHNNY MACK: I was wondering . . . wondering if you could spare me some of them good-looking plums you got behind your house?

CEPHUS: Take all you want. I don't eat the things.

WOMAN ONE/PATTIE MAE (*offstage*): Let's go pick some plums. Come on. We'll take them to the well and wash them off. Let's go pick some plums.

CEPHUS (*focus out*): Pick plums At a time like this?

WOMAN TWO/JOHNNY MACK: What you say?

CEPHUS (*returning focus to* WOMAN TWO): I said . . . whose child are you?

WOMAN TWO/JOHNNY MACK: I'm 'One Arm Ike's' stepson. Johnny
Mack's my name. You know 'One Arm Ike?' He knows you. Likes you
a lot.

CEPHUS: I know Ike. Good guitar man.

WOMAN TWO/JOHNNY MACK: Got his own band now. They play
around to all of the Piccolo Joints in these parts. He's gonna be the
guest artist at the Saturday night fish fry. First weekend in August.

CEPHUS: They've got a live band at the Saturday night fish fry?

WOMAN TWO/JOHNNY MACK: Yup. And a couple of shake dancers too.
From over in Raleigh.

CEPHUS: Lord have mercy. You don't participate do you?

WOMAN TWO/JOHNNY MACK (*Rising*): Yes I do. I be right there.

CEPHUS: You don't stay there too long do you?

WOMAN TWO/JOHNNY MACK: Oh no, sir. Ike say I have to be in the
house by ten o'clock.

CEPHUS: Righteous rascal.

WOMAN TWO/JOHNNY MACK: My job is cleaning the catfish. You ever
clean a catfish?

CEPHUS: Once or twice.

WOMAN TWO/JOHNNY MACK (*sitting on the R wooden box*): Whew!
Tough job ain't it? But I'm good at it, the best. Old Chief, the colored
Indian, he cleans them too. But he's not as good as me. Course
though, you can't talk to him, cause he don't speak nothing but
Indian. Can't nobody never get him to understand plain English.

CEPHUS: I see. Why don't you get yourself a mess of them grapes and
apples, and anything else you see growing back there.

WOMAN TWO/JOHNNY MACK (*rising, shaking CEPHUS's hand*): Oh,
thank you, sir. If you need any help come planting time, I'll be glad to
help you.

CEPHUS: I'll remember that, Johnny Mack.

WOMAN TWO/JOHNNY MACK (*crossing DR on the stage floor*): Thanks
again . . . Mr. Cephus.

CEPHUS: You're welcome. Tell Ike to stop by some time. With the guitar.
We'll sing an old duet that we used to do together.

WOMAN TWO/JOHNNY MACK: I will. Bye Mr. Cephus. (WOMAN TWO
*crosses to the R pipe bannister, puts her cap on it, then crosses and sits on
the R edge of the R platform.*)

CEPHUS (*rising and crossing DC on the platform*): Glad Ike found himself
a ready-made family. He can't make no babies, so they say. Had the
mumps when he was a youngster. They went down on him and
sterilized the poor fellow. Guess that's why he turned to stealing hogs.

(CEPHUS *crosses R on the UC platform*—WOMAN ONE *enters L wearing a flowered shawl and the neck scarf. She crosses along the D edge of the set to D of the R stairs.*) Be nice to have some children running around here. Guess that will never be.

(WOMAN TWO *knocks on the R platform.* CEPHUS *crosses D on the R platform.*)

Who in the world could that be? I ain't expecting nobody. Jesus Christ! P . . . Pattie Mae Wells? What in the world you. It's you. It's you.

WOMAN ONE/PATTIE MAE: Yes. It's been a long time.

CEPHUS: Growed up. Fulled out into a fine woman you did.

WOMAN ONE/PATTIE MAE: Can I come in?

CEPHUS (*leading her up onto the platform*): Sure you can. Come on. I can't get over this. I . . . I don't know what to say.

WOMAN ONE/PATTIE MAE: Neither do I. I had a short speech prepared. I've forgotten what I was supposed to say.

CEPHUS: You are as pretty as ever.

WOMAN ONE/PATTIE MAE: You are as handsome as ever.

CEPHUS: No. Done outgrowed my good looks. If I had known this, I would have washed up. Put on a clean shirt . . . a pair of pants . . .

WOMAN ONE/PATTIE MAE: I'm divorced.

CEPHUS: You been with me day and night. I never stopped . . .

WOMAN ONE/PATTIE MAE: I read about your stand with the army, in the newspapers. I was proud of you.

CEPHUS: You didn't write. Just one word on a piece of paper. Just one. Would have made everything all right.

WOMAN ONE/PATTIE MAE: I've never stopped loving you. It's no kind of life for a person, outside the Cross Roads. They don't understand you.

CEPHUS: You visiting?

WOMAN ONE/PATTIE MAE: Come to stay . . . I hope.

CEPHUS: I hope that . . .

WOMAN ONE/PATTIE MAE: Yes.

CEPHUS: You'll be happy.

WOMAN ONE/PATTIE MAE (*crossing UL on the platform,* CEPHUS *counters C on the platform*): The folks all respect you. They don't understand why you have locked yourself on this farm. Nobody hardly ever sees you.

CEPHUS: I'm not locked in. I go out. I work the land. Go into town. Had a pretty good crop this year. Thought that I had forgotten how to tend the earth. Been away so long. But it come right back to me. Soon as I picked up a hoe and shovel.

WOMAN ONE/PATTIE MAE: Where have you been?

CEPHUS: Oh, all over. This place. That place. Traveling, sort of.

WOMAN ONE/PATTIE MAE: I see. You can tell me about it.

CEPHUS: I will. In time.

WOMAN ONE/PATTIE MAE (*turning toward the UC platform*): Can I . . .

CEPHUS (*leading* WOMAN ONE *to the rocking chair on the UC platform, then sitting*): You're already here. Never left. The old folks matched us up years ago.

WOMAN ONE/PATTIE MAE: Made this calico dress, just for you.

CEPHUS (*crossing L of the rocking chair, kneeling, feeling the fabric of the shawl*): You were always good with a needle and thread. It's soft. The colors won't run, like satin will.

WOMAN ONE/PATTIE MAE: Thanks Cephus Junior.

CEPHUS: One thing though. This is very important. We can be together but you got to do me one great big favor.

WOMAN ONE/PATTIE MAE: Anything.

CEPHUS (*enthusiastically*): Cook me two pecan pies. With lots of butter.

WOMAN ONE/PATTIE MAE: As soon as you chop me some wood and build a fire. I'll shell the pecans.

CEPHUS (*rising, crossing to the R platform*): My ax is sharp and ready. I been waiting honey. I been waiting.

WOMAN ONE/PATTIE MAE: Got my apron and everything.

CEPHUS (*crossing back and kneeling R of the rocking chair—urgently inquiring*): Remember the county fair. Your pies would win first prize every year.

WOMAN ONE/PATTIE MAE: Not every year.

CEPHUS: We'd ride the ferris wheel and the roller coaster.

WOMAN ONE/PATTIE MAE: You were afraid of the roller coaster.

CEPHUS: Still am. But it would always give me a chance to sneak a hug from you.

WOMAN ONE/PATTIE MAE: I only pretended to be afraid so that I could sneak a hug from you.

CEPHUS: Let's go to the county fair this year. It's all integrated now you know. No more white folks days and colored folks days. We'll relive old times. Sixteen again.

WOMAN ONE/PATTIE MAE: That will be fun Cephus Junior. And we'll talk. About everything. And you'll call me a son of a bitch. I know you will. But in time, everything will be fine.

CEPHUS: It has to. A lot of us will never make it back.

WOMAN ONE/PATTIE MAE: I know. But let's you and I wish real hard that they do.

WOMAN TWO (*rising*): All of your luggage is out of the car Mrs. Harper.

WOMAN ONE/PATTIE MAE: Thanks so much for helping me.

WOMAN TWO: You're welcome. You were a good neighbor.

WOMAN ONE/PATTIE MAE: Have a safe trip back to Richmond.

WOMAN TWO: I will. Bye-bye. (WOMAN TWO *exits R.*)

CEPHUS (*rising, softly inquiring*): P. Harper?

WOMAN ONE/PATTIE MAE: Harper was my married name.

CEPHUS (*in dazed astonishment, slowly crossing to the R edge of the UC platform, pointing down to the R platform*): You bought this place. Put it in my name. You bought . . .

WOMAN ONE/PATTIE MAE: Go out and chop some firewood. I'll get to those pecan pies.

(CEPHUS *crosses down to the R platform. Overwhelmed, he hesitates momentarily, starts to cross D, then turns back and begins to cross to* WOMAN ONE. *After a few steps, he stops once again. Finally, he turns, crosses DC on the C platform, looks heavenward.*)

CEPHUS (*saying with controlled jubilance*): You finally came back from Miami. Welcome Home.

(*Lights fade to black. End of play*)

The Sty of the Blind Pig

PHILLIP HAYES DEAN

Left to right: Frances Foster as ALBERTA WARREN, *Moses Gunn (bottom) as* BLIND JORDAN, *Clarice Taylor as* WEEDY WARREN, *and Adolph Ceasar as* DOC *in a scene from* The Sty of the Blind Pig. *Photograph copyright © 1971 by Bert Andrews. Reprinted by permission of Marsha Hudson, the Estate of Bert Andrews.*

Phillip Hayes Dean, a native of Chicago, Illinois, is an actor and playwright who has authored several outstanding works that have appeared at the American Place Theater in New York, such as *Everynight When the Sun Goes Down, Freeman,* and *This Bird of Dawning Singeth All Night Long.* In addition, his *Paul Robeson* appeared on Broadway and the West End of London and was recipient of a Christopher Award. The Negro Ensemble Company production of *The Sty of the Blind Pig,* which was also performed in Munich, Germany, was the recipient of the Drama Desk Award and the Dramatist Guild's Hull-Warriner Award.

The Sty of the Blind Pig was produced in New York by the NEC at the St. Marks Playhouse, and opened November 23, 1971, with the following cast:

Weedy Warren	Clarice Taylor
Doc	Adolph Caesar
Alberta Warren	Frances Foster
Blind Jordan	Moses Gunn

Directed by Shauneille Pery; scenery by Edward Burbridge; lighting by Ernest Baxter; sound by Chuck Vincent.

The Sty of the Blind Pig

CHARACTERS

in order of appearance

WEEDY WARREN

DOC

ALBERTA WARREN

BLIND JORDAN

The setting of the play is the Warren apartment on the south side of Chicago. The apartment shows a definite French influence, which is in sharp contrast to the furniture—signs written in silver on blue cardboard quoting verses from the Bible; and photographs—some faded black and white, some faded in tinted color, showing black people, marrying, standing in fields, standing with horses, etc. This apartment, like many apartments in this neighborhood, once was upper middle-class white. The whites moved out with the mass immigration of blacks coming up from the South at around the end of the First World War.

Two French doors, one with a broken pane of glass, are placed in the back wall. They lead to the two bedrooms. Another French door is downstage left, separating the kitchen and living room. Two large windows are cut into the right upstage wall overlooking the street below. The kitchen is modest and seems a bit too large for the utilities placed there.

The time of the play is the period just before the beginning of the civil rights movement. . . .

ACT ONE

SCENE ONE

The lights fade in on WEEDY WARREN, *sitting before the open window in the living room at dusk. She is an old woman, close to seventy, with hard lines carved in her face. She is dressed in a big black hat and black spring coat. As she sits rocking before the window the light of the dusky evening slowly fades into the night. Down the street, from a little storefront church, a choir can be heard backed by the sound of tambourines.*

CHOIR (*offstage*):
Father alone knows all about it
Father alone understands why
Cheer up, my mama, walk in the sunshine
You'll understand all by and by . . .

(*There is a knock at the door as the choir fades out.*)

WEEDY (*moving to door*): Is that you, Brother . . . ?
DOC (*from other side of door*): You gonna open the door?

(WEEDY *unlocks door and then returns to her rocker.*)

WEEDY: C'mon in.

(DOC *is a little man in his mid-fifties, dressed in the period of another time. There is something of the clown in him . . . both a tragic and a comic quality. A black derby hat sits on top of his head and spats cover his shoes. From the vest of his lifeless gray suit dangle several miniature toy pistols. He carries a walking stick and wears a pair of gray felt gloves.*)

DOC: What'd you sittin' up here in the dark for?
WEEDY: Cooler. Bulb heats up th' room.
DOC (*moving to cupboard*): Hey, Sister . . .
WEEDY: Naw!
DOC: How you gonna naw me before I ask th' question?
WEEDY: Whenever you start that ole "sister" stuff it means you gettin'
    ready to borrow money. And since I ain't gonna give nobody no
    money to play th' numbers with, the answer is naw. Don't aid an' abet
    nobody in gamblin'. An' what are you lookin' for?
DOC: Whiskey.
WEEDY: Lawd, I'm just surrounded by whiskey heads. Keep on . . . be
    done drink your fool self to death.
DOC (*pouring himself a drink*): That's what my wife Nora Lee usta say.
    (*Mimicking Nora Lee*) "Doc Sweet, honey, you gonna keep drinkin'
    that ole whiskey till it kills you." Told her that I would be drinkin'
    whiskey when th' railroad tracks was runnin' over her head. (*Fighting
    off a creeping nostalgia*) Poor woman's been dead now for twenty years.
    Came home one day to find out that th' woman had laid down an'
    died like a dog without any warnin' whatsoever.
WEEDY: You sure gonna haffta give an account of all that ole random
    talk when Jesus gets back here and looks up your record.
DOC: I'm almost sixty an' he ain't made it back here since I been here.
    I'm beginnin' to think maybe he ain't comin' back. Can't say that I
    blame him after th' raw deal he got th' last time he was here. (*Takes his*

tobacco out and rolls himself a cigarette) Hey, Sister . . .

WEEDY: Will you not beg me, please? After doin' all your big talk I sure ain't gonna give you nothin' now. Always beggin'! Hate a beggar! . . . Just hate 'em. Put me in th' mind of a woman named Polly Walker. "Beggin' Polly" they usta call her . . . 'cause she was all th' time beggin'. Got so folks hated to see beggin' Polly comin' so much they locked their doors at th' mentionin' of her name.

DOC: What'd you savin' for anyway? Don't you know money was made round to roll from one hand to another? Suppose to keep it rollin'. It's people like you that stopped th' rollin' of money and brought on th' depression.

WEEDY: I don't see you rollin' around none.

DOC: Did when I had it. Usta fall down to th' Dew Drop Inn on Beale Street . . . down in Memphis. . . .

WEEDY: That's why you ain't got a pot to pee in now or a window to throw it out of . . . sportin' 'em up.

DOC (*at window*): What th' . . . (*raises window*) Hey, you chaps. Those damn kids again. Ev'rytime I come over here they jump all over my car. (*Hollering out of window*) Get your butts off my car before I come down there an' locate my stick in th' vicinity of your hind parts.

WEEDY: Will you not holler outta my window!

DOC: I ain't seen nothin' like these chaps in all my born days.

WEEDY: I reckon they ain't seen nothin' like you before. Dressed like that . . . drivin' that ole car. Walkin' 'round in th' warm weather with gloves on. Told you men don't wear gloves no more.

DOC: Second time today somebody mentioned my gloves. (*Removes dream book and pencil from inside coat pocket*)

WEEDY: Will you please not write your numbers in my house. (*Watches him take gloves off, remove a small bottle from his pocket. Pours a drop or two in his palms, rubbing them together*) What's that mess?

DOC: Lucky oil.

WEEDY: Last month it was incense.

DOC: Hit for twenty-five dollars, didn't I?

WEEDY: Burnin' incense in th' YMCA. Oughta be ashamed of yourself.

DOC: I ain't though. (*He moves to door.*) You'd better get ready if you want me to drive you to church.

WEEDY: I'm ready.

DOC: Then c'mon.

WEEDY: Tryin' to wait for Alberta to get home. (*Looking out of window*) Lawd, don't reckon somebody done hit her in th' head an' dragged her off into one of these old deserted buildin's.

DOC: Sounds like some of Mama's ole random talk.

WEEDY: Mama had second sight.

DOC: She had second sight, all right. Woman once told me she saw Abraham Lincoln's ghost ridin' a gray mule. . . .

WEEDY: Maybe she did.

DOC: If Abraham Lincoln's ghost had nothin' better to do than ride a gray mule on them dark, muddy roads in Mississippi, then they sure shoulda revoked his ghost pass.

WEEDY: Maybe she done run off like her ole no-good father. That's th' way Gardner Warren did . . . just walked outta here one evenin'. . . .

DOC: A nonsmoker who went after th' famous pack of cigarettes an' ain't been heard from since. (*Laughs*) Always liked ole Gardner Warren. Usta love to watch that man eat fish. Never saw anything like it in my life. Man would put fish in one side of his mouth, work his lips, an' th' bones would shoot out on th' other side. Yes, sir, it was like watchin' a machine.

(*A key is heard in the door.* ALBERTA *enters. She is a tall, thin-framed woman in her late thirties. She stands straight and rigid as if she is carrying an unseen burden. She is dressed in a simple print dress that hangs loosely from her body. Her hair is thick, a mixture of gray and black. There is a raw quality about her. She is a woman who has never known pleasure. Pleasure in her life has been equated with sin.*)

ALBERTA: Hello, Mama . . . Uncle Doc. (*Snaps on light*) What are you two sitting up here in the dark for? (*Moves to kitchen table and sets down bag of groceries she has brought in with her*)

WEEDY: Waitin' on you.

ALBERTA: Waiting on me for what?

WEEDY: I told you this morning, before you went to work, that Brother would be over here this evenin' to take you to church.

ALBERTA: Didn't you hear me tell you this morning that I wasn't going to church this evening?

WEEDY: Sister Martin is sittin' down at Mount Hope this very minute waitin' on you . . . to give you the information.

ALBERTA: Did you tell that woman that I was going to write her son's obituary? I don't know why in the world you keep telling people that I am going to write their obituaries for them.

WEEDY: Can't nobody write them like you. Ev'rybody says that. Lettie Wentworth started tryin' to write them an' th' ones she wrote wasn't nothin'. Besides that, she can't read them like you can. Folks still talk about th' one you wrote an' recited for Emanuel Fisher. Reverend Goodlow told me he ain't never heard one like that in all his years of pastoring.

ALBERTA: Well, he's not going to hear it any more.

WEEDY: Brother, would you please tell me what's gotten into her?

DOC: Some sense.

WEEDY (*rising*): Well, give me that one you wrote for Emanuel Fisher. Maybe I can get somebody to change it around. . . .

ALBERTA: I threw it away.

WEEDY: You threw Emanuel Fisher's obituary away?

ALBERTA: Didn't I just say I did?

WEEDY: You mean you don't have a copy of it?

ALBERTA: What does "throw it away" mean?

WEEDY: Can't you remember the way it went and write it out?

ALBERTA: I have erased it from my mind.

WEEDY: Why?

ALBERTA: Because I didn't want to remember it.

WEEDY: An' I promised Reverend Goodlow I'd give him a copy of it. He wanted to make copies of it and send it around to his friends. You should have heard it, Brother. I tell you it was a movin' thing. . . . An' th' way Alberta read it . . . pure poetry.

DOC: Didn't have any figures in it, did it?

WEEDY: Ain't you got no respect for nothin' or nobody? (*To* ALBERTA) I bet if you put your mind to it . . . What did you call it?

ALBERTA: The Flight of the Purple Angels.

WEEDY: Tell Brother what it was about.

ALBERTA: It was about . . . (*Comes into living room*) . . . the purple angels coming to take him home. Coming to take him to the land of glory . . .

WEEDY: Alberta just got carried away, didn't you, Alberta?

ALBERTA: Mama, you're going to be late for church.

DOC: Yeah, you're holdin' me up.

WEEDY: Brother ain't never heard it. Do it for Brother.

ALBERTA: Mama, will you please go to church.

DOC (*opening door*): Will you c'mon, Weedy, if you're goin'.

WEEDY (*halfway out door*): If you're up when I get back I'll bring you some ice cream.

ALBERTA: You don't have to bother.

WEEDY: I thought you liked ice cream.

ALBERTA: All right, Mama, bring me back some ice cream.

DOC (*slightly offstage*): Weedy, are you comin' or not?

WEEDY: Just a minute, please sir. Don't be so impatient. (*Kisses* ALBERTA *on forehead*) Now, be a good girl an' don't open th' door until you hear my voice. Lotta robbin' an' folks gettin' hit in th' head goin' on. Mother'll bring you some ice cream. (WEEDY *exits.*)

(ALBERTA *locks the door behind her. She goes into her bedroom and returns with a brown bag from which she removes several slips of paper. She is about to tear them up when the sound of the* CHOIR *is heard from the storefront church down the street.*)

CHOIR:
Near the Cross
Near the Cross
Keep my soul near the Cross . . .

(*The lights fade on* ALBERTA *holding the obituaries and listening to the* CHOIR.)

SCENE TWO

The lights come up several days later in the afternoon. Beyond the window a heavy downpour of rain is heard along with the sound of thunder and the cracking of lightning. WEEDY *and* ALBERTA *are seated on the couch, both dressed in black, both in naked white light.*

WEEDY: Maybe we should have gone to the cemetery.
ALBERTA (*leaning back, trying to rest*): The cars were all filled up. Every funeral car was packed with his family.
WEEDY: We could have gone in one of the other cars. We could have squeezed in with Mother Hansen and her son.
ALBERTA: And haffta listen to that woman talk that crazy talk she talks. And her ole nutty son, Jimmy. I swear I don't believe he's got good sense.
WEEDY: Isaiah didn't have a load . . . we coulda rode with him.
ALBERTA: Mama, I asked him . . . said he'd be glad to drive us out but that we'd have to find another way back.
WEEDY: Coulda caught th' bus . . . ?
ALBERTA: You know how long it takes to get back from that cemetery by bus? We'd be all night getting back here.
WEEDY: Know Sister Martin'll think it's funny that I didn't go to the cemetery.
ALBERTA: I didn't see her trying to get us a ride. She didn't have our names on the list for the funeral cars.
WEEDY: Woman was upset. (*There is a pause.*) They really did a good job on him. Looked just like he looked in life. I remember when you and him use to be in the Sunshine Band.
ALBERTA: I don't remember him being in the Sunshine Band.

WEEDY: You don't remember being in the Sunshine Band with A. J. Martin?

ALBERTA: I don't remember ever seeing him before today.

WEEDY: Way y'all use to play around th' church when you were little.

ALBERTA: Funny I can't remember him. . . . but he sure was a nice-looking man.

WEEDY: A. J. Martin was a fine-looking man.

ALBERTA: Who was that calling out for him? Kept screaming his name.

WEEDY: That was Lettie Wentworth. She was crazy about him. Hadn't been for Sister Martin I think A. J. might have married her. (*Slight pause.*) She sure did perform this day. I mean she really put on a show.

ALBERTA: The way she was carrying on I thought he was going to raise up in that casket.

WEEDY: She sure did show out . . . just show out. (*Slight pause.*) You sure did read that obituary. You had that whole church just stirred up. One woman just fell out and started kicking. Another one leaped up an' danced the dance of happiness.

ALBERTA: She sure scared me when she let out that scream.

WEEDY: You had her stirred up . . . full of the Holy Ghost. Wasn't one person in that church that wasn't touched by the Holy Ghost. All that hollerin' that Lettie Wentworth did didn't mean nothin'. And the way you read those telegrams . . . I tell you, Alberta, it was somethin' to behold. You have a gift . . . a callin'. Yes, Lord! (*Pause.*) You almost scared me to death when you fell outta th' pulpit like that. You almost fell into th' casket. Fainted like that . . . sure scared me. (ALBERTA *moves to cupboard and pours herself a drink.*) You shouldn't be drinkin' that whiskey.

ALBERTA: I need something for my nerves.

WEEDY: That's what's givin' you them faintin' spells.

ALBERTA: I didn't have a fainting spell. . . . I just lost my balance, that's all.

WEEDY: The ushers had to come an' revive you.

ALBERTA: Mama, they just picked me up.

WEEDY: Keep on drinkin' that whiskey.

ALBERTA: I just lost my balance and fell. Maybe it was Lettie Wentworth doing all that screaming. . . . Got on my nerves.

WEEDY: Did you drink any of that whiskey before we went to the funeral?

ALBERTA: My nerves were bad.

WEEDY: You mean you were up in th' church . . . standin' in th' pulpit drunk as a skunk?

ALBERTA: I was not drunk. I just had a little taste.

WEEDY: No wonder you didn't want to go to the cemetery. Glad now we didn't go. Folks found out you were drunk . . . lawd, th' child, is just turnin' into a whiskey head. A whiskey head!

ALBERTA: I am not a whiskey head! And I wasn't drunk at the funeral.

WEEDY: Then why did you fall out for dead?

ALBERTA: I dunno. I just got weak all over . . . started having heat flashes . . .

WEEDY: Heat flashes?

ALBERTA: Shhhh!

WEEDY: Shhhh, what?

ALBERTA: Don't talk so loud.

WEEDY: Don't talk so loud?

ALBERTA: The walls have ears.

WEEDY: The walls have ears. Alberta, what's wrong with you? I don't know what in this world you're talkin' about. What'd you mean the walls have ears?

ALBERTA: It's just that someone may be listening to us.

WEEDY: Who's listening to us?

ALBERTA (*crossing to door*): Wait a minute . . . (*She places her ear to the door.*) Someone may be out there.

WEEDY (*moving to door*): Ain't nobody out there.

ALBERTA: How'd you know?

WEEDY (*opening door and looking out into hallway*): Ain't nobody out there. Ain't a soul out there.

ALBERTA: I thought I heard something.

WEEDY (*closing door and following* ALBERTA *into living room*): Why don't you go lay down for a while?

ALBERTA: No, I don't want to lie down.

WEEDY: For a half hour or so.

ALBERTA: No! I don't want to lie down.

WEEDY: Don't carry on so.

ALBERTA (*moving to cupboard to refill her glass*): Just leave me alone, please.

WEEDY: You ain't gonna drink no more of that whiskey.

ALBERTA: Mama . . . please! . . . Jesus . . . please! Please! Please, Jesus!

WEEDY: You already not feelin' well.

ALBERTA (*crossing into her bedroom*): I'm all right. (*Slams door behind her*)

(WEEDY, *confused, moves to her rocking chair and looks out of window. She rocks denoting the passage of time.* ALBERTA *comes out of bedroom dressed in a maid's uniform.*)

WEEDY: Where you goin'?

ALBERTA: I promised Mrs. Coutrell that I'd serve a party for her if she let me off for the funeral. I bet she thinks I'm the biggest liar. . . . Everytime she looks around I'm taking time off for a funeral. I sure don't feel like going out there tonight.

WEEDY: Why don't you call her and tell her that you don't feel well?

ALBERTA: No, she'll be stuck. I told her that I would try my best to make it.

WEEDY: Let her serve her own party.

ALBERTA (*moving to door*): I'll see you later.

WEEDY: Alberta?

ALBERTA: Yes?

WEEDY: Never mind . . . nothin'.

(ALBERTA *exits as* WEEDY *rocks at window. The lights fade.*)

SCENE THREE

The lights come up about a week later, at night. ALBERTA *is seated at the table making crepe-paper flowers. She works very intensely, completely involved in her task. Offstage we hear the sound of* BLIND JORDAN *singing and playing his guitar.*

BLIND JORDAN:
Amazin' Grace how sweet it sounds
it saved a wretch like me
I once was lost but now I'm found
was blind but now I see. . . .

(*The voice stops in front of the door. We hear a soft tap.*)

ALBERTA: Who is it?

BLIND JORDAN: It's me, ma'm.

ALBERTA: Who?

BLIND JORDAN: Blind Jordan.

ALBERTA: Blind Jordan? Who do you want to see?

BLIND JORDAN: Grace Waters.

ALBERTA: Grace Waters? You must have the wrong apartment. There's no Grace Waters living here.

BLIND JORDAN: Can I speak to you for just one minute, ma'm?

ALBERTA: What for?

BLIND JORDAN: Please, ma'm . . . please.

ALBERTA: I told you no Grace Waters lives here.

BLIND JORDAN: Please . . . may I speak to you?

ALBERTA: Nobody by that name . . . (*She puts on the night latch and cracks the door open. Seeing that he is blind, she unlatches the door and opens it fully.*) Oh . . . come in . . . (*She leads him across threshold.*)

(*He is a tall, powerfully built man whose age is difficult to judge. He is dressed in a black shirt, with dark trousers, and a black seaman's cap. A pair of dark glasses cover his eyes, and across his shoulder he carries a battered guitar with a silver cup on the stock.*)

BLIND JORDAN: Thank you.

ALBERTA (*closing door*): Now, you say you're looking for a Grace Waters. Do you know which apartment she lives in?

BLIND JORDAN: No, ma'm, I sure don't. Ain't even sure she lives in this buildin'.

ALBERTA: Well, how . . . ?

BLIND JORDAN: I know she lives somewhere on State Street in Chicago. I just been goin' from buildin' to buildin' . . . door to door inquiring about her.

ALBERTA: Grace Waters . . . ? I don't know anybody, off hand, by that name in this building. She could be rooming. What does she look like? Oh, I'm sorry.

BLIND JORDAN: Ain't no need bein' sorry, ma'm. I'm use to it . . . been blind for a long time. That's part of my name . . . Blind Jordan. Don't reckon you've ever heard of me up here, but down home I'm known all th' way from East St. Louis to New Orleans. (*Pause.*) Ma'm, I was wonderin' . . . would you be kind enough to give me a glass of water?

ALBERTA: Surely. (*Crosses to sink and gets glass of water, returns, places it in his hand*) Here you are.

BLIND JORDAN (*drinking*): Thank y', ma'm, thank y' kindly. (*Returns glass to her*) Just about to run dry. Can't seem to get use to this Chicago water. Takes a while, I reckon. (*Another pause.*) You like music, ma'm?

ALBERTA: Yes, I like music.

BLIND JORDAN (*taking guitar off shoulder*): Sure would like to play you a tune.

ALBERTA: I'd like to hear you, but there's no one here but me.

BLIND JORDAN: I don't mean you no harm, ma'm . . . no harm in this world.

ALBERTA (*placing glass in sink*): I'm not afraid, Mr. Jordan.

BLIND JORDAN: Thought I might play a tune for y' in exchange for a little somethin' to eat.

ALBERTA: Are you hungry, Mr. Jordan?

BLIND JORDAN: Ma'm, I'm so hungry I'm weak.

ALBERTA (*starting to help him, hesitating.*): C'mon into the kitchen.

BLIND JORDAN: Could you direct me?

ALBERTA: Certainly. (*Leads him to table*) Let me move some of this stuff out of your way. (*Places vase on sink*)

BLIND JORDAN (*touching one of the paper flowers*): What's this?

ALBERTA: Just something I made.

BLIND JORDAN: Crepe-paper flower?

ALBERTA: You know about crepe-paper flowers, Mr. Jordan?

BLIND JORDAN: Yes'm. Made out of colored crepe paper and paste . . . with pieces of wire for stems. Down home folks don't always have money for real flowers. So they make their own. I never like them . . . same with artificial fruit. . . . Oh, I'm sorry, ma'm. I didn't mean to belittle your gift.

ALBERTA: I'd hardly call it a gift, Mr. Jordan. [*Opens ice box*] Now let me see what's in here.

BLIND JORDAN: Oh, anything'll do me, ma'm. Don't haffta put yourself to no trouble whatsoever. Leftovers from your supper'll do me just fine.

ALBERTA (*removing meat and bread*): I'll make you a sandwich . . . some milk.

BLIND JORDAN: Thank you, ma'm. May I ask your name?

ALBERTA: Alberta. Alberta Warren.

BLIND JORDAN (*singing*):
Alberta, let you hair hang low
Alberta, let your hair hang low
I'll give you more gold than your apron can hold
If you just let your hair hang low
Alberta, what's on your mind
Alberta, what's on your mind
Because you keep me worried and bothered all the time
Alberta, what's on your mind . . .

ALBERTA (*placing sandwich before him. Moving his hands to sandwich and milk*): That was very nice. I don't think I ever heard that song before.

BLIND JORDAN (*eating*): My father taught me that song. He was blind like me . . . runs in our family. He was one of the great street singers. Known all th' way from Vicksburg to Jackson. Yes'm, they all knew Big Blind Jordan . . . king of the twelve-string guitar. (*Slight pause.*) Usta be a lotta blind street singers in them days, but now ain't but a few of us left. They done all passed away . . . faded in time with th' comin' of the piccolo.

ALBERTA: How did you get here . . . to Chicago?

BLIND JORDAN: Part way by car . . . part way by foot. Found th' direction an' just started puttin' one foot in front of the other.

ALBERTA: How long have you been looking for her . . . Grace Waters?

BLIND JORDAN: A long time. Sometimes it seems like I ain't never not been lookin' for her. (*Finishing his sandwich and milk*) Well, I reckon I better be gettin' along.

ALBERTA: Let me get my coat and I'll help you down the stairs.

BLIND JORDAN: No! No, thank y', ma'am. (*Rises from table*) What's th' number of this buildin'?

ALBERTA: Why it's era-era-era-era . . . (*Embarrassed*) It's the . . . I'm sorry. . . . Now, let me see? You want to know the number of this building? The number of this building is . . . 3868 State Street.

BLIND JORDAN: Thank you. I'll know where to start tomorrow.

ALBERTA: Do you have any money?

BLIND JORDAN: I'll walk and play until somebody puts something in my cup.

ALBERTA (*taking dollar from her purse*): Here. (*Puts dollar in his hand*)

BLIND JORDAN: Thank you, ma'm.

ALBERTA (*leading him to door*): And if you're ever hungry or tired . . .

BLIND JORDAN: Good-night.

ALBERTA (*opening door and gently helping him out*): Good-night. (*She closes door behind him.*)

BLIND JORDAN (*offstage, singing*):
Amazing Grace how sweet it sounds
It saved a wretch like me
I once was lost but now I'm found
Was blind but now I see . . .

(*The lights fade on ALBERTA standing watching the door.*)

SCENE FOUR

The lights fade in on a Saturday about a week later at midday. DOC *is seated at the table in the kitchen.* WEEDY *enters from* ALBERTA's *bedroom carrying a bottle of medicine. She places the bottle on the table next to several other bottles of medicine.*

WEEDY: Here's another one.

DOC (*looking off in another direction*): Unhuh.

WEEDY (*taking out her glasses*): This one ain't got the name of no doctor on it either. Now, why should she scratch the label off the bottle?

DOC: Maybe she figured you'd be ramblin' round in her room.

WEEDY: How could she think that? She ain't never caught me ramblin' round in her room. (*Examines bottles*) Pink pills? Lord, what in th' world is th' child doin' with all these pink pills?

DOC: If the voice of the Lord came outta that wall an' told you, I bet you'd break your neck gettin' outta here.

WEEDY: Brother, I want you to help me.

DOC: I ain't puttin' in no numbers for you. Haffta do that yourself.

WEEDY: I'll just wait until you get all through cuttin' th' fool.

DOC (*sighing:*): All right, Weedy.

WEEDY: I want you to help me find out what doctor she's goin' to.

DOC: Why don't you just ask her?

WEEDY: If she intended to tell me don't you think she would have told me by now?

DOC: If she intended for you to know I reckon she would have.

WEEDY: She goes to the doctor on Saturday . . . bound she's there now. Now next Saturday you could be parked outside . . . follow her . . .

DOC: Spy on her?

WEEDY: I ain't askin' you to spy on her. All I'm askin' you to do is to find out what doctor she's goin' to.

DOC: Just how much are you plannin' to pay me for this service?

WEEDY: Pay you?

DOC: As long as I'm goin' into undercover work—which I am told is very dangerous—I feel like I should get paid. Espionage is a very expensive proposition.

WEEDY: You wanna get paid to aid your own flesh and blood?

DOC: Aid? I should've given aid a long time ago. (*Rises, moves to cupboard*) But to that girl . . . not to you. (*Pours himself a drink*) Only she ain't a girl no more. She's gettin' to be . . . You got salvation, but what she got?

WEEDY: I ain't interested in all that ole random talk. All I'm interested in is whether or not you're gonna help me.

DOC: Salvation? What is it exactly you saved folks're saved from?

WEEDY: From plagues like you.

DOC: Y'know, Weedy, for fifteen cents I'd cut off a mop handle, make a short stick and get somethin' done.

WEEDY: Are you goin' to help me find out who her doctor is?

DOC: Ain't nothin' wrong with Alberta.

WEEDY: Oh, you've commence to practice medicine.

DOC: Y'know . . . she's beginnin' to look like you.

WEEDY: Who she suppose to look like?

DOC: Not like you.

WEEDY: Well, y'know you ain't no springtime beauty.

DOC: That ain't what them little, pretty young girls tell me.

WEEDY: They oughta tell you what a big fool you are. What young girl would want your ole gray, rusty behind. Everytime you walk across th' floor your bones done commence to creak.

DOC: Pearl likes it.

WEEDY: Just shows she ain't got good sense. And don't you bring that thing in my house no more. Both of y'all ridin' down State Street on a bicycle . . . her with her dress tucked in her bloomers . . . an' th' both of you drunk. I just held my head in shame when I saw you two fools comin'.

DOC: She sure do look like Nora Lee . . . spittin' image of her.

WEEDY: Woman don't look like Nora Lee . . . nothin' like her.

DOC: You just don't like her.

WEEDY: I ain't got no thoughts about her. Except she's a nut.

DOC: At least she ain't always sick.

WEEDY: Nora Lee couldn't help it 'cause she was frail.

DOC: Is that why you liked Nora Lee? You upheld her in her misery. Now you got Alberta pullin' th' same trick.

WEEDY: I got her . . . (*Mimicking herself*) Oh, now, I done told her, Alberta, you run around and play like you're sick.

DOC: Didn't haffta tell her. Way you moaned an' groaned . . . talkin' all th' time about somethin' bein' wrong with you.

WEEDY: Keep on, you gonna be done made me tell you somethin'.

DOC: Tell me what?

WEEDY: To kiss my foot.

DOC: Better be careful, girl. You'll be swearin' directly.

WEEDY: You're enough to make the angels in heaven swear.

DOC: Why don't you have a little drink?

WEEDY: You better get away from around me.

DOC (*comes to her*): Hey, how about a little sugar?

WEEDY: Will you not be slobberin' all over me, please sir, with that whiskey smell.

DOC: The smell of a happy soul.

(*The door opens and* ALBERTA *enters. There has been a change in her appearance. She wears a tailored suit and hat. Her hair has been combed out and styled.*)

ALBERTA: Hello, Mama . . . Uncle Doc. (*Sees medicine on table*) How did my medicine get out here?

WEEDY: I was just showin' Brother how appetizin' they're makin' medicine nowadays. Wasn't I, Brother?

ALBERTA (*looking at* DOC, *who looks away*): I wish you wouldn't ramble through my room. (*Gathers up bottles*) Stop spying on me.

WEEDY: Ain't nobody spyin' on you, crazy woman. Who'd you think is interested in your medicine? (*Hollering out to* ALBERTA, *who has entered her room with the bottles*) An' you needn' be scratchin' the labels offa the bottles to keep me from knowin' who your doctor is.

ALBERTA (*at door*): Oh, that's why you were rambling through my things? (*Looks at* DOC) You in on this too?

DOC: I was just bein' recruited for the secret service. Detailed to trail you . . .

WEEDY: Well sir, I wasn't sure before you didn't have good sense, but now there is no doubt in my mind whatsoever.

ALBERTA: Will you please not ask people to spy on me?

WEEDY: I ain't askin' nobody to spy on you.

DOC: Didn't you ask me to find out who her doctor was?

WEEDY: Will you shut up? Have you taken complete loss of your mind? Won't be long before the men in the white coats'll be on your tail . . . carryin' you out there to Kankakee insane asylum. I believe you done lost your mind. Got no business runnin' round loose.

DOC: How you gonna stay saved bearin' false witness?

ALBERTA: Why don't you call in the police . . . send a letter to Mr. Hoover? You better stop it, Mama. You just better stop. One day, I swear to God, I'll walk out of here and never look back.

WEEDY: Will you, please, not take the Lord's name in vain in my presence? Sound like some old street woman.

ALBERTA: You have tried my patience for thirty-odd years. Eating up the food I buy. Sleeping out the bed clothes I have to buy. And on top of that drivin' me out of what little mind I have left! I'm so tired of it, sometimes I just wanna run down the street and scream.

WEEDY: Well, now, you just let me straighten out your behind before you go too far. I don't have to stay here an' take this kind of abuse. Before I'll take abuse from a child I birth into the world, I will pick manure with the birds. (*She crosses into bedroom.*) Don't haffta stay here an' take this kinda talk.

(*After a moment* ALBERTA *moves to the bedroom and stands at door.*)

DOC: What she doin'?

ALBERTA: Packing.

DOC: Is she movin' out again?

ALBERTA: Unhuh.

WEEDY (*entering*): Got too much grit in my craw to stay any place I ain't wanted. (*She is carrying a small suitcase.*)

ALBERTA: Where're you going this time?

WEEDY: Anywhere away from here. Before I'll stay where I ain't wanted I'll take up residence in the old folks' home.

DOC: Weedy, you'd worry those folks to death.

WEEDY: Just because I'm concerned with your health that's no reason for you to mistreat me. I never said a harsh word to my mother the longest day she walked this earth. Spyin' on you. You have not heard me say one single, solitary thing about spyin' on you. Have you heard me utter one halfa syllable about spyin' on you? But if you want to listen to the random talk of folks, who are fugitives from the authorities at the Kankakee insane asylum, you go right ahead. (*She has moved into kitchen.*) And you needn't worry about me . . . 'cause I got grit in my craw . . . always did have. I give you up in the hands of the Lord, 'cause I have fought the good fight. (*She moves into the hall near the door.*) If you wanna go sneakin' off to a doctor and not tell nobody about the nature of your complaint, nothin' I can do. (*Opens door*) If you don't tell me, your own mother, who underwent the pains of death to bring you into this world, who struggled with you after your father ran off and left you without a crust of bread on which to exercise your stomach muscles, who worked like the very dog to put shoes on your feet an' give you a place to lay your head. Lord, that's why I got this hurtin' in my side now . . . done almost work myself to death supportin' folks. (*She pauses.*) When I close my eyes in death you're gonna realize that I was the best friend you ever had.

ALBERTA: Good-bye, Mama.

WEEDY: All right. (*Exits*)

DOC: Where'd you think she'll go?

ALBERTA: Around the corner to have some ice cream with some chocolate syrup on it.

DOC (*crossing to window:*) Know what you oughta do? Run like hell! Run like the building was on fire. Run for parts unknown. Satchel up and go if you gotta leave here walking.

ALBERTA: Run? Run where?

DOC: What about Mrs. Coutrell? Ain't she been after you to stay on th' place?

ALBERTA: Yes.

DOC: Get a day off . . . come see Weedy.

ALBERTA: Mrs. Coutrell is almost as bad as Mama. She works my tongue pallet out now. I know what she would do if I was livin' there. She'd be havin' parties ev'rynight . . . to show her friends that she had a gal stayin' on th' place. (*Pause.*) I hear her on the phone now talking about me. Promising people to loan me out to them . . . like I was some kind of thing. (*Pause.*) I don't know what she and Mr. Coutrell think I am. Telling me I'm a member of the family. Just like one of the family. What I oughta do . . . is one night after I fix dinner . . . is to sit down with them at the table. See if they'll let one of the family sit down and eat with them. (*Pause.*) Accusing me of stealing their whiskey?

DOC: I thought they gave it to you.

ALBERTA: No, I steal it. And everything else I can get my hands on that they got.

DOC: Keep on, they're gonna have your behind arrested.

ALBERTA: Mr. Coutrell would never stand for that. He wouldn't have my behind to pinch any more.

DOC: He does that?

ALBERTA: He's been pinching my behind since the first day I walked into that house, fifteen years ago.

DOC (*getting himself another drink*): Sure wish that I could . . . (*Slight pause.*) In the old days down on Beale Street . . . I usta handle a lotta money. Lotta money! Wouldn't been nothin' for me to walk up an' hand you a couple of hundred. Always had that kinda money in my pockct! (*Reflects*) Your ole uncle . . . was a legend on that street. Carried a diamond stickpin an' a pistol in my pocket at all times. Nobody woulda dare mess with none of my kinfolks. Don't care who he was. Cause Sportin' Jimmy Sweet didn't take no mess!

ALBERTA: I can handle Mr. Coutrell.

DOC: You oughta quit . . . find yourself another job. Why don't you quit?

ALBERTA: One place is like another.

DOC: You wouldn't have to take no mess like that. (*Slight pause.*) Is it them brats?

ALBERTA: Janet and Johnny? They're almost grown now. Two or three years and they'll be going off to college. Maybe I'll leave then.

DOC: Why wait for them to leave?

ALBERTA: I promised them . . .

DOC: Promised them what?

ALBERTA: That I wouldn't go away until they got grown. They probably don't even remember that now.

DOC: When did you promise them that?

ALBERTA: When they were little. They use to leave them alone so much.

DOC: You got too involved with those chaps. They'll go on about their business. In a few years th' only thing they'll remember about you is your name. And they'll have to think about that.

ALBERTA: They're forgetting me now. I see. They don't seem to remember things we use to do when they were little. Places I use to take them . . .

DOC: I remember once you brought them around to the shine parlor where I worked. Now, ain't that somethin'? Sportin' Jimmy Sweet—a shoeshine boy!

(*There is a knock on door.*)

ALBERTA: There's Mama now. (*Gets up from couch and moves to door*) Must've forgotten her key. (*Opens door, admits* BLIND JORDAN) Oh, hi, c'mon in. My uncle is here. (*She assists him into living room to meet* DOC.) Mr. Sweet, this is Mr. Jordan.

BLIND JORDAN (*extending his hand*): Please to make your acquaintance, Mr. Sweet.

DOC (*shaking his hand*): How'd y' do?

BLIND JORDAN: You haven't by any chance heard of a woman named Grace Waters, have you, Mr. Sweet?

DOC: Grace Waters?

ALBERTA: Jordan is looking for her. Came all the way up from the old country searching for her.

DOC: Where about in th' big foot country are you from?

BLIND JORDAN: Sort of all over.

DOC: (*Slight pause.*) Grace Waters. Naw, don't recollect meetin' anybody by that name. Chicago's a big place to be lookin' for somebody unless y' know where to put your hand on them.

BLIND JORDAN: I'll find her.

DOC: Well, I reckon I'd better be pickin' up Pearl. Told her I'd pick her up after work. (*He moves toward door.*) Oh, by th' way . . . ain't had no good dreams lately, have y'?

BLIND JORDAN: You play th' numbers, Mr. Sweet?

DOC: Been known to drop a dollar on a figure once in a while.

BLIND JORDAN: Try triple zeros.

DOC (*writing it down*): Triple zero? Sounds good. 'Course, they all sound good.

BLIND JORDAN: Get on it . . . stay on it. It's gonna fall soon.

DOC: How soon?

BLIND JORDAN: Well, I can't give you the exact date . . . but it won't be long.

DOC: All right, I'll get on it for a while. See you, Alberta, Mr. Jordan. (*He exits.*)

BLIND JORDAN: Good-night, Mr. Sweet.

(ALBERTA *closes door behind* DOC, *then comes back into living room.*)

ALBERTA: I didn't know you'd be around this evening.

BLIND JORDAN: Thought I'd try to get through that big buildin' this evenin' . . . th' one we stopped at th' other day.

ALBERTA: That's an awfully big building, Jordan. Might take two or three days to get through it.

BLIND JORDAN: All I got is time.

ALBERTA: And it's Saturday . . . getting late. Folks don't like to be disturbed on Saturday evening.

BLIND JORDAN: They don't have to open the door. All they got to do is to say whether or not Grace Waters is livin' there.

ALBERTA: Suppose she was living in that big building. Suppose we knocked on the right door. All she would have to do is to say that she didn't live there and we'd walk right on away.

BLIND JORDAN: I know her voice too well for that.

ALBERTA: Somebody else could answer the door and say she didn't live there.

BLIND JORDAN: If I come within a hundred feet of her I'll know it.

ALBERTA: You know how many buildings there are in this neighborhood? You know how long it'll take you to knock on every door around here?

BLIND JORDAN: I'll get around to all of 'em. I don't care how long it takes.

ALBERTA: Half the buildings around here are under the order of condemnation.

BLIND JORDAN: That's why I need you to help me. Point out the ones that still got people livin' in them.

ALBERTA: It's not that I don't want to help you, Jordan . . .

BLIND JORDAN: The other evenin' when you went around with me . . . saved me a lot of time.

ALBERTA: You can't find anyone going from door to door. . . . Wandering through these ole, deserted buildings you could fall and hurt yourself.

BLIND JORDAN: That's why I need your eyes.

ALBERTA: Someone . . . some of these kids could attack us . . . try to rob us. There was a pair around here not too long ago—they called them tall and short man—was robbing people in their own hallways.

BLIND JORDAN: Are you afraid?

ALBERTA: No, I'm not afraid.

BLIND JORDAN: You think I can't protect you. Think because of my affliction you ain't safe with me.

ALBERTA: What could you do with two men?

BLIND JORDAN: You don't have to worry none with me.

ALBERTA: Suppose they had a gun? Tall and short man use to hold people up at gun point. That's why so many people won't open their doors.

BLIND JORDAN: Tall and short man with or without a gun don't worry me none.

ALBERTA: Jordan, what could you do against two men with a gun?

BLIND JORDAN: You're saying that you don't want to help me.

ALBERTA: Maybe it's just that I'm tired.

BLIND JORDAN: I reckon it is an exhaustin' thing . . . help me.

ALBERTA: Why don't we wait and do it tomorrow? Tomorrow is Sunday. Tomorrow afternoon would be a good day. About the time people get home from church. People are in a better mood then.

BLIND JORDAN: I had my mind set on this evening.

ALBERTA: Why can't you wait until tomorrow?

BLIND JORDAN: Lose a whole day.

ALBERTA: You said you had all the time in the world to look for her.

BLIND JORDAN: I don't want to lose a whole day.

ALBERTA: All right then, go on! But you can go by yourself. Now, I'm perfectly willing to help you if you wait until tomorrow. Since you can't wait—go right ahead. And I hope you fall and break your neck!

BLIND JORDAN: What?

ALBERTA: I'm sorry, I didn't mean that, Jordan.

BLIND JORDAN: You're upset? Have I done somethin' to you?

ALBERTA: No.

BLIND JORDAN: Then what is it?

ALBERTA: It's got nothing to do with you.

BLIND JORDAN: You want to tell me?

ALBERTA: There's nothing to tell.

BLIND JORDAN (*after a pause*): I reckon I should be getting along.

ALBERTA: Maybe so.

WEEDY (*entering*): Aw, I didn't know you had company.

ALBERTA (*as* WEEDY *comes into living room*): Oh, Mama? Mama, this is Mr. Jordan. Jordan this is my mother, Mrs. Wenella Warren.

BLIND JORDAN: Mrs. Warren.

WEEDY: How do you do.

ALBERTA: I didn't expect you back so soon.

WEEDY: I only came back for a minute. While waitin' for th' bus I had an acute attack of th' miss-meal cramp. You ever had an acute attack of th' miss-meal cramp, Mr. Jordan, sir?

BLIND JORDAN: I've had so many wrinkles in my stomach sometimes it's felt like a prune.

WEEDY: Well, you must stay for supper.

BLIND JORDAN: Wouldn't want to put you out none.

WEEDY (*taking him by arm and leading him into kitchen*): You ain't puttin' us out none. Alberta likes company. (*Seats him at table and sits down herself*) Don't you, Alberta?

ALBERTA (*at refrigerator*): How do you think some warmed-up pork chops would be?

WEEDY: In this warm weather? My stomach wouldn't have time to settle before my bedtime. And I sure ain't goin' to go to bed with no pork unsettled in my stomach to die durin' th' night from an attack of the acute indigestion. Mr. Jordan, sir, did you ever know anybody to die from an attack of th' acute indigestion, brought on by th' eatin' of pork in warm weather?

BLIND JORDAN: Yes'm . . . I knew a man down home once who had a naggin' wife. Lived about twenty-five miles below New Orleans. Well, sir, one night in August he fixed that woman some pork chops. She died that very same night from an attack of the acute indigestion. Of course, later on they found out he fried them in lye.

WEEDY (*uncomfortable*): You know some strange folks.

ALBERTA: Mama, he's joking.

WEEDY: Are you jokin' with me, Mr. Jordan, sir?

ALBERTA: Tell her you're joking. Otherwise she'll swear I'm trying to poison her.

BLIND JORDAN: I'm kidding you, Mrs. Warren.

WEEDY: Oh, you're a kidder, Mr. Jordan. Always liked a kidder. Yes sir, the one thing I always did like was a kidder. How long you been a kidder, Mr. Jordan, sir? Remember a man down in my home who was a kidder. "Kidding Sidney" they use to call him. Always like to kid folks. One day Kidding Sidney kidded the wrong man . . . an' he shot poor Kidding Sidney right dead in his mouth. An' Kidding Sidney didn't kid no more.

ALBERTA (*after a pause*): I'll make some hamburger.

WEEDY: Are you an eater of hamburger, Mr. Kidder? Excuse me, I mean Mr. Jordan.

BLIND JORDAN: I'm not a choosy eater.

WEEDY: Never will I eat the flesh of a horse.

BLIND JORDAN: Hamburger is from a cow.

WEEDY: How do you know? Were you there when they slaughtered th' animal?

ALBERTA: Suppose I just make some pork 'n' beans?

WEEDY: That's what they feed convicts.

BLIND JORDAN: You don't have to fix me nothin', Alberta.

WEEDY: Ain't you gonna eat, Mr. Jordan?

BLIND JORDAN: No, ma'm . . . I reckon I done lost my appetite. (*Rises from table*) Reckon I'll be gettin' along, Alberta.

ALBERTA: All right, I'll see you to the door. (*She leads him through the living room to door.*)

BLIND JORDAN: Good-night, Mrs. Warren. Thank y' kindly for your hospitality.

WEEDY: Good night. Mr. Kidder . . . I mean Mr. Jordan.

ALBERTA (*closing door behind* JORDAN *and coming back into kitchen*): I wish you'd learn how to act nice.

WEEDY: I don't haffta learn how to act nice. I ain't runnin' for office. I've been elected. (*She rises from table and moves to her rocking chair.*)

ALBERTA: I thought you were hungry.

WEEDY: Done lost my appetite too, I reckon. (*Peers out of window*) Well, sir, they're still up there. Alberta!

ALBERTA (*running into living room*): What's the matter?

WEEDY: Come here quick.

ALBERTA (*moving to window*): What is it?

WEEDY: Corner building . . . three windows up. Look at those curtains.

ALBERTA: What about them?

WEEDY: I'm gonna write that woman a letter tomorrow. Dear Miss, whatever you name is, if you would just put a little bleach in your water you could get those dingy curtains you got hanging up there white. Slip down there and put it in her mailbox.

ALBERTA: Be sure to sign it so they can commit you to Kankakee. (*She crosses into her bedroom and returns with a sweater thrown around her shoulders.*)

WEEDY: Where you goin'?

ALBERTA: Catch some air.

WEEDY: With th' blind man?

ALBERTA: His name is Jordan, Mama.

WEEDY: I didn't mean no harm.

ALBERTA: Maybe I'll take a walk with him.

WEEDY: Sure hate to be here all by myself. Suppose I had a stroke while you were galavantin' up an' down th' street?

ALBERTA (*standing in the open door*): You're not going to have a stroke.

WEEDY: Howd'you know? Is the Almighty consultin' you 'bout his plans? Could lay right up here with my mouth all twisted up like poor Molly Ross.

ALBERTA: Molly Ross?

BLIND JORDAN (*from the street below*):
Thro' man-y dangers, toils and snares
I have already come . . .

ALBERTA: That's Jordan singing.

WEEDY: Lived down the block . . . across th' street.

BLIND JORDAN: 'Tis Grace hath bro't me safe thus far
And Grace will lead me home . . .

ALBERTA: Molly Ross?

WEEDY: Died today, poor woman.

BLIND JORDAN: When we've been there ten thousand years
Bright shining as the sun . . .

ALBERTA: I don't think I knew her.

WEEDY: 'Course you didn't! You never paid her no attention. She wasn't none of your equal.

ALBERTA: What did she look like?

BLIND JORDAN: I've so few days to sing her praise
Than when I first begun . . .

WEEDY: Stout woman walked with a cane. Lawd, she sure was fat. Never seen a woman her age that fat before.

ALBERTA: Oh, that woman . . . what was her name? Molly Ross?

BLIND JORDAN: Amazing Grace how sweet the sound
That saved a wretch like me . . .

WEEDY: She sure was a good company keeper. Use to keep me company all day long.

ALBERTA: Mama!

WEEDY: Yes, sir, she sure was a good company keeper.

BLIND JORDAN: I once was lost but now am found
Was blind but now I see . . .

(*The lights fade.*)

ACT TWO

SCENE ONE

The lights fade in on WEEDY *and* ALBERTA *about two weeks later. It is now the first Saturday in September and the sunlight which fills the apartment has a touch of gray in it.* WEEDY, *dressed in a stiff white uniform, is packing a second white uniform into an open suitcase along with several small articles. Throughout her packing she moves to the window and looks out onto the street several times.* ALBERTA *is in the kitchen ironing a third white uniform, alternating that task with the making of sandwiches, which she places in a shoe box on the table.*

WEEDY (*hollering to* ALBERTA *in kitchen*): I wonder if I should take a coat?

ALBERTA (*bringing white dress and sandwiches into living room, beginning to stuff them into the suitcase*): Maybe you oughta take one just in case it turns cold.

WEEDY: Generally, shirt-sleeve weather down there.

ALBERTA (*having difficulty packing suitcase*): This suitcase ain't big enough. You shoulda took mine.

WEEDY: Yours is too big and clumsy.

ALBERTA: You got too much stuff in here.

WEEDY: Same amount I always put in there ev'ry year.

ALBERTA: Maybe the suitcase has gotten smaller. Let me get mine.

WEEDY: Ain't nothin' wrong with that suitcase—not a thing.

ALBERTA (*trying to lock it*): Well, I can't get it closed.

WEEDY: Let me try. (*Struggling with it*)

ALBERTA (*has gone into* WEEDY'*s room, returning with a spring coat*): Get it closed?

WEEDY: Naw. Maybe you better try again.

ALBERTA (*putting spring coat in suitcase*): Never get it closed now. (WEEDY *tries again as* ALBERTA *goes into her room and comes back with a larger suitcase.*) Mama, why don't we just take everything out and pack it in here?

WEEDY (*struggling to close the suitcase*): I don't want that thing. Don't want to be bothered with it.

ALBERTA: Why? Bigger . . . and almost brand new.

WEEDY: I like this one.

ALBERTA: Mama, you can't get this thing closed.

WEEDY (*taking coat out*): Here. (*Sits on it*) Fasten it quick!

ALBERTA (*trying to snap the locks*): This thing is gonna bust wide open.

WEEDY: Ain't never bust on me before.

ALBERTA (*still trying to lock it*): You must have more in there this time.

WEEDY: You just lock it.

ALBERTA (*getting it locked*): Hope it don't jump open on you on the train. All your underwear in the aisle.

WEEDY: Well, if folks ain't never seen underwear before, they won't know what it is.

ALBERTA: What you gonna do about this coat?

WEEDY: I don't reckon I really need it.

ALBERTA: Could carry it over your arm.

WEEDY: I don't feel like foolin' with it.

ALBERTA: Suit yourself. But suppose it turns cold?

WEEDY: It ain't gonna turn cold. (*There is a pause.*) Sure do wish you were comin' with me. You ain't never been to th' convocation. Oughta go once in your life.

ALBERTA: I can't afford to go!

WEEDY: I'd help you on your ticket.

ALBERTA: I can't get off my job for two weeks.

WEEDY: Why don't you just call up Mrs. Coutrell and tell her that you have to go out of town for two weeks, take care of some business?

ALBERTA: I can't afford to lose the money. Besides, I don't want to go down to Montgomery fooling with them crackers.

WEEDY: You don't have to fool with no crackers.

ALBERTA: Here tell they got laughing barrels all over the street down in Montgomery. Negro sees something funny he has to stick his head in the barrel and laugh.

WEEDY: Now, who told you that lie?

ALBERTA: I heard about it.

WEEDY (*after a pause*): We sure would have a good time down there at the convocation. You'd get a chance to hear some of the best preaching you ever heard in your life. Best preachers in the country—from all over these United States—gather down there for th' convocation. An' I don't mean them what's learn it in th' school house. I'm talkin' 'bout them that's got th' callin'. Them that had to go off somewhere an' learn it are so dull an' dry. Near 'bouts puts me to sleep. But them that's got th' callin'—they can stir you up! Yes, Jesus, they can get you so worked up you'll think you're sittin' on your throne in glory. An' th' song battles. You ain't never in your born days heard no singin' like you hear at th' convocation. I tell you, Alberta, it is an inspirin' thing th' way some of them folks sing. I mean they can really sing! It's like Jesus had put th' voices in their mouths. And there's plenty for young folks to do too. Goin' 'round to th' different church socials. An' if th' weather is nice, they have a big outdoor picnic almost every day. Then that evenin' the B.Y.P.U.—Baptist Young People's Union—have their little things in th' basement of th' church. 'Course, now, I don't have no truck with them Baptist folks, but you could go. (*Pause.*) Sure see a lotta folks down there at th' convocation. A whole lotta folks you be done half forgotten—done slipped right outta your mind. Woman came up to me at th' last convocation and said to me, "Ain't you

Wenella Sweet?" Lawd, I looked at that woman an' didn't know who in th' world she was. I couldn't place her to save my life. An' y' know she wouldn't tell me who she was. She just walked on away. (*Another slight pause.*) I was on th' train on my way back to Chicago before it came to me who that woman was. Her name was Flora Jackson. She use to live right next door to me in Clarksdale, Mississippi. I knew her before you were born. Before I was even thinkin' about gettin' married. We went to school together. She sure didn't look like herself. Never would have known her in a million years if she hadn't recognized me. Flora Jackson! Prettiest girl you ever did see . . .

ALBERTA: How long had it been since you'd seen her?

WEEDY: Lawd, I don't reckon I had seen that woman in somethin' like fifty years. She had completely passed out of my mind. You oughta come with me, Alberta . . .

ALBERTA: Mama, I don't want to go to the convocation. We can't even afford for you to go.

WEEDY: Convocation is about the only little pleasure I get out of life. That and church.

ALBERTA: Money you're going down there and throwing away—we could use that money to fix up this apartment.

WEEDY: What's wrong with this apartment?

ALBERTA: The furniture is old—worn out. I'd like to get some new pieces for the living room.

WEEDY: Ain't nothin' wrong with this furniture.

ALBERTA: It's older than the hills.

WEEDY: Whole lot better than the junk they are makin' today.

ALBERTA: At least I could get some slipcovers to put over it. That big chair needs to be reupholstered. And the couch! That thing should have been thrown out years ago.

WEEDY: That couch is still good.

ALBERTA: While you're gone I think I'll have somebody come up and take that thing outta here.

WEEDY: And what we gonna do for a couch?

ALBERTA: I'll try to get a new one.

WEEDY: Now, you leave that couch right alone. Had that couch before you were born.

ALBERTA: The springs are comin' through. Everytime I sit on it it sticks right in my behind.

WEEDY: Then keep your behind off of it.

ALBERTA: Mrs. Coutrell got a couch stored in her garage. Maybe I could buy it from her. It ain't that good, but it's sure better than that one.

WEEDY: Don't let me come back here and find that couch missing!

ALBERTA: Well, I'm sure gonna get rid of it.

WEEDY: No, you ain't! What's gotten into you? Gonna just throw my things out without my permission.

ALBERTA: You love that damned, wore-out ole couch so much, why don't you stay here and watch it?

WEEDY: Now, how am I gonna stay here and watch it if I'm goin' to th' convocation? Talk silly.

ALBERTA: Don't go! Stay here and watch it. Nail it down before you leave.

WEEDY: I don't haffta nail it down. It's mine. You ain't got no business foolin' with it.

ALBERTA (*going into kitchen, getting hammer and nails*): I'll nail it down for you.

WEEDY: What you fixin' to do?

ALBERTA (*bending down to foot of couch*): I'm gonna nail it down.

WEEDY: Don't you be puttin' no nails in my furniture.

ALBERTA: I wanna make sure it's here when you come back.

WEEDY: Give me that hammer.

ALBERTA: No, I'm gonna make sure that nobody can move this piece of junk outta here.

WEEDY: Now, you can put a nail in my furniture if you want to.

ALBERTA: I'm gonna nail every piece of furniture in this house down. Make sure that when you come back it's just like you left it.

WEEDY (*snatching hammer from her*): You better get somewhere an' sit down.

ALBERTA: Then you nail it down.

WEEDY: Just don't let me come back and find nothin' missin' outta here. 'Cause if I do . . .

ALBERTA: What?

WEEDY: You just take anythin' outta here an' you'll see what. Fool around directly and make me mad. (*Moves to kitchen and puts hammer away—hears* ALBERTA *mumbling to herself.*) What's that you're sayin'?

ALBERTA: Nothing.

WEEDY: Well, don't be makin' all them ole funny sounds. 'Cause I think you're talkin' about me.

ALBERTA: I'm talking to myself. Not thinking about you.

WEEDY: Let me know it then. (*There is a pause.* WEEDY *has come back into the living room. She moves to the couch and places the suitcase on the floor.*) Lawd, have mercy.

ALBERTA: What?

WEEDY: I forgot to put on my white stockin's.

ALBERTA: Where are they?

WEEDY: In the suitcase. Think I should open it again? Might not get it closed before Brother gets here.

ALBERTA: I guess I could go out to Thirty-ninth Street and get you another pair.

WEEDY: Would you do that for Mother?

ALBERTA: All right. (*Gets her bag and moves to door*) I'll run down there and get 'em.

WEEDY: Hurry back before Brother gets here.

ALBERTA (*opening door*): I'll get back as quick as I can. (*She exits.*)

(WEEDY *has moved to her rocking chair at the window and begins to rock. The lights dim to denote the passing of a few minutes.* BLIND JORDAN *appears in the door that* ALBERTA *has left open.* WEEDY *senses his presence and turns around to see him.*)

WEEDY: Oh, it's you, Mr. Jordan. C'mon in.

BLIND JORDAN: Alberta here?

WEEDY: She just stepped out for a minute. You can c'mon in an' sit down.

BLIND JORDAN (*making his way to big chair*): Thank y', ma'm.

WEEDY: Seem to make your way around in this apartment pretty good.

BLIND JORDAN: Don't take me too long to get use to a place.

WEEDY: I can see that stickin' out.

BLIND JORDAN: Ma'm?

WEEDY (*slight pause*): You and Alberta done got right friendly.

BLIND JORDAN: Yes'm.

WEEDY: Know I'm goin' to th' convocation?

BLIND JORDAN: You goin' away?

WEEDY: Catchin' th' train tonight for th' convocation. Be gone for two weeks.

BLIND JORDAN: Alberta goin' with you?

WEEDY: No, she's not goin'. (*Slight pause.*) I was wonderin', Mr. Jordan, if you'd do me a favor?

BLIND JORDAN: Anythin' I can, Mrs. Warren.

WEEDY: Would you mind not comin' around here while I'm away?

BLIND JORDAN: You mind if I ask why?

WEEDY: You know why, Mr. Jordan.

BLIND JORDAN: I do.

WEEDY: I know you. You're the devil, Mr. Jordan. An' my daughter done open th' door for you and beckoned you to come in.

BLIND JORDAN: You don't really believe I'm th' devil, Mrs. Warren.

WEEDY: I didn't just come into th' world yesterday, y'know. I know you . . . know who you are.

BLIND JORDAN: Who do you think I am?

WEEDY: I been seein' all you old blind street singers all the days of my life. I know where you been and what you done done. I even know how you got blind, Mr. Jordan.

BLIND JORDAN: I was born blind.

WEEDY: I know that.

BLIND JORDAN: You do?

WEEDY: Probably come from a long line of blind street singers.

BLIND JORDAN: Yes'm, I do. How did you know that? Alberta tell you?

WEEDY: My eye commence to jump th' minute I saw you. An' when my eye commences to jump somethin' ain't right. There's danger afoot.

BLIND JORDAN: Yes'm.

WEEDY: An' this woman you're lookin' for?

BLIND JORDAN: Grace Waters.

WEEDY: You're still lookin' for her?

BLIND JORDAN: I dunno. Lately I ain't sure that I am. All I know is that now when I knock on doors I sorta hope that she won't be there. That thought has crossed my mind several times lately.

WEEDY: You keep on lookin' for her, Mr. Jordan.

BLIND JORDAN: Why?

WEEDY: You know why.

BLIND JORDAN: Alberta?

WEEDY: That's right, Mr. Jordan. You know exactly what I'm talkin' about.

BLIND JORDAN: Ma'm . . . Alberta is . . .

WEEDY: Not for you. No way whatsoever.

BLIND JORDAN: How do you know that?

WEEDY: Because you're a slewfoot! All you're good for is slewfootin' up an' down th' road lookin' for that woman.

BLIND JORDAN: Maybe you're right.

WEEDY: Ain't that I got nothin' against you personally.

BLIND JORDAN: No, ma'm, I just make your eye jump.

WEEDY: Best thing you can do is to leave poor Alberta alone.

BLIND JORDAN: All right, Mrs. Warren, I'll stay away.

WEEDY: As long as you're in th' neighborhood.

BLIND JORDAN: I've worked all th' buildin's in this neighborhood. (*He rises, moves to door.*) Good-bye, Mrs. Warren.

WEEDY: Good-bye, Mr. Jordan. You will keep your promise?

BLIND JORDAN (*at door*): I won't bother Alberta no more.

WEEDY: You've done a ole woman a great kindness.

BLIND JORDAN: Yes'm.

(DOC *enters.*)

DOC: Hello, Jordan.

BLIND JORDAN: Doc? How are you?

DOC: OK

BLIND JORDAN: You been ridin' that number?

DOC: Tell you the truth, I only played it once.

BLIND JORDAN: Came out last week.

DOC: Yes, I know.

BLIND JORDAN: Should've been on it. Was a good number.

DOC: They're all good if they fall.

BLIND JORDAN: It's gonna fall again in a little while.

DOC: Triple zeros?

BLIND JORDAN: I'm tellin' you.

DOC: Why don't you get on it?

BLIND JORDAN: Me?

DOC: Your money is as good as anybody else's.

BLIND JORDAN: Wouldn't ever fall for me.

DOC: Y'mean if you had money on it, it wouldn't have fallen?

BLIND JORDAN: I'm just not lucky. I can give other people numbers but they wouldn't fall for me.

DOC: If a number falls, it falls.

BLIND JORDAN: Not for me.

DOC: Maybe I'm th' same way.

BLIND JORDAN: No, it'll fall for you.

DOC: If I get a few extra dollars, I'll put somethin' on it.

BLIND JORDAN: You broke, Doc?

DOC: Not broke, just fractured.

BLIND JORDAN: You wear a hat?

DOC: A derby.

BLIND JORDAN: Take off your hat.

DOC: My hat? (*Removes hat*)

BLIND JORDAN (*feeling for hat, lowering his hand with hat in it to his pocket level*): Here. (*He removes change from both pockets and pours it into* DOC's *hat.*)

DOC: What're you doin'?

BLIND JORDAN: Fillin' your hat up with change.

DOC: I can't take your money.

BLIND JORDAN: I want you to get on triple zeros.

DOC (*stunned*): Must be thirty or forty dollars here.

BLIND JORDAN: Play it. Every day! You don't even have to box it. No matter what combination it falls in, you win.

DOC: Wait a minute . . .

BLIND JORDAN: See you, Doc . . . Mrs. Warren. (*He exits.*)

(DOC *watches* BLIND JORDAN *go. He moves through the living room to the kitchen.*)

WEEDY: Can't you say good evenin' to folks before you head for th' jug?

DOC (*pouring a drink*): Good evenin'.

WEEDY: Breath strong enough now to knock down folks when you pass.

DOC: You ready to go?

WEEDY: I ain't goin' nowhere with you if you keep drinkin' that whiskey. Never will I ride in a car with a drunkard.

DOC: You're gonna look mighty funny ridin' all th' way down to th' train station standin' on my runnin' board.

WEEDY: You shouldn't be allowed behind th' wheel of a car. Weavin' in an' outta traffic like a wild cowboy. You are a menace to public safety.

DOC: C'mon, you goin' to th' train station or not?

WEEDY: I dunno if I want to ride in that ole car anyhow.

DOC: What's wrong with my car?

WEEDY: Nothin' . . . outside it's a rattle trap ole enough to have driven th' Lawd to th' last supper.

DOC: Look, I ain't got all evenin'. You goin' to Montgomery or not?

WEEDY: If th' gate keep swingin' in th' direction it's swingin' in, I'm goin'. However, if th' gate should decide to swing in another direction, I may haffta change my plans accordin'ly. Lawd, give me th' strength to endure.

DOC: Sister, not only will you endure but you will prevail.

WEEDY: Would you mind takin' my bags into the bedroom. I've decided not to go.

DOC (*coming into living room*): You're not goin'?

WEEDY: Can't go off and leave Alberta here by herself. Y'know she ain't well.

DOC: Maybe a little rest from you will be a tonic for her.

WEEDY (*rising from rocking chair*): 'Course, if you would come over here and stay while I'm gone . . .

DOC: What for?

WEEDY: To see after her. Come here, Brother.

DOC: For what?

WEEDY: Just come here. (*He comes forward to* WEEDY, *who pushes him into rocking chair.*) Now, I need somebody to take care of things while I'm gone. (*She rocks him in chair.*)

DOC: What're you doin'?

WEEDY: Just sit still and listen. I need somebody here to take my place while I'm gone.

DOC: She don't need nobody to see about her.

WEEDY: I say she does.

DOC (*peering out of window*): What's goin' on over there?

WEEDY: Where?

DOC: Across th' street?

WEEDY: What'd you see?

DOC: A milk man. Now, what's a milk man doin' deliverin' milk this time of evenin'?

WEEDY: That's their cloak.

DOC: Who?

WEEDY: Bright woman lives over there on th' first floor. That milk man is in an' outta there all times of day. Poor man out workin' like a dog . . . got two jobs . . . mornin' an' night.

DOC: Y'mean th' poor man is out workin' like a dog on two jobs an' unbeknownst to him he's got another mule kickin' in his stall?

WEEDY: I'd be willin' to get you a little somethin'.

DOC: Pay me to stay over here while you're gone?

WEEDY: A few dollars.

DOC: What's a few?

WEEDY: More than you got.

DOC: Before or after you go to Montgomery?

WEEDY: When I come back.

DOC: Your memory about money matters ain't too good.

WEEDY: Whatever I have when I get back.

DOC (*getting up out of rocking chair*): Naw, I got my own personal life to think about. Pearl keeps me pretty busy.

WEEDY: You still foolin' with that infant?

(ALBERTA *enters with stockings.*)

ALBERTA: I had to go all the way to Forty-third Street to find your size.

DOC: Coulda took your time. Weedy ain't goin' nowhere.

ALBERTA: Not going?

WEEDY: Ain't settled in my mind that I oughta go.

ALBERTA (*taking stocking out of box and taking off* WEEDY's *shoes*): Mama, you're getting on that train.

WEEDY: I ain't made up my mind yet.

ALBERTA: Way you done worried me about going . . . now, you're sure gonna go.

WEEDY: Don't be so rough! You're gonna run th' stockin's.

ALBERTA: Get her suitcase, Uncle Doc.

WEEDY: You're just gonna make me go.

ALBERTA: That's right.

DOC (*at door with suitcase*): Saint Weedy! Will you start marchin'!

WEEDY (*reluctantly*): Well . . . (*Moving to door*)

ALBERTA (*handing her coat*): Take this on your arm.

WEEDY (*taking coat*): Lawd willin', I should be back sittin' at my window two weeks from this very day. I'll send you a telegram and you an' Brother can pick me up.

DOC (*has exited calling*): C'mon, Weedy!

WEEDY: I'll send you a picture postcard from Montgomery. That is, if I get to th' train in one piece. Should get it in a day or so.

DOC (*offstage*): Weedy!

WEEDY (*kissing* ALBERTA *on the cheek*): Be a good girl. Pray for me, I'm off with th' drunkard. (*Exits. From offstage*) C'mon an' make haste. I got a train to catch.

ALBERTA: Jesus? (*She turns off the lights in apartment and moves to rocking chair and looks out of window.*)

BLIND JORDAN (*from the street below*):
Amazing Grace how sweet it sounds
It saved a wretch like me.
I once was lost but now am found
Was blind but now I see . . .

ALBERTA: Jordan! (*Raises window and yells out*) Jordan!!

BLIND JORDAN: Thro' many dangers, toils and snares
I've already come
It's Grace who's brought me safe thus far
And Grace will lead me home . . .

ALBERTA: Jordan! . . . Can't you hear me calling you? Jordan!!!

(*The lights fade with* ALBERTA *at window.*)

SCENE TWO

The sound of the CHOIR *from the little storefront church is heard in the blackout. A thin blue light rises on the half-open window in the living room. Slowly the light widens to envelop the entire apartment.* ALBERTA *and* BLIND JORDAN *are revealed sitting at the kitchen table.*

CHOIR (*offstage*):
Father alone understands why
Father alone knows all about it

Cheer up, my mother, walk in the sunshine
You'll understand it all by and by . . .

BLIND JORDAN: Where's that singin' comin' from?

ALBERTA: That little storefront church down the street.

(*The singing has faded into a hum.*)

BLIND JORDAN: They sing pretty fair.

ALBERTA: Why . . . why didn't you answer me when I called you?

BLIND JORDAN: I reckon I didn't hear you.

ALBERTA: You didn't hear me calling you from the window?

BLIND JORDAN: I reckon not.

ALBERTA: I ran down the street calling after you, and you just kept right on walking.

BLIND JORDAN: There was a lotta noise.

ALBERTA: Where were you going?

BLIND JORDAN: No place in particular . . . just goin'.

ALBERTA: You were . . . going away, weren't you? You were just going to walk away without even saying good-bye to me.

BLIND JORDAN: I promised Mrs. Warren . . .

ALBERTA: Mama? What did you promise Mama?

BLIND JORDAN: That I wouldn't be hangin' around here while she's gone.

ALBERTA: Don't pay Mama any attention.

BLIND JORDAN: She's right. Shouldn't be hangin' round you.

ALBERTA: I don't want you to go away, Jordan.

BLIND JORDAN: You don't know anything about me, Alberta.

ALBERTA: I don't need to know anything about you. I just don't want you to go away.

BLIND JORDAN: I can't stay here forever. Been down here too long as it is. Done been through all the buildin's on this block twice. It's time for me to be movin' on.

ALBERTA: You don't haffta do that. You could stay here.

BLIND JORDAN: With you?

ALBERTA: Be better than walking around begging.

BLIND JORDAN: How could I keep lookin' for Grace and stay here with you at the same time?

ALBERTA: You couldn't.

BLIND JORDAN: You want me to stop looking for Grace?

ALBERTA: You're never going to find her, Jordan.

BLIND JORDAN: Doesn't make much difference whether I do or not.

ALBERTA: Then why do you keep looking for her?

BLIND JORDAN: Because that's what I do.

ALBERTA: Why?

BLIND JORDAN: I dunno any more. Maybe I did when I first started . . . but if I did, I've forgotten. Just seems like I gotta keep lookin' for her. Don't matter none if I find her or not. So long as I keep lookin' for her.

ALBERTA: So you're gonna spend the rest of your days smelling up behind a woman that you ain't never gonna find.

BLIND JORDAN: Maybe so.

ALBERTA: Wouldn't it be better living here with me than stumbling by yourself?

BLIND JORDAN: You're askin' me to live with you?

ALBERTA (*after a moment*): Yes . . .

BLIND JORDAN: For how long?

ALBERTA: No special time.

BLIND JORDAN: But there would be a special time. One day that time would come. Then I'd be back lookin' for Grace again. One day I'd hear it in your voice.

ALBERTA: Hear what in my voice?

BLIND JORDAN: That special time.

ALBERTA: I don't understand what you're saying.

BLIND JORDAN: There's been other women who I've stopped with while I've been lookin' for Grace. Women that had soft, sweet voices. And so I stopped off. Their voice would be little . . . inside of them. After I was there a while I could hear their voices gettin' bigger and bigger. And for a while they would still be sweet . . . but then they would get hard and cracked. Then I would know it would be time for me to move on again. I would be back on the road lookin' for Grace. I don't think I can stop again.

ALBERTA: You're saying that one day I would ask you to leave?

BLIND JORDAN: Not in words.

ALBERTA: You're wrong, Jordan, I wouldn't do that.

BLIND JORDAN: You need somethin' from me . . . and I'd give it to you. But after a while you wouldn't need me any more.

ALBERTA: What is it you think I need?

BLIND JORDAN: Somebody . . .

ALBERTA: You're wrong. I don't need anyone.

BLIND JORDAN: You don't have to lie. It ain't nothin' to be ashamed about. It's nature. Ev'rybody got nature of one kind or another.

ALBERTA: You think I'm talking about nature? You think that's why I want you to stay here? Because of nature?

BLIND JORDAN: Ain't a thing wrong with that.

ALBERTA: I don't have any nature.

BLIND JORDAN: All right.

ALBERTA: If you think that's why I wanted you to stay, you can get out of here right now. That's the only thing that's ever on men's minds. Mama's right. Men are lower than dogs!

BLIND JORDAN: Maybe I better go.

ALBERTA: Maybe you better. (*He rises. She touches his hand.*) Don't go, Jordan . . . I don't want you to go.

BLIND JORDAN: I don't like a whole lotta fussin'.

ALBERTA: I won't fuss. I promise. I won't fuss.

BLIND JORDAN (*sitting back down*): If I'm gonna upset you . . .

ALBERTA: I'm not upset. (*There is a long silence.*) I'm not going to let myself get upset.

BLIND JORDAN: Naw, don't let yourself get upset.

ALBERTA (*after a pause*): I should have gone to church tonight.

BLIND JORDAN: Why didn't you?

ALBERTA: I dunno. I haven't been going too much lately. I guess they'll start thinking I've backslid.

BLIND JORDAN: Have you backslid?

ALBERTA: No, of course not. I'm still saved. After Emanuel Fisher's funeral I haven't been goin' too much.

BLIND JORDAN: Who was he?

ALBERTA: Just a boy . . . man . . . around the church.

BLIND JORDAN: Was he a friend of yourn?

ALBERTA: No . . . no. I admired him from afar.

BLIND JORDAN: Never got close to him.

(ALBERTA *rises, gets herself a drink.*)

ALBERTA: You want a little taste?

BLIND JORDAN: No, thank y'.

ALBERTA: What was she like?

BLIND JORDAN: Grace?

ALBERTA: You know who I mean.

BLIND JORDAN: What's to say?

ALBERTA: Was she pretty?

BLIND JORDAN: Folks said she was.

ALBERTA: Was she nice?

BLIND JORDAN: She had a nice voice.

ALBERTA: What kinda voice is that?

BLIND JORDAN: Raindust.

ALBERTA: Raindust?

BLIND JORDAN: Sorta made you feel . . . Did you ever smell raindust?

ALBERTA: I don't even know what it is.

BLIND JORDAN: Down home when it gets scratchin' hot. So hot you can't stand it any more . . . Then when it rains . . . folks down there call it th' white rain—hard, heavy, coolin' rain you can smell. Like th' ole earth is reborn. Fresh as the mornin' it was created.

ALBERTA: That's what she was like?

BLIND JORDAN: To me.

ALBERTA: Did she have a lot of nature?

BLIND JORDAN: She had a sufficient amount.

ALBERTA (*pours another shot*): I shouldn't have asked you that. None of my business.

BLIND JORDAN: Doesn't bother me.

ALBERTA (*after a moment*): Was she good up under her dress?

BLIND JORDAN: Yes, she was. She was very good up under her dress.

ALBERTA: What's wrong with me? What am I saying things like this for? I sound like some ole street woman.

BLIND JORDAN: You're not a street woman.

ALBERTA: I sound like one.

BLIND JORDAN: No, you're not.

ALBERTA (*after a moment*): Did you ever think . . . that maybe Grace Waters might be dead?

BLIND JORDAN: She ain't dead.

ALBERTA: How can you be sure?

BLIND JORDAN: If anything had happened to her—I'd know it. I couldn't go on lookin' for her and she . . . Why are you tryin' to put that idea in my head?

ALBERTA: It's possible.

BLIND JORDAN: It ain't possible.

ALBERTA: Is she too good to die?

BLIND JORDAN: Yes! Yes, she is.

ALBERTA: That's what they said about Emanuel Fisher. Said he was too good to die. Everybody loved him because he was so good. But that didn't stop him from falling out of the sky.

BLIND JORDAN: He fell out of the sky?

ALBERTA: He was learning to be a pilot. First time he went up by himself—the plane crashed. They had to cut him out of the wreckage. Then they had to cut the metal out of his body. He was so good. He was too good to die. And he had a voice that would make the very angels in heaven weep when he raised his voice in song. Yet God saw fit to let him die. 'S wonder the weeping Purple Angels didn't just swoop down and lift him out of that plane and bring him safely to the ground. Yes, Jesus, yes, Lord . . . he was so good.

BLIND JORDAN: I suppose you went to his funeral.

ALBERTA: Yes, Lord, yes, Jesus, I was there. . . . . It was the biggest funeral in the history of the church . . . (*The lights in the apartment fade on* BLIND JORDAN *and plunge the whole apartment into darkness. A thin white light raises on* ALBERTA.) That place was really packed. They had to rent extra chairs for the people to sit down. And even in the streets, outside the church, people were standing. They came from all over Chicago to say one last good-bye to Emanuel Fisher—he was so beloved.

(*The sound of the* CHOIR *is heard.*)

CHOIR: Father alone understands why
     Father alone knows all about it
ALBERTA: And they really put him away in style. His mother and father must have spent every penny they had putting him away.
CHOIR: Cheer up, my brother, don't you be sad
     You'll understand all by and by . . .
ALBERTA: He had a beautiful powder blue casket, lined with gentle white satin that shined like mirrors. And you never saw so many white roses in your life.
CHOIR: Father alone knows all about it
     Father alone understands why . . .
ALBERTA: There were thousands and thousands of white roses covering his powder blue casket. And his casket was placed so it caught the light from the stained-glass window. The light, the yellow light fell on his face. . . . He looked so much like Jesus. Like a beautiful, sleeping Jesus. They didn't need to paint his face—he was beautiful without makeup.
CHOIR: Cheer up, my mother, walk in the sunshine
     You'll understand all by and by . . .
ALBERTA: He was even more beautiful in death than he had been in life. (CHOIR *is humming "Father Alone."*) The goodness still shined from his face. Then Reverend Goodlow stood up and asked Agnes McLoy to sing "Precious Lord." "Do it once more for Emanuel, Sister Agnes."
SOUND OF WOMAN'S VOICE: Precious Lord, take my hand
     Lead me on, let me stand . . .
ALBERTA (*quietly*): Yes, Lord.
SOUND OF WOMAN'S VOICE: I am weak, I am worn, I am tired
     Through the night, through the storm . . .
ALBERTA: Yes, Jesus!
SOUND OF WOMAN'S VOICE: Lead me on to the light
     Precious Lord, take my hand.
ALBERTA: Then I had to read the telegrams.

(Sound of WOMAN *and* CHOIR *humming "Precious Lord")*

ALBERTA: To the bereaved parents of Emanuel Fisher. Our heartfelt sympathy. Signed, The Reverend Lloyd S. Peters, Clarksdale, Mississippi. To Mr. and Mrs. Joseph Fisher. Our hearts share with you the tragedy of your loss. Signed, The Reverend Doctor John Thomas, 223 Decator Street, Cincinnati, Ohio. From Mr. and Mrs. John W. Lucas of Louisville, Kentucky, to the family of Emanuel Fisher. Please accept our deepest condolences at your loss. From Mr. and Mrs. Richard Matthew and family from Nashville, Tennessee. Our hearts reach out to you at this time of your great loss. To the family of Emanuel Fisher. Our deepest regrets at the passing of Emanuel Fisher. Dr. and Mrs. Harold H. Markus, Augusta, Georgia. *(The humming of "Precious Lord" fades.)* Emanuel Fisher was born in Clarksdale, Mississippi, on the sixth day of June in the year nineteen twenty-five. He was the son of Mr. Joseph Fisher and Marianne Lovelace Fisher. They traveled to Chicago in the year nineteen thirty-two when Emanuel Fisher was six years old. Mr. and Mrs. Joseph Fisher joined this church in the year of its dedication, which was spring of nineteen thirty-three. Emanuel Fisher attended Doolittle grammar school and Wendell Phillips High School, graduating with honors. The year after his graduation he entered Pickering College in the state of South Carolina. While there, he became active in the Christian Young People's Conference and won great recognition for his prize-winning speech, which was later published in the Christian Young People's Conference's annual magazine, called "The Flight of the Purple Angels." In his speech, "The Flight of the Purple Angels," he chose to reconcile life with death. He reminded those who were in the audience that day that we must not become too attached to this earthly life. That our lives here should be preparation for the life that is to come. For it is this life that is to come which is the reason for our being here. And we must earn that life . . . cleanse ourselves in order to earn that life. He tried to give the audience comfort in the knowledge that when the Heavenly Father calls us home we should not be afraid. For the Father has created an orchard for us to live in with life everlasting. That our labors in these vineyards down here is but a prelude to the rest we shall receive when the Purple Angels call us on our final journey. It is a journey that Emanuel Fisher, unlike most of us, looked forward to. Emanuel Fisher asked that when he began that last journey his loved ones and friends not mourn him. That they rejoice for he knows that he will be rejoicing in the bosom of our Savior, Jesus Christ. No, do not mourn Emanuel Fisher for he is this day sitting on the right hand of the Father, the Son and the Holy Ghost. Another has raised his voice in song this day. Another voice sings out with the Heavenly Host. We may not hear that voice because we are too far away. But the Purple Angels hear and they weep and are happy, for Emanuel Fisher flies with them.

VOICE OF REVEREND GOODLOW: I wish to thank Sister Alberta for her words . . . (*The* CHOIR *sings softly "Just a Closer Walk with Thee."*) And I! AND I do not grieve, Emanuel Fisher.

ALBERTA: Yes, Jesus!

CHOIR (*softly*): Just a closer walk with thee
Grant it, Jesus, if you please . . .

VOICE OF REVEREND GOODLOW: For Emanuel Fisher has gone to Glory! Amen. I said Emanuel Fisher is sitting in glory . . .

ALBERTA: Mercy, Jesus! Mercy!

VOICE OF REVEREND GOODLOW: . . . for he has found life everlasting.

(CHOIR *is humming.*)

ALBERTA: Oh, Jesus, have mercy! Jesus, have mercy!

VOICE OF REVEREND GOODLOW: And even though his earthly body was twisted and mangled beyond repair . . . even though man with all his knowledge could not heal his body . . . even though they could not resurrect that body . . . Emanuel Fisher lives! For that motor is still running fine in glory. The breath of life has been blown back into our brother! The breath of life that only God can blow into him has been blown back into him.

ALBERTA: Yes, Jesus, yes Lord!

(CHOIR *is humming.*)

VOICE OF REVEREND GOODLOW: I can see him riding that train to glory! And Jesus is the conductor!

CONGREGATION: Emanuel! Oh, Jesus, Emanuel!

VOICE OF REVEREND GOODLOW: Tell them to get my throne ready, Emanuel! Tell them to get my crown ready, Emanuel! 'Cause I'm coming too!

(*Sounds of* CONGREGATION—*there are screams, moans, and wails.*)

ALBERTA (*being carried away*): Aw, Emanuel! Aw, Jesus. Glory! Take me too, Lord. I said take me too, Jesus!

VOICE OF REVEREND GOODLOW: Tell them I'm coming too, Emanuel. Tell them to get my castle ready! Tell them to get my robes ready. Tell them I'm coming, Emanuel, and I won't be long in getting there. I'm tired of this body! I'm tired of this strife! I'm tired, Emanuel! Whew. Oh, Lawd, How long!

ALBERTA: How long!!

CONGREGATION: How long!!!

VOICE OF REVEREND GOODLOW: How long, oh, Lord.

ALBERTA: How long, Jesus!

CONGREGATION: How long, Lord!!!

VOICE OF REVEREND GOODLOW: How long the night!

ALBERTA: Yes, Lord! Oh, yes, Lord!

CONGREGATION: Mercy, Lord! Lord, have mercy!

VOICE OF REVEREND GOODLOW: How long this darkness!

ALBERTA (*falling to floor*): I wanna shout Jesus! And dance! Amen! (*Lies out on floor*) Fill me with the Holy Ghost. Let me tremble with the Holy Ghost! (*Her body trembling with the Holy Ghost. On her feet*) Let me dance the dance of happiness! (*The* CHOIR *still can be heard humming.*) I want to dance the dance of happiness! (*She goes into a wild, frenzied dance.*) Let me speak in tongues, oh Lord. Twist my words into confusion, Jesus. Let the meaning of my words be withheld even from me. Only you, Jesus, and the beautiful Purple Angels understand my utterances. (*Still dancing, she speaks gibberish.*)

VOICE OF REVEREND GOODLOW: Amen!

CONGREGATION: Amen!!

ALBERTA (*falling to floor*): Amen. (*She is on her knees.*) Then they wheeled his body around for that last, final look. (*Again the "Father Alone" is hummed by the* CHOIR.) Oh, Jesus . . . (*Screams*) Emanuel! You're gone, Emanuel! Let me kiss you once. Never in life did I kiss you. Now in your never-ending sleep . . . I want to climb into the casket with you, Emanuel. (*Slight pause.*) I'm soaking wet, Emanuel! The sweat is pouring out of me! I want to climb in there with you and baptize you with my body fluids. Holy Ghost, take control over me. I can't control myself any more.

BLIND JORDAN (*out of the darkness*): Alberta!

(*The lights rise in the apartment.*)

ALBERTA: Oh, Lord!

BLIND JORDAN (*struggling to find her*): Alberta!

ALBERTA (*at the couch on her knees*): I want to kiss you again!

BLIND JORDAN (*finding her*): Stop it! Stop it, Alberta!

ALBERTA (*confused*): Emanuel?

BLIND JORDAN (*raising her to her feet*): Shhh! Shhh!

ALBERTA: I kissed you.

BLIND JORDAN: Yes.

ALBERTA: You're not Emanuel!

BLIND JORDAN: No.

ALBERTA: I want to kiss him one last, final time.

BLIND JORDAN (*embracing her*): No.

ALBERTA: You're not Emanuel.

BLIND JORDAN: I'm Jordan.

ALBERTA: Jordan?

BLIND JORDAN: The last of a long line of Blind Jordans.

ALBERTA: Jordan.

BLIND JORDAN: Shhh!

ALBERTA: Kiss me. Jordan. Please, kiss me.

(*He kisses her as the lights fade. The* CHOIR *from down the street rings out with "Father Alone."*)

ACT THREE

SCENE ONE

The light comes up on DOC *and* WEEDY, *alone in the apartment, at evening, several days later.* WEEDY *is seated at the window. She no longer rocks from the rhythm of the street below, but from a faraway interior rhythm that we cannot hear. She seems to have begun her process of withering away.* DOC *is in the kitchen, dressed in a brand new gray pinstripe suit and matching felt hat. He removes three bottles of whiskey from a brown paper bag, one of which he opens, and pours himself a drink.*

DOC: This may be the last drink I ever take in this house, Sister.

WEEDY: You done got your little money . . . gettin' ready to get on down th' road. I wouldn't expect you to stay here an' give me th' assistance I need.

DOC: I always said that when I hit th' number and got a few charlies in my pocket I'd be jumpin' back to Memphis.

WEEDY: Prosperity don't sit too well on some folks. Soon as they get a little money got, just go beside themselves, they commence to smell.

DOC: I'd rather have prosperity sit bad on me than have th' poor house sit good on me.

WEEDY: Yes, sir, money done sure made a fool outta you. Done went out here and bought that little sweet water suit. Makes you look like you're seekin' employment on th' chain gang.

DOC: That's th' one thing I ain't seekin'—employment.

WEEDY: If you had anything in you at all you'd throw that money right in Jordan's face.

DOC: I can think of a whole lotta things I'd throw in somebody's face before money.

WEEDY: You ain't nothin', Brother. You just ain't nothin'. You ain't even much what th' birds left.

DOC: I wouldn't give you fifteen cents for all this random talk.

WEEDY (*looking up to ceiling*): I'd rather see her dead and in her grave than turn out this way.

DOC: Stop that, Weedy!

WEEDY: You approve of this kind of conduct?

DOC: I don't approve or disapprove.

WEEDY: No, because you been cloakin' for them right along.

DOC: I ain't cloakin' for nobody. She's a full-grown woman. If you don't like it, all I can say is—move out.

WEEDY: Think you're goin' down to Memphis and be the big shot again, don't y'? Folks down there done forget you ever existed in this world.

DOC: How they gonna forget me? They still remember Sportin' Jimmy Sweet, the Prince of Beale Street!

WEEDY: Folks done forgot you so long ago it ain't even funny.

DOC: They ain't forgot me.

WEEDY: Just wait till you get on down there. You'll see. May as well stay here and help me. You ain't never done nothin' for her.

DOC (*her last remark strikes deep.*): Why did you have to come back? If you had stayed the allotted time out, Jordan might have been gone. Why did you have to come back?

WEEDY: Couldn't stay down there.

DOC: I put you on th' train to Montgomery. You were suppose to stay for two weeks. But you had to bring your behind back and catch 'em.

WEEDY: That wasn't th' convocation I usta know. No sir, Jesus, it wasn't. It wasn't no more th' convocation I usta know than my big toe is.

DOC: Couldn't you have just stayed down there for the whole time?

WEEDY: Them colored folks done gone crazy down there in Montgomery. They had turned that whole convocation all th' way 'round. Had to walk ev'rywhere . . . tellin' colored folks not to ride th' buses. I tell you I don't know what done got into them folks. I had to walk so much my feet was just about to kill me.

DOC: Why wouldn't they ride the buses?

WEEDY: Lawd, don't start me to lyin'. Some young preacher got 'em all stirred up—raisin' sand. They just push out the regular folks at th' convocation. They came into one of our meetin's hollerin' they didn't wanna hear no more fogeyism. Young folk. The mess ain't even wiped good from their behinds an' they're callin' folks fogies. Tellin' folks not to ride th' bus cause they didn't want to sit in th' back.

DOC: People stir up ev'ry once in a while. Ain't nothin' to all that.

WEEDY: They say they gonna carry it all over th' South.

DOC: Carry what all over th' South?

WEEDY: Not ridin' th' buses.

DOC: Let th' fools walk if they don't want to ride.

WEEDY: Bound you it will be in Memphis by th' time you get there.

DOC: Now, how is it gonna be Memphis?

WEEDY: I heard a woman say that when she got to Memphis she was gonna start tryin' to get th' colored folks there not to ride th' buses.

DOC: They better keep that foolishness away from Memphis. If they know like I know, they better. Why can't folks leave things alone? Stirrin' up things . . .

WEEDY: That's why you better stay right on up here in Chicago. There's gonna be a whole lotta troubles down home.

DOC: Not in Memphis.

WEEDY: Didn't I just get through tellin' you . . .

DOC: Them folks come to Memphis with their foolishness and ain't nobody gonna pay them bit more 'tention. They better keep their behinds outta Memphis if they know what's good for 'em. We ain't never had no trouble down there and there sure ain't gonna be none now. Memphis is a sportin' town. It ain't got no time for no mess. Folks is out lookin' to have a good time.

WEEDY: You just go on back down there and see. You'll be right back up here directly.

DOC: Naw, I ain't never comin' back to Chicago. Not in this life anyhow. (*There is a pause. He looks at* WEEDY, *who turns away and looks out of window.*) We're just about th' last ones left, Sister.

WEEDY: Yeap—th' last ones left.

DOC (*moves toward her*): Sister . . .

WEEDY: Brother! (*As he is moving toward her*) Don't kiss me! We ain't never been a kissin' set of folks.

DOC (*retreating*): Naw, we never were a kissin' set of folks.

(*They both are frozen in place as a key is heard in the door.* ALBERTA *enters and comes into living room.*)

ALBERTA: Hello, Uncle Doc.

DOC (*after a moment*): Ain't you two speakin'?

ALBERTA: She doesn't speak to me.

DOC: You two are sittin' up here in this house not speakin' to each other?

ALBERTA (*going into kitchen*): I'll speak to her when she speaks to me.

DOC (*coming into kitchen*): I don't approve of this, Alberta. Not speaking to your mother.

ALBERTA: What'd you want me to do? I've tried to talk to her but she won't answer me. Looks at me like something dirty lying in the street.

DOC: Kinda of a shock to come home an' find you . . .

ALBERTA: Layin' up with a man I ain't married to.

DOC: Your mama don't believe in that sorta thing. It ain't a nice thing to do.

ALBERTA: You got a lot of nerve, Uncle Doc. After all the women you've laid around with in your life.

DOC: But they weren't my flesh and blood.

ALBERTA: What about Mama?

DOC: What about her?

ALBERTA: You think I don't know?

DOC (*taking out his watch*): Listen, I've got to pick up Pearl . . . get my suitcase.

ALBERTA: You're not driving?

DOC: No, I sold my car. Remember—she's your mother.

ALBERTA: I remember. Oh, yes, I remember. (*She follows him to door.*)

DOC: I'll stop back by on my way to the train station. (*He exits.*)

(ALBERTA *looks at* WEEDY, *who is ignoring her.*)

ALBERTA: Mama . . .

WEEDY: I been 'buked and I been scorned
I been 'buked and I been scorned . . .

ALBERTA: Mama . . . I have to talk to you.

WEEDY: Jesus died to set me free . . .

ALBERTA (*getting an envelope out of her purse*): Mama, we have to move. Here's a letter from the city. Says this building has been condemned and they are going to tear it down.

WEEDY: I been 'buked and I been scorned
I been 'buked and I been scorned . . .

ALBERTA: Mama, you're gonna have to loan me the money to find another apartment.

WEEDY: I ain't got no money.

ALBERTA: Mama, you've got some money.

WEEDY: All I got is my little pension money. And I give that to Reverend Goodlow to put in my burial policy.

ALBERTA: We'll have to cash it in.

WEEDY: Cash it in! No, sir, Jesus!

ALBERTA: Mama, we have to move! They are going to tear the building down. Do you understand? This building has been condemned!

WEEDY: I been 'buked and I been scorned
I been 'buked and I been scorned . . .

ALBERTA: We can't stay here. Mama, you don't have to stay here. Papa is not coming back.

WEEDY: I ain't waitin' for him to come back! I wish that thing would come steppin' up here after he ran off. I'd set his soul to rest. I'd spit in his face! Ev'rytime that thing crosses my mind I get mad!

ALBERTA: You silly woman!

WEEDY: Let me tell you somethin', heifer! If you don't know who you foolin' with, you better ask somebody. Don't you be hollerin' at me. 'Cause I'll lay you cold as a milkshake! And you needn' be rollin' your eyes and pokin' out your mouth like you don't like it. And if you don't like it, smile and play like you do. An' you needn' be lookin' like you're gettin' ready to try me. 'Cause if you do, I'll hurt you.

ALBERTA: I'm not getting ready to try you.

WEEDY: I know you ain't. Unless you done lost your mind.

ALBERTA: I'm trying to explain to you we have to move.

WEEDY (*rising, going into her bedroom*): I reckon I'll lie down.

ALBERTA: Mama, the building is condemned!

WEEDY: What you hollerin' about, heifer? I ain't deaf. Ain't you got sense enough to know I hear you? (*Exits into bedroom, closing the door*)

ALBERTA (*flopping down on couch*): That woman's gonna worry me to . . . (*She cups her hand over her mouth. Fade out.*)

SCENE TWO

The lights fade in about an hour later. ALBERTA *and* JORDAN *are seated on the couch, dressed in their coats.* WEEDY, *also dressed in her coat, is seated at the window.*

ALBERTA: What time did Uncle Doc say he'd be coming back? Mama? (WEEDY *does not answer.*) If he doesn't hurry up, he'll be done missed his train.

BLIND JORDAN: What time does his train leave?

ALBERTA: Ten-thirty.

BLIND JORDAN: What time is it now?

ALBERTA: About nine.

BLIND JORDAN: Still got an hour and a half.

WEEDY (*after a long pause*): Mr. Jordan?

BLIND JORDAN: Yes, ma'm.

ALBERTA: Mama, don't start.

WEEDY: I ain't startin' nothin'. I just want to ask Mr. Jordan a question.

BLIND JORDAN: What is it, Mrs. Warren?

WEEDY: Are you plannin' to vacate th' premises anytime soon or have you decided to make this your permanent headquarters?

ALBERTA: Mama!

WEEDY: I only want to know so I can make my plans accordingly.

ALBERTA: He doesn't have to answer you anything.

BLIND JORDAN: Mrs. Warren? What is it you really want to know?

ALBERTA: You don't have to answer her. Don't pay her any attention Jordan. (*To* WEEDY) Why do you always have to keep up the devil?

BLIND JORDAN: What is it you want Alberta to know, Mrs. Warren?

WEEDY (*after a pause*): How many, do you reckon, red-light houses you done played your music box in, Mr. Jordan?

ALBERTA: Red-light houses . . .

BLIND JORDAN: What do you know about red-light houses?

WEEDY: I done covered a whole lotta road.

ALBERTA: You played in red-light houses?

BLIND JORDAN: Quite a few.

ALBERTA: Red-light houses!

BLIND JORDAN: I was born in a red-light house. The same house—same room—exact same bed my father was born in. A place called the Sty of the Blind Pig.

WEEDY: A house down in New Orleans. He's got the smell of blood on him, Alberta. I could smell it the minute he walked into this house.

ALBERTA: How do you know so much about it?

WEEDY: Sure as I'm sittin' here he's got th' smell of blood on him.

BLIND JORDAN: She's right—I do have the smell of blood on me. The smell of butchered pig. That smell gets into your pores—can't wash it off.

ALBERTA: I don't smell anything.

BLIND JORDAN: I can smell it on myself! The smell of the bowels of the pig. All the parts that the others threw away were brought to the sty and cooked in scaldin'-hot water. Sometimes that hot water got thrown into someone's face. You ever hear a man's scream when he had been scalded by the hot water where the pig had been cooked in? It started with the butchering of th' pig . . . men died in th' Sty of the Blind Pig. So did women.

ALBERTA: What kind of women?

BLIND JORDAN: Women who sold their bodies in the Sty of the Blind

Pig. Women who carried knives and cut their pimps when the shame overtook them. And pimps who cut up their women because they had lost their manhood. I've played my music box in places where men and women stood toe to toe and cut each other to pieces while cursin' their own mothers for birthin' them into this world. They've fallen on me with th' blood just oozin' out of them. And I could smell th' flesh of th' pig that had mixed in with their blood.

ALBERTA: You're making this up.

BLIND JORDAN: An' th' ones that was left from Saturday night got up on Sunday mornin' an' went to church to pray for those that had been slaughtered th' night before.

ALBERTA: She told you to say all this, didn't she?

WEEDY: I ain't told him nothin'.

ALBERTA: Lies! You're making this all up! Why, Jordan? Because you want to go back and hunt for Grace Waters again!

BLIND JORDAN (*raising his shirt*): Makin' it up! Haven't you seen this?

WEEDY: Look like somebody tried to cut your guts out.

BLIND JORDAN: Ain't you seen it?

ALBERTA: No! And I don't want to see it!

BLIND JORDAN: Look at it.

ALBERTA: Put your shirt down!

BLIND JORDAN: How could you lay up with me and not see it?

ALBERTA: I've never noticed it.

BLIND JORDAN: You want to know how I got it?

ALBERTA: No!

BLIND JORDAN: A woman gave it to me.

WEEDY: What woman?

ALBERTA: I don't want to hear about it.

WEEDY: What woman put her mark on you, Mr. Jordan?

BLIND JORDAN: A woman that I killed. I choked her to death as she tried to cut me to death.

ALBERTA: Then why ain't you in jail?

BLIND JORDAN: There ain't no punishment for killin' a nigger woman on Saturday night. You just go to church on Sunday mornin' an' pray.

WEEDY: This is what you been layin' up here with! This is what you brought into th' house.

ALBERTA: You any better than he is!

WEEDY: What?

ALBERTA: Running down to the church carrying on with Reverend Goodlow.

WEEDY: What are you talkin' about?

ALBERTA: You been going with him for over forty years.

WEEDY: Where did you get that from?

ALBERTA: Why do you think Papa ran off?

WEEDY: Because he didn't have no grit in his craw.

ALBERTA: He found out about you and Reverend Goodlow.

WEEDY: That fool's accused me of havin' Reverend Goodlow before we even much left th' South. Reverend Goodlow was pastorin' a church down there, and he swore up and down that I was messin' around with him.

ALBERTA: And you kept on when you got up here.

WEEDY: I didn't even know that man was in Chicago when we moved up here. Did that thing tell you all of this?

ALBERTA: Everybody around that church knows it. I guess Papa got tired of everybody pointing at him like he was a fool.

WEEDY: That ain't why he ran off.

ALBERTA: I know better.

WEEDY: He ran off because he didn't believe that you were his.

ALBERTA: Didn't believe I was his.

WEEDY: Kept accusin' me of Reverend Goodlow for so long he commence to see him in you.

ALBERTA: You're a liar!

WEEDY: Don't you call me no liar! I bound I'll slap you clear into next week. Your daddy with his ole strange ways . . . Never did think he could make no baby. When I was carryin' you he use to holler that he was too weak to make a baby.

ALBERTA: Was I . . . ?

WEEDY: What?

ALBERTA: Was I his?

WEEDY: You better get away from me!

ALBERTA: Tell me the truth.

WEEDY (*sitting down*): Go on away from me, gal, before I knock you clear into next week.

ALBERTA (*looking at* BLIND JORDAN, *then at* WEEDY): I wish that I had never laid eyes on either one of you two. What's that Sister Martin always hollers out? How long! How long, oh Lord! How long!

BLIND JORDAN: Alberta?

ALBERTA: Don't come near me, please.

BLIND JORDAN: That life is gone. They done tore down th' Sty of the Blind Pig. Even th' blind street singers are dyin' out.

ALBERTA: Let them all die out. Let us all die out. Make room for somebody else. The sooner the better.

(*There is a pause.*)

DOC (*offstage*): Hey, y'all! (*Bangs on door*)

ALBERTA (*opening door.*): It's Uncle Doc. (DOC *enters. He is in a state of shock. His face is swollen and bloody, and his clothes have been torn.*) What happen to you?

WEEDY: Brother!

DOC (*moving to couch*): They jumped me!

BLIND JORDAN: What is it? What's wrong?

WEEDY (*coming to couch*): What happen to you?

DOC: They tried to rob me.

WEEDY: Who tried to rob you?

DOC: Pearl and some young cat. Tried to take my money away from me. Threw me down th' stairs.

ALBERTA: They get it?

DOC (*almost breaking*): I woulda shared it with her. I would have taken her back to Memphis with me. She woulda been somebody down there with me. (*Pause.*) I sure don't think she'd do me thataway. Wish I never had hit th' numbers. Rather not have hit them than have her do this to me. Them goddamn triple zeros!

WEEDY: You're gonna destroy us all, Mr. Jordan.

(*Fade out.*)

SCENE THREE

The lights come up several hours later. The apartment is dark and empty. We hear the sound of the key in the lock. WEEDY *enters followed by* ALBERTA.

WEEDY: Mr. Jordan? (*Snaps on light*) Mr. Jordan?

ALBERTA: I told you he wouldn't be here.

WEEDY: Maybe he got lost in th' train station. He was standin' right next to me when you went off to get th' magazines for Brother. I looked around an' he was gone. Well, maybe he'll make it back all right.

ALBERTA: I told you he's not coming back.

WEEDY: Did you tell him not to come back?

ALBERTA: No.

WEEDY: But you know he's not comin' back.

ALBERTA: Yes. (*There is a pause.*) Was he ever really here?

WEEDY: Huh?

ALBERTA: I was just wonderin' something out loud.

WEEDY: What was that?

ALBERTA: Just something that passed through my mind.

WEEDY (*after a pause*): Well, Brother's ridin' now.

ALBERTA: Riding South.

WEEDY: I wonder where all them young folks was goin'?

ALBERTA: Young folks?

WEEDY: Didn't you see 'em? Got on th' same train with Brother. Lord, they sure looked a mess. Ev'ryone of 'em had nappy hair.

ALBERTA: Nappy hair?

WEEDY: Look like they woulda gone to th' beauty parlor an' got their hair straighten 'fore they went off visitin'.

ALBERTA: Yes, I saw them. They did all have nappy hair, didn't they? Funny, I didn't even think about it until you brought it up. But now that you mention it . . .

WEEDY: Lord, never would I go off travelin' with my head lookin' like that.

ALBERTA: Sometimes I wish that I hadn't started straightening mine. Maybe it wouldn't be half burned-out now. (*She moves to window and sits in rocking chair.*)

WEEDY: Y'know somethin'—I was thinkin'. You look for another place. I'll talk to . . . Reverend Goodlow and maybe I can draw out somethin' on my funeral savin's plan.

ALBERTA: You don't have to do that.

WEEDY: Well, if they're condemnin' th' buildin' . . .

ALBERTA: They probably won't be tearing it down for a little while yet.

WEEDY: Think we oughta wait until they commence to destroy it right over our heads?

ALBERTA: Ain't no need in getting in a rush now.

WEEDY: Think we got time?

ALBERTA: Time enough, I reckon.

WEEDY: Well, anythin' you want to do is all right with me.

ALBERTA: All right.

WEEDY: From here on in I guess everythin' is up to you.

ALBERTA: Up to me?

WEEDY: If you want to draw all the money out of the funeral plan—all right by me.

ALBERTA: Now you say that. After it's all over and done with you say that.

WEEDY: What's all over and done with?

ALBERTA: Everything.

WEEDY: I don't have the slightest idea of what you're talkin' about.

ALBERTA: Why don't you go to bed, Mama?

WEEDY: Yes, I am tired. (*Moves to door*) What did you mean? Everythin's all over and done with.

ALBERTA: You know what I mean, Mama.

WEEDY: No, I don't.

ALBERTA: You just think about it. Sleep on it. It'll come to you.

WEEDY: Not tired as I am, I won't think about nothin'. All I want to do is lay my head down on that pillow.

ALBERTA: Good-night.

WEEDY: Good-night. (*She enters the bedroom.*)

(*The lights dim to suggest the passing of time.*)

ALBERTA (*rocking at the window*): Well, sir, will you look at that. Look at her strut. Struttin' like she was th' best-lookin' thing on the street. (*She rises, raises window.*) Hey, you! Yes, I'm talkin' to you. You sure oughta go somewhere and take off that red dress and do somethin' about your behind shakin'. It's bouncing like a rubber ball. You needin' be tryin' to ignore me—you hear me! (*Sits down*) Lord, these young folks ain't a bit of count nowadays. They just ain't nothin'. They ain't even much what th' birds left. Like I was sayin' to Mama just th' other day . . . Mama! Mama? (*She rises and crosses to* WEEDY'*s bedroom, opens door.*) Mama? Where are you, Mama? (*She goes into her own room.*) Mama . . . Come back, Mama! (*She comes back to window.*) Oh, Mama . . . you're layin' out there all by yourself. Mama!

(*The sound of a* CHOIR *is heard.*)

CHOIR: Father alone knows all about it
Father alone understands why
Cheer up, my brother, walk in the sunshine
You'll understand all by and by . . .

ALBERTA: I'm all right, Mama! I'm all right! (CHOIR, *humming.*) Because I got grit in my craw. I got a whole lotta grit in my craw!

(*Fade out.*)

Daughters of the Mock

JUDI ANN MASON

Left to right: Barbara Montgomery as ORALIA, *Frances Foster as* MAUMAU, *and Olivia Williams as* MANEDA *in a production of* Daughters of the Mock. *Photograph copyright © 1979 by Bert Andrews, from* In the Shadow of the Great White Way: Images from the Black Theatre *(Thunder's Mouth Press), copyright © 1989. Reprinted by permission of Marsha Hudson, the Estate of Bert Andrews.*

Judi Ann Mason has been writing professionally since the age of nineteen, beginning with the 1975 NEC Off-Broadway production of her Norman Lear Award winning comedy, *Livin' Fat*. Her plays have been produced in theaters across the country, and Ms. Mason has also written for television, including the award-winning *I'll Fly Away* where she served as executive story editor and also as associate head writer for NBC's first interracial daytime serial, *Generations*. Her first full-length feature, *Knockin' At Heaven's Door* was produced by Walt Disney Productions and adapted by Mason to Whoopi Goldberg's *Sister Act 2*. Since, she has written features for Denzel Washington and Disney's upcoming animated adaptation of *The Hunchback of Notre Dame* and is currently adapting a novel to film for the Hallmark Hall of Fame series. She is a theater graduate of Grambling University and has had fellowships from Louisiana State University, Stanford University, and the Ohio State University.

Daughters of the Mock was produced in New York by the NEC at the St. Marks Playhouse, and opened December 20, 1978, with the following cast:

Maumau	Frances Foster
Amanita	Michele Shay
Maneda	Olivia Williams
Oralia	Barbara Montgomery
Gail	L. Scott Caldwell

Directed by Glenda Dickerson; scenery by Wynn Thomas; lighting by Larry Johnson; costumes by Alvin Perry; stage managed by Clinton Turner Davis.

Daughters of the Mock

CHARACTERS
in order of appearance
MAUMAU
AMANITA
MANEDA
ORALIA
GAIL

TIME
The past.
The present.
The future.

PLACE
In southern Louisiana.

SECTION
A region of the mind.

ACT ONE : Scene One

When the lights come up, we see MAUMAU *sitting in her chair making flowers. She seems much into herself when suddenly her ears perk, and she raises her head. Moments later, we see what she reacted to—we hear footsteps coming toward the house and a knock at the door. It is* AMANITA, *her granddaughter.* MAUMAU *rises and moves to the door.*

AMANITA (*entering, kisses* MAUMAU): Hello, Maumau. You okay?

(MAUMAU *nods "no" and beckons toward the kitchen.*)

What? You need something?

(MAUMAU *nods "no."*)

Neda in there? Maumau?

(MAUMAU *nods "no."*)

Maumau, I wish you would talk to me. One of these days, I'm gon make you talk to me. One day, the urge will get too strong for you, and you will have to talk to me.

(MAUMAU *hands her a flower.*)

Thank you, Maumau. They are real pretty. I'll put 'em in my room. They been selling well?

(MAUMAU *nods "yes."*)

At school I set the bouquet you made me right over my bed and everybody wanted to know where I got it.

(MAUMAU *smiles.*)

Is Neda feeling any better?

(MAUMAU *looks at her—not understanding.*)

She been here yet?

(MAUMAU *nods "no."* MANEDA *knocks on the door.* MAUMAU *beckons for* AMANITA *to answer.* AMANITA *moves to the door and opens it. Enter* MANEDA. *She moves to the closet and puts up her purse.*)

Hi.

MANEDA: Evening. Evening, Maumau.

(MAUMAU *nods*)

AMANITA: Where have you been?

MANEDA: Out. . . . I took a walk. I had a headache.

AMANITA: That headache had you looking like you'd lost your best friend!

(MAUMAU *stares.*)

MANEDA (*uncomfortable—*MAUMAU *yet stares*): I just had a headache, Maumau. That's all. Just a headache. It wasn't anything else—

(MAUMAU *rises, moves toward the front door.*)

Maumau, it was just a headache! Maumau—

(MAUMAU *is gone. There is an uncomfortable silence.*)

AMANITA: What was that all about?

MANEDA: I wish you hadn't said anything.

AMANITA: What's going on, Neda?

NEDA: Nothing. (*She sighs heavily and plops down on the sofa.*)

AMANITA: Something is the matter. The few days I've been home, you've been acting like you're in a daze. Why don't you tell me about it?

MANEDA: It's nothing I can't get over. I better get over it.

AMANITA: What?

MANEDA: I keep trying to get it out of my mind, but I can't. I try to forget but I can't forget them!

AMANITA: Forget who?

MANEDA: My husband, my babies. My two little baby boys.

AMANITA: You're not supposed to forget them. Your husband, your children—Why should you forget them.

MANEDA: It's been three years now since . . .

AMANITA: I know. . . .

MANEDA: Three years ago today. Today I went to the graveyard where they are buried. Side by side. I stood there and kept wishing that it was me lying in those graves. Why it had to be them?

AMANITA: I guess God wanted it that way—

MANEDA: Naw, God didn't want it that way. It wasn't his will they were taken away.

AMANITA: I wan't old enough to remember when Daddy died, but I can imagine what it's like. . . . I sympathize for you. I care. I feel. . . .

MANEDA (*hugging her*): Thank you, Amanita. Forgive me these last few days for only thinking about my own feelings. I'm glad you're back home.

AMANITA: Glad to be back—even though it's just for a brief time. . . .

MANEDA: Only a brief time? I thought you said you weren't going back to school. . . .

AMANITA: I'm not.

MANEDA: I'm glad to hear that. You know how happy Mama is about that. She wants you close to home.

AMANITA: Well, I think she better adjust to the idea that I won't be home—

MANEDA: What's that?

AMANITA: I have something to show you— (*She rises and moves to her purse, gets a letter out and returns to* MANEDA.) Read it.

MANEDA: Ohhhh . . . a letter from that history major, huh?

AMANITA: Yeah, read it.

MANEDA: You sure you want me to?

AMANITA: Sure, why not? Go 'head, read it.

MANEDA: Okay. (*She opens the letter and reads:*)

"Dear Nita. School has been out for only four days and I miss you already. Actually nothing is happening here except Professor Jolens has . . ."

AMANITA: Skip that part.

MANEDA: Where do you want me to start?

AMANITA: Read further down . . . where it says "I'm going to try . . ."

MANEDA: Okay. (*Scans letter*)

"I'm going to try to come down there in a week or so. I made a trip to the jewelers the day after you left. I found a ring that I thought would be perfect for you. As soon as you give me the word, I'll come down there to get you and take you as my—" (MANEDA *folds the letter.*)

AMANITA: Finish reading it, Neda.

MANEDA: You write him back and tell him no. Tell him that you don't want to get married.

AMANITA: Do what?

MANEDA: You can't!

AMANITA: What do you mean, I can't?

MANEDA: Mama won't allow it.

AMANITA: Mama has nothing to do with it.

MANEDA: Amanita, listen to me. You're still young with a lot of times ahead of you.

AMANITA: And I want to spend them married.

MANEDA: You just met this boy.

AMANITA: What difference does that make. I've known him since I first started college. Long enough to know I love him.

MANEDA (*with strange force*): No, you don't!

AMANITA: Neda, what's wrong with you?

MANEDA: Mama will never allow it!

AMANITA: Mama could stop boys from coming to see me when I was a little girl, but now I make my own decisions.

MANEDA: Take this letter and burn it, Amanita. We won't talk about it no more, hear?

AMANITA: Why can't we talk about it?

(*Enter* ORALIA. *The girls hush.*)

ORALIA: Talk about what?

MANEDA: Nothing, Mama. How are you?

ORALIA: Just tired, Maneda. My classes were really busy today. What were you girls talking about?

MANEDA: Nothing.

ORALIA: That's a fine thing to spend time talking about.

MANEDA: Just girl talk. (MANEDA *takes the letter and folds it in her bosom.*)

ORALIA: How are you, daughter?

AMANITA: Fine, Mama.

ORALIA: Anything wrong?

AMANITA: Nothing. (*She crosses to the door.*)

ORALIA: Where are you going?

AMANITA: To Gail's house. I need some fresh air. . . . (*She exits.*)

ORALIA: What's that all about? And don't tell me "nothing."

MANEDA: Everyday things get more and more complicated, Mama. . . . I thought they were to be different.

ORALIA: Things are different.

MANEDA: The only difference is that I have no man. . . . I miss him, Mama. There's no fooling myself about it. And it hurts even more because I can't show it. (*She starts to cry.*)

ORALIA: Now you stop that! You know you do not cry!

MANEDA: Then what am I to do?

ORALIA: You are to wipe the memory of that man from your mind. You are to forget you had two sons. Why suddenly bring this up today?

MANEDA: Today is the day they—

ORALIA: They died. . . . It's been three years, Maneda.

MANEDA: Three years I held it in . . . but now—

ORALIA: But now, but now, daughter, but now, you will hold back those tears as you have done for three years. You know what will happen if you don't. And there is nothing I can do to relieve you.

MANEDA: You must have loved Daddy, Mama? When he died . . . you missed him didn't you?

ORALIA (*pausing*): I don't want to talk about it.

MANEDA: Why not, Mama? Doesn't it feel good to think of the days you had with him? Don't your body ache when you remember his touch? I know it does.

ORALIA: It was a long time ago.

MANEDA: Not long enough for you to forget.

ORALIA: I have forgotten. And you will forget, too, Maneda. There is no good in thinking! It only makes things worse for yourself. You are born into this life and that is the way it must be.

MANEDA: Now it is Amanita's turn.

ORALIA: What are you talking, daughter?

MANEDA: She met a man. . . .

ORALIA: Where?

MANEDA: At school.

ORALIA: She didn't tell me that.

MANEDA: I think she knew not to.

ORALIA: How do you know?

MANEDA (*retrieving the letter*): This. (*Hands the letter to* ORALIA.)

ORALIA (*after reading the letter*): She can not. . . .

MANEDA: I told her that, Mama, but she is determined.

ORALIA: She is too young.

MANEDA: We both knew too well that she can not be stopped unless—

ORALIA: Unless what?

MANEDA: Unless Maumau never finds out.

ORALIA: You just said yourself that she can not be stopped. But why couldn't she wait?

MANEDA: Wait for what, Mama? It waits for us. . . . we never wait for it.

ORALIA: Be quiet.

MANEDA: Mama, Amanita is a baby. We can't let this happen to her.

ORALIA: You plan to clean my womb and your grandmother's womb? Even if she is sent away, it will follow her, just as it has followed you and me.

MANEDA: Mama, please! Look at me! I am no good to myself anymore. Are you willing to let another of your flesh and blood suffer as I have?

ORALIA: I suffered! Maumau suffered, too.

MANEDA: But her suffering should not be passed on to us!

ORALIA: Hush, she'll hear you.

MANEDA (*in a whisper*): Please, Mama. Don't tell Maumau. We can try to talk to Amanita.

ORALIA: How can I keep it from her? Do we ever have to tell her anything? She knows things even before they happen. She knows. There has never been a day in my life that I have kept a secret . . . from her.

MANEDA: Just stay away from her until we can deal with Amanita. If she is not around you, she can not read you. Mama, please, Amanita is not ready! (*Pause.*) If you love her, don't let her suffer—

ORALIA: I cannot stop her from suffering. . . .

MANEDA: Not stop it—just delay it. Let her *live*, Mama, let her live a few more years of her life. Don't let her die, so soon.

ORALIA: She does not die.

MANEDA: It is just like death, Mama. I can attest to it. There is nothing else worse.

ORALIA (*pausing, looking at* MANEDA): Daughter, I know how you feel. I know your pain too well. I will try—

MANEDA (*embracing her mother*): Mama, mama. It is too painful. Too hurting. . . . They never did anybody harm. . . .

ORALIA: I know, daughter. *But the blood must be made pure. . . . . And the enemy must be destroyed. . . . .*

(*Enter* MAUMAU)

MAUMAU: *De enemy shall be made weak. De image o' de enemy must be wiped away. And de blood will be made pure. Never to suffer under de hands o' de enemy. Again. To carry de mock . . .*
ORALIA: *To carry the mock—*
MAUMAU: *To carry de mock.*
MANEDA: *To carry the mock.*

(*End of scene*)

(NOTE: *As each scene ends the lights fade to the next. One, two, three-second count*)

ACT ONE : Scene Two

Fade in.

Interior.

As the lights come up, MAUMAU *is seated in her chair making her flowers. She again sits much to herself. Suddenly she throws her work down and grabs her right eye. It pains her, so she cries out in pain. Her cry is at first light, then in a crescendo, it rises to a shrill peak. Then as quickly as the pain came, it goes away.* MAUMAU *slowly brings her hand down from her eye. She stares straight ahead, seemingly taking in the past event. The expression on her face goes from confusion to anger. Suddenly, her head turns and her ears perk toward the door. We hear footsteps moments later and a knock at the door—*MAUMAU *rises and moves to open it. It is* AMANITA *and her friend,* GAIL.

AMANITA: Hello, Maumau.

(MAUMAU *stares at* AMANITA.)

What's wrong?

(MAUMAU *nods "no" and smiles. She hugs* AMANITA.)

GAIL: Hi, Miss Justine. You feeling okay these days?

(MAUMAU *nods "yes," moves to remove her flowers from the table.*)

AMANITA: Did you work your garden?

(MAUMAU *nods "yes."*)

GAIL: Look, Nita, I didn't mean no harm. It's just that you said they all got you worried.

AMANITA: Maumau's not talking doesn't have anything to do with my Mama's feelings.

GAIL: Lotsa folks' mamas don't want them to get married. . . .

AMANITA: My mama has an obsession with it. If it hadn't been for Maumau, I wouldn't have even gone away to college.

GAIL: Nita, let me ask you something. . . . you ever heard anything about your grandma?

AMANITA: Like what?

GAIL: Like what? Well . . . like—

AMANITA: Like what, Gail?

GAIL: Like . . . well . . . it was probably just some crazy talk. . . .

AMANITA: What kinda crazy talk?

GAIL: Well . . .

AMANITA: Gail, what are you talking about?

GAIL: Some folks say your grandma got a curse on her.

AMANITA: What?

GAIL: I told you it was probably just some crazy talk.

AMANITA: Where'd you hear something like that?

GAIL: Around. . . . You know you hear things when you growing up.

AMANITA: How come I never heard anything like that?

GAIL: Who in their right mind would come up and ask you something like that? Besides, all the kids were scared of you. . . .

AMANITA: Gail—

GAIL: They were! They used to call me a fool for hanging around you. They said I had a spell on me—

AMANITA: My grandmother is no more strange than anybody else's.

GAIL: It wasn't that she was strange. . . . They say she tried to make this other lady pay her rent for something and that lady put a curse on your grandmother. . . .

AMANITA: What kind of curse?

GAIL: Ain't you ever noticed nothing odd about your family?

AMANITA: Odd?

GAIL: What don't you have in your family that everybody else got?

AMANITA: What?

GAIL: What do I have in my family that you don't have in yours?

AMANITA (*pausing*): A daddy. . . . But lots of people don't have daddies—

GAIL: Not just daddies . . .

AMANITA: What?

GAIL: Men.

AMANITA: Men?

GAIL: There ain't no men in your family!

AMANITA: So?

GAIL: Don't you find that strange?

AMANITA: So the men in my family have short lives. . . .

GAIL: Short? The men in your family have *no* lives.

AMANITA: Gail, you're not helping me!

GAIL: Don't get upset, Nita. But you hear things like that all the time down here. Louisiana is full of folks that know that stuff—

AMANITA: Know what stuff?

GAIL: Voodoo.

AMANITA: That's just a local bunch of junk, Gail—

GAIL: Naw, it ain't, Nita, I tell ya. People put stuff in your food and put salt over your door, lotsa people down here know roots. I know you done heard of Doctor John in Opelousas—

AMANITA: What does Doctor John have to do with me?

GAIL: Well, you heard about the things he can do. Just don't call it a bunch of junk when you know very well it ain't—

AMANITA: It is a bunch of junk.

GAIL: Nita, you grew up around these bayous! You know—

AMANITA: All I know is that I want to get married to a man that I love, and my mama may not like the idea. . . .

GAIL: Maybe she know about the curse. . . .

AMANITA: There is no curse!

GAIL: It's either a curse or that other thing I heard. . . .

AMANITA: What other thing?

GAIL: Nothing!

(*Enter* ORALIA)

ORALIA: Well, it seems that I have the good fortune of walking in on very interesting conversations these days. . . . did I interrupt something?

AMANITA (*after pause*): No, Mama.

ORALIA (*staring at* AMANITA *then without looking at* GAIL—): Hello, Gail. How are you?

GAIL: I'm fine, Miss Oralia. Just fine . . . uh . . .

ORALIA: Good. And you, daughter?

AMANITA: I'm okay, Mama. (*She moves away, avoiding her mother's stare.*)

GAIL: I'm ready to go, Amanita.

AMANITA: I'll go with you.

ORALIA: Where are you on your way to?

AMANITA: Over to Gail's.

ORALIA: Why don't you visit Gail tomorrow. I want to talk to you.

AMANITA: About what?

ORALIA: Since when do you ask me what I want to talk to you about?

GAIL: I gotta go, Nita, I'll talk to you tomorrow—

AMANITA: Wait, Gail, I'm going with you—

ORALIA: Amanita, I told you to stay.

AMANITA: Mama, I'm going with Gail.

GAIL (*at the door*): We'll talk tomorrow, Amanita. . . .

ORALIA: Good-night, Gail.

GAIL: Good-night, Miss Oralia. (*She exits.*)

AMANITA: Mama, why did you do that? I'm not a child any more—

ORALIA: Under me, Amanita, you will always be a child.

AMANITA: That's just it, Mama. . . . I'll always be a child *under* you. But I'm not supposed to be under you. (*She finds herself yelling at her mother.* ORALIA *just stares, seemingly undaunted. Then, quietly—*) I guess Neda told you?

ORALIA (*now showing some sign of movement*): Yes, she did. . . . and you know my feelings about it so there is no need to discuss it any further.

AMANITA: No need?

ORALIA: Amanita, I suggest that you refrain from raising your voice to me.

AMANITA: I'm sorry, Mama, you made me yell. You never listen to me. You haven't even asked me what I wanted to do—

ORALIA: What you want to do is not important.

AMANITA: Why?

ORALIA (*quickly*): Where is Maumau?

AMANITA: She went to bed. Why?

ORALIA: Are you sure?

AMANITA: I asked her was she going to bed and she nodded yes. But then she could have been saying something else since she never talks to me. . . .

ORALIA: If you had remained here instead of going away to college she may have talked to you.

AMANITA: I didn't want to go to college here.

ORALIA: It was good enough for your sister and me—

AMANITA: I'm different, Mama.

ORALIA: You are not different, daughter! You are the same as we are . . . and that might be your downfall, Amanita.

AMANITA: What does that mean?

ORALIA: It means that you can not and will not marry this man.

AMANITA: Momma, he is a good man. He loves me and I love him.

ORALIA: You are too young!

AMANITA: Too young? Mama I am twenty years old!

ORALIA: I was twenty-eight and your sister was twenty-eight when she married. You will be too—

AMANITA: I don't believe this. My mama just gave me an age to fall in love . . .

ORALIA: It is an age to give you a chance to live—

AMANITA: What are you talking about, Mama?

ORALIA: Do not raise your voice to me, Amanita. Do not raise your voice to me. (*Pause.*) I have spoken to you once about my feelings, daughter. You are to wipe the thought of that man from your mind. You are to forget his name, his face, his features. You are to erase every memory of his existence from your thoughts—

AMANITA: You must be crazy, Mama—

ORALIA: Do not raise your voice to me, Amanita. I will not tell you again—

AMANITA: Mama, I don't know what is going on in this family. I don't even want to think about it, but whatever it is, it is not enough to make me change my mind. So don't even try, please, Mama don't even try! (AMANITA *crosses to the door.*)

ORALIA: Amanita!

AMANITA: Yes, Mama?

ORALIA: I understand more than you think. . . . It is because I love you that I am against it. Please, for your sake, wait, daughter. . . . wait—

AMANITA: No, Mama.

(AMANITA *exits.* ORALIA *moves away slowly, she seems to be begging for some relief. She is on the verge of tears when from what seems like nowhere* MAUMAU *appears. She watches* ORALIA *a moment. Then—*)

MAUMAU (*in a Creole brogue, a lot less polished than her offspring, but her voice strong and quiet*): Your daughter, she find herself a man, eh?

ORALIA: Maumau . . . how long you been standing there?

MAUMAU: Dat one of yours, she start it young, yes. So young . . .

ORALIA: I should have known you would already know.

MAUMAU: Daughter, you worry yourself too much about tings you know don't change. I always know—

ORALIA: But she is so young, Maumau.

MAUMAU: De time now be right, daughter. Right now, no tomorrow no next day. De time be now when she know de truth about de man. Be she blind till she old and worn like I be? No, de time be now—

ORALIA: Maumau—

MAUMAU: De time be now!

ORALIA (*slowly realizing her mother's words*): Yes, Maumau, the time be now.

MAUMAU: Your other one, Maneda. She need you to talk to her, yes.

ORALIA: Why?

MAUMAU: Standing over the grave of dat man and her two boy-chiles. Dropping golden tears on de dirt throwed on dem.

ORALIA: She is still in mourning for them. . . .

MAUMAU: She is of de womb of my womb. After de mock be carried, there be no mourning, daughter. Bring me her—

ORALIA: I will talk to her, Maumau—

MAUMAU: Bring me her!

(*With no further hesitation,* ORALIA *crosses left and calls for* MANEDA.)

ORALIA: Maneda? Come here.

(ORALIA *looks at* MAUMAU *and then crosses to sit in the chair behind* MAUMAU. *Enter* MANEDA)

MANEDA: Yes, Mama? . . . (*She notices* MAUMAU *standing, watching at her every move.*) You called me?

MAUMAU: Granddaughter, you be good. Answer me these questions. Answer me with de trute. Where be de love you had fuh dat man?

(MANEDA *pauses.*)

(MAUMAU *repeats*) Where be de love you had fuh dat man?

(ORALIA *tells* MANEDA *to answer.*)

MANEDA: *The image of the enemy has been wiped away.* . . .

MAUMAU: Why dis love from you be took?

MANEDA: *So that the blood be made pure.*

MAUMAU: And who you be?

MANEDA: *I am a woman.*

MAUMAU: And who you be?

MANEDA: *I am a woman.*

MAUMAU: Why you be here?

MANEDA: *The enemy shall be made weak. And I, as a woman, shall make the blood pure. Never to suffer under the hands of the enemy again. To carry the mock—*

MAUMAU: Close your lips to dose words, granddaughter. Day speak no trute.

MANEDA: *To carry the mock, Maumau—*

MAUMAU: You make your burden heavy, yes, granddaughter. You bring more pain to your soul. You don't see the pain you yet allow dat man to bring you? Each day he be in the bed of yo mind, he bring pain. Yo strent be snatched 'way from you. Your blood be pure, granddaughter, you carry the mock. You be de daughter of de mock . . . of de blood of Justine. No daughter of the mock sheds her golden tears on de ground of a man. De love of the husband be made weak. De love of de boychiles be washed away. Or your suffering be long and never do be ended.

MANEDA: Yes, Maumau.

(MAUMAU *turns away without expression and crosses left. Before exiting, she turns and speaks to* ORALIA.)

MAUMAU: De time be now for your other one. Tomorrow night be fine.

(MAUMAU *exits.* MANEDA *tries to hold her tears in.* ORALIA *stands.*)

MANEDA: Mama. . . .
ORALIA: Hush, daughter. . . .
MANEDA: Mama. . . .
ORALIA: Shhhh. . . .
MANEDA: Mama. . . .
ORALIA: Hold in your pain. . . . With all your strength . . . hold in your pain. I feel that same pain, daughter, only I can not show it. Shhhh. . . .

(*The lights dim slowly, gradually fading into two single lights on* MANEDA, *who is crying, and her mother, who stands on an opposite part of the room. Still, statuesque. The two single spots gradually fade out.*)

(*End of scene*)

ACT ONE : Scene Three

Fade in.

Interior.

As the lights come up, MANEDA *is dusting the table* MAUMAU *makes her flowers on. Moments later,* MAUMAU *enters carrying a crow sack in her hands.* MANEDA *notices her and stops working.* MAUMAU *stops, looks at* MANEDA, *and beckons for her to come to her.* MANEDA *moves to* MAUMAU. MAUMAU *opens the crow sack and* MANEDA *looks in it. Instantly, she goes to a storage area and retrieves a wooden jar with a top. The top of the jar is wrapped in a canvas-type cloth, very tightly sealed.* MAUMAU *pours the contents of her sack into the jar. It looks like just a lot of weeds. After the contents are in the jar,* MANEDA *covers the jar again and wraps the cloth around it and places it in its place again.*

MAUMAU: Jimson weed for the other one. Make a tea. (MAUMAU *crosses to her room.*) When de gull come in dere, I be back.

(MAUMAU *exits.* MANEDA *cautiously waits until she is sure* MAUMAU *is out of earshot and she goes to the sofa to sit. She carefully takes off her left shoe. She removes the inside sole and pulls out a vertically folded photograph. She looks at the picture a moment then brings it slowly to her lips, kissing it. Then she brings it slowly down her face and neck until it reaches her bosom. She holds it to her breast as though it were giving her some source of life.*)

MANEDA: My husband, whose name I can hardly remember, my son, whose tender life was snatched away from him, my baby, whose newborn flesh never lived two full days of his life. . . . those whose flesh became my flesh . . . those whose blood was not pure.

(AMANITA *quietly enters from the entrance door, stands listening to* MANEDA.)

The love I have for you, will never die. I ask forgiveness for my birth because my birth meant your death—

AMANITA (*totally amazed by her sister's words*): Maneda, what does all that mean?

MANEDA (*turning quickly*): Amanita . . .

AMANITA (*moving to* MANEDA): What were you saying, Maneda?

MANEDA: Amanita, you don't understand . . .

AMANITA: What do those things mean?

MANEDA (*folding the picture, quickly putting it back in her shoe*): Hush, you're talking too loud.

AMANITA: Maneda, tell me what's going on here.

MANEDA: Amanita, just forget that you saw me doing that. I was just depressed. . . .

AMANITA: Why?

MANEDA: Because . . . I was thinking about . . . my husband.

AMANITA: Why don't you ever say their names, Maneda? Why is it always "my husband and my sons?" You act like you hardly knew them. You loved Samu—

MANEDA: Hush, Amanita!

AMANITA: Why don't you want me to get married? Is something going to happen to my fiancé? Tell me! (*Pause. She waits for answer.*) Then I'll just have to leave. I'm packing my things and I'll leave this afternoon. I didn't want to run away to get married. . . . I wanted my family to be there. I know there's something going on, but I don't want to be around it.

(AMANITA *turns to leave. Just as she is about to exit,* ORALIA *appears right.*)

ORALIA: You can't run away from it, daughter. It will haunt you and haunt you until the time is up.

AMANITA: You heard my decision, then, Mama.

ORALIA: I have told you that I was against you marrying—

AMANITA: And I would have given your wishes some consideration . . . if I had not been kept in the dark, Mama.

ORALIA: Meaning what?

AMANITA: Tell me why I can't get married? Tell me whether I should listen to the gossip about this family.

ORALIA: Such as . . . ?

AMANITA: Like there's a curse on this family . . . like somebody fixed Maumau. . . .

ORALIA: When you were growing up, Amanita, I told you that those ridiculous wives tales of this area are exactly that, old wives tales.

AMANITA: Mama, I never believed any of them either, until now!

ORALIA: The women of this family are very intelligent, superior female specimens of life, Amanita, we do not entertain trivial thoughts.

AMANITA: Such as men?

ORALIA: Such as men.

AMANITA: Even though we love?

ORALIA: Daughter, you were reared to respect the beauty of the world within yourself. Meaning that at the right time you would be allowed to marry . . . love.

AMANITA: Right time? When is the right time?

ORALIA: Although, I have given you the warning, daughter, there are those of us who feel it is much too soon. But there is nothing I can do.

MANEDA: Mama! Don't give up.

ORALIA: Maneda, hush. . . .

MANEDA: I can not hush, Mama! Why did I have to be born of this family! Death has brought my husband and my two sons closer together while I am left alive. Why, Mama, why did they have to die because I loved them?

ORALIA: It was the will of the mock . . .

MANEDA: The mock is damnation to me, Mama. I held no hate for the man I married. I was given six years to nurture love for my first son and then as quickly as the joy was given me, it was replaced with pain that brings me nothing but more pain . . . while she laughs . . .

(MANEDA *points angrily toward* MAUMAU's *door.* ORALIA *reacts.*)

ORALIA: You do not speak of your grandmother in that tone, daughter. . . .

MANEDA: Then let her take my life from me! Is it because she loves me that she makes me suffer?

AMANITA: What is she talking about, Mama?

MANEDA: Crush my body in the wreckage of a car, Mama. Drain the breath from my lungs. Make my body writhe in pain from my intestines, pull my eyes from my sockets, make my skin red as blood, make my sight weak, and my odor putrid. . . . Let me die the same kind of horrid death that I gave to my loved-ones!

AMANITA: Mama, what's she saying?

ORALIA: Daughter, for your own sake, hush, daughter, hush! Your soul is damned if you do not hold your tongue, daughter!

MANEDA: Why must I suffer, Mama? Why?

(ORALIA *is about to strike* MANEDA *when she notices* MAUMAU *has entered the room. She is visibly frightened by the sudden appearance, but it soon turns to pity for her daughter.* ORALIA *steps away and* MANEDA *turns to see her grandmother.*)

AMANITA: Mama. . . .

ORALIA: Hush, Amanita.

MANEDA: Maumau. . . .

ORALIA: Ask Maumau to forgive you for your tongue, Maneda. . . .

(*A pause. No reply.*)

Daughter, did you hear me? I said ask Maumau's forgiveness for your disobedience!

(*A pause. No reply still.* ORALIA *moves to* MANEDA *and swiftly grabs her arm and turns her to* MAUMAU.)

Ask Maumau to forgive you for your tongue, daughter. . . .

MANEDA: For three years I bore the pain. Not one word. But, I ache at night. My body yearns for a man's touch and my thoughts go to my husband. When I see mothers with their children, I start to cry because I have none. After three years of bearing the weight of their deaths upon my shoulders, I can not bear it any longer, Maumau. I would rather be dead than to endure it any longer. Take the mock away from me . . .

(MAUMAU *turns and walks toward her room.* MANEDA *follows.*)

Do you hear me? Take the mock!

(MAUMAU *stops, but does not turn.*)

I wish to suffer under the hands of the enemy. I wish to love a man! I wish to love a man! I wish to love a man . . .

(*Before* MANEDA *can say the words again,* MAUMAU *turns swiftly and looks directly into* MANEDA'*s eyes.* MANEDA *freezes. Her mouth continues to form the words . . . but no sound comes out. After a moment,* MAUMAU *turns and crosses right. She exits. The lights slowly dim. Single spot on* MANEDA *who stands transfixed facing* MAUMAU'*s exit.*)

(*End of scene*)

ACT TWO : Scene One

As lights come up, AMANITA *is on the phone with* GAIL.

AMANITA: What do you mean you can't get your car started? . . . It was running perfectly before . . . Gail, I called you thirty minutes ago to come get me and you haven't left yet . . . I'm not nervous about anything . . . I'm not screaming at you either! . . . Gail, please . . . I have to get away from here . . . you have to help me. . . . What are you afraid of? . . . Gail? Gail?

(MAUMAU *enters the room, moves to her table, and begins to work the flowers.*)

Gail? . . . Gail? . . . (*She works the phone, then hangs it up.*)

(MAUMAU *does not turn, she continues making the flowers.*)

Maumau, can I ask you something?

(MAUMAU *nods "yes."*)

Do you know I plan to get married?

(MAUMAU *nods "yes."*)

Do you know why Mama and Maneda don't want me to marry?

(MAUMAU *nods "no."*)

Can you . . . will you tell me why?

(MAUMAU *turns away.*)

Maumau, I know you can talk . . . I know you can. Some times I walk into the room when you're alone with Mama or Maneda and I've heard you talking to them. And when I come in the voices hush. Please, tell me. There are so many things I don't understand. . . .

(*There is no reply, no reaction from* MAUMAU.)

Then nod yes to this question for me if it's true . . . is there a curse on this family?

(MAUMAU's *head turns sharply and she looks straight at* AMANITA.)

Is it true, Maumau? Tell me it isn't true. It can't be because Mama said there was no such thing. . . .

(MAUMAU *rises and moves toward her room.* AMANITA *moves to the phone again and tries to dial. It still isn't working. She looks after* MAUMAU *and then crosses to pick up her suitcase and heads for the exit door. Just as she reaches it,* ORALIA *enters.* AMANITA *is slightly startled.*)

ORALIA: Where are you going, daughter?
AMANITA: I am going over to Gail's.
ORALIA: For what purpose?
AMANITA: I'm leaving. I'm going away from all this . . .
ORALIA: All of what?

AMANITA: You tell me, Mama. You tell me what!

ORALIA: Take your suitcase back to your room, daughter. There is no time for such foolishness.

AMANITA: As I told you, Mama, I am leaving. I am going to get married.

ORALIA: You will have to strike me down first.

AMANITA: You know I can't do that . . . so please will you let me go?

ORALIA: It is useless for you to ask.

AMANITA (*looking at her mother a long moment, then—*): Mama . . . how did my father die?

ORALIA: You know those circumstances.

AMANITA: You killed him, didn't you?

ORALIA: What are you saying, daughter?

AMANITA: You poisoned him. Now I know that the doubts I've had all these years are true. You murdered my father!

ORALIA: What possesses you to say such a thing?

AMANITA: That day . . . you gave him some gumbo. I asked you could I have some and you told me no. Daddy was about to give me a little bit but you screamed for me to go outside and play. You wouldn't even let me taste it . . .

ORALIA: Daughter, beware your thoughts. . . .

AMANITA: A while after that, Daddy got sick. His stomach—he was holding his stomach. Then you told me to run here and tell Maumau that Daddy had some pains and to send some medicine. She gave me something wrapped in brown cloth and I took it to you. . . .

ORALIA: It was baking soda. . . .

AMANITA: I remember how brown that baking soda looked, but you gave it to him anyway and he drank it. And the pain went away. He sat down to finish reading a book and then it started . . . that belching, that awful belching. He kept belching up food, then water, then blood. He was crying, Mama. Daddy had never cried. He fell on the floor asking you why? Why? . . . All you said was "I'm sorry—but your task is done . . ." Mama I've been afraid to think of that for a long time—

ORALIA: It is best that you not think about it, Amanita. When the time comes for you to entertain those thoughts, you will regret the day you did.

AMANITA: You killed my father! Why, Mama, Why?

ORALIA: I murdered no one, daughter.

AMANITA: I've got to get out of here— (AMANITA *crosses to the door.*)

ORALIA: There is no place for you to hide.

AMANITA: Anyplace is better than around murderers.

ORALIA: Do not use that word.

AMANITA: What do you want me to use? Voodoo? Juju magic? Which one? Mama, please . . . tell me what is happening to my family? Talk to me.

(AMANITA *is crying.* ORALIA *goes to her.*)

Mama . . . I'm scared.

ORALIA: It will be over soon, daughter. Very soon.

(MANEDA *enters.*)

AMANITA: Maneda . . . are you all right? Can you speak?

(MANEDA *nods "no."*)

Why can't she speak, Mama?

ORALIA: You know she was yelling at the top of her lungs, Amanita. It is only that . . .

AMANITA: But Maumau . . .

ORALIA: Shhh . . . it does not matter. I will give her something to return her voice. You stay here Amanita. The time is now . . .

(MANEDA *and* ORALIA *exit.* AMANITA *sits in the chair. Moments later,* MAUMAU *appears.* AMANITA *does not see her until she speaks.*)

MAUMAU: So . . . you get yo' sef a man dere gran 'daughter?

AMANITA: Maumau—

MAUMAU: You sey dat ole woman she be talkin' all de time, yes. I bet you sey dat woman be lyin' to me, yes she do. No, dis ole ting don' lie to de blood . . . cos de blood be pure. Sit down on dat ting.

(AMANITA *rises and moves to sit on stool.*)

You sey you got de man fuh yo'sef? You sey you want dis man fuh yo' husband. I know dat. My eye be burnin' fuh tree days.

De time be now for you to know 'bout de man. Dese folks down heah dey talk too much de wrong ting, yes. Dey say dere be de cuss on de family. Dey know no ting, no. Nobody put de cuss on me. I be born in de swamps, gran'daughter. Me mama, she be de cajun dat my papa take. She be de seventh daughter o' do seventh daughter. She know de roots well. Nobody put de cuss on me. I put de cuss on me.

Only ting is dat ting don't be no cuss. It be de mock. And yo' mama and yo' sister be daughters o' de mock. When you give yo' consent to de man you be given de mock to carry.

You sey, what be dis ting—de mock? De mock be de cuss o' de

womb. An' de man he be drawed to de woman and he love her. Dis ting happen to me, but de woman be smart, yes. She put de cuss on herself an' de man have de task to give de woman fruit called de gullchiles. An' den he die. An' de mock be passed. De gullchile make two mo' gullchiles an' dey carry de mock an' de mock be carried to de next gullchile when she get de man.

Dis be yo' time, gran'daughter . . .

AMANITA: Is this my family? The people I love? What are you?

MAUMAU: De tongue o' yo' daughter be nasty, Oralia.

ORALIA: Amanita, hush and listen to Maumau's words.

AMANITA: Maneda, is this why you cry in secret, for your husband and sons? You killed them, just like my mother killed my father! No, Maumau. I will not carry the mock. I will not!

MAUMAU: What dat you sey gull?

AMANITA: I will not carry the mock!

MAUMAU: Dis night you will know dis ting dat I fix to make de woman strong. Dis ting be fuh de times he make you cry yo' tears 'cause he do wrong to you, fuh de times you bear de children in pain fuh him, and fuh de revenge o' yo' gran' mutha!

AMANITA: Revenge? You're doing this for revenge?

ORALIA: Amanita, be quiet!

AMANITA: I don't want to hear anymore.

MAUMAU: What be wrong wid dis chile? Be her mind crazy? Let de waters of de alligators wash her mouth. Do she know who I be?

ORALIA: She knows Maumau.

MAUMAU: Den what be dis ting? What be it? Answer me!

(ORALIA *is evidently frightened and amazed at* AMANITA'*s outbursts.* AMANITA *crosses to* MANEDA'*s door and exits.* ORALIA *starts after her, but before she reaches her,* MAUMAU *speaks—*)

Let dat chile be gone!

ORALIA: I'm sorry, Maumau. I don't know what's wrong with her . . .

MAUMAU: Ahnnnn!

MANEDA: I have been given the use of my voice again. With it I express my joy at Amanita's strength. She has taken this deadly curse and thrown it back in your face!

ORALIA: Maneda!

MAUMAU: Leave her be, too, Oralia! In due time both dese gulls will know de trute o' dem tings dat I do. Both yo' gullchiles will suffer from de ignorance o' dey minds. I go, but I come again. . . .

(MAUMAU *exits, leaving* MANEDA *and* ORALIA *alone.* ORALIA *is visibly frightened,* MANEDA—*strange calm*)

ORALIA: This night will bring pain. . . .

(*End of scene*)

ACT TWO : Scene Two

When the lights come up, MANEDA *is cleaning the pieces of fur from the floor. She is somber, perhaps robot-like, while she works. Then,* ORALIA *enters, moves to observe* MANEDA *a moment. There is a silence.*

ORALIA: Where is she now?

MANEDA: In my room—asleep. After all, there are those of us who do not keep such late hours—

ORALIA: Hasn't this night brought enough pain without your adding to it?

MANEDA: There is no pain for me. Not anymore. Tonight has been a night that I hoped would happen for a long time.

ORALIA: Would you please hush!

MANEDA: Oh, you are so scared. Look at you, Mama. The thought of her anger at you makes you tremble like a leaf. What did she give you to put so much fear inside you?

ORALIA: She gave me two daughters that I love very much and both of them have brought wrath upon themselves. Or don't you realize the power she possesses? Look at yourself, daughter. You are a blessed woman. You carry the beauty that others can only envy. Your mind is knowledgeable about history, philosophy, life, death—things that others dare not dream about. Why? Because that woman you curse has prepared this way for you.

MANEDA: What use is this knowledge without love?

ORALIA: You were given a husband and you have *known* love. The knowledge of a thing is more valuable than the thing itself.

(MAUMAU *enters with her flowers and sits at the table and begins to work.*)

MAUMAU: Dat ting you say, daughter, it be good. You try to make dat one of yours see de light, no? Ahnnnn, spit on dat chile. You, Maneda, wid yo' weak mind. Still let dat man make you mind dirty wid his 'membrance! Man not good enough to give you a gullchile and you yet cry ovuh him. You make de air around me stink, granddaughter! Get from around me! Go 'way from here.

(MANEDA *stares at* MAUMAU, *trying not to be afraid.*)

You hear my voice, no? Go, I say!

(MANEDA *exits.*)

ORALIA: She will be all right, Maumau, just give her time—

MAUMAU: Dat ting time be short for your gullchiles, daughter. All my days I no see dis shame in my blood. What kinda man give you fruit like dis?

ORALIA: Why do you bring up my man? He is dead now, Maumau. He has fulfilled his task and has passed from my memory. That was his purpose. Any shame that my daughters have brought is on my account.

MAUMAU: Your tongue speak de trute, daughter. The shame is marked on yo'self. But now, de time be now for me to put my hand in dis. Dat young one of yours, she be strong, but not stronger than de woman. She will take de mock and carry dis blood or I will cuss de very insides of her body. Bring me her—

ORALIA: Yes, Maumau.

(ORALIA *exits*, MAUMAU *goes back to her work.*)

MAUMAU: Maneda!

MANEDA (*standing in the doorway*): Yes?

MAUMAU: Call me by my name, *oui.*

MANEDA: Yes, Maumau?

MAUMAU: Fix de magnolia seeds for de tea.

MANEDA: Yes, Maumau. (*She crosses to prepare the tea.*)

MAUMAU: All my days on dis eart, I never see so ugly. De two from the womb of my daughter deny they own. I fix it, yes! I make you see de light. Dese folks down heah, dey know of me. Ask de old ones . . . dey tell you 'bout the times I make de strong ones weak like de lamb, dey tell you 'bout de times I snatch de breath from de lungs of de livin' and put poison in the gut of de land; makin' de good days bad and de bad days long wid sorrow. I be do one, gran'daughter, and dere be none dat know de roots like me. And you stand in my way!

(*Enter* ORALIA *and* AMANITA. MAUMAU *sees them and beckons for* AMANITA *to sit.*)

Dere be de young one. Come sit to me. Come see—

AMANITA: No, thank you, Maumau. I can stand.

MAUMAU: I got de eyes to see de legs you stand on, gull. Come here to me—

AMANITA: No, thank you.

MAUMAU: What I say, gull? Don't make dat noise to me, gran'daughter, I be no chile dat you speak to. Your days be short on dis eart for your sharp tongue. Now come see!

(AMANITA *reluctantly moves to* MAUMAU.)

Sit down dere on dat ting.

(AMANITA *sits.*)

Strengt be good for de woman. Dat's de ting dat be her food to keep her alive; but dat strengt be no good when pour de water in a well too deep. See my words, gran'daughter, no? It be best for you to heed dese tings I say 'cause dey be de tings dat make you wise.

AMANITA: Wise about what, Maumau? This sickening thing you done for your own spite?

MAUMAU: You be so young, gran'daughter, but I tell you now, after dat man take your heart and walk on it like de ground, you will know de reason dis mock come to be. Dis ting make you sick, eh? Well, I tell you, I be sick, too. Sick o' de slime dat you say ti me, gull. You don't know de tings I can do . . .

AMANITA: I don't want to know. (*She rises.*)

MAUMAU: It make no mind what you want, gull. Sit down dere. (*To* MANEDA) Bring de tea. (*Then to* AMANITA) I don't say dis no more. You sit down—

AMANITA: I am not afraid of you, Maumau.

MAUMAU: You tink I wan you scared of me, yes? Dat ain't de ting I need from you, gull.

ORALIA: Amanita, please sit down.

MAUMAU: How be it you beg your daughter to hear me, Oralia? Tell dis chile dat I will cuss her tongue and make it hang out her mouth like dead meat!

ORALIA: Amanita, please . . .

MAUMAU: Don't you see de ting dat I do to your sister? If I can take de sound o' her voice, I can make you see tings to make you wish for your grave. Look at me . . .

(AMANITA *turns away.* MAUMAU *walks over to her and turns her, facing directly*)

Look at me! You got no strengt over me, chile. None, I say.

(*The fear* AMANITA *has been trying to hide, suddenly overcomes her and she sits.* MAUMAU *moves to sit also.*)

Fix de tea for us all. Like de family we sit. Lock de doors, Oralia. Dis be de time to make tings right again.

(MANEDA *is pouring the tea into cups and giving each one a cup, takes one for herself and they sit quietly a moment.*)

It be wrong, gran'daughter for you to know de sound of my voice before you carry de mock. Dis ting can't be helped, no. Drink de tea.

AMANITA: What is it?

MAUMAU: Don't ask me no ting, gull! Do what I say!

(AMANITA *drinks.*)

Tell me 'bout dis man. Tell me what you feel for him.

AMANITA: I love him. I want to marry him.

MAUMAU: What be de cause?

AMANITA: We have understanding and love between us—

MAUMAU: What be dis understanding?

AMANITA: We share a lot—

MAUMAU: What be it you share?

AMANITA: Love, love—

MAUMAU: What be dis ting love?

AMANITA: What difference does it make?

MAUMAU: If dis be de ting, den tell me, what be dis ting love?

AMANITA: I don't have to tell you—

MAUMAU: Den I will tell you, gran'daughter. Dis ting you say be love, do it make de little jump come to your heart? Do it make you want no food? Do it light de mind? Dat be it? Well, gran'-daughter, that be de sign of your deat. You be sick, gran'-daughter and your body soon be yearn for de ting dat will make it well. And dat ting be de mock. My mind don't be like de others. Dat you want dis man be good, de time be now for you to carry de mock. Dis ting must come to be 'cause de mock be de cuss dat I put on myself and dere be no ting on de face of de eart dat can move de cuss. What dis ting is dat hold you back de tea will tell me, yes. De seed of de magnolia tree make de mind hold trute, I will know dis ting and move it 'way— (MAUMAU *puts her cup down and moves from the table, taking a stem from her work table. She looks at each of the women, then—*) Talk, daughter . . .

ORALIA: Amanita, as you grow older, you will find this knowledge to be the greatest of all that you have gained. Take off your dress—

AMANITA: Mama, I—

ORALIA: You will not be told twice, Amanita.

AMANITA: Won't you listen to me, please? I don't want this! It is ugly, shameful, it is wrong!

ORALIA: It is within ourselves that we choose right or wrong. To us, this is right, and those who stand in our way are cursed.

AMANITA: Then curse me!

MANEDA: Amanita, no.

AMANITA: Did you hear me? I said, curse me! Do the same things to me that you have done to others. Show me your strength, Maumau. Kill your own flesh and blood and see how far your Mock will be carried. Curse me!

MAUMAU: Ah, but dat chile don't know what she say . . .

MANEDA: She doesn't mean it, Maumau.

AMANITA: I do mean it, with all my heart. I'd rather be cursed than to know the wickedness in this family—

ORALIA: What is wrong? Why, daughter, why?

MANEDA: Take it back, Amanita.

AMANITA: No, let her kill me! Go ahead, Maumau, kill me!

MAUMAU (*moving to* AMANITA, *standing directly in front of her*): Death be too good for you, gull—

ORALIA: I will talk to her, Maumau—

MAUMAU: Speak no words to me, Oralia. De time for talk be gone. Your gullchile say she wants de cuss, den she get de cuss. Take off dem tings—

AMANITA: What are you going to do?

MAUMAU: Hush! Be'st dat tongue still! 'Cause you be my gran'chile I show you first what you get when you anger me, yes. Take off dem tings, take dem off!

(MANEDA *rushes to* AMANITA.)

MANEDA: Will you let her be? Please, please, let her be. (*To* AMANITA) Amanita, listen to me, you don't know what you're saying. She can . . .

MAUMAU: Talk, gran'daughter.

MANEDA: Amanita . . . listen. Do you remember that old man they found on Bayou LaFourche? You remember? When they found him, the ants had eaten up his eyes. Do you know who that man was? It was that man who got after you and Gail when you were walking home from school. You came in here crying about him and Maumau left the house . . .

ORALIA: And took the dried canteloupe seeds and buried them with the roots of the amanita plant. Buried them under the steps of that man's house . . .

MAUMAU: And de man . . . he get sick and he come to de Woman and asked me to take de cuss off him. Told him to go down to de bayou and wash dem eyes with dat moss. Man go blind, gran'daughter. De eyes of de man commence to burn like fire. De pain he feel, no man can bear. Den de eyes commence to bleed, blood drap down like sweat. De man die, I tell you, de man die! Or what you want to see? You want to see de blood of your own? (MAUMAU *points to* MANEDA.) You! let de bones inside your head break like de crack of hardwood.

(MANEDA *grabs her head in pain.*)

Let de blood inside your arm run like a mighty stream . . .

(MANEDA's *arm tenses and shakes furiously.*)

Let your throat dry up like scorchin' sand . . .

(MANEDA *makes the sound of a parching throat, gasping.*)

Dat what you want to see, gran'daughter?
AMANITA: What's happening? Maneda? Maneda . . .
MAUMAU: What more you want to see? Tell me quick, gran'daughter!
AMANITA: Maneda, stop it. Stop it!
ORALIA: Don't you see, Amanita, she can't stop it.

(AMANITA *grabs* MANEDA *and shakes her.*)

AMANITA: Stop, please, Maneda. (*Seeing it is useless*) Maumau, stop it now, please. . . .
MAUMAU: Be'st it still, gran'daughter.

(MANEDA's *tantrum subsides. She lies breathless on the floor.*)

I go now, den I come back. De time be now for you to carry de mock.

(MAUMAU *exits.* AMANITA *comforts* MANEDA. ORALIA *stands.*)

AMANITA: How does she do it? You told me there was no such thing, Mama.
ORALIA: There is always such a thing, Amanita. She knows every herb and root that grows in the ground, she knows which to mix with which to create any poison, any cure. It's all strange to you now, but just imagine a person studying the plants of the earth for a lifetime . . . coming up with poisons, deadly poisons, that can create distortions of the mind, and *kill*. She knows all of them, Amanita. Each by name, color, and purpose. No, there was nothing I could do . . . nothing but wait until the tea has run from her body and her blood runs clean

again. Help your sister up, Amanita, and go prepare yourself for your blessing.

MANEDA: Don't do it, Amanita, please. You must not do it.

AMANITA: Do I have a choice, Maneda?

(*There is a silence.* MANEDA *looks at* ORALIA.)

MANEDA: Yes, you do.

ORALIA: I have seen enough pain brought to you already, Maneda.

MANEDA: We mean nothing to her. We are her tools she has used to make her burden lighter. It was *her* man that caused her pain. The men that we loved did nothing to wrong us. Why must we suffer because she had no good memories of him?

ORALIA: She is our blood.

MANEDA: So were my two sons! They were my flesh and blood. I bore the pain for them, not her! It must be stopped. Don't you see, we can do it. Mama, you know what can be done to stop it and if it takes that I will do it.

ORALIA: Maneda—

MANEDA: I will do it, Mama.

AMANITA: Do what?

MANEDA: The only thing that can end the curse is death. I am willing to die if it will stop your pain, Amanita—

AMANITA: Maneda, no . . .

MANEDA: Someone has got to stop this! What do I have to live for? It would mean much more to me to be with my husband and sons—

AMANITA: Is it worth the pain you will bring to us?

MANEDA: No worse than the pain you will feel when the time comes for you to take the life of your loved-ones, when you must carry a child within yourself for nine months full of fear, everyday hoping that the baby inside you is a girl, praying that you can share a life with it, knowing all along that the choice is not yours. If I must die to stop that, then I will—

MAUMAU: Speak you of death, eh, gran'daughter? Dis ting must be ended now. You say you no want dis mock? Den I will tell you de ting dat will stop it, yes. Just as de sun rise ovuh de eart and all de plants dat take de root in de ground, de ting dat cut de life from the plant be death. But to cut de leaves off de plant, don't kill de plant, de root must die . . . (MAUMAU *throws a knife in* MANEDA's *direction.*) Pick up dat knife, gran'daughter, and come to me and rip into my flesh and tear *my* heart. Waste de blood o' yo' gran'mutha to end dis ting.

(MANEDA *is still. She looks at the knife, then at* MAUMAU.)

Pick it up!

(MANEDA *picks up the knife.*)

I be de root dat you must kill. De pain dat I suffer all dese years for your sake—end it now! You don't know what my man did to me, no. Dem times he force himself into me, makin' me give birth to bastards before he come to me with love. Inside my heart was de love fuh my man but he take dat love and play wid it like de chile play wid de toys. I be no toy! I be a woman wid de feelin's, strong feelin's, gentle feelin's dat need de love. I tell him dat. But his heart be hard. Den I say, no more! And I make de way for my daughter to keep her heart from de claws o' de man and her daughters after her. But you spit on dat wish I have fuh you. You cuss de mock! Now I say, kill me and end dis mock. Do de ting dat de man want, gran'daughter, do it now!

(MANEDA *looks at the knife and suddenly plunges toward* MAUMAU. *Just as she reaches her,* AMANITA *rushes and grabs* MANEDA's *hand.*)

AMANITA: Maneda! No, no. Which is worse? The blood of our grandmother or the blood of a man we do not know? I will carry the mock. (AMANITA *takes the knife and places it in front of* MAUMAU.)

MAUMAU: Prepare yo' daughter fuh her blessing, Oralia. . . .

(ORALIA *moves to her daughters and seats* AMANITA *in the chair center. She takes* MANEDA's *hands and guides her to the right of the stage.* ORALIA *goes left. The lights go down, leaving a single spot on* AMANITA. *Using a cyclorama, the colors of the room go from amber to red, to yellow, to blue, to green.*)

ORALIA: Amanita, my daughter, born of the womb of my womb which is of the womb of my mother. I pass on to you the knowledge of the cards. There are four suits of fourteen cards—wands, cups, swords and pentacles and twenty-two extra cards called trumps or major arcana. With these cards you can tell the future and be the protector of the mock—

MANEDA: Amanita, my sister, girlchild born of the womb of my mother. Remember these things for they are passed on to you from the blood of your grandmother. Rise and drink from the juice of the plant, from the blood of your grandmother. Rise and drink from the juice of the plant, from the blood of the mother earth, born on Louisiana soil, wet soil, moist soil, pregnant soil . . .

MAUMAU: And de mock be your father and wid you he will be always. Drink, granddaughter. Dis be de symbol of de blood o' your grandmother, de blood dat be took from her veins. Drink dis blood and you be made pure . . .

(*Slowly, as though she is in a trance,* AMANITA *picks up the cup and slowly brings it to her mouth. As she drinks:*)

MANEDA: *To carry the mock.*
ORALIA: *To carry the mock.*
MAUMAU: *To carry the mock.*

(*As* AMANITA *brings the cup down, she starts to tremble.*)

Tell me what you feel, gran'daughter. . . .
AMANITA: I feel . . .
MAUMAU: What you feel, gran'daughter?
AMANITA: Cold . . . I feel cold. (AMANITA'*s body trembles with cold.*)
MAUMAU: De cold dat you feel be de cold dat de man make you feel when he leave you alone at night . . .
AMANITA: I'm cold. . . .
MAUMAU: De cold be de cold dat de man make you feel when he step on yo hands and hold you down . . . Tell me what you feel gran'daughter . . .
AMANITA: I feel heat. . . .
MAUMAU: What you feel?
AMANITA: It's hot. Hot . . . (AMANITA *seems to feel scorching heat. She tears her dress away from her.*) Hot. . . .
MAUMAU: De heat be de heat dat you feel when de man be inside your body. It be de heat that he make you feel. De cheap heat. De sweat o' de man drap on your body. Dis be de heat from hell. Tell me what you feel, gran'daughter . . .
AMANITA: Pain . . . the pain . . . (AMANITA *starts to writhe.*) It hurts . . .
MAUMAU: Remember dis pain, gran'daughter. Dis pain will always be wid you. You have given your love to de man and he will betray it. He will not live. De man will die. Dis pain be gone, but de pain will come again. De pain will be wid you gran'daughter. . . .
AMANITA: Mama . . . Mama, please, help me, Mama. It hurts me bad, Mama, Mama . . . (*She starts to cry.*) Mama . . . (*The pain starts to subside. She looks up at* MAUMAU.)
MAUMAU: De color o' the moon will be red on the day your man is to die. You will watch de moon. You will take de man as yo husband and he will be given de time on de earth until he give to you two gullchiles. If de boychile be born de first time, he will live till the second chile be born. If no gullchile me born . . . it will be yo task to kill de boychiles. Den yo man will die. It be wise for yo man to give you gullchiles, fuh

den de fruit from yo womb will live. (*Pause. She moves to* AMANITA.) All dese tings we tell you . . . you remember dem. Dey will pass from your mind after dis day till de time you be one wid yo' man. After de organ o' de husband enter yo' crest o' yo' womb, all dese knowledge will come to you again. (*Pause.*) I, Justine being the womb o' yo' mother, give to you de knowledge o' de roots. Dese tings dat grow from de belly o' de ground, be put on de eart fuh healin' de sickness o' de body.

To make de blind man see: Take de water from de bowels o' de man and take a cloth o' cotton and boil de water o' de man wid de water from a spring rain. Dry de cloth in de sun for three days. Let de blind man's tears wet de cloth and de blind man will see.

To free a prisoner: Take the soil from de eart three feet from de door o' de jailhouse. Take de grease from the bacon meat after fryin' black. Mix de grease wid the juice of alfalfa tea and mix wid de dirt. Ball de mud in a lump and place under de step o' de prisoner's house. He will go free in three days.

MANEDA: *To fall out of love:* Take a gift from the man you love and soak it in the juice from the root of a young sycamore tree. Dry the gift and place the gift under the step of the house of the man you love. When the gift is dry, burn it before sundown on the next day, and your heart will run free.

MAUMAU: Yo tongue palate don' touch no unclean chicken meat.

ORALIA: Your lips will touch no wines.

MANEDA: Your stomach will hold no food unless prepared by the daughters of the mock.

MAUMAU: No man shall speak vile words to you face.

MANEDA: No man lay his hands upon you in spite.

ORALIA: No man touch your body except with respect.

MAUMAU: No man shall touch your body during de time o' the seed.

MANEDA: No man shall bear untruths to you.

MAUMAU: You will grow wid de knowledge o' de roots.

MANEDA: You will grow with the knowledge of the physical earth.

ORALIA: You will grow with the knowledge of yourself.

MANEDA: You will grow wid de beauty of the swan.

ORALIA: You will grow with the swiftness of the gazelle.

MAUMAU: You will grow wid de wisdom o' de hoot owl. You feel no weakness under de man. De man be yo' servant 'cause you be de daughter of de mock. You shed no tears fuh de man. Yo bear no pain but de pain o' de womb.

And dis pain

Be de pain

Dat will bring you to yo' place
As
The Mutter o' de Eart.

(*At this moment, the lights go down and the cyclorama appears to "drip" streams of red light.* AMANITA *is alone.*)

ORALIA'S VOICE: My daughter, Amanita, whose name is the deadly mushroom plant—take the oil that was prepared for this blessing, for the salvation and protection of your womanhood. Carry the mock—
MANEDA'S VOICE: Though others may doubt the powers that are given to you, there is none who can escape it. If one believes for one-tenth of one second that he is cursed by your powers, then he is. Carry the mock—
MAUMAU'S VOICE: Take de oil, gran'daughter. Pour it on your body. Make yo' glory known to all de eart. And when de time come dat you and yo' man be one, all knowledge o' de roots will be yours. Carry de mock—

(AMANITA *pours the oil—from her head down. As she pours, the cyclorama is fully red. After she pours,* AMANITA *sits in the chair again. Alone.* MAUMAU'S VOICE *is heard:*)

Now you be de daughter o' de Mock . . . and *woe be to de man who dare hurt a daughter o' de mock!*

(*The End*)

The Offering

GUS EDWARDS

Left to right: Katherine Knowles as GINNY, *Charles Weldon as* MARTIN, *and Olivia Williams as* PRINCESS *in a scene from* The Offering. *Photograph copyright © 1977 by Bert Andrews. Reprinted by permission of Marsha Hudson, the Estate of Bert Andrews.*

Gus Edwards, a native of St. Thomas, Virgin Islands, has had nine plays produced throughout the United States, with most of the works, such as *The Offering, Old Phantoms,* and *Weep Not for Me,* originating from the NEC. His television film credits include the PBS coadaptation (with Leslie Lee) of James Baldwin's *Go Tell It on the Mountain.* He currently serves on the Theater faculty of Arizona State University where he runs the Multi-Ethnic Theatre Program.

The Offering was produced in New York by the NEC at the St. Marks Playhouse, and opened on December 1, 1977, with the following cast:

Bob Tyrone   Douglas Turner Ward
Princess   Olivia Williams
Martin   Charles Weldon
Ginny   Katherine Knowles

Directed by Douglas Turner Ward; scenery by Raymond C. Recht; lighting by Paul Gallo; costumes by Arthur McGee; production stage managed by Horacena J. Taylor.

The Offering

CHARACTERS

in order of appearance

BOB TYRONE

A black man in his late sixties. Physically large and possessed of a commanding presence. An emperor in decay or monster in repose. Old, tired, and gnarled.

PRINCESS

His wife. Black, latter thirties. Suspicious, protective, and constant. There is a residual strength lying dormant in her plain manner and bleak outlook.

MARTIN

Black, early thirties. A twilight person, more comfortable in shadows than in light. Nervous, overeager, slightly shabby, and sometimes strange.

GINNY

White, middle twenties. Her sexuality is explicit and potent but quite unconscious. An odd mixture of vulgarity and innocence.

SCENE

A living room of a basement apartment in West Side Manhattan. Every item in the room (furniture, pictures, etc.) is in a state of decay. Even the air seems stillborn. Dominating all is a sofa that converts into a bed. Other furniture includes a TV, a couple of overstuffed chairs, a coffee table, and some lamps. BOB TYRONE *should have his own chair. Something heavy, ornate, and maybe even thronelike.*

The atmosphere is almost always dim and quite gloomy, even during the day.

TIME

The present.

ACT ONE

SCENE ONE

Evening, about nine o'clock. BOB TYRONE *is seated watching TV (the program is unimportant). Sounds come from the box. Light patterns reflect off him.* TYRONE *is looking at the screen with hardly a change of his expression. (Pause.)* PRINCESS *emerges from the bedroom and in passing stops, looks at the set and then at him.*

PRINCESS: Bob?
TYRONE: Hmmm.
PRINCESS: How can you watch that? It's out of focus. You'll go blind.

(*Pause. No answer from* TYRONE. *Finally* PRINCESS *goes over and adjusts the setting.*)

How's that?

(*No answer.*)

Bob?
TYRONE: Yes. Fine . . . fine.

(PRINCESS *picks up around the room.* TYRONE *watches TV. After a while the front doorbell rings.* PRINCESS *stops, looks at* TYRONE *who doesn't seem to have heard it. Both remain still for a moment, then* PRINCESS *breaks it and continues picking up. Again the doorbell rings. Both ignore it. It stops then rings again.*)

TYRONE: This ain't nothing. Put in a tape.
PRINCESS: Why? Why you want to watch—
TYRONE: Please, Princess.

(*She says nothing, just shrugs then goes over to the VCR and puts in a tape. From the soundtrack it's obviously an adult video he's watching.*)

TYRONE: Turn off the sound. Too much noise.

(PRINCESS *does—*TYRONE *watches it for a while.* PRINCESS *continues what she was doing before. . . .*)

PRINCESS: Who could it be at this hour—
TYRONE: Don't know. . . .
PRINCESS: Should I answer it?

(*No answer from* TYRONE. *He's absorbed in watching the video. The doorbell rings and rings. Then it stops.* PRINCESS *hasn't moved from her position.*)

PRINCESS (*after a pause*): Gone. You want some brandy?
TYRONE (*after a moment*): Hmmm . . . OK.

(PRINCESS *pours a drink into a sniffer and gives it to him. He takes it, goes to drink it, and it slips out of his hand.*)

PRINCESS: Look at that. All over your new robe. Here—let me help you.
TYRONE (*still absorbed in the video*): Don't matter, let it go.
PRINCESS: No. Just stay still. (*She begins to clean him up as the lights fade.*)

SCENE TWO

The next night. Same time.

Positions: TYRONE *seated watching TV. Regular TV, not a video. A cops-and-robber show. We can hear the dialogue.* PRINCESS *seated on the sofa looking at a magazine. Again the doorbell rings. Again they ignore it. It rings twice, then stops. A pause. Another bell rings. It's the apartment door.*

PRINCESS: That's right here.
TYRONE: Oh.
PRINCESS: I wonder who it could be?

(*It rings twice.*)

Who?
TYRONE: See . . . open it.
PRINCESS: I don't know . . . think I should?
TYRONE: Up to you.

(*She considers it, then after a while goes.*)

PRINCESS (*offstage*): Hello?
MARTIN: You don't remember me-huh?
PRINCESS: No.
MARTIN: It's me. Martin . . . Don't let the mustache fool you. Where's the old man?
PRINCESS: Inside.
MARTIN: That's who I come to see . . . my man, big Bob Tyrone. (*He rushes in carrying a suitcase which he puts in a corner.*) Hey Ty, look who's here—it's me, man. Martin.
TYRONE: Who?

MARTIN: Martin, that crazy boy you used to work with.

TYRONE (*after a long moment*): Hey Martin boy. I ain't seen you in years. How you feelin'?

MARTIN: Fine . . . fine. You look good. Ain't changed a lick since the last time I seen you.

TYRONE: No? . . . Put on a few years. More'n a few years.

MARTIN: Don't show. You look fine. Same as ever.

TYRONE: Well, that's nice to hear . . . yes. Nice . . . what's that thing on your face?

MARTIN (*touching the mustache*): This? You like it? I got to shape it a little. Started growing it last year. I like it. It make me look serious . . . mature. People always saying I look like a boy.

TYRONE: Yes, I can see that. . . . One thing I never done to my face. Never let no hair grow on it. Always like my skin smooth and clean like an injun.

MARTIN: Well . . . yeah. (*Laughs a little*) Hey, let me introduce my girl— Ginny. Ginny, this is Mr. Tyrone. Bob Tyrone. Big Bob Tyrone to his friends.

TYRONE: And enemies too.

GINNY (*offering her hand*): Pleased to meet you, Mr. Tyrone.

TYRONE (*standing*): Bob. None a that Mr. Tyrone shit. Bob. Big Bob if you like. (*Appraising her*) Yes . . . yes . . . (*to* MARTIN) Boy you have good taste. She's a lovely lookin' gal.

GINNY: Thank you.

TYRONE: A good looking woman is a pleasure to the eyes. You don't mind me talking like that, do you?

MARTIN: No. You my man, anything you say okay by me. She don't mind neither.

GINNY: No. Not at all. I—

TYRONE: You have to excuse me, miss. I'm an old man. And I hardly get to see anything of real beauty in this room except on TV . . .

GINNY: Thank you, Mr. Tyrone, I mean Bob. That's a nice compliment.

TYRONE: Of course I ain't excluding Princess. She's a true beauty too.

PRINCESS: Stop it Bob.

TYRONE: She being shy today.

MARTIN: Yeah . . . er . . . Princess, you didn't recognize me, did you? You shoulda seen her expression when she opened the door, Bob. She looked at me like I was some kinda ghost or something.

PRINCESS: Well—I hardly knowed you from before and . . .

TYRONE: Ginny. Ginny is your name, right?

GINNY: Yes.

TYRONE: Ginny, this is Princess. Princess is my wife.

GINNY: Pleased to meet you.
PRINCESS (*guarded*): Hello.
GINNY: Yeah—Hello.

(*Pause.*)

MARTIN (*looking around*): Yeah, this is nice. Real nice.
TYRONE: Why everybody standin' around? Sit. We got chairs. Yes, sit. Have a drink? Socialize.
MARTIN: Sure.
TYRONE (*to* GINNY): What about you? Want a drink?
MARTIN: She'll have one. Same as me. Scotch on rocks. If you have Scotch.
PRINCESS: We got it.
GINNY: Yes, please.

(PRINCESS *exits to the kitchen.*)

TYRONE: Well, Martin boy, what bring you around here in the dark of night? I ain't even seen you in ages. What you been doin' with you'self?
MARTIN: Nothing much but, I been everywhere. Texas, California, Florida, Las Vegas. That's where I live now. Me and Ginny we live together. A small place just outside a the strip. It ain't that much, but we like it.
TYRONE: Las Vegas, eh?
MARTIN: Yeah.
TYRONE: That's the other side the world.
MARTIN: It ain't that far.
TYRONE: Maybe not. Just seem far. I guess. What you doing up here?
MARTIN: Just passing through. We was up in Canada for a spell. Had some business to do there. Now we on our way home. So I thought while we in the area, "Why not stop in and see how my man Bob Tyrone is doing."
TYRONE: Why?
MARTIN: You the only person in this whole damn state that I know or even care about anymore.
TYRONE: Oh yeah?
MARTIN: Yeah.
GINNY: It's true. He's always talking about you. Telling me all kinds of stories.
TYRONE: Is that so? . . . How long it been since we last seen each other?
MARTIN: Oh god. More than ten years. I was a boy and you was *the man.* We had some good times in them days. Some real good times.

TYRONE: And you still remember them eh?

MARTIN: Oh man, I didn't forget nothing. And I'll tell you something. A lot a them times out there when I was knocking around, and things wasn't going so good, I used to think about when you and I was together. All them things you used to tell me. And show me. Damn, you don't know how much they helped.

TYRONE: Oh yeah.

MARTIN: I owe you man. I owe you a lot. You don't know.

(PRINCESS *enters with the drinks. Gives* MARTIN *and* GINNY *one.*)

MARTIN: Thanks.

GINNY: Thank-you.

TYRONE: So—you live in Vegas?

MARTIN: Yes.

TYRONE: Ever do any gambling out there?

MARTIN: From time to time.

TYRONE: That's one of the things I never got around to doing. Never got myself to Las Vegas. I always wanted to go in my youth. All them slot machines, roulette tables, show girls kicking up all them pretty legs.

MARTIN: That's what Ginny does for a living. Ginny is a show girl.

TYRONE: Oh yeah?

GINNY: Yes.

TYRONE: Dance in them big floor shows and everything?

GINNY: Sometimes.

TYRONE: Ain't that something? That place always been like a magic land to me. Never really believed it was out there.

MARTIN: It's there all right. You can take it from me. It's there. And there ain't no place like it. Ain't that so, hon?

GINNY: Nope.

TYRONE: Yeah . ... Always wanted to go to Vegas. Always.

MARTIN: Ain't too late. You could come visit us sometime. I don't work days too much so I'd have a lot of time to show you the place and everything.

TYRONE: That would be nice. Real nice. I always wanted to go to Las Vegas . . . Las Vegas, Nevada. You ever been there Princess?

PRINCESS: No.

MARTIN: Then you gotta come. The place we have got an extra room. You could stay a month if you like.

TYRONE: So you work in the floor show at one of them big hotels?

GINNY: Sometimes. I'm a chorus dancer.

TYRONE: Chorus dancer eh? (*He smiles.*) That's a nice line of work. They ever get any black girls in them choruses?

GINNY: Sure. Lots.

TYRONE: See, Princess? That's something you could do after I go. Dance in one of them chorus lines with a big thing on your head and them nice stockings on your legs.

(PRINCESS *snorts.*)

Why not? You a good looking woman.

(PRINCESS *snorts again.*)

And you, Martin boy, you in the entertainment business too?

MARTIN: No—That ain't my schtick. I got a small set up of my own. Private business.

TYRONE: And you makin' it. You look like you making it.

MARTIN: Damn right, I'm making it. I got our place, a car, some clothes . . . you know.

TYRONE: That's good. Good. You always had a smart head on top of your neck.

MARTIN: Yeah. (*Pause.*) And you, Bob. How've these last years been treatin' you?

TYRONE: Me? No complaints. I got enough to eat. A roof over my head. The TV and Princess over there. Now we got that VCR thing, I can watch what I want when I want—no, I ain't got nothing to complain about.

MARTIN: Kinda different from what it used to be, ain't it? You know, the good old days.

TYRONE: Things change Marty boy. Things change. You get old. That's how it is. "Member how I used to love Harlem?"

MARTIN: Oh yeah.

TYRONE (*to* GINNY): I wasn't born there, but I loved that place. Had a lot a good times in that place. Knew some good people, women and men. Even when I left the life, changed my profession, and moved downtown, that place always had something for me. Always. . . . Used to be a time, a week couldn't go by without me going into Harlem looking up some of the old timers, having a drink, talk a little bit, maybe roll some dice. After a while I started doing it once a year. Once a year, New Year's Eve, I'd go up in Harlem, sit in a bar, have some drinks, and laugh with the fellows. I used to like doing it. It made me feel good, you know? . . . But although I didn't know it all the time I was up there hanging out, the place was changing.

Something was happening. I don't know what. New fellows coming up, old boys going out.

Then one New Year's Eve—and this is going back now five, six years I think, I get into my suit like I always do, put some money in my pocket, and take the train as usual. Same bar. I walk in and all the faces were new to me. A lot of young fellows, one or two old timers— but nobody I know. All strangers.

Anyway, went to the bar, got a drink, and took it to a table to sit down. I musta been there maybe twenty minutes looking at all these new faces in the place, listening to the conversations, when the next thing I know, everybody was on the floor. Including me. Some fools had walked in and start shooting up the place like they was crazy. Bam, bam, bam, bam, bam. Bullets flying all over ain't even caring who they hittin'. When it stopped, I see three boys around me dead. Blood, liquor, glass, and furniture all over the place. Smoke in the air.

Everybody was screaming and crying and trying to hide.

GINNY: Oh my god—

TYRONE: But I wasn't hurt. I wasn't even dirty from lying on that floor. Had on a shantung suit and when I stood up it still look like new. Know what I did? (*Pause.*) I put on my hat, straightened my tie, and stepped out of that place. Called a taxi and come straight home, took off my clothes, turned on the TV and watch them clowns crowd Times Square waiting for the ball to drop. Didn't even say nothing to Princess. Just watch the TV and listen for when they play that Guy Lombardo song. . . . I ain't been back up since. (*Pause.*) You ever watch TV?

MARTIN: No. Not much.

TYRONE: You should. You see a whole lot of things, and now with that VCR you see even more. Another drink?

MARTIN: OK.

(PRINCESS *moves to get it.*)

GINNY: Where's the bathroom?

TYRONE: Over there.

GINNY: Excuse me. (GINNY *exits.*)

TYRONE: Good lookin' woman.

MARTIN: She ain't bad. She do anything I tell her.

TYRONE: Oh yeah?

MARTIN: Absolutely.

TYRONE: Where'd you find her?

MARTIN: In the streets, knocking around. She was tending bar this place I used to go. She do that when she can't get dance jobs.

TYRONE: They make good women sometimes, these street girls. Look at Princess.

MARTIN: I know. I know—man, I been wanting to see you for so long. Wanting to talk to you. So much happen to me since I last see you. I see so much. Experience so much. Things only a man like you could understand and appreciate. (*Pause.*) You know I been to jail?

TYRONE (*not surprised*): Yeah?

(PRINCESS *enters with the bottle and some ice.*)

MARTIN: Yeah man. Miami. Thank you, Princess. Eighteen months for pushing. Got out with twelve for good behavior. I thought a lot about you in that prison man. 'Bout all the times we had, all the things we did. I even started writing you a letter. A long letter to tell you 'bout all the things that was going on inside my head—something happened, I never finished it.

TYRONE: How long ago was that?

MARTIN: About two years after I left you. I shouldn'ta left you. We shoulda stuck together. We would've been kings today. You know that? Goddamn city kings.

TYRONE: Maybe.

MARTIN: No maybe, man. I know. We was the best money could buy. You had the head and I had the body. We could've been masters.

TYRONE: That was a lot of years ago.

(GINNY *returns.*)

MARTIN: Thirteen years ago.

TYRONE: Yeah . . . and you still remember? You still come back.

MARTIN: Sure.

TYRONE: Why?

MARTIN: I told you. To see how you is. How you getting on. To talk. You know.

TYRONE: Why?

MARTIN: Because you the only person who ever really teach me anything.

TYRONE: Teach you 'bout what? How to climb a fire escape—go through a window?

MARTIN (*searching*): No man, I'm talking 'bout life. Women, money, that kind of stuff.

TYRONE: I did that? Told you them things?

MARTIN: Hell yes. And more. You told me stories, 'bout your life. Experiences I never heard from nobody else or read in a book even. And them things you tell me. Them lessons you teach me stay with me, man, and helped me when the going was rough and things were bad. You teach me more, prepare me more than any father I ever had. You know that? Lots more.

TYRONE: So you come to see the old man.

MARTIN: Yeah—to tell you thanks. To offer you money or something if you need it. You need any money?

PRINCESS: No.

MARTIN: I ain't trying to insult nobody or nothing. I got money. A whole lot. Look—(*He pulls out a roll of bills.*) Most of these is hundreds. Tell me how much you want. It's yours. (*He waits. No answer.*)

MARTIN: All of it. You want all of it? Here (*He puts the money on the table.*) Take it. There's nearly six thousand dollars there. Take it. It's for you. All of it for you.

(*A long silence.*)

MARTIN: Don't anybody want this money? I'm offering it, I ain't joking. It's yours. You can just take it.

TYRONE (*gently*): Put away your money, Martin boy. Nobody want it. We too old for that kind of money. Put it in your pocket, please.

MARTIN: I want to give you something, Bob. I feel I owe you.

TYRONE: You give us enough coming to see us—talk to us.

PRINCESS: We don't get too many people here—so it's nice for a change.

TYRONE: Yeah. Real nice.

(*Pause.* MARTIN *picks up the money.*)

That's the boy.

MARTIN: This is a funny thing but you know we been here three times looking for you. I ring the bell and ring and ring but couldn't get no answer. I know the bell was workin' because I could hear it from outside. Only reason I got in this time was because the front door was open.

You don't answer your bell.

TYRONE: Lessen we expectin' somebody. It ain't a good policy, these days. Thieves, clowns, all kinds of people try to get in when they feel you old and helpless. Anyhow, people get in the way. I don't mean you—but other people. They come in here, upset you life. Make you do things you don't want to do. Make you get blood on your hands. If you ain't careful.

Had a feller in here a while back. A white boy. Big, with blue eyes and a smooth face. He was okay . . . a lot of personality. Work for an insurance company, selling insurance. Three, four days he came talking about special policies and benefits if I suddenly drop dead, things like that. I didn't pay much attention. Princess talked to him.

PRINCESS: I was bein' polite.

TYRONE: He had manners, so I didn't mind him round the house. Then one day I went out somewhere, I don't remember, and I come back just in time to catch him red-handed trying to touch. (*Pause.*) You see, Princess was bent over putting something in the oven. And this white boy was reaching out trying to touch her butt. He didn't touch her, he was just reaching like when I walked in. I asked him what he was doing and pulled out my knife. He said he was trying to attract her attention.

PRINCESS: I remember that same day he kept telling me how much he looked like Raymond Burr. You know—that fellow on TV? Said people kept mistaking him for Raymond Burr.

TYRONE: So this fellow figger that because he look like Raymond Burr that give him the right to reach out and touch my wife's ass. People are crazy.

PRINCESS: Yeah.

TYRONE: That's why I don't answer the door. You never know what fool you lettin' in.

(GINNY *yawns.*)

That woman fallin' asleep on you.

GINNY: I'm sorry. It's been a long day.

TYRONE: What time is it?

PRINCESS: Nearly twelve.

TYRONE: Listen—that thing turn into a bed if you fold it out right. You could stay the night if you a mind to.

MARTIN (*looking at* GINNY): What do you think, Hon?

GINNY: It's up to you.

MARTIN: Want to stay?

GINNY: I don't mind.

MARTIN (*to* TYRONE): That's what we'll do then. We'll stay the night.

PRINCESS: I'll get sheets and pillows. (PRINCESS *exits to bedroom.*)

TYRONE: I'm going to take the bottle in the bedroom with me. Want a last one?

MARTIN: No—

TYRONE (*to* GINNY): What about you?

GINNY: No, thank you.

TYRONE: Well, you all young, I'm an old man. I need this bottle to help me get to sleep.

(PRINCESS *returns with the sheets.*)

GINNY: I'll take them. Thank you.

TYRONE: See you all in the morning.

MARTIN: Yeah—good-night, Bob.

PRINCESS: Good-night.

TYRONE (*to* GINNY): Good-night, Miss Chorus Girl.

GINNY: Good-night, Tyrone.

(PRINCESS *and* TYRONE *exit to bedroom as* MARTIN *and* GINNY *set up the bed.*)

MARTIN: What'd I tell you. He is something, ain't he?

GINNY: Yes.

MARTIN: He's like the last buffalo. When he goes ain't goin' be no more like him. No sir, not another.

GINNY: How old is he now?

MARTIN: I don't know. Late sixties, I guess.

GINNY: He doesn't look very strong.

MARTIN: No. That's why I'm glad we came.

(*Both strip down to their underwear in preparation for bed.*)

GINNY: But it's interesting, because even in this state, and even if you hadn't told me anything about him, I think I would've still sensed that he was a man who once had a lot of power. There's something about him, I don't know what it is but it's still there.

MARTIN: Yeah . . . he like you. He tell me when you went to the bathroom that you were a fine looking woman. He should know. He had some of the best in his time. And even now. Princess ain't bad.

GINNY: No.

MARTIN: You don't mind us staying over do you?

GINNY: No.

MARTIN: It's just for one night. Make the old man feel good.

GINNY: Sure.

MARTIN: Come here.

GINNY: Martin—

MARTIN: Come here baby.

(GINNY *goes to him. He caresses her all over, then kisses deeply. She kisses back. The embrace becomes more intense; it's starting to lead to other things.*)

GINNY: Martin, what about the lights.

MARTIN: Leave them on.

GINNY: We can't.
MARTIN: You're right.

(*He goes and turns them off. When he does the stage goes black.*)

(*End of scene.*)

Over black

The sound of music comes up. Soft, soothing music. The music plays for a while then begins to fade as the sound of early morning radio takes over. Weather report, traffic report, news report, time checks, and even commercials.
Slowly the lights come up to half. PRINCESS *comes out. By this time* MARTIN *and* GINNY *are out of the room.* PRINCESS *looks at the unmade sofa for a second then goes to the kitchen table where she puts out plates of food.*
MARTIN *comes out.*

MARTIN: Morning, Princess.
PRINCESS: Morning.

(TYRONE *comes out, signals for* MARTIN *to sit. They both do. Lights come up to full.*)

SCENE THREE

Early morning.

TYRONE *and* MARTIN *are silent for a moment after the lights come up.*

TYRONE: So, what was I saying?
MARTIN: You was telling me 'bout the last job you had.
TYRONE: Oh yeah . . . last job I had was waitin' tables in this restaurant. Nice job and I was making money. But my feet went bad on me so I couldn't keep up with the younger boys. Had to limp to get around the floor. It was hard . . . but the money was good.
 The young boys used to help me. Get the drinks, carry the food out, even change the tablecloths when the people left. All I had to do was take the order and pick up the tip.
 They were good boys and kind to the old man, so I felt I should give them something. Something to make up for the way they was helping me.

Couldn't show them nothing serious—so . . . I showed them how to help theirselves while they was helping the owner. How to make themselves silent partners in the business. Know what I'm talking about?

MARTIN: Uh-huh.

TYRONE: That coffee 'bout near ready?

PRINCESS: Coming up in a minute Bob.

TYRONE: Well, Martin boy, I turned on that white-wingless-fairy and told him "Don't you fuck with me, Don't you ever fuck with me, fire me if you like but give me my respect." Then I offer to kick his ass and cut it. He shut up quick and let me walk out like a man.

I come home to Princess and since that day I ain't work for another living soul, white or black or any other color in between.

MARTIN: So how you making it?

TYRONE: Social Security . . . welfare. . . . Sometimes I play the numbers. Sometimes I even hit.

MARTIN: What about Princess? Couldn't she work?

TYRONE: She already got a job. Taking care of me. Plus she done already work hard enough. I'm the man a the house. I take care a things.

MARTIN: Your sons. What about them, don't they send you nothing?

TYRONE: My boys? One's dead, the other is in the army.

MARTIN: Dead? Which one?

TYRONE: Wallace. The oldest one. It was on the front of *The Daily News*. Some F.B.I. or something was trying to arrest him for pushing dope. They broke into his place and he try to shoot it out. . . . I didn't even know that boy was in New York. . . . the other one, Kenny, is a sergeant in the army.

Their mother is still in the Bronx. She was at Wallace's funeral. The oldest black woman I ever seen. Face all dried and wrinkled. Hair all white. But she was a good looking woman in her time. I'll give her that. She blame me for Wallace and call me bad names in front of the preacher and everybody. . . . Then afterwards she send me some money in the mail to pay the rent. My people are strange. You can't ever figure them out. (*Pause.*) Where's your gal?

MARTIN: In the bathroom.

TYRONE: Nice gal . . . nice lookin' too.

MARTIN: Yes . . .

TYRONE: You treat her good?

MARTIN: Yes.

TYRONE: Don't beat her or nothing?

MARTIN: No.

TYRONE: Used to be a time a man could chastise his woman and nobody would say a thing. Not even the woman. But nowadays you raise your hand to a woman she'll get the law on your ass or shoot you herself. And ain't no court in the land gon tell her she wrong. So a man got to be careful how he talk to a woman. Or even look at them.

MARTIN: I—I know . . .

GINNY (*entering*): Good-morning.

(TYRONE *stands up and holds her chair until she sits down.*)

TYRONE: Sleep well?

GINNY: Yes. And you?

TYRONE (*sitting back down*): I always sleep well when I have my bottle.

GINNY: Where's Princess?

TYRONE: Cookin'.

GINNY: I took a shower. I feel refreshed.

(PRINCESS *enters with coffee.*)

Morning, Princess.

PRINCESS: Morning.

GINNY: Can I help you with something?

PRINCESS: It's all done.

TYRONE: Paper come?

PRINCESS: No.

TYRONE: Lottery winners come out today. I got a couple of tickets . . . would be nice to get something outta this city after all these years. (*To* MARTIN) You got any plans for today?

MARTIN: No.

TYRONE: I got to go down to the Social Security office. I don't know why, but they want to see me. Probably to take away some of that little bit they been sending me. Want to come?

MARTIN: No. I think maybe we'll walk around the neighborhood. I want to see what changes went on since I been away.

TYRONE: Suit yourself.

GINNY: Darling, can I go with Tyrone.

MARTIN: Oh . . . ? Sure.

GINNY: I was born in New York but I left here as a little girl. This is the first time I've been back. I haven't seen much of the city. Do you mind, Tyrone?

TYRONE: No, my pleasure.

PRINCESS: You see more a New York if you take a bus tour. What you gon' see with him? The inside of some dirty old office building?

GINNY: I don't mind.

TYRONE: Remember, I ain't as young as I used to be. So walk slow with me. My heart can't take any fast speeds.

GINNY: I'll let you set the pace.

MARTIN: Ginny's father before he died was eighty-nine years old. She used to walk with him all the time. Ginny know how to be careful.

TYRONE: My old man when he die was ninety-one. He was no good and a son of a bitch in the bargain. But he live long. I'll give him that. He live a long evil life.

PRINCESS: What time you plan to be back?

TYRONE: I don't know. Early.

PRINCESS: I'll plan for dinner to be at seven.

TYRONE: All right.

MARTIN: Well, I guess it gon' be you and me today Princess.

PRINCESS: You alone. I got to go to the laundromat in about a half hour.

MARTIN: Breakfast is good.

GINNY: Hmm. Delicious.

MARTIN: You a good cook Princess.

PRINCESS: Thank-you . . . Bob?

TYRONE: Oh yeah. It's good. Like the gal said—delicious.

(*All concentrate on eating as the lights slowly fade.*)

Over black

Sounds of city noise. Traffic, sirens in the distance, etc. Then a clock tolls out the hour.

SCENE FOUR

Nine o'clock that night. PRINCESS *and* MARTIN *are sitting in chairs. She's reading a magazine, he's staring off in space. After a while* MARTIN *rises.*

MARTIN: Look at the hour.

PRINCESS: Hmmm.

MARTIN: Look at the time. They're late.

PRINCESS: Uh-huh.

MARTIN: You hearing me?

PRINCESS: Yes.

MARTIN: I wonder where they could be?

PRINCESS: Who knows?

MARTIN: Goddamn. . . . Is it like Bob to stay out late?
PRINCESS: No.

(*Pause.*)

MARTIN: What time is it?
PRINCESS: Huh?
MARTIN: What time is it?
PRINCESS: Ten after nine.
MARTIN: Ten after nine. Ten after nine. This is a bad city. Ain't you worried?
PRINCESS: About what? Bob is a man able to take care of himself.
MARTIN: Yeah but suppose he got sick or something.
PRINCESS: Then the girl would call. She bright enough to do that, ain't she?
MARTIN: I don't know. She sometimes ain't as bright as she look. Plus I didn't even know you had a phone.
PRINCESS: It's there. We hardly ever use it but it's there.

(*Pause.* PRINCESS *goes back to reading her magazine.* MARTIN *tries to relax but can't.*)

MARTIN: You got any liquor in the house?
PRINCESS: What?
MARTIN: Liquor. You got any in the house?
PRINCESS: Brandy—you want some?
MARTIN: Yes—please.

(PRINCESS *gets it. She returns with the drink. Hands it to* MARTIN *and resumes her former position.* MARTIN, *searching for something to occupy him goes over to the TV-VCR setup and begins to look at the small pile of X-rated tapes next to it.*)

MARTIN: These yours, Princess?
PRINCESS (*looking up from her magazine*): No.
MARTIN: Damn, you'd think a man at Bob's age would be getting some religion instead a looking at these things.

(PRINCESS *doesn't answer or respond.* MARTIN *puts back the tapes and begins to focus his attention on* PRINCESS *who still is absorbed in her magazine.*)

Princess, can I ask you something?
PRINCESS: What?
MARTIN: How old are you?

PRINCESS: Thirty-eight. Why?

MARTIN: And you been married to Bob how long?

PRINCESS: Fifteen years.

MARTIN: Damn, you a young woman. Even when you got married, you was a young woman and he was an old man.

PRINCESS: Ain't nothing wrong with that. Bob is the man I love. Ain't ever love nobody else. Ain't ever had to. Bob Tyrone is a man that know how to please his woman. Ain't a lot of men who know how to do that.

When Bob and I meet I was a child. He take me and he hold me and he show me the way to being a woman. And since that night I been loving him . . . and him alone. That answer your question?

MARTIN: You mean you ain't never—

PRINCESS: Never.

MARTIN: Damn.

PRINCESS: That hard to believe?

MARTIN: No. I suppose not.

PRINCESS: Good.

MARTIN: But what you intend to do when that man goes?

PRINCESS: Go where? Bob ain't got no place to go but here.

MARTIN: That ain't what I mean. I mean when he go for good.

PRINCESS: Oh.

(*Pause.*)

MARTIN: Yeah.

PRINCESS: I ain't ever thought of it.

MARTIN: Maybe you should.

PRINCESS: Yeah.

MARTIN: You got any kin, Princess?

PRINCESS: Outside of Bob, it just me alone.

MARTIN: You ain't never had no children, neither.

PRINCESS: No.

MARTIN: You like me. We got a lot in common. I ain't never had no kin, neither. The day I was born my papa run off to avoid taking the blame for me. My mama lived two years after, and then she died of something or other. From that time to now I've been on my own. (*Silence, but he continues looking at her in an unvarying manner.*)

PRINCESS: Why you looking at me like that?

MARTIN: I don't know. You interest me.

PRINCESS: You interest me too.

MARTIN: Why?

PRINCESS: I keep wondering why you come back here after all this time?

MARTIN: I told you. To see Bob . . . talk to him. See if I could help. Maybe give him some money.

PRINCESS: All that money really yours?

MARTIN: Uh-huh.

PRINCESS: Where you get it?

MARTIN: Earn it.

PRINCESS: What kind of work you do pay you that kind of money all together? You an actor, movie star, something like that?

MARTIN: No.

PRINCESS: Then how you get it? You hit the number, win the lottery . . . what?

MARTIN: Princess, that's my business.

PRINCESS: That ain't legal money. Is it?

MARTIN: It ain't your place to ask me.

PRINCESS: But I want to know. You walk in here and you offer it to us. I want to know where it come from.

MARTIN (*gulping the last of his drink*): Get me another drink.

PRINCESS: Not till you tell me about that money.

MARTIN: Get me a drink woman, damn it. I talk to you now . . .

PRINCESS: Still I ask you a question and you ain't give me back no answer. How, Martin? How?

MARTIN: Princess, stay off—

PRINCESS: You was ready and willing to give it away. It must be easy to get—

MARTIN: What 'bout you? You easy to get? Think I believe that stuff bout Bob being the one and only. Tell me about you Princess.

PRINCESS: You tell me about that money. And I'll tell you 'bout me.

MARTIN: I asked you for a drink before.

PRINCESS: Tell me 'bout your money, Martin.

MARTIN: You looking for something and you goin' get it.

PRINCESS: You jumping around but you ain't fooling nobody. Tell me 'bout that money.

(MARTIN *looks at her. He feels cornered and challenged.*)

MARTIN: Woman you better stay outta my face. You better get outta my way.

PRINCESS: Why?

MARTIN: Why!

PRINCESS: Yeah, why?

MARTIN: B-b-b-because—Because, well b-b-because you mess with me and—Fuck! Just leave me alone, huh? Just leave me be. (*Abruptly he goes into the kitchen and returns with a glass half filled with brandy.*) I don't need you. I can get my own.

PRINCESS: You little sissy. You waste. Chickened out, didn't you?

(MARTIN *sips his brandy, not saying a word.*)

You chicken out! (*Frustrated and tense, she sits down.*) You faggot niggers, make me laugh. Don't know nothin' 'bout bein' men. Just acting up and falling out. That's all you know. That's all. You talk bad but when the time come you only know how to cop a plea and cry for your mama. Ain't that so, little Martin? Ain't that so . . . (*Pause.*) I remember you when you used to hang out behind Bob. You was a fool then and you ain't changed a lick.

Bob, old as he is, he's ten times the man you are now. You know that? Ten times the man. (*Pause.*) Now do something for me. Get me a drink. And make it goddamn quick.

(*Pause. Then* MARTIN *rises and gets* PRINCESS *a drink. He hands it to her. She looks at him.*)

That's the way, Martin boy. That's the way.

(MARTIN *returns to his chair—another pause.*)

MARTIN: The money I make is for killing people. I do it and I get paid good pay for it. It's a job like any other job. You have your tools. And you have your way of going about getting the job done. No two jobs are the same, but every one is interesting.

Like any other job you got to first go through a training period, then working with somebody else before you go out on your own. Some people have the knack, some don't. (*Pause.*)

The people you kill don't always have to be important people. Most of the time they're not. Just some dumb son of a bitch who mess with the wrong man or the wrong woman and didn't even know it. Some people is just dangerous to be around and that's how it is. (*Pause.*)

That trip to Canada. That was a job. The man was fifty-five and bald and funny looking. He didn't look like he could upset anybody but he must've. So—now he ain't no more. (*Pause again.*)

I always do my business with a knife because it quiet and it's the tool I know how to use best. (*Pause.*)

I stuck a knife in his kidneys four times and left him in the alley behind his store. The money I showed you and Bob was half the payment for that job. When I go back the other half will be waiting. (*Long pause.*) When Ginny come back I'm going to kick her ass because she should know better than to stay out this late without telling me. What you looking at?

PRINCESS: Nothing.

MARTIN: Then look at something else.

PRINCESS (*standing up*): You want another drink?

MARTIN: Yes.

(PRINCESS *exits and returns with the drink.* MARTIN *takes it and puts it on the table.* PRINCESS *turns away.*)

MARTIN: Princess.

PRINCESS: What?

MARTIN: Come here.

PRINCESS: Why?

MARTIN: Come here.

(*She goes to him. Without a word* MARTIN *takes her in his arms and kisses her. They break and watch each other. Before either can say a word the front door opens. Both turn and wait.* TYRONE *and* GINNY *enter. Both are slightly high or drunk.*)

TYRONE: Hey, Martin boy—

GINNY: Hello darling.

MARTIN (*to* GINNY): Where were you?

GINNY: At the Social Security office. (*She giggles at her own joke.*)

MARTIN: Till ten o'clock at night.

TYRONE: We did a few bars, had a few drinks.

PRINCESS (*to* TYRONE): You eat anything?

TYRONE: Yes—I had some roast beef. . . .

MARTIN (*to* GINNY): Couldn't you call . . . say something. Princess and I was here worrying.

GINNY: I didn't know we would be this late.

MARTIN: What were you doing?

GINNY: Honey—

TYRONE: Leave the woman alone, Martin—

MARTIN: Keep out of this, Bob. I'm talking to her.

TYRONE: But she ain't done nothing wrong.

MARTIN: She out all day and half the night, and you say she ain't done nothing wrong.

GINNY: I'm sorry darling. I didn't know. . . .

MARTIN: Didn't know? Didn't know. (*Viciously he slaps her across her face.*) That'll teach you to think next time.

TYRONE: Now, that's wrong. That's goddamn wrong. I ain't having it in my house. That girl ain't done nothing wrong.

PRINCESS: Bob—

TYRONE: If she did something wrong I'd understand. But that girl ain't done nothing. You hearing me boy! That girl is innocent.

MARTIN: Bob, I told you to stay the *fuck* out of this. This don't concern you.

TYRONE: Yes it does. It mother-fucking does. I ain't standing for no woman being beat in my house for no reason. You gon' apologize to that woman for what you done just now.

MARTIN: Apologize?

TYRONE: Damn right you better apologize.

MARTIN: Bob—do me a favor and go—

TYRONE: Boy, hear me! I's talking to you now. I ain't goin' have this in my house. I ain't (*He moves in front of* MARTIN.) Now tell the girl you sorry and this will all be over.

MARTIN: Bob, I'm only going to tell you once. You're an old man. Get out of my face.

TYRONE: And if I don't?

MARTIN: I'm fucking warning you.

PRINCESS: Bob . . . Bob, be careful with this man. He makes his living killing people.

TYRONE: And I's the man who teach him. All right, Martin, boy. You want a showdown? Now is the time. Apologize to this woman or face up to me.

(*A tense pause.*)

You hear me!

GINNY: Tyrone—

TYRONE: Keep out of this. I'm waiting on you boy.

MARTIN: Waiting? Waiting? You, you, you—Ahhh—What's the point? What's the whole fucking point? (MARTIN *once again becomes nervous and upset. Again he seems ready to attack but then for some inexplicable reason decides not to.*) You an old man, Bob, an old man looking to get hisself killed. But I ain't goin' be the one. No. Hell no. Die on your own. I get paid for who I kill. (*The tension passes.*) Come on, Ginny, let's go?

GINNY: Go where?

MARTIN: Back to the hotel.

GINNY (*waiting a long moment, then saying*): You go. I'm not ready just yet.

MARTIN: What?

TYRONE: You getting hard of hearing? Girl ain't finish visiting yet.

MARTIN: She finished when I say she finish.

TYRONE: I don't think so Martin boy, that woman look like she got a mind of her own.

MARTIN: What's goin' on here? You going crazy? What happened between you two today?

TYRONE: Nothing.

MARTIN: No?

GINNY: No.

PRINCESS: Bob?

TYRONE: Nothing.

MARTIN: Then what's the problem? Let's go.

TYRONE: The girl don't want to go.

GINNY: Not just yet.

MARTIN: Why?

GINNY: No reason. I just want to stay a little longer.

MARTIN (*totally confused*): How much longer?

GINNY: A few more days—that's all. You go.

MARTIN (*sitting down*): I don't understand.

TYRONE: What's so hard about what the woman just said?

MARTIN (*a different tone, lightly*): Honey—let's go.

GINNY: No. . . . Not just yet.

MARTIN: Why?

GINNY: I don't know. I don't want to go, that's all.

MARTIN: But why?

(GINNY *shrugs*.)

MARTIN: Then that settles it. I'm not going either. . . . I go when you go. We come together, we're leaving together. That's it.

PRINCESS: Bob—? (*No answer.*) Bob.

TYRONE: It's getting late and I'm tired. Let's call it a night.

PRINCESS: Night?

TYRONE: Yes. Let's call it a night.

(*The tension broken, all begin to move. Wearily* MARTIN *goes toward the sofa.* TYRONE *gets to the door of the bedroom and turns to* PRINCESS.)

Hold it a minute. . . . Princess, you sleep out here tonight. Ginny— in here.

(MARTIN *looks at him numbly.* GINNY *moves past* TYRONE *and enters the bedroom.*)

See you all in the morning. (*Tyrone exits.*)

(PRINCESS *and* MARTIN *stand as though in a trance for a moment. Then* MARTIN *pulls out the bed and begins fixing the sheets.* PRINCESS *in the meantime starts removing her dress. The light in the bedroom clicks off.* MARTIN *considers it for a moment and then turns to see* PRINCESS *standing in her underwear.*)

MARTIN (*resignedly*): Well, like it or not. It's you and me, ain't it Princess. You and me and this sofa bed.

(PRINCESS *doesn't answer. He goes to her and takes her in his arms. She doesn't resist. Roughly he smears his thumb over her lips.*)

PRINCESS: Don't hurt me, please.
MARTIN: Shut up!
PRINCESS: Martin—
MARTIN: You been curious about me, I been curious about you. Now I guess is when we find out. (*He goes to kiss her roughly but she stops him.*)
PRINCESS: Be nice—please.

(*Pause.*)

MARTIN: All right. . . . I'm sorry.

(*They embrace and kiss gently as the lights fade.*)

(*End of Act One*)

ACT TWO

SCENE ONE

Early the following morning. The light from outside gives the place a bleak and austere look. The sofa is still pulled out into an unmade bed. All the positions of the glasses are still the same as the previous night.

MARTIN, *fully dressed, is sitting on the bed, staring into space—waiting. His wait isn't long. A moment later* GINNY *enters. She is dressed but not as completely as* MARTIN. *She has no shoes on.* MARTIN *jumps up when he sees her.*

GINNY: Hi, Martin . . .
MARTIN: Morning—(*one beat*) Sleep well?
GINNY: Yes . . . thank you.

MARTIN: Er—er—where's Bob?

GINNY: In there—still sleeping.

MARTIN: I guess he slept well too.

GINNY: Yeah.

MARTIN: Well . . . I didn't sleep well. Tossed and turned all night. Must've been the bed. I never sleep well in strange beds.

GINNY: You didn't complain the night before. It was the same bed.

MARTIN: That's true . . . that's true . . . maybe it wasn't the bed.

GINNY: Where's Princess?

MARTIN: I don't know . . . out . . . somewhere.

GINNY: Did she sleep well?

MARTIN: You care?

GINNY: Yes.

MARTIN: I guess so. Yeah. She slept—

GINNY: I slept like a baby.

MARTIN: Yeah—you said so.

GINNY (*remembering the pleasure*): Hmmm . . .

MARTIN (*after a beat*): You ready?

GINNY: Ready for what?

MARTIN: To go.

GINNY: Go—where?

MARTIN: Home. Las Vegas—the place where we live.

GINNY: Oh . . . Er . . . no. No. Not yet.

MARTIN: When?

GINNY: I don't know.

MARTIN: You—don't? Okay, okay—fine.

GINNY: What's that mean?

MARTIN: We'll go when you ready.

GINNY: You plan to just stay and wait, just like that?

MARTIN: Yes.

GINNY: Why?

MARTIN: Because I ain't going without you.

GINNY: But suppose it's long? Suppose I decide to stay for a long, long time.

MARTIN: Doesn't matter.

GINNY: But what about . . . the money you're supposed to collect?

MARTIN: That can wait.

GINNY: You sure?

MARTIN: Yes, it can wait.

(*A long pause.*)

GINNY: Martin—I don't know if I can ever go back.

MARTIN: What? What you talking about?

GINNY: It's not the same. Things have changed. It won't be the same as it was before.

MARTIN: What you talking about? Of course it'll be the same. Same as it always been. You and me.

GINNY: No it won't. I know it won't. It can't ever be the same.

MARTIN: Why?

GINNY: It just can't. That's all.

MARTIN: Ginny—

GINNY: Martin I'm trying to be straight with you.

MARTIN: So, what's the next move?

GINNY: You're asking me?

MARTIN: Yes. I'm asking you what's the next move for you and me.

GINNY: Breaking up, I suppose. You going one way. Me going the other.

MARTIN (*shaking his head*): No.

GINNY: It's the only way, Martin.

MARTIN: No. There must be some other way. Think of another way.

GINNY: I don't want another way. I want it this way. Our next step has to be good-bye.

MARTIN: Why? Why we got to break up? Why we got to say good-bye?

GINNY: Martin—

MARTIN: You and me, baby, we been together. We live together.

GINNY: Things have changed.

MARTIN: Nothing's changed.

GINNY: I went into that room last night. I was with that man. I slept with him. Made love to him. Kissed his body and he kissed mine. Did things with him I never did with anybody else. . . . and when it was all over I slept like I haven't slept in years.

MARTIN: This—this is a game, Ginny. A joke, a dream. Some kinda hot weather mood that will pass. People get crazy in a city like this when the weather turn hot. We'll get back to where we used to be. Back to when we were close—when you was lonely and we was close. Like . . . like . . . like the time when your father died.

GINNY: He was an old man like Tyrone is an old man. And he needed me. He needed me and I was there, but you didn't come to the funeral.

MARTIN: You wouldn't let me come. You said you didn't want me there.

GINNY: He was nothing to you. He was my father. My own flesh and blood.

MARTIN: You needed me then Ginny. In those days you needed me— bad. And you gon need me again. You'll see.

GINNY: Funny, I have nobody left now—no parents, nobody . . . (*She steps away and begins to move.*) I'm a dancer. A good dancer. I should practice more. Everybody says I have talent, but I should practice more. (*She begins doing dance exercises.*)

MARTIN: Ginny, listen to me. (GINNY *doesn't answer, she just continues her movement, lost in the reverie of her thoughts and movement.*)

(MARTIN *watches her for a while, thinking, then he reaches into his pocket and produces a knife.* GINNY *doesn't see it. He positions himself and is about to do something violent, when* PRINCESS *walks in.*)

PRINCESS (*not seeing the knife either*): He up yet? (*She means* BOB.)
GINNY: No.
PRINCESS: He sleep quiet all night?
GINNY: Yes.

(PRINCESS *looks at* MARTIN *who's put away the knife and looks exhausted.*)

PRINCESS: You staying or going?
MARTIN: Staying.
PRINCESS (*to* MARTIN): I think you should go.
MARTIN: I'm staying.
PRINCESS (*to* GINNY): You too.
GINNY: I'm not ready just yet.
PRINCESS: I don't care. I don't give a good goddamn. And that's the truth.
MARTIN: Me either.

(*A pause while everyone waits for the other to say something. Suddenly* PRINCESS *begins to laugh.*)

PRINCESS: What a mess. What a goddamn mess. . . . Anybody want coffee?
GINNY and MARTIN (*in unison*): Yes, please.
PRINCESS: It's in there. (*She points to the kitchen.*) You all got to get it for your damn self. I'm done being the servant. You all ain't guests anymore. (*With that she leaves.*)
MARTIN: It's every man for himself I guess.
GINNY (*distantly*): Yes.

(MARTIN *rises and goes toward the kitchen.* GINNY *turns her back to him and once again begins dance exercises.* MARTIN *looks at her for a while, then exits to the kitchen.*)

(*Lights fade. End of scene*)

SCENE TWO

Later that same day. Afternoon.

GINNY *is sitting around watching daytime television (a soap opera or game show), when* PRINCESS *walks in carrying laundry or groceries. She stops, looks at* GINNY *(who doesn't see her) then puts down her package. Then she goes over very deliberately and turns off the TV.* GINNY *looks at her.*

PRINCESS: What do you want from us?
GINNY: Want?
PRINCESS: Yes. Want.
GINNY: I don't want—I don't want anything.
PRINCESS: Then why don't you leave? Just go.
GINNY: I'm going to go.
PRINCESS: When? Why don't you go now?
GINNY: I'm not planning to stay here forever. I'm going to go. When the time is right I'm going to leave, and you won't ever have to look at me again.
PRINCESS: Why'd you come here in the first place? We was doing fine, just me and him. We didn't have nobody. And didn't need nobody. . . . So why'd you have to come. Just to make trouble?
GINNY: We weren't coming here. That wasn't the plan. We went to Canada, Martin and me. He had something to do up there. Some kinda work. And he asked me to go with him. Most of the time I never go on trips with him. I had my job. And I don't like to travel that much. But this time I said okay. You see, things weren't going so well with us, and we thought maybe this trip would help. I mean— when things ain't going too well for two people, sometimes a long trip together in a car might help. And, since I wasn't working I had a lot of free time.

You see—I—had been working but then I quit. Las Vegas is a strange place sometimes. A weird town full of strange, weird people. Doing weird, strange things. And they make you do them too. Especially if you work in the chorus of one of those big casinos.

That place isn't normal. It's all turned upside down. The clocks run funny. It's always night wherever you are. Never day. Always, always night. And it affects you after a while if you live there.

Martin lives there. And he is kinda strange. But not as strange as most of the people you meet. He was the nicest of everybody I knew. That's how we came to live together. Because he was nice. And still is. But now it's time for a change. Time for it to be over.

PRINCESS: I don't care about you or Martin. I care about Bob—And when this is over—after you leave—what am I supposed to do? Go back into that bedroom and lie down next to that man and forget about all of this? Act as if you didn't come and invade our home—

GINNY: I didn't—

PRINCESS: Behave as if this was some kind of nightmare that didn't really happen. (*Pause.*) When I met Bob I was still a girl, and he was already getting old. People warned me against him. Said he was evil, but I didn't care. They said he would close off the world for me. And so he did. But Bob was what I wanted and what I had. Till you came in. You and that goddamn Martin pushing and pushing and pushing on that bell. Not taking no for an answer. Coming in here with your noise and your money. And all that talk about Vegas . . . and about lights. . . . I wish I'd never seen you. Never knew you exist. and I wish you would go home—and leave us. Me and my man. Just leave us—alone.

GINNY: I can't.

PRINCESS: Why?

GINNY: I don't know why. I can't, that's all. I just can't. Don't hate me Princess. Just give me a little while longer, a little while longer and I'll be gone, I promise.

PRINCESS (*after a pause*): I want you to die. You know that. I want you to die real soon.

GINNY: Why?

TYRONE (*entering*): Princess? . . . Ginny? Oh there you are. (*Looking around*) Where's Martin?

GINNY: Out. I don't know. Out somewhere.

TYRONE: What you two up to? Talking? That's nice. What I like to see. It's nice for women to get along especially in a household as small as this one. (*Pause.*) Well, I'm going out to sit on the stoop for a while. Call me if you need anything.

PRINCESS (*softly*): Yes. Bob, we will. We'll call you if we need anything.

(*Lights fade. End of scene*)

SCENE THREE

Ten o'clock that night, a radio in the distance is playing something soulful and plaintive. Seated about the room are GINNY, MARTIN, PRINCESS, *and* TYRONE. TYRONE *is wearing a jacket and bow tie, the style of a long gone era.*

The music plays. All have drinks in their hands sitting around—almost in a tableaux gathering—represents a party of some sort. . . . Silence while the music plays. . . . Finally Tyrone speaks.

TYRONE: The music that you hear nowadays ain't that good to dance to. Not like the old days when songs were only so that people could get themselves together. (*Pause.*) That's how I met my first wife. She was a dancer, and I was thinking 'bout becoming one. I had a good body then. Slim and hard. I used to move with style, and people were always telling me I should be on the stage. Jennifer was a dancer. A good one, too. She had a hard little body with strong nice-shaped legs. But no chest area to speak of.

She was the smartest woman I knew, so I married her. I figured that she was the only one who could help me straighten myself out. I was getting in trouble a lot. Broke all the time. So I figure this woman could help me. She had a good brain.

(*Pause.*)

We was married for only a short while when I found out that the woman had a freaky nature. I should have recognized it sooner, but I was young and a little ignorant about those things. So I had to walk in unexpected one day and catch her hot—laid up in bed, naked as a barbeque chicken with this other friend—a girl named Wilma who used to come to the house all the time—they was so deep into their freaky business that I walked right in the room and nobody heard me.

When they see me Jenny start to cry, and the girl, that goddamn Wilma, start to call me a no-count nigger, mother fucker, and things like that. . . . I turned over the bed and kicked the freaky bitch in her butt. Then I took my belt and whipped both a them till the police come. Somebody called them because of all the noise and screaming. Judge give *me* thirty days for disorderly conduct. He didn't give them a thing for being freaky. Anyway, when I come out I divorced that bitch. Told her I was a man who didn't need no freak in his life. About a week after the divorce wouldn't you know she hit the numbers for something like *ten thousand dollars*. My luck! . . . I tried to get back with her, but she won't have nothing to do with me. She said I was an evil nigger.

(*A long pause as he sips his drink*)

I never went in for that freaky stuff. Never felt it paid. I once knew a boy who was taking money from a sissy and sleeping with a woman on the sly. The sissy catch wind of what was happening and sneaked in the house one night when the boy was on top of the woman. What he did to that boy was a terrible thing. He chop off his dick with a bread knife and threw it out the window. A friend of mine—Malcolm Reilly, was walking on the street. The dick nearly hit him on his head.

The boy died and the sissy went to jail. I don't know what ever happened to the woman.

(*Pause.*)

GINNY: Bob?
TYRONE: Yes.
GINNY: Dance with me.
TYRONE: Sure.

(*They move closer together.* TYRONE *encloses her in his embrace.* GINNY *presses herself deeply into his chest.* MARTIN *and* PRINCESS *sit absorbed in their own thoughts, almost unaware of the dancing couple.* MARTIN *finishes his drink and goes to get another. When he returns, the music has stopped and* TYRONE *goes back to his chair.* GINNY *hesitates then joins* TYRONE. *She sits on his knee.*)

TYRONE: I ever tell you about the time when I was working in this place in Harlem and this man asked me to get a spade for his wife? (*He waits. No answer.*) Eh, Martin boy? Ever tell you about that?
MARTIN: No, Bob.
TYRONE: He was a funny looking little white dude that used to come in all the time in the club. He used to tip me good and talk to me. Then one night he put the question to me. He told me he wanted a black man to work his wife for him and wondered if I knew any. Of course I knew a hundred boys including myself who would jump at the opportunity. He said he couldn't use me because I knew him too well, but if I knew somebody he would pay that man good money.

I brought him a fellow so ugly, so big, and so black, a ape would run from him. He say the boy was perfect and carried us in his car to his apartment somewhere around Central Park. I don't remember exactly where. When we get there the man poured us liquor and sit with us for a spell. After the booze, the man excused himself and took my friend to the bedroom to meet his wife. I had to stay outside. They didn't want me in their business. So I sat and I wait. And when I felt the time was right I cracked the door to see what was going on.

Know what I saw? I saw two white legs and a big black butt. I saw the little white man giggling and watching. When the thing got hot he would take his hand like this and slap my friend's behind calling out "Faster, nigger, faster!"

Afterwards when he came back he gave us each fifty dollars and told us we were nice people. That was in the twenties. At that time fifty dollars was a lot of money.

Money is a thing that always rule my life. Can't think of a time when money wasn't important to me. Can't think of a thing I wouldn't 've done for money. Didn't have to be big money either. Any kind of money. Just as long as it fold and you could spend it.

(*Pause.*)

PRINCESS: So this is how it going to be tonight? Everybody gon' just sit here being sociable, drinking and talking, acting like nothing happen? Huh?

(*She looks from* MARTIN *to* TYRONE *and* GINNY *and back to* MARTIN *for a response but gets none.*)

Well, something *did* happen. To us. It happen last night. It happening again now. (*Pause.*)

This (*She indicates* TYRONE *and* GINNY) and this (MARTIN) and me over here.

(*To* TYRONE) Bob, I'm your wife. Me. Princess Ellen de Witt. That woman, these people—outsiders—strangers. Coming in here busting up our home. Throw them out, Bob. Send them away. We didn't invite them. We don't even know them.

What they doing here? What they want from us? Huh?

(*To* MARTIN) What? What?

MARTIN (*automatically*): I don't want nothing, Princess. Nothing at all. I come to see Bob. Maybe give him something—money—something.

PRINCESS: Ain't you done give enough?

MARTIN: I don't know what you talking 'bout, Princess.

PRINCESS: Oh Bob . . . Bob . . . Bob . . . what's happening to us? What happening to our house?

TYRONE (*stroking* GINNY's *legs*): You got a nice body under them clothes.

GINNY: Thank-you.

TYRONE: It come from dancing, don't it?

GINNY: And exercise. When I'm home I always make a point of exercising every day. To limber up and to keep the muscles supple.

TYRONE: I bet you're a good dancer.

GINNY: I can follow choreography, and I can keep time in a chorus. And—I have good legs.

TYRONE: Strong legs.

GINNY: Well—yes.

TYRONE: Do something. A dance. A chorus number like you do for all them tourists in Las Vegas.

GINNY: Here?
TYRONE: Why not?
GINNY: But suppose—
TYRONE: Do it for me . . . please.
GINNY: OK.

(GINNY *stands before* TYRONE, *does a ballet turn and begins a movement. It is one of her chorus movements. It is subtle, and obvious, refined and loose and very sexy all at the same time.* TYRONE *sits watching her attentively while* MARTIN *looks the other way, and* PRINCESS *is watching* GINNY. *When she stops* TYRONE *takes her in his arms and kisses her. Slowly, while still kissing, they move across the room and into the bedroom.*)

MARTIN: The army taught me how to use a gun but I always found a blade so much nicer. The blade don't get hot and make a noise. It just stick in your hand and do your job quiet and quick. People's body, when they get a blade stuck in it, tremble and shake. The muscles tense up and then wait. With the second and third jab you feel them relax. Their whole weight lean against you. And if you touching their skin, you could already feel the life starting to slip out of that body.

I once had a woman to kill, she bother somebody, and they put the money out for her head. She was a good-looking woman and I managed to get in her bed a few times. I cut her throat when she was sleeping. She didn't even know she was dead till it was too late.
PRINCESS: You ever kill an old man?
MARTIN: I only kill people for money, Princess.
PRINCESS: How much?
MARTIN: A lot. A whole, whole lot.
PRINCESS: What about Ginny. You planning to kill her? You should. Ain't no reason she should live. Not after what she done.

(MARTIN *moves to indicate he doesn't want to answer her.*)

You don't want to talk or act, so I guess we gon' have to stay like this tomorrow and the next day till that girl decides she had enough. . . . What a life. What a goddamn life. (*Pause—somewhere in the distance a clock strikes the hour.*) Nighttime. Sleeptime again. Day is over. Move so's I can pull out this bed.

(*He moves and* PRINCESS *begins pulling out the bed in the sofa. After she pulls the bed out,* MARTIN *sits on it.* PRINCESS *removes her dress. She is stepping out of her half-slip when* TYRONE *enters the room dressed in his underwear.*)

TYRONE (*with a strange expression on his face*): My mama was half Indian. My poppa was the ugliest black man you ever did see. People used to ask my momma all the time, "Louise—Louise, why you let that ugly man touch you?" My momma only used to smile and shake her head.

"I love him," she used to tell me. "I love that no-good nigger—your father."

When I was fourteen I was big for my age. A teacher named Miss Andrews, a white woman, took a liking to me and give me a job beating her rug. One day she let me into the house and up 'gainst her body. After that every Thursday I'd beat the rug and pump the woman. I-I-I-I-I-I-I-

(*This continues for a while.* TYRONE *seems to be gasping for breath.* MARTIN *and* PRINCESS *sit and watch him in a frozen position.* GINNY *appears at the door. She too is in her underwear. The sight of* TYRONE *stuck like the needle on a phonograph stops her too. But she is the first to recover and say something.*)

GINNY: Martin! Princess! For God's sake, somebody do something!

(*Her short scream jolts them out of their stupor and both rise to go toward him. Before they can reach him* TYRONE *abruptly falls to the floor in a heap.* MARTIN *goes to him while* PRINCESS *and* GINNY *look on from afar.* MARTIN *touches* TYRONE's *forehead, feels his pulse, listens at his chest and his mouth for sounds of life. Finally he stands up and looks from one woman to another.*)

MARTIN: Gone.

(*Nobody moves.*)

MARTIN: Gone. (*Like a bell tolling*) Gone . . . gone . . . gone . . . gone.
PRINCESS: And it's about time. It's about goddamn time.

(*Everybody remains in their positions as though frozen. Slowly the lights fade.*)

SCENE FOUR

Two days later. That afternoon about six o'clock. Approximately one hour after the funeral.

Lights come up on the empty set. Moments later the key is heard in the door.

Enter PRINCESS, *followed by* MARTIN *and* GINNY, *all dressed in dark clothing.*

PRINCESS *goes into the bedroom while* MARTIN *and* GINNY *wait in the living room.* GINNY *is looking at* TYRONE'*s empty chair,* MARTIN *is looking at her. . . . A long pause.*

MARTIN: Ain't no chance a you changing your mind, I suppose.

GINNY: No.

MARTIN: What you plannin' to do?

GINNY: I'm not sure. Dance, I guess. Maybe get married, settle down. Have some children.

MARTIN (*quietly*): Yeah?

GINNY: Yeah . . . that's the plan. At least for now anyway. What about you?

MARTIN: Don't worry about me. I'm going to be fine. Better than fine.

GINNY: Good.

MARTIN: But, you be careful in this city, hear? You keep a eye out. Walk on bright streets. People in this place—some a them crazy out their head. One of these nights, if you ain't careful, somebody might jump out of a corner with a knife after your money. And he'll cut your throat just because he want your two dollars. So be careful, baby. Don't let that happen because I worry about you. You used to belong to me.

GINNY: I'll be careful.

(MARTIN *picks up one of the adult video tape boxes.*)

MARTIN: He used to like to look at these things. Can you imagine, a man of his age.

GINNY: Hmmm.

MARTIN: He was an evil old creature when you come to think of it. Can't think of a thing he ever did for anybody but himself. Ever. Just an evil old creature right up to his last day.

GINNY: He wasn't so bad.

MARTIN: Yes he was. He was the worst.

GINNY: If you say so.

MARTIN: I think I hate him. I hate the old sonofabitch. I wish he was here. You know what I would do? I'd put my knife in him. Put my knife right through his heart. But it's too late ain't it? That's always the story. Too damn late. (*Pause.*)

(PRINCESS *emerges from the bedroom carrying two suitcases.*)

PRINCESS: That's it for me. You ready?

MARTIN: Yeah.

(MARTIN *takes both suitcases from her, and both move toward the door.* GINNY's *still standing there distracted.*)

PRINCESS: You leaving or staying?

GINNY: Leaving. (*She hurries past them.*)

MARTIN: Feel welcome to drop by and see us anytime.

GINNY: I will.

PRINCESS: What about your things?

GINNY: Keep them or throw them away.

PRINCESS: All right.

(GINNY *exits.* MARTIN *and* PRINCESS *are about to leave also when he stops, goes back, and takes the tapes.*)

MARTIN: What the hell.

PRINCESS: Don't forget the lights.

MARTIN (*after a moment*): Leave them on.

(*Both exit with the suitcases. Lights remain on the set for a while, then slowly fade out.*)

(*End of play*)

The First Breeze of Summer

LESLIE LEE

Left to right: Moses Gunn as MILTON EDWARDS, *Ethel Ayler as* HATTIE, *Frances Foster as* GREMMAR, *and Barbara Montgomery as* AUNT EDNA *in a scene from* The First Breeze of Summer. *Photograph copyright © 1974 by Bert Andrews. Reprinted by permission of Marsha Hudson, the Estate of Bert Andrews.*

Leslie Lee, a native of Bryn Mawr, Pennsylvania, earned a B.A. from the University of Pennsylvania, and an M.A. from Villanova University. He received his initial experience with the professional theater by working at Ellen Stewart's La Mama E.T.C. where his earliest plays were produced. He later taught playwriting at the College of Old Westbury, New York, and the Frederick Douglas Creative Arts Center in New York, served as playwright-in-residence at the University of Pennsylvania, and was playwriting coordinator at the Negro Ensemble Company. He is the recipient of grants from the Shubert Foundation, the Rockefeller Foundation, and the National Endowment of the Arts, as well as a playwriting fellowship from the Eugene O'Neil Playwriting Conference in Waterford, Connecticut. His film credits for public broadcasting include *Almos' a Man,* an adaptation of a Richard Wright short story; *A Killing Ground,* which won first prize at the National Black Film Consortium; and a co-adaptation (with Gus Edwards) of James Baldwin's novel, *Go Tell It on the Mountain.* Other significant plays include his history play, *Colored People Time,* and *Hannah Davis.* Included among the awards garnered by *The First Breeze of Summer* are an Obie Award for Best Play (1974–75), a Tony nomination, and a John Gassner Medallion for Playwriting awarded by the Outer Circle Critics.

The First Breeze of Summer was produced in New York by the NEC in association with Woodie King, Jr., opening at the St. Marks Playhouse on March 2, 1975, and later reopening on Broadway at the Palace Theatre on June 10, 1975, with the original cast:

Gremmar	Frances Foster
Nate Edwards	Charles Brown
Lou Edwards	Reyno
Aunt Edna	Barbara Montgomery
Milton Edwards	Moses Gunn
Hattie	Ethel Ayler
Lucretia	Janet League
Sam Green	Carl Crudup
Briton Woodward	Anthony McKay
Reverend Mosely	Lou Meyers
Hope	Petronia
Joe Drake	Peter DeMaio
Gloria Townes	BeBe Drake Hooks
Harper Edwards	Douglas Turner Ward

Directed by Douglas Turner Ward; scenery by Edward Burbridge; lighting by Sandra L. Ross; costumes by Mary Mease Warren; production stage managed by Horacena J. Taylor.

The First Breeze of Summer

TIME

Contemporary

PLACE

A small city in the Northeast

ACT ONE

Thursday afternoon through Friday night in June

ACT TWO

The following Saturday afternoon through Sunday night

ACT ONE

It is mid-June, Thursday afternoon, the Edwardses home. A porch, stage left, takes up only a small area of the stage. It has a cement floor. A bench in the center of the porch constitutes the porch furniture. A door at the right of the porch leads into the living room, a modest area larger than the porch, with a writing desk, upstage right; a dining table with chairs, stage center; an armchair, downstage right; and an armchair, upstage left. Upstage right is an upright piano; up center, a low bench; and up left, a small side table. A flight of stairs, up right, leads to GREMMAR'S *room, which is also the room where the flashbacks take place. The room contains a bed, stage right; a chair, stage center; and a dresser, down left.*

At rise, GREMMAR *is standing at the bed, removing a pair of house slippers from a suitcase, which is on the bed. She is singing a hymn as she moves around the room. She puts on the slippers and closes the suitcase and puts it under the bed. As she does, she has an attack of dizziness and falls on the bed. She rises finally and crosses to the dresser to get a fan, discovering a photograph and a string of pearls. She fondles the picture affectionately.*

GREMMAR: Sam Green, Sam Green. (*Stands the photograph on the dresser and looks at the string of pearls longingly*) Sam, Sam, I've never had something like this in my whole life—pearls, real pearls.

(*She puts the pearls on, picks up the fan, which she had placed on the dresser top, and starts out of the room. As she does, lights rise in the living room and porch areas. Simultaneously we hear the sounds of* LOU *and* NATE *playing a game of sidewalk tennis, offstage right. As* GREMMAR *reaches the bottom of the stairs* LOU *and* NATE *enter from downstage right.*)

LOU (*following* NATE): Where are you going?
NATE (*at stage center*): Man, later for that—it's too hot!
LOU: Come on, Nate, we've not finished the game yet!
NATE: It's too hot, Lou!
LOU: Nate, its only 18-15. The game goes up to twenty-one!—
NATE: I know what the game goes up to!
LOU: Come on, Nate, it's not that hot!—
NATE (*lying on the couch, pulling at his clothing and fanning*): The hell it isn't!
LOU: Three more points!—
NATE: You beat me, man—you won—all right?
LOU: One more serve then—one more.
NATE: Later, nigger. Shoot!—no way. That's why the old man and me

quit early today, because of this heat, and I am playing that stupid game like some fool! I beat you twice already—what else do you want?

LOU: Just because I'm leading—

NATE (*crossing to the porch and sitting, stage right end of bench*): So you beat me, all right?

LOU (*moving slowly toward the porch and sitting on stage left floor*): Tomorrow don't say the game wasn't over because the score was only 18-15 either!

NATE: Man, I am smothering! . . . Shit! . . . No air—Nothing! Haven't had a decent breeze all summer, if we've had any! Stuff's enough to make you want to slap Jesus on Easter Sunday! (LOU *laughs despite being miffed.*) Can't eat . . . sleep . . . can't half breathe . . . itching all the time. Take a bath and you're still itching. . . . Can't even get worked up over my woman Hope. You know I'm in trouble. (*Laughing despite his discomfort*) You know what I oughta do? I ought to form me a march . . . get me some folks together and march on this crap! Demonstrate! Sit down in the street! "Down with heat! Heat ain't too cool! . . . Ban the good old summertime!"—a march! . . . Even in the wintertime, when somebody mentions the word *summer*, I begin to sweat. I hate the word, man!

(GREMMAR, *inside the living room, is seated on the piano stool, commencing to play a hymn.* LOU *crosses to the doorway. He pauses for a moment, listening. Finally he crosses stage left of porch.*)

LOU: Gremmar's been good to us, you know that, Nate? (NATE *nods.*) I mean, when you think of older people—right? She's so easy to talk to—I mean, you can—sit down and talk to her about . . . anything just about, you know? . . . Anything . . . more than Mom and Pop. (*Pause.*) You know what I mean, Nate?

NATE: Yeah . . . yeah.

LOU (*sitting stage left end of bench*): Nate, do you remember that scooter Gremmar brought you a long time ago?

NATE (*shifting to his back, fanning*): Yeah, I remember . . .

LOU (*pause, smiling, reminiscent*): She brought me that cowboy outfit, too—remember? (NATE *nods.*) Two guns and a holster . . . and silver bullets! (LOU *rises.*) And that ten-gallon hat!

NATE (*hot, shifting again*): Yeah, Mr. Bad Nigger—the Lone Ranger himself! Damn hat falling down all over his eyes . . . running and bumping into shit and wondering why. . . . Couldn't half see. . . . Running to Mom and crying about hurting yourself.

LOU (*laughing*): Yeah, I'd have worn them to bed at night if Mom hadn't ripped them off me. (*Pause.*)

NATE: Man, this humidity's a regular bitch! (*They are interrupted by the appearance of* AUNT EDNA, *moving up to them laboriously from offstage left.*)

LOU: Hi, Aunt Edna.

EDNA: Lord Jesus, I'm telling you! The Lord is punishing somebody today, child! I just wish he wouldn't include me in on the whipping, though. I didn't do nothing! Just minding my own business! (*She kisses* NATE *and* LOU *on the cheek. They assist her as she sits and begins to wipe her face with her handkerchief.*) I'm telling you boys, it's hot out here today! Just let me catch my breath a minute! (*Hearing* GREMMAR *playing the piano*) I see Mama's home from work for the weekend a day early! . . . Lord, it feels good to get off them feet! Things was killing me! Dogs was hurting! Yes sir! . . . (*With feigned indignation*) Louis looks so cool! How come you look so cool, Louis?

NATE: You know them colored people, Aunt Edna—just love the heat!

LOU (*slightly embarrassed*): I can feel it! . . . I mean . . . it's hot, but—

NATE: Listen at Lou, Aunt Edna—doesn't want to be accused of being a nigger for the life of him!

LOU: I just said—

EDNA: Well, I guess I must not be one, because I can't stand it—never could! No sir! Yes, Lord, this must be Egypt—can't be the United States!

NATE: Got your flowered dress on today, huh, Aunt Edna?—all fixed up, trying to turn some heads today? I know—I know what you're trying to do!

EDNA: I'm glad you do, son, because I'm a wilted flower today! My leaves done dried out today!

NATE: Oh no!

EDNA: Gets a little cooler now, then you're talking about something else!

NATE: You don't have to tell me!—

EDNA: Might be snow on the roof, son, but there's plenty of fire inside! (*All laugh.*)

NATE: All right, all right now!

EDNA: *Plenty* of fire inside!

NATE: Oh, I know that! I can see that! I been watching you! "Look at old Aunt Edna fluttering and flapping her eyes at old Mayberry."

EDNA: Lord, children, don't put that old man on me, now! I don't deserve that now, do I? I don't want no old man. I want a *young* man! Yes, a young man!

NATE: I don't know, Aunt Edna, maybe you'd better stick with Mr. Mayberry. One of these young cats might be too much for you!

EDNA: Well, too much is better than too little, and Henry Mayberry is too little!

(*They all laugh uproariously. During the laughter, the blackout drop is flown in and the three walls—for the flashbacks—*SAM, BRITON, *and* HARPER *are sneaked in behind it.*)

Well, I got my breath here now. (*Having difficulty rising.*) Give me a hand, son. These dogs of mine ain't cooperating!
NATE (*moving to help her*): I'm going to take another damn shower.

(*They begin toward the door.* LOU *lingers outside before exiting downstage right across the apron.* GREMMAR *is playing and singing "Leaning on the Everlasting Arms."* NATE *and* EDNA *enter the living room;* EDNA *gives her shopping bag to* NATE *to hide it from* GREMMAR. NATE *heads upstairs and exits stage right.* EDNA *starts singing and* GREMMAR *looks around and sees her. They hug and* EDNA *crosses to down right armchair and sits.* HATTIE *enters from kitchen, which is up left. She is carrying a tray with four glasses of iced tea. She gives one to* EDNA *and one to* GREMMAR *and stands stage left of the piano—joining the singing.* MILTON *enters from kitchen area, carrying a garden spade and gloves. He crosses to the table and sits in stage left chair, also joining the singing.*)

GREMMAR (*finishing*): I just love that hymn!—such a beautiful song!
HATTIE (*crossing to the desk and putting the tray on it*): Yes, it was. (MILTON *and* EDNA *agree.*)
EDNA: Sounded like Mrs. Armstrong down at the church, Momma.
GREMMAR (*laughing*): Oh child, I'm just sitting here banging—just banging, that's all. I could play like that, child, I'd be doing something.
HATTIE (*crossing downstage between* EDNA *and* GREMMAR): Yes, for somebody that's so disagreeable, she's certainly a good organist—and just loves Milton!
MILTON: Oh now, Hattie!
EDNA: A little sweet on Milton, huh, Hattie?
HATTIE: Yes, Jesus! The first thing Sunday morning, here she comes, "Hello, Hattie," and then just gab, gab, gab to Milton!—
MILTON: Hattie—
HATTIE: The two of 'em just chin to chin! Tickles me!
EDNA (*winking at* HATTIE, *who laughs*): Better keep your eye on him, Hattie—keep your eye on him! I know Lucille—

MILTON: Hattie, you shouldn't be telling stories like that!—

HATTIE (*crossing to the table, giving a glass to* MILTON, *and sitting in stage right chair*): I'm just teasing you, Milton.

GREMMAR: Yes, yes, she is, son, just teasing.

MILTON: Well, I wish she wouldn't. I'm in the Lord's house . . . wouldn't be right to be . . . nasty to the woman . . .

GREMMAR: No, that's right . . . that's right . . .

HATTIE: Milton can tease but can't stand nobody to tease him.

EDNA (*laughing*): Just chin to chin, huh, Hattie? Lucille is something else! Yes, Lord! (*They are silent a moment as* LOU *crosses apron from stage right to sit on porch bench.*)

HATTIE: Well, did Tom show up today?

MILTON: Half drunk as usual. . . . I'd just as soon do without the man. . . . Been advertising for somebody for two weeks now, and we haven't had one call—not one! (MILTON *rises, and crosses to* GREMMAR *stage right between the armchair and piano.*) Can't get young people interested in plastering today. . . . Don't want to do a day's work— want something for nothing—fast cars and loud radios! . . . Haven't had one call! (LOU *rises, enters, and stands at the door.*) Louis comes this summer, that'll be somebody at least. Lord knows we need the help. (LOU *frowns, sighing heavily.* HATTIE *looks at him.*)

HATTIE (*starting toward the kitchen with two empty glasses from the table, seeing* LOUIS, *and stopping*): Louis, what are you frowning about? You aren't coming down with something, are you?

EDNA: This kinda weather—

LOU (*sighing heavily again*): I was . . . thinking about . . . about working someplace else this summer.

(*There is a moment of strained silence, and glances are exchanged by the others.* HATTIE *puts the glasses on the small side table up left.*)

MILTON: Somewhere else? Where else?

LOU (*shrugging, peeved*): I don't know . . . just . . . somewhere . . . else, that's all . . .

MILTON: Lord knows, Louis, I certainly was depending on you. Nathan and I could use all the help we can get, for all Tom is worth.

LOU: For goodness sakes, do I have to plaster every summer?

HATTIE (*stepping to* LOU): You don't have to do anything but die, Louis.

MILTON: Is there something wrong with the way I make my living?

LOU: I didn't say that!—

HATTIE (*as* EDNA *concurs*): He certainly didn't, Milton, now don't start exaggerating—

GREMMAR: No, he didn't now . . . he didn't . . .

LOU: It's . . . it's—all I said was—

MILTON: All the work we have—people calling me up and me promising, and here I am trying to plan ahead—can't get nobody to work for me and—

EDNA: Milton, if the child don't want to—

MILTON: It's not a question of wanting to—

LOU: Pop—

MILTON: His brother didn't want to drop outa school to help me, but he did. Louis is only in high school. It's not like I was asking him to sacrifice his education—

LOU: Well, I'm not Nate—

GREMMAR: Louis, son—

MILTON: What's the matter, don't I treat you right?

LOU: Pop, I'd rather do something else—

MILTON (*stepping toward* LOU): I can't help what you want to do. You're working with Nate and me this summer! (*Cutting him off as he starts to speak.*) I'm still the father of this house!

LOU: How can anybody forget it!

MILTON: Now, that's enough back talk from you, young man!—that's enough! Here—here I am sweating to put food on the table—providing—we need the help—you wanting me to help you with your college tuition next year and—

LOU (*crossing downstage center to the dining table*): All right, I'll pay for it, then!—

GREMMAR (*trying to lighten the atmosphere*): Come on, you all. Let's not fight. Let's be happy—let's be happy now. (*She begins playing softly.*)

LOU: Gremmar, I will pay for it!

MILTON (*crossing downstage center to* LOU): I don't care what you do next summer—that's your business! This summer you're working for me, and I don't want to hear another word about it! (MILTON *starts toward kitchen.*) Louis just wants to be the black sheep of the family—

LOU (*starting for the porch*): Oh, for goodness sakes! Just because—(LOU *storms out.* MILTON, EDNA, *and* HATTIE *exit kitchen arguing about* LOU.)

GREMMAR: Louis! Son?—Sam! Sam!

(GREMMAR *crosses to stage center. She stops suddenly, faint, and sits in the stage center chair at table—holding the pearls. The lights dim in living room to special on* GREMMAR, *and blackout drop is flown out to reveal wall no. 1* [SAM]. *As lights rise in the bedroom,* LUCRETIA *enters from stage left—stands at the dresser holding a hand mirror.* SAM *enters from upstage right and crosses to stand at foot of bed.*)

LUCRETIA: Oh, Sam, these are lovely!—they really are! They're so pretty!

SAM: You like 'em, huh, babe?

LUCRETIA: Oh, Sam, you know I do—I really do! (*Looking almost in awe at herself.*) They're so pretty!— What are these—pearls, Sam? Is that—

SAM (*proudly, cockily*): They're pearls . . .

LUCRETIA: Oh . . . (*Continuing to look at herself and then giggling nervously.*) I—I've never had something like these before, Sam—real pearls. . . . Makes me feel like a . . . a . . . rich lady or something . . . (*She laughs, glancing at him for his approval, and then looks again in the mirror, gently fingering the pearls.*) They're so beautiful . . . tiny . . . sparkling-like . . . Pearls! (*She stops, a look of horror on her face.*) Sam, how much did these things cost you?

SAM (*laughing*): Come on, babe, you're not supposed to be asking me no questions like that! What's the matter, don't you have no manners? Your momma didn't bring you up no better than that? Don't worry about it!

LUCRETIA (*laughing*): Lord, Momma's eyes'll pop wide open when she sees this. She thinks everything's supposed to be so simple. Nothing flashy. These certainly would be flashy to her. Probably just jealous, I guess, Poppa not being able to give her nothing like this . . . (*Pause, stepping to* SAM.) They didn't cost a lot, did they, Sam? Just tell me that. You don't have to tell me nothing more—all right? They weren't, were they?

SAM (*shrugging, nonchalant*): Oh . . . not too . . .

LUCRETIA (*watching him*): That's the truth?

SAM: Baby, you asked me, and I just told you—

LUCRETIA: All right, all right— (*Looking down at the pearls again.*) Sam . . . I—I'm going to have to hide these things—

SAM: Hide 'em? . . . Huh? . . . Baby, what are you talking—

LUCRETIA: Sam, I know—I know they'll make me give 'em back to you. I know they will!—

SAM: Give 'em back? How come you're going to have to give 'em back? It's my money. I do with it what I want. Nobody—

LUCRETIA: Sam, it's not that! . . . That's not it . . . not it at all. . . . Sam, I'm only seventeen. . . . They—they might think I shouldn't be . . . be having things like this—so expensive-looking. I mean, you know the way things are around here—work so slow—you know what I mean? I mean, they're kinda funny that way. . . . So afraid somebody's going to be showing off with something new—

SAM: For Pete's sake, babe! I—I didn't buy them things for you to have to hide—

LUCRETIA: I—I'll wear 'em only around you, Sam. (*She hugs him.*) When we're together—all right? Momma and them don't ever have to know. Sam, it's either that or I'm going to—to have to give 'em back to you. (*She crosses to the dresser and looks in the hand mirror.*) I mean . . . pearls, Sam! Who around here has some pearls?

SAM (*sighing heavily, helplessly*): Lu, baby. . . . Look, sugar . . .

LUCRETIA: What's the matter?

SAM: Well . . . (*Pausing, shrugging, and then blurting out.*) Look, sugar, they—they ain't—ain't no real pearls! (*He sighs, looking at her and then dropping his eyes, expecting the worst.*) They . . . ain't . . .

LUCRETIA (*surprised*): Oh . . . they're not?

SAM (*sighing heavily*): They're not real. . . . They're . . . imitation—that's what the woman said—imitation . . .

LUCRETIA: You mean they're . . . fakes or something?

SAM (*quickly*): No, they're not fakes. . . . I mean, you know, they're supposed to be pearls, but they're not, you know? . . . I mean, they look like 'em, but they're not. You know what I mean, babe? I mean, they're supposed to look like pearls, but they're something else— (*Stopping, exasperated.*) Oh, I don't know, baby, they're just—just . . . imitation, whatever the hell that is! How should I know! (*Pause.*) I—I just . . . I just don't want you to think you got something you don't, that's all. . . . And there's no sense anybody else thinking it too. . . . I certainly don't want you hiding them . . . (*Sighing heavily.*)

LUCRETIA (*turning to the mirror again*): They sure do look real if they aren't. . . . They cost a couple of dollars, then?

SAM (*turning and stepping stage right*): Yeah . . . yeah . . . a couple, you know . . .

LUCRETIA: Well, Sam, that's better then, isn't it? I mean, if Momma and Poppa think they're fakes—I mean, imitation—then they won't mind then, will they?

SAM: I don't know. You know your people better than I do.

LUCRETIA: Oh, Sam, thank you!— Thank you, Sam! (*Rushing to, embracing, and kissing him.*) I'll wear 'em—okay?

SAM (*somewhat bewildered*): Damn, lady, you sure did put me through the mill over them things—

LUCRETIA (*pulling away*): Sam, where's your uniform? I thought there was something funny about you! Sam, how come you're not at work? It's not time yet for—

SAM (*turning downstage*): They—they give me the afternoon off—

LUCRETIA: The afternoon? How come?

SAM (*hesitant, shrugging*): I—I don't know, baby. . . . Man come up and told me. . . . Some . . . some kinda slow-up on the tracks somewhere—accident—trains wasn't coming in . . . tied up. . . . Didn't need all the porters in the station. . . . Said to take the afternoon off. So I took it. (*Laughing nervously.*) Didn't have to tell me twice . . .

LUCRETIA (*not really comprehending*): You get paid for it, don't you?

SAM (*boldly*): Oh yeah . . . oh yeah. . . . Something like this . . . wasn't our fault . . . they pay us . . .

LUCRETIA (*watching him*): Oh . . .

(LUCRETIA *starts to the dresser as* SAM *sits dejectedly on the foot of the bed. She crosses to him.*)

Sam . . . are you all right? What—what are you telling me? I know—I know you're trying to tell me something—

SAM (*rising*): Yeah . . . yeah, I'm trying to tell you something! . . . Yeah! . . . I'm trying to tell you I ain't been to work in two days, babe—two days! . . . Yeah, I got the afternoon off. Yeah, I get the rest of my life off as far as those people are concerned down there— (*He crosses left center.*)

LUCRETIA (*sighing heavily and then looking away*): Oh, Sam! . . . Sam, what happened? Sam, you haven't been to work in—in . . . *two* days, and you're just telling me?—

SAM: There wasn't no need, baby—

LUCRETIA: What do you mean no need? Don't you think—

SAM: I thought I could get another one! . . . I thought I could . . .

LUCRETIA: Sam, what happened? (*With great consternation.*)

SAM (*slowly*): Babe, do you remember me telling you about Pop?

LUCRETIA: You mean that old man at the station—the porter?

SAM: The man's a doctor, Lu! (*She looks at him, amazed.*) He's a doctor, baby! So help me! You should hear him rattle off that stuff! I mean the man knows it backward and forward—he is! He doesn't have no reason to lie to me, babe! Look, I see his—whatever they call the damn thing—his degree—all in Latin and junk! He carries it with him—no lie!—in his back pocket! He showed me!

LUCRETIA: A doctor? Lord Jesus!

SAM: You never heard nothing like that in your whole life, have you? A porter!

LUCRETIA: What—what in the world is he doing down there at the station, Sam?

SAM (*crossing stage right to the foot of the bed*): He told me one day—quietlike. . . . We was sitting there eating lunch. He likes me, you see.

I don't know why. We just kinda took a shine to one another—right away. I don't know. . . . Maybe because I didn't ask him to explain hisself, you know? I mean, I didn't try to take nothing away from him, that's what he told me . . . (*Pause.*) He couldn't get no work, babe—

LUCRETIA: Sam, there's plenty of need for doctors around here—

SAM: He couldn't make it, baby. You have to eat. What are you going to eat—promises? Damn right we get sick. But who the hell can pay for it? He couldn't make it. The man had to eat! A hell of a lot of sick people, but no cash, babe!

(LUCRETIA *sits on the bed as* SAM *crosses stage center.*)

Colored people weren't ready for colored doctors, or maybe colored doctors weren't ready for colored people. I forget the way he put it, but something like that. . . . He said he didn't mind helping folks, but he didn't realize how much it was necessary for him not to be hungry—to not be worrying about next month all the time. . . . (*Pauses.*) Wanted it simple, he said . . . just plain simple, you know, babe. . . . Didn't want to have to think . . . or feel . . . or even care . . . the hell with it. . . . Gave it up. . . . He's a porter, so help me God, a porter, down at the station. (*Pause.*) He was . . . you know . . . doing his job. . . . He's pushing this cracker's bags. . . . Cracker's got enough bags for everybody in this whole town piled up on top of Pop's cart. He's pushing the damn thing, and it's heavy, but he's pushing, smiling and whistling, happylike. . . . And I don't know, for some reason one of the bags comes tumbling down and falls on the floor. The thing is, it splits— A couple of things break. The cracker claims they're from— I don't know whether he's lying or not—from Paris or Europe, one of them damn places. And all of a sudden he's getting red in the face. He's yelling and making a big stew, calling Doc names! Calling him boy this and nigger that, and Pop—Pop is just . . . just standing there—like he's supposed to take it, smiling and apologizing. (*Pause.*) He's got his mind—Pop—on what he is now, not what he was. He ain't no goddamn porter, but he don't want nobody to change it. He's got it all figured out! So that stupid, dumb, doctor-porter is taking all the cracker's crap! Taking it, talking to himself, reciting that stuff from his medical books! . . . Well, I couldn't take it! So I hightail it over to where they standing, and—and before I could catch myself, I'm telling this cracker off! I got my hand, my fist, my nose into his, and I'm screaming at him—yelling at him—calling him the names he's calling Pop. And that stupid Pop—Doc—is pulling at me—yanking at me, because he knows, because he's made it all so simple! And he's struggling with me! And I'm yelling at the cracker: "This man's a doctor, goddammit! You oughta be carrying his bags, you sonofabitch! Don't you talk to Dr. Savage that way! And Pop is crying almost, because I promised I wouldn't say nothing to nobody! That's what's getting him! He's begging me and half crying for me to shut up! And then all of a sudden he pulls out that damn piece of paper and tears it into shreds—just rips it up! (*Pauses.*) Well . . . to make a long story short . . . that's it. I mean, that's it. . . . I wasn't worth a good minute after that. . . . Right on the spot . . . on the damn spot! (*Pauses.*) I turn around . . . on my way out . . . and there's . . . *Pop* . . . doing penance for me . . . cleaning up that bastard's shit . . . smiling, apologizing . . . kissing ass! . . . If he's mad, he's mad at me and not at the cracker—for messing up his goddamn, stupid world. . . . (*Laughing suddenly and sitting in the chair stage center.*) Baby, I'm so miserable, it's funny . . . miserable . . .

LUCRETIA (*taking the beads off and crossing to* SAM): You—you take these things right back where you got it from! I—I'm not going to take your last penny! (*She gives the pearls to him.*) I don't care if they are fakes! (*Crosses to stage right.*)

SAM (*going to her with the pearls*): They're yours, now put 'em on! I bought 'em for you! I wanted you to have 'em! I wasn't thinking about no money! I just wanted you to have 'em—because you'd look nice in 'em! . . . Now come on! (*He places them around her neck.*) That's it . . . that's it, baby. . . . Yeah, now you're looking good . . . just like—like a—a plate of fried tomatoes and gravy, huh? . . . Huh? (*He forces a laugh. She crosses back to the dresser. He turns away.*) Yeah, yeah, he's got it all figured out . . . figured out. . . . To him it's so simple. . . . The rest of us make it so complicated . . . (*Turning to* LUCRETIA.) Lu . . . baby . . . I'm going to have to . . . to . . . pull out for a while.

(*She groans softly, turning away.*)

There's . . . there's nothing here, babe—nothing. Two days I been looking and hating, babe. . . . But the word's out—everywhere . . . down in the fields too. They got me, babe . . .

(*She is silent, choking back tears.*)

Just for a while . . . won't be long . . .

LUCRETIA (*taking a step to him*): Will you—will you take me with you?

SAM: Come on now, babe . . . come on! It ain't no kinda life for you, not the way—

LUCRETIA (*crossing to* SAM): Sam, I want to go with you!—

SAM: No! No! . . . No! . . . You may as well stop—stop talking! It's no life, now take my word for it! . . . Running here . . . running there . . .

riding that damn boxcar . . . (*Sighing, shaking his head.*) It'll only be a little while . . .

LUCRETIA: Oh Sam . . . Sam— (*She crosses upstage between the bed and chair.*)

SAM (*crossing to* LUCRETIA): Just a while. . . . What am I supposed to do, babe—stay here and . . . and . . . starve? There's nothing here! Pop's seen to that! (*Sighing.*) You think I want to go? I'll just be a . . . while, baby. You know I'm not going to stay away. (*Again trying to laugh.*)

LUCRETIA: That's probably what you told the last one where you've been.

SAM (*turning away and crossing downstage*): Come on, will you, babe—

LUCRETIA: You probably got a whole string of 'em waiting for you to come home to—probably. You . . . black . . . nigger!

(*He turns and slaps her face. She turns away, holding her face.*)

SAM (*sighing heavily*): Oh, goddammit!

(*Pause.* LUCRETIA *crosses to the dresser.*)

Look, sugar, I'm sorry. . . . I'm sorry. . . . Don't call me stuff like that, huh? . . . Not stuff like that. . . . It ain't that simple for me, babe—not like Pop . . . like Pop.

LUCRETIA (*crossing to* SAM): Sam? . . . Sam, I—I want to talk to you about . . . something—

(*She starts to speak, but he kisses her. They embrace, passions rising, and fall on the bed.*)

(*Blackout. In the blackout* NATE *can be heard singing offstage. The lights rise in the living room and porch, where* LOU *sits brooding.* GREMMAR *rises and crosses to the stairs—meeting* NATE *as he moves down the steps to the porch. He pinches her cheek lightly.* GREMMAR *exits upstairs and offstage right, carrying her glass and fan.*)

LOU (*tersely, upon* NATE'S *arriving*): You've given it all up for Daddy, haven't you, Nate?

NATE (*stopping*): Given what up?

LOU: School. I thought you wanted to teach so much. That's what you said you wanted to do before.

NATE: I know what I said—I know it. The man needs help, Lou. So what am I supposed to do, huh? Yeah, I wanted to be one. (*Crosses stage left of the porch.*) So what the hell, everybody can't be one. Besides, they have enough people doing it without me.

LOU (*shaking his head disconsolately*): Gremmar told me about . . . about your dropping out of—quitting school because of me.

NATE (*shrugging, sitting*): Yeah, well, I figured as long as one of us went, what the hell's the difference. You were smarter than me . . . in the long run . . . had the best chance of making it, so . . . (*Pause, wiping perspiration from his forehead.*) I suppose I was pissed off at first. You know the way the old man can make you feel guilty—like if you don't help him you're going to be cast into the fiery furnace . . . you know. . . . So, who knows, maybe I didn't have any other choice. What the hell, it's a . . . trade. . . . It's honest . . . making my own living . . . not cheating anybody. I don't know, I might go back someday.

LOU: You've been saying that for three years now, Nate.

NATE: And I might be saying it for five more! I *might* go back—I might! I . . . I think about it. . . . Anyway, it's not that important anymore . . . not like it used to be. . . . You get out of school, and you see some things different. . . . Those people don't make that much bread anyway. Oh, who knows! I'm plastering—it's all right—it is. . . . I'm outside a lot. . . . Nobody but the old man standing over me, and . . . I can handle him. . . . I'm better than he is anyway. He knows it. He may not admit it, but damned if he doesn't know it! . . . He knows it. . . . So I'm no teacher. . . . I'm a plasterer.

LOU (*softly, intensely*): I . . . I could've gotten a job in the hospital this summer—in the lab maybe . . . an orderly or something. . . . Instead I—I have to do what?—plaster! I could be picking up some experience maybe—something that has to do with what I want to do in . . . college. But no . . . I have to fool around working for him—

NATE: That's between you and him, Lou. I—

LOU (*rising, crossing to downstage edge of porch*): Don't remind me! (*Softly, agitated.*) Riding in the back of that . . . truck . . . like some . . . dope!

NATE (*crossing downstage to level with* LOU): So ride in the front—all right? I'll ride in the damn back! I don't give a shit if people think I'm a dope! Let 'em think what they please!

LOU: Oh, it's—it's not just . . . that! (*Sighing heavily.*) Plaster . . . you get sores all over your hands . . . stuff all in your eyes! . . . Damp . . . dirty! . . . It's—

NATE: Man, you can wear some gloves—and we have a pair of goggles, if that's what's bothering you. I used to wear 'em when I first started.

(LOU *sits on the edge of porch downstage.*)

It's not too bad, Lou. . . . Shit, I have a business. . . . I'm saving a little bread. . . . Don't have the damn bill collectors on my tail. . . . I have enough threads and all that. . . . It's no big deal . . . not worth all that. Shit, you are what you are, you know?

(*There is a sudden, loud, crashing noise—the sound of breaking glass.* NATE *and* LOU *both jerk around, startled, toward the noise.*)

What the hell—

(*The noise also startles* MILTON, *who is just entering from the kitchen.*)

MILTON (*crossing stage center of living room*): What in the world?—

(NATE *moves quickly off the porch, around the side of the house, exiting downstage right from apron.*)

NATE: Come on, man!

(LOU *follows, as* HATTIE *rushes into the living room from upstage right, followed by* GREMMAR.)

HATTIE: Milton, a rock! A rock! Just come flying through the window, breaking glass all over the place!
MILTON: A rock?
GREMMAR: Lord have mercy!
HATTIE: A big piece of rock!
MILTON: Those two boys! Louis! Nate!

(NATE, *again followed by* LOU, *moves back onto the porch and into the living room, meeting* MILTON.)

NATE: Pop, it was Tom!
LOU: We just saw him running down the street!
MILTON: Tom? What in the world is Tom throwing stuff through my window for?—
GREMMAR: Trash, nothing but trash, that's all. It's a shame!
NATE: I don't know. He's mad, that's all, I guess. I stopped down at the Picket Post for a couple of seconds after work. Tom was there—drunk, as usual. Already drunk up his pay. And he started bugging me to lend him some money. I told him I wasn't going to give him one red cent. I told him you weren't either, so there was no sense asking. He got teed off, and I guess he still is.
MILTON: That man! I'm going to break his neck!
NATE: He's probably back at the Post.
MILTON (*moving toward the kitchen area exit with* NATE *and* LOU *leading*): Break his neck! Fool man!
HATTIE: Milton!

GREMMAR: Come on back, son.

MILTON: I—I'm just going to talk to the man, Momma. (*He continues out with the boys.*)

HATTIE: Milton, Tom ain't worth you getting in trouble about.

GREMMAR (*rising, moving after him, preceded by* HATTIE): Milton, there's no sense going down there and getting yourself in a lot of trouble over that man. It's not worth it, son. Just because he wants to show his ignorance is no reason why you have to. Use your head now, Milton. Use your head.—Don't leave with anger in your heart, son— Don't go—don't go—(*She stands in the kitchen area looking helplessly after them. Her thoughts turn inward as she continues to mutter softly, "Don't leave." The lights fade to special on* GREMMAR. *Lights rise in* LUCRETIA'S *room. She enters from stage left and stands at the dresser in same position as* GREMMAR, *then crosses to the bed, as special on* GREMMAR *fades out. She sits on the bed, staring emptily.* SAM *appears at the door, upstage right, a traveling bag in his hand. He stands with uncertainty before stepping into the room and setting down the bag.*)

LUCRETIA (*without looking up*): Are you leaving now, Sam?

SAM: In—in a minute.

LUCRETIA (*rising and crossing to the dresser*): I . . . I know . . . I know you'll be gone forever.

SAM (*attempting lightness, stepping to* LUCRETIA): I'll be back . . . just as soon as I get me a job. . . . Won't take me long. (*Laughing.*) Soon as I get me a job . . . be right back here! . . . Maybe—maybe in one of them brand-new buggies! (*Forcing more laughter.*)

LUCRETIA (*despondently, crossing to the bed*): You must be getting touched in the head, Sam. (*She is silent for a moment, and then quickly without looking.*) Sam?

(*He stops. She places her hand on her belly and sits on the foot of the bed.*)

Sam, feel here please!

SAM: Do what?

LUCRETIA: Feel here—right here. . . . Come on, feel it, Sam!

SAM (*frowning, sitting beside her on the bed and putting his hand on her belly*): What—what is it I'm supposed to be feeling?

LUCRETIA: It's your child there, Sam.

SAM: You . . . you got a . . . a . . . child in there?—a . . . baby? (*She nods.*) How you—how you—you seen a doctor?

LUCRETIA: No, but—

SAM: Then how the hell you know if you haven't—

LUCRETIA (*rising, crossing to the dresser*): Sam, I know! . . . I mean . . . I know! . . . I'm a woman, ain't I? I ought to know—

SAM (*rising, following her*): Don't play with me now, Lucretia! I don't like for people to play with me like that—

LUCRETIA: Sam, I know—I know! . . . I told you!

(*He turns away and crosses stage right.*)

SAM (*turns to* LUCRETIA): Shit! . . . Shit! . . . Baby—baby, I have to go! . . . I—I can't stay here! I stay here . . . what . . . what's that . . . child going to live on, huh? I mean, what's he going to feed on if I don't have no work? . . . Can't have no starving child in there, now. You got one, you sure of it? (*Turning to face her.*) You ain't just . . . just doing it to me?

LUCRETIA: Sam, why do I want to lie?

SAM (*moving to her and sitting with her on the foot of the bed*): Look, baby, now look . . . look. . . . You—you just get in touch with me, you hear? You . . . you get on over to that doctor in town, and when you're sure—real sure—you just get in touch with me—

LUCRETIA: Sam, don't change on me—people change—

SAM: I ain't people, dammit! I'm Sam Green. . . . Ain't nobody but Sam Green! Now . . . now you do what I tell you, Lu, you hear? I'll—I'll let you know where I am, and you get word to me the first thing—

LUCRETIA (*standing, moving away from him stage left*): Oh, man, just . . . just . . . just . . . get out of here before I start bawling, please! Please? . . .

SAM (*watching her for a moment, and then rising and crossing downstage right*): Yeah . . . yeah. . . . Trains don't slow down much for niggers. (*He hesitates.*)

(*She suddenly turns away from the dresser and rushes to him, embracing him.*)

Soon—soon, sugar lump, you'll look over at that goddamn old door—

LUCRETIA (*whispering*): Please don't swear, Sam—not right now . . .

SAM (*matching her softness*): You'll look at that old door, and you know who'll be standing there? . . . Yeah, that's right—me! Yeah, me! And you know what? You know what, baby? I'm going to have me a brand-new buggy outside—all shined up and ready to take you back—

LUCRETIA: Don't talk simple, Sam. Just—just come back on a mule if you have to.

SAM: I'll be back. You'll see. . . . You just keep watching. (*Brings* LUCRETIA *downstage center.*) Every once in a while, you look out that old window . . . look way down the road there—way down there. You'll see me . . . see me coming back. Done struck it rich! Yeah!

(He smiles and then kisses her. She clings to him for a moment and then lets go. At first somber, he straightens and swaggers toward the door.)

SAM *(turning to her)*: See you, sugar, when I'm rich! *(He moves jauntily out the door. He is gone, enveloped by the darkness.)*

LUCRETIA *(crossing to the doorway upstage right)*: You're touched in the head! . . . You know that, Sam? *(She stares into the darkness.)* And don't you go messing with all them other women neither, man! You're supposed to be working hard and providing for Little Sam—that's what I'm going to call him! *(She crosses back into the room, looks at the photograph on the dresser, and then sits on the bed and stares emptily.)* Sam, I'm scared . . . all of a sudden I'm scared!

(Lights fade, and LUCRETIA clears upstage right. Laughter is heard. The lights rise on the porch. It is the afternoon of the next day, and wall no. 1 is flown out to reveal wall no. 2 [BRITON]. GREMMAR and LOU sit on the porch front, playing Scrabble. GREMMAR is stage right, and LOU is stage left on bench.)

LOU *(quickly)*: That's a word!

GREMMAR: It is?

LOU: Yep—cilia.

GREMMAR: Cilia? What in the world—you mean *silly*, don't you?

LOU *(laughing)*: No, Gremmar—*cilia*.

GREMMAR: Now, Louis, what kind of word is that? I never—

LOU *(straightening, reciting proudly from memory)*: Okay, let's see. It's the . . . hairlike outgrowths of certain cells, capable of vibrating—no!—vibratory movements, or the . . . small . . . hairlike . . . processes extending from certain plant cells . . . often forming a fringe or hairy surface . . . as on the underside of some leaves . . . that's a term in biology.

GREMMAR *(smiling, impressed)*: Yes, I figured it was something from all you were saying about it. That's what it means, huh? Yes, well, that's right, baby, learn all you can about it—learn all you can. Lord, just spouting it out like butter! *(She studies the letters on her rack and then begins to fit them into the maze.)* Is that right? . . . I don't want you to think I'm cheating now.

LOU *(teasing)*: Gremmar, I'm really impressed! And another thing—you didn't cheat! Yes, that's right.

GREMMAR: I know it's right. . . . Beseech! . . . Bee-seech! . . . I beseech you therefore, brethren, by the mercies of God, that ye present your bodies . . . a living sacrifice, holy, acceptable unto God, which is your reasonable service. . . . And be . . . and be not confirmed to this world: but . . . be ye . . . transformed by the renewing of your mind, that ye may prove—that ye may prove what is good . . . and acceptable . . . and perfect . . . will of God! . . . That's Romans, twelfth chapter—St. Paul talking . . . ! Yes, Saint Paul . . . ! Yes sir! . . . And that's what I've been trying to do all these years, abiding by the will of the Master— doing the right thing—all my life. . . . Yes, abiding by the will of the Master. . . . Making myself acceptable unto the Lord, which is my reasonable service! Yes sir!

LOU (*pausing*): Gremmar, sometimes, you know, you—you try to do the right thing—I mean, I've been trying to—just like you did—

GREMMAR (*reaching, patting his hand*): I know you have, baby. I see you trying, and the Lord'll bless you—he will.

LOU: I mean, I want to be a doctor or scientist—right? And you have to study hard—right?

GREMMAR: That's right. Oh yes!

LOU: I don't know. . . . The colored kids at school . . . most of 'em . . . they fool around. They don't care! And just because I don't act silly as they do—because I know what I want to do—they call me a bookworm and really—I mean, *really* get jealous because I study hard. I mean, they try to make me feel guilty. You know what I mean?

GREMMAR: I know, I know.

LOU: And next year, half of 'em, after graduation, won't be able to get near a college, and then they'll be complaining about having to work in a . . . a . . . gas station! or . . . or . . . doing construction work . . . or being a . . . garbage collector, maybe—things like that. . . . Well . . . I just don't want to do things like that. . . . I mean, it's . . . it's . . . you know . . . de . . . grading . . . (*Shrugging.*) I mean, it's all right and all, but . . . I want to be . . . better than that. You—you know what I mean, Gremmar?

GREMMAR: I know. . . . Oh yes, child, yes, I know. But that's right . . . that's right. You strive, you hear? You just strive on for the highest you can get. There's nothing wrong with that. No, you've got the brains. Lord yes, you can see that playing this here old game with me. Yes, you have the brains. No reason why white folks have to get it all—no reason at all! (GREMMAR *rises and crosses downstage.*)

LOU: I know . . .

GREMMAR: Yessir, keep right on striving, you hear? (*Lights fade down to special on* GREMMAR.)

LOU (*nodding softly*): Yes, ma'am.

GREMMAR: That's it, baby . . . that's it.

(*Special fades out, and* GREMMAR *and* LOU *clear stage left. The lights rise on* LUCRETIA'S *room.* LUCRETIA, *an apron on, runs into the room, followed by* BRITON. *He attempts to kiss her.*)

LUCRETIA (*resisting*): Mr. Briton, I—I haven't finished my cleaning, and—and I got cooking to do—

BRITON: You've got plenty of time for that!—

LUCRETIA: Mr. Briton, please! Your father—your father finds out—he's got a mean temper! I—I can't afford to lose my job—my child!—

BRITON: They're gone, and you know it!—you know it! You want to see? I'll show you, and then what kind of excuse will you have? (*He goes to the door upstage right.*) Hey, you old sonofabitch, are you down there? You're gone, aren't you, you and your old bitch?—to another one of your goddamn parties! Tell this black woman here who won't kiss me that you're gone and won't be back until after she kisses me at least once! Tell her so she won't be scared. Tell her, Daddy! (*He stands, feigning listening, and then laughs, moving back to her.*) You see, they're gone!

LUCRETIA: Sometimes they come back early.

BRITON (*crossing downstage and into the room stage center*): And most of the time they don't. You think they get all fixed up like they do just to come running back to spy on us? (*Attempting to kiss her again, but she resists.*)

LUCRETIA: Mr. Briton, I—

BRITON: You've been . . . been teasing me, that's what you've been doing—teasing this little white boy ever since you came into this house draggin' your knapsack and little kid behind you—

LUCRETIA: Mr. Briton, I haven't. . . . I most certainly haven't—

BRITON: The hell you haven't! . . . You know damn well what you've been doing—the way you look at me. Those quick little glances. . . . That sneaky little smile you've got—when you're serving the table—rubbing yourself against me—

LUCRETIA: Mr. Briton, you're lying, that's not true!

BRITON: Oh yes, it is!

LUCRETIA: Shhhhhh. (*Turning and stepping stage right.*) I think—

BRITON: They're gone, goddammit! (*Crossing to the chair.*) I could do something, you know? . . . I could . . . I damn sure could. . . . I could tell my old man about you. . . . I could walk up to him and say, "Old man, I got something to tell you, about your servant girl. . . . It's about her teasing, old man. She isn't no servant girl, she's nothing but a great big tease, that's what . . ."

LUCRETIA: Mr. Briton, I'm nothing of the kind. I never did anything to make you think . . .

BRITON (*sensing her fear, teasing her more*): Yep, I just might tell him — old bird. . . . You can never tell about me. I'm adopted, you see, I ain't really one of theirs. They all think I'm half crazy anyway. Yeah, who knows, I might just walk on down these steps when he comes and tell him —

LUCRETIA: I'll . . . I'll . . . I'll leave. . . . I'll take Little Sam, and I'll leave right now! — (*Moving toward the dresser and removing clothing from it.*)

BRITON (*stopping her*): Jesus Christ! — you — you — Oh, Jesus Christ! (*Looking at her in amazement.*) Do — do you *really* think I'd do something like that — You know I wouldn't dare, don't you? (*Pause.*) Don't you? What do you take me for, huh? I'm teasing you — just teasing you, that's all! My daddy — which he really isn't — he's the one that holds threats over folks here in Roanoke. He's the one that does stuff like that! (*Pause.*) You didn't believe I was serious, did you? . . . Did you, Lucretia?

LUCRETIA (*softly*): Yes . . .

BRITON (*in animated disbelief*): Oh, man! . . . Oh, man, I mean, what the hell do I look like — some . . . goon or something? Is that what I look like? Jeee-sus God, are you gullible! . . . I mean . . . I mean, is that why you wouldn't let me kiss you, is that why?

LUCRETIA (*turning away*): Things would start. . . . Things would start . . . (*Crosses stage right.*) Mr. Briton, I have to get back to work —

BRITON (*stopping her*): Why do you call me that?

LUCRETIA: Your daddy said —

BRITON: My daddy, my daddy, hell! Well, he's not my daddy. He's nothing of the kind! He says he is, but he's not! My father, I don't know where the hell he is — who the hell he is! My mother either! I don't give a good damn either, for that matter! . . . My daddy thought he was impotent. That's why it's "Briton, you do this; Briton you do that!" I remind him of his impotence! . . . Every time he looks at me, that's what he sees — and he hates . . . he hates to think of it! (*Laughing ruefully.*) They never thought they were going to have anything. Ten years they did it — humping each other. They didn't give a good goddamn about each other. Ten years! And nothing, not even a dribble from his cock! . . . And so, it was me . . . me! "That one over there!" — me! . . . And then, through some miracle, Jamie comes along! No more use for me now! You — you should just see the way they go on and on about that little bastard! I'm a mistake. . . . "My daddy" hates to think of himself as possibly having been so much of a weakling for so long—no, not with all his illusions of grandeur! But that's what the hell he thought, until they finally managed to scrape the bottom of the barrel of their sexual powers and dug up Jamie. . . . He looks dug up too!

LUCRETIA (*trying to push him out of the room*): Please go, Mr. Briton, and let me get to my work.

BRITON (*grabbing her arm, stopping her*): You're . . . you're really a pretty woman, Lucretia . . . you really are. You're not . . . artificial—like those high-society dames they try to set me up with. (*Pause, looking tenderly at her.*) We have a lot in common, you and me, Lucretia! You know that? Both of us are outcasts! That's what we are around here. No wonder it's—

LUCRETIA: I—I have to go. . . . I—I have to clean the upstairs and the downstairs too. And your father—Mr. Woodward likes a bite to eat when he comes in—

(*He grabs her and kisses her. She starts to struggle but yields, embracing him—pulling away after a moment, turning away downstage.*)

BRITON (*frowning*): What—what's the matter? . . . You—you didn't like it? . . . I—don't kiss like your . . . black friends out on the grounds?

LUCRETIA: Shhh! (*Crossing toward the door.*) It's them—I told you! I told you! And I haven't got nothing done!

BRITON (*following her*): This isn't the last time, is it, Lucretia?

LUCRETIA (*in near panic*): I have to go! Mr. Briton, please don't let them catch you in my room!

BRITON (*at the door, whispering*): Tomorrow, Lucretia, do you hear? . . . Lucretia? . . . Tomorrow! We're outcasts—okay?

(*Lights fade to black offstage, we hear* REVEREND MOSELY, HATTIE, *and* MILTON *talking. As lights rise,* GREMMAR *is crossing from kitchen area into the living room, where she reaches stage center.* REV. MOSELY *enters from the kitchen carrying a cup of tea followed by* HATTIE, MILTON [*carrying a Bible*], *and* LOU, *also entering from the kitchen.* GREMMAR *sits down right armchair;* MILTON *sits stage right at table;* HATTIE *stage left of table, and* LOU *on the piano stool.*)

MOSELY: Therefore, I said, therefore doth my soul keep them!

GREMMAR (*simultaneously with* MILTON *and* HATTIE): Amen, Reverend.

(NATE *and* HOPE *enter from porch—see* REV. MOSELY *and start to leave.*

They are stopped by HATTIE, *who indicates for them to sit in up left armchair.*)

MOSELY (*a slight reasonance in his voice*): The mercy of the Lord is everlasting to *everlasting.* . . . Just think of it—everlasting, children, upon them that fear him—*fear* him and his righteousness unto children's children! (*Again, "amens" from the three adults.*) For no other—no *other* foundation can any man—*any* man lay than which is in the Savior! ("*Amens.*") We're here to give testimony . . . to give thanks—to say, "Thank you, Mr. Jesus, for the many blessings you bestowed upon this household this past week. Thank you, Jesus!"

MILTON: That's right, Reverend.

GREMMAR: Thank you, Jesus.

MOSELY (*crossing downstage in front of the table*): And he has—oh yes, he has! Yes sir! We must count our blessings tonight, children. Let's count 'em—count 'em—each in his own way, each in his own time. For surely, children, we are pilgrims in this strange and weary land!—

MILTON: All right, Reverend!

GREMMAR: Amen, sir—amen!

HATTIE: Have mercy, Jesus—have mercy! (*Softly.*)

MOSELY (*crossing upstage center behind the table*): And *he* is our refuge and strength, though the waters, young people, roar and be troubled, the Scriptures says: "And the mountains *shake* with the swelling thereof!"

(*"Amens" from* HATTIE, MILTON, *and* GREMMAR.)

All right now, children, each in his own way . . . in his own time . . . let the spirit of God—let his spirit move you—let it move you, and give thanks for his bountiful goodness this past week. . . . Perhaps sister Lucretia will play something on the piano now to help us feel the spirit of God moving.

GREMMAR (*rising, going to the piano*): Certainly, Reverend, be glad to.

(LOU *rises from the piano stool and sits on the bench.*)

MOSELY: Softly now . . . softly. . . . Let Jesus come into your hearts tonight, now. Let him in. . . . Open up your hearts now. . . . Give him the key. . . . Let him unlock the door of your heart and steal softly in and move you, children.

(*She begins to play "Blessed Assurance," humming softly as she does. The others join in, singing softly.*)

Softly . . . softly . . . each in his own way . . . his own time . . . softly . . .

(NATE *coughs, shifting nervously, attempting to mask his reluctance to be present. He glances from the corner of his eyes at* HOPE, *who is less nervous.* LOU, *like* HATTIE *and* MILTON, *is pensive and stares down at the floor.*)

Let him move you now . . . *move* you. Let the Father, Son, and Holy Ghost walk on into your hearts, my friends, and move you. Don't fight him . . . don't fight him. . . . Let him in.

MILTON (*reading strongly*): Yea, though I walk through the valley of the shadow of death, I will fear no evil, for thou art *with* me! —

MOSELY (*softly but intently*): Yes, yes! (*Resuming humming.*)

MILTON: Thy rod and thy staff comfort me! . . . Thou preparest a table before me in the presence of mine enemies; thou anointest my head with oil; my cup . . . *runneth over! (Closing the Bible.)*

MOSELY: Yes, yes! (*In response* GREMMAR *sings louder.*)

MILTON (*rising and crossing behind stage right armchair.*): I want to thank the good Lord for walking with me the past week.

MOSELY: Uh-huh . . . uh-huh . . .

MILTON: As he has done each week in the past. He has been by my side—I know it!—because I know him—I know the Lord—yes, I do!

GREMMAR: All right, son! All right! (*Singing again.*)

MOSELY: Yes, yes! (*Singing.*)

MILTON: Been by my side! I know him! Many have fallen by the wayside since last we've gathered together, through death or through the wages of sin, but the good Lord has spared this family to see another week! —

MOSELY: All right now, sir—all right!

GREMMAR: Amen, amen!

HATTIE (*softly*): Have mercy, Jesus!

MILTON: And I want to let Jesus into my heart now, and I want to say, "Thank you, Jesus!"

MOSELY: Thank you, Jesus!

GREMMAR (*echoing him and then singing louder*): Thank you, Jesus!

MILTON: And I want to thank you, Lord, for preparing a table . . . preparing a table and providing . . . and providing . . . (*Unable to control his emotions, stopping and crying slightly.*)

MOSELY: Take your time, brother . . . take your time . . . take all the time the spirit gives you—

GREMMAR: Bless you, son—bless you!

MILTON (*with difficulty*): Thank you, Lord, for . . . preparing a table and . . . and providing for me and my family (*Crosses to* GREMMAR *and hugs her.*) and looking after Momma—

GREMMAR (*Stops playing, but everyone continues to sing.*): That's right, son . . . that's right now. . . . "Looking after Momma"—that's right— (*Resuming singing.*)

MILTON (*standing stage left of* GREMMAR): And . . . taking care of her needs and all. . . . And we . . . we ask your continued blessings, Lord—your continued blessings . . . and ask your help—help us to grow stronger—stronger in your way, Savior—stronger, so that—

(*His voice cascades into soft sobbing,* REV. MOSELY *crosses to* MILTON *and helps him to sit at table stage right chair.*)

MOSELY: That's all right, brother, that's all right. . . . It's good to let the Lord fill up your heart—it's good! Let him fill up your heart as he filled up your table! Let him fill it up! For I will fill up your heart if you let me, he said! Fill it up! (*Crossing behind stage right armchair.*) Each in his own time . . . his own way . . .

HATTIE (*after a moment, rising quickly*): I just want to say, "Thank you, Jesus—your continued blessing!" (*Sitting.*)

MOSELY: Amen . . . amen. . . . That's right, sister Hattie. Thank you, Jesus, and your continued blessings! (*Humming and then stopping.*) Softly . . . softly . . . each in his own time . . . own way . . . (*As the others sing.*) Maybe one of the young people would like to . . . would like to say something—testify.

MILTON: Amen.

MOSELY: Maybe one of the young people would like to say something . . . remember his kindness—his goodness. You don't have to be embarrassed in front of Jesus—no sir!—not in front of the Savior! No sir, children, because he understands us all . . . understands us all!

(NATE *is more uneasy and sinks down in his seat.* MILTON, *attempting not to be too obvious, looks at* NATE, *who shrugs, keeping his head down.* MILTON *glares at him.*)

Trust in the Lord, young people! Let him do the talking for you. Give him the key! Can't unlock your hearts unless you give him the key now! Give him the key, young people!

(HATTIE *looks at* NATE *and gestures for him to rise.* HOPE *nudges him.*)

GREMMAR: All right! All right! Give him the key! All right, sir!—

(NATE *stands finally, reluctant, angry, nervous, trying to conceal his feelings. He begins to mumble his words. The others continue singing.*)

NATE: I'd . . . I'd like to say . . . as a . . . young person . . . I'd like to say . . . thank God for . . . for . . . for . . .

MOSELY: Take your time, son. . . . Give him the key now . . . Don't forget the key! He'll move you!

GREMMAR: That's right, Nathan—that's right.

NATE: For all his blessings . . . this week . . . (*Sighing heavily.*) And . . . last week . . . And . . . for safety . . . and . . . good health . . . and . . . for all his . . . continued blessings . . . (*He sits dropping his eyes, embarrassed.*)

MOSELY (*crossing stage left toward* NATE): All right, son, all right. . . . You don't have to feel no shame in front of Jesus—no shame! He promised us that! He is willing and able to do your talking if you ask him. (*Crosses stage center.*)

GREMMAR (*suddenly, zealously*): Yes, he will! Yes, he will! I know—I know, 'cause I'm a child of the King!—(*She rises, crosses downstage right, in front of the armchair.* LOU *watches her, entranced and intrigued.*) A child of the *King!* And I want you to know—I want you to know that I'm walking up the *King's* highway!

(*The others sing throughout her testimony, stopping to comment but always resuming singing.*)

MILTON (*picking up her enthusiasm*): That's right, Momma!

MOSELY: Uh-huh, uh-huh!

GREMMAR: And ain't nothing—nothing going to stop me from making heaven my home, because he promised me a room—

MOSELY: All right, sister, let him move you!

MILTON: Go ahead, Momma!

HATTIE (*softly*): Have mercy, Savior.

GREMMAR: Promised me a room in one of his many mansions!—

MOSELY and MILTON (*in unison*): Yes, yes!

GREMMAR: And though the way has been long and weary, I want you to know, Lord Jesus, that I will persevere!

MOSELY: Persevere!

MILTON: Amen, Momma!

GREMMAR: Persevere, because I am sustained in *his* strength that has made me whole! Because he alone—He alone can sustain. He is the King!

MOSELY: Yes!

GREMMAR: The King! And I want to thank my King—thank you, Jesus, for your blessings—for your tenderness. Thank you, Jesus, for being a rock in a weary land full of sin and destruction! Thank you, Jesus, for letting me *lean.* You've let me lean, Jesus, on your mighty arm, and let me lay my tired body against your soft bosom!

MOSELY: Let him talk to you, sister!—let him talk!

GREMMAR: I am weak, but you are strong, Lord! And heaven is my
eternal home! And I will be there—I will *be* there on Judgment Day,
because I have tried to fulfill your ways! I have walked the straight and
narrow path, keeping my eyes on the sparrow—on the sparrow!—
ignoring the temptations along the way! I'm marching on up the
King's highway with nothing but heaven on my mind—my feeble
mind. I will be there!—standing in front of your judgment bar to
listen—
MOSELY: To listen—
GREMMAR: To listen to your sweet and mighty voice say—
MOSELY: Tell him what it's going to say, sister!
GREMMAR: To hear your sweet and mighty voice say: "Well done, good
and faithful servant—well done!" Have mercy, Jesus, and bless your
precious name!

(HATTIE *starts singing "Well Done"; the others join in.* LOU *has watched*
GREMMAR'S *demonstration in awe and reverence. Caught up in the
fervor of the moment, he stands suddenly—crosses downstage behind*
MILTON *mesmerized, trembling, almost oblivious to the others. The others,
somewhat shocked, stop singing for a moment and watch him.*)

LOU: I—I want to—to thank God. . . . I want to thank God! I do—I
really do!

(NATE *looks at him in disbelief.*)

I want to thank him . . . thank him! . . . I want to thank him for
sparing my family . . . for food and strength . . . for school . . . for
church . . . for Gremmar . . . (*Turns to* GREMMAR *and hugs her.*) For
providing a table. . . . For helping me to . . . to keep Satan out of my
life . . . and . . . letting me into his heart . . . and touching me!—(LOU
crosses downstage right in front of the armchair.)

(NATE *frowns, suddenly realizing* LOU'S *seriousness. He shifts in his seat,
disturbed. The others resume singing.*)

For giving me the key and . . . and . . . unlocking the door to my heart
to serve him. . . . And . . . and nothing's going to stop me, like
Gremmar said—Satan—nothing! Because I—I want a room in one of
your mansions, Jesus—I really do! And I promise—I promise to serve
you, because I love you, because . . . because I . . . I love you, Lord. . . .
I love you and—I give myself to you, and I'll continue to do what you
want me to do . . . and pray . . . and not sin . . . and obey your
commandments—I really will! Because I . . . I want to go to college
and study medicine and . . . science . . . and biology . . . and keep my

eye on the sparrow, and pray and . . . and not get tempted . . . and trust and . . . and . . .

(GREMMAR, HATTIE, MILTON, *and* REV. MOSELY *move to him, comforting him, and take* LOU *off into the kitchen, with* GREMMAR *following.* HOPE *starts to follow, but* NATE *tugs at her and they exit stage left off porch area.* GREMMAR *stops up left and turns stage right as lights fade down to special on her. The lights rise on* LUCRETIA'S *room and special fades out.* GREMMAR *clears stage left.* BRITON *and* LUCRETIA *lie together on the bed, their clothing awry.*)

BRITON (*silent, and then sitting up suddenly and crossing stage center*): I've decided, goddammit, Lucretia! Just now, laying here with you! I'm not going back to school! I don't have to! Christ, I'm over twenty-one! I don't have to go back unless I want to! The only reason I went was because he wanted me to. He wanted me to because my brother Jamie, which he's not really, didn't want to be a lawyer like him. That's why I went—to please him. Somebody—somebody in the family had to be a lawyer. Somebody—one of us—just *had* to be a lawyer because he is! Well, to hell with him! He's so proud of Jamie, let Jamie do it for him! . . . What do you think of that, lady?

LUCRETIA: If . . . if that's what you want . . .

BRITON: Well, that's what I want, lady. I want you! (*He crosses to the bed—kisses her.*) That's what I want. . . . I don't want to be a crooked lawyer like him. He's a crook—I know he is! He—he carries himself too perfect—too stiff—too proud—too much like a—big shot! (*He hops out of bed and begins strutting around the room in imitation.*) Like some—some . . . proud-assed turkey! That's how he walks. (*She laughs.*) Doesn't he?

LUCRETIA (*laughing*): Yes!

BRITON: Man, you talk about somebody not knowing how to have any fun, it's that man! (*Sobering suddenly.*) Not unless he's with Jamie . . . then he laughs. (*Strutting again, laughing only slightly.*) Big, powerful, important man like him just couldn't have taken ten years to have a kid. (*He is silent and then sits on the side of the bed next to her, thinking.*) I'm not going back. (*Rising again and pacing.*) No sir. . . . I'm going to . . . I'm going to . . . to just . . . I don't know—just get the hell out of here and—and . . . *bum!*—and fly high! I'm going to be like a great big bird, Lucretia, and fly all over this world! (*He spreads his arms like a bird and spins around the room, "flying."*) Fly until I get dizzy—until I see it all, and then—then I'll come flying back to wherever you are! (*He "flies" toward her, leaping on the bed beside her and tickling her.*)

LUCRETIA (*laughing, again resisting*): Briton, stop!

BRITON (*nestling close to her*): You like me, don't you, Lucretia?

LUCRETIA (*softly*): Yes . . .

BRITON: That's good . . . yeah, that's what I need . . . yeah. . . . You need it too, you know . . . outcasts like we are . . . (*He lies down with his head on her lap.*) You're soft, Lucretia . . . good and soft . . . like a pillow. (*Pretending to snore.*)

LUCRETIA: Briton . . . if . . . if you don't like them people out there in the field . . . how . . . how come—how come you like me. . . . I'm no different.

BRITON (*sitting up*): The hell you're not! . . . You're. . . . good-looking . . . (*Rises and crosses down left center.*) And besides . . . besides . . . your face isn't always screwed up and pissed-off-looking like theirs—like they want to kill me and not my *daddy!* I'm nice to 'em. I'm polite. . . . I'm always talking with them and clowning around when I'm down there—just like I do with you. . . . It pisses the old man off! It really does! You should see his face, Lucretia! You've seen his face when he gets pissed off!

LUCRETIA (*standing suddenly at the foot of the bed*): Shhhhhhh!

BRITON (*crossing to* LUCRETIA): Oh, come on now! Every time we're together!—They went out to dinner. . . . And . . . she'll get drunk and sloppy sick with her *Southern charm*, of course. And so will he. When he's ready, they'll come home bound by their drunkenness and flop into bed. We could stay here the whole night, so stop worrying. (*Sits on the bed and pulls* LUCRETIA *down beside him, and kisses her.*)

BRITON: Your mouth is really sensual, you know, Lucretia? You Negras really have sensual mouths—not like us white people—

LUCRETIA (*with difficulty*): Briton . . . when I was gone today—

BRITON: Hey, I was wondering where the hell you were. I was getting lonesome.

LUCRETIA: I . . . I was at . . . I was at the doctor, Briton.

(*He frowns.*)

He . . . he says I'm . . . going to have another baby—

BRITON (*turning sharply to her, stunned*): He says you're . . . what?

LUCRETIA: That's what he told me, Briton. I—

BRITON (*staring hard at her and then rising*): You—you're not saying it's . . . *mine,* are you? You're not—

LUCRETIA: Briton, it can't be nobody else's. I don't see nobody but you. I don't hardly go out of this house—

BRITON: Who—who the hell did you go to—some colored doctor across town?

LUCRETIA: Yes, but—

BRITON: Well, you—you just get yourself to a white doctor! (*Turning away, angry, trembling.*) You just get yourself to a *white* doctor!—

LUCRETIA: Briton, the man did a test or something! He—

BRITON (*rising and crossing stage left center*): But I made sure!—

LUCRETIA (*looking toward the door*): Briton, not so loud!

BRITON: They're gone, goddammit! I keep telling you that! I'm not going to that goddamn door again! (*Pacing.*) I made sure! I took precautions with you—every time! Unless . . . unless the—the last time—or—sometime you told me it was all right!—

LUCRETIA: I—I thought it was!

BRITON: What do you mean, you thought? Jesus Christ, Lucretia!—

LUCRETIA: I thought . . . I thought it . . . was . . .

BRITON: You're trying to trick me, aren't you? You black—

LUCRETIA: Briton, I'm not—

BRITON (*turning angrily away downstage center*): Trying to trick me!— One of those—those . . . *people* out there knocked you up and now you're trying to blame it on me!—

LUCRETIA (*rising, straightening, and crossing to* BRITON): I ain't one of those flighty girlfriends you bring around here, boy!—

BRITON: Wait . . . just wait . . . just let me get my mind together. . . . Sometimes I have trouble getting my mind together, you know? (*Pacing.*) I have a little trouble. . . . These people around here! . . . Look, Lucretia . . . that—that white doctor . . . (*Sitting on the foot of the bed and easing her downstage right of him.*) Look, we'll get you over to him—or the black one, if that's what you want, and . . . and we'll get a job done on you.

LUCRETIA: Briton, I'm not going to get rid of it, if that's what you mean—

BRITON: Oh, come on, Lucretia, you have to—

LUCRETIA: I don't believe in that kinda stuff—

BRITON: Well, you better believe in it! . . . You have to do it, Lucretia, because—Lucretia, don't tie me down to thoughts. . . . Don't tie me down to something I'm not ready to think about.

LUCRETIA (*rising, crossing down right*): Briton, I've thought about it— I'm going away from here—

BRITON (*rising*): Where?—and saddled with two kids? Look—

LUCRETIA: I'm not going to do what you want me to! . . . I'll tell your father I have to quit—I have to go on up North, but . . . I'm not going to do it! . . . I'm not going to tell nobody if that's what you're worried about—I won't.

BRITON (*stepping to* LUCRETIA): No . . . no, I know you wouldn't. . . .

You should, but you wouldn't. (*Pacing, stage center.*) So many things I want to do . . . so many goddamn places I want to be—sometimes all at the same time. I won't have any money—just a knapsack probably, but I know I have to go, Lucretia. I know I have to get away from this goddamn place—not you—here! And . . . and even if I stayed . . . even if I did . . . you know it would be impossible, don't you?

LUCRETIA: Briton . . . don't . . . don't say no more, please?

(*He crosses to bed, sits facing downstage. She crosses to him, and he lays his head against her belly. The lights fade out.* LOU *enters the porch in darkness, and* GREMMAR *enters to the foot of the bed. The lights rise in a special on* GREMMAR *and on* LOU, *as* LOU *sits on the bench.* NATE *moves slowly up to porch from stage left.* GREMMAR *exits upstage right.*)

NATE: What's up?

(LOU *shrugs.*)

Everybody in bed?

(LOU *nods as* NATE *moves onto the porch.*)

Oh brother, I thought it would have cooled off a little by now anyway! (*He is silent a moment and then turns his head toward* LOU. *He speaks softly because of the lateness of the hour. His tones are suggestive rather than angry.*) Lou, man, I'm telling you. (*Shaking his head.*)

LOU (*turning, looking at him*): Telling me what?

NATE (*shrugging, pausing*): Tonight. . . . All that carrying on in there—

LOU (*tense*): What do you mean "carrying on"?

NATE (*slight pause*): All that . . . testifying, crying and falling-out nonsense. Man, come off that stuff, will you? That's . . . old folks' bullshit . . . breaking down all over the place and acting like asses!—

LOU (*defensively*): I couldn't help it, Nate! I—I wasn't . . . trying to! . . . It just . . . happened, that's all! . . . I can't help it if you don't believe in it! . . . I do—all right?

NATE: I didn't say I didn't believe in it, man. You just don't have to get so carried away with it, that's all. Shit, you can do all the believing you damn well please, but it still doesn't call for all them shenanigans. No, indeed!

LOU (*rising and crossing downstage*): Look, Nate, let's drop it! . . . It's my business! . . . If—if I'm supposed to be ashamed of myself, then I'm not! . . . You just do what you want, and I'll do what I want!—

NATE (*crossing to the bench and sitting*): So be an ass—all right? . . . Maybe you should've seen yourself.

(LOU *turns partly toward* NATE, *speaking with extreme difficulty, tension, yet softly.*)

LOU: Nate . . . you know what? . . . I . . . I . . . I really think there's . . . something wrong with me—I really do.

NATE (*turning slowly, frowning*): What do you mean?

LOU: I . . . I don't know. . . . There's something wrong . . .

NATE: What do you mean, you don't know? You just said there was something wrong with you, so what the hell are you talking about?

LOU (*crossing to the bench and sitting stage left*): It's just that . . . Last week . . . Peggy and I, well, we went out . . . parking, you know . . . in the woods . . . near Martin's Dam . . . and, well, we were there and . . . one thing led to another, and . . . we started fooling around—

NATE: Well, that's not it, is it? What the hell's wrong with that?

LOU: I'm not finished.

NATE: Because I was going to say, man—

LOU: We started . . . fooling around . . . all that stuff, and, well, you know . . . she wanted me to . . . you know? . . . I guess I wanted to . . . I guess . . . (*Pause.*) So . . . when it was time . . . even before it was time . . . before . . . she took my hand and put it . . . down there . . . and . . . I got sick . . . I got sick! . . . I vomited! I just . . . puked all over the place! . . . I just all of a sudden got this . . . sick feeling in the pit of my stomach, and . . . and it all came up—and I just couldn't do it! I couldn't! . . . I don't know what was wrong—why I got so sick—

NATE (*laughing*): So you got sick—so what?

LOU (*angrily*): What do you mean, "so what?" I threw up!—(LOU *crosses downstage left.*)

NATE: Tell me the honest to God's truth, Lou—have you ever had any nookie before?

(LOU *doesn't answer, turning away.* NATE *rises and crosses.*)

I know you ain't—knowing you, you haven't. Shit, there's nothing wrong with you, nigger—not a damn thing! . . . Shit, I know your problem. Shit, man, you just have to get on that stuff and just start working out! Work out, nigger, and don't ask no questions—don't even think about it, brother. Just get on it and get the job done! That's your problem, man. You think too much about it! Just let nature take over and forget all that . . . fiery furnace stuff. Stuff'll mess you up every time, when you want some of it. Indeed, it will! I'm sorry, but that's just not the time for it. Hell, worry about it after you've busted your nuts. Get guilty later, if you want to. It'll pass, believe you me, it will pass! Just get on it and knock that shit out and chalk it up, and square it with your conscience later—much later, if that's what's bothering you. (*Sits downstage center on the edge of the porch.*) Yeah, be ready for that stuff when it comes, man because sometimes it's far and few between! Indeed!

LOU (*speaking softly but intensely*): Nate . . . some—sometimes I get . . . I get so sick and tired of it all! . . . I really do! . . . Honest to God!

NATE: What's that—nookie? Shit! I don't . . . I don't never get tired of it man—never!—

LOU: Sometimes I'd . . . I'd like to . . . to . . . take a knife and . . . and just . . . rip this black stuff off!—just . . . skin myself clean! I—

NATE: You'd just bleed, man, that's all . . . just bleed . . . (NATE *rises after a moment, and then goes up to* LOU *and claps him on the shoulder, shaking him gently.*) Ease up, man . . . just ease up! . . . Fuck it, you know? I mean, just plain fuck it all! . . . Just keep moving and you don't get hurt. . . . And don't let some of it hang out, let it all! You know what I mean? (NATE *puts his arm around his shoulder.*) Fuck it—just plain fuck it all! You know?

(*Lights begin slow fade.*)

LOU (*sighing heavily, shrugging*): Yeah . . . yeah . . .

(*Lights out and curtain falls. During act break, no. 2 wall is flown out to reveal no. 3 wall for* HARPER *flashback.*)

ACT TWO

Curtain rises. It is Saturday afternoon. The set is the same except for a tablecloth on the dining table. The Bible, cup and saucer, and tray have been struck. The bed upstairs has been made up. At rise, LOU *is sitting on the floor of the porch at the entrance to the house reading a biology book.* MILTON *and* NATE *are downstage of the desk in the living room, discussing a bid for a plastering job.*

NATE: Pop, the bid is way too low, for Pete's sake!

MILTON: Nathan, you don't have to get greedy about it!

NATE: Who's getting greedy? Pop, the trouble with you is you always bid too low!

MILTON: Look, Nathan, I got it figured down right here! That's why I called you in here!

NATE: Pop, you don't have a thing here for—for profit—not a thing! . . . for time and aggravation!

MILTON: Nathan, that house isn't going to take anymore than two weeks!

NATE: Pop, by the time we buy material, pay everybody, what do we have left?

MILTON (*giving the bid to* NATE): Nathan, look at these figures down there again, will you?

NATE: I'm looking at them! All they're saying is that we're going to have to scramble and charge at the lumberyard for the next job, instead of charging what the job is worth. (*Crosses stage center.*) You always underbid because you're afraid of not getting the job!

MILTON (*stepping to* NATE): I charge what the job is worth, and that's what I've been doing all these years!—

NATE: And that's why we don't have any capital now!

MILTON (*crossing stage right*): I've been able to provide for this family, haven't I? Nobody's in need of anything here, are they?

NATE (*stepping to* MILTON): Pop, just tell me—why do we always have to submit the lowest bid, huh? No wonder we always get the job. They know they're going to get a first-class job for the least amount of money. Those white contractors, they see us coming, and they laugh all the way to the bank. (*Crosses stage center.*) As far as I'm concerned—

MILTON (*grabbing the bid again and studying it*): All right, all right, let me see the paper. (*Sits at the desk and opens the ledger, which is on the desk.*)

NATE: I'd rather risk not getting the job than to—Things are going up, and here we are charging the same thing we did last year. That house has got—

(JOE DRAKE *moves up to walk onto the porch from stage left.*)

DRAKE: Hello, Nate.

LOU (*rising quickly, polite but attempting to mask the indignation at the mistake*): I'm not . . . Nate . . .

DRAKE: Oh, I'm sorry. . . . I—I thought you were. (DRAKE *forces a smile.*) Is . . . your father in? . . . It's Joe Drake.

LOU (*moving toward the porch door*): Just a minute . . . (*Going to* MILTON) Pop, it's Joe Drake.

(NATE *crosses upstage at the desk, hovers over* MILTON.)

MILTON: Tell him I'll be there in a minute—I'm finishing up on the bid. (*Gestures for* NATE *to sit;* NATE *sits anxiously on the piano stool.*)

LOU (*returning to the porch*): He'll be here in a second.

(DRAKE *stands hesitantly.*)

Won't you have a seat?

DRAKE: Thank you. (*He sits stage right on the bench.*)

(LOU *crosses stage left and sits on the floor. Throughout the scene with* DRAKE, LOU *tries to be polite, though he is somewhat ill at ease.*)

You must be Lou, then?

(LOU *nods, grinning somewhat shyly.*)

Your father and Nate are good plasterers. (*Pause.*) That Nate is the best I've ever seen—a first-class perfectionist! I have work, I try to make certain they get it.—So, how's school going?

LOU (*reluctantly, shrugging*): Okay . . . so far . . .

DRAKE (*nodding, pause*): Your brother tells me you want to be a doctor some day.

LOU (*looking directly at him*): I hope so . . .

DRAKE: Well, that's great . . . that's great. . . . Who knows, maybe someday I'll be getting a checkup from you. (*He laughs, pausing as* LOU *forces a polite smile.*) My kid's in school too—Yale. . . . Every once in a while he sends me stuff home to read—things he's been studying. . . . Wants to make sure I don't get too complacent—wants some intelligent conversation when he comes home on vacations . . . doesn't want a dunce as a father. (*Laughing again.* LOU *is stoic.*) Your . . . father tells me you don't like plastering very much . . .

LOU (*softly, hesitantly*): It's . . . all right . . .

DRAKE: Well, it's hard work . . .

LOU: I'd just . . . rather be doing . . . something else—

DRAKE: Well, I don't blame you, son—no, I don't. . . . I don't blame my own kid for not wanting to go into the building business. No, let him make up his own mind what he wants to be—

MILTON (*turns to* NATE): All right, seventeen hundred—(*Rises.*)

NATE (*rising*): It's still not enough!

MILTON (*crossing stage right*): Nathan, I can't charge that man no more than that!—

NATE (*following*): Drake's got it.

MILTON: Now you're being ridiculous!

NATE: It ought to be at least two thousand!

MILTON: Nathan, I'm sorry, but I'm just not going to do it!

NATE: That old place has got closets and pipes galore—

MILTON: I know what it's got! I can see! I'm not going to charge Drake any two thousand, so you may as well stop!—

NATE: Well, I don't know why you asked my opinion in the first place.

MILTON (*crossing stage center*): Nathan, I appreciate your help, but I thought you'd use better sense.

NATE: Well, maybe you'd better figure out the bids yourself from now on! (*He angrily crosses downstage right, sits in the armchair.*)

(MILTON *stops, looks at him for a moment, and then studies the bid. Going to the table, he writes a figure on it and steps to* NATE.)

MILTON: All right, I got it up to eighteen hundred, but I certainly can't charge the man any more than that—absolutely not! (*Crosses to the porch.*)

NATE (*without looking up*): Pop, it's your business . . .

MILTON (*appearing at the door*): Hello, Mr. Drake, I'm sorry to keep you waiting.

DRAKE (*rising*): Oh no, that's all right. Your boy and I were just out here talking.

MILTON: Come on into the living room, Mr. Drake, where it's more comfortable. It's so hot out here.

DRAKE (*following him*): Okay. Nice talking to you, Lou.

(*The two men go into the living room.* DRAKE *sees* NATE.)

How are you doing, Nate?

NATE (*sullenly*): Okay, Mr. Drake, how are you?

DRAKE: Oh, fair to middling. (*Sitting at the table stage left.*)

MILTON (*handing him the bid and then sitting opposite him*): I tried to make it as fair as I could.

DRAKE (*putting on a pair of glasses*): Oh, I know that—I know that. Just let me take a quick gander at it. I'm sure it'll be all right. (*He looks at the bid and then frowns.*) Milton . . . this is a little high, isn't it?

MILTON: Mr. Drake, like I said, I tried to be fair.

DRAKE (*reexamining the bid*): I'm sure you did, but—

MILTON: And I'm still not making any money. . . . Material's gone up. I've got my men to pay, and they have to get union scale—

DRAKE: My expenses are up too, Milton.

MILTON: I have to make some money, Mr. Drake. Both of us are after some kind of profit—

DRAKE: Agreed, Milton, but it's just that your other bids were so much lower.

MILTON: I really didn't charge what I should have then.

DRAKE: I thought you said it would take two weeks. Here you have three—

MILTON: Mr. Drake, I don't like to rush things. I want to give you a first-class job—

DRAKE: And you always do, but—

MILTON: There's a lot to be done in that house, Mr. Drake.

DRAKE: Milton, you know I have other bids?

MILTON: I'm aware of that.

DRAKE (*pausing*): This one is pretty steep. Milton, you know I'm not trying to beat you out of money—you know that?

MILTON: Well, I certainly hope you wouldn't.

DRAKE: Well, I wouldn't. . . . And I really would like you and Nate to have this job because you do such damned good work. (*Looking slowly at the bid again.*) But . . . on the basis of this . . . I . . . I really have to consider some of the others.

MILTON (*shrugging*): Well, I'm sorry, Mr. Drake. . . . I gave you the figures I . . .

DRAKE: You wouldn't consider dropping it a little, would you? Sixteen hundred—how does that sound?

MILTON: Mr. Drake, I already gave you what I thought—

DRAKE (*rising, crossing downstage of the table to stand between* MILTON *and* NATE): Milton, I'm trying to arrive at something equitable for both of us—so both of our purposes can be served. I really want you and Nate to have the job, and that's no joke! Sixteen hundred—no higher, no less. (MILTON *is silent, thinking.* NATE *watches anxiously.*)

MILTON: Let me see the bid.

DRAKE: I'm not trying to pressure you now—(*Handing him the bid and crossing up center behind table.*)

MILTON (*studying the bid*): You're not pressuring me.

DRAKE: Sixteen hundred.

MILTON: Sixteen hundred?

DRAKE: Sixteen. . . .

MILTON (*a lengthy pause*): All right . . . but . . . Lord knows I can't do it any cheaper.

DRAKE: I'm not asking you to. Sixteen hundred. We have a deal then? (*Offering his hand, which* MILTON *shakes.*) Good. Have it typed up, and we'll both sign it. I'm really glad we could compromise, Milton. You guys have me spoiled when it comes to your work. (*Looking at his watch.*) Okay, then . . . I've got to get out of here. The wife and I are having some friends over tonight, and if I'm not back on time, she'll hit the roof.

(MILTON *follows him to the door.* NATE *disgustedly crosses up stage to the desk.*)

When do you think you can get started, Milton?

MILTON: Oh . . . Monday, I suppose . . .

DRAKE: Good . . . sounds good. (*Looking for* NATE *who is out of view.*) Okay, Milton, I'll be talking to you a little later in the week, all right?

MILTON: All right.

DRAKE (*shaking his hand again*): Good night, Milton.

MILTON: Good night.

(DRAKE *moves onto the porch, leaving* MILTON *in the living room studying the bid again.*)

DRAKE: Good night, Lou. Lots of luck in school, son.

LOU (*softly*): Thank you.

(DRAKE *leaves stage left.* MILTON *moves into the living room and sits at the table, stage left.* NATE *turns and glares at him.*)

NATE: Pop, you had him! Why did you let that man beat you down?—

MILTON: Now, Nathan, nobody beat nobody—

NATE: Pop, he most certainly did!

(*Hearing* NATE's *loud responses,* LOU *rises and moves into the living room and sits in stage left armchair, listening.*)

MILTON: Nathan, I got a hundred dollars more than I started with! Now we can at least be thankful for that!—

NATE: Pop, you were asking for eighteen hundred, not sixteen! Maybe that's how that man can afford to send his son to Yale—by beating us down!

MILTON: Nathan—

NATE: You had him! You should've just told him to go and get somebody else if he didn't like it! Who needs—(*Turns stage right.*)

MILTON (*rising and crossing upstage center*): Nathan, you don't know anything about bargaining. In business sometimes you have to compromise. Now, you know that—

NATE: Oh, for goodness sakes, Pop, if that white man had asked for nine hundred, he'd have beaten you into less than that!

MILTON: I wouldn't have done anything of the kind! I'm getting sick and tired of you telling me what I'm supposed to do with white people!—

NATE: Maybe if you'd just listen to me just once—just once!

MILTON: I've been dealing with these people longer than you were born! And you're trying to tell me! (*Pacing, ranting.*) Took my trowel long before you were born! Brought it across that man's face—Jake Ricker—man calling me out of my name! Jumped on him and beat

him to the floor—slurring me—the white devil! Beat him down! And
you trying to tell me about white people!—

NATE: I'm giving you my opinion—all right?

MILTON: I didn't ask you for any opinion! I know what you're
calling me!

NATE: Oh, let's just forget it—forget it! I'm trying to tell you how I feel!
If you don't appreciate it, then—

MILTON: I don't want to know how you feel! . . . I'm trying to feed and
clothe you—I don't want to hear another word! I don't want you to
bat an eye around here from now on! (*Pacing.*) Here I am trying to
work and keep my dignity—I'm spending a year in jail beating up that
man . . . learning to keep my dignity—keep my reputation—and I
have to get some smart lip from you! I'm surprised at you, Nathan!
You ought to be ashamed of yourself! Well, I don't want to hear
another word!

(MILTON *turns, sees* LOU, *and crosses to him.* LOU *rises and backs onto the
porch.* GREMMAR, *who has heard the noise, starts down the stairs,
carrying the Scrabble game.*)

And you are working for me this summer, young man—as long as I
need some help—next summer too, whether you're willing or not! You
don't have nothing to say about it! I'm your father, and you are going
to respect me! You hear me?

(GLORIA *appears at the porch, interrupting* MILTON'S *tirade.* GREMMAR
moves toward the porch, but stops just inside the living room entrance.)

Can I help you?

(LOU *crosses upstage on the porch behind the bench.*)

GLORIA: Mr. Edwards?

MILTON: Yes?

GLORIA: I'm Gloria Townes . . . Tom's wife.

MILTON: Yes?

GLORIA: Can—can I talk with you a minute?

MILTON (*pause, frowning*): Would . . . would you like to come in?

GLORIA (*glancing nervously at* LOU): No, I . . . I . . . (*Pause.*)

MILTON (*looking strangely at her*): What—what can I do for you,
Mrs. Townes?

GLORIA: Well . . . (*Again looking at* LOU.) Could I . . . could I . . . see you
down here a minute?

MILTON: Please come inside, Mrs. Townes.

(GLORIA *enters the living room, nodding to* GREMMAR *as she passes.* MILTON *follows.* GREMMAR *goes to the porch and sits on the bench with* LOU *to play Scrabble.*)

GLORIA (*standing up center behind table*): I don't have much time, Mr. Edwards, I just come over for Tom's pay.

MILTON (*behind stage right armchair*): His what?

GLORIA: I said, his pay, Tom says you haven't given him his pay—the last three weeks before you laid him off, you haven't given that man nothing!

MILTON: Oh now, Mrs. Townes!—

GLORIA: And that's not right!

MILTON (*crossing to* GLORIA): Mrs. Townes, I'm a deacon in the church now—

GLORIA: Mr. Edwards, you shouldn't be hiring nobody if you can't afford to pay them—

(LOU *and* GREMMAR *stop playing to listen to the conversation.*)

MILTON: Mrs. Townes, your husband is lying—

GLORIA: My husband hasn't got no right to lie to me—

MILTON: I paid Tom every cent he earned—every cent!—

GLORIA: Well, he said—

MILTON: And some days he wouldn't even show up, and I'm depending on him—

GLORIA: Mr. Edwards, I think it's a shame for colored people to treat other colored people the way you're treating my husband—

MILTON: Mrs. Townes, why would I want to cheat Tom, huh?

GLORIA: I don't know! That's up to you to answer. All I know is—

MILTON: The man coming to work drunk half the time—half can't do his work—

GLORIA (*her voice rising*): I beg your pardon! I beg your pardon! Tom hasn't never left my house drunk—hasn't never! Mr. Edwards, if you have the money, I'd appreciate having it. My children's get colds, I'm running out of things. We are poor Negroes, Mr. Edwards—

MILTON: Now, wait a minute—wait just a minute! I want to show you something here! (*Moving quickly to the desk to get the ledger.*) Isn't that something?

GLORIA: It's a shame!—a damn shame!—It's awful!

(MILTON *crosses to the table, carrying the ledger; puts it on the table and attempts to show it to her.*)

MILTON: Every cent! My boy Nathan puts it in here promptly every week—doesn't miss a one. Now, look here, Mrs. Townes—

GLORIA (*turning away*): Mr. Edwards, Tom needs his money!

MILTON (*turning to the payroll section of the ledger*): I'm trying to show you, woman. Look—here it is! I have to pay taxes! You think I want the government down on my back?

GLORIA: Mr. Edwards, I ain't hardly interested in reading no book!—

MILTON: You want to know the truth, don't you? (*Pointing to the page.*) Here's the last week the man worked—right here!—all his pay! And the week before that . . . and before that. It's all in here! Now, if you don't want to believe that, then I feel sorry for you! (MILTON *crosses stage right.*) Right in here!

(*She reluctantly looks as* MILTON *crosses back to the table and points to the page again.*)

Right there!—and there—and right there!—I'm not trying to cheat your husband, Mrs. Townes.

(*She looks closely at the page.*)

And then coming up to this house—my house—and throwing a brick through my window because my boy Nate wouldn't lend him some money—drunk!

GLORIA (*stunned, stepping to* MILTON): Tom did?

MILTON: Yes, ma'am—that's right!

GLORIA (*softly*): He didn't get laid off?

MILTON: Indeed, he did not! . . . I had to fire your husband!

(*She is silent, fighting back tears.*)

Did Tom send you up here, Mrs. Townes?

GLORIA (*after a moment, softly, her voice breaking slightly*): No . . . I . . . I . . . just come . . .

MILTON: Well, I'm sorry you did. . . . He should've told you not to. . . . I'm sorry . . .

(*She stands for a moment, sighing heavily and resisting the desire to cry. Turning, she hurries out, exiting stage left off the porch.*)

GLORIA: That bastard!

(GREMMAR *rises and enters the living room.*)

MILTON (*standing, looking after her*): Isn't that something? . . . Tom's nothing but a fool!—nothing but a plain fool!

GREMMAR (*crossing to* MILTON): Milton, I don't want to meddle now—I never did do that with you children—but why don't you give the woman a few dollars—just a couple. She's in trouble, son—

MILTON: Momma, I feel sorry for the woman, but—

GREMMAR: It's not her fault, Milton. I'm not taking the blame off him, but the Lord will deal harshly with him. She does have some little children. Be charitable, Milton. You know the Bible talks about being charitable to others. Others, son. Go on over there, or send one of the boys and just give her a little present. It doesn't have to be much—just a little present. She'll appreciate it. She will. Remember your Bible, son. Remember it, and trust in it. . . . Trust in it . . .

MILTON (*after pausing thoughtfully, nods his head*): I'll do it myself, Momma.

(*They both move to the porch, and* MILTON *exits stage left.* GREMMAR *looks after him, her thoughts again turning inward; lights fade to special on* GREMMAR. *The lights rise simultaneously in* LUCRETIA'S *room as the special fades out.* GREMMAR *and* LOU *clear stage left.* LUCRETIA *enters.* HARPER *follows from upstage right as she puts her purse on the dresser.* HARPER *puts his hat on.*)

LUCRETIA: You have to go now, Harper?

HARPER: Yes, ma'am. . . . Have to go to work in the morning.

LUCRETIA: What time do you have to be up?

HARPER: Oh, four o'clock thereabouts . . .

LUCRETIA: You have to be down in the mines at four o'clock?

HARPER: 'Round about then . . . four . . . four-thirty.

LUCRETIA: Lord, at four o'clock I won't be thinking about waking up, unless Little Sam or Edna does it.

HARPER: Yeah, well, it's . . . early, all right—it's early. Can't say I like it, but that's when my shift has to go down.

LUCRETIA (*crossing to* HARPER): Well, you can stay a bit longer if you want. It won't be imposing on me none. Mrs. Darden, my landlady's got the children for the evening, and she don't mind keeping 'em as long as it's not too late. You sure you won't stay a minute?

HARPER (*shyly*): All right . . . if—if it won't be imposing too much.

LUCRETIA (*crossing stage center*): Heavens no! I'm always up late. Mrs. Darden says I must be a night owl or something, my light's on so much. (*Pulls a chair downstage center.*) Have a sit-down, and I'll be right with you. (*Takes his hat, goes to the dresser, and takes off her hat; puts both on dresser.*) I want to thank you for taking me to the services down at the church tonight. Harper, I really enjoyed it.

HARPER: You're certainly welcome.

(*She primps at the dresser, catching him staring admiringly at her. He smiles bashfully, dropping his glances.*)

LUCRETIA: You like my beads, Harper? . . . Pretty, aren't they?

HARPER: Yes, they are . . . yes . . .

LUCRETIA: Thank you. My husband gave them to me before he passed on—Sam Green? I hope you don't mind me mentioning his name.

HARPER: No, ma'am, go right ahead.

LUCRETIA: He was good to me, Sam was. . . . Yes, he was. (*Moving away to the bed and sitting opposite him.*) There now, I feel better now that I freshened up a bit. (*She smiles, and he shyly returns it.*) A woman should freshen up as much as she can. . . . One thing I can't stand is a woman who don't keep herself cleaned up and looking nice. Of course, they get jealous of you if you do—swearing you're trying to steal their menfolk—but it's just being jealous, that's all. (*She smiles again, pleased at herself, a silence following.*) Would you like some tea or something? . . . Won't be no trouble. I usually have some this time of night. . . . Helps me to stay awake. I just hate to go to sleep at nights, it seems. I don't get company that often—gets kind of lonesome for a widow like me. (*She rises.*) You're welcome to have some.

HARPER: No, thank you. . . . I—I appreciate the offer.

LUCRETIA (*pause as she sits on the bed*): How . . . how's your studying for the ministry coming along now, Harper?

HARPER: Fine, just fine . . .

LUCRETIA (*pausing*): Reverend Lockwood going to make you a preacher soon?

HARPER: Well . . . I preach my trial sermon and . . . and he says I'll be just about ready. (*Pleased.*)

LUCRETIA: You—you have a church all lined up when you finish your practicing?

HARPER: Reverend Lockwood says he get me one over in Greensborough—folks over there, they needs somebody.

LUCRETIA: Lord Jesus, you must be excited, aren't you?

HARPER: Yeah . . . yeah, I guess I am. . . . Yeah . . . it's . . . it's kinda scary, a little. One day I'm just a man way down in the mines, mining coal . . . wasn't even thinking about religion hardly—just making a living—hating it—hating it! And the next day I'm hearing the call of the Lord—hearing it as clear as I'm hearing you now—

LUCRETIA: What'd it sound like?

HARPER: Just as . . . as clear as a bell!—and pretty—just as pretty! The voice of the Lord is sweet! . . . And it's saying to me—saying to me: "I need you, Harper Edwards, to do my will—to preach the gospel—my gospel! I need you!" Well, I'm thinking at first—I'm going crazy or something, and I'm trying to shut it out!—

LUCRETIA: Ain't that something!—

HARPER: "Go 'way from here," I'm saying, "go 'way!" But it wouldn't. Kept after me—a couple of weeks, I guess. And . . . well . . . here I am . . . ready to preach and do his will . . . a shepherd looking after his own flock. . . . Yeah, I—I get kinda tense when I think about it.

LUCRETIA: Oh, Harper, you're going to be a good preacher—I know you will!

HARPER: Well . . . I'm going to do my best, Miss Lucretia—with the help of God.

LUCRETIA: Sure you will . . . (*Pause as she rises and steps to the mirror and primps.*) You . . . you go on over there to Greensborough, and I bet I won't be seeing you no more, I bet, will I?

HARPER (*with difficulty*): I—I was going . . . I was going to . . . to ask you . . . I—

LUCRETIA: Ask me what?

HARPER: Well . . . if . . . if I could come a-courting—

LUCRETIA: Oh, Harper—isn't that lovely! That's lovely! Of course you can!—

HARPER: You're a fine woman, Miss Lucretia—

LUCRETIA: Oh, Harper, I haven't done nothing special. I'm . . . I'm just a . . . a widow trying to look after her children with the little bit of money her husband left her—that's all.

HARPER: Well, you been doing a fine job—yes, ma'am. . . . Little Sam's a fine-looking boy—a fine-looking lad! And Miss Edna's just as pretty as a picture—

LUCRETIA (*crossing to the foot of the bed and sitting, facing audience*): I done my best, Harper—with the Lord's help. He's watched over us. Yes, he has, ever since I come here—the kids too young for me to work much, and hardly no women's jobs at all in this little mining town. He's made it possible for me and the children to make it somehow on the little bit of savings I had.

HARPER: Well, a man—especially if he's going to be a preacher—needs a fine woman—somebody who's gonna be an inspiration to his soul and light to his path and his children's path. And—and I been praying a long time, Miss Lucretia. And I see you at the church . . . and the Lord spoke to me and told me . . . the same voice I heard in the mine—told me as clear as a bell—you was the one.

LUCRETIA: That's so kind of you, Harper. (*Pleased.*) I know the children are wild about you. Yes, they are! They know a good man when they see one.

(*Both laugh softly, nervously and are silent, groping for words.*)

HARPER (*pleased with himself*): Well, I best be going. . . . I—I done stayed past my time.

LUCRETIA: I'm not sleepy if that's what's troubling you. But . . . if you have to go, since you have to be up so early.

HARPER: Yes, ma'am—four o'clock.

LUCRETIA: Lord, I'm telling you—four o'clock!

HARPER (*rising and standing awkwardly*): Well . . .

LUCRETIA (*also standing*): I want to thank you again for the time at the church, Harper. It was real nice.

HARPER: You're more than welcome, Miss Lucretia—more than welcome.

HARPER: Well, good night . . . (HARPER *crosses stage right.*)

LUCRETIA: Aren't—aren't you going to . . . kiss me good night, Harper?

(HARPER *stops and turns to* LUCRETIA. *She reacts quickly to his being taken aback.*)

You can . . . we're courting now, aren't we? You're going to court a woman, you have to learn to kiss her on the cheek or hand or something. (*Holding out her cheek.*) Right there—just a little peck, that's all.

(*He does so, shyly.*)

There now, that wasn't so bad, was it?

HARPER (*smiling*): Good-night . . . Miss Lucretia . . .

LUCRETIA: Your hat, Harper, don't forget it!

(*She moves quickly to the dresser and gets the hat and places it on his head, simultaneously kissing him. He exits upstage right, stunned. She laughs gaily. Blackout. In the blackout* LUCRETIA *clears stage left.* GREMMAR *and* LOU *get into place as the lights rise again on the porch; a special on* GREMMAR. MILTON *enters from stage left, the special goes out on* GREMMAR.)

GREMMAR: You get it straightened out with her, baby?

MILTON: Yeah . . . yeah . . . couldn't help feeling sorry for the woman, though . . .

(GREMMAR *begins coughing suddenly—heavy, wracking coughing.*)

Do . . . do you feel all right, Momma? (*Sitting beside her as* LOU *stands, equally concerned.*)

GREMMAR (*slowly*): Oh, I'm all right, son . . . just a little headache . . . a little one. . . . The heat, I guess. . . . I'm a little tired. . . . Probably should go on upstairs and rest some. . . . No sir, can't do like I used to . . . not like I used to . . .

MILTON: Oh, Momma, you're still as spry as—

GREMMAR (*decisively*): Oh no . . . no . . . no, sir. . . . No, I can't lie to myself. . . . Not going to do me one bit of good. . . . No, son, I'm not a young woman no more. . . . I know the road. . . . Momma used to recite a poem to me. She used to say:
"Oh, the old sheep, they know the road,
The old sheep, they know the road.
The old sheep, they know the road;
Young lambs must find the way."
Yes, the young lambs must find the way. . . . I know the road. . . . Well, let me get up from here with this Scrabble and go upstairs for a while. . . . A little rest may help me.

(MILTON *helps* GREMMAR *to her feet, and she crosses into the living room with* MILTON *and* LOU *following.*)

You all don't bother about waiting for me for dinner. I'll eat something a little later on.

MILTON: Put the fan on up there, Momma. Louis, help her upstairs, will you?

(LOU *rises, crosses to* GREMMAR, *takes her arm, and they move up the stairs.* MILTON *follows to the foot of the stairs and stands watching— concerned.*)

GREMMAR: The old sheep, they know the road . . . the young lambs must find the way . . . find the way . . .

(GREMMAR *stops at the top of the stairs, gives the Scrabble game to* LOU, *who exits stage right. She exits upstage right.* MILTON *returns the ledger to the writing table. He stands, thinking for a moment, then sits at the table stage right chair, staring distantly, painfully.* HATTIE *enters from the kitchen and crosses stage center.*)

HATTIE (*softly*): Milton, are you all right?

MILTON (*sighing*): Yeah . . . I'm all right. (*She frowns curiously at him, then begins to remove the tablecloth.*)

HATTIE: Milton, I'd like to set the table.

MILTON (*turning to look up the stairs as* HATTIE *is folding the tablecloth*):

I don't know, Hattie, but . . . every time I think about . . . (*Pause.*)
Momma used to be so . . . active . . . spry . . . cutting up and on the
go—going here and there—just had to be doing something—doing
something! Busy! . . . It just doesn't seem to . . . make sense! (*Sighing
again—pause.*) I look at her now and . . . in some ways . . . she's . . . not
even the same person. . . . It's . . . somebody else—not Momma . . .
somebody else. . . . Somebody almost like her, but like a stranger—
Somebody that—that reminds me of her . . . has the same walk . . .
same kind of laugh . . . same way of talking, but—

(HATTIE *crosses behind* MILTON *and puts her hands on his shoulders.*)

HATTIE: Your mother's not a young woman now, Milton, she—
MILTON: I know, I know. (MILTON *rises, sighing.*) Well, I guess I'll go on
outside for a while. Weeds are taking over the string beans.
HATTIE (*crossing down to a level with* MILTON): Milton, do you know
how hot it is out there?—do you? You'll get yourself a stroke! (*Wiping
his brow.*) Look at yourself now—sweating and all! You already
worked half the day, plastering! It ought to be enough for you! Sit
down and rest and be sensible! You're not one of the boys!
MILTON: I used to . . . used to be able to work out there in that heat
when I was younger . . . didn't think nothing of it—
HATTIE: Well, you certainly aren't younger now!—
MILTON: Momma would—would come all the way out to me . . . a mile
near . . . worrying about me, trying to get me to slow down or stop.
"Sun can't hurt me, Momma—can't hurt me!" Always so worried
about me.
HATTIE: Milton, you can't stop living now. If I'd stopped the day I
realized my mother and father were old people, I'd be no more good
today. Now, all of us, if the Lord spares us, has to grow old and leave
this world, and your momma's one of them. So just make up your
mind to it. Besides, there's nothing more beautiful than somebody
that's grown old as gracefully as that woman has.
MILTON (*turning to* HATTIE): Yeah, I suppose you're right.
HATTIE: If you're a Christian, I'm right.
MILTON: You're right, you're right, Hattie.
HATTIE: I know I'm right.

(*They hug.* HATTIE *picks up the centerpiece,* MILTON *the tablecloth. As
they exit to the kitchen,* MILTON *repeats: "The old sheep they know the
road; young lambs must find a way." Blackout to denote passage of time. As
lights rise on the porch and living room,* GREMMAR *enters from downstage
left, wearing a straw hat and carrying the garden spade. She crosses into*

the living room, but suddenly suffers a dizzy spell stage center. She pauses, regaining her composure, and crosses to the piano, putting her hat and spade on top of the piano, and sitting on the stool. As she does, LOU, NATE, *and* HOPE *enter from kitchen carrying a birthday cake, a pitcher with punch, and glasses. They are singing "Happy Birthday." As* LOU *and* NATE *hug* GREMMAR, HOPE *lights the candles, and* HATTIE *and* MILTON *enter from kitchen.)*

LOU, NATE and HOPE (*in unison*): Speech—speech!

GREMMAR (*crossing to upstage center and sitting at the table*): Oh now, you all didn't have to go to all this trouble!—

MILTON: Wasn't any trouble, Momma—

(EDNA *enters slowly from stage right, down the stairs carrying a gift-wrapped package.*)

GREMMAR: And me looking a mess!—

NATE (*teasing*): That's all right, Gremmar, you're among kinfolk.

GREMMAR: Well, I want to thank you—all of you. Thank you so much.

EDNA (*crossing to* GREMMAR *and giving her a gift*): Happy birthday, Momma! (*As they exchange kisses.*)

GREMMAR: Thank you, baby. When'd you get here? Nobody told me.

EDNA: Couldn't spoil the surprise, Momma. Anyway, you was out in the garden just a piddling and poking around.

GREMMAR: Well, it's good to see you, baby—yes, it is. (*Seeing* HOPE.) Lord, what a pretty face. How are you, dear?

HOPE: Fine, Mrs. Edwards. Happy birthday.

(HOPE *gives* GREMMAR *a kiss and then a small gift which she brought in on the tray.*)

GREMMAR: Thank you, sugar.

NATE: Okay, Gremmar, it's time to blow out the candles!

GREMMAR: Lord have mercy, I'm not that old, am I? How many of these things you have on there?

LOU: Just sweet sixteen, Gremmar.

GREMMAR: Oh child, I know that's not true. No, sir—a long time since I was that!

HATTIE: Come on now, Momma, time to blow now.

GREMMAR: Now, I know I'm not that big a bag of wind, am I? You all trying to tell me something?

EDNA (*to the laughter of the others*): You have to try anyway. Come on, Momma. There isn't that many.

GREMMAR: All right . . . lemme see here. . . . Where'll I start? . . . All right. (*She blows—*)

(*Blackout, the lights rising upstairs.* LUCRETIA *sits on the bed and* HARPER *in the chair.* LUCRETIA *looks at him with excitement and admiration.*)

LUCRETIA: I keep saying to myself: That's Reverend Edwards— Reverend Edwards!

HARPER (*smiling, trying to restrain his joy*): Yeah . . . yeah, I—I guess that's me, all right.

LUCRETIA: Yes, and that was a wonderful sermon you preached for your trial one—a wonderful sermon!

HARPER: Yeah, it felt good . . . yeah. . . . After it was all over, Reverend Lockwood grins and says, "Well, looks like you made it, son. You're a preacher now!"

LUCRETIA (*exuberant, crossing downstage left of the chair to the dresser and putting her hat down*): Lord, you had them folks just a-shouting and carrying on—getting happy! And you were just a-preaching on— a-preaching on!

HARPER (*laughing, pleased*): Couldn't help myself. The Lord was talking to me.

LUCRETIA: Well, he certainly must've been! And—and the collection basket was full up too! Some of them folks was putting in dollar bills! That shows you! Colored folks ain't going to put nothing in the collection basket unless they enjoys it—put in a lot of pennies maybe—

HARPER (*pleased*): Yeah . . . yeah . . . they don't like something, they'll let you know about it one way or another. (*Looking at her with admiration as she takes his hat and puts it on the dresser, then crosses to bed and sits.*) You was a hit too, little lady—all the folks looking at you—

LUCRETIA (*frowning*): They . . . they were looking at me?

(*He nods. They exchange smiles and a lengthy stare.*)

HARPER: Yeah. . . . "That man certainly couldn't've done no better for somebody who's going to be a preacher's wife! She's a pretty thing!" (*Laughing nervously.*) They're . . . right about that.

LUCRETIA (*crossing to* HARPER): I—I didn't hear nothing. I—I was so busy watching you after the service—making sure none of those other ladies was trying to steal you. (*Laughing coyly.*)

HARPER: No need to worry about that . . . no . . . !

(*They exchange a lengthy, warm stare. He drops his eyes and rises, crossing downstage right as* LUCRETIA *crosses downstage left.*)

And . . . and one of the members ups to me after the service and says, "That sure is a pretty child, Reverend. . . . Used to be a child that looked like that in Roanoke a while back. Belonged to a family—

LUCRETIA (*quickly, fearfully—turning to* HARPER): I—I've never been to Roanoke—never. I—

HARPER: That's what I told him. . . . I couldn't imagine nobody in Roanoke as . . . pretty as you. (*He grins, pleased with his boldness.*)

LUCRETIA: Never in my life . . . (*Crossing to the dresser, avoiding contact with him.*) Who—who was this . . . gentleman that was asking?

HARPER (*crossing to chair*): Oh, a short little dark fellow. He's been around White Rock off and on since I been attending. Drops in and out—

LUCRETIA (*attempting to collect herself*): Who—who—what was this girl's name—the one he thought I was?

HARPER: He plum forgot, it's been so long since he's been back there.

LUCRETIA: Oh . . . (*Feigning gaiety.*) Well, it couldn't have been me, since I've never been there! Must've been my double or something.

HARPER: "Sure is pretty and familiar-looking pretty."

(HARPER *sits as* LUCRETIA *crosses behind the chair to sit downstage on the bed.*)

LUCRETIA: Well . . . the next time, thank the gentleman for me. (*Nervously.*) It's—it's been so hot out . . . seems like . . . we haven't had a breeze all summer. (*Pause, silent, breathing more heavily and reacting nervously to* HARPER'S *admiring look.*) I . . . I think I hear the children . . . downstairs . . . I think. . . . Did—did you hear 'em? Little Sam probably wants me now. . . . Edna wakes up because he does.

(*He rises reluctantly, and she does also.*)

HARPER: Well, I best be going. . . . It—it don't seem possible I won't be going down in that mine tomorrow. . . . I been going down in all that blackness for so long, it just seems strange, you know? . . . Lord knows I'm glad I don't have to . . . you've been a blessing to me, Lucretia. The Lord's done answered my prayers all the way 'round, he has.

LUCRETIA (*sighing heavily*): Thank . . . thank you, Harper. . . . You've been a blessing to me too. Well, I guess I'd better be getting to the children. (*She crosses to the dresser and gets his hat.*)

HARPER (*starting to go, but stopping stage right at the foot of the bed*): Won't be long before you'll be the good reverend's wife—

LUCRETIA (*crossing to* HARPER): Yes, yes, that's right. . . . I'd better . . . go, Harper. (*Giving the hat to* HARPER.) You—you have a good time over there in Greensborough. And—and don't you let none of them pretty-looking sisters over there turn your head, now—

HARPER (*wanting to kiss her fully, but restraining*): No need to worry about that . . . no need at all. (*Staring at her and then turning to go, his reluctance visible.*) Well . . . good night . . .

LUCRETIA: Harper? (*He stops.*) That—that man—the one that asked you about me?—the girl he thought I was?—Well, I'm . . . I'm glad it was me and not her that has you.

(*He smiles and then kisses her almost fearfully on the cheek. He looks at her warmly and then leaves. She watches his departure and then turns and crosses stage center.*)

Never . . . never been to Roanoke in my life—not even near it . . . wouldn't know it if I stumbled over it!

(*As the lights black out on* LUCRETIA, *exiting stage left, applause is heard, and lights rise on the living room.* GREMMAR *leans over the candles, having blown them out. The others are applauding. She begins to cough slightly.*)

MILTON: You all right, Momma?

GREMMAR (*feigning*): I'm all right. . . . Just a little cough . . .

HATTIE: Sit right there, dear, I'll cut the cake for you.

GREMMAR: After all that huffing and puffing, I need to.

HATTIE (*cutting the cake*): You all come and help yourselves. I'm not waiting on nobody but Gremmar tonight. This is her night!

(*They respond, moving to the table and helping themselves to punch, cake, and the other food. After getting various items,* NATE *and* HOPE *sit in stage left armchair.* LOU *sits at the table in stage left chair.*)

EDNA (*crossing between the table and stage right armchair*): You don't have any "tea" in here, do you, Milton?

MILTON (*standing behind stage right armchair*): Tea? . . . What "tea" are you talking about?

EDNA: The "tea" that makes you high.

MILTON (*crossing downstage and sitting in the chair*): Girl, you better go 'way from here!

EDNA (*laughing along with the others*): Lord, Milton would have a fit if some "tea" was in here.

HATTIE (*crossing downstage of the table to upstage left of* MILTON):

Milton's not fooling nobody. Doctor Walker told Milton he should take some of that mess for his cold—said it would help him—and, Lord Jesus, there wasn't any trouble at all getting that man to take his medicine.

MILTON: Hattie—

HATTIE: Three o'clock in the morning and Milton's getting out of bed, creeping downstairs. "Where are you going, Milton, this time of night?" "Have to take my medicine!"

MILTON: Hattie, now, why you want to—

HATTIE: Three o'clock! Usually you have to get the law almost to get him to take some medicine! (*Sits on upstage arm of stage right chair.*)

NATE (*teasing*): I heard him going downstairs.

MILTON: You all know I was just doing what the man told me—

EDNA: Tasting away, huh, Milton? Making sure to get his medicine *on time!*

(*He waves away her laughter.* GREMMAR *begins coughing again.*)

So how you feel, Momma? Milton says you haven't been feeling too well.

GREMMAR: Oh, I'm all right, baby—just a little cough . . . little cold or something. I'm all right.

EDNA: Well, besides that, you're looking good.

GREMMAR: I ought to go up and change this old rag I got on.

MILTON: Momma, you look fine. Stop worrying. . . . Momma's always worrying.

EDNA: Well, it wouldn't be her if she didn't. (*She crosses downstage left of* LOU.) Well, Louis, Nathan's got his girlfriend—where's yours?

LOU (*slightly embarrassed*): Oh, I have more important things to do, Aunt Edna.

HOPE: Well, I like that, Louis!

LOU (*as the others laugh, again embarrassed; rising and crossing upstage to* HOPE):

(EDNA *sits in the chair he vacated.*)

No, I mean . . . I mean, I have to do a lot of studying if I want to be a doctor . . . or a . . . scientist. . . . I mean . . . after I finish up there'll be lots of time. . . . Being a doctor's the most important thing right now. . . . We need a lot of doctors and things. I mean . . . someday . . .

HOPE: That's right, Lou—try and squirm out of it.

GREMMAR (*reaching out to take* LOU's *hand*): He's right. . . . Yes, plenty of time. . . . No need to rush things. . . . He's such a handsome boy, the Lord'll send him one when he's ready.

EDNA: Yes, him and Nathan's good-looking boys—good-looking!

NATE: I keep telling Mom that.

HATTIE (*as the others laugh*): Lord Jesus! Hope, don't pay no attention to Nathan now. He's just showing off!

HOPE: Don't worry, Mrs. Edwards—I don't.

(NATE *frowns mockingly at her.*)

EDNA: Yes, good-looking!

GREMMAR (*patting* LOU's *arm. They exchange smiles*): No, no need to rush . . . no need . . . plenty of time!

(*Lights fade down to special on* GREMMAR. LUCRETIA *enters the bedroom from stage left and moves the chair upstage as lights rise.* HARPER *enters from upstage right, shouting happily.*)

HARPER: I got my church, Lucretia! I got me . . . a . . . church! (*He laughs unrestrainedly, crosses stage center and puts his hat on the chair.*) Those folks in Greensborough, they liked me! . . . They . . . they said . . . "You're the one we want, son! You're the one the—*good* Lord sent us!" That's what they said, Lucretia! I got me a church, woman! (*Laughing happily.*)

LUCRETIA: Harper . . . that's—that's beautiful—that's beautiful!

HARPER (*happy, wanting to let go fully*): I'm telling you . . . I'm telling you . . . I'm just so . . . tickled. . . . I . . . I just want to . . . I just want to holler again!

LUCRETIA: Why don't you just go on?

HARPER: Yeah . . . yeah. . . . The Lord won't mind if I holler a little, will he?

LUCRETIA (*laughing*): Of course not! Go ahead, man—holler! (*He lets out a yell.*) Do it again! Feel real good about it, Harper—go ahead!

(*He yells again, and then stops. They exchange glances, laughing softly at first. Their laughter begins to build. They rush suddenly toward each other, laughing, holding hands and swinging almost childishly in a circle, dancing. They stop suddenly, continuing to hold hands, and stare at each other. They rush suddenly at each other, embracing, kissing, feeling, and touching. He starts to break away but cannot, continuing to react to his passions. As they begin to sink slowly toward the floor, the lights fade out and as they clear, the stage left lights rise in the living room, where everyone is laughing.* EDNA *takes a piece of cake and crosses downstage of the table, up to the piano.*)

EDNA: Hattie, this is some scrumptious cake, girl! (EDNA *sits on the piano stool.*)

HATTIE: Thank you, dear.

MILTON (*after a slight pause*): Hired me a white fellow Saturday.

EDNA: Yesterday?—A white man? Lord Jesus! Milton Edwards, my brother, is carrying on some! Going big time! Has it turned around! Got them working for him!

MILTON (*restraining his pleasure, crosses to the table and puts his plate down*): Come around looking for work, so I tried him out. (*Crosses upstage to* NATE.) Works pretty good, doesn't he, Nate?

NATE: Yeah, at least we don't have to prop him up after lunch like we did Tom.

MILTON: Lord, no! . . . Quiet. . . . Don't say much. . . . Just does his work . . .

EDNA (*rises*): Maybe he's afraid of you niggers!

MILTON: I wish you wouldn't use that word, Edna.

EDNA: Well, that's what we are, aren't we?

MILTON: Well, maybe that's what you are!

EDNA: Well, whether we are or not, I'm going to have another piece of cake! (*Going to the table and getting a piece of cake.*) I can't help it if I like to eat. I guess it don't matter. The Lord takes 'em fat, skinny, short, and tall. He ain't prejudiced. That's one thing about him.

NATE (*rising and taking* HOPE's *hand*): We have to run over to Hope's house. We'll be right back.

EDNA: Getting tired of us old heads, huh?

NATE: No, we'll be right back—just a couple minutes. Hope's got an errand to tend to.

GREMMAR: All right, you all have a nice walk now.

HOPE (*as they leave*): We'll see you later.

(*They leave, exiting off the porch.* EDNA *sits in stage right armchair.*)

EDNA: Yes, Lord, I'm telling you! Momma don't come over to see me no more!

MILTON (*crossing to stand behind* GREMMAR): Edna, you know Momma hasn't been well all weekend. I told you that.

EDNA: I don't mean this weekend! I'm talking about before. Kids say to me: "Where's Grandma? How come she don't come over and stay here like she does at Uncle Milton's?" I say: "I don't know, you have to ask her!"

GREMMAR: Oh now, Edna, child—

LOU: She really has been a little tired this weekend like Pop said, Aunt Edna.

(GREMMAR *reaches down and pats his hand, holding it.*)

MILTON: And you know you don't have room over there like we have.

EDNA: Burgess died last year. Momma could sleep with me. The kids they can double up. Yes sir, they wouldn't mind for Momma. No, Momma's just got to be with her baby! (*Laughing, a trace of bitterness contained.*)

MILTON: Edna's just messing now.

EDNA: Well, Milton, you are the baby of the family!

GREMMAR: Oh, child, you know your momma didn't play no favorites. Treated all my children equal—even Little Sam before he passed on—

EDNA: Oh no! One of us messed with Milton, and we liked to've got the devil knocked out of us!

MILTON: Edna, Momma used to spank us all!

EDNA: Me maybe—but not you and Sam much. (*Rising, getting another piece of cake.*) Yes, Jesus. Momma comes home on the weekends, and before I know it, she's gone on back to work.

MILTON (*crossing to stage left armchair and sitting*): Edna's just trying to start something on Momma's birthday—

EDNA: I'm not trying to start nothing, Milton! I'm just wishing she'd come over and visit me a little more than she does! That's all I'm talking about!

GREMMAR: I will, baby, I will. . . . Just as soon as I get over this cough—little headache. All right?—

(*Lights fade to specials on* GREMMAR *and* LUCRETIA. HARPER *enters in darkness from stage left and drops his coat and tie on the floor, upstage of dresser. The lights rise fully upstairs.* LUCRETIA *sits on the stage left foot of the bed, her clothing awry.* HARPER, *equally disheveled, sits next to her—stage right—his face buried in his hands.*)

LUCRETIA: You shouldn't fault yourself, Harper, you shouldn't—

HARPER: I let him down, that's what I did! I let him down!—

LUCRETIA: Harper, you didn't. . . . Harper, you're . . . you're a—a man!

HARPER: I'm a minister! You hear me? I'm a minister!

LUCRETIA: You're a man too!—

HARPER: A weak one—

LUCRETIA: Harper . . . Harper . . . we both—we both have feelings—

HARPER: We only had a couple of weeks to wait—just a couple more!—

LUCRETIA: Oh, Harper, what's the difference? A couple of weeks is supposed to make it right? . . . Harper, it just happened! It can't make us wrong the rest of our lives—

HARPER (*standing slowly and crossing stage center*): I . . . I went to Greensborough today. . . . Lord knows, it was a pretty day! Lord knows! The sun . . . just shining . . . birds flying and jack-rabbits running. . . . And I'm sitting in that old buggy, and I'm scared. I'm scared, but I'm happy! I'm scared and happy and filled with the . . . (*turns to* LUCRETIA) the spirit of God! . . . It's his day . . . and yours too . . . and the children's, because I'm thinking about all of you and just hoping to God those folks'll accept me into their fold—just hoping. . . . Scared some. . . . And—and I gets there . . . and they're waiting for me . . . just waiting! Can't wait for me to get down to the ground—can't wait—hands reaching for me—starved to hear the word of God, I'm telling you! Just a-thinking, thanking God for sending me to them! (*Turning to face her.*) I just . . . I just got me a church, Lucretia!

LUCRETIA: Harper, I know . . . I know! And . . . and you're going to be a wonderful minister!—

HARPER (*turning away*): No sooner than I leave 'em . . . here I am . . . acting . . . acting like I don't have the first bit of sense, like some—

LUCRETIA (*rising and crossing to him*): Harper, stop it! . . . Stop! . . . Don't—don't make me feel wrong! I'm not going to let you make me feel wrong! . . . I . . . you . . . you were so happy! I looked at your face and you were so . . . so happy!

(HARPER *takes* LUCRETIA'S *arms and turns; they counter cross.*)

HARPER: Pray with me, Lucretia, and—and ask for his forgiveness. It's a guilty stain against our record, girl, and we have to—have to . . . wipe it clean—

LUCRETIA: Oh, Harper! . . . it—it just happened! We—we were just happy about you getting your church. It—it just happened!

HARPER (*sighing*): Get on your knees with me, Lucretia. . . . Will you do that with me?

LUCRETIA (*trying to prevent him from assuming a prayerful position*): Harper, don't—please!

HARPER: Do you want to be banished from the Kingdom, Lucretia? Is that what you want? Do you want his thunder and lightning to . . . to come down here in this room and—and strike us down?—do you?

LUCRETIA (*crossing down left center*): Harper, I don't *want* . . . I don't want to be a part of no kingdom like that!—

HARPER (*following, shaking her*): Don't you say that! Don't you say that to me! You're talking about the Kingdom he called me to lead folks to! That's what you're talking about! Don't you ever say that to me again!

We're going to pray—right now—you and me! (*Assuming a prayerful position at the foot of the bed.*) Our Father, who art in heaven . . . hallowed be thy name . . . Thy kingdom come . . . Thy will be done . . . on earth as it is in heaven . . . Give us this day our daily bread . . .

LUCRETIA: Harper—please!

HARPER: And forgive us our trespasses, as we forgive those who trespass against us—

LUCRETIA (*again trying to break his position*): Harper, we don't have to be doing this—we don't!

HARPER: And lead us not into temptation . . . but deliver us from evil, for thy name's sake—

LUCRETIA: It isn't wrong—it's not! You—you're just making it wrong yourself!

HARPER: For thine is the power and the glory, forever and ever . . . amen. (*He rises quickly, straightening his clothing, and moves and picks up his coat and tie from the floor, and his hat from the chair.*)

LUCRETIA: Harper, where are you going?

(*He doesn't respond.*)

Harper—Harper, you're not . . . leaving me, are you? (*Rushing, grabbing him.*)

(*He wrenches away.*)

Harper, don't be silly! Come on back here, please!

(*He exits upstage right. She follows as the lights fade out. Lights up in the living room.*)

EDNA (*laughing*): Sometimes . . . sometimes I think the only reason Momma don't come over is because my daddy was *white!* And Milton and Sam had black ones!

(LOU *looks up slowly at* GREMMAR, *his face registering shock. He slowly slides his hand away from hers and glances at her.*)

HATTIE (*also looking at* LOU): Edna . . .

MILTON (*rising and angrily, crossing stage center*): Now, that isn't right, Edna! That's not a nice thing to say to Momma at all!

EDNA (*as* LOU *turns away in deep thought*): I'm just teasing Momma. . . . He *was* white, wasn't he? Momma knows I was just teasing, don't you, Momma?

GREMMAR: Edna always did like to tease.

MILTON: Just as determined as she can be to spoil Momma's birthday with her foolishness! (MILTON *crosses stage left to the armchair.*)

EDNA: Milton—

HATTIE (*crossing upstage of the table to* LOU): Let's have a good time now, you all . . . (*Looking at* LOU, *who is more absorbed in thought.*) Louis, you want some more to eat? . . . He eats like a bird now.

GREMMAR: You should eat, son. That's how you get your strength now. (*Reaching over and rubbing his arm.*)

LOU (*rising suddenly and moving away from the table*): I—I'm . . . going on the . . . porch for a while. . . . It—it's hot in here . . . (*He smiles tautly at* GREMMAR *and then moves out to the porch, where he stands mesmerized.*)

MILTON (*crossing to* EDNA): I certainly wish to heaven you'd stop your tomfoolery sometimes, Edna.

EDNA (*rising and crossing downstage of the table to stage left*): I don't know why everybody is so down on me. The man was white, wasn't he? Momma knows—

GREMMAR: All right, baby. Momma'll be over her next day off—next weekend—all right?

HATTIE: Momma, why don't you play us a little song? You feel like it?

MILTON: Edna is just jealous!

HATTIE: Milton!

EDNA: Milton knows I'm telling the truth!—

MILTON (*crossing to the kitchen with* HATTIE *following*): Why don't you stay home sometime, and don't come over to my house no more!

EDNA (*following*): Now, wait a minute! I'll come over and see my momma any time I want to.

GREMMAR: All right, children, don't fuss. Momma's going to play now.

(*She goes slowly to the piano and collapses suddenly on the stool. The lights fade to special on* GREMMAR. *Lights also rise in the bedroom as* LUCRETIA *enters from upstage right with a basket of clothes and sits in the chair. As she sits,* HARPER *enters from upstage right, where he stands staring icily at* LUCRETIA.)

LUCRETIA (*rising and crossing down to* HARPER): Harper—Harper, what's the matter? . . . Don't . . . you feel good? . . . Something happened?

(*He continues to stare and then begins toward her, seething, stopping near her.*)

HARPER: You . . . you lied to me, didn't you?

LUCRETIA: I what?

HARPER: You lied to me, didn't you?

LUCRETIA (*avoiding his stare*): Lied?

HARPER (*taking a step closer*): *Didn't you?*

LUCRETIA: I—I don't know what you're talking about. (*Attempting to pass him.*) I—I better go now . . . the . . . the children—

HARPER (*lunging, grabbing her arm and twisting it*): You tell me the truth!

LUCRETIA (*screaming in pain*): Harper, you're—my arm, Harper! Harper, what's wrong—what's the matter with you?

HARPER: You ain't never had no husband!—you *never,* did you?

LUCRETIA: Harper, I did—

HARPER: Liar! . . . You liar! . . . You *never!* You never! Now you just tell me the truth!

LUCRETIA: Oh God!—my arm!

HARPER (*exerting more force*): You been to Roanoke before, haven't you? Haven't you?

LUCRETIA: I told you—

HARPER: And they run you out, didn't they?—made fun of you and run you out—because you was a . . . a—whore, wasn't you? That's what you was, wasn't you?

LUCRETIA: I wasn't. . . . I wasn't, Harper—Harper . . . I . . . can't . . . breathe!

HARPER: That little old dark man remembered—just upped and remembered!—

LUCRETIA: He's a liar, that's what he is! . . . Sam Green was!—he was! He just—just got killed, that's all! . . . He—was coming back . . . and—

HARPER: Just another lie! Just another . . . lie! That little old dark man. . . . He wrote your momma a letter.

(GREMMAR *rises and crosses downstage to stage right arm chair.*)

LUCRETIA: Momma?

HARPER: Yeah, your momma! And she wrote him back . . . asking you to . . . to come back home with your sinful self!—your lying, sinful self! You ain't never been no widow! You ain't never been nothing, have you? (*Twisting her arm fully and making her scream, and then letting her go.*)

(*Simultanously, as* LUCRETIA *falls,* GREMMAR *sits in the chair.*)

LUCRETIA (*dropping to the floor and whimpering softly*): No, no, no, no, no—no, no!

HARPER (*crossing downstage right*): People laughing . . . calling the preacher a fool! . . . a fool! . . . The preacher!—

LUCRETIA (*rising*): Oh, nigger, why—why don't you stop thinking!—stop your . . . your . . . *thinking* and feel something—just . . . just . . . *feel* something!

HARPER: I—I don't deserve no church!—don't deserve none! . . . Making them laugh. . . . Nothing but a fool! . . . a . . . a fool! Don't . . . don't even deserve . . . God! . . . Not even him! . . . (*Pausing, breathing heavily, thinking.*) He's . . . he's telling me . . . telling me . . . telling me. . . . He's. . . . Don't even want me! . . . Don't even want me! . . . Don't want me! Don't want me!

(*He stands mesmerized—"listening." He turns, stares at her, and then starts suddenly toward her. She rises quickly, trying to retreat. He lunges, missing, and then chases her, catching her and ripping her clothing—pawing and mauling and kissing her roughly.*)

LUCRETIA: Harper, don't—don't be crazy! Please don't be crazy!

(*He forces her down on the bed. She screams.*)

(*Blackout, except for special on* GREMMAR. *The no. 1 blackout drop is flown in, the no. 3 wall and no. 2 blackout drop are flown out.*)

GREMMAR (*softly, distantly*): He . . . he never did become no minister—Harper. . . . Never did. . . . Went back to the mines again . . . way down in them mines . . . (*Pause.*) Folks . . . folks told me—told me they never did see much of that man again . . . except that when they did, he was drinking a lot . . . always . . . always . . . drunk. (*Pause.*) He . . . fell out one day. . . . Fell out dead. . . . Harper . . . drink on his breath . . .

(*The lights rise slowly in the living room and on the porch as* GREMMAR *rises and crosses to the piano stool and sits. After a moment* HOPE *and* NATE *walk up on the porch, where* LOU *sits staring blankly.*)

NATE: What's the matter, the party over?

LOU (*softly*): No, it's . . . still going on.

(NATE *takes* HOPE'S *hand and brings it close to* LOU'S *face.* LOU *looks at the ring, forcing a smile.*)

Con—congratulations . . .
HOPE: Hey, don't I get a kiss?
LOU: Sure . . . (*Kissing her cheek.*)
NATE: Getting a sister-in-law, man!

(*They go inside,* LOU *again caught up in thinking.*)

Hey, everybody, I have an announcement to make!

(MILTON *enters from upstairs,* HATTIE *from the kitchen, with* EDNA *following.*)

We're engaged!—

(*Everyone reacts happily—*GREMMAR *rises and applauds. She grasps her head suddenly and slumps to the floor, groaning. There is a brief moment of stunned silence, and then near panic as* MILTON, NATE *and* HATTIE *rush toward her, calling her name.* EDNA *begins to cry, while* HOPE *stands uncertainly.* LOU, *hearing the noise, rushes into the room.*)

HATTIE (*as* NATE *and* MILTON *hover over* GREMMAR, *trying to revive her, calling her name*): Louis—quick!—call the doctor! Hurry! Lord, let me get some water! . . . water! (*Rushing toward the kitchen.*)
MILTON: Wake up, Momma!—Momma, wake up!

(MILTON *and* NATE *pick* GREMMAR *up and carry her up to bed, with* EDNA *following—crying.* HOPE *precedes them and turns back the bed covers. As they place* GREMMAR *in bed,* HATTIE *enters and crosses upstairs with a glass of water. The lights fade to black. In the blackout,* EDNA *continues crying as* GREMMAR *puts on a bed jacket and the no. 1 blackout drop is flown out. When the change is complete,* EDNA *stops crying, and the lights rise slowly in the bedroom.* LOU *stands outside the door to the room.*)

LOU (*entering and crossing stage center—pulling the chair up to the head of the bed and sitting*): Gremmar? . . . Gremmar!

(*She opens her eyes slowly, weakly, dazedly, seeking him, and looks foggily at him for a moment.*)

GREMMAR: Nathan? . . . Is . . . is that you, Nathan?
LOU (*softly, hesitantly, somewhat anxiously*): No . . . it's me . . . Louis . . . Louis . . .
GREMMAR: Louis? . . . Yes . . . yes . . . (*Beginning to fade away.*) Yes . . . yes . . . come up to see me . . . come to see me . . . yes . . .
LOU (*quickly*): How—how do you feel? . . .

GREMMAR (*still drifting*): Come up to see me . . . knows I'm not . . . not feeling well . . . yes . . .

LOU: Gremmar . . . (*Pause.*) Gremmar . . . why . . . why didn't you . . . didn't you . . . tell me?

GREMMAR (*opening her eyes*): What—what's that, child . . . ?

LOU: Why didn't you . . . tell me? Why—(*Stopping, having difficulty.*) Why did you lie to me?

GREMMAR (*speaking partly to herself*): No . . . no . . . no . . . I never . . . I never lied to you, son . . . oh, no . . .

LOU: Gremmar, you did. . . . You did . . . (*Smoothing the covers and then watching her sympathetically.*)

GREMMAR: Not knowingly . . . no . . . no . . . not knowingly . . . no sir. . . . I wouldn't do that, child . . . no, no . . . (*Coughing.*)

LOU: Are you . . . all right? (*Pause.*) Gremmar?

GREMMAR (*distantly*): I'm all right . . .

(*He takes her hand and begins to stroke it.*)

LOU: You—you always did the right thing . . . always . . . your . . . whole life. So perfect . . . never did anything . . . wrong . . . never . . . lying . . .

GREMMAR: I had my needs, son—yes, I did, child . . . oh yes . . . (*Silent again, tired.*) I had my men—yes. . . . I was a young woman once, child—yes, I was. . . . Wasn't always your grandmother, wasn't always tired. . . . No, child . . . wasn't always tired . . . (*She reaches for his hand, grasping it.*) No, baby, don't . . . don't close your eyes to my needs. Don't close your eyes. They were real. . . . God knows they didn't have nothing to do with right or wrong . . . nothing to do with them . . .

LOU: Gremmar . . . don't . . .

GREMMAR: Don't make me no more than what I was, son. . . . Don't fault me for my feelings. . . . That's what you're doing . . . that's what you're doing . . .

LOU: Gremmar . . . Gremmar . . . you could have—have said . . . something . . .

GREMMAR (*speaking softly*): Some things are mine, baby . . . mine . . . just mine. . . . I had feelings. . . . Yes . . . needed loving . . . touched . . . held—

(LOU *rises and steps stage left.*)

Held in my men's arms. . . . That's what my body was for—oh yes! Wasn't easy to be all by yourself in them backwoods. . . . No, no . . . I had my feelings—

LOU (*crossing stage center*): Gremmar . . . just . . . just . . . stop. . . . That's

just what they think . . . just what they think. . . . That we're so
dumb. . . . Nothing but . . . dumb and . . . stupid and inferior! . . . Sex
maniacs . . . degenerate, and all that crap! . . . Lazy . . . black . . .
coons! (*Pause.*) You . . . you . . . call them liars and . . . and . . . punch
them out and . . . for what? . . . (*Pause, angrier, crossing to the bed.*) All
this time . . . all this time . . . you were just the opposite, weren't
you? . . . just the opposite . . . just another one of those . . . those
old . . . phonies . . . Just another . . . phony—
GREMMAR (*sitting up*): I was nothing of the kind! (*Pause.*) Nothing of
the kind! I was a colored woman!—life in my bones! And they were
tender to me! . . . tender to me! . . . They . . . they understood. . . .
They knew! Yes, they did! I'm still your grandmother, Louis—I still
am! . . . That's something different, baby—something different,
child—didn't have nothing to do with you—nothing to do with you
and me—
LOU: Gremmar . . . Gremmar, it . . . did! . . . It did! . . . I—I—who . . .
who do you think I was listening to . . . around here, Gremmar?
(*Pause.*) Doing things. . . . Testifying. . . . Telling those white kids
off! . . . I'm . . . I'm . . . behaving . . . going to church . . . all that—
GREMMAR: Lord, Louis—Louis, child, get off your high horse, son. . . .
Don't be some old . . . old . . . goody-goody—some old—
LOU (*angrily*): Gremmar, I'm not! (*Hurt.*) I'm not!
GREMMAR: Yes, you are—that's what you are—some old goody-goody!
Talk like some old maid, some—some little old sissy! Some little
old . . . prude—that's what you are!

(LOU *is shocked by her words.*)

Lord, Louis, you're a man, son! You're a man! He gave you something
to use—to use! Don't you know it?

(*He looks at her in disbelief, and with embarrassment.*)

It don't have nothing in this world to do with what you want to be—
don't let folks tell you that!—no, it don't!

(LOU *turns away, shaking his head, trying to find a way to shut out
her words.*)

Stop thinking there's something so special about it, Louis—stop
thinking so much and . . . and . . . *feel*, son. That's what you're
missing—that's it . . . It's there, baby. . . . Don't deny it's there—don't
deny what it's for.
LOU (*turning away*): I . . . I . . . know what it's for. . . . Don't you think
I . . . haven't . . . done . . . some—some things? Just because I—I

haven't said anything. . . . I know . . . what—what it's for! I . . . don't
have to go . . . boasting about it—

GREMMAR: You're ashamed, son—

LOU: Ashamed of—of what?

GREMMAR: Ashamed of us, Louis. . . . Ashamed of your family—your
father . . . your mother . . . Nathan . . . and me, too. That's—

LOU (*turning to face her, stricken*): Gremmar, I'm not ashamed! . . .
When—when was I ever—ever—ashamed? When—when was I . . .
ashamed? . . . I—I have a right to my opinion! Does everybody have to
be—to be the . . . same? What do you mean, ashamed? . . . You—you
didn't mean that, did you? Huh? (*Going to her, grasping her hand.*)

GREMMAR: Yes, I did, son—oh yes . . . yes. I seen you. . . . I seen you
when I come to your school—I come there looking for you—I seen
you . . . eating your lunch with your hand in your bag so's nobody
could see what you were eating. I knew what you were doing!

(*He starts to protest.*)

You're ashamed—ashamed of being a black boy! I know it! I can sense
it in you—you're ashamed!

LOU (*jerking away from her*): I was not! I just—it—it was . . . nobody's
business, that's all! I keep telling you I'm not! . . . I'm not! . . .
You're . . . you're just a . . . a—

(*HATTIE hearing the noises, enters from the kitchen and crosses upstairs.*)

just a . . . nigger, that's all! That's all you are! Just a . . . a . . . a . . .
sex . . . pot, that's all! . . . Just a nigger!—

GREMMAR (*her breathing more difficult*): Ashamed of your skin . . . your
skin—your family . . . me—

LOU (*angry*): Just a . . . lying . . . nigger! You're a nigger, that's what!—

(*She begins gasping. LOU looks at her in horror, yet is caught up in his own
rhythm.*)

GREMMAR (*gasping*): Ashamed! Ashamed!

(*He moves to her, sitting, grasping her hand, holding it tightly.*)

LOU: Will you stop saying that! (*Moving closer to her, his arms around her,
rocking her*) Stop saying that!

GREMMAR: Ashamed!

LOU (*crying, rocking her*): A black . . . nigger, that's all!

(*MILTON scurries down the hallway, meeting HATTIE. Together they rush
into the room. Unaware of them, LOU huddles close to GREMMAR,*)

continuing to rock her and sob. HATTIE *and* MILTON *look at him in horror.*)

HATTIE (*with* MILTON): Louis!

LOU: A nigger! . . . Just a nigger! . . . A nigger! . . . A nigger!

MILTON (*lunging, trying to wrestle him away*): Let—let go of her, boy! You—

HATTIE (*trying to assist him*): Be careful now, Milton!—Unhand her, Louis! . . . Louis!

LOU (*resisting*): She knows what she is!

(MILTON *wrenches him away and begins to half drag, half push him across the room.*)

GREMMAR: Ashamed!—yes! Ashamed! . . .

LOU (*screaming*): Nigger! . . . Nigger! Nigger, nigger, nigger!—

(MILTON *drags* LOUIS *to the stairs and pushes him down them.*)

MILTON: Break your neck—break your neck!

LOU (*gasping, crying, muttering*): Just a . . . nigger, that's all—

(HATTIE *takes* GREMMAR *in her arms and begins to fan and mop the perspiration from her face.* MILTON *pushes* LOU *through the living room onto the porch. As they appear,* NATE *approaches.* MILTON *shoves* LOU *to the upstage left corner of the porch.* NATE *moves quickly onto the porch to prevent a possible continuing altercation.* MILTON *hovers near* LOU.)

MILTON: You big . . . dummy! . . . Going in there . . . going in there and—and disturbing her and calling her names, and . . . and . . . doing the things you were doing to her! I'll break your neck!

(GREMMAR *groans wrackingly. Both* MILTON *and* NATE *turn in horror.* MILTON *moves quickly toward the door.*)

Don't you move—don't you move off this porch! You hear me? (*As he goes up the steps.*) Break your neck! (*He hurries upstairs into the room. He and* HATTIE *talk in whispers.* MILTON *takes* HATTIE's *place, rubbing her arms, while* HATTIE *begins fanning and patting her face.*)

(*Stunned,* NATE *glares at* LOU, *who rises, turning his back and glancing at him from the corner of his eye.*)

LOU (*after a moment, softly, intensely*): Three of them!—three! . . . Just another—another . . . nigger, that's all! Didn't even marry any of them—not even—not even—one!

NATE: Oh man! . . . You—Lou—You stupid idiot!

(LOU *turns and lunges at him, swinging.* NATE *ducks and retaliates, knocking him down.* LOU *rises, charging back. They grapple,* NATE *getting well the better of it.*)

You dumb bastard!

LOU (*crying, shouting*): You nigger! . . . black nigger!

(NATE *knocks him down again.* LOU *is ineffective as* NATE *pummels him.* GREMMAR *begins to suddenly sing, blurting out a song—a spiritual.* HATTIE *and* MILTON *react with surprise and then join her. Oblivious to it at first,* NATE *jerks up, listening.*)

NATE: What the hell. . . . They're . . . singing. . . . They're . . . they're singing, Lou. . . . Lou, listen!

(*On his back,* LOU *groans, covering his face.*)

Listen—listen, goddammit! . . . It's . . . her! . . . It's . . . it's—yeah! I swear to God, it's her singing, man! (*He moves to* LOU *and pulls him to a sitting position.*) You hear her, man!—the coarse one? . . . the crackly one?—the one coming—coming in behind . . . behind Mom's and Pop's. . . . You hear it?

(LOU *nods vigorously.*)

She—she hasn't done that—I mean, since . . . since yesterday, you know? I mean—hey—hey—maybe she's gonna make it, huh? Maybe she's . . . she's gonna be—be all right. You know, I think she's gonna do it, man!

LOU (*laughing, half sobbing, half crying*): Yeah . . . yeah . . . yeah!

(*The singing stops.* GREMMAR *gasps and is still.* HATTIE *and* MILTON *stare at her in shock. After a moment* MILTON *nudges her, calling her name several times. He then sits, dazed.*)

NATE: They've . . . they've stopped singing.

MILTON (*slowly rising from the bed, crossing to the stairs*): Killing my mother! . . . Killing my mother!—Killing her!

HATTIE (*moving after him*): Milton—Milton, now wait a minute!

MILTON: Killing her!—

HATTIE: Milton, will you listen to me! (*As they move down the steps.*)

MILTON (*moving onto the porch and confronting* LOU): Killing my mother! Going upstairs, upsetting her and—and—killing that woman!

HATTIE (*moving in front of him*): Now calm down, Milton—just calm down. She was—

(NATE *gasps slightly and stands between* MILTON *and* LOU. LOU *stands transfixed, tears welling.*)

MILTON (*his voice breaking*): Calling her names . . . calling her names and killing her! (*Lunging toward him.*) I'll kill you, nigger!

(*He grabs* LOU. *As he does,* NATE *grasps and struggles with him.*)

NATE: Come on now, Pop—ease up now! He didn't know what he was saying!—

HATTIE (*trying to assist* NATE): Lord God!—fighting and killing, and she isn't hardly gone! Let go of him, Milton!

MILTON: I'll break his neck!

LOU (*gasping, crying*): I'm . . . sorry . . . I'm sorry . . . (*Crying, whispering to himself.*) Oh God! . . . I'm—I'm sorry! . . .

MILTON: No good! . . . No good! . . . You lie! . . . You lie—do nothing but lie! . . . Good as that woman was to you! You ought to be thankful to her as long as you live! You ought to be thankful! I'll make you remember this night . . . *nigger!*

(*He wrenches away from* NATE *and glares at* LOU. LOU *flings himself off the porch, stumbling and falling and crawling a few paces away. Hesitant,* HATTIE *moves quickly off the porch and stands near him.* MILTON *turns and rushes quickly upstairs, where he sits beside the bed, holding* GREMMAR's *hand. Dazed,* NATE *stands emptily for a moment and then crosses upstairs and sits at the foot of the bed.* HATTIE *sighs heavily, trying to catch her breath, unnerved. She looks toward the house.* LOU *is in a kneeling position on the ground, gasping and crying softly.* HATTIE *turns again to him and sighs, softening somewhat. She moves slowly to him, hovering a moment.*)

HATTIE: Louis, why didn't you do what I told you? . . . I told you to leave it down the drain—that's exactly what I told you!—exactly! (*She turns away, sighing heavily and shaking her head. She looks out into the street, staring blankly, whispering to herself.*) Lord have mercy! . . . (*Taking a step toward him.*) Louis—

LOU: I didn't . . . I didn't . . . mean to . . . to . . . to kill her!

HATTIE (*sighing*): She . . . she was on her way out, Louis . . . She was. . . . We all . . . knew it . . . we knew it. . . . She was going. . . . It didn't help any—what you did, but . . . she was . . . going . . .

LOU (*almost uncontrollably*): I didn't mean to. . . . I was . . . I was just . . . just . . . trying to tell her how—how I felt. . . . That's all. . . . I wasn't trying to . . . to *kill her!*

HATTIE (*sighing heavily again*): Well . . . (*Pause.*) I don't know, Louis. . . . I don't know . . . (*Pause.*) All I know is there's been a lot of trouble around here tonight.

LOU (*standing crossing to downstage right of apron*): I wasn't trying to cause any trouble!—

(HATTIE *crosses stage right to* LOU. LOU *whispers to himself, trying to control his sobbing but failing.*)

I wasn't trying to kill her!

HATTIE (*suddenly tired, numb, sounding almost emotionless*): That's your father talking, Louis—

LOU: I . . . I . . . loved her. . . . I wasn't trying to hurt her. (*Pause.*) More than . . . than . . . anybody! . . . Anybody! . . . She—she should've known that! Anybody around here! . . . She knew that . . . Nate . . . Pop and—and—any of you! She knew that!

HATTIE (*hurt, trying to mask it*): I'm . . . I'm sure she did, Louis, . . . I'm sure . . . (*Turns* LOU *around and embraces; he sobs silently.*) It always . . . always comes so hard when it comes. . . . Crashes down on you no matter what you say you are—like a fist!—no matter how prepared you think you are for it . . . (*Sighing again.*) She was a good person, Louis . . . a good person . . .

(LOU *nods slowly.* HATTIE *looks toward the house and then crosses stage left.*)

Such . . . such lovely hands . . . lovely. . . . Long, pretty fingers. . . . You wouldn't have thought it, all the housework and things she did over her life. . . . But she did . . . (*Looking at her own hands.*) Much as I try, I can't get mine like that. . . . Soft, pretty hands. . . . She liked her hands—took pride in them . . . (*Both are silent, thinking.*) And such . . . a pretty laugh. . . . Just as clear as a bell . . . came from way down inside. . . . Made her shake all over . . . (*Pause.*) Face would light up . . . eyes would shine . . . (*Both are silent, thinking.*)

LOU (*after a moment crossing stage left to* HATTIE): She used to . . . to wear that . . . floppy-looking hat out in the sun . . . in the garden . . .

(HATTIE *nods.* NATE *rises from bed. He moves to* MILTON, *patting his shoulder, and then crosses down the steps through the living room to the porch and sits on the bench.*)

Made her look like some . . . some creature from outer space . . . some Martian in the garden . . .

(HATTIE *smiles slightly, murmuring agreement.* LOU *pauses, looking out into the street.*)

We used to . . . to . . . sit out here at night and . . . see things. . . . Make up things. . . . Listening to the crickets and things and . . . and staring out into the woods . . . into the dark.

(HATTIE *turns, following his glance.*)

We'd conjure up things and . . . all sorts of things . . . cowboys . . . Indians . . . monsters . . . tanks, ships, castles . . . pirates . . . all kinds of . . . crazy things. . . . A game . . . just a game . . . (*Pause.*) It's so dark out there now . . . just seems so . . . dark. . . . Hardly see anything out there . . . Like—like there was a . . . a . . . power failure and the whole town is blacked out . . . nothing. . . . So small . . . so little . . . a big power failure . . .

(LOU *and* HATTIE *cross onto the porch.* NATE *rises suddenly, reacting to a breeze that has suddenly begun to blow. He opens his shirt, throwing his head back.*)

NATE: Oh man! . . . Oh man, it's about time! . . . It's about time!

(*The lights fade out slowly as* LOU *and* HATTIE *turn toward the direction of the breeze.*)

Dream on Monkey Mountain

DEREK WALCOTT

Left to right: Ester Rolle as MARKET WIFE, *Roscoe Lee Brown as* MAKAK, *Antonio Fargas as* MOUSTIQUE, *Anita Wilson as* VILLAGE WOMAN, *David Downing as* MARKET INSPECTOR PAMPHILION, *Ester Bailey and Freda Teresa Vanterpool as* VILLAGE WOMEN, *Afolabi Ajayi as* SOURIS, *and* SICK MAN, *in a scene from* Dream on Monkey Mountain. *Photograph copyright © 1971 by Bert Andrews. Reprinted by permission of Marsha Hudson, the Estate of Bert Andrews.*

Derek Walcott, a native of St. Lucia, is an internationally acclaimed poet whose work has been collected in several distinguished volumes such as *Collected Poems 1948–1984* and *Omeros,* which led to his being awarded the Nobel Prize for Literature in 1992. As a dramatist, much of his earlier work, such as *The Sea at Dauphin, Ti-Jean and His Brothers, O Babylon, The Joker of Seville,* and the 1970–71 Obie Award winning *Dream On Monkey Mountain,* originated in Trinidad where he spent nine years developing the Trinidad Workshop Theatre. In addition to being a Nobel laureate, he is also a recipient of a MacArthur Foundation Fellowship, and currently teaches poetry at Boston University.

Dream on Monkey Mountain received its celebrated NEC production in New York at the St. Marks Playhouse, and opened in 1971 with the following cast:

Tigre	Lawrence Cook
Souris	Afolabi Ajayi
Corporal Lestrade	Ron O'Neal
Makak	Roscoe Lee Brown
Apparition	Margaret Spear
Moustique	Antonio Fargas
Basil	Robert Jackson
Market Wife	Ester Rolle
Market Inspector Pamphilion	David Downing
Village Women, Wives of Makak	Ester Bailey
	Charliese Drakeford
	Freda Teresa Vanterpool
	Anita Wilson
	Alma Woolsey
Village Men, Warriors	K. Lawrence Dunham
	Laijba Durr
	Noel Hall
	Alexander O. Sallid

Directed by Michael A. Schultz; choreographed by Mary Barnett; scenery by Edward Burbridge; lighting by Ernest Baxter and Oyamo; costumes by Lewis Brown; production stage managed by Nate Barnett.

Dream on Monkey Mountain

for Errol Jones and the Trinidad Theatre Workshop

> *If the moon is earth's friend,*
> *how can we leave the earth?*
>   *Noh Play*

CHARACTERS

In order of appearance

TIGRE, *a felon*

SOURIS, *a felon*

CORPORAL LESTRADE, *a mulatto*

MAKAK, *a charbonnier or charcoal-burner*

APPARITION, *the moon, the muse, the white Goddess, a dancer*

MOUSTIQUE, *a cripple, friend to Makak*

BASIL, *a cabinetmaker, figure of death*

MARKET INSPECTOR PAMPHILION, *a government servant*

A DANCER, *also* NARRATOR

LITTER BEARERS

SISTERS OF THE REVELATION

MARKET WOMEN, WIVES OF MAKAK

WARRIORS, DEMONS

A SINGER, A MALE CHORUS, TWO DRUMMERS

A NOTE ON PRODUCTION

The play is a dream, one that exists as much in the given minds of its principal characters as in that of its writer, and as such, it is illogical, derivative, contradictory. Its source is metaphor, and it is best treated as a physical poem with all the subconscious and deliberate borrowings of poetry. Its style should be spare, essential as the details of a dream. The producer can amplify it with spectacle as he chooses, or, as in the original production, switch roles and limit his cast to a dozen or so. He will need dancers, actors, and singers, the same precision and vitality that one has read of in the Kabuki. He may add songs more recognizable to his audience once he can keep the raw folk content in them. SCENE II, *the healing scene, owes an obvious debt to "Spirit," choreographed for the Little Carib Company by Beryl MacBurnie.*
     D.W.

SETTING

A West Indian island

PART ONE

PROLOGUE

A spotlight warms the white disc of an African drum until it glows like the round moon above it. Below the moon is the stark silhouette of a volcanic mountain. Reversed, the moon becomes the sun. A dancer enters and sits astride the drum. From the opposite side of the stage a top-hatted, frock-coated figure with white gloves, his face halved by white makeup like the figure of Baron Samedi, enters and crouches behind the dancer. As the lament begins, dancer and figure wave their arms slowly, sinuously, with a spidery motion. The figure rises during the lament and touches the disc of the moon. The drummer rises, dancing as if in slow motion, indicating, as their areas grow distinct, two prison cages on either side of the stage. In one cell, TIGRE *and* SOURIS, *two half-naked felons are squabbling. The figure strides off slowly, the* CONTEUR *and* CHORUS, *offstage, increase the volume of their lament.*

CONTEUR:
Mooma, mooma,
Your son in de jail a'ready,
Your son in de jail a'ready,
Take a towel and
               band your belly.

CHORUS:
Mooma, mooma,
Your son in de jail a'ready,
Your son in de jail a'ready,
Take a towel and
               band your belly.

CONTEUR:
I pass by the police station,
Nobody to sign de bail bond.

CHORUS:
Mooma, don't cry,
Your son in de jail a'ready,
I pass by de police station,
Nobody to sign de bail bond.

CONTEUR:
Forty days before the Carnival, Lord,
I dream I see me funeral.

CHORUS:
Mooma, mooma,
Your son in de jail a'ready,
Take a towel and band your belly.

(*The* CORPORAL, *in Sunday uniform, enters with* MAKAK, *an old Negro with a jute sack, and lets him into the next cell.*)

TIGRE:
Forty days before the Carnival,
Lord, I dream I see me funeral . . .

TIGRE and SOURIS:
Mooma, don't cry, your son in de jail a'ready . . .

TIGRE:
Take a towel and band you' belly,
Mooma, don't cry, your son in de jail a'ready.

(MAKAK *sits on the cell cot, an old cloth around his shoulders.*)

SOURIS: Shut up! Ay, Corporal. Who is dat?
TIGRE (*singing*):
Mooma, don't cry, your son in de jail a'ready.
CORPORAL: Dat, you mange-ridden habitual felon, is de King of Africa.
TIGRE (*singing*):
Your son in de jail a'ready,
Your son in de jail a'ready . . .
SOURIS: Tigre, shut your trap. It have Majesty there.

(*The* CORPORAL *elaborately removes a notebook and gold pencil.*)

CORPORAL: Now before I bring a specific charge against you, I will require certain particulars . . .
TIGRE, SOURIS, and CORPORAL: You are required by law to supply me with certain data, for no man is guilty except so proven, and I must warn you that anything you say may be held against you . . .
CORPORAL (*turning*): Look!

SOURIS: Don't tell him a damn thing! You have legal rights. Your lawyer! Get your lawyer.

TIGRE (*singing*):
  I pass by de police station,
  Nobody to sign de bail bond,
  Mooma, don't cry . . .

SOURIS (*shrilly*): What he up for, Corporal? What you lock him up for?

CORPORAL: Drunk and disorderly! A old man like that! He was drunk and he mash up Alcindor café.

SOURIS: And you going cage him here on a first offence? Old man, get a lawyer and defend your name!

(*The* CORPORAL *bends down and removes a half-empty bottle of rum from the bag, and a white mask with long black sisal hair.*)

CORPORAL: I must itemize these objects! Can you identify them?

SOURIS: O God, O God, Tigre! The king got a bottle! (SOURIS *and* TIGRE *grope through the bars, howling, groaning.*) O God, just one, Corporal. My throat on fire. One for the boys. Here, just one swallow, Corp.

TIGRE: Have mercy on two thieves fallen by the wayside. You call yourself a Catholic?

(*Inchoate, animal howling, leaping and pacing*)

CORPORAL: Animals, beasts, savages, cannibals, niggers, stop turning this place to a stinking zoo!

SOURIS: Zoo? Just because you capture some mountain gorilla?

(*The* CORPORAL *with his baton cracks* SOURIS's *extended wrist.*)

CORPORAL: In the beginning was the ape, and the ape had no name, so God call him man. Now there were various tribes of the ape, it had gorilla, baboon, orangutan, chimpanzee, the blue-arsed monkey, and the marmoset, and God looked at his handiwork, and saw that it was good. For some of the apes had straighten their backbone, and start walking upright, but there was one tribe unfortunately that lingered behind, and that was the nigger. Now if you apes will behave like gentlemen, who knows what could happen? The bottle could go round, but first it behoves me, Corporal Lestrade, to perform my duty according to the rules of Her Majesty's Government, so don't interrupt. Please let me examine the Lion of Judah. (*Goes towards* MAKAK) What is your name?

TIGRE: (*singing softly*):
  Oh, when the roll

Is called up yonder,
When the roll
Is called up yonder,
When the roll
Is called up yonder,
When the roll is called up yonder,
I ain't going!

(CHORUS: *When the roll . . .*)

(*Spoken*) And nobody else here going, you all too black, except possibly the Corporal. (*Pauses, points*) Look, is the full moon.

CORPORAL (*as moonlight fills the cell*): Your name in full, occupation, status, income, ambition, domicile or place of residence, age, and last but not least, your race?

SOURIS: The man break my hand. The damn man break my hand.

TIGRE: Well, you can't t'hief again.

MAKAK: Let me go home, my Corporal.

SOURIS: Ay, wait, Tigre, the king has spoken.

TIGRE: What the king say?

SOURIS: He want to go home.

CORPORAL: Where is your home? Africa?

MAKAK: Sur Morne Macaque . . .

CORPORAL (*infuriated*): English, English! For we are observing the principles and precepts of Roman law, and Roman law is English law. Let me repeat the query: Where is your home?

MAKAK: I live on Monkey Mountain, Corporal.

CORPORAL: What is your name?

MAKAK: I forget.

CORPORAL: What is your race?

MAKAK: I am tired.

CORPORAL: What is your denominational affiliation?

(*Silence*)

SOURIS (*whispering*): Ça qui religion-ous?

MAKAK (*smiling*): Cat'olique.

CORPORAL: I ask you, with all the patience of the law, what is or has been your denominational affiliation?

MAKAK: Cat'olique.

CORPORAL (*revising notes*): You forget your name, your race is tired, your denominational affiliation is *Catholique,* therefore, as the law, the Roman law, had pity on our Blessed Saviour, by giving him, even *in extremis,* a draught of vinegar, what, in your own language, you would call *vinegre,* I shall give all and Sunday here, including these two thieves, a handful of rum, before I press my charge.

(TIGRE *and* SOURIS *applaud loudly. The* CORPORAL *takes a swallow from the bottle and passes it through the bars to* TIGRE *and* SOURIS; *then, holding it in his hand, paces around* MAKAK)

TIGRE: How a man like that can know so much law? Could know so much language? Is a born Q.C. Still every man entitle to his own defence.

SOURIS: The wig and gown, Corporal. Put on the wig and gown!

TIGRE: You have a sense of justice, put on the wig and gown.

CORPORAL: I can both accuse and defend this man.

SOURIS: The wig and gown, Lestrade. Let us hear English!

(*The* CORPORAL *strides off.*)

SOURIS (*sings*):
Drill him, Constable, drill him,
Drill him, Constable, drill him,
Drill him, Constable, drill him.
He t'ief a bag of coals yesterday!

CHORUS (*repeats*): Drill him, Constable, drill him . . .

SOURIS: Drill him, Constable, drill him,
He mash up old Alcindor café!

(*The* CORPORAL, *isolated in a spot, with counsel's wig and gown, returns with four towels, two yellow, two red.*)

TIGRE: Order, order, order in de court.

(*A massive gong is sounded, and the* CORPORAL *gives the two prisoners the towels. They robe themselves like judges.*)

CORPORAL: My noble judges. When this crime has been categorically examined by due process of law, and when the motive of the hereby accused by whereas and ad hoc shall be established without dychotomy, and long after we have perambulated through the labyrinthine bewilderment of the defendant's ignorance, let us hope, that justice, whom we all serve, will not only be done, but will appear, my lords, to have itself, been done . . .

(*The* JUDGES *applaud*)

Ignorance is no excuse. Ignorance of the law is no excuse. Ignorance of one's own ignorance is no excuse. This is the prisoner. I will ask the prisoner to lift up his face. *Levez la tête-ous!*

(MAKAK *lifts up his head. The* CORPORAL *jerks it back savagely.*)

CORPORAL: My lords as, you can see, this is a being without a mind, a will, a name, a tribe of its own. I shall ask the prisoner to turn out his hands. *Montrez-moi la main-ous!*

(MAKAK *turns his palm outward*)

I will spare you the sound of that voice, which have come from a cave of darkness, dripping with horror. These hands are the hands of Esau, the fingers are like roots, the arteries as hard as twine, and the palms are seamed with coal. But the animal, you observe, is tamed and obedient. Walk round the cage! *Marchez! Marchez!*

(MAKAK *rises and walks round the bench, as the* CHORUS *begins to sing.*)

CHORUS:
    I don't know to say this monkey won't do,
    I don't know what to say this monkey won't do.

(*As the* CORPORAL, *like an animal tamer, cracks out his orders, the choir of* JUDGES *keeps time, clapping.*)

CORPORAL: About turn!

(MAKAK *turns around wearily.*)

CHORUS:
    Cause when I turn round, monkey turn around too,
    I don't know what to say this monkey won't do.
CORPORAL: On your knees!

(MAKAK *drops to his knees.* SOURIS *shrieks with delight, then collects his dignity.*)

    I kneel down, monkey kneel down too,
    I don't know what to say this monkey won't do.
    I praying, monkey praying too,
    I don't know what the hell this monkey won't do.
CORPORAL: Stand up! Sit down! Up on the bench! Sit down! Hands out! Hands in!

(MAKAK *does all this. The* CHORUS *sings faster, and the* JUDGES *keep time.*)

CHORUS:
    Everything I say this monkey does do,
    I don't know what to say this monkey won't do.

I sit down, monkey sit down too,
I don't know what to say this monkey won't do.

(MAKAK *sits wearily on the bench.*)

CORPORAL (*Holding up a palm*): The exercise, my lords, proves that the prisoner is capable of reflexes, of obeying orders, therefore of understanding justice. Sound body. Now the charge!

(*Drum roll*)

(*To the sound of martial drums*) His rightful name is unknown, yet on Saturday evening, July 25th, to wit tonight, at exactly three hours ago, to wit at 5:30 P.M., having tried to dispose of four bags of charcoal in the market of Quatre Chemin, to wit this place, my lords, in which aforesaid market your alias, to wit Makak, is well known to all and Sunday, the prisoner, in a state of incomprehensible in toxication, from money or moneys accrued by the sale of self-said bags, is reputed to have entered the licenced alcoholic premises of one Felicien Alcindor, whom the prisoner described as an agent of the devil, the same Felicien Alcindor being known to all and Sunday as a God-fearing, honest Catholic. (*He rests the bottle down.*) When some intervention was attempted by those present, the prisoner then began to become vile and violent; he engaged in a blasphemous, obscene debate with two other villagers, Hannibal Dolcis and Market Inspector Caiphas Joseph Pamphilion, describing in a foul, incomprehensible manner . . .

(*The* JUDGES *posture: Hear no evil. Hands to their ears*)

a dream which he claims to have experienced, a vile, ambitious, and obscene dream . . .

(*The* JUDGES *mime: See no evil. Hands to their faces in horror*)

elaborating on the aforesaid dream with vile words and with a variety of sexual obscenities both in language and posture! Further, the prisoner, in defiance of Her Majesty's Government, urged the aforementioned villagers to join him in sedition and the defilement of the flag, and when all this was rightly received with civic laughter and pious horror . . .

(*The* JUDGES *mime: Speak no evil. Their hands to their mouths*)

the prisoner, in desperation and shame, began to wilfully damage the premises of the proprietor Felicien Alcindor, urging destruction on

Church and State, claiming that he was the direct descendant of African kings, a healer of leprosy and the Saviour of his race.

(*Pause. Silence.*)

You claimed that with the camera of your eye you had taken a photograph of God and all that you could see was blackness.

(*The* JUDGES *rise in horror.*)

Blackness, my lords. What did the prisoner imply? That God was neither white nor black but nothing? That God was not white but black, that he had lost his faith? Or . . . or . . . what . . .

MAKAK: I am an old man. Send me home, Corporal. I suffer from madness. I does see things. Spirits does talk to me. All I have is my dreams and they don't trouble your soul.

TIGRE: I can imagine your dreams. Masturbating in moonlight. Dreaming of women, cause you so damn ugly. You should walk on all fours.

MAKAK: Sirs, I does catch fits. I fall in a frenzy every full-moon night. I does be possessed. And after that, sir, I am not responsible. I responsible only to God who once speak to me in the form of a woman on Monkey Mountain. I am God's warrior.

(*The* JUDGES *laugh.*)

CORPORAL: You are charged with certain things. Now let the prisoner make his deposition.

MAKAK:

(*During this speech, the cage is raised out of sight.*)

Sirs, I am sixty years old. I have live all my life
Like a wild beast in hiding. Without child, without wife.
People forget me like the mist on Monkey Mountain.
Is thirty years now I have look in no mirror,
Not a pool of cold water, when I must drink,
I stir my hands first, to break up my image.
I will tell you my dream. Sirs, make a white mist
In the mind; make that mist hang like cloth
From the dress of a woman, on prickles, on branches,
Make it rise from the earth, like the breath of the dead
On resurrection morning, and I walking through it
On my way to my charcoal pit on the mountain.
Make the web of the spider heavy with diamonds

And when my hand brush it, let the chain break.
I remember, in my mind, the cigale sawing.
Sawing, sawing wood before the woodcutter,
The drum of the bullfrog, the blackbird flute,
And this old man walking, ugly as sin,
In a confusion of vapour,
Till I fell I was God self, walking through cloud.
In the heaven on my mind. Then I hear this son.
Not the blackbird flute,
Not the bullfrog drum,
Not the whistling of parrots
As I brush through the branches, shaking the dew,
A man swimming through smoke,
And the bandage of fog unpeeling my eyes,
As I reach to this spot,
I see this woman singing
And my feet grow roots. I could move no more.
A million silver needles prickle my blood,
Like a rain of small fishes.
The snakes in my hair speak to one another,
The smoke mouth open, and I behold this woman,
The loveliest thing I see on this earth,
Like the moon walking along her own road.

(*During this, the* APPARITION *appears and withdraws. Flute music.*)

You don't see her? Look, I see her! She standing right there. (*He points at nothing.*) Like the moon had climbed down the steps of heaven, and was standing in front me.

CORPORAL: I can see nothing. (*To the* JUDGES) What do you see?

JUDGES: Nothing. Nothing.

MAKAK: Nothing? Look, there she is!

TIGRE: Nothing at all. The old man mad.

SOURIS (*mocking*): Yes, I see it. I can see it. Is the face of the moon moving over the floor. Come to me, darling. (*He rolls over the cell floor groaning.*)

CORPORAL: My lords, is this rage for whiteness that does drive niggers mad.

MAKAK (*on his knees*):
Lady in heaven, is your old black warrior,
The king of Ashanti, Dahomey, Guinea,
Is this old cracked face you kiss in his sleep

Appear to my enemies, tell me what to do?
Put on my rage, the rage of the lion?

(*He rises slowly and assumes a warrior's stance. Drums build to a frenzy.*)

Help poor crazy Makak, help Makak
To scatter his enemies, to slaughter those
That standing around him.
So, thy hosts shall be scattered,
And the hyena shall feed on their bones!

(*He falls.*)

Sirs, when I hear that voice,
Singing so sweetly,
I feel my spine straighten,
My hand grow strong.
My blood was boiling
Like a brown river in flood,
And in that frenzy,
I let out a cry,
I charged the spears about me,
Grasses and branches,
I began to dance,
With the splendour of a lion,
Faster and faster,
Faster and faster,
Then, my body sink,
My bones betray me
And I fall on the forest floor,
Dead, on sweating grass,
And there, maybe, sirs,
Two other woodmen find me,
And take me up the track.
Sirs, if you please . . .

(*The two prisoners carry him.*)

CORPORAL: Continue, continue, the virtue of the law is its infinite
patience. Continue . . .

(*The cells rise, the others withdraw.* MAKAK *lies alone in the hut.*)

MAKAK *remains on the ground, the mask near him. We hear a cry far off, echoing.* MOUSTIQUE, *a little man with a limp, a jute bag over his shoulder, comes into the morning light around the hut, puffing with exhaustion.*

MOUSTIQUE: Makak, Makak, wake up. Is me, Moustique. You didn't hear me calling you from the throat of the gully? I bring a next crocus bag from Alcindor café. Today is market day, and time and tide wait for no man. I tie Berthilia to a gommier tree by the ravine.

(MAKAK *has stirred.*)

MAKAK: Berthilia? Which Berthilia?

MOUSTIQUE: Listen to him! Which Berthilia? The donkey you and I buy from Felicien! Every Saturday is the same damn trouble to wake you! You have the coals ready, eh? Spare me a little to light this fire. (*He helps* MAKAK *into the hut.*) Ay, what? What happen? (*He stoops near him.*) Eh! Negre? (*He rests the back of his hand on* MAKAK's *forehead.*) No fever. No sweat. (*He walks around the hut, distressed.*) What we going to do? The last time this happen, I find you outside the hut, trembling with fever. What we going do? (*He throws down the bag.*)

MAKAK: Go alone.

MOUSTIQUE: Go alone? Tcha, go alone.

MAKAK: I going mad, Moustique.

MOUSTIQUE: Going mad? Go mad tomorrow, today is market day. We have three bags at three-and-six a bag, making ten shillings and sixpence for the week and you going mad? You have coffee?

MAKAK: I don't want.

MOUSTIQUE: Well, I want, I cold like hell. (MOUSTIQUE *prepares coffee and sits down pensively by the small fire, watching the water boil. He takes out a pipe and sighs.*)

MAKAK: Moustique?

MOUSTIQUE: Eh?

MAKAK: How many years I know you now?

MOUSTIQUE (*shrugging*): Three, four. Why? (*He is making the coffee.*)

MAKAK: You find that long?

MOUSTIQUE (*turning, staring at him*): No. (*Pause.*) Look, we going to the market?

MAKAK: Yes. We will go.

MOUSTIQUE (*crouched on his heels, poking the fire*): Well, I just getting you something hot to drink. (*Leans back, puffs on his pipe*) Four years. And I remember how you find me.

MAKAK: True?

MOUSTIQUE: True. Drunk. Soaking drunk, with this twist foot God give me. Sleeping anywhere, and one morning when you come to market, you find me in the gutter, and you pick me up like a wet fly in the dust, and we establish in this charcoal business. You cut, burn and so on, and I sell, until we make enough to buy the donkey. (*Stretches for the coffee.*) Here, pass the cup. (*Pours*) Yes. You was the only one to make me believe a breakfoot nigger could go somewhere in this life. Four years gone last August. Drink. (*He passes the cup.*) Drink. But after that is zwip! down the mountain!

MAKAK (*staring into the cup*): Moustique . . .

MOUSTIQUE (*patiently*): Ehhh?

MAKAK: Listen. You take the same shortcut to come up here?

MOUSTIQUE: *Oui.*

MAKAK: The one with the wood-bridge and white falling-water?

MOUSTIQUE: The one with the wood-bridge and white falling-water.

MAKAK: The one that so narrow, two men cannot pass?

MOUSTIQUE: The one that so narrow, two men . . . Drink.

(*Sound of a flute, bird noises*)

MAKAK (*rising*): This morning, early, the moon still up, I went to pack the coals in the pit down the mountain. I will tell you. Make a white mist in the mind; make that mist hang like cloth from the dress of a woman, on prickles, on branches; make it rise from the earth, like the breath of the dead on resurrection morning, and I walking through it on my way to my charcoal pit on the mountain. Make the web of the spider by heavy with diamonds and when my hand brush it, let the chain break. I remember, in my mind, the cigale sawing, sawing, sawing wood before the woodcutter, the drum of the bullfrog, the blackbird flute, and this old man walking, ugly as sin, in a confusion of vapour, till I feel I was God self, walking through cloud, in the heaven of my mind. Then I hear this song. Not the bullfrog drum, not the whistling of parrots. As I brush through the branches, shaking the dew, a man swimming through smoke, and the bandage of fog unpeeling my eyes, as I reach to this spot, I see this woman singing, and my feet grow roots! I could move no more. A million silver needles prickle my blood, like a rain of small fishes. The snakes in my hair speak to one another, the smoke mouth open, and I behold this woman, the loveliest thing I see on this earth, floating toward me, just like the moon, like the moon walking along her own road. Then as I start to move, she call out my name, my real name. A name I do not use. Come here, she say. Come, don't be afraid. So I go up to her, one step by one step. She make me sit down and start to talk to me.

MOUSTIQUE: Makak.

MAKAK (*angrily*): Listen to me, I not mad. Listen!

MOUSTIQUE: I have all day. (*Exasperated*)

MAKAK: Well, well . . . .the things she tell me, you would not believe. She did know my name, my age, where I born, and that it was charcoal I burn and selling for a living. She know how I live alone, with no wife and no friend . . .

MOUSTIQUE: No friend . . .

MAKAK: That Makak is not my name. And I tell her my life, and she say that if I want her, she will come and live with me, and I take her in my arms, and I bring her here.

MOUSTIQUE (*looking around*): Here? A white woman? Or a *diablesse*?

MAKAK: We spend all night here. Look, I make something for she to eat. We sit down by this same fire. And, Moustique, she say something I will never forget. She say I should not live so any more, here in the forest, frighten of people because I think I ugly. She say that I come from the family of lions and kings.

(*Drum roll*)

MOUSTIQUE: Well, you lucky. (*Rises wearily*) Me and Berthilia have three bags of coal to try and sell in the market this morning. We still have eighteen shillings for Alcindor for the shovel, and Johannes promise us a bag of provisions in exchange for half a sack. You had a bad dream, or you sleep outside and the dew seize you.

MAKAK: Is not a dream.

MOUSTIQUE (*exasperated*): Is not a dream? Then where she? Where she gone? (*Searches mockingly*) Upstairs? *Gadez!* You had a dream, and she is here (*Touches his own head*), so, bring her to market. Sun hot, and people making money.

MAKAK: I tell you is no dream.

MOUSTIQUE: You remember one morning I come up and from the time I break the bush, I see you by the side of the hut, trembling and talking, your eyes like you crazy, and was I had to gather bush, light a fire and make you sweat out that madness? Which white lady? You is nothing. You black, ugly, poor, so you worse than nothing. You like me. Small, ugly, with a foot like a "S." Man together two of us is minus one. Now where you going?

MAKAK: I going to get the coals (MAKAK *goes out*, MOUSTIQUE *cleans up, talking to himself.*)

MOUSTIQUE: The misery black people have to see in this life. (*Rummaging around, blowing out the fire, putting away the cups*) Him and his damned fits. A man not only suppose to catch his arse in the daytime but he have to ride nightmares too. Now what the hell I looking for? (*He puts his hand under the bench, then withdraws it slowly in horror.*) Aiiiiiiiiiiie. (*He turns his head and shakes his hand in frenzy as* MAKAK *comes running into the hut.*)

MAKAK: Moustique!

MOUSTIQUE (*shaken*): A spider. A spider was on the sack. A big white one with eggs. A mother with white eggs. I hate those things.

MAKAK: Where it?

MOUSTIQUE: Look it. Kill it, kill it. (*Grabs his hat and pounds it*) *Salop! Salop!* When it pass over my hand, my blood turn into a million needles. (*He sits back panting.*) Well. What you looking at? (*Pause.*) Is a bad sign?

MAKAK: Yes, is a bad sign.

MOUSTIQUE: Well?

MAKAK: You know what it mean.

MOUSTIQUE: Yes. (*Holds out his hand, which is trembling*) To hell with that! I don't believe that. I not no savage. Every man have to die. It have a million ways to die. But no spider with white eggs will bring it. (*Silence*) You believe that, of course. You . . . you . . . you living like a beast, and you believe everything! (*Points at the spider*) That! (*Stamps on it*)

MAKAK: She say I will see signs.

MOUSTIQUE: Yes, every damned full moon.

MAKAK: I must do what she say, which is . . .

MOUSTIQUE: Which is to sell coals! Now, where the next sack? (*He searches under the bench and withdraws a white mask with long coarse hair.*) This is she? eh? This cheap stupidness black children putting on? (*He puts it on, wiggles and dances.*) *Chatafunga, deux sous pour weh, Chatafunga, deux sous pour weh.*

(MAKAK *steps back.*)

MAKAK: Where you get that?

MOUSTIQUE: You ain't see?

MAKAK (*slowly*): I never see it before.

MOUSTIQUE: She leave her face behind. She leave the wrong thing. Ah, *Mon Dieu.* (*He sits by the fire, puffing his pipe angrily, pokes the fire.*) And the damned fire out.

MAKAK: I never see this before. (*Pause.*) Saddle my horse!

MOUSTIQUE: Eh?

MAKAK: Saddle my horse, if you love me, Moustique, and cut a sharp bamboo for me, and put me on that horse, for Makak will ride to the edge of the world, Makak will walk like he used to in Africa, when his name was lion!

MOUSTIQUE: Saddle your horse? Berthilia the jackass? When you will put sense in that crack coal-pot you call your head? Which woman ever look at you, once, much less a white one? Saddle your horse? I could put this beat-up tin pot on your head, cut a bamboo for a spear, make a cup of my two hands and put you on that half-starve jackass you call a horse and send you out for the whole world to laugh. But where we going? Where two black, not-a-red-cent niggers going? To war?

MAKAK: *Non.* To Africa!

MOUSTIQUE: Oh-o! Africa? Why you didn't tell me? We walking? (*He stands in the doorway.*)

MAKAK (*hurling him away*): Out of my way, insect!

MOUSTIQUE (*on the floor*): You mad. To God, you mad, O God, the day come, when I see you mad.

(MAKAK *crouches over him.* MOUSTIQUE *is weeping.*)

MAKAK: I hurt you, little one? Listen, listen, Moustique. I am not mad. To God, I am not mad. You say once when I pick you up like a wet fly from the dust that you would do anything for me. I beg you now, come. Don't cry! You say we will be friends until we dead. Come, don't mind the spider. If we dead, little one, is not better to die, fighting like men, than to hide in this forest? Come, then, lean on Makak. Bring nothing, we will live. (MAKAK, *who has helped* MOUSTIQUE *to his feet, takes up the bamboo spear, and goes out of the hut.*)

MOUSTIQUE: Yes, yes, master. (MOUSTIQUE *puts out the fire, picks up the sacks, stool, then the mask, and looking at the squashed spider, shudders.*) What is to come, will come. Come on, down the mountain.

(*The hut rises out of sight,* MAKAK *striding with his spear,* MOUSTIQUE *riding ahead.*)

MOUSTIQUE:
Is the stupidest thing I ever see
Two jackasses and one donkey,
Makak turn lion, so let him pass,
Donkey gone mad on pangola grass,
Haw haw haw haw haw haw haw hee,

A man not a man without misery,
Down the mountain!

(*Sound of the jackass braying*)

(MAKAK *and* MOUSTIQUE *set out*, MAKAK *striding ahead;* MOUSTIQUE, *to the rhythm of flute and drum, miming the donkey. The dancer doing the* burroquite, *or donkey dance, circles the stage and turns the disc of the sun to moonlight. The lights dim briefly, just long enough to establish a change of mood.*)

SCENE TWO

There is a sound of wailing. White-robed women, members of a sisterhood, bearing torches, swirl onto the stage, which is now a country road. Behind them, carrying a shrouded SICK MAN *in a bamboo hammock, are four bearers and a tall frock-coated man in black silk hat,* BASIL, *his face halved by white makeup. The* SISTERS, *shaking their heads, dancing solemnly and singing, form a circle described by their leader. The bearers turn and rest the* SICK MAN *down. Around him, the* SISTERS *kneel and pray, swaying, trying to exorcise his sickness. A small fire is lit by the bearers. The silk-hatted man stands back quietly, watching, while the* SISTERS *clap and sing.*

SISTERS:
Before this time another year
I may be gone, Lord,
In some lonesome graveyard
Oh Lord, how long?
MOUSTIQUE (*entering*): Good night. God bless you, brother.
FIRST PEASANT: Shh. God bless you, stranger. Pray with us.
MOUSTIQUE (*crossing himself, prays swiftly, then in the same whisper*): . . .
And give us this day our daily bread . . . and is that self I want to talk to you about, friend. Whether you could spare a little bread . . . and lead us not into temptation . . . because we are not thieves, stranger . . . but deliver us from evil . . . and we two trespassers but forgive us brother . . . for thine is the kingdom and the power and the glory . . . for our stomach sake, stranger.
FIRST PEASANT (*keeping the whisper*): Where you come from, stranger . . . now and at the hour of our death, amen.
MOUSTIQUE (*whispering*): From Monkey Mountain, in Forestiere quarter . . . and forgive us our trespasses . . . amen, is me and my

friend and old man . . . in the name of the father . . . and we was sleeping in a hut by the road there, when we see you all coming, with all those lights, I thought it was the devil.

FIRST PEASANT: . . . Now and at the hour of our death, amen. . . . It ain't have much to eat, stranger. We taking the sick man down to the hospital, and it have just enough for all of us here . . . forever and ever, amen.

MOUSTIQUE (*in a fiercer whisper*): . . . Our daily bread, and forgive us our trespasses . . . Anything, brother. Three days now we traveling on these roads. What is wrong with him, stranger?

FIRST PEASANT: A snake. He was working in the bush, and a snake . . . but deliver us from evil . . . and no medicine can cure him.

MOUSTIQUE: So what they doing him now?

FIRST PEASANT: . . . And at the hour of our death, amen . . . they putting coals under his body to make him sweat. To break the heat in his body so he can sweat . . . forever and ever, amen . . . so they making a small fire to break the sweat with coals.

MOUSTIQUE: Coals?

FIRST PEASANT: Charcoal. You ent know charcoal?

MOUSTIQUE: Charcoal is my business, stranger.

FIRST PEASANT: They bring priest, doctor they still have no hope. He have a bad fever, and he cannot sweat.

MOUSTIQUE: And who is the man there, in the tall black hat. . . . Now and at the hour of our death, amen.

FIRST PEASANT: He is Basil, the carpenter, and cabinetmaker. He going down to hospital too, just in case . . . amen.

(*A* WOMAN *begins singing. A* SECOND PEASANT *comes over.*)

SECOND PEASANT: Who is he, what he want?

FIRST PEASANT: He say he hungry, and could we spare him some food?

(*The* WOMEN *have begun rubbing the* SICK MAN.)

SECOND PEASANT: It have only enough for us here, brother.

(*The* WIFE *lets out a cry.*)

MOUSTIQUE: Look, I know an old man, he been living in the forest, he know all the herbs, plants, bush. He have this power and glory, and if you want, and it have no harm in that, I could fetch him for you. Look, before you pick him up again, before you choke him with that stinking medicine, before Basil the cabinetmaker get another job . . . Forever and ever, amen . . . Just something to eat and I will go and fetch him. He don't want no money, but he could cure this sick man.

SECOND PEASANT: How far he is?

MOUSTIQUE: Around the next bend, brother. All we ask is a little bread, a little piece of meat . . . for thine is the kingdom, the power and the glory . . .

FIRST PEASANT: I will ask his wife. Give him some bread. (*He goes over to the* WOMAN, *whispers, then returns.*) All right. But if you . . . (*Goes for his cutlass*)

MOUSTIQUE: . . . At the hour of our death, amen.

(MOUSTIQUE *scuttles off. The women resume wailing, and the other men are about to raise the litter when the* FIRST PEASANT *stops them. Enter* MAKAK; *behind him,* MOUSTIQUE)

MOUSTIQUE: Here they are, Master. (*Hurriedly gesticulating, eating the bread, he removes his hat*) Here he is, my master. I have explain everything. Go ahead, master.

(MAKAK *enters, stands by the litter*)

MAKAK: Let all who want this man to heal, kneel down. I ask you. Kneel! (*They kneel, after some delay, except one or two men, whom* MOUSTIQUE *gently forces down*)

MOUSTIQUE: The man say kneel. Kneel!

MAKAK: Now I want a woman to put a coal in this hand, a living coal. A soul in my hand. (*He places one hand on the* SICK MAN's *forehead and holds out his palm. A* WOMAN *hesitantly places a coal in his palm.* MAKAK *winces, closing his eyes. We hear him groan, then silence.*) We will wait for the moon.

(*A pause, then the full moon emerges slowly out of a cloud. We hear the dying man breathing hard.*)

Like the cedars of Lebanon,
like the plantains of Zion,
the hand of God plant me
on Monkey Mountain.
He calleth to the humble.
And from that height
I see you all as trees,
like a twisted forest,
like trees without names,
a forest with no roots!
By this coal in my hand,
by this fire in my veins
let my tongue catch fire,

let my body, like Moses,
be a blazing bush.
Now sing in your darkness,

(*The* WOMEN *sing "Medelico."*)

sing out you forests,
and Josephus will sweat,
the sick man will dance,
sing as you sing
in the belly of the boat.
You are living coals,
you are trees under pressure,
you are brilliant diamonds
In the hand of your God.

(*They continue singing softly.*)

Sweat, Josephus will sweat.
The fever will go!

(*They wait. Nothing happens.*)

More coal. Hotter coal.
Sweat, Josephus, sweat.

(*They put more coals in his hand.*)

And believe in me.
Faith, faith!
Believe in yourselves.

(*Silence.*)

MOUSTIQUE: (*Furious at the failure, and frightened, he circulates among them, angrily.*) Faith, faith! what happen to you? You didn't hear the man? You ain't hear the master. Sing, sing. Come on, Josephus, let that forehead shine, boy. Sing . . .

(*But the singing peters out.* MAKAK, *broken, moves away from the body. He looks at his dry palm.*)

MAKAK: Let us go on, *compère*. These niggers too tired to believe anything again. Remember, is you all self that is your enemy.

(*The* WIFE *comes forward with a gift of food, bread, vegetables, etc.*)

WIFE: I want to thank you, stranger. But what God want, nobody can change.

FIRST PEASANT: Come, come, put back on the medicine.

(*A* WOMAN *goes over to the pall and lets out a loud cry. The others turn. Laughing and weeping, she holds up her hand, which is wet from the* SICK MAN'*s brow.*)

WOMAN: *I'suat! I'suait! I'suait! I'suait!* Sweat! He sweat!

(MAKAK *and* MOUSTIQUE *are apart, watching. The others rush up and in turn touch the freely sweating body and hold up their hand and rub their faces and taste the sweat, laughing and crying. One or two begin to dance. The* WIFE *bends over the man's body. The drummer and* CHORUS *join in the rhythm.*)

ALL: *I'suait!* He sweat! *I'suait! Aie ya yie!*

(*The* CHORUS *picks up the sibilance. In the dancing and drumming to* "*Death, Oh Me Lord!*" MOUSTIQUE *takes over and, mounting a box, shouts above the celebration.* MAKAK, *dazed at his own power, is kneeling.*)

MOUSTIQUE:
Ah, ah, you see, all you.
Ain't white priest come and nothing happen?
Ain't white doctor come and was agony still?
Ain't you take bush medicine, and no sweat break?
White medicine, bush medicine,
not one of them work!
White prayers, black prayers,
and still no deliverance!
And who heal the man?
Makak! Makak!
All your deliverance lie in this man.
The man is God's messenger.
So, further the cause, brothers and sisters.

(*He opens his haversack and holds it before him.*)

Further the cause,
drop what you have in there.
Look! Look! Josephus walking.
Next thing he will dance.

(*They laugh. The* WIFE *makes him do a little dance.*)

I tell you he dancing!
God's work must be done,

and like Saint Peter self,
Moustique, that's me,
is Secretary-Treasurer.

(*During all this, they bring him gifts of food, some put money in the haversack, one man gives him the shoes he had slung around his neck.*)

Now dance out in the moonlight,
let him breathe the fresh air,
let him breathe resurrection,
go forth, and rejoice . . .

(*They take the* SICK MAN *out, dancing and singing "Death, Oh Me Lord!"* BASIL *hangs behind.* MOUSTIQUE *removes the tall hat from* BASIL *as he passes.*)

MOUSTIQUE: You don't mind, friend? Only a black hat, in exchange for a life. You see, the man heal, you ain't going to need it.

BASIL: My work never done, friend. And that hat is my business.

MOUSTIQUE: And mine, from now on.

BASIL: We go meet again, stranger.

MOUSTIQUE: Oh, I sure of that friend. But only at the sign of a spider. (*He is counting the take in the hat.*) Three coins, earrings. Ah, a dollar. In God we trust. Like you, brother, I don't believe in credit. Now, if you was a spider . . . The coat too, pardner.

BASIL: You know where you are? (BASIL *surrenders the coat.*)

MOUSTIQUE: At a crossroads in the moonlight.

BASIL: You are standing in the middle. A white road. With four legs. Think what that mean, friend. I can wait for my hat. (BASIL *exits.*)

MOUSTIQUE: A white road. With four legs. A spider. With eggs. Eggs. White eggs! (*Shouting after* BASIL) But I still here! And I still alive! (*Laughing, he counts again.* MAKAK *comes toward him, mistaking him for* BASIL; *he stiffens.*)

MAKAK: Moustique, Moustique. Oh, is you. You frighten me. What you doing there?

MOUSTIQUE: Counting. (*He continues.*) And believe me, as the politician said, this better than working. Well, which way now, boss?

MAKAK: You see? You see what I do there? This power, this power I now have . . .

MOUSTIQUE: I see a sick man with snake bite, and a set o' damn asses using old-time medicine. I see a road paved with silver. I see the ocean multiplying with shillings. Thank God. That was good, that was good. (*Mimes the healing*) By this power in my hand. By this coal in my hand. You ain't playing you good, nuh. Here, take what you want.

MAKAK (*striking the hat away*): Move that from me. You don't understand, Moustique. This power I have, is not for profit.

MOUSTIQUE (*picking up the hat*): So what you want me to do? Run behind them and give them back their money? Look, I tired telling you that nothing is for free. That some day, Makak, swing high, swing low, you will have to sell your dream, your soul, your power, just for bread and shelter. That the love of people not enough, not enough to pay for being born, for being buried. Well, if you don't want the cash, then let me keep it. 'Cause I tired begging. Look, look at us. So poor we had to sell the donkey. Barefooted, nasty, and what you want me to do, bow my head and say thanks?

MAKAK: You will never understand. (MAKAK *kneels again.*)

MOUSTIQUE: What you kneeling again for? Who you praying for now? (MAKAK *says nothing.*) If is for me, partner, don't bother. Pray for the world to change. Not your friend. Pray for the day when people will not need money, when faith alone will move mountains. Pray for the day when poverty done, and for when niggers everywhere could walk upright like men. You think I doubt you, you think I don't respect you and love you and grateful to you? But I look at that moon, and it like a plate that a dog lick clean, bright as a florin, but dogs does chase me out of people yard when I go round begging, "Food for my master, food." And I does have to stoop down, and pick up the odd shilling they throw you. Look, turn your head, old man, look there, and that thing shining there, that is the ocean. Behind that, is Africa! How we going there? You think this . . . (*holds up mask*) this damned stupidness go take us there? Either you let me save money for us, or here, at this crossroads, the partnership divide.

MAKAK (*rising*): All right, all right. But don't take more than we need. All right, which way now?

MOUSTIQUE (*spinning around blindly, pointing*): This way, master. Quartre Chemin Market!

(*Music. Exeunt*)

SCENE THREE

CORPORAL *in wig and gown enters the spotlight.*

CORPORAL (*infuriated*): My lords, behold! (*Arms extended*) Behold me, flayed and dismayed by this impenetrable ignorance! This is our reward, we who have borne the high torch of justice through tortuous thickets of darkness to illuminate with vision the mind of primeval peoples, of backbiting tribes! We who have borne with us the texts of the law, the Mosaic tablets, the splendours of marble in moonlight, the affidavit and the water toilet, this stubbornness and ingratitude is our reward! But let me not sway you with displays of emotion, for the law is emotionless. Let me give facts! (*He controls himself.*) It was market Saturday and I, with Market and Sanitation Inspector Caiphas J. Pamphilion, was on duty at Quatre Chemin crossroads. I was armed because the area was on strike.

(*Sounds of the market: cries, etc., as the market scene, baskets, cloth, etc., is lowered*)

(*A village market, at a crossroads, before dawn. Vendors, crates, carts, wares slung from rope. The* FIRST VENDOR'S *cries, flute music. In one corner, setting up their basket-stall, a* WOMAN, *her* HUSBAND, *and two other* VENDORS *in near-rags, drinking coffee.*)

WIFE: He will tell you he see it, of course, but don't mind him, he wasn't there.

MAN: You was not there yourself. (*Piles the basket*)

WIFE: It was on the high road. The old woman husband Josephus, well, snake bite him, and they had called the priest and everything. From the edge of his bed he could see hell. Then Makak arrive—praise be God—and pass his hand so, twice over the man face, tell him to walk, and he rise up and he walk. And before that, he hold a piece of coal, so (*demonstrates*), in his bare hand, open it, and the coal turn into a red bird, and fly out of his hand.

MAN: Hear her. (*Sucks his teeth*)

(*The market is waking around them, the light widening.*)

WIFE: Then, the next day, this I cannot kiss the Bible that I see it myself, there had a small boy, he have, you know, a . . . a . . . what you call it?

MAN: Abscess.

WIFE: Right. A abscess. And he was in serious, serious pain, and the boy father bring him, and he rub a piece of bluestone on the boy . . . on the boy . . .

MAN: Cheek. By his cheek.

WIFE: Who telling the story, me or you? By the boy cheek, and the tooth fall out of the boy mouth, and he was well again. You want some more tea? (*She turns away.*)

SECOND WOMAN: I hear that in Micoud he hold a stone in his hand and it turn into fire.

THIRD WOMAN: Not Micoud, it was by La Rivière.

SECOND WOMAN: *Eh, bien.* Wherever it was then.

MAN (*to his wife*): *Gardez,* Agafa! is work you working or is talk you talking?

WIFE: What happen to you? You have no manners?

SECOND WOMAN: And for all that, he not asking for nothing.

THIRD WOMAN: They say it is a dream he have.

MAN: It have man so. It have men that have powers and nobody don't know where they getting it from. I did have a uncle so.

WIFE: If you did have a uncle so, you think is basket I would be selling? (*The* WOMEN *laugh.*) It have more than a week now that thing happen with the man on the high road. Then the next day, the boy with the . . . with the . . .

SECOND WOMAN: Abscess.

WIFE: Whatever you calling it, at Micoud . . .

SECOND WOMAN: At La Rivière. He going to the sea, he must pass there.

(*The* CORPORAL, *wearing a pistol; and the* MARKET INSPECTOR, *issuing certificates to the* VENDORS)

INSPECTOR: So hence, the pistol?

CORPORAL: No, Market and Sanitary Inspector Pamphilion. *Mens sana in corpore sano.* The pistol is not to destroy but to protect. You will ask me, to protect who from what, or rather, what from who? And my reply would be, to protect people from themselves, or, to put it another way, to preserve order for the people. We are in a state of emergency.

INSPECTOR: Is not because of the strikes and the cane-burning taking place in the district?

CORPORAL: No, Market Inspector Pamphilion, it is to prevent more strikes and cane-burning happening in the district. You understand?

INSPECTOR: No.

CORPORAL: Well, the law is complicated and people very simple. (*To a* VENDOR) Morning. That's a nice pawpaw, sir.

VENDOR: *Oui, mon corporal.* (*They move on.*)

CORPORAL: You see?

INSPECTOR: That was a melon.

CORPORAL: I know. But in the opinion of the pistol, and for the preservation of order, and to avoid any argument, we both was satisfied it was a pawpaw.

INSPECTOR: I am beginning to understand the law.

CORPORAL: And if you know how much I would like to do for these people, my people, you will understand even better. I would like to see them challenge the law, to show me they alive. But they paralyse with darkness. They paralyse with faith. They cannot do nothing, because they born slaves and they born tired. I could spit.

INSPECTOR: They must believe in something.

CORPORAL: Believe? Let me tell you what happen. I following this rumour good. And is the same as history, Pamphilion. Some ignorant, illiterate lunatic who know two or three lines from the Bible by heart, well one day he get tired of being poor and sitting on his arse so he make up his mind to see a vision, and once he make up his mind, the constipated, stupid bastard bound to see it. So he come down off his mountain, as if he is God self, and walk amongst the people, who too glad that he will think for them. He give them hope, miracle, vision, paradise on earth, and is then blood start to bleed and stone start to fly. And is at that point, to protect them from disappointment, I does reach for my pistol. History, Mr. Pamphilion, is just one series of breach of promise. (*They have reached the basket* VENDORS) That's a nice set of cages you have there.

VENDOR: Is a basket, Corporal.

CORPORAL: Good! I like a nigger with spirit.

WIFE: They say that he on a long walk, going through every village, on his way to the sea, looking across to Africa, and that when he get there, God will tell him what to do. (*She sings a hymn. The others join her, working.*)

INSPECTOR: They know he is coming. The rumour like a cane fire. Faith is good business. I've never seen the market so full. It's like a fair.

(*And indeed the market is filling with vendors, cripples, the sick.*)

From all parts of the district.

CORPORAL: The crippled, crippled. It's the crippled who believe in miracles. It's the slaves who believe in freedom.

INSPECTOR: And with music too! It's so beautiful I could cry, but I'm in uniform. My wife has rheumatism. I wonder.

(*In a corner of the market, an improvised music of sticks, clapping, and a tin grater begins under the cries of the* VENDORS. *Two men dance as another sings a bongo. The men mime a healing.*)

SINGER: I'll show you how it happen: *Il dit Levez, Makak.* [He said Rise, Makak.]

VENDOR: Pepper, pepperrrrr.

VENDOR: Plantainnnn!

DANCER: Woy, woy, Makak.

SINGER: *Quittez charbon en sac.* [Leave your bags of coal.]

DANCER: Woy, woy, Makak.

SINGER: *Negre ka weh twop misere.* [Niggers see too much misery.]

VENDOR: Cassava, cassavaaah.

SINGER: *Ous kai weh ou kai weh.* [You'll see it for yourself.]

DANCER: Woooh, Makak.

SINGER: *Il dit Levez, Makak.* [He said Wake up, Makak.]

DANCER: Woiee, Makak.

SINGER: *Il dit Descendre, Makak.* [He said Come down, Makak.]

DANCER: Woy, Makak.

SINGER: *Descendre Morne Makak.* [Go down Monkey Mountain.]
Il dit . . .

(*He stops, suddenly, as a small boy, a fishing pole in his hand, comes screaming into the market, huddles behind the* SINGER *and points. In the distance we hear the sound of a stick beating on a kerosene tin, and a voice roaring.*)

SINGER: What happen? What happen, son?

BOY: I went down by the bridge by the river. I was looking in the water, down so, in the water, when I turn my head and . . . and I see a man alone singing and coming up the road, beating on a pan, and singing. With a long stick in his hand, and with a big white hair on his head, and . . . and a tall black hat, coming up the road so, one by one. I drop everything and I run like monson.

SINGER: *C'est lui. C'est Makak.*

CROWD: *Makak. C'est Makak.*

(*A woman screams.* MAKAK *enters leaping, whirling in black coat and tall hat and spear. This is in fact* MOUSTIQUE *impersonating* MAKAK.)

MOUSTIQUE: *Oui. C'est Makak.*

CROWD: *Makak, c'est Makak!*

MOUSTIQUE: *Oui.* It is Makak.

(*Limping in his stride, he moves among the* CROWD.)

Let the enemies of Africa make way.
Let the Abyssinian lion leap again,
For Makak walk in frenzy down Monkey Mountain,
And God send this message in lightning handwriting
That the sword of sunlight be in his right hand
And the moon his shield.

CORPORAL: You there!

MOUSTIQUE: Who it is dare to call Makak by name? Which man dare call the lion by his name?

CORPORAL: A corporal of police.

MOUSTIQUE (*turning to the* CROWD): I laugh. I laugh. A corporal of police? Makak have come to Quatre Chemin Market and neither corporal nor spiritual stopping him today! (*Pointing at the* CROWD) *Dire, Abou-ma-la-ka-jonga.*

CROWD (*defiantly*): *Abou-ma-la-ka-jonga.*

MOUSTIQUE: *Faire ça.* (*Gestures, with a stance*)

CROWD: Hunh. (*They gesture like him, many laughing.*)

MOUSTIQUE: Now sing monkey! All you.

(*Sings*)

I don't know what to say that monkey won't do. . . . Sing!

(WOMEN, *laughing, sing "monkey" as they strut around the* CORPORAL.)

MOUSTIQUE: Take note, Corporal.

INSPECTOR: This is ignorance!

MOUSTIQUE: Ignorance? It seem to me I hear a voice, a voice, the color of milk, cry ignorance. (*Cups his ear. More laughter*) But that voice is not the whispering of God who does pour counsel in the cup of great men ears, but just the usual voice of small-time authority. What is your name?

INSPECTOR: I am Market Inspector Caiphas J. Pamphilion.

MOUSTIQUE: Market Inspector? Well then, inspect with respect, do not be suspect, or you will be wreck. (*To* CROWD) They calling that English, but the color of English is white. Inspector of milk! (*The* CROWD *is delirious.*) Yes, find room in your heart to laugh, find room inside you to be happy, because Makak shall not pass this road again. His dream call him to the sea, to the shore of Africa. And he hungry and tired. The dust of thirty roads is in his throat. (*A woman brings him water.*) Daughter of heaven, Makak will remember you. But I prefer cash, as I traveling hard. Zambesi, Congo, Niger, Limpopo, is your brown milk I drink, is your taste I remember, is the roots of your trees that is the veins in my hand, is your flowers that falling now from my tongue. (*He takes the bowl from the woman.*) By belief, I make blessing. But even the black sheep of God cannot go hungry. And they shall be fed. So, children of darkness, bring what you can give, make harvest and make sacrifice, bring whatsoever you have, a shilling, a yam, and put here at the mouth of God, that Makak is the tongue, and then, when all is in one bag, we shall pray. You shall fast, and I shall pray. (*He lifts the bowl high above their heads as they place a few offerings at his feet.*) Kneel, and listen while I deliver the revelation of my experience. They say I can cure. Well, I cannot cure, except you want to be, except you believe that I can cure. . . . Just put it down there, brother. Seven days and seven nights me and my friend, that great man, Moustique, who fal sick by the wayside, six days and six nights we leave Monkey Mountain, crossing hot pasture and dry river, like two leaves blowing in the hot wind. You will say how the divine sadness can fall on such men? A poor charcoal-seller that cannot see the light? *Eh bien,* listen, listen, Inspector of milk, and corporals of the law. One billion, trillion years of pressure bringing light, and is for that I say, Africa shall make light. And now . . . now . . . Makak shall sprinkle you with this water, for the cure is in yourself, and then, then he must go where his feet calling him. First, Makak will drink.

(*They look to him. He lifts the bowl reverently to his mouth, then drops it with a cry. He seems shaken.*)

Is nothing. A spider. A spider over my hand. I cannot bear these things.

CORPORAL: A spider? A man who will bring you deliverance is afraid of a spider?

MOUSTIQUE: I not 'fraid of nothing. It just make me jump.

CORPORAL: Then show us. You. You, Basil, the carpenter, take it and bring it for the warrior Makak. Take it.

(BASIL *looks for the spider, holds it in his cupped palm and brings it toward* MAKAK *and places it on his body.* MAKAK *winces, enduring it. Shuddering*)

BASIL (*as he gets nearer, looking into his eyes*): You cannot run fast enough, eh? Moustique! That is not Makak! His name is Moustique!

MOUSTIQUE: Eh?

(*A man comes nearer.* MOUSTIQUE, *for that is who it is, stares at him, sweating.* BASIL *steps forward.*)

LABORER: Wait! Wait! It is Basil the carpenter. Let him speak.

(*A rustling stillness*)

BASIL: I have little to say. Why should I talk? Look for yourselves. The tongue is on fire, but the eyes are dead.

(MOUSTIQUE *cowers, mumbling.* BASIL, *sometimes moving the spider around* MOUSTIQUE'*s body, circles him, talking slowly, slowly waving his arms. During this, he removes the silk hat.*)

You have seen coals put out by water. What comes from that mouth is vapor, steam, promises without meaning. The eyes are dead coals. (*The* CROWD *mutters*.) And the heart is ashes. (*He confronts* MOUSTIQUE.) Ah, friend, when the spear of moonlight had pinned the white road till its legs were splayed like a spider (*he opens one palm*), I tried to direct you. Everywhere you were shown signs. In the hut that first morning, in the white shrieking of the funeral procession, in the mask of the cold moon, but you would not listen.

MOUSTIQUE: Who in hell is he? What he want? What he want?

BASIL: I want nothing, pardner. And I go get it. You have one chance! If this is Makak, if this man will deliver the revelation of his experience, then let him show you your hope! Ask him to share it with you! Show them! Show them what you have learnt, *compère!*

CROWD: Yes! Show us! Show us!

CORPORAL (*shouting*): What is your name? Your name not Moustique?

CROWD: Show us! Show us!

MOUSTIQUE (*pushing* BASIL *aside*): You know who I am? You want to know who I am? Makak! Makak! or Moustique, is not the same nigger? What you want me to say? "I am the resurrection, I am the life"? "I am the green side of Jordan," or that "I am a prophet stoned by Jerusalem," or you all want me, as if this hand hold magic, to stretch it and like a flash of lightning to make you all white? God after god you change, promise after promise you believe, and you still covered with dirt; so why not believe me. All I have is this (*Shows the mask*), black faces, white masks! I tried like you. Moustique then! Moustique! (*Spits at them*) That is my name! Do what you want!

LABORER: And you come here to rob your own people? What is one more mosquito? What is one more man?

MOUSTIQUE: Die in your ignorance! Live in darkness still! You don't know what you want!

(CROWD *grows angrier*.)

LABORER: Well then take that from us! (*Clouts him.* MOUSTIQUE *falls*.)

CROWD: Kill him! Break his legs! Beat him! Kill him!

(*They beat him to a noise of sticks rattling, tins banging and screaming women. The* CORPORAL *stands apart, then he moves toward them*.)

CORPORAL: All right, all right! *Assez, assez!* I say enough. Go home. Go home before I arrest all of you. Go home!

(*They disperse, leaving* MOUSTIQUE *crumpled among the heap of offerings.* BASIL *picks up his hat, puts it on, then waits*.)

INSPECTOR: Why you didn't stop them?
CORPORAL: All those people. Do you want me to get killed? Come on.
I'll buy you a drink. You look afraid. Funny, I can't stand cockroaches
myself.
INSPECTOR: It was a spider. Harmless.
CORPORAL: Well, whatever it was. Come on, let's go.

(MAKAK, *dusty and tattered, enters the market.*)

MAKAK: Moustique? Moustique? (*He looks around, among the wreckage,
and then discovers* MOUSTIQUE, *sprawled on a heap.*) Moustique. What
happen? What happen to you? What they do you? (*He lifts up*
MOUSTIQUE'*s head.*) Oh God, what they do you, little man?
MOUSTIQUE: Pardon, Makak. Pardon. To see that this is where I must
die. Here, in the market. The spider, the spider. (*He shudders.*) Go
back to Monkey Mountain. Go back, or you will die like this.
MAKAK: You will not die.
MOUSTIQUE: Yes, I will die. I take what you had, I take the dream you
have and I come and try to sell it. I try to fool them, and they fall on
me with sticks, everything, and they kill me.
MAKAK: How you could leave me alone, Moustique? In all the yards and
villages I pass, I hear people saying, Makak was here, Makak was here,
and we give him so and so. If it was for the money, I didn't know.
MOUSTIQUE: No. You didn't know. You would never know. It was always
me, since the first time in the road, where . . . always me who did have
to beg . . . to do . . . (*He passes out.*)
MAKAK (*shaking him*): Moustique, Moustique.
MOUSTIQUE: Go back, go back to Monkey Mountain. Go back.
MAKAK: No, she tell me what I must do.
MOUSTIQUE: Let me die, Makak, I hurting and I tired, tired . . .
MAKAK: You will not die, you must not die!
MOUSTIQUE: Every man have to die . . . (*He faints again.* MAKAK
shakes him.)
MAKAK: Then look. Look then. . . . Open your eyes, try and open your
eyes, and tell me what you see. Look, look, then, if you dying, tell me
what you see. Open them. Tell me and I will preach that. Tell me!
MOUSTIQUE: I see . . . I see . . . I see a black wind blowing. . . . A black
wind . . . (*He dies.*)
MAKAK (*forcing his eyes open*): And nothing else? Nothing? Let me look
in them, let me look, and I will keep the last picture of your eyes in
mine, let me be brave and look in a dead man eye, Moustique . . . (*He
peers into* MOUSTIQUE'*s gaze and what he sees there darkens his vision.
He lets out a terrible cry of emptiness.*)

MAKAK: Aiieeeeee. Moustique!

(*In the darkness the drums begin, and shapes, demons, spirits, a cleft-footed woman, a man with a goat's head, imps, whirl out of the darkness around* MAKAK, *and the figure of a woman with a white face and long black hair of the mask, all singing. They take the body on a litter.*)

CHORUS: Death, O death, O me Lord,
When my body lie down in the grave,
Then me soul going shout for joy.

(*To a frenzied climax as* MAKAK *writhes on the ground in a fit, and the music dies*)

PART TWO

Let us add, for certain other carefully selected unfortunates, that other witchery of which I have already spoken: Western culture. If I were them, you may say, I'd prefer my mumbo-jumbo to their Acropolis. Very good: you've grasped the situation. But not altogether, because you aren't them — or not yet. Otherwise you would know that they can't choose; they must have both. Two worlds; that makes two bewitchings; they dance all night and at dawn they crowd into the churches to hear Mass; each day the split widens. Our enemy betrays his brothers and becomes our accomplice; his brothers do the same thing. The status of "native" is a nervous condition introduced and maintained by the settler among colonized people with their consent.*
    Sartre: Introduction to "The Wretched of the Earth," by Frantz Fanon*

SCENE ONE

The cell. Night. TIGRE *and* SOURIS *in their cell.* MAKAK *in his. The* CORPORAL *enters, banging a tin plate with a cup.*

CORPORAL: All right, all right! Chow time! Stand back. Up against the bars there! I ain't want you all chewing up my hand for three green figs and a sliver of salfish. Hold this plate. (TIGRE *steps forward, accepts plate, steps back*) You next. (SOURIS *steps forward, accepts plate and cup, then steps back*) How is the old king?

SOURIS: He's been there moaning, muttering to himself, since he come in. Sometimes he sing, sometimes he letting out a cry, sometimes even a little dance, and half the time in gibberish. One more green fig, Corporal?

CORPORAL: No more figs. Any more you get will have to be in your mind. A figment of your imagination, so to speak.

SOURIS: Look at him. Just look at him. I feel sorry for him. Let him go, Corporal.

CORPORAL: I am an instrument of the law, Souris. I got the white man work to do. Besides, if he crazy he dangerous. If he is not, a night in jail will be good for his soul. (*Goes over to the old man's cell*) Is chow time, King-Kong. Hey. Food, food, old man.

TIGRE: Bring me damn supper, Lestrade! I have me rights, you know!

CORPORAL: Your rights? Listen, nigger! according to this world you have the inalienable right to life, liberty, and three green figs. No more, maybe less. You can do what you want with your life, you can hardly call this liberty, and as for the pursuit of happiness, you never hear the expression, give a nigger an inch and he'll take a mile? Don't harass me further. I didn't make the rules. (*To* MAKAK) Now, you. Come for this plate!

(MAKAK *gropes forward.*)

TIGRE: So what? Is against the law to be poor?

CORPORAL: Here, hold this. (*Turns to* TIGRE) Don't tell me about the law. Once I loved the law. I thought the law was just, universal, a substitute for God, but the law is a whore, she will adjust her price. In some places the law does not allow you to be black, not even black, but tinged with black.

TIGRE: And that is what eating out your soul, Lestrade. That is why you punishing this man. You punishing your own grandfather. Let him go home.

MAKAK: Let me go home. I will pay you. I have money. I have money that I hide . . . all of you.

CORPORAL: Bribery! (*Pulling the old man through the bars*) Listen, you corrupt, obscene, insufferable ape, I am incorruptible, you understand? Incorruptible. The law is your salvation and mine, you imbecile, you understand that. This ain't the bush. This ain't Africa. This is not another easygoing nigger you talking to, but an officer! A servant and an officer of the law! Not the law of the jungle, but something the white man teach you to be thankful for.

MAKAK: It is the law that kill my friend. You let them kill my friend.

CORPORAL: I don't know what you talking about.

MAKAK: You lie. . . . You lie. Right here, in the market . . . you let them kill my friend.

SOURIS: My figs, Corporal, my figs!

CORPORAL: Shut up! Shut up, nigger!

SOURIS (*dancing*): O you beast! You filt'y fascist beast! I hungry!

MAKAK: I will give you all the money I have to go back home.
O Moustique, you did warn me. I open my eyes and I see nothing. I
see man quarreling like animals in a pit. The spider there for all of us.
I see us in this pit . . .

CORPORAL: How long he been like this?

TIGRE: Since you bring him in. After the first fit. Is like he is living over
and over a bad dream he had.

SOURIS: I hungreeeeeeeeee!

CORPORAL: All right! All right! The law says I must feed you. I will feed
you. But God, remind me to ask for a transfer to civilization. (*Exit.*)

TIGRE (*in a single spot*): You hear what he say? Ain't I tell you old men so
does have money hide away. We must help the old bitch escape, track
him to Monkey Mountain, then put him out of his misery. Eat your
food when it come, but dream about money, Souris. Dream hard and
good. Shhhhhh.

TIGRE: Tell us about the money. About that . . . and Africa.

MAKAK: You will laugh at me.

SOURIS: Where is it?

TIGRE: We believe your dream, Makak. Tell us . . . and . . . look. . . . You
want to get out of here?

MAKAK: Yes, yes, but how?

TIGRE: Never mind how. You want to get out?

MAKAK (*wearily*): Yes . . .

TIGRE: Listen. First we must kill the Corporal.

SOURIS: I know now you crazy.

TIGRE: You know why you must kill him? Because she tell you to, old
man, remember, in the dream? Lion, she call you. And lion don't stop
to think. The jaw of the lion, that is the opening and closing of the
book of judgment. When the moon in quarter, you know what
Africans say . . .

SOURIS: Where you get all that?

MAKAK: Tell me, my son, what?

TIGRE: That the jaw of the sun, that is the lion, has eaten the moon.
The moon, that is nothing, but . . . a skull . . . a bone . . .

(MAKAK, *growling, begins to pace his cage.*)

SOURIS: Pappy! Eh?

TIGRE: How else can you prove your name is lion, unless you do one
bloody, golden, dazzling thing, eh? And who stand in your way but

your dear friend, Corporal Lestrade the straddler, neither one thing nor the next, neither milk, coal, neither day nor night, neither lion nor monkey, but a mulatto, a foot-licking servant of marble law? He cause Moustique to die. He turn his back on that. Believe me, like your friend saw the spider, I see it clearly. You bastard son of a black gorilla, you listening?

SOURIS: Look, look, he standing still.

TIGRE: He have something in his hand.

SOURIS: The same mask again.

TIGRE: No. No . . . friend. . . . As the moon unsheathe its blade, I swear by the crucifix of the handle, the old black gentleman has unclouded . . .

SOURIS (*in wonder*): A knife!

TIGRE: Look how it shines, old man. Like the sea. Like silver. Think of the bright blood! Think like the lion that is dazzled by pity for only a second! Call the Corporal. . . . Then, when the moon come out again, pretend you going mad. . . . Yes. You are in the forest now, you are hunted, tired. Your heavy, hanging tongue is dry as sand. Your muscles thunder with exhaustion. You want to drink. Fall down, ask for water . . . a drink. . . . Pretend you catch a fit. And then the keys, the keys! (*Loudly*) Corporal! Corporal! Shhhhh. . . . Go back to sleep . . . Corporal!

(CORPORAL *enters with a red towel, wiping his hands*)

CORPORAL: What you want, Tigre?

TIGRE: I cannot sleep. . . . I . . . I thirsty. . . . And the old man over there, groaning and coughing like a sick lion all night. . . . Between him and the moon they keeping me up. The night hot like a forest fire. He must be thirsty too.

(*The* CORPORAL *comes to* MAKAK's *cell*)

CORPORAL: Old man . . . you thirsty? (*He goes nearer*)

TIGRE: For blood, perhaps. Not you who call him lion?

CORPORAL: He who? that ape? What you want to drink, old man . . .

MAKAK (*with a cry*): Blood! Blood! Blood! Lion . . . Lion . . . I am . . . a lion (*He has grabbed the* CORPORAL, *stabbing him. Then he hurls him to the floor*)

TIGRE: The keys! The keys!

(MAKAK *takes the keys and opens the cells*)

MAKAK (*holding* TIGRE *and* SOURIS *and near-weeping with rage*): Drink it! Drink it! Drink! Is not that they say we are? Animals! Apes without law? O God, O gods! What am I, I who thought I was a man? What have I done? Which God? God dead, and his law there bleeding. Christian, cannibal, I will drink blood. You will drink it with me. For the lion, and the tiger, and the rat, yes, the gentle rat, have come out of their cages to breathe the air, the air heavy with forest, and if that moon go out . . . I will still find my way; the blackness will swallow me. I will wear it like a fish wears water. . . . Come. You have tasted blood. Now, come!

TIGRE: Where? To Monkey Mountain?

MAKAK (*laughing*): Come! (*Looks at body*)

(*They exit.*)

CORPORAL (*clutching the towel to his wound, rises. Single spot*): Did you feel pity for me or horror of them? Believe me, I am all right. Only a flesh wound. Times change, don't they? and people change. Even black people, even slaves. He made his point, you might say. (*Drawing out a knife*) But this is only what they dream of. And before things grow clearer, nearer to their dream of revenge, I must play another part. We'll go hunting the lion. Except . . . (*Takes down a rifle*) They're not lions, just natives. There's nothing quite so exciting as putting down the natives. Especially after reason and law have failed. So I let them escape. Let them run ahead. Then I'll have good reason for shooting them down. Sharpeville? Attempting to escape. Attempting to escape. Attempting to escape from the prison of their lives. That's the most dangerous crime. It brings about revolution. So, off we go, lads! (*Drums. Exit chanting*)

SCENE TWO

The forest. Enter MAKAK, SOURIS, TIGRE.

MAKAK: Come, we will rest here. I know this forest. Smell it. Smell it, it speaks to your blood.

SOURIS: Yes, it saying, your damn foot bleeding. It saying, "You hungry?" And the answer is yes. You know where we are, in all this damn darkness?

MAKAK: I can read the palm of every leaf. I can prophesy from one crystal of dew.

SOURIS: Good! Then read what we having for supper.

MAKAK: I know the nature of fire and wind. I will make a small fire. Here, look, you see this plant? Dry it, fire it, and your mind will cloud with a sweet, sweet-smelling smoke. Then the smoke will clear. You will not need to eat.

TIGRE: You crazy ganga-eating bastard, I want meat. Flesh and blood. Wet grass. Come on, come on, show us the way to Monkey Mountain. The Corporal hunting us.

MAKAK: The first quality of animals is stillness. Keep still. I can hear the crack of every leaf. I know all the signals of insects. It will be a small fire. (*He moves off.*)

TIGRE: Come on, come on, old man. We have to reach Monkey Mountain.

MAKAK: Monkey Mountain?

TIGRE: I . . . I mean Africa.

SOURIS: We should 'a eat first, then killed the Corporal. (*Whispers*) You really think he have money? Look at him! Half-man, half-forest, a shadow moving through the leaves.

TIGRE: Just do as he say. That's all. This is his forest. He could easily lose us. You didn't see how he stabbed the Corporal? He coming back. Let's mix ourselves in his madness. Let's dissolve in his dream. (*As* MAKAK *returns with twigs, bush, etc.*) Ah, Africa! Ah, blessed Africa! Whose earth is a starved mother waiting for the kiss of her prodigal, for the kiss of my foot. Talk like that, you fool.

SOURIS: How you will take us to Africa? What we will do there? In the darkness, now that I can see nothing, maybe, it is there I am. When I was a little boy, living in drakness, I was so afraid, it was as if I was sinking, drowning in a grave, and me and the darkness was the same, and God was like a big white man, a big white man I was afraid of.

MAKAK: Here, you are at home, my son. One of the forest creatures.

SOURIS: And in the darkness, big man as I am, I still afraid of him. You 'fraid God, Tigre?

TIGRE: I not 'fraid no white man.

SOURIS: Well, God help us. I really frighten. Like a child again. (MAKAK *lights the fire. They watch him.*) And that is what they teach me since I small. To be black like coal, and to dream of milk. To love God, and obey the white man.

TIGRE (*whispering*): Enough! Enough! You going crazy too?

SOURIS: How we will go, old man? How we will go?

MAKAK: Once, when Moustique asked me that, I didn't know. But I know now. What power can crawl on the bottom of the sea, or swim in the ocean of air above us? The mind, the mind. Now, come with me, the mind can bring the dead to life, it can go back, back, back, deep into time. It can make a man a king, it can make him a beast.

Can you hear the sea now, can you hear the sound of suffering, we are moving back now . . .

(*The* CHORUS *chants, "I going home."*)

Back into the boat, a beautiful boat, and soon, after many moons, after many songs, we will see Africa, the golden sand, the rivers where lions come down to drink, lapping at the water with their red tongues, then the villages, the birds, the sound of flutes.

SOURIS: Yes, yes, I see it. I see it!

MAKAK: When your eyes open, you will be transformed, as if you have eaten a magic root.

(SOURIS *moves off.*)

TIGRE: We will need money to go there, uncle. To buy a boat. A big, big boat that will take everybody back, or otherwise, is back into jail. Back where we were! It's drizzling. Where Souris gone? Where that damn thief? Is drizzling and I cold. And the light of the coals making figures in the forest. The trees take one step nearer. The leaves are eyes and tongues. And there are eyes or diamonds winking in the bush. Old man, if I go with you, what will I find? If they don't hang us for killing the Corporal.

MAKAK: Look at those coals. When I look in the fire, I see visions. The fire will talk with its bright tongue. Tell me what you see?

TIGRE (*huddled, shivering*): I see hell. I see people black like coals, twisting and burning in hell. And I see me too. The rain will put it out. Where Souris? I hungry. By tomorrow they will catch us, and three of us will hang. *Tiens,* what is that? But you, they will let you go, because you old, ugly and crazy. Where that mouse? Where that damn Souris? What I will find in Africa?

MAKAK: Peace.

TIGRE: Peace? Piece of what? (*The squawk of an animal*) What was that? What in hell is happening? Where Souris gone? For the first time in my life, I feeling frighten. Come, come on, you old bastard, let us move on.

MAKAK (*suddenly grabbing him*): Then, when we get there, I will make you my general. General Tigre, and when my enemies come, I will say fight with him, because he is a man, a man who know how to hate, to whom the life of a man is like a mosquito, like a fly. (*Claps his hands at an insect, and drops it in the fire.* TIGRE *laughs.*) And the fire is up to God.

(SOURIS *enters, holding up a dead chicken.*)

SOURIS: Well then, God best keep the fire going, 'cause look what drop in through the garden. (*Drops chicken*) And then, ay, what is this, what is this? (*Feels around in his large coat*) O Blessed Saviour, a miracle. Ground provisions, look, potatoes, one yam, never take more than you need, for the Lord will provide, a hand of small onions, and a little pepper. (*Spills them onto the ground*) So, how is the king?

(MAKAK *has drawn apart, talking to himself.*)

TIGRE: Mad like a ant. He just make me general.

MAKAK (*trotting up to them*): Good, my men. Good, my men. The Lord on the day he dead (*Opening his arms*) had two thief by him.

SOURIS: Only one went in heaven. (*Plucking the chicken*)

TIGRE: You. Because I look in the fire, and I see myself burning there, forever and forever, amen.

SOURIS: Amen. (MAKAK *walks away again, regally, mumbling.*) So what we will do with him?

TIGRE: Let us eat first. I will peel the yams. (*He takes out a knife and they watch* MAKAK *as they work.*)

SOURIS: Mad, mad, mad.

TIGRE: You see his eyes? That is the eyes of a man who will kill you in your sleep. They looking at you, and like you not there. Once we letting him believe what he is, is all right. Otherwise . . . (*Draws the knife across his throat*) Look, his blanket fall off.

SOURIS: I will fix it.

(MAKAK *has sat down on a log.* SOURIS *gingerly goes up to the fallen blanket and places it around the old man's shoulders.*)

MAKAK: My crown.

SOURIS (*twisting a vine and crowning him*): Crown. And don't bother call me for your sword, until the damn yams boil.

MAKAK (*in a thundering voice*): Feed my armies!

SOURIS: Pardon?

MAKAK: Feed my armies! Look, look them there. (*Rises and gestures beyond the fire*) They waiting for their general, their king, Makak, to tell them when to eat. Salute them. You see them where they are? Salute them. Let my generals salute them. Like me.

TIGRE: *Salute, Couillon.* (SOURIS *salutes.*)

MAKAK: General Tigre?

TIGRE: Look me, general. (*Rises, salutes*)

MAKAK: Attention, and listen. I want to speak to my men. I want to tell my armies, you can see their helmets shining like fireflies, you can see their spears as thick as bamboo leaves. I want to tell them this. That now is the time, the time of war. War. Fire, fire and destruction. (*He takes his spear and dips it in the fire.*) Fire, death. (SOURIS *and* TIGRE *withdraw in the darkness, and the sky grows red.*) Fire. The sky is on fire. Makak will destroy.

SOURIS (*still saluting*): Eh, bien. We reach Africa.

MAKAK: Shh! Somebody coming. The fire! Come. Into the bushes! Shh! Somebody coming.

(*Enter the* CORPORAL *armed, alone*)

CORPORAL: Ho! Ho! My beaters, ho! My head. My wound. Dusty blade. Gangrene. Delirium! Thrash that bush there! Build a fire for my safari. Set down the white man's burden. My back is breaking. Whisky and soda, you smoke-black sod. And start smoking out the mosquitoes. Bwana Lestrade is tired. Once I knew this jungle like the back of my hand. What-ho, chaps, more lights. Come dawn like thunder and we'll blow their brains out. (*He kneels down beside the fire.*) Ah! Ashes! Ashes and naked footprints! Black footprints. Let me stalk and think. Aha! Oho! Over here! Over here, bring me my Mannlicher, then a gimlet. (*Looking down*) Uh-huh. Footpad of tiger, ferrule of rat, spoor of lion, and all leading up the garden path to . . . (*Looking up*) To Monkey Mountain.

(*Wild cackling laughter*)

Gibberish! No fear, lads! Steady on! A calm blue eye acquired this Empire. Mine, a tawny yellow. English! You animals! English! English!

(*More laughter, coughs, howls*)

Animals! Savages! (*Quietly*) My wound! I'll pack my wound with earth! Niggers? God, the fire's gone out, lads! The light of civilization's finished. M'tbutu! Zola! Who's there? The moon, the moon, the pockmarked moon alone, the siphylitic crone. Who's that?

(*In the moonlight,* BASIL *comes out of the bushes.*)

Who are you? I'm going mad, goddammit. Stiff upper lip. Who're you in that ridiculous gear? Shoot! Or I'll stop! Stop or I'll run. It's Basil, is it? Time up. Twilight of Empire, eh? Night of the what's what? Who in hell are you? *Qui moune?* (BASIL *waits, his face hidden.*) You speak Swahili? Creole? Papiamento? Urdu? Ibo? Who you?

BASIL: I am Basil, the carpenter, the charcoal seller. I do not exist. A figment of the imagination, a banana of the mind . . .

CORPORAL: Banana of the mind, figment of the . . . ho! That's pretty good. Good-bye. (*He goes.*)

BASIL: You have one minute to repent. To recant. To renounce.

CORPORAL: Repent? Renounce what?

BASIL: You know, Lestrade. You know.

(TIGRE *and* SOURIS *emerge.*)

CORPORAL: My mind, my mind. What's happened to my mind?

BASIL: It was never yours, Lestrade.

CORPORAL: Then if it's not mine, then I'm not mad.

BASIL: And if you are not mad, then all this is real.

CORPORAL: Impossible! There is Monkey Mountain. Here is the earth. Banana of the mind . . . ha . . . ha . . . ha . . .

TIGRE: What happen to him? What he looking at?

SOURIS: I don't know, but he look crazy. It must be the wound. Or. . . . Is the moon. Is the moon . . .

BASIL: Confess your sins, Lestrade. Confess your sins. Strip yourself naked. Look at your skin and confess your sins.

CORPORAL: Which sins? What sins?

TIGRE (*stepping nearer*): At the edge of death you'll remember them. Confess!

CORPORAL (*as the creatures circle him*): Mooma, don't cry, your son in the grave already. Our son in the grave already, Mooma, don't cry. . . . But he's crying, Mother. Mother India, Mother Africa, Mother Earth, he is crying. Why? Why? (*Tries to sing*) "By the light of the silvery moon." (*Weeps*) Whistle, boys, it's only death. (*Whistles weakly*) The earth, the earth was a black child holding a balloon, and somebody cut it.

BASIL: Fifteen seconds.

TIGRE: Who de hell he talking to? I see nothing.

SOURIS: I see nothing too.

MAKAK: He is talking to nothing.

BASIL: Ten seconds.

CORPORAL (*flatly, like an accustomed prayer*): All right. Too late have I loved thee, Africa of my mind, *sero te amavi*, to cite Saint Augustine who they say was black. I jeered thee because I hated half of myself, my eclipse. But now in the heart of the forest at the foot of Monkey Mountain (*The creatures withdraw.*) I kiss your foot, O Monkey Mountain. (*He removes his clothes.*) I return to this earth, my mother. Naked, trying very hard not to weep in the dust. I was what I am, but now I am myself. (*Rises*) Now I feel better. Now I see a new light. I sing the glories of Makak! The glories of my race! What race? I have no race! Come! Come, all you splendors of imagination. Let me sing of darkness now! My hands. My hands are heavy. My feet . . . (*He rises, crouched.*) My feet grip like roots. The arteries are like rope. (*He howls.*) Was that my voice? My voice. O God, I have become what I mocked. I always was, I always was. Makak! Makak! forgive me, old father.

MAKAK (*stepping forward*): Now he is one of us.

CORPORAL (*looking up*): Grandfather. Grandfather. Where am I? Where is this? Why am I naked?

MAKAK: Because like all men you were born here. Here, put this around you. (*He covers him with the sack.*) What is this?

CORPORAL: A gun.

MAKAK: We don't need this, do we?

(TIGRE *and* SOURIS *approach cautiously.*)

They reject half of you. We accept all. Rise. Take off your boots. Doesn't the floor of the forest feel cool under your foot? Don't you hear your own voice in the gibberish of the leaves? Look how the trees have opened their arms. And in the hoarseness of the rivers, don't you hear the advice of all our ancestors. When the moon is hidden, look how you sink, forgotten, into the night. The forest claims us all, my son. No one needs gloves in his grave.

TIGRE: Tie up the bastard and let him find his way back.

SOURIS: So how it feel to be a nigger, Corporal? Animals. Savages! Niggers! Stop turning the place into a stinking zoo! (*Hops around*) Who is the monkey now, Lestrade? You bitch! I long had this for you. (*Jumps on him, wrestling*) And this! And this!

MAKAK: Enough! You hearing me? Enough! I came unto my own and they turned me away. Fighting, squabbling among yourselves. I have brought a dream to my people, and they rejected me. Now they must be taught, even tortured, killed. Their skulls will hang from my palaces. I will break up their tribes.

TIGRE (*picking up the rifle*): All right. Up till now I been playing this game. Shadows and shapes been crossing my mind, I have felt my body altered by firelight, and I watched all three of you, like animals paralysed by the glare of a headlamp. About three miles back there is Quatre Chemin jail, remember that, Souris, is where you and I come from. Up there is the damn mountain, I don't know if you have money, uncle, but I intend to find out. (*Cocks trigger*) Come on now, move! Souris, get the Corporal belt, and tie up his hands. Souris! You ent hear me?

SOURIS: No, Tigre.

TIGRE: What happen to you? You know who talking to you? You know what you are? Don't make me have to shoot.

SOURIS: You can't shoot us all, Tigre.

TIGRE: Whose side you on, nigger?

SOURIS: I believe this old man.

TIGRE: What the hell you talking about?

SOURIS: I believe I am better than I am. He teach me that. (*Picks up a rock*) Now you know me, Tigre. You will have to shoot.

TIGRE: You know what you saying? You going break up our friendship for one worthless, lunatic old charcoal burner?

SOURIS: He teach me more than you ever teach me, Tigre. His madness worth more to me than your friendship. Are you sure where you are, Tigre, are you sure who you are?

TIGRE: I'm a criminal with a gun, in the heart of the forest under Monkey Mountain. And I want his money.

MAKAK: Money. . . . That is what you wanted? That is what it is all about . . . money . . . ?

TIGRE: Shut up! Africa, Monkey Mountain, whatever you want to call it. But you first, father, to where the money buried. Go on. You too, Lestrade. Walk.

MAKAK (*moving forward, then stopping*): I am lost. I have forgotten the way. Who are you?

TIGRE: My name is Tigre.

MAKAK: But you, like him, had your own dream of money. The tiger eats and lies down content, but tomorrow he must rise again. Think, Tigre, money is not what you want. I know now you cannot reach that rainbow weighted like scales with your bags of fool's gold, no more than I can ever reach that moon; and that is why I am lost.

SOURIS: You will bring us so far, then abandon us? You will surrender that dream?

MAKAK (*holding out the mask*): I was a king among shadows. Either the shadows were real, and I was no king, or it is my own kingliness that created the shadows. Either way, I am lonely, lost, an old man again. No more. I wanted to leave this world. But if the moon is earth's friend, eh, Tigre, how can we leave the earth. And the earth, self. Look down and there is nothing at our feet. We are wrapped in black air, we are black, ourselves shadows in the firelight of the white man's mind. Soon, soon it will be morning, praise God, and the dream will rise like vapor, the shadows will be real, you will be corporal again, you will be thieves, and I an old man, drunk and disorderly, beaten down by a Bible, and tired of looking up to heaven. You believe I am lost now? Shoot, go ahead and shoot me. Death is the last shadow I have made. The Carpenter is waiting.

(BASIL *waits in the shadows.*)

SOURIS: But your dream touch everyone, sir. Even in those burnt-out coals of your eyes, there is still some fire. Dying, but fire. If a wind could catch them again, if some wind, some breath. (*He looks into his eyes.*)

MAKAK: And these tears will put them out. I have left death, failure, disappointment, despair in the wake of my dreams.

(*The* CORPORAL *has picked up* MAKAK'S *spear. He faces* TIGRE. *A dance begins.*)

The tribes! The tribes will wrangle among themselves, spitting, writhing, hissing, like snakes in a pit.

CORPORAL: I seen death face to face, Tigre, look! He's behind you. Turn, and he turns with you!

TIGRE: You turn savage, red nigger?

SOURIS: Stop them, stop them.

(*They are circling each other.*)

MAKAK: Locked in a dream, and treading their own darkness. Snarling at their shadows, snapping at their own tails, devouring their own entrails like the hyena, eaten with self-hatred. O God, O gods, why did you give me this burden?

SOURIS: For God sake, Tigre!

CORPORAL: Look, he's behind you!

TIGRE: Ha, ha, there's nothing behind me.

BASIL: Tigre!

(TIGRE *turns. The* CORPORAL *leaps onto him with a cry and drives the spear through him.*)

MAKAK (*over* TIGRE'S *body*): The tribes! The tribes! One by one, they will be broken. One will sink, and the other rise, like the gold and silver scales of the sun and the moon, and that is named progress.

CORPORAL: Now we must press on, old man. He is out of the way. This is jungle law. Come on, come on.

MAKAK: Yes, but where?

CORPORAL: Where? Anywhere! Onward, onward. Progress. Press on. We need that cry, and those who do not bend to our will, to your will, must die. You, help him up.

SOURIS: He doesn't know where to go.

CORPORAL: Put him in front. He's a shadow now. Let him face the moon and move towards it. Let him go forward. I'll take over. Come on. Go. Drag that thing there into the bush.

(SOURIS *takes away* TIGRE'*s body and* BASIL *helps him.*)

Now, where to, old father? No. We cannot go back. History is in motion. The law is in motion. Forward, forward.

SOURIS: Where? The world is a circle, Corporal. Remember that.

(*They move off, wearily. The* CORPORAL *remains behind in a single spot.*)

CORPORAL: Bastard, hatchet-man, opportunist, executioner. I have the black man work to do, you know. I breathe over the shoulder of your leaders, I hang back always at a decent distance, but I am there to observe that the law is upheld, that those who break it, president or prince, will also be broken. I have no ambition of my own. I have no animal's name. I simply work. And if a niche in history opens for me, what else can I do, for the sake of the people, Vox Populi, but to step into it? I don't know where we are going. But forward, progress! When you reach the precipice, simply step aside. That right, Basil? You see, he is not here. Now, let splendor, barbarism, majesty, noise, slogans, parades, drown out that truth. Plaster the walls with pictures of the leader, magnify our shadows, moon, if only for a moment. Gongs, warriors, bronzes! Statues, clap your hands you forests. Makak will be enthroned!

SCENE THREE

Apotheosis. Bronze trophies are lowered. Masks of barbarous gods appear to a clamor of drums, sticks, the chant of a tribal triumph. A procession of warriors, chiefs and the wives of MAKAK *in splendid tribal costumes gather, chanting to drums.*

CHORUS:
These are the conquests of Makak,
King of Limpopo, eye of Zambezi, blazing spear.
WARRIORS: Aieeee!
CHORUS:
Who has bundled the tribes like broken sticks,
Masai, Zulu, Ibo, Coromanti,
Who has scattered his enemies like grain in the wind.
WARRIORS: Aieeee!

CHORUS:

Drinkers of milk from the Mountains of the Moon.
Who has held captivity captive,
Who has bridled the wind,
Who has fathered the brood of the crocodile.
Whose eye is the sun,
Whose plate is the moon at its full,
Whose sword is the moon in its crescent.
Praise him!

WARRIORS (*chanting in antiphon*): Aieeee!

CHORUS

And we are his wives
For whom the sea knits its wool,
Robes without seam
Who is brother to God.

(*The volume increases.*)

WARRIORS: Aieee!

CHORUS:

Drinker of rivers,
In whom Gods waken,
Die, are reborn.

WARRIORS (*leaping in the air*): Aieeee!

CHORUS: Borne by the hands of the four corners of the earth on his
golden stool.

(MAKAK, *carried on a magnificent litter, enters. A golden stool is set down.
The* CORPORAL, *also garbed magnificently in tribal robes, enters, with*
SOURIS *some distance behind.*)

CORPORAL (*softly*): He whose peace is the counsel of the sea, gentler
than cotton.

CHORUS:

Whose hands are washed continually in milk,
Whose voice is the dove,
Whose eye is the cloud.

CORPORAL:

Who shall do unto others as to him it was done.
Behold too, Basil, a dark ambassador,
Behold Pamphilion, apotheosised.

CHORUS:

Who drew the thief to his bosom,
The murderer to his heart,

Whose blackness is a coal,
Whose soul is a fire,
Whose mind is a diamond,
Dispenser of justice,
Genderer and nourisher to a thousand wives,
Praise him!

(*All have assembled. The* CORPORAL *steps forward, then addresses*
MAKAK.)

CORPORAL: Inventor of history! (*Kisses* MAKAK's *foot*)
MAKAK: I am only a shadow.
CORPORAL: Shh. Quiet, my prince.
MAKAK: A hollow God. A phantom.
CORPORAL: Wives, warriors, chieftains! The law takes no sides, it
    changes the complexion of things. History is without pardon, justice
    hawk-swift, but mercy everlasting. We have prisoners and traitors, and
    they must be judged swiftly. The law of a country is the law of that
    country. Roman law, my friends, is not tribal law. Tribal law, in
    conclusion, is not Roman law. Therefore, wherever we are, let us have
    justice. We have no time for patient reforms. Mindless as the hawk,
    impetuous as lions, as dried of compassion as the bowels of a jackal.
    Elsewhere, the swiftness of justice is barbarously slow, but our
    progress cannot stop to think. In a short while, the prisoners shall be
    summoned, so prepare them, Basil and Pamphilion. First, the accused,
    and after them, the tributes.

(*The prisoners are presented.*)

Read them, Basil!
BASIL: They are Noah, but not the son of Ham, Aristotle, I'm skipping
    a bit, Abraham Lincoln, Alexander of Macedon, Shakespeare, I can
    cite relevant texts, Plato, Copernicus, Galileo and perhaps Ptolemy,
    Christopher Marlowe, Robert E. Lee, Sir John Hawkins, Sir Francis
    Drake, The Phantom, Mandrake the Magician. (*The* TRIBES *are
    laughing.*) It's not funny, my Lords, Tarzan, Dante, Sir Cecil Rhodes,
    William Wilberforce, the unidentified author of The Song of
    Solomon, Lorenzo de Medici, Florence Nightingale, Al Jolson,
    Horatio Nelson, and, but why go on? Their crime, whatever their plea,
    whatever extenuation of circumstances, whether of genius or
    geography, is, that they are indubitably, with the possible exception of
    Alexandre Dumas, Sr. and Jr., and Alexis, I think it is Pushkin, white.
    Some are dead and cannot speak for themselves, but a drop of milk is
    enough to condemn them, to banish them from the archives of the

bo-leaf and the papyrus, from the waxen tablet and the tribal stone. For you, my Lords, are shapers of history. We wait your judgment, O tribes.

TRIBES: Hang them!

BASIL: It shall be done. The list continues *ad nauseam*. (*His voice fades under a medley of screams and a drum roll of execution.*) So much for the past. Consider the present. Petitions, delegations, ambassadors, signatories, flatterers, potentates, dominions and powers, sects, ideologies, special dispensations, wait politely on him fearing revenge. (*Reads from a ledger*) An offer to the Pope.

(MAKAK *shakes his head.*)

TRIBES: No!

CORPORAL: Unanimous negative. (*He throws away the letter.*)

BASIL: An invitation to be President of the United States?

(MAKAK *shakes his head.*)

TRIBES: Impossible!

(CORPORAL *throws away the letter.*)

CORPORAL: Unanimous negative.

BASIL: An apology in full from the Republic of South Africa.

(MAKAK *shakes his head, the pace increases.*)

CORPORAL: Unanimous negative! (*Throws away the letter*)

BASIL: An offer to revise the origins of slavery. A floral tribute of lilies from the Ku Klux Klan. Congratulations from several Golf and Country Clubs. A gilt-edged doctorate from the Mississippi University. The Nobel Peace Prize. One thousand dollars from a secret admirer. An autograph of Pushkin. The Stalin Peace Prize. An offer from the U.N. A sliver of bone from the thigh of Lumumba. An offer from Hollywood. (*Throws all the letters away*)

TRIBES: No!

CORPORAL: Unanimous negative! Now, the prisoners.

(MOUSTIQUE, *bleeding and broken, is brought in.*)

MOUSTIQUE: How am I guilty?

CORPORAL: You have betrayed our dream.

MOUSTIQUE: I am talking to you, Makak. (MAKAK *looks away.*) Again, I must die, again?

CORPORAL: This is a lion. You are an insect whining in his ear.

MOUSTIQUE: Look around you, old man, and see who betray what. Is this what you wanted when you left Monkey Mountain? Power or love? Who are all these new friends? You can turn a blind eye on them, because now you need them. But can you trust them for true? Oh, I remember you, in those days long ago, you had something there (*Touching his breast*), but here all that gone. All this blood, all this killing, all this revenge. So go ahead, kill me. Go ahead. Is for the cause? Go ahead then.

MAKAK: I will be different.

MOUSTIQUE: No, you will be no different. Every man is the same. Now you are really mad. Mad, old man, and blind. Once you loved the moon, now a night will come when, because it white, from your deep hatred you will want it destroyed.

MAKAK: My hatred is deep, black, quiet as velvet.

MOUSTIQUE: That is not your voice, you are more of an ape now, a puppet. Which lion? (*Sings: I don't know what to say this monkey won't do . . .*)

CORPORAL: You waste time, your Majesty. We have other cases, and justice must be done. Even tribal justice. What says the tribunal?

TRIBES: Next!

MAKAK: Take him away! (*Softly*) Moustique! Moustique!

CORPORAL: And now a pale, pathetic appeal for forgiveness.

(*The* APPARITION *is brought in.*)

MAKAK: Who are you? Who are you? Why have you caused me all this pain? Why are you silent? Why did you choose me? O God, I was happy on Monkey Mountain.

CORPORAL: She, too, will have to die. Kill her, behead her, and you can sleep in peace.

MAKAK: The moon sinks in the sea and rises again, no sea can extinguish it. I will never rest. Tell me please, who are you? I must do what my people want.

CORPORAL: Bring me a blade, Souris. This is a job for a king, and, your Majesty, you cannot escape it. (SOURIS *brings him a curved sword.* CORPORAL *puts it in* MAKAK's *hand.*) You will displease your wives, your sons, the vision is exhausted, her silence is enough.

MAKAK: Let the rest go. Leave us alone.

CORPORAL: You don't mind, I have to record this for history. For the people. If General Souris and I remain behind. I understand, I understand. It is a private matter. Out, wait outside. We will show you her head.

(*All withdraw except* SOURIS, CORPORAL, BASIL, MAKAK *and the* WOMAN.)

MAKAK: Is she there? Do you see her now?
CORPORAL: Of course. Don't you, General?
SOURIS: Plain as the moon.
CORPORAL: Time, time, your Majesty.

(MAKAK *steps down and stands over the* WOMAN, *whose back is toward him.*)

MAKAK: I remember.
CORPORAL: We have no time. We have no time.
MAKAK: Please. (*He looks at the moon, then he lifts the back of her hair.*) I remember, one day, when I was younger, fifty years old, or so, I wake up, alone, and I do not know myself. I wake up, an old man that morning, with my clothes stinking of fifty years of sweat. My eye closing with gum, my two hands trembling, trembling when I open them, so, and I look in them, with all the marks like rivers, like a dead tree, and I ask myself, in a voice I do not know: Who you are, *negre?* I say to the voice and to my hands, with the black coal in the cuts, I say, your name is what—an old man without a mirror. And I went in the little rain barrel behind my hut and look down in the quiet, quiet water at my face, an old, cracked, burn-up face, with the hair turning white. And it was Makak. So I say, if you dead now, if you dead now. Well what? No woman will cry for you, no child will look at your face in death, as if it was the first time. The water in the rain barrel will show the cloud changing, and, as it have no memory, will forget your face. It will show the hawk passing smaller than a fly, and it will lick a dead leaf with its tongue, but you will go under this earth and burn and change as if you were a coal yourself, *charbonnier.* A big, big loneliness possess me, as if I was happy once, and strong, but could not remember where, as if, in some way, I was not no charcoal burner, God be blessed, but a king, and I feel strongly to go down the mountain, and to reach the sea, as if the place I remember was across the sea. Before I do this thing, tell me who she is.
CORPORAL: She, she? What you beheld, my prince, was but an image of your longing. As inaccessible as snow, as fatal as leprosy. Nun, virgin, Venus, you must violate, humiliate, destroy her; otherwise, humility will infect you. You will come out in blotches, you will be what I was, neither one thing nor the other. Kill her! Kill her!
MAKAK: I cannot! I cannot!
CORPORAL: She is the wife of the devil, the white witch. She is the

mirror of the moon that this ape look into and find himself
unbearable. She is all that is pure, all that he cannot reach. You see her
statues in white stone, and you turn your face away, mixed with
abhorrence and lust, with destruction and desire. She is lime, snow,
marble, moonlight, lilies, cloud, foam and bleaching cream, the
mother of civilization, and the confounder of blackness. I too have
longed for her. She is the color of the law, religion, paper, art, and if
you want peace, if you want to discover the beautiful depth of your
blackness, nigger, chop off her head! When you do this, you will kill
Venus, the Virgin, the Sleeping Beauty. She is the white light that
paralysed your mind, that led you into this confusion. It is you who
created her, so kill her! kill her! The law has spoken.

MAKAK: I must, I must do it alone.

CORPORAL: All right!

(SOURIS, CORPORAL *and* BASIL *withdraw.*)

MAKAK (*removing his robe*): Now, O God, now I am free.

(*He holds the curved sword in both hands and brings it down. The*
WOMAN *is beheaded.*)

(*Blackout*)

EPILOGUE

The cell bars descend. TIGRE, SOURIS *and* MAKAK *in jail.*

MAKAK: Felix Hobain, Felix Hobain . . .

(*The* CORPORAL *returns into the spotlight, holds up the mask.*)

TIGRE:
Mooma, don't cry,
You son in the jail a'ready
You son in the jail a'ready . . .

CORPORAL: What is your name?

MAKAK: Hobain. . . . My name is Felix Hobain . . .

CORPORAL: I must itemize these objects. What is your race? What is or
has been your denominational affiliation?

SOURIS: What he in for, Corporal?

MAKAK: My name is Felix Hobain . . . Hobain, I believe in my God. I have never killed a fly. And I cannot sleep. Where is General Tiger? Where is General Rat?

TIGRE: All night, with no sleep.

CORPORAL: Your name is Hobain. I must mark that on the charge.

MAKAK: Charge? What charge?

SOURIS: Drill him, Constable, drill him . . .

CORPORAL: Shut up! Charge? The reason why you in jail. It is only for a night, and the moon is growing thin. When the sun rises, I will let you go. You live up there? on Monkey Mountain?

MAKAK: Yes. *Oui*. Hobain. Sur Morne Macaque, *charbonnier*. I does burn and sell coals. And my friend . . . well, he is dead. . . . Sixty-five years I have. And they calling me Makak, for my face, you see? Is as I so ugly.

TIGRE: Get a lawyer, old man, to fix your face.

CORPORAL: I see uglier than that already, friend.

MAKAK: Then why am I here? What happen to me?

CORPORAL: Drunk and disorderly. You break up the shop of Felicien Alcindor yesterday, Saturday, on market day. I watch you quarreling, preaching in the market. You insulted a friend of mine, Market Inspector Caiphas J. Pamphilion. You called a poor carpenter an agent of death. Then you start drinking, and before you cause more damage, I bring you in here. You had a rough night, friend. But is a first offence. Now, what is this? (*Holds up the mask*) Everybody round here have one. Why you must keep it, cut it, talk to it?

TIGRE: You like white woman, eh, old man? I can imagine your dreams . . .

SOURIS: Look, look, look, I see it. The face of the sun moving over the floor. Is morning . . .

CORPORAL: Niggers, cannibals, savages! Stop turning this place into a stinking zoo. Believe me, old man (*Unlocking the cell*), it have no salvation for them, and no hope for us. (MAKAK *steps out*.) You want this? (MAKAK *looks at the mask*.)

MAKAK: And what day is this?

CORPORAL: It is market Saturday, it was, when you came. It is Sunday morning now. (*Singing can be heard*) That noise is from the Church of Revelation. You want this?

(MAKAK *shakes his head*.)

SOURIS: Go with God, old man.

TIGRE: What happen, nigger, you going soft in your old age?

CORPORAL: Go on. Go home. There, Monkey Mountain. Walk through the quiet village. I will explain everything to Alcindor. Sometimes, there is so much pressure. . . . Go on. You are free. It is your first offence.

MAKAK: Moustique. . . . There was a man called Moustique.

CORPORAL: Listen to them, listen to the sisters. All night. Well, some find it in rum, some find it in religion.

(*A voice outside: "Corporal! Corporal!"*)

MOUSTIQUE (*entering with crocus bags*): You have a man here named Felix Hobain. They calling him Mak . . .

MAKAK: Is you? Is you, Moustique?

MOUSTIQUE: Time and tide wait for no man. What happen to you? What he do, Corporal? You must forgive him. He live alone too long, and he does catch fits. When the full moon come, a frenzy does take him. Ah, Felix Hobain, poor old Felix Hobain. Since yesterday morning I looking for you. I went up the Mountain, you wasn't at home. And you know Alcindor promise us two bags? What happen? I hear how you mash up Alcindor café. . . . I have Berthilia outside. . . . If is any damage, Corporal, I will pay you for it. Sometimes, in life, Corporal, a man can take no more. . . . He don't know why he born, why he suffer, and that is what happen . . .

CORPORAL: He had a fit here. I thought he was drunk. A night in jail, I thought, would fix him.

MOUSTIQUE: He is a good man, Corporal. Let me take him where he belong. He belong right here.

CORPORAL: Here is a prison. Our life is a prison. Look, is the sun.

The River Niger

JOSEPH WALKER

Left to right: Douglas Turner Ward as JOHN WILLIAMS *and Roxie Roker as* MATTIE WILLIAMS *in a scene from* The River Niger. *Photograph copyright © 1972 by Bert Andrews. Reprinted by permission of Marsha Hudson, the Estate of Bert Andrews.*

Joseph Walker, a native of Washington, D.C., earned a B.A. in philosophy from Howard University and an M.F.A. in drama from Catholic University of America. His play, *Harangues,* opened the 1969 season of the Negro Ensemble Company; his *Ododo* opened the 1970 season; and *The River Niger* opened the 1971 season and transferred in 1973 to Broadway where it was awarded the Tony Award for Best Play of the season. He was the cofounder and artistic director of The Demi-Gods, a Dance and Music theater repertory company which he had personally trained. He has also taught playwrighting at Howard University and City College of New York and served as playwright-in-residence at the Yale University School of Drama. He is currently the chairman of the theatre program at Rutgers University, Camden, New Jersey.

The River Niger was produced in New York by the NEC; its world premier opened on December 5, 1972, at the St. Marks Playhouse and later reopened on Broadway at the Brooks Atkinson Theatre on March 27, 1973, with the original cast:

Grandma Wilhelmina Brown	Frances Foster
John Williams	Douglas Turner Ward
Dr. Dudley Stanton	Graham Bronn
Ann Vanderguild	Grenna Whitaker
Mattie Williams	Roxie Roker
Chips	Lennal Wainwright
Mo	Neville Richen
Gail	Saundra McClain
Skeeter	Charles Weldon
Al	Dean Irby
Jeff Williams	Les Roberts
Voice of Lt. Staples	Morley Morgana

Directed by Douglas Turner Ward; scenery by Gary James Wheeler; lighting by Shirley Prendergast; costumes by Edna Watson; incidental music by Dorothy Dinroe; stage managed by Wyatt Davis.

The River Niger

This play is dedicated to my mother and father and to highly underrated black daddies everywhere.

CHARACTERS
in order of appearance
JOHN WILLIAMS, *in his fifties, an alive poet*
MATTIE WILLIAMS, *in her fifties, an embittered but happy woman*
GRANDMA WILHEMINA BROWN, *eighty-two, very alive,* MATTIE's *mother*
DR. DUDLEY STANTON, *in his fifties, cynical, classic Jamaican, lover of poetry*
JEFF WILLIAMS, *twenty-five,* JOHN's *son, thoughtful, wild, a credit to his father*
ANN VANDERGUILD, *twenty-two, strong black South African girl, lover of quality*
MO, *twenty-four, young black leader of underlying beauty and integrity*
GAIL, *twenty-one, very much in love with* MO
CHIPS, *sexually perverted, a young fool*
AL, *the closet homosexual, capable, determined, very young*
SKEETER, *basically good, but hung on dope*
LIEUTENANT STAPLES, *police officer (voice only)*
BASS PLAYER, *highly skillful at creating a mood (not seen), provides musical poetry for the play*

ACT ONE

TIME
February 1, the present: 4:30P.M.

PLACE
New York City—Harlem

SETTING
Brownstone on 133rd between Lenox and Seventh. Living room and kitchen cross section. Living room a subdued green. Modest living-room suite consisting of coffee table, two easy chairs, and a sofa. The chairs and

sofa are covered with transparent plastic slipcovers. There is a television set with its back to the audience.

The kitchen is almost as large as the living room. There are a large kitchen table and four chairs. Stage right is an entrance from the back porch to the kitchen. Stage left is an entrance that leads from a small vestibule to a hallway—to the living room. In the hallway is a stairway that leads upstairs.

The house is not luxuriously decorated, of course, but it is not garish either. The "attempt" is to be cozy. Even though the place is very clean, there are many magazines and old newspapers around—giving the general appearance of casual "clutter."

(*At rise, a bass counterpoint creeps in, and* GRANDMA WILHEMINA BROWN, *a stately, fair-skinned black woman in her middle eighties is in the kitchen. She is humming "Rock of Ages" and pouring herself an oversized cup of coffee. She drops in two teaspoons of sugar and a fraction of cream, which she returns to the refrigerator. For a moment she stops humming and looks around stealthily. She goes to the kitchen window and peeps out into the backyard. Satisfied that she is alone, she opens the cabinet under the sink. With one final furtive glance around, she reaches under the cabinet and feels about till she finds what she's been looking for—a bottle of Old Grand-dad. Apparently, she unhooks it from under the top of the cabinet, glances around once more, then pours an extremely generous portion into her coffee. There is a sound from the backyard—as if someone or something has brushed by a trash can. She freezes for a second. With unbelievable speed she "hooks" the bottle back into her secret hiding place, snatches her coffee, and hurries out of the kitchen.* GRANDMA *pauses on the stairs. In the next moment we hear a key in the back door.* GRANDMA *hurries out of view. The back door opens cautiously. It is* JOHN WILLIAMS, *a thin, medium-sized brown man in his middle fifties. His hair is gray at the temples and slicked down. He has a salt-and-pepper mustache. He wears a brown topcoat, combat boots, corduroy pants—on his head a heavily crusted painter's cap. He is obviously intoxicated but very much in control. From his topcoat pocket he removes a bottle of Johnnie Walker Red Label, which he opens, and takes a long swallow, grimacing as he does so. He then stuffs the bottle into his "hiding place," behind the refrigerator. He pushes the refrigerator back in place and removes his topcoat. Pulling out his wallet, he begins counting its contents. Extremely dissatisfied with the count, he sits heavily and ponders his plight. A second later he takes out a piece of paper.*)

JOHN (*reading aloud to himself as bass line comes back in*):
I am the River Niger—hear my waters.

I wriggle and stream and run.
I am totally flexible—
Damn!

(*He crumples the paper and stuffs it into his pants pocket. In the very next instant, he remembers something—goes out the back door and returns with a small cedar jewelry box which he places on the table with great pride. There is a rapping at the back door. Bass fades out.* JOHN *is startled. He begins sneaking out of the room when he hears . . .*)

VOICE (*softly but intensely*): Johnny Williams! Open the damn door. (*Raps again*) It's me, Dudley. Open up!

(JOHN *goes to the door.*)

It's Dudley Stanton, fool.

(JOHN *opens the door.* DUDLEY STANTON, *a thin, wiry, very dark black man—in his late fifties—graying. He is impeccably but conservatively dressed. The two men stare at each other. Much love flows between them.*)

JOHN: Well, I'll be a son-of-a-bitch.
DUDLEY (*in a thick and beautiful Jamaican accent*): Yeah, man, that's what you are, a son-of-a-bitch. Now, will a son-of-a-bitch let a son-of-a-whore in? It's very cold out here, man! Did I ever tell you my ma was a whore?
JOHN: Only a thousand times. Come on in, ya monkey chaser.
DUDLEY (*coming in*): Now, you know I can't stand that expression. Why do you want to burden our friendship with that expression?
JOHN: Where in the hell you been?
DUDLEY: Can I take off my coat first?
JOHN: Take off your jockstrap for all I care. Where in the hell you been?
DUDLEY: To Mexico on vacation—fishing, man. And oh, what fishing. Man, I tell you.
JOHN: Did it ever occur to you that your old buddy might like to go fishing too? Did that ever cross your mind?
DUDLEY: You ain't never got no vacation time coming. You use it up faster than you earn it.
JOHN: Well, at least you could have let a buddy know you were going. (*Sees the bottle under* DUDLEY's *arm*) Give me a drink?
DUDLEY: Sure thing. (*Hands* JOHN *the bottle*)
JOHN: Vodka! I be damned! You know I can't stand vodka.
DUDLEY: You don't want my vodka, go on behind the fridge and get your Scotch. I saw you hide it there.
JOHN: You been spying on me with that damn telescope again.

DUDLEY: *Yeah.* I saw you coming in. Closed my office.

JOHN: You old monkey chaser.

DUDLEY: One day, I'm going to brain you for that expression.

JOHN: Goddamn black Jew doctor. You make all the money in the world, and you can't even buy your poor buddy a bottle of Scotch.

DUDLEY: Hell, I shouldn't even drink with you. (*Pause.*) If you don't stop boozing the way you do, you'll be dead in five years. You're killing yourself bit by bit, Johnny.

JOHN: Well, that's a helluva sight better than doing it all at once. Besides, I can stop any time I want to.

DUDLEY: Then why don't you?

JOHN: I don't want to. (*Changing the subject purposely*) Dudley, my son's due home tomorrow.

DUDLEY: Jeff coming home? No lie! That's wonderful! Old Jeff. Let's take a run up to the Big Apple and celebrate!

JOHN: That's where I'm coming from. I left work early today—I got so damned worked up, you know. I mean, all I could see was my boy— big-time first lieutenant in the United States of America Air Force— Strategic Air Command—navigator—walking through the front door with them bars—them shining silver bars on his goddamn shoulders. (*He begins saluting an imaginary Jeff.*) Yes, sir. Whatever you say, sir. Right away, Lieutenant Williams. Lieutenant Jeff Williams.

DUDLEY: Johnny Williams, you are the biggest fool in God's creation. How in the name of your grandma's twat could you get so worked up over the white man's air force? I've always said, "That's what's wrong with these American niggers. They believe anything that has a little tinsel sprinkled on it." "Shining silver bars." Fantasy, man!

JOHN: He's my son, Dudley, and I'm proud of him.

DUDLEY: You're supposed to be, but because he managed to survive this syphilitic asshole called Harlem, not because he's a powerless nub in a silly military gristmill. What you use for brains, man?

JOHN: I'm a fighter, Dudley. I don't like white folks either, but I sure do love their war machines. I'm a fighter who ain't got no battlefield. I woke up one day, looked around, and said to myself, "There's a war going on, but where's the battlefield?" I'm gonna find it one day— you watch.

DUDLEY: In other words, you'd gladly give your life for your poor downtrodden black brothers and sisters if you only knew where to give it?

JOHN: Right! For my people!

DUDLEY: I wonder how many niggers have said those words: "For my people!"

JOHN: Give me the right time and I'd throw this rubbish on the rubbish heap in a minute.

DUDLEY: Cop-out! That's all that is!

JOHN: Ya goddamn monkey chaser—you're the cop-out!

DUDLEY: Cop-out! The battlefield's everywhere. That's what's wrong with niggers in America—everybody's waiting for *the* time. I don't delude myself, nigger. I know that there's no heroism in death—just death, dirty nasty death. (*Pours another drink*) The rest is jive, man! Black people are jive. The most unrealistic, unphilosophical people in the world.

JOHN: Philosophy be damned. Give me a program—a program!

DUDLEY: A program!?! We're just fools, Johnny, white and black retarded children, playing with matches. We don't have the slightest idea what we're doing. Do you know, I no longer believe in medicine. Of all man's presumptions medicine is the most arrogantly presumptuous. People are supposed to die! It's natural to die. If I find that a patient has a serious disease, I send him to one of my idealistic colleagues. I ain't saving no lives, man. I treat the hypochondriacs. I treat colds, hemorrhoids, sore throats. I distribute sugar pills and run my fingers up the itching vaginas of sex-starved old bitches. Women who're all dried up, past menopause—but groping for life. They pretend to be unmoved, but I feel their wrigglings on my fingers. I see 'em swoon with ecstasy the deeper I probe. Liars—every one of them who would never admit their lives are up—what they really want is a good dose of M and M.

JOHN: M and M?

DUDLEY: Male meat! Old biddies clinging to life like tenants in condemned houses, and medicine keeps on finding cures. Ridiculous! Nature has a course. Let her take it!

JOHN: But what I do is part of nature's course, ya idiot!

DUDLEY: Go on, Johnny, be a hero and a black leader, and die with a Molotov cocktail in your hand, screaming, "Power to the People." The only value your death will have is to dent the population explosion. You can't change your shitting habits, let alone the world.

JOHN: You know what your trouble is, Dudley? You're just floating, man, floating downwind like a silly daisy.

DUDLEY: Come on! What the hell are you rooted to?

JOHN: To the battlefield. To my people, man!

DUDLEY: You ain't got no people, nigger. Just a bunch of black crabs in a barrel, lying to each other, always lying and pulling each other back down.

JOHN: Who do you suppose made us that way?

DUDLEY: You want me to say *whitey*, don't you?

JOHN: Who else?

DUDLEY: You goddamn idealists kill me. You really do, you know. No matter what the *cause* is, the fact remains that we *are* crabs in a barrel. Now deal with that, nigger!

JOHN: Aw, go screw yourself.

DUDLEY: There you go. Hate the truth, don't you? The truth is, you're a dying wino nigger who's trying to find some reason for living. And now you're going to put that burden on your son. Poor Jeff! Doesn't know what he's in for.

JOHN (*pausing*): The fact remains, monkey-chasing son-of-a-bitch, the fact remains that I got a son coming home from the air force tomorrow and you ain't got nobody— (*A loving afterthought*) but me—

DUDLEY: You are a big fool! Jessie wanted children. Every time she missed her period, I'd give her something to start it over again. Poor lovable bitch, till the day she died she never knew. But I knew—I knew it was a heinous crime to bring any more children into this pile of horse shit.

JOHN: You're sick, you know that, monkey chaser—sick. To satisfy your own perverted outlook, you'd destroy your wife's right to motherhood. Sick!

DUDLEY: The day Jessie died she made me promise I'd marry again and have children, and I lied to her—told her I would—Didn't make her dying any easier, though. She still died twitching and convulsing, saliva running from the corners of her mouth—death phlegm rattling in her throat. She still died gruesomely. That's the way it is. That's life! I'm the last of my line—thank God. No more suffering for the Stantons. Thank God—that cruel son-of-a-bitch.

JOHN: You depress the shit out of me, you know that, monkey chaser— but you can still be my friend, even if you're just a chickenhearted rabbit, afraid to make a motion.

DUDLEY (*genuinely angry*): Look, nigger—any motion you make is on a treadmill.

JOHN: Aw, drink ya drink. What's the matter with you? It don't take no genius to figure out that none of this shit's gonna matter a hundred years from now—that the whole thing's a game of musical chairs—so what? What's your favorite word—presumptuous? Well, man, it is presumptuous as hell of you to even think you can figure this shit out.

DUDLEY: Ain't that what we're here for, stupid? What we've got brains for? To figure it out?

JOHN: Hell no! To play a better game, fool. Just play the motherfucker, that's all. And right now the game is Free My People. Ya get that!

And if you don't play it, nigger, you know what you're gonna become—what you *are*—you know what you are, Dr. Dudley Stanton? You're a goddamn spiritual vegetable. Thinking's for idiots—wise men act; thinking is all dribble anyhow, and idiots can do a helluva damn better job at it than you can. My advice to you, Mr. Monkey Chaser, is fart, piss, screw, eat, fight, run, beat your meat, sympathize, and criticize, but for God's sake, stop thinking. It's the white folks' sickness.

DUDLEY: I'm talking to a bloody amoeba.

JOHN: Amoebas are the foundation, man, and they ain't got no blood. Now loan me one hundred and ninety dollars.

DUDLEY: What?

JOHN: A hundred and ninety dollars—shit. Don't I speak clearly? I had two years of college, you know.

DUDLEY: You drank all your money away?

JOHN: Hell yes.

DUDLEY: At the Apple?

JOHN: Right!

DUDLEY: Setting up everybody and his ma?

JOHN: Uh huh!

DUDLEY: Bragging like a nigger about how your first lieutenant, Air Force, Strategic Air Command son is due home tomorrow?

JOHN: Right!

DUDLEY: And they all smiled, patted you on your back, and ordered two more rounds of three-for-one bar slop?

JOHN: Right, nigger. Now, do I get the bread or not—Shit, I ain't required to give you my life story for a measly handout—

DUDLEY: Of a hundred and ninety dollars—

JOHN: Shit! Right!

DUDLEY: You already owe me three hundred and forty.

JOHN: That much?

DUDLEY (*taking out a small notebook*): See for yourself—

JOHN: Well, a hundred and ninety more won't break you. Do I get it or not?

(*There is a knock on the front door.*)

Come on, man, that's Mattie.

DUDLEY: Well, well, well, look at the great warrior now—about to get his ass kicked!

JOHN: Come on! Yes or no?

DUDLEY: But here's your battlefield, man. Start fighting! I tell you one thing though, I'm putting my money on Mattie, man.

(*Again there is a knock on the front door.*)

JOHN: See ya later. (*Starts for the back door*)
DUDLEY: Wait a minute! If it were Mattie, she'd use her key, right?
JOHN (*coming back*): Hey, yeah, that's right. Didn't think of that!
DUDLEY: You don't believe in thinking.

(JOHN *goes to door and sneaks a look through the pane.*)

JOHN (*coming back*): Hey, it's a young chick. Good legs—like she might
have a halfway decent turd cutter on her.
DUDLEY: Let her in, man, let her in!
JOHN: Look—am I going to get the money?
DUDLEY (*interrupting him*): We'll talk about it. I ain't saying yes and I
ain't saying no.
JOHN: Sadistic bastard!

(*A more insistent knock*)

DUDLEY: Open the goddamn door, nigger!

(JOHN *opens the door.* ANN VANDERGUILD—*a very attractive black
woman in her early twenties—enters. She sparkles on top of a deep
brooding inner core. A bass line of beautiful melancholy comes in.*)

JOHN: Yes, ma'am.
ANN: I'm Ann—
JOHN: Uh huh.
ANN: I'm a friend of Jeff Williams's. This, uh, is his, where he lives,
isn't it?
JOHN: When he's home, yes. He won't be here until noon tomorrow.
ANN: Yes, I know—may I come in?
JOHN: Oh, I'm sorry. Come in.
ANN: Would you help me with my suitcases? They're in the cab.
JOHN: Suitcases!
ANN: Yes, I'd like to spend the night—if I may.
JOHN: Spend the night—
DUDLEY (*coming in from the kitchen*): Go get the young lady's suitcases,
man. And close the damn door. It's colder than a virgin's—(*Catches
himself*)
JOHN: Suitcases!

(JOHN *exits.* DUDLEY *and* ANN *size each other up.*)

DUDLEY: Come on in. Let me have your coat.
ANN: Thank-you.

DUDLEY: So you're Jeff's intended?

ANN: Well, not exactly, sir. We're very good friends, though.

DUDLEY: But you intend to make yourself Jeff's intended. Am I right?

(ANN *smiles.*)

What a nice smile! Then I am right. Have a seat—

(JOHN *staggers into the room with an armful of suitcases, plops them down, stares at* ANN *for a second. Bass fades.*)

JOHN: There's more. (*Exits*)

DUDLEY: Planning a long stay?

ANN: I'll go to a hotel tomorrow.

DUDLEY: I wasn't saying that for that. I'm merely intrigued with your determination. Young women—strong-willed young women—always fascinate me.

(JOHN *enters with a small trunk on his back which he unloads heavily.*)

JOHN: That'll be three dollars and fifty cents, young lady.

DUDLEY: I've got it, Miss—What's your last name?

ANN: Vanderguild.

DUDLEY: Miss Vanderguild.

ANN: I wouldn't think of it.

DUDLEY (*hurriedly pays* JOHN, *who is somewhat bewildered*): I told you about my weakness for strong women. My mother was strong. Lord, how strong. Could work all day and half the night.

JOHN: Flat on her back! Anybody can do that.

DUDLEY: Only a strong woman, man. Besides, who says she was always on her back. I'm certain she was versatile. Sorry, dear. We're two very dirty old men. Stick out your tongue!

ANN: What is this—

DUDLEY (*grabbing her wrist, examining her pulse*): Stick out your tongue, young lady!

(*She obeys like a child.*)

Had a rather severe cold recently, girl?

ANN: Why yes, but . . .

DUDLEY: You're all right now. Can tell a lot from tongues.

JOHN: There you go, getting vulgar again. You can take a man out of his mother, but you can't take the mother out of the man.

DUDLEY: That's just his way of getting back at me. Actually, I loved my mother very much. She worked my way through college and medical school, though I didn't find out how until the day I graduated.

JOHN: Stop putting your business in the street!

DUDLEY: I'm not. It's all in the family. Miss Ann Vanderguild here's a part of the family, or almost. Ann, here, is your prospective daughter-in-law, and she'll make a good one too, Johnny. I stamp her certified.

JOHN (*to* ANN): Jeff never wrote us about you.

ANN: Well, he doesn't exactly know I'm here, sir. I mean we never discussed it or anything.

JOHN: Where you from, little lady?

ANN: Canada, sir—I mean, originally I'm from South Africa, sir.

JOHN: This gentleman here is Dudley Stanton. Dr. Dudley Stanton.

ANN (*to* DUDLEY): My EKG is excellent too, sir.

DUDLEY: Excellent?

ANN: I mean it's within normal limits, sir. I guess my pulse is very slow, because I used to run track—the fifty-yard dash. I'm a nurse. Perhaps you can help me find a job, sir?

DUDLEY: Oh, these strong black women!

ANN: I'm only strong if my man needs me to be, sir.

JOHN (*genuinely elated*): You hear that, Dudley, a warrior's woman! A fighter—

DUDLEY: Women always were the real fighters, man, don't you know that? Men are the artists, philosophers—creating systems, worlds. Silly dreams and fictions!

JOHN: Fiction is more real, stupid.

DUDLEY: You see, young lady, your prospective father-in-law here is a philosopher-poet!

JOHN: A poet!

DUDLEY: Philosopher-poet!

JOHN: I'm a poet! A house painter and a poet!

DUDLEY: Then read us one of your masterpieces.

JOHN: Do I have to, Dudley?

DUDLEY: A hundred and ninety bucks' worth—hell yes! You don't think I come over here to hear your bull, do you? Your poems, man, by far the better part of you—now read us one—then give it to me. (*To* ANN) You see, I'm collecting them for him, since he doesn't have enough sense to do it for himself—One day I'm gonna publish them—

JOHN: Probably under your own name, you goddamn Jew.

DUDLEY: Read us your poem!

(JOHN *fumbles through his pants pockets and comes up with several scraps of paper, which he examines for selection. He smooths out one piece of paper and begins reading.*)

JOHN: *I am the River Niger—hear my waters—*
   No, that one ain't right yet.
ANN: Please go on!
JOHN: No, it ain't complete yet. Let's see, yeah, this one's finished.

   (*Begins reading from another scrap of paper as lights fade to a soft amber.
   A bass jazz theme creeps in.* JOHN *is spotlighted.*)

   "Lord, I don't feel noways tired."
   And my soul seeks not to be flabby.
   Peace is a muscleless word,
   A vacuum, a hole in space,
   An assless anesthesia,
   A shadowy phantom,
   Never settling anyway—Even in sleep.
   In my dreams I struggle; slash and crash and cry,
   "Damn you, you wilderness! I will cut my way through!"
   And the wilderness shouts back!
   "Go around me!"
   And I answer,
   "Hell, no! The joke's on both of us
   And I will have the last laugh."
   The wilderness sighs and grows stronger
   As I too round out my biceps in this ageless, endless duel.
   Hallelujah! Hallelujah! Hallelujah!
   I want a muscle-bound spirit,
   I say, I want a muscle-bound soul—'cause,
   Lord, I don't feel noways tired.
   I feel like dancing through the valley of the shadow of death!
   Lord, I don't feel noways tired.
ANN: Beautiful!

   (*Bass fades.*)

DUDLEY (*taking sheet of paper*): This is a blank sheet of paper!
JOHN: I made it up as I went along. Hell, I'll write it down for you.

   (*Holds out his hand insistently for the money.* DUDLEY *counts it out. The
   doorbell rings suddenly and* MATTIE's *voice is heard—"Mama—John."*
   JOHN *takes the money eagerly, stuffs it in his pocket, then starts for the
   door. En route he stops suddenly, looks at* ANN *as if in a dilemma, thinks
   quickly, then crosses to* ANN *and whispers urgently.*)

   Look, Ann, if my wife thinks for one minute that you're trying to get
   Jeff hooked, she and her crazy mama'll reduce the whole thing to

ashes. Tell 'em you're just passing through—you and Jeff were friends up there in Canada—just friends, see—

DUDLEY: Gradually—you've got to ease in gradually. They think Jeff fell off a Christmas tree or something. No one's good enough for Jeff— Not even Jeff.

JOHN: Act like a good-natured sleep-in—

ANN: Sleep-in?

DUDLEY: A maid!

MATTIE: Will someone please open the door! I can't get to my key.

GRANDMA (*at the top of the stairs; slightly intoxicated*): I'm coming, daughter. I'm coming—(*Starts humming "Rock of Ages" as she descends the stairs*)

JOHN (*to* ANN): Now remember. (*Opens door*) Hello, Mattie!

MATTIE: The groceries—help me with the groceries.

ANN: Let me give you a hand, Mrs. Williams.

(DUDLEY *gestures to* ANN *approvingly.* MATTIE *takes off her coat, kicks off her shoes, and settles in an easy chair while* ANN *and* JOHN *take the groceries to the kitchen.*)

MATTIE: Who's that young lady?

DUDLEY: A friend of the family.

GRANDMA: How you feeling, daughter? Look a bit peaked to me.

MATTIE: Not too well, Mama; almost fainted on the subway. Was all I could do to get the groceries.

JOHN (*coming back*): Just need a little soda and water, that's all.

MATTIE: That's what you always say. Something is wrong with me, John. I don't know what, but something's wrong.

DUDLEY: Tomorrow's Saturday. Why don't you come into my office around eleven, let me take a look at you?

MATTIE: No thanks, Dudley. You always manage to scare a person half to death. Have you ever heard of a doctor who ain't got no bedside manner at all, Mama? (*Laughs*)

DUDLEY: Well, what do you want—the truth or somebody to hold your hand?

GRANDMA: Both, fool.

MATTIE: Mama!

GRANDMA: Well, he is a fool.

DUDLEY: Well, I guess that's my cue to go home!

JOHN: I'll be damned! Mrs. Wilhemina Brown is going to apologize—

GRANDMA: Over my dead husband's grave—

MATTIE: Mama. You must not feel well yourself.

GRANDMA: I don't, child, I don't. Planned to have your dinner ready, but I been feeling kinda poorly here lately.

JOHN: That's what she always says.

MATTIE: Come to think of it, Mama, your eyes—

GRANDMA (*defensively*): What about my eyes?

MATTIE: Well, they look kinda glassy—

JOHN (*knowingly*): I wonder why?

GRANDMA (*on her feet*): And what in the Lord's name is that supposed to mean?

MATTIE (*raising her voice*): Will you stop it—all of you.

GRANDMA (*to* MATTIE): Are you talking to me? You screaming at your mama?

MATTIE: At everybody, Mama.

GRANDMA: My own daughter, my own flesh and blood, taking a nogood drunk's part against her own mother.

MATTIE: I'm not taking anybody's part. I just want some peace and quiet when I come home. Now I think you owe Dr. Stanton an apology.

GRANDMA: I'll do no such thing. (*Starts humming "Rock of Ages"*)

MATTIE: I apologize for my mother, Dudley.

DUDLEY: That's okay, Mattie, I wasn't going anywhere anyway.

GRANDMA: I got two more daughters and two manly sons. They'd just love to have me. Maybe I should go live with Flora.

JOHN: Good idea! Plenty of opportunity to get glassy-eyed over at Flora's. Yes, indeed.

MATTIE: John, what are you agitating her for?

DUDLEY: Are you afraid, Mattie? To have a checkup, I mean?

MATTIE (*pausing*): Stay for dinner, Dudley.

DUDLEY: Thanks, I will.

ANN (*at the door*): Would you like for me to fix dinner, Mrs. Williams? (*Pause.*)

MATTIE: Who is this child?

JOHN: Ann Vanderguild. She's from South Africa. She's a friend of Jeff's—just passing through. I asked her to spend the night.

GRANDMA: Where's she going to spend it—the bathroom?

MATTIE: Mama, what's wrong with you tonight?

JOHN: She had a little too much, that's all.

MATTIE (*to* ANN): You're welcome, dear. You can stay in Jeff's room tonight. I got it all cleaned up for him. He'll be her tomorrow, you know? Thank the Lord.

ANN: Yes, ma'am! It certainly will be pleasant to see him again.

(MATTIE *looks at* ANN *curiously.*)

I make a very good meat loaf, ma'am. I noticed you've got all the ingredients as I was putting the food away.

MATTIE: You put the food away?

ANN: You seem so bushed.

MATTIE: What a nice thing for you to do. And you read my mind too. Meat loaf is exactly what I was planning to fix. Yes, indeed. Such a pretty girl too.

JOHN (*to* DUDLEY): Why don't we make a little run and leave these black beauties to themselves. To get acquainted—

GRANDMA: Don't be calling me no black nothing. I ain't black! I'm half-full-blooded Cherokee Indian myself. Black folks is "hewers of wood and drawers of water" for their masters. Says so in the Scriptures. I ain't no hewer of no wood myself. I'm a Cherokee aristocrat myself.

JOHN: Go on, Grandma, show us your true Cherokee colors, yes, indeed.

GRANDMA (*obviously inebriated—singing at the top of her voice*)
Onward, Christian soldiers,
Marching on to war,
With the cross of Jesus
Going on before!

(*Begins shouting as if in church*)

I'm a soldier myself. I ain't no nigger. A soldier of the Lord. I ain't no common nigger. So don't you be calling me no black nothing. Bless my Jesus. Don't know what these young folks is coming to, calling everybody black!
I'm going home to see my Jesus.
This little light of mine,
Let it shine, let it shine, oh, let it shine. Do Jesus!

(*Shouting gestures*)

DUDLEY: What I tell you, Johnny. Crabs in a barrel, waiting for a hand from Canaan land to lift 'em out. Each one shoving and pushing, trying to be first to go. And if Jesus was to put his hand down there, they'd probably think it belonged to just another nigger crab and pinch it off.

JOHN: Ain't that poetic. I can just read the headlines: "Jesus extends his hand to bless his chosen"—'cause we are the chosen, Dudley—"and a hustling dope addict takes out his blade and cuts it off at the wrist."

DUDLEY: For the ring on his little finger. Rub-a-dub-dub, niggers in a tub. Christ extends a helping hand and (JOHN *joins in and they deliver the end of the line in unison*) draws back a nub.

MATTIE: WILL YOU TWO PLEASE STOP IT!

(GRANDMA'S *still singing.*)

Mama, why don't you go upstairs and take a rest. Ya'll 'bout to drive me crazy.

GRANDMA: My own daughter treats me like a child. Sending me upstairs. Punishing me 'cause I got the spirit.

(*Starting for the stair. Starts singing once again, but in a more subdued and soulful manner*)

I know his blood will make me whole.
I know his blood will make me whole.
If I just touch the hem of his garment
I know his blood will make me whole.

(JOHN *tries to help her up the stairs.*)

Don't need no help from nobody but Jesus. (*Starts up steps*) I got Minerva and Flora, and Jacob and Jordan—fine children. Any one of 'em be tickled pink to have me—tickled pink! I don't have to stay here.

MATTIE: Mama, go lie down for a while.

GRANDMA: And ain't none of 'em black either. Christian soldiers every last one of 'em. Mattie's the only black child I ever spawned—my first and last, thank Jesus. (GRANDMA *starts up the steps—on the verge of tears*) I don't have to stay here— (*Sings*)
I ain't got long,
I ain't got long
To stay here.
Ben Brown was black though. Looked like an eclipse—sho' nuff.
Lord, my God, hallelujah and do Jesus—he was the ace of spades.
And a man, afore God, he was a man—you hear me, Johnny Williams? My man was a man.

(*Exits, humming "Steal Away"*)

MATTIE (*to* ANN): She gets like that every now and then.
JOHN: More like every other night.
MATTIE: We have a guest, John.
JOHN: Come on, Dudley, let's make that run!
MATTIE: Hold on, Johnny Williams. Where is it?

JOHN: Where's what?

MATTIE: Don't play games, John. This is rent week—remember. Now give it to me.

DUDLEY: All right, great African warrior, do your stuff.

JOHN: Mind your business—

MATTIE: John, I don't feel well. Now, do we have to play your games tonight—Now give it to me.

(JOHN *counts out the money and gives it to her. She counts it rapidly.*)

It's ten dollars short, John.

JOHN: Come on, Mattie. I got to have train fare and cigarettes for the next two weeks.

MATTIE: Stop playing, Johnny. You know if I don't keep it for you, you'll drink it up all at once. Come on, now.

(*He gives her the ten.*)

JOHN: Look, let me have five at least. There's more than enough for the rent. (*Pause.*) Good God, woman, Jeff'll be here tomorrow. Dudley and I just want to do a little celebrating. Five, woman, hell.

MATTIE: Promise you won't be out late. We got a lot of gettin' ready to do tomorrow morning.

JOHN: I got this chick, see, sixteen years old, and she is as warm as gingerbread in the wintertime, and we gon' lay up all night—

MATTIE: We have a young lady here, Johnny.

JOHN: Jeff'll be here by noon. Now, let's see! My little mama just might let me out of the saddle by noon. Yes, indeed—she just might!

MATTIE: JOHN!

JOHN: But if I'm not back in time, Jeff'll understand—ain't too often a man my age gets himself into some young and tender, oven-ready, sixteen-year-old stuff what can shake her some tail feathers like the leaves in March.

(*She hands him the five.*)

MATTIE: Get out of here, Johnny Williams.

DUDLEY: Whew! What a warrior—have mercy! You sure do win your battles, man!

JOHN: Oh, shut up! Why fight when you know you're wrong. Let's go!

MATTIE: Dudley—don't let him overdo it. Tomorrow's gonna be a long day.

(JOHN *gets their coats from the hallway.*)

DUDLEY: I'll do my best, Mattie . . .

JOHN (*coming back*): Don't worry—this black-ass Jew ain't gon' spend enough to even get a buzz—he'll watch over me—just like an old mongrel hound dog I used to own. Damn dog stayed sober all the time—wouldn't even drink beer. He was the squarest, most unhip dog in the world! Come on, monkey chaser, let me tell you 'bout that dog. Named him Shylock!

DUDLEY: Niggers invented name-calling. Mouth, that's all they are, mouth. Good night, ladies. Ann, see you tomorrow.

JOHN: Come on, sickle head. See ya, Ann!

DUDLEY: I'm coming, O great African warrior!

(*They exit.*)

MATTIE: Well, Ann, now you've met the whole family. I hope Johnny's cussing don't bother you too much.

ANN: No, ma'am I think he's delightful—he and Dr. Stanton. My father had a friend like him—always attacking each other something terrible.

MATTIE: Sometimes they get to going at each other so hard you think they're gonna come to blows.

ANN: But when they put my father in prison—

MATTIE: In prison—for what?

ANN: They accused him of printing these pamphlets which criticized the government—

MATTIE: Lord, you can't criticize the government over there?

ANN: No, ma'am. Anyway, just after my father was jailed, his friend just pined away. God—those two men loved each other.

MATTIE: Men can really love each other, and the funny thing about it is, don't nobody really know it but them.

ANN: Women don't seem to be able to get along with each other that way—I mean that deep-loving way. You know what I mean, Mrs. Williams?

MATTIE: Of course I do. It's all 'cause women don't trust one another. Your father? Is he still in prison?

ANN: Yes, ma'am. This is going on his ninth year.

MATTIE: Nine years in prison, my God! How does your mother take it?

(*Bass melancholy enters.*)

ANN: Quietly. Ma takes everything quietly. Dad turned himself in to protect my two brothers. They were the ones operating the press. Dad was just as surprised as the rest of us when the police found the setup in an old chest of drawers in the attic. Before anyone could say a word, Dad was confessing to everything. This dirty old sergeant got mad and hit him in the stomach with his billy club. Dad had a violent temper, but when he got back on his feet, I could see it in his eyes, the decision, I mean. He turned and said, "Boss, if I said something offensive, please forgive an old black fool." And you know what that sergeant did? He hit him again. He hit him again, Mrs. Williams! (*Overcome with rekindled grief*)

MATTIE: Oh, I'm sorry, Ann. I must write your mother.

ANN: She'd like that. (*Pause. She collects herself.*) My brothers escaped though—stole their way across the border. At first they didn't want to go, they wanted to turn themselves in for Dad, but Ma made 'em go. They live in England now and have families of their own. It wasn't long before the authorities found out that Dad was really innocent, but just because my brothers got away and are free, and just to be plain mean, they kept him in prison anyway. Nine years—nine long years. Those bastards! I despise white people, Mrs. Williams.

MATTIE: Let's talk about something nicer. Tell me about Jeff—

(*Bass fades.*)

ANN: Yes, ma'am.

MATTIE: And you—

ANN: Ma'am?

MATTIE: About Jeff and you . . . or you and Jeff.

ANN: I was nursing in Quebec when they brought him into the hospital. He had fractured his ankle skiing. Every time it started paining him, he'd laugh—

MATTIE: He's such a fool.

ANN: Said his dad had taught him to do that. The second night there were some minor complications and he was in so much pain until the doctor ordered me to give him a shot of morphine. Then he got to talking. Very dreamily at first, like he was drifting in a beautiful haze. He told me all about you and Mr. Williams and Grandma Wilhemina Brown and Dr. Stanton. I almost lost my job—I kept hanging around his room so much, listening to one episode after another.

MATTIE: And that's when you started loving him half to death.

ANN (*pausing*): Yes, ma'am.

MATTIE: That boy sure can talk up a storm. He'll make a fine lawyer. Don't you think so?

ANN (*pausing*): I won't get in his way, Mrs. Williams.

MATTIE (*after a long pause*): No, I don't think you will. (*Pause.*) Well, let's see if we can trust each other good enough to make that meat loaf. Why don't you chop the onions while I do the celery? (*Starts to rise*)

ANN (*stopping her*): Oh, no, ma'am, this one's on me.

MATTIE (*laughing*): I'm very particular, you know.

ANN: I know you are. Jeff's told me a lot about how good your cooking is.

MATTIE (*happy to hear it*): That boy sure can eat—Lord today. Well, all right, Ann. Let me go on up and get myself comfortable. I'll be right back. (*She sees the jewelry box on the table—opens it up—takes out a card.*) What's this? (*Reads card*) "Big-legged woman, keep your dress tail down. Big-legged woman, keep your dress tail down, 'cause you got something under—"

ANN: Go on, Mrs. Williams.

MATTIE: Lord, child, that man of mine.

ANN: Read it, please ma'am.

MATTIE: "Big-legged woman, keep your dress tail down, 'cause you got something under there to make a bulldog hug a hound."

(*They laugh.*)

Tomorrow's our anniversary, you know.

ANN: Congratulations!

MATTIE: He made this. Can do anything with his hands, or with his head for that matter, when he ain't all filled up on rotgut. (*Pause.*) He's killing himself drinking. I guess I'm to blame though.

ANN: Oh, you don't mean that, Mrs. Williams.

MATTIE: It's true.

ANN: But he seems so full of life.

MATTIE: Is it "life" he's full of—or something else?

(MATTIE *exits up the steps.* ANN *busies herself about the kitchen. There is a knock on the front door.*)

MATTIE'S VOICE: Will you get that, please, Ann?

ANN: Yes, ma'am.

(*She crosses and opens the door. A tall, rangy young man in his early twenties rudely pushes his way in. He looks around boldly. He has an air of "I'm a bad nigger" about him*)

CHIPS: Jeff here?

ANN (*sarcastically*): Come in!

CHIPS: I'm already in. Is Jeff home yet?

ANN: Are you a friend of Jeff's?

CHIPS: Could be. You a friend of Jeff's?

ANN: Yes.

CHIPS (*looking her over lewdly*): Not bad! As a matter of fact, you look pretty stacked up there.

ANN: Jeff's not home.

CHIPS: Hey, what kinda accent is that? You puttin' on airs or something—

(*She opens the door.*)

Yeah, yeah, I'm going. Tell him Chips came by. Big Mo wants to see him at headquarters as soon as possible. Like it's urgent, ya dig it?

ANN: He won't be here until noon tomorrow.

CHIPS: That's what he wrote the family. He wrote Mo—

ANN: Who's Mo?

CHIPS (*laughing*): Who's Mo? Mo's the leader.

ANN: The leader of what?

CHIPS: The leader! Wrote Mo he'd be here tonight. Tell him we'll be back around midnight. (*Leers at* ANN) Yes, sir—just like a brick shithouse.

(CHIPS *slaps her on the rear.* ANN *instinctively picks up a heavy ashtray.*)

Now, don't get rambunctious! If there's anything I can't stand it's a rambunctious black bitch.

ANN: You get the hell out of here!

CHIPS (*taking out a switchblade*): Now, what's that ashtray gonna do? If I wanted to, I could cut your drawers off without touching your petticoat and take what I want. Now, dig on that?

ANN: Over my dead body.

CHIPS: I made it with a corpse once. Knew a guy that worked in a funeral home. Pretty chick too—looked something like you. Wasn't half bad either—once I got into it.

ANN: You damn dog—get out of here!

CHIPS (*laughing*): Yeah, little fox. I'm going, but I'll be back tonight with Big Mo. (*Exits*)

(ANN *slams the door. She is obviously shaken.* MATTIE *comes down the step wearing a robe and house slippers.*)

MATTIE: Who was that, honey? (*Sees* ANN'*s fear*) What happened?

ANN: Some fellow to see Jeff. Called himself Chips.

MATTIE: Chips! That bum! If he or any of them other bums show up around here again, you call somebody. They're vicious! Come on, sit down. Catch your breath.

ANN: I'm fine.

MATTIE: Do as I say now!

(ANN *sits.*)

I wonder what they want with Jeff. Jeff used to be the gang leader around here when he was a teenager. By the time he go to college, Jeff and his friend Mo had made the gang decent—you know, doing good things to help the neighborhood. But I heard lately, the bums gone back to their old ways. I wonder what they want with Jeff now. . . . Well, let's get this thing ready and into the oven so we can eat, and you can get a good night's rest. You must be exhausted. Bought a new bed for Jeff. You'll sleep like a log.

ANN: Doesn't the couch in the living room let out into a bed, ma'am?

MATTIE: Why, yes.

ANN: Then I'll sleep on the couch. If it's all right with you.

MATTIE: Jeff wouldn't mind a bit you sleeping in his new bed, child! He'll probably say something vulgar about it. Chip off the old block, you know.

ANN: Let it be fresh for him, ma'am, let him christen it with that pretty long frame of his.

MATTIE (*laughing*): Is he skinny, Ann?

ANN: As a rail.

MATTIE: You're welcome to stay as long as you want. But no tomfoolery between you two, ya understand?

ANN: Oh, no, ma'am.

MATTIE: And another thing. Between you and me and the lamppost, don't let on to my mother how you feel about Jeff. She don't think nobody's good enough for Jeff. Says he's the spittin' image of my father. Lord, child, she sure loved my father. I'm very lucky in a way, Ann. I come from very loving parents—in their fashion.

ANN: Yes, ma'am, I can see that!

MATTIE: I've often wondered why my sisters turned out to be such hogs.

(*They start on food preparations as lights fade out. When the lights come up once more, the house is in darkness.* ANN *is asleep on the living-room couch. It is 2 A.M. There is a low rapping at the front door.* ANN *bolts upright. The knocking becomes insistent. Sleepily she answers the door.*)

ANN: Is that you, Mr. Williams?

(*No response*)

Mr. Williams?

(*No answer. She opens the door.* MO, *an athletic-looking young man in his mid-twenties; his girlfriend,* GAIL, *sincere and very much in love with* MO; SKEETER, *who seems constantly out of it and desperate;* AL, *who appears to be intensely observant; and* CHIPS—*all force their way in.*)

CHIPS: Ann—Big Mo. Big Mo—Ann.

MO: Hello, Ann.

CHIPS: Ain't she fine, Mo?

GAIL: Why don't you hush your lips! Simpleton!

MO (*to* GAIL): Cool it! (*To* CHIPS) Get yourself together, Chips!

AL: Yeah! Get yourself together, nigger. It's past the witching hour.

MO (*ferociously to everybody*): Ease off! Ease off me! (*Silent respect*) Is Jeff home?

ANN: No!

MO: No! How ya mean—no?

ANN: Just what I said—no!

CHIPS: She's a smarty, Mo.

MO: Okay. You sound like you're for real!

CHIPS: She is, Mo, baby—she is! Let me squeeze up on her a bit.

MO (*intensely*): Shut the fuck up! Excuse me, Ann. (*To* CHIPS) And sit down somewhere. (*To* SKEETER, *falling asleep in the chair*) You fall asleep—I'm gonna crack your skull, nigger!

SKEETER: Just meditating, chief—just meditating.

MO (*to* ANN): Pardon that dumb shit, baby, but, er, we gonna wait right here till your man shows—all right?

ANN: Look! It is 2 A.M. in the morning. Jeff won't be here until noon. Now what is it that can't wait till noon?

MO: I can't wait. (*Pause.*) Besides—said he'd be here tonight!

ANN: You know what I think? I think you're being very rude—a bunch of very rude bastards! That's what I think.

CHIPS: Let me squeeze up on her a bit, Big Mo!

(*The conversation is interrupted by the somewhat noisy entrance of* JOHN *and* DUDLEY *through the back door*)

DUDLEY: That's all you ever do! Blow off at the mouth! Blow off! Blow off! Pardon me, but kiss my brown eye!

JOHN: Looks too much like your face.

DUDLEY: You gimme a royal pain. Give me one for the road, and let me go home.

JOHN: One for the road! Why didn't you buy one for the road before we hit the road. Shylock stingy bastard.

ANN: Mr. Williams! Mr. Williams!

JOHN (*coming into the living room—closely followed by* DUDLEY): Yes, Ann—sweet Ann? (*Sees the crowd*) Company, I see.

ANN: Unwanted company, sir.

MO: We're gonna wait for Jeff, Mr. Williams—that's all.

JOHN: Is that Mo—Mo Hayes?

MO: Yes, it is.

JOHN: Well, well, well—I ain't seen you since Skippy was a punk.

MO: I've been around, Mr. Williams.

JOHN: Nice to see you again, son. Who're your friends?

MO (*introducing them*): Well, sir, this is Gail—my girl. Chips and
Skeeter, remember? And Al.

JOHN: Nice to meet you.

(*They exchange greetings.*)

Now go home, gentlemen. It's the wee hours of the morning.

MO: We're gonna wait for Jeff.

GAIL: Let's go, Mo, we can come back later.

JOHN: What'd you say, Li'l Mo? Aint that your nickname? Li'l Mo?
Ain't that what we used to call you?

MO: I said, "We're gonna wait for Jeff."

JOHN: We're planning a celebration for Jeff noon tomorrow, and you're
welcome to come—all of you. But that's noon tomorrow.

MO: Can't leave until I see Jeff. Sorry.

JOHN: You're "sorry." You wait until you see how sorry I am when I get
back—okay. (*Exits*)

GAIL: Mo, baby, let's go. Jeff ain't gon' run nowhere. I mean, what's
the hurry?

CHIPS (*eyeing* ANN): Yeah, what's the hurry?

GAIL (*turning on him*): You should be in the biggest hurry, nigger, 'cause
when Jeff finds out how you been insulting his woman, you're gonna
be in a world of trouble.

DUDLEY: Gentlemen, I'd advise you all to leave. Before something
presumptuous happens. Can never tell about these black African
warrior niggers.

AL (*pushing* DUDLEY *into a chair*): Shut up.

DUDLEY (*blessing himself*): Father, forgive them, for they know not what
they do.

(JOHN *comes back with an M-1 and a World War II hand grenade.*)

JOHN (*highly intoxicated but even mor deadly serious because of it*): Yeah—
well, Father may forgive 'em, but I don't, not worth a damn.

CHIPS: You ain't the only one in here with a smoking machine, man.
(*Opens his coat to reveal a shoulder holster and a revolver*)

MO: Close your jacket, stupid.

JOHN: Come over here, Ann. Dudley, get your drunk self outta that
chair and make it on over here.

(*They follow his instructions.*)

(*To them*) I don't know if this old grenade'll work or not, but when I pull the pin and throw it at them niggers, we duck into the kitchen — all right.

AL: This old stud's crazy as shit.

MO: Shut up.

CHIPS: I bet he's faking.

(*Reaches for his revolver.* JOHN *instantly throws the bolt on the M-1. They all freeze for a long moment; finally . . .*)

MO (*laughing*): You win. You win, Mr. Williams. Dig it? We'll see ya 'round noon. Let's go.

(*They file out.* MO *stops at the door, still laughing.*)

Ya got some real stuff going for you, Mr. Williams.

DUDLEY: Impressive. Presumptuous as hell, but impressive.

(*At this moment* GRANDMA *comes down the steps. She pretends to be sleepwalking. She hums "Rock of Ages" under her breath.*)

JOHN: Shh. The old bag's dreaming.

DUDLEY: What?

JOHN: I've been waiting for this a solid week, Dudley.

DUDLEY: What?

JOHN: Shh. You said you wanted one for the road, didn't you? Then be patient, nigger, be patient.

(GRANDMA *makes her way into the kitchen — seeing nobody. Bass line enters.*)

GRANDMA: Possum ain't nothing but a big rat. I used to say so to Big Ben Brown. "Call it what you want, wife." Always called me wife, you know. "Possum sure got a powerful wild taste to it." (*She finds her hiding place, pours herself a huge glass of whiskey — talking all the time.*) That big old black man of mine. Sure could hunt him some possum. Always knew exactly where to find 'em. I sure hated picking out the buckshot though. Sometimes I'd miss one or two, and I'd jes' be eating and all a sudden I chomp down on one. Lordy, that was a hurting thing. Felt like my tooth was gonna split wide open. Sassafras root — and burning pine cones. Do Jesus! Possum's got a wild taste.

(*Bass line fades out.* JOHN *throws his keys into the hall. Startled,* GRANDMA *caps the bottle, hides it, and mumbles her way back up the*

steps, intermittently humming "Rock of Ages." When she's out of sight,
JOHN *lets out a yelp, gets* GRANDMA's *bottle, and pours each of them
a drink.)*

JOHN: Here's to Grandmammy.

(*They drink as* JEFF *enters silently, loaded down with duffel bags and
luggage. He sees them, sneaks into hallway without being seen, and hides.*)

Here's to us. (*Again*) Here's to Jeff. (*Again*) Here's to his daddy.
(*Again*) Here's to his sweet old mama. Here's to Jesus Christ—one of
the baddest cats to ever drop.

(*They exchange "good nights."* DUDLEY *exits front door.* JOHN *goes
upstairs.* ANN *goes back to sofa—switches off light. Lights fade to night.
Music covers.* JEFF *enters, sees* ANN *on sofa, and is very pleased. He is a
lanky young man in his middle twenties. There is a heavy seriousness about
him, frosted over with the wildness he has inherited from his father. His
presence is strong and commanding. He is dressed casually in a turtleneck,
bell-bottom slacks, boots, and long-styled topcoat. Magazines protrude
from his overcoat pocket. His hair is a modified or shortened afro. His face
is clean. He takes off his coat, sits directly opposite* ANN, *fumbles in his
pockets, comes up with a plastic bag of marijuana, rolls a joint, and lights
up. After a couple of puffs, he leans over and kisses* ANN *on the lips. She
groans; he then takes a heavy drag on the joint and blows it full in her face.
She awakens with a soft sputter. She is overwhelmed at seeing him.
Without saying a word, he extends the joint to her. She sits upright and
drags on it. He grabs her foot and gently kisses the arch.*)

JEFF: Three whole days—um, um—and I sho' have missed them big old
feet of yours.
ANN (*handing him the joint*): Are my feet big?
JEFF: Why do you think I always walk behind you in the snow? You got
natural snowshoes, baby. (*He grabs her roughly but lovingly and
kisses her.*)
ANN: I had to come, Jeff.
JEFF: I know. Now, let's get down to the nitty-gritty. How 'bout some
loving, mama?
ANN: Oh, Jeff—I promised your mother.
JEFF: She won't know. And whatcha don't know—(*Starts taking off his
clothes, talking as he does*) My dad taught me that where there's a will,
there's a way.
ANN: Your dad taught you a lot of things.
JEFF: Yeah. Now we're banging away, right. Oo, ahh, oo, ahh. And it's

sweet—like summertime in December, right? And just when it really gets good, right? And we're about to reach the top of the mountain, down the steps comes Grandma—on one of her frequent sleepwalking things. And what do I do? I roll over to the wall and drop down to the other side. Like this— (*Demonstrates*) And nobody knows but us.

(*She kisses him.*)

Daddy Johnny says before a man settles down—which shouldn't oughta be until he'd damn near thirty or more—

(*She kisses him.*)

a young man's mission is the world.

ANN: Well, isn't that what you've been trying to do? (*She kisses him.*)

JEFF: You keep taking up my time.

ANN: Uh huh. (*Kisses him as the lights begin to dim. Bass line plays under*) You like my feet?

JEFF: Is the Pope Catholic? Can a fish swim? Do black folks have rhythm? Do hound dogs chase rabbits? Your feet got more beauty than sunshine, mama.

(*They kiss as the lights fade to black. Bass line fades.*)

ACT TWO

It is 10:45 the next morning. JOHN, *wearing coveralls made rough with dry paint and a painter's cap, is sweating heavily as he sits pondering his poem. It is obvious that he has suspended the activity of mopping the kitchen floor.*

(*Bass enters.*)

JOHN: I am the River Niger—hear my waters!
    I wriggle and stream and run.
    I am totally flexible.
    I am the River Niger—hear my waters!
    My waters are the first sperm of the world—
    When the earth was but a faceless whistling embryo
    Life burst from my liquid kernels like popcorn.

Hear my waters—rushing and popping in muffled finger-drum
staccato.
It is life you hear stretching its limbs in my waters—
(*To himself*) Yeah.

(*Quietly he gathers his multiple scraps of paper, folds them neatly, stuffs
them into his pocket. Bass fades. He rises to continue mopping the still-
half-wet floor. Abruptly he decides to quit and starts for the closet to get his
overcoat. He stops as a knock is heard at the kitchen door. He answers it. It
is* DUDLEY.)

JOHN: Man, you just in time.
DUDLEY: For what?
JOHN: To make it with me to the Big Apple. The labor's too deep
around here for me. Mattie's gon' off her head. Do you know that, I—
me—Lightnin' John Williams—more powerful than a speeding
locomotive—do you realize that I have mopped this entire house by
myself? And now I am making it.
DUDLEY: Without telling the captain?
JOHN: What's that suppose to mean?
DUDLEY: It means that the African warrior is always sneaking around
like Brer Rabbit instead of walking up to the captain and saying,
"Captain Mattie, I's worked hard 'nuff—I's taking a rest and a mint
julep at the Apple!" I mean, I want to see some evidence of your
spear-throwing, baby—not just words. Words are outta style.

(JOHN *goes to closet in living room. Gets overcoat, comes back, stepping
lightly on wet floor.*)

JOHN: Look, my West Indian corn roaster, I accept the fact that you're a
gutless black aristocrat, going thumbs up or thumbs down while your
brothers and sisters are being fed to the Lion's Club— So beat your
meat while Rome burns—I don't give a piss. Just allow me to paint my
own self-portraits—okay, ugly?
DUDLEY: It's pretty chilly out there, man, you better put on a sweater or
something, you know.
JOHN: You mean it's pretty chilly for you—that's what I'm trying to tell
you. That's you, man, not me!
DUDLEY: Johnny—
JOHN: And don't step on my floor—
DUDLEY: Mattie came over this morning—early. I examined her—and,
well, I felt a lot of—irregularities—Anyway—
JOHN (*sardonically*): Well, what're you quacks gonna do now—remove
her other tit?

DUDLEY: Johnny. (*Pause.*) Maybe even worse. I don't want to alarm her until I'm sure. I made an appointment for her at Harlem—they'll do a biopsy—anyway, I'll know as soon as the lab gets done with it. (*Pause.*)

JOHN (*stricken but defensive*): Why you telling me all this if you don't know for sure? (*Pause.*)

DUDLEY: She came over while you were still asleep—she doesn't want you to know. I promised I wouldn't tell you.

JOHN: Does she suspect?

DUDLEY: I was very honest with her.

JOHN: That figures! Honesty sticks to some people's mouths like peanut butter.

DUDLEY: Like you just said, man, I have to deal with things the way I think best.

MATTIE'S VOICE (*from upstairs*): Johnny—Johnny—have you finished the kitchen?

JOHN: She just keeps going, Dudley. I don't know how in hell, but she keeps on keeping on. (*Pause.*) When'll you know for sure?

DUDLEY: By Friday evening.

MATTIE'S VOICE: If you've finished the kitchen, John, how about taking out those bags of trash.

JOHN: Just keeps on keeping on! (*Pause.*)

MATTIE'S VOICE: John! Johnny!

JOHN (*quietly*): Johnny's gone to the Apple, you amazing bitch, to celebrate an amazing bitch.

(*He and* DUDLEY *exit just as* MATTIE *and* ANN *come down the steps.*)

MATTIE (*on the landing, followed by* ANN): Ann, I do believe that man's gone! Sneaked out!

ANN: I'll finish, Mrs. Williams.

MATTIE: Ann, thank-you so much for your help. I don't think we coulda finished without you, and that's a fact. (*Pause.*) Mama, will you please hurry! (*To* ANN) The store will be jam-packed when we get there.

GRANDMA'S VOICE (*from upstairs*): If you can't wait for your mother, then go on without me!

MATTIE: Please, Mama!

GRANDMA: Just go on without me, just go on!

MATTIE (*to* ANN): There's too much drinking in this house. That's the problem. She's probably hungover.

ANN: Pardon me, Mrs. Williams, but you know about your mother's drinking?

MATTIE: Of course! It's all in her eyes.

ANN: But last night I thought—well—

MATTIE: Child, you got to swallow a lot of truth 'round here to give folks dignity. If Mama knew I knew—I mean really knew I knew—she'd be so embarrassed. Don't you know, I even pretend that John ain't the alcoholic he really is?

ANN: But you're not helping them that way.

MATTIE: Helping them! Who says I ain't? Johnny soon be pushing sixty. He ain't got but a few more years left. If he wants to spend 'em swimming in a fifth a day, who am I to tell him he can't? And Mama, she'll be eighty-three this September. I'm supposed—as the youngsters on my job say—"to blow their cool?" Honey, all we're doing in this life is playing what we ain't. And well, I play anything my folks need me to play.

ANN: I guess that makes sense.

(Bass enters.)

MATTIE: That man had two years of college, Ann. Wanted to be a lawyer like Jeff wants to be, you know. He had to stop school because my mother and my two sisters—Flora and Minerva—came up from the South to live with us—for a short time, so they said. Ignorant country girls—they weren't trained to do nothing. I got a job, and together Johnny and I fed 'em, clothed 'em. In a couple of years, John was ready to go back to school, raring to go, don't you know. Then Flora's boyfriend came up from good old South Carolina and didn't have a pot to piss in or a window to throw it out of. He and Flora got married, and where do you think they stayed? *(Yells upstairs)* MAMA! *(Back to* ANN) On top of it all, Minerva got herself pregnant by some silly, bucktoothed nineteen year old who just vanished. So here comes another mouth to feed—Child, Johnny was painting houses all morning, working the graveyard shift at the post office, and driving a cab on his days off. *(Again yells)* MAMA PLEASE! *(Back to* ANN.) He kept on reading though. And I mean heavy reading. Smart, Lord knows that man is smart. Student friends of his were always coming 'round here getting his help in stuff like trigonometry, organic chemistry, philosophy—stuff like that—heavy stuff, you know. They used to call him Solomon. Some of his bummified wino friends still call him that at the Apple. Solomon!

ANN: Every other word out of Jeff's mouth is "Daddy Johnny says—"

MATTIE: That's what he did. He poured himself into Jeff. Lord, had that boy reading Plato and Shakespeare when he was thirteen years old. *(Yelling upstairs)* I gonna leave without you, Mama.

GRANDMA'S VOICE: I'm a child to be told when to come and go!

MATTIE: You can be too good, Ann. I was actually proud of the way

John worked himself. I read somewhere—in one of John's psychology magazines—where it's called a Christ fixation, or something like that.

ANN: But that's kinda nice, isn't it?

MATTIE: Honey, the meek ain't never inherited nothing. No, Ann, if I had to do all over again, I'd do it a whole lot different, believe me. What did we get for it? A chest full of bitterness, that's all. These past few years I've had nothing but bile in my mouth. No, Ann, we got nothing, honey. I mean you'd think they'd call every once in a while.

ANN: My mother used to say, "The giver receives all."

MATTIE: Not in this world, child.

ANN: Somewhere! It must be somewhere—some place—

MATTIE (*growing heated*): In heaven, honey?

ANN: In a manner of speaking. Treasures—

MATTIE (*brooding with anger*): In heaven! Treasures in heaven! My man is an alcoholic, the city's trying to condemn this firetrap we ain't even finished paying for yet, and Flora's got a fancy house and a fancy lawn mower upstate. There were times, Ann, times when I wanted John to get mad—really mad—get a bullwhip and whip 'em out—just whip 'em right on out. Johnny woulda done it, ya know. Started to several times, but I'd always managed to cool him down. I got nobody to blame but myself. (*Pause.*)
Treasures in heaven—shit. A good man is a treasure. White folks proclaim that our men are no good and we go 'round like fools trying to prove them wrong. And I fell right into the same old dumb trap myself. That's why I can't get angry with that man no more. Oh, I pretend to be, but I'm not. Johnny ran a powerful race with a jockey on his back who weighed a ton. So now he's tired. Do you hear me? Tired—and he's put himself out to pasture—with his fifth a day; and I say good for Johnny. I knew he was a smart man. Good for Johnny. (*On the verge of tears*)
If our men are no good, then why are all these little white girls trying to gobble 'em up faster than they can pee straight? I rejoice in you young people, Ann. You're the spring rains we need, 'cause we as a people got a lot of growing to do. Bless our young folk.

GRANDMA (*down the steps*): Well, I ain't young like them people you blessing. Them steps is mighty steep.

(*Bass line fades.*)

ANN: Morning, Mrs. Brown.

GRANDMA: You still here?

MATTIE: Mama, she's here on my invitation. Let's go.

GRANDMA: The gall of a young girl, planting herself right on the boy's doorstep. (*Crosses to the kitchen*)

ANN: I'm leaving as soon as Jeff's party's over—

MATTIE: You'll do no such thing. Mama, hush! (*Embarrassed*) Ann, would you kinda give Jeff's room a once-over? I started to do it myself, but for some strange reason the door was locked. Been searching for the key half the morning. (*Hands* ANN *the key from her apron pocket*)

ANN (*exiting up the stairs*): Yes, ma'am.

(MATTIE *goes to the hall closet, which gives* GRANDMA *a chance to check her bottle in the kitchen.* MATTIE *gets their coats, plus an old creaky shopping cart.*)

MATTIE: Mama, will you stop insulting that child!

GRANDMA (*astonished to see empty bottle*): That boy needs some time to grow up.

MATTIE: Who's stopping him?

GRANDMA: That audacious girl! That's who.

MATTIE: Mama, she's a nice girl. Besides, Jeff has a mind of his own.

GRANDMA: Ain't no such thing. Not when it comes to a pretty face. And I got a feeling she's animal-natured.

MATTIE: Then you admit she's pretty?

GRANDMA: Well, she's halfway light skin—got good hair. You know what that does to a colored man's mind!

MATTIE: Not today, Mama. (*Yelling upstairs*) Ann, Ann, would you come here a minute.

GRANDMA: Young niggers—old niggers—they all the same! High yellows is still what they want! Young girls these days just like vipers! Anyhow, why you rushing the boy?

MATTIE: I'm not doing a thing, Mama. It's all in your mind.

(ANN *appears at the top of the stairs. She looks like a cyclone has hit her.*)

My God, child, what on earth—is the room that dirty?

ANN: It's a very strong room, ma'am, I can tell you that.

MATTIE: Listen, honey, I got a roast in the oven. Take it out in twenty-five minutes exactly.

ANN: Yes, ma'am.

MATTIE: Come on, Mama.

(*Ice wind hits* GRANDMA *full in the face as* MATTIE *opens the door*)

GRANDMA: Do Jesus!

(MATTIE and GRANDMA exit. JEFF appears at the top of the stairs.)

JEFF: How your feets feeling this morning, mama?

ANN: You're insane, you know that—trying to pull my clothes off with your mother right downstairs.

JEFF: Hey, ain't I got a groovy mama?

ANN: She's wonderful.

JEFF: You ever look at her feet? She's got some boss dogs—

ANN: Jeff, I'm moving into a hotel this evening—your grandma's a little too much—even for me.

JEFF: Look, today's my homecoming and tomorrow's Sunday—a day of rest. Monday we'll find you a place—okay? Now, why don't you cool your heels and let's get a quickie before the inmates return— *(Pause)* Don't worry! Dad won't be back for at least an hour, and Mama always gets carried away shopping—

(Knock on the front door)

And you will not be saved by the bell. See who it is.

(ANN goes to peephole in door)

ANN: It's Mo's friend—Skeeter, and I believe the other one's called Al.

JEFF: Skeeter! Send them away! No! That wouldn't be cool. That means Mo's not far behind. Let them in! Tell them to make themselves comfortable, that you've got some last-minute cleaning to do upstairs, and come on up. For all they know, I'm not here yet.

ANN: As simple as that, huh?

JEFF: Right!

(Another knock)

ANN: You're crazy.

JEFF *(starting upstairs)*: Can I help it if I'm in heat for your feet? *(Exits)*

(ANN answers the door.)

SKEETER: Hey, we come for the party. Mo wanted us to break in early so's we could rap a taste before Jeff's folks gits into him, ya dig.

ANN: Come on in. Skeeter, isn't it?

SKEETER: Ain't it.

ANN: And Al?

(AL nods. They enter. SKEETER is jittery. It is obvious he is in heavy need of a fix, but he's clever enough to hide the chilling cold running through him.)

Can I take your coat?

(AL *gives her his coat.*)

What about you?

SKEETER: That's okay—I mean, I'm cool.

ANN: Can I get you a beer or something?

AL: Not right now, thanks.

ANN: Skeeter?

SKEETER: I'm cool, sister, I'm cool. Is Jeff here?

ANN: Not yet.

(*There is a pounding from upstairs.*)

SKEETER: What's that?

ANN: Please make yourselves comfortable. Jeff's due shortly, and I've got
to get his room cleaned up a bit. (*Starts up the stairs*) There's beer and
stuff in the fridge. Just call if you need me.

SKEETER: Yeah. Everything's everything.

(ANN *exits.*)

I hate smart-ass black bitches. (*Lights a cigarette*)

AL: So do I, sweet baby.

SKEETER: Stop being so obvious. If Mo ever finds out about your
sweet shit—

AL: He won't, sweet baby.

SKEETER: Don't give me that sweet-baby jive. Have you got it?

AL: Well, fuck you. I hate smart-ass dope fiends.

SKEETER: Aw, come on, Al, don't catch an attitude.

AL: I'll catch a 'tude if I so desire. I got the shit and you want it, so walk
soft or go to Phoenix House, nigger man.

SKEETER (*shivering*): Come on, man. I'm sorry.

AL: You sure is. You the sorriest motherfucker I ever run across.

SKEETER: Come on, man. Mo'll be here in a minute.

AL: Finish telling me 'bout Buckley.

SKEETER: Gimme the stuff first.

AL: I want to know 'bout Buckley.

SKEETER (*shivering*): I'm cold, man—cold.

AL: Then talk to me, sugar baby.

SKEETER: What you want to know?

AL: Who ripped him off?

SKEETER: Why you so anxious to know?

AL: Those motherfuckers in Queens claim they did it. They always
claiming credit for what we do.

SKEETER: We? You weren't even heard of when it happened.

AL: Well, it's we now, ain't it? Had to be you, Chips, or Mo!

SKEETER: Why's that?

AL: Well, I know you cats wouldn't trust none of the young bloods in the organization to do an important job like that.

SKEETER: Why you want to know 'bout Buckley? You sure you from the home office, nigger? Ever since they sent you here, you been bugging me 'bout Buckley!

AL: Look, I fight for niggers, 'cause I hate the devil pig—but I don't trust niggers as far as I can spit. If there's a finger man on the team, I want to know who it is. Somebody might make a mistake and put him on my ass. You sure get heated up 'bout simple party gossip. So heated up, sugar baby, you clean forget all 'bout that deep-freeze chill slipping and sliding through your bones. You even bite the hand that lights your fire, don't you, sugar baby?

(*In furious desperation,* SKEETER *suddenly reaches inside his coat, but* AL *is too quick. At about the same time they both produce their revolvers.*)

Don't make the mistake of thinking a sissy can't play that Gary Cooper shit if he want to, nigger man.

(*They face each other.*)

SKEETER (*seething*): I hate your guts.

AL: All that's cool. But I got what it takes to get your guts together, and don't you forget it. I can draw a gun like Sammy Davis, and I was a Golden Gloves champion two years in a row. I got all the hole cards, baby. I could even pull the trigger faster than you right now, 'cause I stays in shape, baby, and you is a dope fiend.

(SKEETER *puts his gun away.* AL *follows suit.* SKEETER *paces about the room, clutching his stomach as* AL *watches, underneath enjoying* SKEETER'S *pain. Finally,* SKEETER *turns to* AL, *pleading in anguish.*)

SKEETER: Give me the shit, Al.

AL: I had it for you all the time. You just been running backward and now you're facing the right way, that's all, sugar baby. Just answer me one teeny-tiny little question. Was it you?

SKEETER: No.

AL: Chips?

SKEETER (*almost screaming*): It was an outside dude.

AL: Who?

SKEETER (*clutching his stomach*): He wouldn't give his name. He just did it and split. Last I heard he was in Frisco.

(*Satisfied,* AL *searches his pockets. Unknown to* AL, SKEETER *suppresses a chuckle.*)

AL (*handing him a package of wrapped tinfoil*): Here, snort on this. It oughta hold you till after the meeting. It's strong as a horse's ass.

(*Using the tip of his little finger,* SKEETER *snorts greedily—first one nostril, then the next.*)

Later on we can really take care of business. (*Watches* SKEETER *awhile*) Why'd ya'll hate Buckley so?

SKEETER (*calming down rapidly*): He was on the narco squad. Useta raid and steal scag and push it to the school kids. Always little girls. He'd get 'em hooked, strung out, then make em do freakish shit for a fix. Any one of us woulda blown him away. (*Pause.*) Hey, I seen you trying to feel up on Chips's little brother.

AL (*excitedly*): You lie, nigger.

SKEETER: If you'd make it with Chips, you'd make it with anybody. Don't give me that funny look, nigger.

AL: You lie!

SKEETER: If I tell Mo 'bout it, he'll bust both of you mothers. Ain't that some shit. And you mean to tell me you don't know 'bout Chips? He stuck his joint in an embalmed cunt. And he brags about it! You know what Mo calls him when he really gets mad at him? Femaldehyde Dick. (*Laughs*)

AL: That shit you just snorted ain't gon' last forever, you know.

SKEETER: Oughta call you Femaldehyde Brown Eye.

AL: Ya never miss the water till the well runs dry.

SKEETER: Don't give me that shit. We got a working relationship—the three of us.

AL: What three?

SKEETER: You, me, and Chips. You give me scag 'cause you know I know where you at—I don't tell Mo where you at 'cause I need the scag. Chips don't tell him 'cause he digs fags. That's where he's at! Now, you keep your eye—your brown eye—on that relationship 'cause all three of us is walking on the same razor blade, sugar baby, and don't you forget it, 'cause our asses could get cut in half! (*Laughs uproariously.*)

(*There is a knock on the door.*)

AL: Answer the door, dope fiend!

(SKEETER *goes to the door, peeks through*)

SKEETER: It's Femaldehyde himself.

AL: Flake off, nigger—I'm warning you!

SKEETER: You want to know something else, Alfreida? That shit about an outside man ripping off Buckley—I made that up.

AL: Your ass is gon' be mine. Wait and see!

SKEETER (*laughing*): You wanta know something else? I'm supposed to pick up some good stuff as soon as we finish rapping with Jeff. I don't really need your shit. (*Laughs and opens the door*)

CHIPS (*to* AL): What's this clown laughing about?

SKEETER (*holding his sides*): Gary Cooper here just got some lemon in his sucker— (*Laughs.*)

(*The front door is left slightly ajar.*)

CHIPS: Dig these happenings. A young dude who said he was from the *Times* was hanging around headquarters all morning, asking questions about you know who.

SKEETER: Buckley!

CHIPS: Dig it!

SKEETER (*eyeing* AL): Ain't that interesting! (*Laughs*)

CHIPS: The pigs is restless. So you cats be careful.

(ANN *appears at top of stairs.*)

Well, bless my soul—if it ain't foxy mama. How 'bout a hug and a squeeze, foxy mama? (*To* SKEETER) Who else is here?

SKEETER: Just us chickens.

CHIPS: You mean foxy mama is by her little old self—in this big house?

ANN (*trying to ignore him*): Jeff'll be here in a minute, everybody.

CHIPS: Then we got to git it before he gets here, right, mama? All I want you to do is show me the upstairs. (CHIPS *starts up the steps after her.*)

ANN: What are you trying to prove?

AL: Chips—

SKEETER: Man, can't you act civilized?

CHIPS: Mind ya business.

SKEETER: Chips—come on, man.

ANN: It's all right—he wants to see upstairs—I'll show him.

CHIPS (*swatting her on her rear*): Now you talking, foxy mama. All I wants is a hug and a squeeze. You dudes take it easy now. And call me when you see MO coming.

(ANN *hesitates, and he shoves her ahead of him.*)

He who hesitates is lost, mama.

(They exit upstairs)

AL: Some niggers ain't got no couth—

SKEETER: There goes Femaldehyde!

(In the next moment we hear a loud yell from JEFF and much commotion. A second later JEFF comes down the stairs with CHIPS's revolver pressed against CHIPS's head. ANN brings up the rear.)

Here comes Femaldehyde!

CHIPS: Come on, Jeff, man, I was only fooling, man. I mean, you know me, Jeff. I didn't know she was your woman, man. Honest!

(JEFF smacks him brutally across the face.)

SKEETER: Lighten up, Jeff.

AL: Yeah, like you made your point, man.

(JEFF turns and looks at them, saying nothing. The ferocity of his stare silences them.)

ANN: Jeff—it's okay.

(JEFF wallops CHIPS in the pit of his stomach. CHIPS's knees buckle to the floor.)

CHIPS: It's your world, baby! It's your world!

ANN: He's not worth it, Jeff. Please, baby, for me—okay?

(MO and GAIL enter, almost unseen.)

CHIPS: I was only fooling, Jeff. Honest.

JEFF: Fooling with a gun at my woman's head?

CHIPS: I wouldn't hurt ya woman, man. It ain't even loaded.

JEFF *(placing gun against CHIPS's temple)*: So if I pull the trigger, it won't matter. *(Cocks hammer)*

CHIPS *(hysterical)*: Oh shit—oh shit—Don't do that, Jeff. Please don't do that.

JEFF: The next time I catch you looking cross-eyed at my woman, I'm gonna rid the world of one more jive-ass nigger. Now, get out of here.

MO: Let him stay, Jeff. As a favor to me.

JEFF *(turning to see MO)*: I despise irresponsible niggers, Mo.

MO: I'll be responsible for him.

JEFF: Then he'd better become shy, quiet, and unassuming. 'Cause that's the only kind of nigger I tolerate in my house.

MO: Well, you sound like the Jeff I used to know back when.

GAIL *(to CHIPS)*: You act more like a pig than the pigs.

MO: Old Femaldehyde!

SKEETER (*laughing*): Rides again.

MO (*referring to the revolver*): Is that your steel, man?

SKEETER: It's Chips's. (*Laughs*)

MO (*collaring* CHIPS *angrily*): What! Not only do you insult a personal friend of mine—but you let him take your steel! That's unforgivable, cluck. You better get it back or another one just like it—posthaste— you dig me. Loss of a weapon is a crime against the organization. Do you dig them apples, Femaldehyde?

(SKEETER *holds his sides laughing.*)

(*To* SKEETER) Shut up!

GAIL (*extending her hand to a still angry* JEFF): I'm Gail.

JEFF: Hi!

MO: This is my woman, Jeff. And of course you know Skeeter—

JEFF: Hey, Skeets.

SKEETER (*shaking* JEFF's *hand*): What's happening, big Jeff?

MO: And Al here I wrote you 'bout.

(*They shake hands.*)

Now, can we all settle down awhile and rap?

(*Everybody finds a comfortable spot, and there is an uneasy silence.*)

ANN: Who wants a beer?

(*Everybody nods.*)

MO: Why don't you help her, Gail?

GAIL: Sure.

(ANN *and* GAIL *cross the room to the kitchen.*)

MO: Now, dig this, Brother Jeff. What I'm about to run down to you is only to make a point, and stop being so pissed. Everybody's edgy.

JEFF: I'm not edgy, baby, I'm about to draw blood.

CHIPS: Look, man, I'm sorry—okay.

JEFF: Negative, baby—not okay, not okay worth a damn.

MO: Jeff—Jeff—why do you think Chips had the nerve to shoot on your woman like he did? I think it's because of your letters, man!

JEFF: You showed *them* my personal letters to you?!

MO: Yeah! And you know why? 'Cause they sounded like you were turning, man, dig it—turning into a weak, halfway-in-between, neither here nor there Oreo cookie. I mean, the last thing we expected was Big Brother, badass Jeff, our main man who we been waiting to welcome back to the trenches suddenly deciding to go trip off to law school, rapping 'bout the Constitution and a whole lot of the upside of the wall shit. . . . Jeff, remember the time I had to fight Billy Richardson? Remember how his brothers kept clipping me and pushing on me every time it looked like I was winning? Remember that shit?

JEFF: What's the point?

MO: It was supposed to be a fair fight to see who was to gain control over St. Nicholas Avenue, right? I mean we parlayed and parlayed, and it was agreed upon—we had a verbal contract. And what they do? Billy's older brothers held you against the fence while he and the younger punks in his gang went to work on me. I was ready to give up, man, I mean all the wind was outta my sail, baby. And I looked up, and there you were, crying, baby, crying—trying to break loose from cats twice your size, can you dig it? Trying to break loose to help your main man, your brother, and crying, and somehow your shit got into me, and I beat Billy until he was screaming for mercy—his own boys let up when they dug what was happening!

Well, a dumb-ass nigger and a pig are one and the same! They don't understand agreements and contracts; they're beasts—the only thing a beast understands is guts and determination. We ran the whole goddamn neighborhood after that, and we had one motto, "Keep on keeping on!" And anybody who gave up in a fight got his ass kicked when he got back to the club.

All that shit about legal pressure, the democratic process bullshit. I tell you, man, the law ain't never helped the black man do nothing. The law is the will of the prevailing force, which is the pig in this country—and you want to be a lawyer? That Constitution ain't nothing but bullshit, don't you know that yet, man?

JEFF: Make it work and you've got a formidable weapon.

MO: I say, burn the motherfucker! Look, man, we've gone all those routes. We've petitioned, we've sat in, shitted in, demonstrated until we got fallen arches, etc., etc., etc., and where did it get us, huh? Things are worse! Contracts!? I'm talking 'bout revolution, man.

JEFF: That word's been talked to death. The revolution ain't nothing but talk, talk, talk, and I ain't gonna waste my life on talk. Niggers are jiving, man, can't you see it? That's all I heard from the black troops in the air force—revolution. Where's the gun factory, the bomb-assembly plant? We're shucking and jiving, man—that's all. Law is something concrete, something I can *do*, not talk about.

MO: To a certain extent, you're right, Brother Jeff. Black people have been shucking and jivin', passing the buck. Well, we are the buck-ending committee. We ain't just talking, baby. We proving it. And in a few days we gonna serve notice on whitey that the shit has only begun to hit the fan. We want you with us, man.

JEFF: You've got it all figured out, Mo. You don't need me.

MO: We don't need nothing, baby, we just *want* you with us.

JEFF: Maybe I'm out of it, Mo. Maybe I don't know what's really happening any more. Yes, I'm still for whatever advances the cause of black folks, but I reserve the right to choose my own weapons. I don't have to fight with yours, Mo, and I respect your right not to have to fight with mine. . . . All I know is that right now my convictions rest elsewhere. . . . Now, gentlemen, my folks will be making it back pretty soon and I'd like the atmosphere to change into something a little bit more groovy, ya dig?

MO: Yes, sir, Lieutenant Williams, sir.

JEFF: Or *leave.*

MO: Is that an order, sir?

JEFF: You're in my house, nigger.

MO: I don't play that word, man. You throw it 'round a little too much.

JEFF: Oh yeah, well, you pat your foot while I play it, nigger.

MO: You either gon' be with us or against us, Brother Jeff. Nobody stays uncommitted in this neighborhood. Besides, we can make you do anything we want you to do.

JEFF: How you gonna do that, brother?

MO: Every time you poke your head out your door, you can be greeted with rocks, broken glass, garbage bags, or doo-do. And if that don't work . . .

(ANN *and* GAIL *return from kitchen.*)

And if that don't work . . .

JEFF (*furious*): If that don't work, what?

MO: We can work on your moms and pops. They might come home and find the whole house empty, no furniture or nothing, motherfucker.

JEFF: Oh no, baby, you're the motherfucker. You really are the motherfucker! (*Controlling his fury at* MO) You jive-ass nigger. Mr. Zero trying to be Malcolm X. List' old world, list' to *the* revolutionary. See him standing there with his Captain America uniform on. Look at his generals. Skeeter the dope head and Chips the sex pervert. Mo the magnificent, playing cops and robbers in his middle twenties, trying to be somebody and don't know how. The one advantage I have over you, Mo, is my daddy taught me to see through my own bullshit, to believe that I don't need bullshit to be somebody. Go back to school, Mo, you're smart enough.

GAIL: Don't talk to him like that!

MO: You been thinking this shit for a long time, ain't you, nigger?

JEFF: Affirmative. And if you try any shit on my folks, your ass is mine, nigger. Or have you forgotten what a mean, evil, black bastard I can be, how you could whip everybody in the neighborhood and how I could whip the piss out of you, how I got more determination in my little toenail than you got in your whole soul, nigger!

MO: At least you still talk bad.

JEFF: I ain't bad. I'm crazy, motherfucker. Now you, your dope fiend, and Marquis de Sade, get the fuck outta here, and don't call me—I'll call you.

MO (*not too frightened but impressed*): Let's go. This ain't the end, Jeff. I suggest you think about what I said and think hard.

JEFF: Just make it, man. And remember (*Places gun to* CHIPS*'s temple*) I'm fully armed, thanks to General Chips here.

MO: Don't make fun of me, Jeff.

JEFF: Why should I do that, you're a self-made comedian.

CHIPS: I think we should—

MO: You ain't had a thought in your life, cluck.

(*They all exit.*)

JEFF (*walking around the room*): Goddamn, goddamn! . . . Where's the hootch? I know Pop got some somewhere. (*Looks around frantically*) I know the fridge used to be one of his favorite places. (*Finds it*) Damn! Almost half full! Lawd hep me! 'Cause these niggers don' gon' crazy. (*Takes a drink*) Hep me, Lawd. Hep me, hep me, Lawd. (*Takes another drink and sings the words . . .*) " 'Cause the niggers don' gon' crazy!"

ANN: That's enough.

JEFF: Ann, my love, the most glorious bitch I ever don' run across—let's get married. Let's get married and screw right at the ceremony. Monday we'll get the license. There's a three-day wait—Tuesday, Wednesday, and Thursday—Friday we'll get high off this badass smoke I been saving and fly on to the preacher.

ANN: Are you serious?

JEFF: Indubitably.

ANN: Oh, Jeff, why so sudden?

JEFF: Honey, with the way these niggers is acting up 'round here, I figure I better get me some hep.

ANN: Jeff, I—

JEFF: I know you love me to pieces, and I don't blame you one bit.

ANN: You conceited—

JEFF: The problem is, I don't really love you. (*Pause.*) I glory for you, baby. Besides, you got the bossest dogs I ever seen.

(*They kiss and embrace. There's a knock at the door. It's* GAIL.)

GAIL: Can I come in?

ANN: Of course. (ANN *brings her into the kitchen.*)

GAIL: Mo thinks I stopped at the store to get cigarettes.

ANN: Would you like a drink?

GAIL: No, I don't drink.

ANN: Relax, Gail.

GAIL: Jeff, when I was a little girl, all I used to do was watch you and Mo running everything, the whole neighborhood together, always cool— no strain, ya know what I mean? You two cats were so beautiful together. . . . Maybe it was wrong for Mo to come down on you so hard tonight, Jeff, after three years—but you the only person he trusts, Jeff. Writing to you the years you were away was his way of forgetting you had ever left. Now he needs you more than ever, Jeff. The organization has gotten to be a real hassle.

JEFF: How could it be anything else with those nothings he's got at his back? I mean, it's hard to be out front when you got shit at your back.

GAIL: That's why he needs you bad, Jeff. Mo only looks at the good in people. Skeeter and Chips been with you cats ever since you started gang-bopping. Mo's not dumb, he knows their hang-ups. But they swore to him they'd stay clean. Anyway, when you trying to build an army outta people who been buried in garbage all their lives, you can't expect they gon' all of a sudden start smelling like roses. In time, Mo believes, the movement will straighten 'em out for good.

JEFF: Mo's a saint. I'm a realist.

GAIL: Then help him, Jeff, help him.

JEFF: It's not just those okeydoke creeps 'round him, Gail. We don't see eye to eye. Mo thinks he's still back in the old days, leading a gang. Times have changed.

GAIL: You could influence him, Jeff.

JEFF: He doesn't need me, Gail. He's sure about where he's going and confident about how to get there—

GAIL: That's not true, Jeff.

JEFF: And all that bull about threatening me and my folks—I'd jump in an elephant's chest behind that jive.

GAIL: He was only saying that for them—

JEFF: Why crucify me for a bunch of nothings, baby?

GAIL: Do you know Mo, Jeff?

JEFF: I thought I did.

GAIL: If you really know him, Jeff, then you know he didn't mean what he said. He's desperate, Jeff. Things are all mixed up. A few years ago, everything was straight up and down—simple—*right on for the people.* Now everything's falling apart, splitting up, people going every which way. And Mo's gotten into some heavy, scary things, Jeff. Right now the heat's on 'cause a pig cop was wasted a few months ago. And this Friday Mo plans to destroy a new state office building going up, or else mess with one of the police stations. You think he's so cocksure? Well, he ain't. He don't even know if what he's doing is right any more. I know—'cause I see him get up in the middle of the night and stare out the window and talk to himself— talk to his demons. Don't let his tough act fool you, Jeff. Behind his real together front, he's about to snap. You hear me, Jeff, he's gonna snap. I know it. Lord God, help him, Jeff Williams. Even if you don't see eye to eye with him, find a way to help him. The hell with the movement, help HIM! Help him, please, before he breaks apart. Help him, Jeff.

(*She sobs uncontrollably.* ANN *comforts her.*)

ANN: He will, Gail, he will—I know he will. (*To* JEFF) I like him, Jeff. His approach may be all wrong, but he's fighting. He's honest and he's fighting. He's a determined black man, just like you, Jeff.

JEFF: All right. I'll try, Gail, I'll try. I promise you.

(*The front door swings open. It's* MATTIE *and* GRANDMA, GRANDMA *pushing a shopping cart,* MATTIE *loaded down with grocery bags. Bass line enters.*)

MATTIE: Lawdamercy. The door's wide open!

GRANDMA: That hussy girl's doings!

(MATTIE *sees* JEFF.)

MATTIE: Lawdamercy! Lawdamercy! Jeff! (*She rushes to embrace him*) You big old good-for-nothing thing.

(GRANDMA *starts for him.*)

GRANDMA: Ben Brown! The spitting image of Ben Brown. Ben Brown all over again. (*She embraces him.*) Ain't black like Ben Brown, but he sho' do carve himself out a fine figure, don't he, Mattie?

JEFF (*eyeing her lewdly*): You don't do so bad yourself, sweet meat!

GRANDMA: You ought to be ashamed of yourself. (*Hugs him once more*)

MATTIE: You weren't supposed to be here till noon.

JEFF: I'll go back and come at noon.

MATTIE: Go on, boy, stop acting so simple.

JEFF: Can't help it, Mama. I got my two foxes back again—Cleopatra— (*Referring to* GRANDMA) and her sidekick. (*Referring to his mother*)

MATTIE: I'll sidekick you.

JEFF (*hugging them both at the same time*): Got my two womens back again.

MATTIE: Stop being so rough with your simple self. What they been feeding you—bread and water? You too thin to say grace over.

JEFF: Know what I wants for dinner? Some corn bread, yeah. And some of Grandma's mustard greens, Mama.

GRANDMA (*saluting him*): Yes, sir.

JEFF: And black-eyed peas. And some of your candied sweets, Grandma, with lemon and raisins all over 'em, yeah!

GRANDMA: And roast beef!

JEFF: Do Jesus, and bless my soul, Grandma Brown! And don't forget the lemonade.

GRANDMA: A gallon of it. Made it myself.

JEFF: And some sassafras tea.

GRANDMA: Got it fresh from that new health-food store. (*Pause.*)

JEFF: Ma, do you realize that I'm home for good—

MATTIE: Thank God!

JEFF: No more okeydoke. No more time outta my race against time. No more stuff, messing with my mind. I'm me—Jeff Williams, because Daddy Johnny named me—before ya'll claimed me on your income tax! And ya'll sho' is looking gooooooood—good God, good!

MATTIE: Go on, boy!

JEFF: Mama, this is Gail. Mo Hayes's girl friend.

MATTIE: Nice to know you, Gail.

GAIL (*extending her hand*): Heard a lot about you, Mrs. Williams.

JEFF: And this is my grandma, Gail. Grandma Wilhemina Geneva Brown.

GRANDMA: There you go, acting the fool, Jeff Williams. You know I can't stand "Geneva."

GAIL: My pleasure, Mrs. Brown.

GRANDMA: What? Oh, yes. How do, child.

JEFF: And this is Ann!

GRANDMA (*disapprovingly*): We've met.

MATTIE: The best—of—friends!

(GRANDMA *grunts.*)

JEFF (*ignoring* GRANDMA): Well, I'm glad 'cause this foxy mama here and your son—me—the baddest dude to catch an attitude—God's gift to the female race—"for God so loved the world that he gave—"

MATTIE: I'll take off my shoe and knock holes in your head, boy!

JEFF: Mama, what I'm trying to tell you—

GRANDMA: You gon' marry this here brazen gal?

(*Bass fades.*)

MATTIE: Mama!

JEFF: Indubitably!

GAIL: That's beautiful! Just beautiful!

GRANDMA: Do Jesus, Uncle Sam don' took my child—

MATTIE: Your child—

GRANDMA: And turned him into a cockeyed ignoramus.

MATTIE: Don't pay any attention to her, Ann.

ANN: Jeff, I think I'll walk to the corner with Gail.

JEFF: You will not!

GRANDMA: You too young to fart good—talking 'bout getting married.

JEFF: I'm twenty-five!

GRANDMA: Stop lying! You ain't outta your teens.

JEFF: I was twenty-two when I left, Grandma.

GRANDMA (*to* MATTIE): Lawd, Mattie, is my child don' got that old on me?

MATTIE: Your *grandson* is that old, Mama.

GRANDMA: Do Jesus! Time sho' do fly, don't it? 'Tweren't yesterday I was getting myself all sprayed up changing your diapers.

JEFF (*slowly, deliberately*): That was twenty-five years ago, Grandma.

GRANDMA (*coming out of her reveries*): Don't make no difference. You're too young to get yourself saddled with a wife. Next thing you know, here comes one crumb snatcher—then two—

JEFF: Then three—then four. It's pretty lonely not having any brothers and sisters, I can tell you.

GRANDMA: A lodestone! A lodestone 'round your neck, a-dragging you down.

MATTIE: What about law school, Jeff?

JEFF: Oh, we gon' do that too. I mean them crumb snatchers ain't coming until we are ready for 'em. Ann's gonna use the loop, birth-control pills, the rhythm method, and the diaphragm, and Emko!

GRANDMA: There sure is a whole lot Emko babies walking 'round here.

MATTIE (*to* JEFF): Well, you certainly seem to know an awful lot 'bout it.

JEFF: Like I said before, I'm *twenty-five*. Be twenty-six the twenty-fourth of this month, Mama.

MATTIE: You still don't have to know so much in front of your mother.

JEFF: I apologize.

GRANDMA (*blurting out a long-pent-up reality*): Look at your father. He wanted to be a lawyer, didn't he? Then I jumped on his back, then them two no good daughters of mine, then their two empty-headed husbands—then you. The load was so heavy till he couldn't move no more. He just had to stand there, holding it up.

MATTIE (*very serious*): Then you know about it?

GRANDMA: What do you think I am? A sickle-headed, lopsided, cockeyed ignoramus like your son here?

MATTIE: Oh, so you admit he's my son?

GRANDMA: He's your son, but he's my child.

MATTIE (*turning to* ANN): Have ya'll given it serious thought, Ann?

ANN: He just asked me, Mrs. Williams.

GRANDMA: Is that all you gon' do? Talk? You gon' let this brazen hussy just take my child away?

MATTIE: Mama, why don't you go to your room and cool off a bit.

GRANDMA: She is brazen. Camping right on his doorstep. I call that bold, brash, and brazen! And conniving too! A pretty face'll sho' kill a man—even a good man. (*To* ANN) And not even mean to! You gon' take that on your shoulders, child, you gon' kill your man before he can stand up good yet? Is that what you gon' do? I did it. Mattie did it. She let me help her do it.

MATTIE: Mama!

GRANDMA: Don't mama me. Where's my medicine? I don't want to be here and watch my child leap into deep water. Lawdamercy, no! Where is my medicine? Where's my pocketbook?

JEFF (*to* MATTIE): Is Grandma sick, Ma?

MATTIE: In a manner of speaking.

(GRANDMA *finds her purse. There is a large bulge in it. She seems satisfied. She starts up the stairs, singing "Rock of Ages."*)

GRANDMA: Hep him, Lawd! Hep my child! (*She exits, singing.*)

JEFF (*to* ANN): Is this what you've been putting up with?

MATTIE: Ann's a fine girl, Jeff. You know I believe that, don't you, Ann?

ANN: Thank-you, Mrs. Williams.

MATTIE: And you know women get silly over their sons and, well, grandsons.

ANN: Yes, ma'am.

MATTIE: My personal opinion—if ya'll are interested—is that you should wait awhile—at least until Jeff's finished law school.

JEFF: Ever since I got home, people been telling me what to do and what not to do. You talking about a lodestone—that's the heaviest lodestone in the world. . . . I want to marry Ann 'cause she is a fine girl, Mama. Something rare—came home and found my sweet baby here—it was like God was saying, "This is your woman, son. I can't let you do nothing that dumb. I can't let you leave her. I made her for you!" And goddamn it—

MATTIE: Jeff!

JEFF: I'm following what I hear inside my soul!

MATTIE (*pausing for a long moment, finally embracing him strongly, on the verge of tears*): Then you do that, baby. You follow the Lord. As mad as He makes me sometimes, I don't think He's ever really told me wrong. (*Hugs* ANN *lovingly*) Come on in here and help me fix this food, girl. You're one of the family now. I guess I knew you were the moment I laid eyes on you. (*To* JEFF) Why do you like to shock people so? You know how your grandmother dotes on you. (*She exits into the kitchen.*)

GAIL: A beautiful black brother and sister, doing a beautiful thing. (*She embraces* ANN.)

JEFF: Gail, I'll try to talk to Mo. I'm not certain it will do any good, but I'll try to talk to him—when he's alone—Just him and me. Okay?

GAIL: I appreciate it, Jeff.

(*She exits as* JOHN, *very intoxicated, and* DUDLEY, *still in control of himself, enter. They are arguing some philosophical point.* JOHN *sees* JEFF.)

JOHN: Jeff! Well, I'll be goddamned. Jeff! (*He ruffles* JEFF's *hair.*)

JEFF: How you been, Pop?

JOHN: Where's your uniform?

JEFF: Dr. Stanton.

DUDLEY: You're looking fine, boy! Just fine. Skinny, but fine.

JOHN: Where's your uniform?

MATTIE (*coming back in, followed by* ANN, *with a cake*): John, you're drunk.

JOHN: Yes, my love.

(GRANDMA *comes down the stairs. She too is loaded. She's singing* "Onward, Christian Soldiers.")

JEFF: Why don't you take the load off your feet, Pop.

JOHN: Where's your uniform, Jeff? Go put it on.

JEFF: If it's all the same to you, Pop—

JOHN: I've got a theory, Dudley—Dr. Dudley Stanton—

MATTIE: Why don't you go sleep it off—

JOHN: My theory is that if you as a doctor don't try to keep the living from dying, then you're dead yourself. You're a dead doctor.

(GRANDMA *crosses to* JOHN *and sings directly into his ear.*)

Mrs. Brown, I have never hit an old lady in my life—

GRANDMA: Ya hit this old lady—

JOHN: And what?

GRANDMA: She's gon' jump down your throat—

JOHN: And what?

GRANDMA: Straddle your gizzard—

JOHN: And what?

GRANDMA: And gallop your brains out!

(*He picks her up and whirls her around the room, laughing.*)

JOHN: Grandma, you are the biggest fool in the world, but I sure do love me some Grandma Wilhemina Geneva Brown.

GRANDMA: Stinking old wino.

JOHN: I love you too, Dudley—Dr. Dudley Stanton—even if you do walk through life with a broomstick up your ass. (*To* ANN) And even though we just met, I loves me some Ann—sweet fighting lady that you are. Jeff, ya got yourself a mama—a mama who's gonna protect your flanks—a sweet fighting lady.

JEFF: I know, Pop.

(GRANDMA *grunts disapprovingly.*)

JOHN: And my son I loves better than I love myself. My big old big-time United States Air Force lieutenant son. He's coming home today—

JEFF: I'm here, Pop.

JOHN (*really annoyed*): No, you ain't—you ain't here. 'Cause if you were, you'd have on your uniform—

JEFF: I don't like to wear it, Daddy Johnny.

JOHN: Why not?

JEFF: Well, I guess—

JOHN: Spit it out.

JEFF: I feel ashamed of it. I feel that it's a kinda cop-out, Pop—it makes me feel like a buffoon every time I put it on. I should have burned my commission, not shown up, made it to Canada or something. I really don't believe in this country any more.

DUDLEY: Boy, you don't believe in the United States of America—land of the free, home of the brave, this democratic, constitutional, industrial giant?

JEFF: I don't believe in lies any more, Dr. Stanton.

DUDLEY (*jokingly but meaning it*): Welcome home, Jeff. Welcome home, Brother Jeff. (*Pats him on the back*)

JOHN: Have I been waiting around here, waiting to see you in that goddamn uniform—for you to—Go put it on!

JEFF: I made a vow with myself, Daddy Johnny.

JOHN (*getting angry*): It's an accomplishment, fool. How many of us ever get there—to be an officer? God knows, this country needs to be torn down, but don't we want it torn down for the right to be an officer if you're able? It's an accomplishment. And I'm proud of your accomplishment.

DUDLEY: A dubious accomplishment.

JOHN: Laugh and ridicule the damn thing all you want, goddamn it, but recognize that it's another fist jammed through the wall.

DUDLEY: Man, he became the protector of a system he believes should be destroyed.

JOHN: So we're contradictions—so what else is new? That could apply to every black man, woman, and child who ever lived in this country. Especially the taxpayers. They been financing the system for a long time. Besides, who ever said we wanted total destruction anyway? If you get right on down to the real nitty-gritty, I don't want to totally destroy what, by rights, belongs to me anyway. I just want to weed out the bullshit. Change the value system so that the Waldorf has as many welfare tenants as Rockafellows.

JEFF: The Rockafellows will never allow it.

JOHN: They will if you put *them* on welfare.

DUDLEY: How in the hell you gonna do that, fool?

JOHN: By finding the battlefield—like I told you—like I been telling you—each and every motherfucker—

MATTIE: John!

JOHN: Whoever dropped from a pretty black poontang has got to find his own battlefield and go to war. In his own way—his own private war.

DUDLEY: All hail to the philosopher-poet.

JOHN (*grabbing* DUDLEY *roughly in the collar and screaming as bass line enters*): I'm a poet, ya hear me, a poet! When this country—when this world, learns the meaning of poetry—

Don't you see, Jeff, poetry is what the revolution's all about—never lose sight of the true purpose of the revolution, all revolutions—to restore poetry to the godhead!

Poetry is religion, the alpha and the omega, the cement of the universe. The supereye under which every other eye is scrutinized, and it stretches from one to infinity, from bullshit to the beatific, the rocking horse of the human spirit—God himself. God himself is pure distilled poetry.

DUDLEY: Bravissimo!

JOHN: Preserve the Empire State Building—if you can. It was built from over three hundred years of black poetry, 'cause sweat is poetry too, son. Kick out the money changers and reclaim it. Ain't none of us gonna be free until poetry rides a mercury-smooth silver stallion. (*Pause.*) Seeing you in your uniform with bars on your shoulders and them navigator wings on your chest is a kinda—

(*Bass fades.*)

DUDLEY (*undaunted*): Heresy!

JOHN: Poetry, Jeff. Black poetry.

JEFF: Pop, I didn't make it through navigator school—I washed out—flunked out—whatever.

JOHN (*furious*): My son flunked out—You lie—Go get that uniform!

JEFF: No, Daddy Johnny, no!

MATTIE: Leave him alone, Johnny.

JOHN: I'm the head of this house.

MATTIE: Ain't nobody disputing that.

JOHN: And when I ask my son—who I ain't seen but three or four times in three years—to do me one simple favor—

ANN: But if it's against his principles, Mr. Williams—

JOHN: There goes the little fighting lady, protecting your flanks.

JEFF: I don't need nobody to protect my flanks.

ANN: I know you don't, baby.

GRANDMA (*half high*): "I know you don't, baby!" Brazen hussy.

JEFF: Don't call her that again, Grandma!

GRANDMA: I calls 'em as I sees 'em. My Ben Brown told me—

MATTIE: Hush, Ma!

JEFF: I'll leave, Pop. I'll leave now—tonight—ya dig that? 'Cause I've had me enough homecoming for a lifetime.

JOHN: Ain't nobody asking you to leave—

JEFF: Ya telling me what to do like I was sweet sixteen or something. Everybody 'round here wants to tell me what to do.

MATTIE: You didn't write to us about flunking out, Jeff.

JEFF: Ya want to know why I didn't write home about it, Mama? 'Cause every single letter I got from you or Pop was telling me how proud you were of your navigator son.

JOHN: We thought you were doing all right.

JEFF: You thought that because that's what you wanted to think!

JOHN: What else could we think?

JEFF: About me, Daddy Johnny, about Jeff—damn your pride! You coulda thought about me. (*Strained pause.*) I hated navigation! You know how I hate figures, Pop.

JOHN: You never worked hard enough!

JEFF: So you say, Daddy Johnny—'cause that's what you want to believe. "Jeff Williams is my son, everybody! Just like me. Anything I can do he can do."

JOHN: You can! It's all in how you think of yourself—

JEFF: Right, Pop, right. As a matter of fact, I may be able to do a few things you can't do. But not math, Pop. That's you, not me. Don't you dig that?

JOHN: Say what you got to say.

JEFF: Haven't I said it already? You said it yourself! We got to find our own battlefields. Don't you dig how that statement relates to what I'm saying?

JOHN: No! Hell, no, I don't. You flunked out. My boy, my boy failed. That's all I can see.

JEFF: Ya'll had a piece of my big toe, Pop. *Everybody* had a piece of my toe. Not just those white-pig instructors who kept checking and rechecking my work, 'cause I was what they called a belligerent nigger. There were only eight black officers out of three hundred in that school, and they kept telling me, "Man, you got to make it. You got to be a credit to your race."

JOHN: What's wrong with that?

JEFF: Then there was this girl I was shacking up with.

MATTIE: Shacking up!

JEFF: Shacking up, Mama!

GRANDMA: Another brazen hussy!

JEFF: She was the fox to end all foxes, Pop. An afro so soft and spongy, until my hands felt like they were moving through water. And she kept telling me, "Honey, we needs that extra hundred and thirty a month flight pay to keep me in the style to which you have made me accustomed."

JOHN: Come to the point!

JEFF: Don't you see the point, Pop? Everybody had a piece of my nigger toe—my fine fox, my fellow black brother officers, the pig instructors, you and Mama, Pop—everybody had a piece—but me—Jeff Williams!

JOHN: Jeff Williams is Johnny Williams's son, goddamn it!

JEFF: You mean none of me belongs to me, Pop?

JOHN: I want to see you in your uniform! Now, what is all this talk about?

JEFF: It's about you and me and the battlefields. About who is Jeff Williams, Pop.

JOHN: Then tell me who in the hell is he!

JEFF: A dude who hated navigation to the point where he got migraines. Who wanted to throw up on every flight—motion-sickness pills notwithstanding. Whose ears pained him from takeoff to landing. Do you know what it feels like when your ears don't clear?

MATTIE: My baby!

(*Bass enters.*)

JEFF: Don't baby me, Mama. I still think I'm the baddest, but I ain't— nor do I want to be a supernigger, 'cause that's all a supernigger is, a *super*nigger. Someone who spends his life trying to prove he's as good as the Man. On my last flight exam—a night celestial—I wound up eighty miles into Mexico, according to my computations, while everybody else's figures put us at Harlingen Air Force Base, Texas. We were circling the field. The sun was coming up, soft and pastel like someone had sprinkled red pepper all over the clouds. I tore off a piece of my flight log and began writing a poem. You see, Pop, I do believe in poetry. It was a simple poem—all about the awe of creation. Anyway—along came this Lieutenant Forthright—a Texas cracker whose one joke, repeated over and over again, was "Hee, haw, students, never worry about being lost. At least you knows ya'll is in the airplane. Yuk, yuk." This creep caught sight of my poem, and this big Howdy Doody grin spread all over his face, and he started laughing. This Howdy Doody pig started laughing. This subhuman, caveman, orangutan was laughing at something he couldn't even understand. Then he showed the poem to the other instructor orangutans, and they started laughing. And that did it, Pop. I said to myself, "This ain't my stick. What am I doing this for? What am I doing this shit for? This navigator jive ain't for me." They sent me before a board of senior officers. You see, this was the second time I'd failed my night celestial flying exam, and they gave me a flat-ass white all-American lieutenant for counsel, and you know what he told me? He told me to cop a plea, to cop a plea, Pop, to express my love of country and dedication to the air force! To lick ass! That way, he said, they'd only wash me back a few months and I could still come through. But I told that board, "Let go my toe!" And they replied, "What?" You know, the way white people do when they don't believe their ears. So I screamed at the top of my voice, "Let go my nigger toe so I can stand up and be a man." . . . I guess they thought I was insane. They hemmed and hawed and cleared their throats, but they let go my toe, Mama. I had cut loose the man. Then I went right home and I cut loose my fine fox, and I cut loose my so-called black brother officers, and I felt like there was no more glue holding my shoes to the track; I felt I could almost fly, Pop, 'cause I was a supernigger no more. . . . So I ain't proving nothing to nobody— white, black, blue, or polka dot—to nobody! Not even to you, Daddy Johnny. . . . Mama, you give that thing—that uniform thing to the Salvation Army or to the Goodwill or whatever, 'cause it will never have the good fortune to get on my back again.

DUDLEY: *Bravo! Bravissimo!*

(*Bass fades.* GRANDMA *sings "Onward, Christian Soldiers," and for some time no one says anything.*)

JEFF (*quietly*): It's all about battlefields—just like you said, Pop.

(JOHN *pauses for an infinite time, looking at* JEFF, *then at* MATTIE *and the others. With great deliberation he then collects his coat and starts walking out slowly.*)

MATTIE (*trying to stop him*): John! It's Jeff's coming-home party!

(*He doesn't stop, exiting through the front door—leaving everyone suspended in a state of sad frustration. Lights fade as they all avoid looking at each other.*)

ACT THREE

It is Friday evening, DUDLEY, MATTIE, GRANDMA, *and* JEFF *are seated in the living room.* ANN *is in the kitchen busily putting away dishes. The air is very heavy. After a long pause,* JEFF *rises, moves toward the window.*

JEFF: I noticed the kids tore down the baskets on the basketball court, Ma.

MATTIE: Yeah, well, they weren't made to be swung on, that's for sure.

JEFF: Why are we so damn destructive, Ma?

MATTIE: I guess 'cause we're so mad. . . . Lord, where could he be?

GRANDMA (*intoxicated*): Ain't nothing strange about a man staying away from home. Does 'em good.

MATTIE: Mama, it's Friday. He's been gone since Saturday.

DUDLEY: Oh, he'll be all right, Mattie.

MATTIE: It's like he just disappeared—

JEFF: Mama, have you checked the police station today?

MATTIE: Five times!

DUDLEY: Well, won't do any good to worry. He's a strong, capable man with a whole lot of sense. He's probably in some hotel writing.

GRANDMA: You mean *drinking!*

DUDLEY: Well—both then.

MATTIE (*on the verge of tears*): Anything could happen to him. All these dope fiends running 'round Harlem, banging people in the head for a quarter. He could be laying in some vacant lot—hurt—or, or—

JEFF: No, Mama—he's all right!

MATTIE: Six days!

DUDLEY: I'm gonna have to give you a sedative if you don't calm down, Mattie.

GRANDMA: I like sedatives myself.

DUDLEY: You starting on your medicine a little early, aren't you, Grandma?

GRANDMA: I takes my medicine whenever I need it. It opens up my chest and cuts the phlegm.

MATTIE: Poor thing—he could be seriously injured—

(*Bass enters.*)

GRANDMA: Now, that's exactly what happened to my Ben Brown. He was wild as a pinecone and as savage as a grizzly, and black! Black as a night what ain't got no moon. He'd stay out in the woods for days at a time—always come back with a mess of fish or a sack of rabbits, and possums—that man could tree a possum like he was a hound dog. I guess he was so black till they musta thought he was a shadow, creeping up on 'em. (*Pause.*) One day he just didn't come back.

MATTIE: Mama, do we have to hear *it* again?

GRANDMA: A load of buckshot ripped his guts right out—right out on the ground!

MATTIE: Mama!

GRANDMA: It was an old redneck cracker named Isaiah what been poaching on our land. Ben said he'd kill any white man he caught hunting on our land. So there they were—both dead—Ben musta been strangling him. I guess Isaiah figured a load of buckshot would put a stop to him. But there was Ben, still holding on to that cracker's throat when we found 'em. Couldn't nothing stop my husband from doing what he had a mind to do. They had to pry his hands loose. Folks come from miles around to attend his funeral. White folks too. Yes, they did. He was a king in his own right, and they knew it. Gawdamercy, my man was a king. And I know he's in *Glory!* Just awaiting for his Wilhemina. I knows it. (*Starts humming "Rock of Ages." Bass fades.*)

DUDLEY: The reason I asked to see you all tonight—well—well— because Mattie and I have something very serious to discuss with you.

MATTIE: Do they have to know, Dudley?

DUDLEY: It's only fair that they should know, Mattie. Mattie is going to have to be hospitalized. I guess that's why Johnny hasn't been home— I guess he's off somewhere—brooding.

MATTIE: Dudley! You promised me you wouldn't tell him—

DUDLEY: I made a decision, Mattie. It was either keep my promise to you or prepare Johnny ahead of time for what might kill him—if he heard it too sudden-like . . .

MATTIE: Then you're responsible—If anything's happened to him— you're responsible.

DUDLEY: I made a judgment—

JEFF: Will somebody please tell me what's going on?

DUDLEY: Jeff, we got the report today. Mattie's got, well, several growths—malignant growths. Mattie's got cancer.

MATTIE: There you go again—about as gentle as a sledgehammer.

JEFF: How serious?

DUDLEY: Very serious, but not hopeless—the location prevents removal, but radium treatments might arrest the—

MATTIE: Jeff, you don't see me upset, do you, son?

JEFF (*cupping her face in his hands lovingly*): Mama!

MATTIE: I'm gonna die—that's all there is to it.

GRANDMA: No such thing! You know Dudley here's a cockeyed quack—

MATTIE: Mama, the only thing I'm worried about is the whereabouts of my man.

JEFF: But you can't think negative like that—

(GRANDMA *sings loudly, "For His eye is on the sparrow, and I know He watches me."*)

MATTIE: Hush, Mama.

(ANN *comes to the door. Bass enters.*)

Now, what old negative? Look at me! I've had a full life with an extraordinary man who fell upon me and fed my soul like manna from heaven—bless him, God bless him wherever he is—And you—where could I get a finer-looking, stronger-looking, more loving son than my Jeff? And I'll be around to see you marry Ann—a gift to you, Jeff, and don't you abuse her. I got my mother beside me, still alive and kicking. And Dudley Stanton—a mainstay—your father's and my spiritual brother—

DUDLEY: Thank you, sweetheart—

MATTIE: No, Dudley! Thank you. Now, what old negative thinking? If Johnny were to come through that door right now, I'd be the happiest woman in God's creation—and like my Johnny says, "Lord, I don't feel noways tired—I could go on for another century."

JEFF (*very upset*): You will, Mama. You will.

MATTIE: But it's my time, baby. I guess maybe I've done whatever He put me here to do.

(*There is a knock on the front door.* ANN *answers it. It is* MO *and* GAIL. ANN *shows them into the living room.*)

MO: Dr. Stanton! Mrs. Williams—Grandma—

MATTIE: How've you been, Li'l Mo? Lord, you sure have grown.

GAIL: Mrs. Williams—everybody—

(GRANDMA *grunts.*)

MO: I got to see you, Jeff.

JEFF: Is it important?

MO: I need your help, Jeff.

JEFF: Let's go into the kitchen. I'll be right back, Mama.

(JEFF, MO, GAIL, *and* ANN *move toward kitchen. Livingroom conversation continues.*)

MATTIE: Looks like rain.

GRANDMA: I sure hate this dirty city when it rains—looks like a cesspool.

DUDLEY: One thing good about rain in February—it means an early spring.

JEFF (*from the kitchen*): Look, man, I know I promised Gail—but that's gonna have to wait. My folks are in heavy trouble.

MO: Yeah, I heard about your father.

ANN: We just found out Mrs. Williams has cancer.

GAIL: Oh, Jeff, I'm so sorry.

MO: Wow, me too, man—I see what you mean. Wow!

MATTIE (*from the living room*): Don't you think—well—we could go on without Jeff, Dudley? He's just a child.

DUDLEY: He's a man now, Mattie, and with Grandma getting up there and Johnny—taking it so hard—

GRANDMA: Who's getting up where? A body ain't no older than their toes, and mine twinkle a damn sight better than yours—

DUDLEY: When you've had your medicine.

GAIL (*from the kitchen*): How serious is it, Jeff?

ANN: It's inoperable. The only hope is radium treatment.

MO: I'm sorry, man. I really am.

JEFF: Thanks.

MATTIE (*from living room*): Mama, sing that song for me.

GRANDMA: Which song, daughter?

MATTIE: "Rock of Ages."

(GRANDMA *begins singing soothingly.* MATTIE *joins her from time to time.*)

MO (*from kitchen*): All them years we was running together, Mrs. Williams was like a mother to me too, remember, Jeff?

JEFF: Yeah.

MO: I guess that changes things 'round. I wouldn't want to put more weight on you now, especially behind news like that.

ANN: What is the problem, Gail?

GAIL: There's a stool pigeon in the organization. It's gotta be either Chips, Skeeter, or Al.

ANN: Oh no.

GAIL: If we don't find him out quick, everything's liable to blow up in our faces. Remember what I told y'all 'bout that cop Buckley?

ANN: What can Jeff do?

GAIL: Mo's laying a trap tonight where the stoolie's gonna hafta phone his boss. He'll hafta do it from either the pool-hall phone next to headquarters, or the bar phone down the street. Mo's got both phones bugged, ready to be monitored. I'll be listening in the pool-hall basement, and we wanted Jeff to cover the phone in the bar. Jeff's the only person we can trust.

MO: What about it, Jeff?

JEFF (*angrily*): I got no time for this cloak-and-dagger shit—my folks are hurting, man, didn't you hear?

MO: Okay, man. Okay, I dig.

ANN: What about me?

JEFF (*adamantly*): Hell, no. I won't let you or my family get implicated in this shit—

ANN: Jeff, I don't intend to get implicated—but what Gail and Mo are asking doesn't seem unreasonable. Remember?—my brothers were betrayed once, Jeff. My father is still in prison as a result. Nine years with still no release in sight. No matter what you and I might think about Mo's activities, he certainly does not deserve betrayal. I could not live with myself knowing that I had an opportunity to help and didn't.

MO: Thanks for the offer, baby. But I'm afraid it's no good. What has to be done and where it's gotta happen, a woman would only draw suspicion.

JEFF: How long would it take, Mo?

MO: No more than an hour's time, Jeff. All together, you should be back here three hours from right now. I promise you, Jeff, it'll be no sweat. I just need to know, you dig?

JEFF: Why you sure he'll make contact?

MO: He's gotta. Tonight is the night of our big thing, Jeff. I'm ordering a change of plan at the last minute that's gonna make the rat hafta contact the pigs. Meanwhile, nobody but me knows that I'm crossing everybody up by following through with my original plan. Nobody's gonna get hurt, Jeff, just some property damaged. While everybody is on their way to the police station, I'll be headed—

JEFF: I don't want to know, Mo. I'll monitor the phone for you, but I don't want to know nothing. Don't crowd me, Mo, you understand?

MO: That's cool, Jeff.

JEFF: This is as far as I go, Mo.

MO: I gotcha, Brother Jeff. I dig.

ANN: And I will sit with Gail at the pool hall.

JEFF: No!

ANN: She shouldn't be alone, Jeff.

JEFF: I SAID NO!

MO: It's safe, Jeff. I swear. You know I wouldn't have my woman doing anything that would put her in a trick. No jeopardy, man, I promise.

MATTIE (*from living room*): What time you got, Dudley?

DUDLEY: Five after seven.

MATTIE: You think he's had his dinner?

DUDLEY: Sure, sweetheart. Keep singing, Grandma.

JEFF (*from the kitchen*): All right, Ann.

MO: Groovy. Make it to the bar about 8:45, Jeff. Take a cab so you'll be seen as little as possible. The bartender, a buddy of mine, will take you to the setup. About the same time Jeff leaves here, Gail will pick you up outside, Ann. Okay, we'll split now—by the back door. So we won't disturb—Like I said, Jeff, I really am sorry about Mrs. Williams. I really mean it.

JEFF: Yeah, later, Mo.

MO: Okay.

(MO *and* GAIL *exit out the kitchen door.* JEFF *and* ANN *return to the living room.*)

MATTIE: What happened to Mo and his girl?
JEFF: They went out the back, Mama.

(*There is an awkward silence.*)

DUDLEY: Jeff, Mattie will be admitted to the hospital on Monday.
MATTIE: Couldn't I be treated at home, Dudley? Ann's a nurse. She could—
ANN: You need special equipment, Mrs. Williams, but of course I'll be your nurse.
MATTIE: Would you, Ann? I hate those nurses at Harlem. They're so indifferent and snooty.
JEFF: Goddamn!
GRANDMA: Watch your mouth! Can't even pee straight and using that kind of language.

(*There's a second sound at the back door.* JOHN: "*I'm all right! I can make it!*" JEFF *and* ANN *rush to open the door, exiting. We hear voices outside—* MO *and* GAIL *explaining.* JOHN *enters, assisted by* JEFF *and* ANN. *He has a week's growth of beard. His eyes have the deep-socket look of an alcoholic who's been on a substantial bender. His overall appearance is gaunt and shoddy. His clothes are filthy ahnd wrinkled. He obviously smells. His hands have a slight tremor. There is a deep gash above his left eye. Bass enters.* JOHN *is helped into a chair,* MATTIE *embracing him.*)

MATTIE: Johnny, sweet Johnny! We've been so worried about you.
JOHN: Don't, Mattie! I smell something awful.
DUDLEY: Move, Mattie. Let me take a look at that cut. (*Moves* MATTIE *aside*) Jeff, bring my bag. It's in the hallway there.

(JEFF *exits to hallway.*)

Hand me a towel, Grandma.
GRANDMA: Old wino, nigger.
DUDLEY: Wet it with cold water. Maybe we can stop the bleeding.
ANN: I'll hold it, Dr. Stanton.
DUDLEY: Good girl.

(ANN *presses the folded paper towel to* JOHN'S *cut.*)

JOHN: Fighting lady Ann. I sure needed me a fighting lady out there. You shoulda seen me, Mattie, when them young hoods jumped me.

MATTIE: I saw you, baby. Every second.

JOHN: I was like a cornered wildcat. I was battlin' 'em to a draw. Then Li'l Mo and his fighting lady came up.

DUDLEY: It's a bird, it's a plane, it's a Supercullud Guy!

JOHN: Super Black Man, sicklehead. I ain't been hanging out with them militant winos for nothing.

DUDLEY: Folks, take a look at an aging African warrior, trying to make a comeback.

JOHN (*singing to a made-up tune*):
When I get home to Africa
I'll buy myself a mango.
Grab myself a monkey gal
And do the monkey tango.

DUDLEY: When'd you eat last?

JOHN: Can you imagine. The great Marcus Garvey.

DUDLEY: Niggers used to sing that to make fun of Marcus Garvey. Can you imagine. The great Marcus Garvey.

DUDLEY: Answer my question! When was the last time you had a decent meal?

JOHN: Wednesday. Or was it Tuesday?

DUDLEY: What are you trying to do, Johnny?

(JEFF *returns with the bag.*)

ANN: I'll do it. (*She swabs the wound and bandages it.*)

MATTIE: Where've you been, baby?

JOHN: In the desert, Mattie. Out in the desert, like Christ, talking to myself.

GRANDMA: Christ was talking to the devil, ya old wino.

JOHN: Same difference. But I took care of the old bastard. I said, Get thee behind me, Prince of Darkness! Then I got thirsty and came home. I wanted to see me some angels.

JEFF: Pop, you okay now? I mean, for real?

JOHN: Yeah, Jeff. Welcome home, son. My son is really home. And I'm happy he's found his battlefield.

MATTIE: You won't do it again, will you, Johnny? If something's troubling you, let's talk about it. Okay? Now promise!

JOHN: I was all right, Mattie—really. Dulcey gave me a room over her store. I told her I wanted to think—to write some poetry. I wanted to write a love poem—to you, Mattie. Words are like precious jewels, did you know that? But I couldn't find any jewels precious enough to match you, Mattie. So I took to drinking, and before I knew it, I was drunk all the time. I couldn't stop. Then yesterday these little men came to visit me—about one foot tall. They both had a T-shirt on with a zero on the chest. And they carried two little satchels. I asked 'em what they were carrying in 'em, and they opened up the satchels, and they were empty. I asked them their names, and they said, "The Nothing Brothers." That's when I figured it was time to go home.

DUDLEY: Delirium tremens—D.T.'s from not eating.

JOHN: Whatever. I knew it was time to come home. I knew it was Friday too. Dudley told me he'd have some information for me on Friday.

(*Tense silence.*)

DUDLEY (*avoiding it*): What kind of information?

JEFF: We all know, Pop.

JOHN: You all know? Then—

DUDLEY: Mattie will be admitted Monday morning.

(*At this point,* JOHN *goes berserk. Screams at the top of his voice. Racing around the room, whipping with an imaginary whip, and screaming, "Get out, get out, you motherfuckers. Get out of my father's house!" He falls to the floor—somewhat exhausted, looks up as if to heaven. Bass counterpoint increases.*)

JOHN: You son-of-a-bitch, why do you keep fucking with me? What do you want from me, you bastard?

MATTIE: Johnny, don't talk like that. That's blasphemy.

JOHN: He keeps fucking with me, Mattie. When I was a kid, the bigger kids used to always pick on me. I had to fight every day. They said it was because I was a smart aleck. (*To the heavens*) Is that why, you bastard, 'cause I'm a smart aleck?

MATTIE: You can't talk to Him like that. He'll turn His back on you.

JOHN: You know what I'm gonna do on Judgment Day? I'm gonna grab that motherfucker by the throat and squeeze and squeeze and squeeze until I get an answer.

MATTIE: He doesn't have to give you an answer. I thought you said, "Get thee behind me—" I thought you took care a Satan!

JOHN (*breaking into tears*): I tried, Mattie. I tried—you don't know how fucking hard I tried.

MATTIE (*embracing him*): I know, baby. I see you every second.

JOHN: You shoulda let me whip 'em out, Mattie. You shoulda let me whip out the bullshit.

MATTIE: We weren't made that way, baby.

JOHN: You shoulda let me whip out the money changers. You deserve so much more than this nothing. I wanted to do so much for you, Mattie.

MATTIE: I got *you*, baby. I got the kindest, sweetest man in the world. I got the Rolls-Royce, baby.

JOHN: I coulda done it, Mattie. God knows, I coulda done it!

MATTIE: I know, baby. I put it on you. I stopped you and I'm sorry. I'm sorry. Will you forgive me, sweet baby? Please forgive me! I was selfish, Johnny. I've been so goddam happy! All I ever cared about was seeing you walk, stumble, or stagger through that door. I only complained because I felt I should say something—but I never meant it, Johnny, I never meant a word. You couldn't have given me nothing more, baby. I'da just keeled over and died from too much happiness. Just keeled over and died.

(*Lights begin to dim as bass rises. Music remains as long as it takes actors to exit and get into place for next scene. When lights finally rise again,* MATTIE *and* DUDLEY *are sitting in living room,* MATTIE *under heavy sedation, intermittently knitting, nodding from time to time.* DUDLEY *is watching TV, smoking a cigar. Silence ensues for a long time. Finally* MATTIE *addresses* DUDLEY.)

MATTIE: What'd you give me, Dudley? Sure is strong. Can hardly keep my head up.

DUDLEY: Do you feel any pain?

MATTIE: Not now.

DUDLEY: Then it's doing its job. You'll rest good when you go to bed.

MATTIE: Which can't be too long from now. The way I'm feeling.

(JOHN *appears at the top of the stairs; descends slowly, as he is absorbed in reading some pages. He enters the living room and announces quietly . . .*)

JOHN: I finished it.

MATTIE: What?

JOHN: A poem I been working on, Mattie. It's your poem, Mattie. "The River Niger." It ain't a love poem, but it's for you, sugar, dedicated to my superbitch, Mattie Jean Williams.

DUDLEY: Read it to us, nigger.

(ANN *and* GAIL *are seen entering the back door.* JEFF *too.* JOHN *begins to read, and bass begins low with African motif and gradually rises.* JEFF *and girls begin to engage in conversation, but desist when they hear* JOHN. *They drift to living room.*)

JOHN:
I am the River Niger—hear my waters!
I am totally flexible.
I am the River Niger—hear my waters!

My waters are the first sperm of the world.
When the earth was but a faceless whistling embryo,
Life burst from my liquid kernels like popcorn.
Hear my waters—rushing and popping in muffled finger-drum
    staccato.
It is life you hear, stretching its limbs in my waters—
I am the River Niger! Hear my waters!
When the Earth Mother cracked into continents,
I was vomited from the cold belly of the Atlantic
To slip slyly into Africa
From the underside of her brow.
I see no—
Hear no—
Speak no evil,
But I know.
I gossip with the crocodile
And rub elbows with the river horse.
I have swapped morbid jokes with the hyena
And heard his dry cackle at twilight.
I see no—
Hear no—
Speak no evil,
But I know.

I am the River Niger—hear my waters!
Hear, I say, hear my waters, man!
They is Mammy-tammys, baby.
I have lapped at the pugnacious hips of brown mamas.
Have tapped on the doors of their honeydews, yeah!
I have shimmered like sequins
As they sucked me over their blueberry tongues,
As they sung me to sleep in the glittering afternoon, yeah!
I have washed the red wounds of clay-decorated warriors—
Bad, bad dudes who smirked at the leopard.
I have cast witches from gabbling babies, yeah!
Have known the warm piss from newly circumcised boy.
Have purified the saliva from sun-drenched lions—
Do you hear me talking?
I am the River Niger!
I came to the cloudy Mississippi
Over keels of incomprehensible woe.
I ran 'way to the Henry Hudson

Under the sails of ragged hope.
I am the River Niger,
Transplanted to Harlem
From the Harlem River Drive.
Hear me, my children—hear my waters!
I sleep in your veins.
I see no—
Hear no—
Speak no evil,
But I know, and I know that you know.
I flow to the ends of your spirit.
Hold hands, my children, and I will flow to the ends of the earth,
And the whole world will hear my waters.
I am the River Niger! Don't deny me!
Do you hear me? Don't deny me!

(*Pause. Bass fades.*)

MATTIE: That's very beautiful, Johnny.
JEFF: Yeah, Pop, that's pretty nice.
DUDLEY (*sarcastically*): Interesting!
JOHN: Ya monkey chaser.
JEFF: How you feeling, Mama?
MATTIE: Okay, I guess. A little woozy, but I'm going to bed now, and I couldn't think of a better time than after Johnny's poem. Thank you, dear.
JOHN: Be up soon, Mattie.
MATTIE: Take your time.
DUDLEY: Yeah, I'd better get home, too.
JEFF: Good-night, Mama.
ANN and GAIL: Good-night, Mrs. Williams.
MATTIE: Good-night. (*She exits.*)

(GRANDMA *enters, humming "Rock of Ages." They pass each other on the stairs.*)

Good-night, Mama.
GRANDMA: Sleep tight! Don't let the bedbugs bite.

(MATTIE *exits, shaking her head.* GRANDMA *hums throughout this scene. She comes into the living room.*)

JEFF: How ya feel, Pop?
JOHN: Fine! Fine, still a little shaky, but all right.
JEFF: Ya got any booze, Pop?

JOHN: No, I'm drying out. Doctor's orders.

GRANDMA: Where's the *TV Guide?* (*She searches for it.*)

DUDLEY (*finding it underneath him*): Oh, here it is, Mrs. Brown. I was sitting on it.

GRANDMA: It was under you all this time?

DUDLEY: I guess so.

GRANDMA: Then let it cool off a little bit before you give it to me.

JEFF (*to* ANN *and* GAIL): Let's make it into the kitchen.

ANN: I'm still cold from outside.

DUDLEY (*to* JEFF): Has it started raining yet?

JEFF: It's raining and snowing at the same time.

(*They move to kitchen.*)

JOHN: See, Dudley, life's full of contradictions.

DUDLEY: Ain't nothing contradictory about nature, man. Nature is everything. It's human beings who are contradictions.

JOHN: Well, ain't human beings a part of nature?

DUDLEY (*seriously*): Guess so, now that you mention it.

JOHN: That's why we're so messed up. We forget that we're just a part of nature. (*Pause.*) Put on the TV, Dudley.

DUDLEY: I should be going home.

JOHN: Relax, man.

(DUDLEY *switches on the TV.*)

JEFF (*from the kitchen*): What'd *you* hear, Gail?

GAIL: Nothing but Skeeter, making a horse connection.

ANN: We thought it might be a code, but it sounded innocent enough.

GAIL: What about you?

JEFF: I heard something all right. But I couldn't identify the voice. The bartender was no help; he was somewhere else when the call was made.

GAIL: What did the caller say?

JEFF: Plan B.

GAIL: That's all—"Plan B"?

JEFF: Right. And the voice on the other end said, "You sure?" The caller said, "Yes—Plan B."

GAIL: You couldn't recognize the voice?

JEFF: No, but I might if I heard it again.

GAIL: I shouldn't have let you talk me into coming here. Mo might need me.

JEFF: Calm down, baby. We'll hear soon.

GAIL: But something might have happened.

ANN: He wanted you to come with us.

JEFF: Stop worrying, Mo's all right.

GAIL: I can't help it . . . (*She attempts to calm herself, crossing to the back door and looking out.*) It sure is beginning to come down. Beginning to stick.

ANN: I've been away from South Africa for a long time, but I still can't get used to snow.

GAIL: Snow makes everything so quiet. It's spooky.

GRANDMA (*entering the kitchen*): Ya wants some spirits?

JEFF: We sure do, Grandma.

GRANDMA: Turn your backs. (*She produces a bottle of Old Grand-dad from her new hiding place on top of the cabinet—pours each of them a drink.*) The way things been happening 'round here today, a body needs some spirits. Here! Besides, this child's so fidgety—(*Referring to* GAIL)— done got phlegm acting up again.

(GRANDMA *downs hers. For a second they watch in amazement—then down theirs. There is a noise at the back door.* JEFF *goes to the door.*)

JEFF: It's Mo and Skeets.

(JEFF *opens door.* MO *drags* SKEETER *in. It's obvious he's been hurt.*)

MO: Pigs are swarming all over headquarters!

(DUDLEY *enters, followed closely by* JOHN. DUDLEY *examines* SKEETER.)

DUDLEY: Gunshot wound. What's going on 'round here? Bring me my bag, Ann. You're very lucky, young man—no bones broken. Put a tourniquet on that arm, Ann, while I clean it out.

(ANN *and* DUDLEY *work on* SKEETER. JEFF *pulls* MO *into the living room.*)

JEFF: Why in the hell did you bring him here?

MO: I figured Dr. Stanton would be here—

JEFF: I told you I don't want my family implicated in this shit—Why didn't you take him to your place?

(JOHN *comes to the door.*)

MO: I live over headquarters! The pigs—

JEFF: Oh, shit—shit—what happened?

MO: It's stupid—stupid. I mean, we had just crossed the street. I mean, we were just walking 'round the fence when this pig started blowing his whistle and yelling at us.

JEFF: They musta been alerted.

MO: Fucking Skeeter panicked—started running—what the hell am I supposed to do? I'm carry a tote bag with four sticks of dynamite. So I start running too. Next thing I know, there're four pigs chasing us. One fires and spins Skeets clean 'round. Skeets is screaming and shit, and they're gaining, so I blast off a couple and knock trigger-happy on his ass.

JEFF: What—you crazy motherfucker, coming here after that?

JOHN: You mean, they just started shooting? You didn't shoot first?

MO: Why would we do that?

JOHN: You sure?

MO: I don't want to hurt nobody if I can help it, Mr. Williams.

JOHN: You think he's dead?

MO: I don't know. He hit the ground so hard I could almost feel it.

JOHN: I sure hope you killed the bastard. But if you call yourself a revolutionary, then you supposed to know where you gonna take your wounded. Takes more'n wearing a goddamn beret.

DUDLEY (*from the kitchen*): Yeah! Why don't I set up another office over here?

(*There is a wild banging on the front door.* JEFF *answers the door.* AL *enters, followed closely by* CHIPS.)

JEFF (*angrily*): What's going on?

AL: There are wall-to-wall pigs at headquarters. And Mo said—

JEFF (*to* MO): And you told them to come here if that happened—

(*Silence.*)

Didn't you? Didn't you? Didn't I tell you not to crowd me, ya stupid bastard?

MO: I was wrong, Jeff. I'm sorry.

JEFF: You're sorry.

(JEFF *leaps on* MO *and is separated by* JOHN.)

I'll kill him, Pop, so help me. I'll kill him!

JOHN: You'll wake up your mother.

(*In the next second, a confusion of sirens and police whistles—lights shining through the front windows and the back door, and a policeman on a bullhorn*)

LIEUTENANT STAPLES'S VOICE (*from outside*): This is Lieutenant Staples from the Thirty-second Police Precinct. We know you are in there and who's in there. We gotcha front and back, plus men on the roof. You got five minutes to throw out your weapons and come out of there. And let me remind whoever else is in there not to harbor criminals from the law. You got five minutes. If there're innocent people in there, their blood will be on your hands.

JOHN: Give me those goddamn guns. (*Pause.*) Come on, come on! They can't prove a thing—except those guns. Dudley, get Skeeter's. Come on, Mo, give it to me.

(MO *hesitates, but gives it to him.*)

CHIPS: Al's the one, Mo. A fucking Judas faggot.

AL: You lie!

CHIPS: There were cops everywhere. You said not to do nothing when we got to the police station until you and Skeeter showed, right? Well, when you didn't show, he ran across the street and deliberately bumped into one of 'em—

AL: He's lying.

CHIPS: And whispered something in his ear. Next thing I know, every pig and his mother is jumping into a car—that's when it hit me you was pulling a trick, and the state office building plan was still on.

AL: I didn't have a damn thing to do with that.

CHIPS: You shoulda heard the squawk boxes, "State office building—emergency—emergency." The block was vacant inside of a minute.

AL: You're not believing this shit?

CHIPS: Then he tried to shake me, Mo. Caught a cab, and you know what he told him? Told him to go to the state office building.

AL: I gave him the address of headquarters.

CHIPS: You lie, nigger. I overheard you.

SKEETER (*coming out of the kitchen*): And the way you keep questioning me about Buckley—

MO: Why didn't you tell me about that?

AL: He's your informer, Mo. He'd do anything for horse. (*Pause.*) He told them pigs to go to the state office building. He's the one.

MO: He was with me.

JEFF (*to* AL): It was you. I heard you.

AL: Heard me what?

JEFF: The phone—you phoned. It was your voice. You said, "B." The voice at the other end said, "Are you sure?" and you repeated, "B!"

AL: That don't prove nothing—Skeeter left too—we both went to the phone.

JEFF: Okay, if it wasn't you then, suppose I were to tell you I killed Buckley?

AL: What do you know about Buckley?

JEFF: I did it. I killed him.

AL: How'd he die?

JEFF: Two slugs in the chest.

AL: What caliber?

JEFF: Forty-five. I stole it from the air force.

AL: Don't shit me. Buckley was killed almost a month ago. Ya only been here a week.

JEFF: What makes you so sure?

MO: What are you doing, Jeff?

JEFF: I was released from active duty exactly one month from last Friday.

AL: Bullshit!

JEFF: Wanta see my release papers?

ANN: Jeff!

JEFF: Stay out of it, Ann!

(JEFF *fumbles through wallet and gives* AL *his release papers.* AL *reads them.*)

AL (*pulling out his revolver*): All right, stand still, all of you! I took this assignment for one reason and one reason only, to find out who killed Buckley. And now I know. (*To* JEFF) You killed Buckley. He was worth ten of you Brillo heads. Now his friends out there are gonna take this place apart, and all of you are in trouble, you hear. You motherfuckers, fucking up the country with your slogans and your jive-ass threats. Militants, ain't that a bitch. Black cripples, trying to scale a mountain. I hate the smell of you assholes.

MO: Jeff's lying, can't you see that? I killed Buckley.

SKEETER: I did it.

CHIPS: I did it.

AL: No, no, it fits. It fits. I know where each of you mothers were when Buckley was killed. None of you coulda done it. He did it. Why didn't I think of good old Jeff? All I heard about was good old Jeff. Jeff this—Jeff that—till you bastards staged your phony scene to throw me off the track when he got here.

MO: Don't be stupid. It was an outside job.

AL (*to* JEFF): Yeah—him.

ANN: What are you doing, Jeff? You know you were with me that whole month in Canada!

(*This causes* AL *to pause for a moment in frozen doubt.* JOHN *seizes the opportunity to raise the gun still in his hand, pointing it at* AL.)

JOHN: Drop it, son.

(AL *whirls and shoots. There is an exchange of gun play between the two* men. AL *goes down, killed instantly.* JOHN *also goes down, mortally wounded.*)

JEFF (*rushing to his father's side, followed closely by* DUDLEY): POP!
JOHN: The guns, Jeff—put 'em in the drain in the basement. Al's still holding his? Good.
JEFF: Pop!
JOHN: Hurry, you don't want Daddy Johnny to die for nothing, do you?

(JEFF *grabs* SKEETER'*s and* CHIP'*s, tries to take* MO'*s.*)

No! We need Mo's—this is yours, ain't it, Mo?
MO: Yes, sir.
JOHN: Go on, son.

(JEFF *exits.*)

(*To* DUDLEY, *who's been trying to get at* JOHN'*s wound*) Don't worry about that, ya monkey chaser. They'll be in here in a second.
DUDLEY: You're hurt, man. Ann—my bag—

(ANN *starts off.*)

JOHN: Fuck your bag, Dudley. Go to the door—tell that Lieutenant Staples—tell him—to give us five more minutes—just five more— then he can make his arrests—
DUDLEY: You'll die if I don't—
JOHN: I'll die anyway. Do as I say! Before they shoot up Mattie's house.

(ANN *comes back with bag, starts preparing dressings.* JEFF *returns.* MATTIE *appears at the top of the stairs.*)

MATTIE (*extremely drowsy.* JEFF *and* GAIL *run to her, the rest are stupefied.*): I had a dream, and I heard this noise in the middle of it.
DUDLEY (*waving a handkerchief out the front door and shouting*): Lieutenant Staples—Lieutenant Staples.
STAPLES'S VOICE: This is Lieutenant Staples—what's going on in there?
DUDLEY: I'm Dr. Dudley Stanton—next-door neighbor. A man's been seriously wounded in here. Call an ambulance.
STAPLES'S VOICE: Throw out your guns.
DUDLEY: I think it would be best for you to see the situation for yourself.
JOHN: Good boy, Dudley. They don't care nothing 'bout niggers killing themselves nohow.

DUDLEY (*to* STAPLES): Both weapons are secured. I have them. Give us five minutes, then come in.

STAPLES'S VOICE: If anyone tries to escape, my men have orders to shoot—

MATTIE: What on earth's going on?

DUDLEY: No one will. I give my word. Five minutes. (*Closes the door*)

CHIPS: We *got* to get outta here!

MO: Shut up, and stay tight!

JEFF (*to* MO): Do you see what you brought in here tonight? (*Leaps for* MO *once again*)

JOHN: Jeff, stop it. Don't make a mockery out of my death. Sit down, all of you, and listen to me.

MATTIE (*for the first time realizing* JOHN's *hurt*): Johnny! Johnny!

JOHN: Keep Mattie away, Dudley—keep her away—

DUDLEY (*restraining her*): Try and be calm, Mattie.

JOHN: Wipe off the handle on Mo's gun, Jeff.

(JEFF *does it.*)

Okay, now give it to me. (*He grips the gun firmly several times.*) I don't want nobody's fingerprints on it but mine.

MATTIE: Johnny, you're bleeding—

JOHN (*with savage power*): Mattie, I love ya, Mattie. I ain't got much life left.

MATTIE: Johnny, no!

JOHN: I got to get our children straight before I go—now be my superbitch and shut the fuck up.

(MATTIE *understands and obeys.*)

Now you youngbloods listen to me. Here's the story: I am the real leader of the organization—ya got me. I was with Skeeter when he got shot. I fired the shot which hit the cop at the office building. I made it back here—found out that Al here is a Judas, and we had a shoot-out. The rest of you have never owned a gun—only your leader—me! Ya got that?

(GRANDMA *drunk, and in a state of shock, comes strangely alive. She thinks* JOHN *is her Ben. She rushes up and falls at* JOHN's *knees.*)

GRANDMA: BEN—BEN BROWN! (*Reaches for* JOHN's *gun*) Gimme that shotgun.

(MATTIE *blocks her.*)

MATTIE (*very calm and solemn, almost eerie*): No, Mama.

GRANDMA: I'll just shoot right into the crowd, daughter. See 'em, look at their faces! They's glad to see my Ben dead. Lawdamercy! He's dead! (*Crying from an ancient wound*) Gimme that shotgun, child. Ten for one, ten for one—my man is a king—you crackers—ya dirty old redneck crackers. (*Breaks into "Rock of Ages." Bass counterpoint seeps in.*)

JOHN: Hear that, Mattie. The old battle-ax finally gave me a compliment. Where's my Mattie? Let me see my Mattie.

(MATTIE's *let through. They embrace.*)

MATTIE: I'm with you every second, baby.

JOHN: I knew she'd slip one day. I'm sorry, Mattie.

MATTIE: What for, baby?

JOHN: I'm cheating ya, honey—going first this way.

MATTIE: Hush now!

JOHN: Don't suffer long, honey. Just give up and take my hand. The children—the children will be all right now. (*Pause.*) Look at Dr. Dudley Stanton down there. Trying to save my life. Ain't that a bitch! See what a big old fake you've been all along. Don't worry, Dudley—fighting lady Ann—Jeff—ya got a fighting lady to protect your flanks, son—don't worry, I don't feel nothing now. Just sweetness—a sweet sweetness.

DUDLEY: Your poems—I'll get 'em published.

JOHN: Fuck them poems—this is poetry, man—what I feel right here and now. This sweetness. Sing on, Grandma. (*Pause. He shivers.*) I found it, Dudley—I found it.

DUDLEY: What, Johnny?

JOHN: My battlefield—my battlefield, man! I was a bitch too, ya monkey chaser. See my shit! I got two for the price of one.

DUDLEY: Yeah, chief.

(JOHN *dies. Pause.*)

CHIPS (*whimpering*): Oh God, oh my God!

MATTIE: Shut up! And tell it like Johnny told ya. He ain't gonna die for nothing, 'cause you ain't gonna let him! Jeff—open the door, son! Tell 'em to come on in here!

(JEFF *crosses to the door.*)

And you better not fuck up!

The Great MacDaddy

PAUL CARTER HARRISON

Al Freeman, Jr. (center) as SCAG, *surrounded by the* FAST LIFE CHOURUS *(left to right): Marjorie Barnes, Dyane Harvey, Bebe Drake Hooks, and Phylicia Allen-Ayers (Rashad). Photograph copyright © 1977 by Bert Andrews. Reprinted by permission of Marsha Hudson, the Estate of Bert Andrews.*

Paul Carter Harrison, a New York native, is a playwright, director, and author of *The Drama of Nommo*, which essays the African foundations of Afro-American aesthetics, as well as the editor of two collections of African diaspora plays, *Kuntu Drama* and *Totem Voices*. He is the recipient of a 1995 NEA Playwright's Fellowship. In addition to his 1973–74 Obie Award winning play, *The Great MacDaddy*, his *Tophat* and *Abercrombie Apocalypse* have also been part of the NEC repertory. Other significant plays include *Tabernacle, The Death of Boogie Woogie, Ameri/Cain Gothic,* and the blues operetta, *Anchorman*. He is the recipient of a 1985 Rockefeller Fellowship and 1993 Meet-the-Composer Reader's Digest Commission for his operetta, *Goree Crossing*. He is currently playwright-in-residence at Columbia College in Chicago where he is developing his new opera, *Doxology Opera/the Doxy Canticles*.

The Great MacDaddy was produced in New York by the NEC at the St. Marks Playhouse in 1974, and later revived at the Theatre De Lys on April 5, 1977, following a tour of the Virgin Islands. The original cast members, including the ensemble playing multiple roles, were:

Principals

Wine	Graham Brown
Macdaddy	David Downing
Scag	Al Freeman, Jr.
Leona	Hattie Winston

Ensemble

Phylicia Allen-Ayers (Rashad)
Marjorie Barnes
Adolph Caesar
Dyane Harvey
BeBe Drake Hooks
Sati Jamal
Alton Lathrop
Howard Porter
Alvin Ronn Pratt
Martha Short-Goldsen
Freda T. Vanterpool
Charles Weldon
Victor Willis

Music composed by Coleridge-Taylor Perkinson; directed by Douglas Turner Ward; choreographed by Dianne McIntyre; scenery by Gary James Wheeler; lighting by Ken Billinton; costumes by Mary Mease Warren; production stage managed by Clinton Turner Davis.

The Great MacDaddy

AUTHOR'S NOTE

The Great MacDaddy is a ritualized African-American event inspired by the African storytelling technique advanced by Amos Tutuola in his world famous novel, *The Palm Wine Drinkard*. While the event is developed in such a way as to parallel the continuity of the story, no attempt has been made to seek a representative identification with its content. Rather, the content of the event might be considered a translation of African mythic and cosmic references as they appear in the African-American modes of experience which receives cosmic focus from the black church, and gives expressive weight to such mythic heroes as the Great MacDaddy, Stagolee, Shine, John Henry, and the Signifyin' Monkey. The intention of the ritual, then, is to identify, rather than simulate African sensibilities as perceived in the context of African-Americans.

The ritual is rhythmically developed in a force-field. All the forces in the event are recognizable aspects of African-American existence, with SCAG being a force that appears in several inimical manifestations; and Song, Dance, and Drum appearing as the civilizing forces. MACDADDY experiences the forces as personified realities: they are not to be considered aspects of his fantasy or subconscious life, thus, should not be construed as cartoons. Nor is he bound by the strict definition of linear Time, since his progress forward is *backward:* wherever he might be located during any Beat of the ritual is a result of his contextual relationship to Time, since Time, as conceived here, is never static, and merely serves the transitional Beats of the event.

Stylistically, the ritual is conceived as rhythmical pulses, rather than scenes: Primal Rhythm, Beats, Transitional Beats, and Terminal Rhythm all contribute to lock the ritual, compositionally, into the changes of the musical mode. Song and Dance are used to heighten the mode, as any dramatic device should, rather than as specialty numbers, as described by American musical forms. The set should have enough plasticity to be orchestrated within the rhythmical pulses, allowing for quick magical changes of the environment which is never static. And while the music may be described by the American 1920s — secular and sacred — its underlying designation is rhythmically African.

The environment is total: at no times must the audience/participator feel separated physically/emotionally from the event. When plausible, and without strained efforts at improvisation, certain texts may be delivered directly to the audience/participators, inviting their response. And while the ritual may seem composed of innumerable characters, it may be adequately executed with twelve to fifteen players and a five-piece band. All aspects of the ritual must be in harmonious relationship to the rhythmic pulse so as to assure—spiritually—revelation of the event.

PRIMAL RHYTHM

Los Angeles, California. No curtain. The room is covered with a pliable plastic material, including exits, to create a total environment. Upstage, raised level, MUSICIANS *are vaguely seen behind material. They are playing a 1920s jazz riff as audience/participators enter the house.*

The time is the twenties, during Prohibition; the space is a funeral parlor speakeasy: upstage right is a door; left of the door, two candelabra stands; further left, an empty coffin. Downstage left is a large wine cask and an ornamental gold tray with long-stemmed glasses upon a small table. Down right, an old-fashioned box-camera on tripod. Plastic flowers laden around the area.

With houselights still on, MACDADDY *enters through the door upstage right, signals for the others to follow as he ambles over to the wine cask to pour a glass of wine. A gathering of black people (*CHORUS/COMMUNITY*), stylishly dressed, enter as if having returned from a burial; they speak to a few people among the audience/participators about the passing of Big Mac as the* SCAG PHOTOGRAPHER, *who has entered downstage right, dressed in duster and cap, his face painted like a skull—a white-faced death mask—adjusts the lens of the camera.*

Houselights begin to fade out, as well as the music; lights up in a sepia tone on the CHORUS/COMMUNITY *who are now posed in a gay still-life photographic attitude; the* SCAG PHOTOGRAPHER's *head under the camera's black cloth as he raises a powder-flash instrument.* MACDADDY *is the only one animated, sipping from a glass as he observes the scene.*

SCAG PHOTOGRAPHER's *flash instrument flashes sending up a cloud of smoke, breaking the frozen attitude—lights changing and music playing instantaneously—as the* CHORUS/COMMUNITY *commences to dance a vigorous Charleston, the steps, however, indicating an African influence. A party is in progress: the occasion is a wake for Big MacDaddy, who has*

just been buried, leaving his fortunes to his son who is now the GREAT
MACDADDY, *great lover, great patriarch, great hustler.*

The SCAG PHOTOGRAPHER *moves unobtrusively through the dancing group, exiting with a smile of contentment. The flamboyant, young*
MACDADDY *looks on with an air of confidence owing to the social prestige
attendant to his recent acquisition of power. He is offered condolences and
congratulations from his friends, both in the same breath, for inheriting
his father's business status. The tone of the festivities indicates a greater
concern for the party than the recent burial of Big MacDaddy. Everybody
seems to be enjoying a certain vicarious sense of pride through having an
association with the* GREAT MACDADDY'S *money/power. Women smother*
MACDADDY *with affection, though his charm is merely superficial, his
worldliness not yet tested. He is generally indolent, never having worked
for a living, having always been dependent upon his father or others. He is
not, however, naive: he understands that the gathering's loyalty is directly
proportionate to his money/power.*

DEACON JONES (*after dance ends*): Sure hated to see Big Mac go.
MACDADDY (*patting flirtatious* YOUNG WOMAN *on her bottom*): I know.
DEACON JONES: He sho' was a good man!
MACDADDY (*casually*): I know that too, Deacon.
DEACON JONES (*attempting to inject humor*): But he didn't go 'way mad,
   did he, young Mac?
MACDADDY (*correcting* DEACON JONES): Great . . . MacDaddy!
DEACON JONES: Yes suh, yes suh! I guess that's what you bees now. The
   Great MacDaddy, son of the Big MacDaddy who is dead, making you
   the greatest Daddy of all the MacDaddies who can do anything in
   this world.
MACDADDY: Every day that God send, Deacon!
DEACON JONES: Naw, Big Mac didn't go 'way mad. He done left you
   the world, MacDaddy. Ain't many of us gon' get our hands on the
   world like you got it. Yup, you sho' nuff got it made!
MACDADDY (*pouring a glass of wine*): As long as the wine flows, the
   barrels will roll, and my dough will glow in the eyes of the world. Got
   plans, Deacon. Grand plans. Gonna start movin' my wine across
   country. Lotta niggas in Chicago and New York that ain't never had
   their lips on my Palm Wine.
DEACON JONES (*anxiously*): You mean, you movin' outta Los Angeles?
MACDADDY: And give up all this sun? You talk like a fool, Deacon. I'm
   just movin' my wine. Spreadin' out a lil taste. So don't worry, Deacon,
   I'll be around to scratch your plate on Sundays.

YOUNG WOMAN (*sassy*): C'mon, let's dance, Junior Mac!

MACDADDY (*emphatically*): Great . . . MacDaddy!

YOUNG WOMAN (*compliantly*): Sure . . . sure, honey. The greatest
MacDaddy of 'em all. C'mon, let's dance, nigga!

MACDADDY (*patting her bottom*): Not now, sugar. You just run along
now and keep the mustard hot 'til MacDaddy finishes talkin' business.
Go on, now! (*Observes* DEACON*'s worried expression*) Hey, Deacon, I
know you loved Big Mac, but you ain't got to be lookin' down in yo'
mouth. Everything's gon' to be everything. Just like it always been,
only greater. Go on and have some more wine.

DEACON JONES: MacDaddy, you might be great, but maybe you better
give this movin' out . . . or movin' in . . . a bit more thought. After all,
I don't know if your movin' around gon' sit right with the Man.

MACDADDY: The Man? What Man? You lookin' at the Man . . . who
can do anything in this world he pleases. And if I'm the Man, can't be
no other Man runnin' my game.

DEACON JONES: Now, MacDaddy, you know as well as I know, the ways
of the Man. He don't like ugly. And as long as you don't make a wave
there won't be no ugliness. It's the law of the land. And on his land,
the fruits of the land must pass through his hands.

MACDADDY (*unconcerned*): Uh-uh!

DEACON JONES (*sermonizing*): Ain't never been a man, on this land, who
didn't have to come by the Man, at least once. Who didn't have to pay
by hook or crook, for his benevolence. And he that don't know 'bout
sacrifice, I say sacrifice, I mean sacrifice, can only know the back-hand
of the Man's patience.

MACDADDY: Well, we'll save the bones for Deacon Jones! How's that?

YOUNG MAN (*exuberantly*): Hey yawl, I'm makin' a toast to my man
MacDaddy, my main man, my ace boon coon, my horse if he never
wins a race, my nigga if he never gets bigger . . .

YOUNG WOMAN (*interjects*): The jelly in my roll, honey!

YOUNG MAN (*to the gathering's delight*): MacDaddy with pimps as
caddies, blame all the young 'hoes for his new game. . . . Big Bear
hugger, Momma plugger . . . the maker of crumb snatchers, the
smasher of crummy crackers . . . carved the world out of a wooden
nickel and called it the Bucket of Blood . . . my main stem under a
lady's hem and a gangster's brim, MacDaddy!

(*Everyone drinks to the toast: the festive moment is interrupted by an
urgent rhythmical rapping at the door. An anxious hush comes over the
room.* MACDADDY *suggests everyone be cool as he approaches the door and
a* WOMAN *collects all the glasses and returns tray to table.* MACDADDY

taps a rhythmical signal on the door; there is a feeble response. He repeats the gesture; again, the response. Cautiously, he opens the door: in sprawls WINE, *the keeper of the illegal still and the possessor of the precious Palm Wine formula that has produced* MACDADDY's *greatness.* WINE *appears to be badly beaten and delirious as he collapses in the arms of* MACDADDY *and a few* MEN.)

WINE: Turn me loose . . . turn me loose.

MACDADDY (*befuddled; embarrassed*): Bring him down here! Hurry! Make room for him!

YOUNG WOMAN (*as other guests stare anxiously*): Who's that old dude?

YOUNG MAN: That's Wine! He runs the still. It don't look too good.

WINE: Turn me loose . . .

MACDADDY (*bending over* WINE *and holding up his head*): It's all right, Wine, it's just me.

WINE (*practically prostrate*): Yeah . . . yeah . . . young Mac . . .

MACDADDY: Great Mac! . . . What happened?

WINE: The Man . . . he done come down on Wine . . .

MACDADDY: What man?

WINE: Thee Man . . . you know? . . . like man-in-the-moonshine? . . . Thee Man. And I'm a dead man, Mac.

MACDADDY: Don't worry 'bout a thing, Wine. You gonna be awright. But what about the still?

WINE: He . . . he just swoop down on me . . . you know how he do . . . he just swoop down on me when I wasn't lookin' . . .

MACDADDY: Sure . . . sure . . . but who's lookin' after the still?

WINE: I ain't give him no cause to do that! I ain't botherin' nobody back there in the bush . . . back there in the bush where the spirit come to me . . . where the spirit come to me and fix my hand on the tree . . . fix my hand on the palm leaf . . . fix my soul on the palm leaf juice . . .

MACDADDY: Yeah. Sure, Wine. Nobody should be botherin' you. But who's watchin' the operation?

WINE: I'm a dead man now, MacDaddy. The Man done gone too far with Wine. He done fix Wine so that he a dead man now. Wine ain't got no time. He done swoop down on me and dragged me away from the tree . . . dragged me away from the tree that fix my soul . . . the soul that fixed my mind . . . he done taken advantage of Wine . . .

MACDADDY (*annoyed, grabbing* WINE *roughly*): On yo' feet, Wine, you goin' back to the bush!

WINE (*resisting as other guests reproach* MACDADDY, *exhorting him to leave* WINE *alone*): Turn me loose! I'm a dead man now.

MACDADDY (*complying momentarily to his guests' demand; unable to cope with the situation, grabbing* WINE *once more*): Get up, nigga, get up! You ain't gettin' paid to lay on yo' ass!

WINE (*gagging, as guests reproach* MACDADDY *once more*): Wine ain't got no time. He gon', MacDaddy . . . he gon' 'way from here!

MACDADDY (*complying once more to guests' irritation: suspecting that* WINE *is actually upon his last breath, he tries desperately to extract the formula from him*): You can't go, Wine. You hear me?

WINE: I'm gone! And by-the-by, the Man will come to you in curious ways and you'll see why Wine is a dead man.

MACDADDY (*shaking* WINE): The formula, Wine. What about the formula? C'mon, quick, write it down. (*He fixes a pencil in* WINE'*s hand and urges him to write, but is unsuccessful.*) C'mon, I'll help you. Write it down, nigga, before I get mad. Okay. Okay, whisper it to me. . . . Whisper in my ear. Louder . . . louder!

(WINE *struggles to whisper something into* MACDADDY'*s ear, but collapses dead.*)

Wine? Wine, are you still there? Wine! (*He releases* WINE *and postures as if he has at least secured the formula: adjusting his composure, he commands a few of the men to place* WINE *into the casket.*) A couple of you dudes make Wine comfortable over there. (*He begins to light the candelabras.*) I think it's time to pay our respects to Wine. Deacon, you preside, if you will, over the remains of this wasted brutha.

(*Transitional Beat:* MUSICIANS *play a hymn as* DEACON JONES *moves in between the candelabras to face the gathering downstage for his eulogy;* MACDADDY *resting his elbow on the casket appearing to be in deep thought; lights change.*)

DEACON JONES: Wine was good. Wine was great. Wine was everybody's mistake! Though Wine was a gift of God. Wine is of the Blood . . . and the Father . . . and the Weary Spirit . . . but Wine was abused. It's a mistake to abuse the gift of God. It's a mistake to let Blood bleed blind when wine is plentiful and adversary deep. Wine, in a good time, would never bleed Blood blind. But these are bad times, brethren, these are not the times of wine. I say, these are not the times of wine, those earthly times when Wine was host to the ancestral spirit, those good times when Blood would catch fire and the Body would rock with Dance, and the heart would burst with Song, and the ground would rumble under our stomp like Drum, those real times, those vital times that soothed our minds with revelation, those revelations that revealed the mystery of Hell on Earth, I say reveal the mystery of Hell on Earth. . . . (*He becomes progressively more incantative, causing the*

COMMUNITY/CHORUS *to respond with shouts, sighs, and jerking motions.*) I say, those revelations that come down from the wisdom of wine, the Blood River rolling over its banks, rolling over the Dikes of Time, rolling over Creation, movin' with the magic of Wine, out of Time but movin' down the line anyhow, like the ancestors say, Wine is good, Wine is great, Wine is everybody's mistake. I say, it's a mistake to abuse the gift of God. Right here in Los Angeles, from the tastiest palm trees in the West, Wine brought the gift of God . . . put his life on the line in the name of the Father, the Blood and the Weary Spirit, brought joy to the wasteland and peace to the mind in these sad and merciless times. And now Wine done passed. I say, now that Wine done passed, what has this scorched land in store for us now? Lawd, what on earth is in store for us now, since it was a mistake to abuse po' Wine, a gift of God. Lawd . . . Lawd . . . Lawd . . . how we gonna miss our Wine!

(MUSICIANS *continue playing as sanctified atmosphere settles;* MACDADDY *looks up from his disengaged posture. Lights normal.*)

MACDADDY (*perfunctorily opening casket*): At this time, I would like to invite everybody to review the remains of Wine.

(*As the* COMMUNITY/CHORUS *lines up and slowly approaches the casket,* MACDADDY *goes over to* DEACON JONES *to shake his hand and eases some money into his palm: the first* WOMAN *to approach the casket screams with great consternation etched upon her face.*)

What's wrong with you, woman?
WOMAN (*greatly agitated*): Nothin' remains of the *remains!*
MACDADDY (*anxiously runs over to the casket, and with great agitation and bewilderment, searching interior and exterior*): Where did he go? Where'd he go? (*To perplexed* COMMUNITY/CHORUS) What happened to Wine?

(*Silent astonishment is the response.*)

Well, he ain't here, where in Hell is he?
OLD WOMAN (*nodding head sagaciously*): Gone back!
MACDADDY (*eyes searching audience*): Back where?
OLD WOMAN (*to bewildered* COMMUNITY/CHORUS): Back to the source! He done gone back to the source. Just like Wine to do a thing like that. Always knew he had the power. Poof! Evaporate in thin air. Just like a spirit. He done left here and gone back to the source, chile!
MACDADDY (*irritated; searching audience*): Uh-huh! Like Hell he did! Not with my formula.

(COMMUNITY/CHORUS *respond with amazement.*)

If he ain't in this casket, he's out here somewhere. And when I find the low-life sucker with my formula, I'm takin' it out his ass.

YOUNG MAN (*pursuing* MACDADDY): Wait-wait-wait, hold on, MacDaddy. You mean . . . he didn't tell you nothin' before he split? . . . I mean, he got away . . . and you ain't got no wine?

MACDADDY (*boastfully*): There's plenty wine, dude! Just keep drinkin' while I get it together.

YOUNG MAN (*pursuing* MACDADDY): Wait-wait-wait, hold on, ain't got no formula, you ain't got no wine. And if you ain't got no wine . . .

YOUNG WOMAN: You ain't got shit!

MACDADDY (*reaching for* YOUNG WOMAN): Let me tell you somethin', lil momma . . .

YOUNG WOMAN: Uh-uh! Don't be puttin' your fumblin' hands on me. Don't you ever do that! And the next time you put your hands on my backside, just be lookin' out for a heel upside your jaw. In fact, I jes' left!

(*As* YOUNG WOMAN *exits, she takes off a bunch of plastic flowers, thereby prompting the rest of the* COMMUNITY/CHORUS *to leave, each removing some aspect of the room; flowers, rolling off casket and wine cask, and finally, one man removes the door in one motion as he exits.*)

MACDADDY (*as everyone is leaving*): Where yawl goin'? Yawl ain't got to leave. I said I'd find him. Wine can't be too far. Just wait awhile. I'll bring him back. Just stick around one minute!

(*The room is empty. Abandoned,* MACDADDY *stands in the middle of the stage adjusting his clothes while the stage darkens and* MUSICIANS *play calamitously: sounds of wild beasts, screams, hoots, and hollers, suggesting a perilous mood.* MACDADDY *tightens up his appearance/attitude, adjusting hat on his head to the "perfect" degree of angularity: a light downstage focuses on a heavy wooden cane, bedecked like a fetish and shaped like an elephant's head at the top. It has the appearance of a carved tree branch. The object is a cane inherited from his father:* MACDADDY'S *juju stick. He moves down to hold up the juju cane for inspection of its power. Confident, his attitude locked into place, he now looks out into the audience as if frontally confronting the dangers in the world lurking behind their eyes.*)

BEAT ONE

Nevada desert. MACDADDY *moves upstage right, returns downstage left to discover a young blood on the desert with a bell around his neck sitting by a shoeshine box. He is surprised to find someone on the desert giving shoeshines, but places his foot up on the stand and issues a command.*

MACDADDY: Shine!

SHINE (*popping rag rhythmically*): On the job, suh!

MACDADDY: What's a young blood like you doin' out here on the desert shinin' shoes?

SHINE: Workin' my way 'cross country, suh.

MACDADDY: Now, Blood, that's sho' 'nuff simpleminded. Ain't nobody gettin' no shine on the desert.

SHINE: You gettin' one right now, suh.

MACDADDY: Well . . . that's different!

SHINE: Don't make me no difference. Any shoe will do . . . right along through here.

MACDADDY: Well, you'll never make it, June. Ain't that many shoes out here to carry you 'cross country.

SHINE: Guess I'll jes' work up a sweat 'til I get there.

MACDADDY: What you 'spect to find 'cross country?

SHINE: A better job!

MACDADDY: Don't see what you got to be worryin' 'bout workin' so hard for . . . as young as you are. Shit, when I was your age, party-time occupied my mind . . . and I sho did party!

SHINE: Well, I'm growin' fast. By the time I get across country, I'll probably be a man.

MACDADDY: What you figure on doin' by the time you become a man?

SHINE (*popping rag*): Well, I'm pretty good with my hands. And I hear they layin' train track back East. So I figure they gon' need some pretty strong men to shape that steel . . . and I got a callin' that means me!

MACDADDY: Shit, you gotta be plenty cock-strong to be thinkin' 'bout bendin' steel.

SHINE: Oh, I'm plenty strong. Used to work in a mill back home in Milltown. Could tote quite a load for a young nigga. That's what the mill captain used to say.

MACDADDY: Hell, you oughta be glad you gave up that job.

SHINE: Oh, I didn't give it up. Mill caught fire and I ran for my life. Had to keep gettin' up, though, 'cause the captain and his daughter

got burned to death and you know how 'em white folks get't pointin'
the blame.

MACDADDY: You got that right, every day that God sends. A nigga's
story ain't worth two cents when a cracker judge strokes his chin.

SHINE:
Yeah, I knew they wouldn't hear it
    though I was littler then;
how I look talkin' 'bout sniffin' 'round for smoke
    when the fire broke in.

(SHINE *leaps to his feet and begins detailing the story demonstratively.*)

I run to the captain shoutin',
    "there's a fire all about!"
He say, "nothin' to it, Shine,
    the automatic sprinklers will put it out."

The fire raged and the sprinklers pumped,
    filled the room with smoke and a whole lot of funk.
I say, "Captain, captain, those sprinklers ain't worth a damn."
He say, "You talk like a fool, Shine, they were made by Uncle Sam."

But that fire told me captain's talk was some jive,
    I leaped outta the window without any alibis.
I say, "There was a time your word might've been true,
    but this is one Goddamn time your word won't do!"
I hit that window so unbelievably fast
    I passed right through without ever breakin' the glass.

Then I hear captain shoutin', "Shine, Shine, please save poor me.
    I'll give you more money than any black boy ever did see."
I say, "You ain't got enough money to get me for hire,
    not if I've got to get back in that fire!
If money ain't on land, I'll find it at sea,
    so you'd better get out here and boogie like me!"

Then captain's daughter start to shoutin',
    drawers in her hand, brassiere 'round her neck;
she gon' put me to the test
    by steppin' out her dress.
She say, "Shine, Shine, save poor me,
    I'll give you more bootie than any black man ever did see."
I say, "Hoe . . . you know my color, you know my race.
    you'd better get out here and give these rats a chase.

'Cause bootie ain't nothin' but meat on a bone;
   you can kiss, fuck it, or leave it alone."

I even ran up on captain's dog, you know,
   one of 'em German shepherds whose teeth snap logs.
I say, "You may be man's best friend,
   catcher of squirrels, even smart as him;
but before I let you sink your green teeth in my knee,
   you gonna have to be a runnin' sombitch to outrun me."

And that's how I lived to tell the story that wasn't told!

MACDADDY: You must be a pretty mean young dude, Shine. I guess
   that's why you wear that bell 'round your neck, you know, just to let
   people know you comin'.

SHINE (*resuming shoeshine*): Aw, shoot, that ain't nothin'.

MACDADDY (*inspecting bell*): Where'd you get it?

SHINE: I made it. I told you, I'm pretty good with my hands.

MACDADDY: Let me see that. (*Closer inspection*) Could you make
   another one?

SHINE: Sure, anytime. Ain't nothin' to it really.

MACDADDY: Look, I'll give you the price of two shines if you let me
   have it.

SHINE: Two shines don't add up to one, mistah. But you can have it just
   the same. Like I said, I can make another bell. But you can only get
   one shine. Anyhow, it was nice talkin' to somebody for a change. It do
   get lonely out here.

MACDADDY (*taking bell; paying for shine*): You know, you're a good lil'
   nigga, Shine. You'll make it! By the way, what's your real name?

SHINE: Well, my friends call me Shine, but my real name is John Henry!

(MUSICIANS *play.* MACDADDY *stares at* SHINE *curiously as he departs
upstage. Transitional Beat:* MACDADDY *comes upon* OLD GRANDAD *and*
MOMMA *sitting around a fire in the evening chill. Curiously, he
approaches them.*)

MACDADDY: Hey now! How you folks doin'? (*No response.*) See you got
   your fire. (*No response.*) Been warm out here on the desert, but I guess
   yawl know somethin' 'bout night I don't know. (*No response.*) Yeah, I
   guess it do be chilly! (*No response.*) I said, yeah, it do get chilly on the
   desert. (*No response.*) Dry too! (*No response.*) Yawl been here long? (*No
   response.*) Hey, what's wrong with yawl? It don't get that cold that you
   can't warm up to a cousin. Look here, I'm lookin' for somebody, so
   why don't you give cuz a hand? I gotta find Wine.

(OLD GRANDAD *chuckles.*)

You seen Wine?

OLD GRANDAD (*a manifestation/personification of* WINE): On the desert?

MOMMA: Ain't nothin' out c'here but Old Grandad and me, son.

OLD GRANDAD: Don't tell the ig'nant oil rough-tail nothin'!

MACDADDY: What's your problem, Grandad, what you got against me?

OLD GRANDAD: Nothin'!

MOMMA: But you ain't no cousin, and you don't look like our kind. He
bees a pretty lil' nigga, Grandad, but his shoes ain't shined.

MACDADDY: Hey now, Momma, all I'm tryin' to do is find Wine. Can't
help it if I kick up a bit of dust. But we ain't got to fuss about it,
do we?

MOMMA: Don't rain every time the pig squeal, do it?

OLD GRANDAD: But it sho' 'nuff look like stormy weather comin' 'round.

MACDADDY: Look here, what you people doin' out here anyhow?

OLD GRANDAD: Livin'!

MACDADDY (*slapping at flies*): On the desert?

OLD GRANDAD: Only way I know to get my nuts outta the sand is to get
as close to the sand as I can.

MOMMA: We done give up on 'em crackers with wheat on their land,
and come out here to make somethin' out the sand. 'Course, I'd rather
be a nigga than a poor white man!

MACDADDY: Well, yawl jes' keep right on gettin' up!

OLD GRANDAD: Got to! Nigger got to keep movin' the way these
grasshoppers be eatin' up everything. Move or die.

MOMMA: Back there in Backwater, the grasshoppers be eatin' up your
britches and spittin' up yo' shirts. And got an appetite that's growin'
mo' bigger. So we packed up and hit the dirt before they starts in on
the nigga.

MACDADDY (*slapping at flies*): Hell, yawl sure can't come to much out
here on the desert. Plenty of flies out here. White flies! They sting and
stick to yuh too. You can slap at 'em all day, but they get to yuh. Ain't
nothin' nastier than a fly, and there bees plenty sand flies out here.
Can't stand flies myself.

OLD GRANDAD: Don't blame you, son. But like I was gonna say, soon as
I get my nuts outta the sand, we pushin' on for Diddy-Wah-Diddy.

MACDADDY: Where that bees?

OLD GRANDAD (*with self-titillation*): Way off somewhere, but I'll find it.
'Spose to be a place where you ain't got to work or worry 'bout man
nor beast . . . a restful place where every curbstone is like an easy chair.
And when you gets hungry, all you gots to do is sit on that curb and

wait. Pretty soon you hear something hollerin', "Eat me! Eat me!" and is bees a big baked chicken come struttin' along with knife, fork, and bread too. After you done eat all you want, there's still plenty left over for neighbor. And before you know it, a great big, deep, sweet potato pie comes shoving itself in front of you with a knife stuck up the middle so you can cut the size that fits your mouth. Can't nobody ever eat it all up, though. The mo' you eats, the bigger it gets! (*Laughs with* MOMMA *joyously.*)

MACDADDY: C'mon, Old Grandad, you sure you ain't been dippin' in your bottle?

OLD GRANDAD: Now, I ain't got to lie to you. Not out here on the desert.

MOMMA: 'Sides, a nigga don't sing much when plowin' on a hillside!

MACDADDY: Come off it, Momma. Yawl don't even know the way. So I guess ain't nobody gonna live there today.

OLD GRANDAD: It is said that everybody would live in Diddy-Wah-Diddy if it wasn't so hard to find and so hard to get to, even after you know the way.

MACDADDY: In the meantime, cousin, since yawl ain't goin' nowhere, maybe you can point out the direction of Wine.

OLD GRANDAD: I ain't seen no Wine in many a day.

MACDADDY: But you must have seen him, cousin. I'm sure he passed this way.

MOMMA: Old Grandad ain't got nothin' to do with Wine. And stop gettin' familiar, 'cause you ain't no cousin of mine.

MACDADDY: Damn! Talkin' to you old folks is like gettin' blood out of a stone.

OLD GRANDAD: Watch your mouth, son. Don't like no talk like that 'round Momma.

MACDADDY: Listen, I'll walk, talk . . . bark anyway I want to!

OLD GRANDAD: Not around here you won't!

MACDADDY: You must not know who I am.

OLD GRANDAD: I ain't gon' lie! Naw, and don't care much if I do!

MACDADDY: Well, get hip, Old Grandad. I am the Great MacDaddy, son of the Big MacDaddy who is dead, making me the greatest Daddy of all the MacDaddies who can do anything in this world.

OLD GRANDAD (*unimpressed*): So?

MACDADDY: So I wanna know about Wine!

OLD GRANDAD: Well, I don't know now. You be the greatest of the great, don't see what Old Grandad can do for you, though few have ever gotten past Old Grandad without calling his name. All I can tell you is go-for-yuh-self, mistah . . . er . . . how you call yo' name . . . ?

MACDADDY: MacDaddy!

OLD GRANDAD (*he and* MOMMA *tickled*): Uhm-hmm . . . !

MACDADDY (*threateningly*): And I'm gettin' tired of foolin' with yuh!

MOMMA: Mole ain't 'fraid of the moonshine, now!

MACDADDY: You'd better tell yo' ole lady somethin'!

OLD GRANDAD: Naw, I'm gonna tell you somethin'!

MACDADDY: You can't tell me nothin'!

OLD GRANDAD: Uh-huh, that's jes what I thought. I guess Wine will be mellow without yo' company anyhow.

MACDADDY: C'mon, Old Grandad, I ain't got no time to lose. Can you turn me onto Wine or can't you?

OLD GRANDAD: I guess I could.

MACDADDY: Then give him up!

OLD GRANDAD: What have you done for me lately?

MACDADDY: What . . . ?

MOMMA: Folks on the rich bottom stop braggin' when the river rise.

MACDADDY (*hesitantly*): Okay. Okay, how much dough you want?

OLD GRANDAD: What kinda dough do I be needin' on the desert? Now, that's sho' 'nuff dumb. And if you that dumb, I don't see what you can do for me.

MACDADDY: What do you want? Just tell me, what is it?

OLD GRANDAD: That bell!

MOMMA: Can you deal with that?

MACDADDY: I can deal with anything! But, uh-uh, that ain't gonna get it, ole lady. If Old Grandad wants this bell so bad, he gonna have to run down Wine right here and now. Okay, you want this bell, let me see you foam at the mouth. Go on!

OLD GRANDAD: Look here, son, I'm tired. I ain't gonna argue with yuh. You see, I know why I need that bell and you don't. Ever since I saw the red clay breakin' 'foe a pale face moon, I knew I had to have that bell. And the moon is plenty pale this night. Now, Old Grandad through talkin' to yuh. You jes do what you wanna do!

MACDADDY (*reluctantly gives up bell;* OLD GRANDAD *snatching it anxiously*): Okay. Now you give up Wine!

OLD GRANDAD (*gleefully tying bell around neck*): Well, now, you see, it ain't as easy as all that. Wine is hard to find in stormy weather. Maybe you'd better come with us to Diddy-Wah-Diddy, son.

MACDADDY: What you puttin' down, Grandad? Don't bring that jive to me.

OLD GRANDAD: I ain't jivin'! In Diddy-Wah-Diddy there bees a powerful man, the most powerful man in the land. He bees the Moon Regulator. He can make the moon do what he wants it to do. And I just got to thinkin', since the moon do be kinda pale around 'bout now, maybe he been sick lately. Ain't easy to find nothin' in pale moon.

MACDADDY: Hold it right there, Grandad. You ain't slick! I don't wanna know nothin' 'bout Ditty-Witty, 'less it's mommas with fat titties. Ou-blah-dah and ou-blah-dee don't mean nothin' to me, 'cause I ain't goin' there. Just turn me onto Wine and we can forget we ever met. (*He draws back his juju cane threateningly.*) Now break it down for me!

OLD GRANDAD (*withdrawing*): Ain't no need in all that, young fella . . .

MACDADDY: MacDaddy . . . the Great MacDaddy.

OLD GRANDAD: Uhm-hmm, I know a fella greater than you. He bees on the other side of the moon. That's why we gettin' stormy weather for sure. But I didn't want you to get mixed up with that fella . . . 'cause he be bad . . . mean as leftover Death! But he knows how to get around in stormy weather.

MACDADDY: Ease up, Old Grandad. You ain't crackin' no ice with me.

OLD GRANDAD: I mean what I say. It's the only way we gonna find Wine in this weather. But then, if you ain't that bad . . .

MACDADDY: If I ain't, Skippy is a faggot! Who's the dude? Spoke up!

MOMMA: Needun be walkin' 'round c'here with yo nose all snotty. When you don't know, jes ask somebody!

OLD GRANDAD: Scaggarag! Ain't never met him, but I hear'd 'bout him. But I can't blame you for not wantin' to deal with Scaggarag. He's mean!

MACDADDY: Where bees the dude?

OLD GRANDAD: Out there somewhere with the other desert rats, I guess.

MACDADDY: Awright, Old Grandad, this is the only time I'm gonna go for this shit. When I get back, you'd better have some facts.

MOMMA (*as MACDADDY leaves*): The distance to the next mile post depends on the mud in the road.

(*Transitional Beat:* MUSICIANS *play traveling music as* MACDADDY *peers through the audience and calls "Scaggarag" three times. He then supports himself on his juju cane as if napping.* SCAG *appears—in death mask as earlier—and dances adroitly around the napping* MACDADDY.)

SCAG (*curiously inspects*): Uhm-hmmmm . . . Uhm-hmmmm . . . Uhm-hmmmm! Could this man still be alive or dead?

MACDADDY (*quickly spins and fronts* SCAG; *brandishing his juju cane*): I'm very much alive . . . and ain't thinkin' 'bout dyin'! (MACDADDY *enters dance rhythm of* SCAG.)

SCAG: Yeaaaaah, you look pretty live to me. Maybe you can tell me, just who you be?

MACDADDY: I'm the Great MacDaddy, son of the Big MacDaddy who is dead, making me the greatest Daddy of all the MacDaddies who can do anything in this world!

SCAG: Oh yeaaaah? That's good enough for me!

MACDADDY: Then run it on back, Jack, before I jump into the third degree.

SCAG (*making intricate dance movement*): Uh-uh, that won't be necessary, Cherry! (*Negotiates another intricate movement*) Scag! I'm the one. . . . I'm the one. . . . I'm the one. . . . (*Repeated rhythmically*)

MACDADDY (*interpolating each of the last phrases and maintaining a simple dance movement*): Yeah, you the one!

SCAG: Where you from?

MACDADDY: Where they scrapple-at-the-apple not far from your place.

SCAG: And what did you come to do?

MACDADDY: Been hearin' 'bout you on the drum . . . the talk of the town . . . thought I best get to know you personally!

SCAG: Well, here I bees. . . . Let's do-the-do . . . do-the-do . . . do-the-do . . .

MACDADDY (*interpolating between each phrase of "do-the-do"*): Doo-aaaaaah! Doo-aaaaaah! Doo-aaaaaah!

(SCAG *begins song/monologue about himself while engaging* MACDADDY *in a dance designed to capture him within* SCAG's *influence. While* SCAG's *dance is quite supple, yet intricate,* MACDADDY's *dance is rudimentary, but intense, with a few improvisations on the basic step as he dances furiously, using his juju cane as a support, to offset* SCAG's *challenge.*)

SCAG:
You're talkin' to one of the meanest Sidewinders
    in Babylon.
They call me Scag, but my real name is
    Heroin;
    a cousin to the Caesars,
    a nephew of Napoleon,
    got a Spartan pedigree.

I came to these borders in a cellophane bag!
    mess with me a taste, if you wanna waste;
    I'll make your liver quiver,
    your body sag like a rag.

But I'm a thrill, you see
    yeah, thrill you to death;

as you ride into the lower depths,
that adventure into unreturnable Seas.

I can put a hex on your sex;
put your mind under arrest;
make a young girl sell her body,
for failin' the acid test

Reality!
Reality is called Miss Jones.
When the Jones come down strong
she can make you
shake, rattle,
and throw up your bones.

You may sigh until your nose bleeds,
but there ain't much you can do
with her stew,
'cept CRY my misery blues.

You be hooked!
Hooked on me,
and ridin' a race through Hell.
We ridin' together,
at breakneck speed;
til that day you fall off the pace
and you SCREAM your death knell!

(*"Scream" is repeated three times with response from* MUSICIANS. *At the end of song/monologue,* SCAG *and* MACDADDY *dance furiously until* SCAG *is overtaken by the intensity of* MACDADDY's *determination to win. He raises his juju cane triumphantly and a net falls from above which is used to cover the fallen* SCAG. *Transitional Beat:* OLD GRANDAD *and* MOMMA *approach the net trepidly yet curiously.*)

OLD GRANDAD: Back so soon, son?

MACDADDY (*downstage tightening up his appearance with his back on net which is upstage*): What do it look like to you?

OLD GRANDAD: Looks like you been pushed outta shape a little bit. (*Curiously*) What you got in that net?

MACDADDY: Just what you asked for. Scag!

OLD GRANDAD (*he and* MOMMA *are alarmed*): No. You didn't! How could you do a thing like that? (*Fearfully, he begins to shake the bell furiously toward the audience as if sending out an alarm signal, while* MOMMA *withdraws from net.*)

MACDADDY: What's wrong with you, Grandad? Stop actin' simple! (*He grabs* OLD GRANDAD *on collar desperately.*) You hear me, nigga? What in the world are you tryin' to do?

OLD GRANDAD (*as* MOMMA *tries to separate* MACDADDY'*s grip from* OLD GRANDAD): You done brought Scag among the livin', son. That ain't right! Ain't even wrong. That's Death!

(*As* MACDADDY *deals with* OLD GRANDAD, SCAG *stealthily escapes the net and creeps away from the scene smiling.*)

MOMMA (*prayerful attitude*): Only a blind mule ain't 'fraid of darkness. Lawd, oh Righteous Father!

MACDADDY (*furious*): You asked for him, now you got him.

OLD GRANDAD: Naw we ain't. You ain't even got him no more. Look, see there, the net's empty!

MACDADDY (*viewing empty net with astonishment*): But I had him!

OLD GRANDAD (*picking up net and backing away with* MOMMA): And you let him go! It's yo' fault! All yo' fault! You done taken Scag outta Hell and turned him loose to roam with decent people.

MACDADDY: Where you goin'?

OLD GRANDAD: Naw, don't come near us. Stay back! We leavin' here.

MACDADDY (*as they prepare to exit*): We had a deal!

OLD GRANDAD: Find Wine on your own time. We gon'!

(*They exit briskly.*)

MACDADDY (*bitterly; shouting after them*): Nigguhs . . . and flies . . . I do despise. The more I see nigguhs, the more I like flies!

(MUSICIANS *respond.* MACDADDY *appears annoyed with himself for having made such a harsh indictment, compensating for the self-hate by tightening up his appearance/attitude, then moving on. Transitional Beat:* MACDADDY *comes upon a weary looking First World War veteran — another manifestation/personification of* WINE — *togged in remnants of "battle" dress. He is drinking from a canteen.*)

Hey! Soldier! How far is the next town?

SOLDIER (*sitting on an old suitcase*): Next town? Hmm, far as you wanna go, and even farther than that as far as I'm concerned.

MACDADDY: Well, how far is that?

SOLDIER: On the otherside of Far, in the land of Zar. Ever been to Zar? Naw, I guess you too young to have been that far.

MACDADDY: Look, can you jes get me to the next town?

SOLDIER: Who, me? I can get you farther than that. I been to West Hell and back. 'Course, you know 'bout West Hell, don't yuh? Where the soul bounces 'round like a rubber ball cause the Devil ain't gon' carry you through, you know what I mean?

MACDADDY (*preparing to leave*): I'm sorry I asked. So, if you don't mind, I'll just get off your trip and make my own way, thank you!

SOLDIER: Hold on there, sonny . . .

MACDADDY: MacDaddy . . . the Great MacDaddy!

SOLDIER: Yeah, sure, but before you start trippin', you'd better have a sip outta my canteen . . . 'cause what you got before you is a trip and a half which might not even be worth the trip!

(MACDADDY *accepts the offer: turns up canteen, sips, tastes, drinks gluttonously.*)

Ever been to war? Now there's a trip that tripped me halfway 'round the world to trip on some hellified trippers who weren't just trippin', but stompin'! And after nearly gettin' stomped, I didn't realize what a trip that was until I got back on this trip and got my butt kicked by the dudes I was trippin' for. Now ain't that a blip!

MACDADDY (*removing canteen from mouth; face expressing astonishment*): Wine!

SOLDIER: 'Nuff to last me the rest of my trip, though it's one trip I hate to make.

MACDADDY (*anxiously*): Where'd you get this wine, Soldier?

SOLDIER: Over in the next town.

MACDADDY: Well, where is the next town?

SOLDIER: Oh, it's a trip and a half, son.

MACDADDY: That's what you said before!

SOLDIER: And that's what it still is!

MACDADDY: Okay, then show me, I'll follow. (*Sipping wine*)

SOLDIER: No suh-ree-suh! I ain't ready for the trip. I'm tired. So I'm gonna sit here with this wine 'til I'm ready to get back in the world. Got enough problems. And I got that wine from a man who didn't have a care in the world.

MACDADDY: Was he 'bout your height . . . your color . . . with a scruffy beard . . . kinda walk, you know, like you . . . even talks like you?

SOLDIER: Sho 'nuff sound like him!

MACDADDY (*raising juju cane threateningly*): Get steppin', Soldier!

SOLDIER (*unimpressed*): Now, hold on just a minute. (*Snatches canteen from* MACDADDY) And give me back my canteen! I done told you I ain't ready to go into the world, and I ain't got no intentions of goin'. Ain't nothin' in the world I ain't seen, so you don't scare me. I done lived too long with fear, and there ain't nothin' more fearful in the world than fear. So as long as we gon' be in the world, why don't we sit down here and have a drink in the world, so we can ease up on the world quietly together.

MACDADDY: Fuck the world! You talkin' to the Great MacDaddy, son of the Big MacDaddy who is dead, making me the greatest Daddy of all the MacDaddies who can do anything!

SOLDIER: Is that right? Is that the God's truth or are you trippin'?

MACDADDY: I done told you, didn't ah?

SOLDIER: Well, looka here, God-son, you may be the answer to my worldly problem.

MACDADDY: You got a problem for real if you don't get steppin'!

SOLDIER: That ain't no problem. When I'm ready to step . . . (*Self-mockery*) . . . I be marking the cadence of time. But I do have a little girl in the world who givin' me a big problem. My daughter done let herself get swallowed up in the jaws of some evil dude in the world. And since I'm tired and you can do anything, maybe you can go into the world and bring her outta that world so she can get hooked up with some nigga in the world who is sittin' on the world. That should be like stuff for you, God-son.

MACDADDY: No good, cousin. I can do anything, but I ain't goin' for that! So, start markin' time!

SOLDIER: I ain't ready yet! So you might as well put that weapon away. Hell, I guess you ain't as interested in this wine as I thought.

MACDADDY (*lowering juju cane to ground*): That wine probably done gone to yo' head anyway. You don't know nothin'. Later!

SOLDIER (*as* MACDADDY *starts to leave*): MacDaddy . . . Great MacDaddy!

(MACDADDY *stops*.)

Just listen to my story. Have a little sip of wine so I can tell you 'bout the world. You got time for that, ain't cha?

MACDADDY (*taking canteen*): Where's the place?

SOLDIER: Las Vegas!

BEAT TWO

Las Vegas: Dramatization of SOLDIER's *tale about daughter.* MUSICIANS *play fast-life music: downstage, several men stand around in formal attire outside gaming room craps table which has been moved onto stage on a wagon from upstage behind plastic; several* FAST-LIFE WOMEN *carouse around table. Impressionable* LEIONAH *appears, doing her best to make a worldly appearance among the "fast" men outside the gaming room who flirtatiously pursue her.*

FAST-LIFE CHORUS:
Hey now, gurlie,
wha'cha doin' foolin' 'round
    here so early
you sho' look bright and dandy
    in the noon day sun;
you a long way from yo' mammy
    but we playin' for fun.

Yeah,
    you sho' look good gurlie
    feathery as my rooster;
    if I could wear you in my hat
    you'd give my soul a booster.

Gurlie,
    it's early
    didn't you know?
If you dance to the music
    you gotta pay to the piper.
    Yo' mammy must have told you so!

And
    if you lookin' for a daddy,
    you ain't got far to go.
Cause here I am lil momma,
    to show you everything I know.

Yeah,
    you sho' look bright and dandy
    in the noon day sun;
you're a long way from yo' mammy
    but we playin' for fun.

So,
    what you gonna do
    when the sun goes down,
    gurlie?

(*Repeat three times as they head for gaming table, leaving* LEIONAH *to ponder the question as she trepidly advances toward the gaming room to join the men with the* FAST-LIFE WOMEN. *As she approaches the area,* LEIONAH *encounters the resplendent* SKULL—*another manifestation/ personification of* SCAG—*who has entered from upstage right, dressed in white-on-white ensemble: awestruck, she gazes at him, though* SKULL *merely glances at her and continues onto the game-room platform to join the others at the craps table; he is greeted enthusiastically by the gathering as he takes over the dice.* LEIONAH *enters the gaming room, attracted by* SKULL's *magnificence; he is impeccably dressed, fingers laden with jewelry, and owns a smooth, cold, countenance as he observes his ladies' handling of the men around the table, hustling them into betting, while generating applause for each pass made with the dice.* LEIONAH *tries to make her presence felt, but is ignored by* SKULL *and pushed aside by the* FAST-LIFE WOMEN. *After his last pass,* SKULL *signals for the women to leave with the men. As he collects and counts his winnings,* LEIONAH *searches for a cigarette from her purse, then follows him outside the gaming room which is rolled away.*)

LEIONAH (*affected deep voice*): You got a match, mistah?

(SKULL *looks off his shoulder, then coldly turns away to continue counting money downstage;* LEIONAH *approaches awkwardly.*)

I said, do you have a match, mistah?

(SKULL *repeats gesture/attitude and walks down a bit further stage left;* LEIONAH *makes another attempt, somewhat aggressive, but coquettish.*)

A girl's feet could get tired lookin' for a match!

SKULL (*harshly*): Piss off home, kid! You ain't ready for the pace!

(*He gestures as if opening a car door, enters, and postures himself in a frozen attitude as if leaning at the wheel.* LEIONAH *backs off, but doesn't leave, hovering in the shadows as if spying upon* SKULL. MUSICIANS *playing. A* CAR DEALER *in white mask appears.* SKULL *steps out of the "car" and counts off some bills while the man inspects the "car." Satisfied, the* CAR DEALER *takes the bills, climbs into the "car," and stylistically "drives" off.* SKULL *walks across to down right,* LEIONAH *close behind without his knowledge, where he comes upon a white-masked* PAWN BROKER *with three gold balls suspended above his head from a rack attached to his shoulders.* SKULL *takes off the lovely white suit, returning it to* PAWN BROKER, *now exposing his shabby garments underneath as well as a reduced body size. After paying off the* PAWN BROKER, SKULL *moves up stage,* LEIONAH *following, where he comes upon a shaddy* STREET HUSTLER *to whom he returns all the jewelry; after the jewelry is inspected, the* STREET HUSTLER *accepts the money, and* SKULL *moves on with* LEIONAH *in pursuit.* SKULL *now responds to a hissing sound from behind upstage plastic material: a suspicious looking character,* ALLEY RAT, *pokes his head through, then the rest of his body.* ALLEY RAT *collects the lovely white hat and shoes from* SKULL, *accepts a few dollars, then alerts* SKULL *to a "shadow" in the alley. As the* ALLEY RAT *darts out of sight,* SKULL, *now reduced to a less awesome spectacle, spots* LEIONAH *who is now less impressed and, in an effort to conceal her fear, as well as get away, assumes a "hardened" disposition.*)

SKULL (*as* LEIONAH *attempts to leave*): Hey, lil girl, that you?

LEIONAH (*stops, catches breath, turns*): You who?

SKULL: You, baaaaabeeeeeee! You and me makes two of us!

LEIONAH: Us? What us? I don't know nothin' bout us! You here alone, and I'm on my way home!

SKULL (*reaching out to grab her*): Hold on, lil momma!

LEIONAH (*withdrawing forcefully*): Don't put yo' hands on me, nigga! You don't know me! Don't you e-e-ever put yo' funky hands on me.

SKULL: Come down, momma, I told yuh you couldn't stand the pace.

LEIONAH (*trying to out-maneuver* SKULL): I ain't even in the race, nigga. So you can't tell me nothin'!

SKULL: Be cool, fool, and don't break no rules. 'Cause I see I'm gonna have to send you back to school.

LEIONAH: School who? Don't talk crazy, baby. How a broke-down, low-life, no-count fool like you gonna teach me some rules? If you asked me, you need to do some bookin' on how to survive, as bad as you look, out here on the corner beggin' and stuff!

SKULL (*forcing her upstage right*): I ain't beggin', momma!

LEIONAH: Sure, you beggin'! Yeah, you beggin', honey. Ain't no need in me lyin' . . . and you neither, for that matter.

SKULL: What matter's, lil momma, is that you are here. And there ain't nowhere for you to go.

LEIONAH (*somewhat nervous now*): Like I been trying to tell you, I'm on my way home.

(*Upstage-right wagon/platform moves on with bed and clothes rack, indicating shabby effects of* SKULL'*s room.*)

SKULL (*urging* LEIONAH *onto bed*): Rest yo' mind at ease, Honey Chile, 'cause you gonna stay here for a little while.

LEIONAH (*fretful; almost tearful*): But I can't stay. I . . . I . . . I got thangs to do!

SKULL: Ain't no way, lil momma. You had yo' chance to go. Now you gots-to-get-down!

(*Transitional Beat.* LEIONAH *reclines tearfully, somewhat nervously on bed, as* SKULL *reduces himself further by taking off his "conked" wig, exposing a stocking cap underneath, and removing his shabby clothes until he is down to underwear.*)

You'll see, lil momma, once you get hip to me, I ain't bad. I'm jes baaaad, that's all. But everybody knows I'm a ball. Ain't never in a mood to be crude, which is why any chick who is slick, and does what she's told, can get my gold. Shit, I don't need no boost, but I do be the King of the Robber's Roost. When the world gets uptight in some bad action, I give everybody satisfaction. Even Uncle Sam wanted me 'cause of what I am. I'm a cool fool, to say the least. I've climbed Rocky Mountains, fought grizzly bears, even tracked wild panthers to their hidden lair. Lissen! I've crossed the Sahara Desert, momma, and swam the Rio Grande, fought with Pancho Villa and every Wasp in the land. I've knocked down doors, and broken gorilla's jaws. Used tiger teeth for toothpicks, drunk lion's blood for soup. I'm a player and parlayer when I come across a chicken coop. Yesterday, a rattlesnake bit me, crawled away, and died, and you know, pretty momma, I ain't got no reason to lie. And when you see a hurricane or cyclone breezing through a city, you can bet everything you got that Skull, me, is drivin' it. So that's what you got to deal with here, momma. So get down, and get-up somethin' quick!

(*As* SKULL *leans over the frightened* LEIONAH, *he reaches into his underwear: lights out, leaving only* SKULL's *head to glow in the dark; he is now reduced to a greater state of unnatural imperfection, a skull.* LEIONAH *screams;* SKULL *curses. Lights up; she had bolted away, but is now restrained at the edge of the bed by two figures appearing skull-masked who block her retreat.*)

Bring her sweet buns right back up here!

(*The* TWO SKULETONS *force her down onto the bed.*)

Okay! we might as well break her in right, right?
SKULETONS (*in unison*): Rhhaaaight!

(*Wagon/platform wheeled off as lights dim. Transitional Beat. Entering from downstage,* MACDADDY *seeks out* SKULL, *thus approaches* FAST-LIFE MEN *and* WOMEN *gathered around the craps table upstage left.* MUSICIANS *playing fast-life blues theme. Without uttering a word,* MACDADDY's *forceful appearance commands the dice. He rubs his juju cane and makes three quick passes to the gathering's delight.* SKULL *enters the gaming room. He usurps all the attention from* MACDADDY *who, also apparently awestruck by* SKULL'S *completely together potent appearance, humbly gives up the dice, then leaves the gaming room to sing the blues.*)

MACDADDY (*blues/ballad, i.e. "Stormy Monday"*):
Who could blame the woman
   who would follow
   when she can
the complete gentleman.

Who could blame the woman
   who would follow
   when she can
the complete gentleman

If I were that woman
   I too would wanna be the feather
   in the hat
   of the man
   who's got it all together.

Yeah,
   he's mean
   as the eye can see
   if he were in battle
he wouldn't get touched by a war machine.

Yeah,
   he's mean
   as the eye can see
   if he were in battle
he wouldn't get touched by a war machine.

If a bomb would dare to fall
   it would not want to touch him at all
   it would rather explode in Hell
than touch a thread on that man's lapel.

Yeah, he's mean!

Oh,
   it hurts the eyes to see him
   bringing tears to my eyes
   wonderin' why
God had not blessed me with such beauty.

Yeah,
  it hurts the eyes to see him
  bringing tears to my eyes
  wonderin' why
God had not blessed me with such beauty

But,
  on the other hand,
  since this beauty is only
  a Skull,
I thank my God
  I was created a man.

Yeah, yeah, yeah,
  I thank my God,
  to beat the band,
  since this beauty
  is only a Skull,
I thank my God
  I was created a man!

(*Confidence recovered through singing the song,* MACDADDY *approaches the craps table once more, and, with the head of his juju cane, stops the roll of* SKULL's *dice abruptly: everyone gasps; music stops. He boldly stares at* SKULL *as the gathering quickly disperses, leaving the two men alone. Having made the confrontation,* MACDADDY *then leaves and positions himself downstage right. With a cold, and calculated countenance,* SKULL *picks up his winnings and leaves the gaming room which is rolled away.* SKULL *stops, spies* MACDADDY, *and approaches with deliberation. He taps* MACDADDY *on the shoulder, but as he turns around, he appears now to be a "gray cat," a cat mask having emerged from the juju cane and held up before* MACDADDY's *face.* SKULL *ignores him. Now, as earlier, confident that he is alone,* SKULL *postures in the "car" and waits for* CAR DEALER, *the "gray cat" lurking behind him as the lights fade downstage. Transitional Beat. Upstage right,* LEIONAH *lays indecorously spread across the bed with a large ring in her nose. She is mounted by a* SKULETON *who wears a chain around his waist, the end of it connected to the ring in* LEIONAH's *nose; making carnal gestures, he grunts and groans while the other* SKULETON *squats in front of the bed posts.* SKULL *enters—reduced to a* SKULL *as earlier—with the unsuspecting "gray cat"—*MACDADDY— *at his heels. The* SKULETON *mounting* LEIONAH *stops and disconnects the chain from her nose, and wearily dismounts.* SKULL, *also with chain* *around his waist, squats next to the squatting* SKULETON *as the "gray cat" moves around bed inspecting* LEIONAH.)

SKULL (*to* SKULETON *dismounting* LEIONAH): How you doin', boon coon?

FIRST SKULETON: Just about wore this one down to the nitty gritty!

SECOND SKULETON: And just about wore me out!

SKULL: What's yo' story, Mornin' Glory?

SECOND SKULETON: Tired!

SKULL: Wha-choo-say?

SECOND SKULETON: Whupped!

FIRST SKULETON: Me too! So move over and let me squat awhile.

SKULL (*squatting with them*): Damn!

FIRST SKULETON: Ain't much fun no more. All she do is lay up on her ass.

SKULL: Wha-choo-say!

SECOND SKULETON: She ain't movin'! We gotta do all the goddamned work.

SKULL: All I wanna know is did you do yo' job?

SECOND SKULETON: If you ask me, I think we overdid it!

SKULL: Wha-choo-say?

FIRST SKULETON: She got an overdose of the treatment. She done played out!

SECOND SKULETON: We did everything you told us to do, Skull. Got her hooked with a ring in her nose that won't let go. She hooked up pretty good, but I don't know what she's good for.

SKULL: Anything we want her to do!

FIRST SKULETON: Well, she ain't actin' right, so I ain't gonna bust myself up on her dead ass no more today.

SKULL: She ain't dead, just dead-alive. But when the Jones comes down on her funky butt, she'll make a livin' for all of us.

(*Shouts at "gray cat" who is stroking* LEIONAH's *forehead, trying to revive her.*)

Get away from there, pussy!

SECOND SKULETON: I think I'm gonna nod!

FIRST SKULETON: Me too!

(*The three of them, squatting at the foot of the bedposts, nod into sleep: the "gray cat"—*MACDADDY—*furtively takes the ends of their chains and locks them to bedposts. He then leads* LEIONAH *away from the bed/platform, past* SKULL *and* SKULETONS *who suddenly awake.*)

SKULL *and* SKULETONS (*shouting*): Hey, pussy, come back here with our snatch!

(*As they shout furiously, the bed/platform wagon is withdrawn, and lights dim out. Transitional Beat.* MACDADDY *observing* SOLDIER'*s efforts to fully revive daughter, vainly trying to remove ring in her nose as she leans forward on ground.*)

SOLDIER: Leionah! Leionah, chile, come on back. This is yo' daddy talkin'. Leionah! What in the world have they done to yuh, honey? Can you hear me, chile?

MACDADDY: Ain't no use. Nothin' else to be done about it, Soldier.

SOLDIER (*anxiously; pacing*): You gotta do somethin', God-son. You promised to bring my baby back.

MACDADDY: And I did! Now, I gotta go catch up with Wine . . .

SOLDIER: Uh-uh, no good, God-son. My baby ain't even nearly back. If she can't come to herself she ain't got a hope in the world.

MACDADDY: It ain't my fault! I did the best I could.

SOLDIER: Well yo' best ain't worth a damn. All the trouble I got in the world keepin' my nose off the grindstone, and you talk 'bout yo' best. Hell, I can't even leave here on time.

MACDADDY: Awright, goddammit, just don't cry on my shoulder. I'll try one more thing. Any natural weed around here?

SOLDIER: Got some dippin' snuff here, will that do? (*He pours a bit into* MACDADDY'*s palm.*)

MACDADDY: Got any wine left? Pour a little into my palm. (MACDADDY *works mixture into his palms, raises clenched fist and juju cane in other hand upward and chants.*) Like your son, God, you can do no wrong! (*He repeats phrase.*)

(*He leans over* LEIONAH *and gestures as if feeding her some of the mixture; then, as she quickens, with great deliberation, he slowly begins to remove the ring in her nose.* LEIONAH *stretches her arms and yawns as if having had a deep sleep.*)

LEIONAH: Uhump! Don't you get tired!

SOLDIER (*elated*): Well, I'll be damned, God-son, you sho know how to do yo' stuff! How you feelin', daughter?

LEIONAH: Fine, Daddy, jes fine!

(*As* LEIONAH *stands up, it is now apparent that she is pregnant as she rubs her stomach.* MACDADDY, *ignoring the scene, prepares to leave.*)

SOLDIER (*inspecting her stomach*): What you got there, chile?

LEIONAH: Got a little surprise for Daddy.

SOLDIER (*elated; patting* MACDADDY *on shoulder*): Well, I'll be God-damned, MacDaddy. You sho 'nuff for real know how to do yo' stuff.

MACDADDY (*as* LEIONAH *smiles affectionately*): Look, I don't know nothin' 'bout all that . . .

SOLDIER: Oh, I understand, MacDaddy. You ain't got to boast when you got the most!

MACDADDY (*to* LEIONAH): Look here, girl, you'd better tell your Daddy somethin'!

LEIONAH (*smiling affectionately*): He sho is fine, ain't he, Daddy?

MACDADDY: Wha . . . ?

SOLDIER (*to* LEIONAH): Ain't you the sweetest thang! Hate to lose you, chile, but I don't mind steppin' down for the Great MacDaddy, the greatest Daddy of 'em all!

MACDADDY: You ain't lost nothin', Jack, 'cause Mac ain't goin' for that!

SOLDIER (*offering canteen*): Maybe you can go for some of this wine, son?

MACDADDY: That's exactly what I had in mind. Which way did he go?

SOLDIER: Take yo' time, MacDaddy. Consider' Leionah's condition and all, she might not be ready for travelin'.

MACDADDY: Look, that's up to Leionah, but I'm damn sho gonna!

SOLDIER: How you feelin', chile?

LEIONAH (*beaming at* MACDADDY): Feelin' fine as wine, Daddy.

(*As* MACDADDY *and* SOLDIER *discuss the issue to one side,* LEIONAH *sings a lively blues—Ma Rainey style.*)

I'm feeling fine
   with the man
   I call mine.
He's the host
   of my life,
   and I'm glad
   to be his wife.

He's the man
   with the most
   that is why
   I call him boss.
I don't care
   what people say
   cause they gon'
   say it anyway.

I'm gonna walk
 hand in hand
  with my man.

I'm gonna walk,
 walk, walk,
no matter how they
 talk, talk, talk.
Can't give a damn
 long as my man
  has got my hand.

He's the host
 with the most
and in my belly
 is his jelly;

So if anybody ask you
 when I'm gone
 how I 'spects
 to get along,
tell everybody
 to rest their minds
 cause I am
 feelin' fine.

 (SOLDIER *embraces* LEIONAH *as* MACDADDY *looks on perplexed by the unresolved solutions.*)

SOLDIER (*handing* LEIONAH *his suitcase with all his worldly possessions*): Take care of yourself, chile. I'm on my way.

MACDADDY: Where you think you goin'?

SOLDIER: Outta this world! Where I should've been long time ago. You see, I was jes passin' through. Bye yawl!

MACDADDY: What about Wine?

SOLDIER (*as he exits*): Just lay with Leionah. She'll show the way through!

LEIONAH (*holding suitcase*): Guess we can leave now, Mac.

MACDADDY: What you mean, *we*? *We* ain't goin' nowhere. But MacDaddy is leavin' here, dig it?

LEIONAH: What about *our* baby?

 (*Members of the* OUTRAGED COMMUNITY/CHORUS *drift onto stage within earshot of the dispute and take notice: they whisper and signify about confrontation.*)

MACDADDY: *Our* baby, is *your* baby . . . which ain't got nothin' to do with me.

LEIONAH: Well, I sho didn't make this baby by myself.

MACDADDY (*trying to exit quietly*): It's been done. Just ask Jesus!

LEIONAH (*grabbing* MACDADDY's *arm*): You ain't goin' nowhere, nigga! You ain't leavin' me with this baby!

MACDADDY (*conscious of* OUTRAGED COMMUNITY): Let me go, woman! Find yourself another sponsor! Let go!

LEIONAH (*directly to* OUTRAGED COMMUNITY): Who's gonna take care of my baby? Who's gonna take care of my baby?

MACDADDY: Shut up, woman, you're drawin' a crowd!

LEIONAH: All you niggas wanna lay with Leionah, but when the shit goes down, yeah, when her belly gets round, all she ever gets from yawl is frown. Well frown done drowned in my tears, 'cause, let's face it, Mac, you ain't as slick as all that! You gonna take care of my baby and all 'ems that come back-to-back!

MACDADDY (*angered, he violently strikes her in stomach with juju cane*): Goddamn your baby!

(*The* OUTRAGED COMMUNITY *gasps: out pops the* SIGNIFYIN' BABY *through the plastic environment upstage center, adult-sized and wearing a diaper.*)

SIGNIFYIN' BABY (*dancing about frenetically*): Hoo-popsie-doo, how do you do! What you see is what you got! Oooooo!

LEIONAH (*rubbing flat stomach as she rises*): Ahhhh, Mac, ain't he cute? Go on, Mac, say somethin' nice to him.

SIGNIFYIN' BABY: If you ain't got nothin' nice to say, don't say nothin' at all. Ooooo!

MACDADDY: Yawl ain't puttin' me in no trick. I ain't got no claim on that boy!

SIGNIFYIN' BABY: You got that right, so come down, MacBrown, you know I'm outta sight.

MACDADDY: MacDaddy! The Great MacDaddy!

SIGNIFYIN' BABY: You gotta prove it to me, MacGee! Weeeeeeee!

LEIONAH (*admiringly*): Shall we name him after you, Mac?

(*The* OUTRAGED COMMUNITY/CHORUS *responds to the frenetic child with astonishment and titillation, shaking their heads admonishingly.*)

SIGNIFYIN' BABY:
Hold on, momma, put yourself at ease;
I got a name and pedigree.

MACDADDY: How somethin' like you get a name?

SIGNIFYIN' BABY:
What's it to yuh, momma screwer,
you ain't 'ceptin' no blame.
But if anybody asks you
what's my name,
you go on tell 'em,
Puddin'nin Tain!
MACDADDY: What's yo' name?
SIGNIFYIN' BABY:
Puddin'nin Tain!
Ask me again, I'll tell you the same!
OUTRAGED COMMUNITY (*together*):
Better do somethin' 'bout that child,
he don't be natural;
better do somethin' 'bout that child,
he be a foundless foundling;
better do somethin' 'bout that child,
he gonna turn havoc loose on the block!
SIGNIFYIN' BABY (*breaking his frenetic motion to assail member of the*
OUTRAGED COMMUNITY):
Don't none of yawl be bad moufin' me,
'cause I'll raise my leg and on yawl I'll pee!

(SCAG *enters scene laughing. Now being led around by* SCAG *whom*
MACDADDY *watches closely, directing* SIGNIFYIN' BABY'*s attack on
members of the* OUTRAGED COMMUNITY.)

Ugly? Who you callin' ugly? You got some nerve to call me ugly! You
so ugly that yo' momma got to put a sheet over your face so sleep can
creep up on you. And yo' wife ain't no cuter. Man, is yo' wife ugly! Me
and yo' wife went out to get a lil drink, before I got my bit, and she
was so ugly she had to put on sneakers to sneak up on the drinks. (*To*
SCAG *who laughs raucously*) Now you know that don't make no sense.
She look like somethin' I used to feed peanuts to in the zoo.

(LEIONAH *is unable to restrain* SIGNIFYIN' BABY *and is quite concerned
about the growing hostilities ignited in* OUTRAGED COMMUNITY *who
begin to chorally utter, "Uhm–umm–uhmp!"*)

LEIONAH: Good Lord, MacDaddy, can't you do somethin'? You gotta do
somethin' quick for the baaa-bah!

(LEIONAH *tries desperately to break up a fight instigated by* SCAG *whom*
MACDADDY *studies more intently as he ruminates over the options of what*

must be done: SIGNIFYIN' BABY *assails a man who is being contained by his wife.*)

SIGNIFYIN' BABY:
   Don't you be givin' me no evil eye!
   I saw the last fight you were in
      and you were truly jive.
   You 'member when I had to stop you the other day
      to tell you what this dude had to say down the way.
   The way he talked 'bout yo' was a goddamned shame;
      even heard him curse 'bout yo' grandmammy's name.
   So you go runnin' off with an uproar, beatin' yo' chest like an ape;
      and the dude just beat yo' ass all outta shape.
   You made this chickenshit pass,
      the dude stepped back and kicked your natural ass.
   He put knots on yo' head, and kicked your ribs outta place,
      the way he messed over yo' eye was truly a disgrace.
   Now, you get back here more dead than alive
      and got the nerve to be signifyin'.
   Shit, if you had called me, I would have fought the dude myself,
      cause anybody could see you needed a helluva lot of help.

(MACDADDY *points his cane at* DRUM *among the* MUSICIANS, *who plays a rhythmic pulse that grips the* SIGNIFYIN' BABY.)

Ooooooooowweee! Oooooweeeeee!

(*As the* SIGNIFYIN' BABY *moves around frenetically,* MACDADDY *points juju cane at* DANCE, *a member of* OUTRAGED COMMUNITY, *who dances with* SIGNIFYIN' BABY, *occupying his energies.* MACDADDY *then points to* SONG, *another member of the community who sings a song to civilize the force of* SIGNIFYIN' BABY *while the rest of the* OUTRAGED COMMUNITY, *at a different rhythm, utter "Uhm-umm-uhmm": a polyrhythmic mode.*)

SONG/WOMAN (*gospel*):
   Oh, lead me on, I pray, Savior divine,
   Let me commune with Thee, and let me find.
   When storms of life appear

   That Thou wilt linger near
      to quell each rising fear
   and lead me on.

Oh, lead me on, I pray, Lord, God of Light,
When deep'nin' shades I see, when coming night;
Engulfs the path I go,
I feareth naught I know
   Thou still doth go
before to lead me on.

(SIGNIFYIN' BABY *becomes occupied and absorbed by all three modes,*
SONG, DANCE, *and* DRUM, *until his energies dissipate: at this point, the*
MICKEY MOUSE ORDERLY, *wearing white hospital attendant's jacket,*
enters and begins to wrap SIGNIFYIN' BABY *in a straitjacket;* LEIONAH
protests, but MACDADDY *restrains her as the child is led off.*)

LEIONAH: Mac, they're takin' away my baby. No! No! Not my baby.
Mac, do somethin'! I love my baby. Oh, Mac, please don't let them
take my baby!

(CHORUS, SONG, DANCE, *and* DRUM *continue their activity until the*
baby is taken offstage. SCAG *blocks* MICKEY MOUSE ORDERLY's *exit*
momentarily, but moves aside when stared down, and retreats.
MACDADDY *still holding the sobbing* LEIONAH *as the* OUTRAGED
COMMUNITY *slowly disperses; stage empty,* MACDADDY *releases*
LEIONAH *and prepares to leave once more.*)

MACDADDY: Stop cryin', woman! You'll get over it!
LEIONAH: My baby . . . the only thing I had in the world.
MACDADDY: Look! He's better off where he is. You would've lost him
anyhow. That baby didn't have a chance out here. So, forget
about him!
LEIONAH (*plaintively*): How you 'spect me to forget about my child?
MACDADDY (*tightening up appearance/attitude*): Yeah! Okay! But there'll
be others. (*Prepares to leave*) Well, anyway, I'm gone.
LEIONAH: What am I supposed to do?
MACDADDY (*stopping*): I don't know. Do what you been doin'!
LEIONAH: Alone?
MACDADDY (*tightening up his jaws: disgruntled, and without turning*
around, shouting): Shit! C'mon, woman!!!

(*She picks up suitcase and follows.*)

BEAT THREE

Arizona: Dog Races. ANNOUNCER'S VOICE *at a greyhound dog race-track announcing last call for placing bets. Downstage,* FOUR JACKALS, *local Arizona types in white masks, sit on their haunches passing money between them. Upstage,* MACDADDY *stands wearily next to* LEIONAH *on wagon/platform watching the scene; she now wears a simple, full-length sheath and a matching shawl around her head as she sits on suitcase.*

ANNOUNCER'S VOICE (*offstage*): Hurry . . . hurry . . . hurry . . . place your bets. Put your money on the line for the bitch of your kind. Hurry . . . hurry!

MACDADDY: We gotta make some dough quick, baby, before we go another fu'ther!

LEIONAH: Dog racin' jes ain't yo' game, Mac!

MACDADDY: Don't worry 'bout it, Momma, I still got a few games to play.

ANNOUNCER'S VOICE (*offstage*): The doges are eeeeaaadee . . . theeeiirrr goes the rabbit . . . and they're off!

(*Sound of a bell. General crowd noises as* ANNOUNCER'S VOICE *calls the race. The* FOUR JACKALS *rise up off their haunches and enthusiastically follow the course of the dogs in a circle. As the race ends, a final cheer, the* JACKALS *sit once more on their haunches, facing downstage, and pass money between themselves.* MACDADDY *hits upon an idea; he urges* LEIONAH *to stand, place one leg upon her suitcase, and raise the hem of her dress above the knee, and assume a seductive attitude. He now moves downstage in front of the* JACKALS *who, upon seeing him, scramble to pick up their money, yet remain on haunches.*)

MACDADDY (*salesman pitch*): 'Afternoon, gentlemen, how-do-you-do? On a bright sunny Sunday like today, I can tell by your winnings you're having your way. But would you believe it if I told you I've got somethin' new for you.

(*The* JACKALS *begin to slowly rise off their haunches, but are checked in place by* MACDADDY, *despite their suspicions.*)

Now, don't crowd me! There's enough to go 'round for everybody. It may be sweet or sour, but there's sure enough for anybody whose dough is big enough for a taste. The biggest dough, of course, goes first. But make up your minds, I ain't got no time to waste. What's it gonna be, gentlemen? Money talks, nobody walks! And just to put yo' minds at ease, so yawl don't think I'm a tease, turn around and look for yo' self!

(*The* JACKALS *swivel around on their haunches and lasciviously gaze at* LEIONAH, *making comments about her with local attitudes.*)

There she bees, gentlemen, some of the best black bottom in these parts. Her name is Leionah. Now, when have yawl seen such sweet meat in Arizona? Who got the thirst to lay with Leionah first? Money talks, nobody walks! The firmest black bottom in Sodom, right down to the bone. But hold it! Just hold onto your seats! Yawl ain't heard 'bout the special treat. A sleeve job! Leionah gives the best sleeve job in Gomorrah!

(*The* JACKALS *look at each other perplexed.*)

Now, I know yawl heard about the sleeve job. (*No response.*) Ain't yawl heard 'bout the sleeve job?

(JACKALS *shake their heads.*)

Now, now, now, think of that . . . we got some gentlemen here who ain't never had a sleeve job. Well, yawl got a friend in MacDaddy indeed. 'Cause once you've had a sleeve job you won't settle for no more chicken feed. So roll up yo' sleeves and step right up. Don't miss yo' ebony opportunity!

FIRST JACKAL: I'll buy one of 'em!

SECOND JACKAL: Me too!

THIRD JACKAL: Me three!

FOURTH JACKAL: Make that four!

MACDADDY (*collecting money*): Like I said, gentlemen, money talks, nobody walks! But being as much as yawl never had no sleeve job, I'm gonna help yawl get over the embarrassment of the first time. So as not to spoil the fun, I'm gonna introduce yawl one-by-one. Roll up those sleeves. Higher. Higher! And to make sure everybody gets the most outta Leionah without any alibis, we gonna tie a cloth around everybody's eyes.

(MACDADDY *uses the kerchiefs around the* JACKALS' *necks to blindfold them.*)

It just ain't righteous to peek on a fellow when the sleeve job starts to get mellow.

(MACDADDY *moves the* FIRST JACKAL *upstage right with his bare arms outstretched, stations him, and constantly exhorts the anticipating*

JACKALS *to "roll sleeves higher," "spread yo' legs," "stretch out those arms,"
"easy does it," etc. Moving the* SECOND JACKAL *to the same location, he
places his hands on the arm of the first, and commands "hold on tight"; the*
THIRD JACKAL'*s outstretched hands are placed on the arm of the second;
the fourth on the arm of the third so that they appear to be locked into a
square formation.*)

Hold on tight, yawl, and don't let go. By the time yawl count to ten,
the fun will just begin.

(JACKALS *begin to count in unison, and with much agitated anticipation,
as* MACDADDY *steals away with* LEIONAH: *sound of a train passing
faintly heard.*)

JACKALS: One . . . two . . . three . . . four . . . five . . . six . . .

(*Lights fade on* JACKALS. *Transitional Beat. Sound of a train passing over
a track with loud whistle. It is dark.* MACDADDY *and* LEIONAH *stand by
a railroad track, eyes following a passing train, as if contemplating
"hopping" a freight. A figure upstage of them approaches with a searchlight
which breaks the darkness:* WHITE TRACK MAN, *wearing white mask,
white shirt, and trousers, white straw hat, and carrying shotgun.*)

WHITE TRACK MAN (*pointing shotgun*): Who's that?
MACDADDY (*spinning around startled*): Who's that?
WHITE TRACK MAN: Who's that, say who's that, when I say who's that?
MACDADDY: Ain't nobody here but us chickens, Jack.
WHITE TRACK MAN: And you sho 'nuff in for a roastin', Bub, 'less you
    got some explanation for bein' out here on this track.
MACDADDY: Hey, lissen, we just passin' through . . . when we stumbled
    up on this track.
WHITE TRACK MAN: Uh-huh, you just stumbled up on this track, just
    like that, huh? Well it's my business to see that you stumble right on
    back where you came from, 'cause we don't allow no messin' 'round
    with our track.
MACDADDY: Ain't nobody messin' 'round. As a matter of fact, we only
    out searchin' for wood.
WHITE TRACK MAN: What kinda wood?
MACDADDY: Firewood!
WHITE TRACK MAN: Now, you folks wouldn't be figurin' on usin' no
    track for your fire, would yuh? Let me have a look here! (*He
    checks track.*)
MACDADDY: Nawwwww, we wasn't figurin' on nothin' like that! But you
    got to admit, Mistah Track Man, it do get cold out here at night.

WHITE TRACK MAN (*dropping guard momentarily*): You sure as Hell got that right. Can't stand the night. Only part of my job I don't like. But yuh gotta keep your eye on the railroad day and night. Even if the wind do bite. It's all about progress. An eye on the future. Can't look away from the track even if it is a cold damn night. But that's the kinda sacrifice we Americans gotta make, or the Injuns will steal the track right out from under our feet. They ain't like us, you know. When it comes to progress, they ain't got an ounce of sympathy.

LEIONAH: That sho is cold!

WHITE TRACK MAN: Yeah! and me without a coat. Misplaced my coat somewhere along the track. And you know, that's a whole lotta track. Been searchin' out here all night. Yawl didn't happen to stumble up on my coat, did yuh?

MACDADDY (*shaking head*): Uhm-uhmmmm! But if we could get this fire thang goin', we could make it big enough for three.

WHITE TRACK MAN: Guess we could, Bub, but we ain't got no wood.

MACDADDY: There's plenty wood in 'em tracks.

WHITE TRACK MAN (*greatly agitated*): Take that back! Take that right back! That ain't no way for no American to be talkin'!

MACDADDY (*backing off from shotgun*): Raise, Track Man, I just thought you said you were cold.

WHITE TRACK MAN: Colder than a witch's tit! Blood done chilled up in my veins so bad I'm afraid to turn my head too fast without breakin' my neck!

LEIONAH: That sho is cold!

MACDADDY: Well, no wood, no fire. Guess we'll be movin' on down the line.

WHITE TRACK MAN: Hold up there, Bub! What's the big hurry?

MACDADDY: Ain't no use in all of us standin' 'round out here. Somebody's got to find some wood.

WHITE TRACK MAN: Now, you wouldn't be holdin' out on a fellow American, would yuh?

MACDADDY: You gotta believe me, Track Man, I ain't holdin' nothin'!

WHITE TRACK MAN (*gesturing at juju cane*): What's that you got in your hand?

MACDADDY: My daddy's juju!

WHITE TRACK MAN: Looks like right good kindlin' to me.

(MACDADDY *unresponsive.*)

LEIONAH: That sho is cold!

WHITE TRACK MAN (*agitated*): I said, it looks like mighty fine kindlin'!

MACDADDY: Yeah. Yeah, I guess it could be. Too bad I ain't got no match.

WHITE TRACK MAN (*pumping shotgun*): I got yuh match, Bub . . . right down in this barrel. Now you folks beginnin' to act as cold as night. Yuh didn't have it in your mind to be actin' like no Injun, did yuh? Maybe sneak up on us Americans and burn up our track?

MACDADDY: Hey, why would I do a thing like that? Us Americans got to stick together, right?

WHITE TRACK MAN: Well *us* is just about to have a bust!

LEIONAH: That sho is cold!

WHITE TRACK MAN: Never figured no nigga to be actin' like no Injun since yawl do speak our tongue, even though you do lie and cheat . . .

MACDADDY: We speak in many tongues!

WHITE TRACK MAN: There you go lyin' again! Well you won't trick me. (*Levels shotgun*) So for the sake of progress, let me see how fast you can work up on that fire. And I hear tell you niggas got plenty of it!

(*Responding to the urgency of the threat,* LEIONAH *sits on the end of her suitcase, spreads her legs, snaps her finger and invites* MACDADDY *to place his juju cane between her thighs: when he removes the cane, the tip is "glowing" red.*)

MACDADDY (*raising his juju cane*): How's that for fire, my man?

(*He takes* LEIONAH *around the shoulder and starts up the track with* WHITE TRACK MAN *in pursuit.*)

WHITE TRACK MAN: Hold up, Bub, let me next to that fire!

MACDADDY: Make your own!

WHITE TRACK MAN: Don't talk loco! I already own that fire.

MACDADDY: You mean, you used to own it!

WHITE TRACK MAN: Yuh outta line 'er, Bub. I own everything on this side of the track!

MACDADDY: And what about the other side?

WHITE TRACK MAN: That's the other fella's business. I ain't got no business over there.

(MACDADDY *and* LEIONAH *gingerly cross over to the other side of the track.*)

Hey, what yuh doin'? That's trespassin'! Come back here with that fire!

MACDADDY: C'mon over and get some!

WHITE TRACK MAN: That's trespassin'! Ain't supposed to trespass on your neighbor's property. Come back, it's cold over here. Don't be like no Injun! Yuh wouldn't desert a fellow American, would yuh?

MACDADDY: Wouldn't I?

LEIONAH: That sho is cold!

(As lights dim, sound of passing "freight" along track drowns out WHITE TRACK MAN'*s voice, while* MACDADDY *and* LEIONAH *gesture as if "hopping" the train, their leaping attitude frozen as lights dim out.)*

BEAT FOUR

Texas. MUSICIANS *playing country-western rhythm. Upstage right, the swinging door of a saloon; downstage left, a bar on which sits a white-masked* COWBOY *who sings a country-western tune while a black* WAITER *does a "jig" dance for the amusement of the white-masked* BARTENDER *and* SHERIFF — SCAG *in another manifestation/personification.*

COWBOY (*singing*):
I got a boy and his name is Blue,
bet ten dollars he's a good boy too.
Never talks back like some coons do,
works like a horse and well trained too.

Hey Blue, you good boy, you!

Ain't nothin' shiftless 'bout my boy Blue,
'cept when he's out playin' with his girlfriend Sue.
Heavy as molasses is sweet Sue's rump,
bet'cha Blue can cut it with his ole tree trunk.

Hey Blue, you good boy, you!

Happy as a Blue Jay sittin' on a fence,
dancin' for his supper like he's got some sense.
Ain't nothin' in this world that Blue won't do,
to keep me off his buttocks with my hob-nob shoes.

Hey Blue, you good boy, you!

(COWBOY *starts to repeat the first verse, but trails off as* MACDADDY *intrudes forcefully through the swinging doors and stands boldly: his attitude/appearance tightened up, though showing signs of wear, he surveys the scene. Everyone's attention, except that of* NIGGERTOE, *the waiter, is at the door.*)

BARTENDER: Check out that dude!

SHERIFF: That ain't no dude. That's a niggah!

COWBOY: Hah, you must be gettin' color blind!

MACDADDY (*signaling outside*): C'mon in, baby!

LEIONAH (*entering and standing with trepidation by the door*): I better wait, Mighty Mac, 'til you make the path straight!

(MACDADDY *checks out* NIGGERTOE *as he makes his way toward the bar.* LEIONAH *also observes him with apparent disgust.*)

BARTENDER: Niggertoe! Who tole you to stop dancin'?

NIGGERTOE: If yuh please, suh, the music stopped.

BARTENDER: So what? Keep on dancin'!

NIGGERTOE: If yuh please, suh, yes suh! (*He continues "jig."*)

(*Everyone pretends to ignore* MACDADDY's *presence as he stands at the bar.*)

MACDADDY (*shouting*): Bartender!!!

BARTENDER (*begrudgingly moves toward him*): You want somethin', boy?

MACDADDY: What you got to drink?

BARTENDER: Sheriff, this boy here wants to know what we got to drink.

SHERIFF: Then tell 'im!

BARTENDER: Sass-parilla!

MACDADDY: Ain't you got no wine?

BARTENDER (*to* SHERIFF): You reckon somethin' wrong with this boy's hearin'? Y'll hear-d me say sass-parilla, didn't yuh?

COWBOY (*as* MACDADDY *observes* NIGGERTOE): Maybe the boy is deaf!

SHERIFF: And dumb! Everybody knows we don't 'llow no cuffy put their lips on alcohol 'round o'here.

MACDADDY (*to* BARTENDER): Sassparilla!

BARTENDER: Did you say somethin'?

MACDADDY: I said sassparilla. And two glasses.

BARTENDER (*to* SHERIFF): Did you hear this boy say two glasses of sass-parilla?

SHERIFF: And that's all I heard!

BARTENDER: Maybe you'd better try that one more time, boy. Don't wanna make no mistake 'bout what I'm hearin'.

MACDADDY (*emphatically*): Sass-parilla! Two . . . glasses!

BARTENDER: If you . . . ?

MACDADDY: What?

BARTENDER: If you . . . ?

MACDADDY: If you *got 'em*, Peckerwood!

(BARTENDER, SHERIFF, *and* COWBOY *recoil;* LEIONAH *sighs, suspecting trouble, and* NIGGERTOE *mumbles toward the ceiling as if in silent prayer, but continues dancing.*)

SHERIFF (*subdued confidence*): Now, boy, you ought 't know better than to sass the man like that over a lil sassparillee. The man asked you a civilized question and all he wants is a civilized answer. Cause, you see, you ain't that tall in the rump that you can't get thumped, follow me?

MACDADDY: Sassparilla! Two glasses! Do I get 'em, or don't I?

SHERIFF: Boy, let me tell you a little story. I 'member when the Dodge Boys came through. Had plenty horsepower too. They started kickin' up their heels the way a lotta niggas do. But they didn't count on my fire power! No, boy, they didn't count on that! Had to run 'em outta town before sundown. And without their sassparillee. Now, if you act right, and cause me no strife, you might even get outta here with your life.

MACDADDY: Well, might had damn sho better be right!

BARTENDER: That settled it right there! The cuffy ain't gettin' served. Can't get nothin' here but a barrel of trouble.

SHERIFF: Now, see there, boy, huh? See what yuh done gone did? You done gone made the man mad, 'er, see? Boys like you make it tough on other niggas to come in here and drink, you know.

COWBOY: Jes can't treat 'em right! Never could!

MACDADDY: Ain't no big thang, Sheriff. Yawl ain't got no wine, and I don't know too many niggas who wanna drink that funky sassparilla yawl drink no how. I thought I was doin' yawl a favor comin' in here, but since yawl ain't got nothin' better to do than fuck with me, I'll jes leave!

SHERIFF (*blocking* MACDADDY's *passage and looking him over*): Now, now, now, hold on, boy!

COWBOY: That there's one cuffy I wouldn't bet a Buffalo nickle on. He ain't nearly true as Blue!

SHERIFF: Have I ever seen you in these parts before?

MACDADDY: Maybe! Maybe not! But in case you didn't, have a good look so you can recognize me when I come back through.

SHERIFF: Hold your horses, boy. (*To* BARTENDER) Give the boy a drink on me.

BARTENDER: Yuh gotta be kiddin', Sheriff.

SHERIFF: Yuh heard me, Prairie Dog, give the boy a drink! (*Beckons to* LEIONAH.) C'mon gurlie, you too.

(LEIONAH *approaches with trepidation.*)

MACDADDY (*as* BARTENDER *pours*): Don't do me no favors.

SHERIFF (*handing* LEIONAH *and* MACDADDY *drinks*): Don'tcha bet on it, boy. That ain't no favor. That's a drink for the road . . . with the signpost warnin' *get outta town!* When you get on that road, jes keep gettin' up, you understand, 'cause I done seen the bad of the bad without ever blinkin'. You name 'em, I've seen 'em. When the West was at its best, Jesse James and his brother Frank put everybody to a test, 'cept me who they tried to make a pal, hearin' 'bout my reputation at the O.K. Corral. You 'member the Dalton Brothers, don'tcha? They were four of a kind. Shot a poor sombitch for a raggedy dime. And there's one mean renegade I'm sure you must know . . . thinks they calls him Geronimo! Even came across a few bad coons before, and you don't nearly measure up to what I saw.

MACDADDY: You must not know who I am!

(LEIONAH *arches eyebrows.*)

SHERIFF: Don't have to! If you've seen one cuffy, you've seen 'em all.

MACDADDY (*turns on* NIGGERTOE): Stop dancin', nigga, you makin' me tired!

(NIGGERTOE *stops.*)

BARTENDER: Who . . . ? Boy, who told you to stop dancin'?

(NIGGERTOE *points meekly, confusedly, at* MACDADDY.)

Wha . . . Boy, you'd better get back up on your toes!

(NIGGERTOE *dances.*)

MACDADDY (*as* SHERIFF *stands by benignly knotting a rope*): Stop! (*Stares angrily*) And I'm not gonna tell you again.

COWBOY: Somebody corral that cuffy before Texas gets a bad name.

BARTENDER: Ain't no cuffy gonna stand on my grandpappy's grave and run my show. The Niggertoe will do what I want it to do. Get movin', boy!

(NIGGERTOE *moves once more and is clearly confused, as* LEIONAH *anxiously tries to get* MACDADDY *to leave the saloon.*)

MACDADDY (*his back to* NIGGERTOE): When I turn around, you'd better still be standin', nigga. And tall! Straight up on your feet!

BARTENDER (*shaking finger*): Now you gonna get it! You really gonna get it!

LEIONAH (*urging* MACDADDY *to leave*): Well, time done passed outta my cup, Mac. Time do fly!

MACDADDY: Have another drink!

COWBOY: Boy, I'm gonna sing a song about yuh when we drag yuh carcass up Boot Hill.

MACDADDY: All I wanna know is who would dare to put it there?

BARTENDER: Who do you think you are, huh? Just who do you think you are, cuffy?

MACDADDY: 'Bout time you asked, Shoefly, 'cause if you knew you wouldn't be fuckin' with me. I am the Great MacDaddy, son of the Big MacDaddy who is dead, making me the greatest Daddy of all the MacDaddies who can do anything in this world!

SHERIFF (*holding up end of knotted rope*): You know what kind of knot this is?

MACDADDY: Ain't interested!

SHERIFF: You should. It's a nig-knot! Think you great enough to slip it?

(*They stare at each other momentarily.*)

MACDADDY: Shiiidddd! If you can't show me nothin' better we might as well split. C'mon baby. And you too, Niggertoe!

SHERIFF (*ruffled; draws gun*): Don't you walk away from me, boy, when I'm talkin' to yuh. Hear me, boy? You ain't jes talkin' to no redneck trash. I ain't no trash, boy, hear me . . . ?

(LEIONAH *and* NIGGERTOE *stand by nervously.*)

MACDADDY: I smell every word you say, Sheriff. And I can see from the ring around your collar that yo' neck is as red as sour grapes. Furthermore, I got a graveyard disposition and a tombstone mind. . . . I'm a bad muthafuka that's why I don't mind dyin'! So go on, shoot!

BARTENDER (*as trio heads for doors*): Stop 'em, Sheriff! They stealin' my niggah!

SHERIFF (*flustered; waving gun, shouting incantatively*): In the name of Jehovah. . . . In the name of Jehovah. . . . In the name of Jehovah . . .

(*Before* MACDADDY, LEIONAH, *and* NIGGERTOE *can reach the swinging doors of the saloon, the* BEASTS OF PREY *emerge from upstage: three enormous, demonic figures—raised on platformed shoes—covered like Ku Klux Klanners with a single eye/light which blinks on and off as room darkens. They direct their beam of light toward the retreating trio as if trying to brand them, causing them to scurry about the stage desperately in an effort to stay out of range of the flashes of light.* NIGGERTOE, *though afraid, begins to dance in an effort to distract the beams of light away from* MACDADDY *and* LEIONAH *so that they might escape: he dances furiously as the* BEASTS OF PREY *close in on him with their flashing, branding eyes.* NIGGERTOE *absorbs all the light, sustains the abuse courageously, dancing until he is broken down by the beams of light, sacrificing his life while* MACDADDY *and* LEIONAH, *who had hesitated a moment before leaving, make good their escape, and the* SHERIFF, BARTENDER, *and* COWBOY *stand by in a frozen, hostile, attitude.* MUSICIANS *play calamitously.*)

BEAT FIVE

A suburb in Arkansas. Upstage right, on wagon/platform, a white-masked woman, MRS. MIDDLESEX, *sits in a wicker rocker knitting, while her husband,* MR. MIDDLESEX, *also in white mask, sits in a wicker chair and reads the* Wall Street Journal. *They are sitting on a porch. At center stage is the* SCARECROW, *another manifestation/personification of* SCAG. MR. MIDDLESEX *bemoans the decline of the stock market;* MRS. MIDDLESEX *bemoans the black intrusion in Heavensville.* MACDADDY *and* LEIONAH *enter downstage right, their backs to the* SCARECROW, *anxiously surveying the audience, as if looking for traces of the* BEASTS OF PREY. *Their vigil is interrupted by the voice of the* SCARECROW.

SCARECROW: Stop!

(MACDADDY *and* LEIONAH *turn around quickly; observe* SCARECROW, *then turn away.*)

MR. MIDDLESEX (*eyes riveted to his newspaper*): Prices are smokin', and money is frozen!
SCARECROW: Stop!

(MACDADDY *and* LEIONAH *spin around again to seek out voice; observe* SCARECROW, *then turn away.*)

MR. MIDDLESEX: Things look bad for this country, Mrs. Middlesex.
SCARECROW: Stop! Go! Blow! Ain't gonna tell yuh no moe!

(MACDADDY *and* LEIONAH *stare incredulously at* SCARECROW.)

MR. MIDDLESEX: This land was built on blood, sweat, and tears, Mrs. Middlesex. It jes don't seem fair!

MACDADDY (*pointing toward* SCARECROW): That voice came from over there.

LEIONAH: Ain't nothin' there to know but an old scarecrow!

SCARECROW: And I ain't no doormat, so go!

(MACDADDY *and* LEIONAH *size up the* SCARECROW, MRS. MIDDLESEX *stops knitting, slowly stands, and stares out as if inspecting her property for intruders.*)

MACDADDY (*jocularly*): You know, for a minute, I thought I heard this scarecrow say go!

SCARECROW: And I did!

LEIONAH (*sensing trouble, attempting to lead* MACDADDY *away*): Ain't nothin' here to know but an old scarecrow!

SCARECROW (*as* MACDADDY *searches for gimmick*): That jes goes to show how much you know 'bout ole Jim Crow. Better flap your wings away from this door!

MACDADDY (*incredulously*): A talkin' scarecrow!!??

SCARECROW:
Eenee, meenee, minee, moe,
beat a nigger with old Jim Crow;
if he hollers, snap his collar,
eenee, meenee, minee, moe!

LEIONAH (*attempting to draw* MACDADDY *away from his inspection of* SCARECROW): Ain't nothin' here to know but an old scarecrow!

MACDADDY (*pulling away; annoyed*): Wait a minute!

MRS. MIDDLESEX: You know somethin', Middlesex . . . ? I could swear I see nigras in our yard.

MR. MIDDLESEX (*eyes on* Wall Street Journal): Who'd ever believe it could happen here in Heavensville!

MACDADDY (*absurdly defiant to* SCARECROW):
Hickery dickery dock,
the mouse ran up the clock;
the clock struck ten,
the mouse broke wind,
and if you open yo' mouth once again,
I'll flatten you with my cane!

(MACDADDY *raises juju cane threateningly over* SCARECROW *who is now silent.*)

MRS. MIDDLESEX (*alarmed*): They is nigras in our yard. And they meddlin' with our scarecrow!

MR. MIDDLESEX: Heavensville can't stand this pressure much longer.

(MACDADDY *seems satisfied, lowers cane, and starts to walk away.*)

SCARECROW:
Fly, Blackbird, fly away home!
   Fly, fly, fly!
Fly, Blackbird, fly away home!
   Fly, fly, fly!

(MACDADDY *turns on* SCARECROW *furiously with raised cane but is restrained by* LEIONAH *who grabs his arm.*)

LEIONAH: Don't waste your energy down to the wick. Ain't nothin' here but spittle and sticks!

MRS. MIDDLESEX (*greatly alarmed*): Middlesex, 'ems some evil nigras out there. And it looks to me like they stayin'.

MR. MIDDLESEX (*absorbed in* Wall Street Journal): This is a dark day for Heavensville!

MACDADDY (*lowering cane once more*): Hell, I ain't studin' the bag of hay. But I ain't gonna let no scarecrow make a fool outta me.

SCARECROW: You a fool if you stay! Better flap your wings while you got a chance to get away.

MACDADDY: You still got something to say?

SCARECROW: Yeah, I got plenty to say! We don't allow no carousin' out here, pissin' in doorways, squattin' on the grass, or playin' stink-finger with the moon. This ain't Coontown. Ain't no way a spade can stay, spade for spade!

MACDADDY: Look, if you don't shut up, I'll dig you today, and spade you all the way up into next week!

SCARECROW: Two little blackbirds sittin' in the thicket, tryin' to get to Heaven on a jive wolf-ticket!

MACDADDY (*searching pockets*): Where're my matches? (*To* LEIONAH) Look in your bag for some matches! (*To* SCARECROW) When I find my matches, I'm burnin' yo' ass down to the ground.

MRS. MIDDLESEX (*alarmed*): Middlesex! They squattin' on our property! That lil heffer down there with that buck, done opened up her suitcase. Next thin you know they'll have a string of dirty drawers strung across the yard.

MR. MIDDLESEX: Looks bad. That's what an open door policy will get'cha!

(LEIONAH *closes suitcase and shakes head, having not found any matches.* SCARECROW, *who only a moment ago watched them anxiously, now smiles.*)

MACDADDY: I don't know what you're smilin' at! I'm jes two minutes off
yo' stack without a match!
SCARECROW (*singing*):
  'Tis better that you steal on home,
  than get your feathers tarred-to-the-bone,
    bye, bye, Blackbird!

(MACDADDY *absurdly irritated;* LEIONAH *tries to pull him away.*)

LEIONAH: Let's split, Mac. Ain't nothin' here a good drought can't fix!
MACDADDY (*pulling away from her*): Uh-uh, naw, I ain't goin' nowhere!
SCARECROW: Shoo-shoo, fool, before I call my man the eagle down
on you!
MACDADDY (*incensed*): What goddamn eagle?
SCARECROW: The Great American Eagle!
MACDADDY: Well, I'm the Great MacDaddy, you understand?

(LEIONAH *sighs.*)

Son of the Big MacDaddy who is dead, making me the greatest
Daddy of all the MacDaddies who can do anything in this world. So
call yo' sad-assed eagle, Jim, I'll ride his back until he grins! Go on,
call him!

(SCARECROW *murmurs toward the sky as* MACDADDY *directs* LEIONAH
to keep an eye out for EAGLE. *They circle* SCARECROW *vigilantly.*)

MRS. MIDDLESEX: It jes ain't American what these nigras do. They
understand nothin' 'bout private property.
MR. MIDDLESEX: Done placed a lotta stock in Heavensville too.
SCARECROW (*shouting*): C'mon Eagle, come on through. Gotta show
these blackbirds what Eagle can do!

(EAGLE *appears from upstage flapping his wings: a grotesquely featured
creature covered with soiled money, dancing menacingly around*
MACDADDY *and* LEIONAH.)

Sic 'em, Eagle. Sic 'em!

(*Retreating from* EAGLE, MACDADDY *and* LEIONAH *back into*
SCARECROW. *For the first time,* SCARECROW *moves from his stationary
position, causing* MACDADDY *and* LEIONAH *to fall to the ground.*)

MRS. MIDDLESEX: What those nigras need is a good thrashing. The
heffer's layin' down on the ground with that buck. Bet they ain't even
married or nothin'.

MR. MIDDLESEX: It's a sin and a shame for a God-lovin' country to sink so low!

(MACDADDY *and* LEIONAH *lay stretched out on the ground.* SCARECROW *places straw-clips on their wrists and ankles as if anchoring them to the ground, while* EAGLE *dances about menacingly. A large, oversized, hypodermic needle and a plastic bag of white powder "fly in" from above and is suspended over the couples' heads.* EAGLE *becomes excited.*)

SCARECROW (*reaching toward "works"*): Now, we keeps something up our tree that always makes the Eagle happy! (*Detaching hypodermic needle from wire*) Get back, Eagle! Just so you birds don't think we're without humanity, I'm gonna show you a little Christian pity, just to ease your pain.

(*As* MACDADDY *and* LEIONAH *struggle vainly,* SCARECROW *injects them with the hypo-needle, then replaces it on wire to be suspended over their heads like bait to urge* EAGLE *to dance ferociously at their feet.*)

Go on, Eagle, work yo' show! Yeah, do it to 'em!

(MACDADDY, *in an effort to overcome the influences of the drug, and the imminent attack by* EAGLE, *begins to shout incantatively as if trying to awaken a stronger source of power to free them.*)

MACDADDY: God is so great! God is so great!

(MACDADDY *repeats this phrase which is interpolated with a response from* LEIONAH *of "Thank yuh, Jesus!"*)

MRS. MIDDLESEX: Did you know that nigras use the Lord's name in vain?
MR. MIDDLESEX: Can't happen here in Heavensville!

(*As* MACDADDY *and* LEIONAH *repeat their phrases with varying rhythmic tonalities, improvisationally, a work gang, the* SPIRIT OF WOE, *suddenly appears from upstage left, chained together, pounding their sledge hammers rhythmically, punctuating their song, "My Country 'Tis of Thee," which is sung with a gospel inflection. Leading the* SPIRIT OF WOE *is the manifestation/personification of* WINE.)

MRS. MIDDLESEX: Oh no, good God! It's happening, Middlesex. Exactly what folks always say 'bout nigras. The moment you let one in they start bringing their friends around.
MR. MIDDLESEX: Heavensville will never be the same after this!
SPIRIT OF WOE: (MACDADDY *and* LEIONAH *shouting in between the*

phrases which reinforces the dynamics of the musical mode with call'n response):

My
   coun-try 'tis
   of thee
sweet
   land of
   lib-erty
for
   his I
sing.
Land
   where my
   fa-thers died!
land
   of the
   Pil-grims pride;
from
   ev-ery
   moun-tainside,
O Lord,
   let free-dom
   let free-dom
   let-it-ring!

MRS. MIDDLESEX: Before you know it, they'll be havin' all-night parties out there.

MR. MIDDLESEX: Heavensville, my Heavensville!

(*The* SPIRIT OF WOE *repeats the same verses one more time, along with the interlocking invocations of* MACDADDY *and* LEIONAH, *thus intensifying the musical mode which distracts* EAGLE *from his "bait," actually wears him out, his "killing dance" becoming subdued by the spiritual force of the work song.* SCARECROW *scolds* EAGLE *to keep dancing. He is now astonished and chagrined to see* EAGLE *"peck," pull up the clips that had fastened* MACDADDY *and* LEIONAH *to the ground. As the* SPIRIT OF WOE *exits, dragging its chains and singing vigorously,* EAGLE *trails docilely behind them.*)

SCARECROW: What's wrong with you, Eagle? You supposed to be my partner. Come back! You makin' a fool outta the whole goddamned nation! Come on back here! This ain't no time to go soft-on-the-job. Lotta people dependin' on you and me, Eagle, come-on-back!

(MACDADDY *stands while* LEIONAH *remains in a state of grace for having been freed by the spirit, and tips up behind* SCARECROW *who faces the exit.*)

MACDADDY (*as* SCARECROW *turns around*): Booo!

(*Horrified,* SCARECROW *runs offstage.*)

MRS. MIDDLESEX (*despairingly*): Ain't there somethin' we can do, Middlesex?

MR. MIDDLESEX (*looking away from the* Journal *for the first time to stroke his chin reflectively*): They tell me cyanide is colorless, odorless, and painless.

(MRS. MIDDLESEX *collapses in her chair with a horrified expression on her face, gazing at her husband as wagon/platform is wheeled offstage.* MACDADDY *detaches hypo-needle and bag of powder from wire.*)

MACDADDY: Wonder what this is?

LEIONAH: Ain't nothin' more fearful than idle curiosity!

MACDADDY: Nothin' wrong with bein' curious. That shit he shot into us was powerful. For a minute, I thought I was in the valley of the shadow of Death. Always was afraid of needles, though I fear no evil. Here, put this in your bag. The only way to beat fear is to get used to having it around.

LEIONAH (*forewarning as she takes hypo and powder*): The cheapest way to help a man through the world is to pile up flowers on his tombstone!

(*Lights fade out as* MACDADDY *seems puzzled by her response.*)

BEAT SIX

St. Louis. Lights up on MACDADDY *and* LEIONAH *looking at a sign upstage left which reads* THE FAITHFUL REST, *hanging over a boarding-house "stoop" upon which sits* MOTHER FAITH, *wearing a housedress, bedroom slippers, and fanning herself with a church fan as she casually leans forward to observe the street scene. Downstage right is* STAGOLEE *standing around with a "street corner" attitude.* MACDADDY *and* LEIONAH, *both appearing quite tired, approach the "stoop."*

MOTHER FAITH (*responding congenially*): 'Afternoon, children!

MACDADDY: How you doin'? You know who runs this place?

MOTHER FAITH: Why, sho . . . Mother Faith!

MACDADDY: Where she bees right about now?

MOTHER FAITH: You lookin' at her, chile. Anything I can do for you?

MACDADDY (*hesitantly*): Well . . . er . . . that depends. Got any beds free?

MOTHER FAITH (*business attitude*): Why sho! Got plenty beds . . . but they ain't *free!*

MACDADDY (*somewhat embarrassed*): Well . . . er . . . how much are they?

MOTHER FAITH (*surreptitious tone*): For . . . two?

MACDADDY (*uncomfortably*): Hmm? . . . er . . . yeah!

MOTHER FAITH: Ah dollar and ah half ah day! Clean linen and two meals!

MACDADDY (*apparently broke*): I see . . . well . . . er . . . we'll be back a bit later, okay?

MOTHER FAITH: Why, sho, anytime yawl ready. Mother Faith ain't goin' nowhere.

(*She begins to fan once more and follow* MACDADDY *and* LEIONAH *with her eyes as they hesitantly approach* STAGOLEE.)

MACDADDY (*tentatively*): How you doin', cousin?

STAGOLEE (*spinning around; suspiciously*): Don't *cousin* me! My name is Stagolee!

MACDADDY: That's awright with me. I jes thought I'd see if you could spare a dime.

STAGOLEE:
A dime! Man, you must be outta yo' mind.
Do I look like some kinda money tree?
Ain't nothin' out in these bushes free!

MACDADDY: Look here, brutha . . .

STAGOLEE: Uh-uh, I ain't got no brutha! My momma only made one like me!

MACDADDY: Well anyway, dig on what I got to say. Me and my ole lady ain't had no sleep nor somethin' to eat for nearly ah week!

STAGOLEE:
So what you want from me, pity?
My middle name ain't Charity!
Out here it's every man for hisself.
If you wanna keep yo' game in check,
    you gotta get yo'self a rep,
    by any means necessary.

Hell, I done fucked over every nigguh alive
  so that I might survive.
So don't be askin' me for no sympathy,
  you'd better get out here
  and beat these bushes like me.
Or pick up yo' stick
  and split.
Cause you'll get nothin' here
  but yo' head shook,
  yo' pennies took,
  and yo' name put
  in the St. Louis General
  Hospital book!

(MOTHER FAITH *observes the scene downstage with great consternation.*)

MACDADDY: So yo jes gonna over us, huh? What kind of city you
  nigguhs livin' in without no pity? Can't you see this sista is hungry?
STAGOLEE:
  I ain't got no sista, either. And before you try to make a
  sissy outta me, I'm gonna tell you somethin' 'bout bein' hungry.

Back in '22 when times was hard,
  had a sawed-off shotgun with a crooked deck of cards;
  had a pin-striped suit, and a broke-down hat;
  had a T-model Ford without a payment on that.

Had a cute lil 'hoe who throwed me out in the cold.
  When I asked why, she said, "Our love is growin' old."
So I walked on down to Market Street,
  down where the baddest nigguhs in town used to meet.
Walked through water and waded through mud,
  'til I came to a place called "The Bucket of Blood."

I walked in, asked the man for somethin' to eat.
He brought me a stale glass of water
  and a fucked-up piece of meat.
I said, "Raise, chicken-shit, do you know who I am?"
He said, "Frankly, sad ass, I don't give a damn!"
I said, "This is me, bad Stagolee!"
He said, "Yeah, been hearin' 'bout you 'cross the way,
  but I feed hungrier and badder nigguhs each and every day."
I knowed right then that this bird was dead;
  threw a thirty-eight shell right through the sucker's head.

And if I'm lyin', I'm flyin'!

LEIONAH (*insinuating disbelief*): Countin' the stars don't help the meal-box!

MACDADDY (*responding pragmatically*): Look here, Stagolee, we ain't got much . . . (*Opens* LEIONAH's *suitcase*) but maybe we can sell you somethin' . . . like a pretty dress for your woman or somethin'.

STAGOLEE (*checking out suitcase*): Lissen, chump, my name is Stagolee, not Sugar Daddy. Any buyin' to be done, will be buyin' for me! What's that in the corner, somethin' to eat?

(MACDADDY *holds up plastic bag of white powder.*)

MACDADDY: This? Uh-uh, don't think you can handle it, Stagolee. Much too mean. Even meaner than you.

STAGOLEE (*taking bag; dipping finger in for a taste*): Ain't nothin' that mean! And if it is, I oughta get to know it. (*Tastes*) Ooooweeee! it sho do have a bite. But I damn sho ain't gonna let a little white stuff give me no fright. What's the price?

MACDADDY: I'm tellin' yuh, Stag, that stuff will grab you like death-dipped-in-misery!

STAGOLEE: How you sound, Clown? I know all about misery. Just give up the price!

LEIONAH: A blind mule ain't hardly 'fraid of darkness!

MACDADDY: Ah dollar and ah half!

STAGOLEE (*as he counts out money*): You got it! Now, how do you get next to this white stuff without using yo' fingers?

MACDADDY (*holding up hypo-needle*): Here's the shot, but I'm afraid I can't sell it to you 'cause it's such a fearful thing and I'm still gettin' used to havin' it around. But . . . er . . . I guess I could rent it to you for another dollar.

STAGOLEE (*taking hypo-needle*): Fifty cents! and that's all you get.

(MACDADDY *accepts money;* STAGOLEE *walks off.*)

MACDADDY: Hope that white stuff don't knock you down, Stagolee.

STAGOLEE (*exiting*): If it's that bad, we'll jes have to lock assess 'til one of us falls dead, and you know, I ain't been beat lately!

(MACDADDY *and* LEIONAH *look away from* STAGOLEE *and discover* MOTHER FAITH *vigorously beckoning them; they approach.*)

MOTHER FAITH (*admonishingly*): C'mon over here, chile, and let me talk to yuh! Whay you children doin' talkin' to that bad Stagolee. He ain't gonna do you no good.

MACDADDY: Ain't nothin' to it, really. We jes had to hit on Stag for some bread so we could ease up on that meal and bed you be advertisin'.

MOTHER FAITH (*directing them inside*): Stagolee is the last person in the world yawl should have to go see. I got eyes, ain't ah? I can see yawl need a rest. If you didn't have no money, why didn't you say so.

(LEIONAH *sulks as she leads them onto stoop in preparation to go inside.*)

Now, yawl just come on in here. Mother Faith ain't never turned nobody 'way from her door. C'mon in, chile!

(*Wagon/platform rolled offstage. Transitional Beat. Lights up on stage right while* MUSICIANS *play honky-tonk. Several black people,* THE COMMUNITY AT REST/CHORUS, *seated at a long table. At one end,* WOMEN *eating from soup bowls and dipping bread; at the other end,* MEN *are playing cards noisily while the* WOMEN *chat with abandon.* MOTHER FAITH *enters with* MACDADDY *and* LEIONAH. *She directs them to a table.*)

MOTHER FAITH: That's right, yawl jes come right in here and rest yo' souls. We ain't got much, like everybody else out here, but yawl jes make yo'selves at home. Stay as long as you like, we'll find a way. (*To others*) Yawl make room for these children. (*To* MACDADDY *and* LEIONAH) And after supper, yawl be sure to get some sleep, even though the bed do take two! Keep the faith, children.

FIRST CARDPLAYER (*to* MACDADDY): Hey man, you wanna take my hand? I'm 'bout to give it up!

POPPA (*another manifestation/personification of* WINE; *grouchily*): You oughta! Can't play no way!

(MACDADDY *starts to accept the offer, but looks over at* LEIONAH *and is reminded through a glance the limitations of his monies, thus merely sits next to* POPPA.)

MACDADDY: Naw! That's awright! Kinda hungry right through here.

(LEIONAH *enters into lively conversation with the other women.* MACDADDY *suddenly becomes aware of the grouchy* POPPA.)

POPPA (*signifyin'*): Can't none of yawl play. Uhmmp! looka there!

FIRST CARDPLAYER: Stay out the game!

POPPA: What game? Yawl ain't got no game. (*Poking* MACDADDY'S *elbow*) They never could play the Man's game down front!

(MACDADDY *merely nods placatingly.*)

Trump card! Uhump! that sho was po'!

SECOND CARDPLAYER: Didn't the man say stay outta the game?

POPPA (*poking* MACDADDY'*s elbow*): Can't tell these young squirrels nothin'! They think they know it all. (*Re-intrudes the game*) Trump 'im! Ain't that somethin'!

THIRD CARDPLAYER (*having just played the wrong card*): Now, we ain't gonna tell yuh no moe'. . . . keep yo' cottonpickin' nose outta my cards!

MOTHER FAITH (*admonishingly*): Uh-uh, wait one minute here. Yawl know yawl ought'n do Poppa like that. He's only tryin' to tell you somethin'!

FOURTH CARDPLAYER: How he gonna know what I know when he ain't even in the game?

POPPA: I know you got a handful of trumps, Short Change, and you don't even know it. (*To* MACDADDY) And if he did know it, he wouldn't know what to do with 'em.

FIRST CARDPLAYER (*waving* POPPA *off*): Awwww, man, you ain't said nothin'! Let's play cards!

POPPA (*to* MACDADDY): 'Em fellas ain't learned nothin' 'bout the Man's game.

(MACDADDY *merely nods placatingly.*)

I know, 'cause I done seen 'em all. Ain't no new game. Only the card deck is new and the stakes higher. Same old shuffle, though. (*Becomes more agitated*) Common sense will tell you that the man with the biggest trump will thump everytime. Trump card is powerful, you know. Every niggah's got one! If we put 'em all together and use 'em right, we'd all be powerful. (*He stands up, moves down the end of table, looks away as he takes a swig from his half pint of Old Grandad. Suddenly he spins, slams his fist down on the table, and ejaculates a statement that stuns the whole table into silence. His speech and attitude is redolent of Marcus Garvey.*) Saw seven bust eleven in the pants . . . (*Everyone is startled.*) . . . and make snake-eyes give him some respect! A trump can bust anybody in the rump. That's the true test of Time. I know about Time!

(*They stare at him as one does a man who speaks with a drunkard's tongue, but possesses wisdom.* MACDADDY *is particularly curious as the women reinforce his speech with responses.*)

There was a time when black people had all the trumps, and white folks got bumps on their behinds sittin' in caves. And that's a fact! And the time when black women were to men what daylight is to darkness, a change for the better, shedding light on the mysteries of life. Couldn't do without her then, and no real man can do without her now. But you gotta have your trump card! It ain't no virtue to be poor all yo' life. It's a crime! When you poor, you be hungry without hope of food, sick without a drop of medicine, tired without a bed to lay your sleepy head, naked without clothes to hide your sores. Without that trump card you be despised! Hell, ain't nothin' left but crime! Yeah, the trump card is power! If you don't believe me, ask the Man . . . you always askin' him for somethin'! I know what I say, cause I been hungrier longer than anybody here today. The Man got the trump card, and his family too! That's why he got more power than you. They done played full house and got a nation. A nation! hear me, a nation! Is that trump enough for you? If you want yo'self a nation, you'd better figure out how he stacked that deck and get you some trump cards too. Cause the man who can't play the game is cheatin' on God's image. Hear me? God wanted you . . . to be the complete master of yo'self, so he could go on bein' the Almighty trump card!

MOTHER FAITH (*she repeats the last few words, then launches into song "Amazing Grace" as* POPPA *words improvisationally—call'n response—throughout phrases of the song*):

T'was grace that taught my heart to fear
and grace my fears relieved;
Oh, how precious did that grace appear
the hour I first believed.

    Amazing grace
    how sweet the sound
    that saved
    a wretch like me;

    oh, I once was lost
    but now I'm found
    was blind
    but now I see.

(MOTHER FAITH *repeats the verses once more. Her song has restored spiritual harmony at the table as* POPPA *braces himself with another swig of Old Grandad.* MACDADDY, *confidence restored, moves in closer to card game.*)

MACDADDY: Deal me in . . . brutha!

(*Lights fade out. Transitional Beat.* MACDADDY *and* LEIONAH *encounter the nerve-wracked figure of* STAGOLEE, *now* SCAGOLEE, *on the "street corner." He scratches and talks to himself as they approach him.*)

Wuz happenin', Stagolee?

SCAGOLEE (*spinning around nervously; suspiciously*): Who you talkin' to? You don't know me. My name is Scagolee!

MACDADDY: Hey, man, this is me, MacDaddy.

SCAGOLEE (*vacantly*): Yeaaaaah! (*Almost nodding*)

MACDADDY: Look, I got some bucks. I thought I'd buy that stuff back.

SCAGOLEE (*snapping upright*): Ain't no moe'! I done whupped Death's ass. I put fist all in white stuff's face. Dude tried to do Scagolee dirty. I put a hurtin' on him, Jim.

LEIONAH (*signifyin'*): Hard for me to see who hurts the worse!

MACDADDY: You sho 'nuff been in a fight, Scagolee. How the dude get yo' jaws so tight?

SCAGOLEE: The dude did this funny thing, Braaaahhh! You know me, Scagolee, I always keep some bread for my shit, you understand. Ain't nobody ever caught me beggin' for nothin'! So I'm sittin' out there by my ride when ole white stuff slid up on me with this ghostly lookin' dude. Yeah, right down here in the Jetto!

(SCAG *appears upstage and mimics the literal, as well as the visceral, levels of the story.* LEIONAH *responds with utterances and gestures to indicate her contempt for what is implied by the carnal level of the story; she insinuates, while punctuating the story, that she rejects such experiences which are merely "typical" and the consequences of such events she almost welcomes.*)

First, I thought he was the Man, so I was cool, but he kept on rappin', you know, leanin' on my ear, fillin' my head up with white stuff. Said she was his ole lady, you know. Said he was tryin' to get into somethin', right down here in the Jetto, Jim! And I say, that's cool, not wantin' to act-the-fool, you understand. So he say, "how 'bout some little-girl?" Now, I lean back on my ride and checks the dude out. I checks out some more of white stuff too. Then I say, no, I ain't interested in no little girl. So he looks at me kinda funny and say, coke? And I say, I don't drink no coke. He say, "you mean you don't like white stuff at all?" Then he reached down in his pocket and come out with the little girl, Jack! I start sniffin' a little bit of her right there on the corner, you understand, and it was good.

(MUSICIANS, SCAG, *and* LEIONAH *all making impressions which heighten the story rhythmically.* SCAGOLEE, *quite frenetic in his pacing;* MACDADDY *subdued.*)

Now we cuts down to the dude's hotel, outside the Jetto, cause we gonna party! No sooner do we get there, ole white stuff start doin' strange, takin' off her clothes and shit! Before I know it, she done stretched out on the bed neckid! But I don't pay no 'tention, cause all I wants is some moe' of that little girl. Still, he asked me just the same 'bout his ole lady, asked me how I liked her. I say, she ain't bad, where's the little girl? And he say, with his hands strokin' white stuff's thighs, "in the hay," you know, like you tell somebody on-the-cuff, "in the hay is your little girl, white as snow, sweet as cotton candy." So, now I sees what's comin' down, and I say, "No good, Jim, your ole lady can't do nothin' for me. Just give me my taste of coke and I'll split. I'll even pay for it!" He say, "That won't be necessary, Buddy." . . . he called me Buddy . . . cause if I could get down with johnson and give white stuff a turn, I could have a whole bunch of little girl free.

(LEIONAH *furious;* SCAG *dancing gloatingly.*)

MACDADDY: Now, I know a bad nigguh like you didn't go for that!
SCAGOLEE: Didn't I? Sure I did! What else could I do? But that ain't the worse of it, that ain't really what burned Scagolee. You see, it wasn't easy talkin' johnson into that kind of action, the dude standin' over me and shit. But we gets it together, like Scagolee always do, and johnson is hard as Chinese 'rithmetic! And I start pile drivin' into ole white stuff like I was breakin' ground for a projects. I was doin' it to death, Jim, but now she really puts me in a trick, you understand.

(SCAG *becomes almost orgiastic in his movements;* LEIONAH *more embittered.*)

She got both my legs pinned down to the bed. And when I raised my head to peek out the corner of my eye, my heart almost stopped. This dude is standin' over me with his own johnson choked around the neck. And he is pumpin', Jim, jes-a-pumpin'! (SCAG *mimics fiercely.*) Now I know it's time to get up from here, but this white stuff is strong, she got me all strung out. She starts moanin' and stuff, and I struggle to break free, almost breakin' my back! But her grip is a monster. And jes when I was about to crack her upside her head, I felt it, Jack, all up and down my back. All up and down my spine, you understand!!! The dude had blown his whole load up and down my back!

(MACDADDY *laughs.*)

That shit ain't funny!!! The dude might as well had fucked me in the ass!

(SCAG *indicates his pleasure;* LEIONAH, *great disappointment;*
MACDADDY, *dismay.*)

MACDADDY: What did you do about it?

SCAGOLEE (*more subdued, as in music*): I went crazy on 'em. Took out my razor and went crazy on 'em muthafukas!

MACDADDY: Before, or after the little girl?

SCAGOLEE (*vacantly*): Yeeaaaaaah!

(*Lights dim on a nodding* SCAGOLEE.)

BEAT SEVEN

Louisiana. Lights come up red. Percussion rhythms. MACDADDY *and* LEIONAH *standing in same area downstage as earlier, searching the empty redness that surrounds. They become startled by the sudden appearance of* RED WOMAN *who dances on and toward them with sensual, Afro-Caribbean movements as if trying to get* MACDADDY's *attention.*

MACDADDY: Who's that?

(LEIONAH *checks out* RED WOMAN *with a 'tude.*)

She callin' you?

(LEIONAH *shakes her head.*)

She callin' somebody, and I don't even know the lady. You sure you don't know her?

(LEIONAH *looks up at* MACDADDY *with a 'tude.*)

Then what she want with me?

LEIONAH (*as* RED WOMAN *comes in close, then backs away rhythmically, beckoning* MACDADDY *the while*): Maybe we oughta see jes what she's puttin' down!

MACDADDY: Uh-uh, you never see me followin' no strange 'hoes around!

LEIONAH (*hand on hip; curious*): C'mon! fear is only dangerous for the heart when you let it get yo' mind. Let's go!

(LEIONAH *struts arrogantly on top of* RED WOMAN *who tries to look around her as she backs away, so as to maintain* MACDADDY's *attention, as he follows, peering over* LEIONAH's *shoulder. They move upstage to a certain point where* RED WOMAN *stops, looks past them, reacts fearfully, and runs away.* MACDADDY *and* LEIONAH *spin around sharply. They encounter the grotesque features of* BENNY *and* RED, *two drug forces.* BENNY *is hyperactive and fast talking;* RED *is slow, dawdling, hesitant in speech.*)

BENNY (*startled by* MACDADDY's *swift spin*):
Look out, nigger, and hold your ground,
ain't nobody told you to turn around!
RED (*slowly*): No-body told you nuthin'!

(*No response from* MACDADDY *who ushers* LEIONAH *to one side, then stands firm, his appearance/attitude tightened up, supporting himself on his juju cane.*)

BENNY:
And don't be actin' cute,
'cause you all dressed up
  in yo' Sunday suit.
Don't wanna hear no cryin'
  this time!
RED: Don't wanna hear it!

(*No response.* LEIONAH *upstage vigilantly.*)

BENNY:
  And don't be givin' me no glass eye;
    ain't never met a nigguh
    who wasn't 'fraid to die.
You might not be the usual pick
    but that don't matter
    one damn bit!
RED: Don't be matterin' no way!
BENNY:
Maybe you don't know who I am?
My name is Benny;
    this here is my
    girlfriend Minnie!
RED: Awww, Benny man, drop dead! You know my name is Red!
MACDADDY (*with arched deliberation*): And I am the Great MacDaddy,
    son of the Big MacDaddy who is dead, makin' me the greatest Daddy
    of all the MacDaddies who can do anything in this world.
BENNY:
Oh yeah?

Then you must be the goddamned meat
     for my goddamned cat.
Not too
     goddamned lean;
nor too
     goddamned fat.
Ready to be packed in a neat sack!
MACDADDY:
Yeah,
     I'm your goddamned meat
     for your goddamned cat.
Not too
     goddamned lean,
nor too
     goddamned fat.
And if you don't get
     your goddamned ass
     outta here quick,
I'm gonna break it
     with this goddamned stick!
RED: Ooooooooohhhh! Wwwweeeeeeee!
BENNY:
Who you think you playin' with, Jack?
I couldn't give a damn if yo' momma calls you Mac!
RED (*slow reaction, but titillated*): Hah . . . Momma Mac!
BENNY (*excitedly*):
You don't know what you doin' messin' with me.
Messin' with me will make your nerves twitch,
     your backside itch,
     and your bowels switch
     so badly they
     empty out yo' mouth
     so you only talk shit!
RED: Phewwwweeeeee!
BENNY: That's right, Mac, you'd rather be locked up in a phone booth
     sandpaperin' a lion's ass than to be messin' with me. Dig it? You'd be
     better off suckin' milk outta a gorilla's left breast than to be thinkin'
     'bout jumpin' in my chest.
RED: Beat 'im to death, Benny!
BENNY: Let me tell you one more goddamned thing. Don't you know I
     ain't worried 'bout you . . . 'cause I'll run up yo' goddamned throat,
     jump down yo' goddamned lungs, tap dance on yo' kidneys, do-the-

grind on yo' liver, stomp yo' balls into a nod, then kill yo' goddamned rod, even die in yo' funky but 'til yo' heart stops beatin'!

RED: And you gets double-trouble messin' with Red!

MACDADDY (*cold and deliberate*): I'm gonna turn around and count to three. And if yawl still here when I look back, thunder and lightnin' will close your traps!

BENNY (*stalking* MACDADDY *cautiously*): Ain't that some bitch!

MACDADDY (*searching* LEIONAH's *eyes which register their positions*): One . . . !

BENNY: Move in on 'im Red, he's as good as dead!

MACDADDY (*holding juju cane firmly*): Two . . . !

RED: Not so fast, Benny!

MACDADDY: Three!

BENNY: Grab that stick!

(MACDADDY *spins around with the juju cane extended with both hands: a single, loud blast from the juju cane and* BENNY *and* RED *fall dead. Lights change to normal as* MACDADDY *and* LEIONAH *stand over the bodies. The* BLOOD FOLK *community rush on to review the outcome of the confrontation. They are horrified by what has transpired, and fear reprisals.*)

BLOOD LEADER (*manifestation/personification of* WINE): What did you do? Is that Benny and Red that you've slammed dead? Don't you know you can't get away with a thing like that in Louisiana?

MACDADDY: Look, Blood, it's over and done with. Ain't no moe' problem.

BLOOD LEADER: When 'em cracker-flies see this, they gonna give us a fit for real. Let's get outta here. Everybody out quick!

(*Fear causes everyone to panic. Strobe light indicates calamity as everyone runs in different directions, and in the confusion, even* LEIONAH *is swept off, leaving* MACDADDY *alone. Transitional Beat. Lights back to normal,* MACDADDY *frantically searches audience for* LEIONAH. *He is worried.*)

MACDADDY: Leionah! Leionah! Leionah!

(HUMDRUM, *another manifestation/personification of* SCAG, *enters upstage right carting a large, stuffed, burlap bag load on a rolling dolly.*)

HUMDRUM (*street-crier rhythm*):
Got Black Cat
Got Black Cat
Got Black Cat today-oh
  catch me now

while I'm givin'
'im away-oh!
Dry lo-ad!
Dry lo-ad!
Dry load for pine
Dry load passin' time.
Make up yo' mind
take up my cry-oww!
Make up yo' mind,
'foe I pass by-oww!
I'll sell it to the rich
I'll sell it to the poor
I'll sell it to the baby girl
standin' in the door-oww!

MACDADDY (*approaching* HUMDRUM *anxiously*): Hey, man, you see some people pass this way?

HUMDRUM (*settling load*): Humdrum sees people each and every day.

MACDADDY: I'm lookin' for some particular people. Some Bloods! See some Blood go by?

HUMDRUM: Humdrum do all he can not to miss them. Best customers I got out here in the street.

MACDADDY (*impatient*): Yeah . . . yeah, that's cool. But which way did they go? My woman is with them? Gotta find them now, you understand?

(*Two* TREES *appear.* BLOOD LEADER *and* RED WOMAN *each with large umbrellas with strips of plastic material draped over the side obscuring their faces. The* TREES *enter from stage left and right, come together briefly upstage of* HUMDRUM *and* MACDADDY, *then exit upstage right and left. They seem to be humming.*)

HUMDRUM: Sure, I understand. You lookin' for your woman, and you in a hurry. Well, I'm in a hurry too. So if you help me with this load we can get to them even faster.

MACDADDY (*agreeing*): Ain't no big thang! Which way do we go?

HUMDRUM: Jes follow those trees!

(*As they move upstage, the* BLOOD FOLK, *including* BLOOD LEADER *and* RED WOMAN *appear.* LEIONAH *is with them.* MACDADDY *leaves* HUMDRUM *to deliver the load at the feet of the* BLOOD LEADER *as he embraces* LEIONAH. *As they query about the contents of the load, and prepare to inspect it upon the invitation from* HUMDRUM, MACDADDY *sings one brisk chorus of a blues/ballad.*)

MACDADDY:
Leionah!
Leionah, bab-ee!
you sure
are a sight
for sore eyes.

Leionah!
Leionah, momma!
you sure
did open
my eyes.

A man ain't worth a quarter
without some other man's
daughter,
I'm glad
you're at
my side!

(*Throughout the brief song,* HUMDRUM *prods the* BLOOD FOLK *community to open the sack. Upon doing so, they discover the body of the* BLOOD SON.)

BLOOD LEADER (*stridently*): Blood Son! It's my Blood Son! Who would do a thing like this to my Blood Son? (*Searching faces in the audience*) Somebody tell me, who would do such a thing to my Blood Son? Huh? Do you know? (*Shouting toward audience*) Somebody tell me, why should my Blood Son be the victim of this scaggy life?
HUMDRUM: That's a goddamned shame, ain't it? If I had known that load was such a burden, I never would've helped that fellow!
BLOOD LEADER: Who?
HUMDRUM (*pointing finger at* MACDADDY): Him! How could I know? I was jes helpin'!

(*The* BLOOD FOLK *angrily seize* MACDADDY, *while* HUMDRUM *feigns innocence, but are stopped by* BLOOD LEADER.)

BLOOD LEADER: Wait! We have no time to chastise that man. We must celebrate the Blood Son's spirit before it becomes cold. Let's dance and sing 'til seven bells ring, so that his spirit will be assured of rest. And this man will join us!

(BLOOD LEADER *moves toward* MACDADDY *to relieve him of his juju cane.* MACDADDY *withdraws, but under the pressure of the community, he gives up the juju cane.* BLOOD LEADER *now places the cane on the chest of the* BLOOD SON.)

Get up, Blood Son, and show us the way!

(MUSICIANS *play New Orleans funeral procession music.* BLOOD SON *rises, takes the juju cane, and solemnly leads a double line, men on one side, women on the other, across stage in the first line.* HUMDRUM, *anxious to join them, takes the dolly and sack offstage, cries out for them to wait for him, and joins the back of the line to pick up the rhythmic handclap. From upstage center,* BLOOD SON *leads group downstage forming a "strip" as men and women now face each other.* BLOOD SON *now gestures toward the* MUSICIANS *with the juju cane, and the tempo of the rhythm is accelerated for the beginning of the second line.* BLOOD SON *dances vigorously up the "strip": on his way down, he hands the juju cane to the man at the top of the line who now enters the "strip" with the woman facing him, initiates a dance step which she follows, gives juju cane to next man, then moves on down the "strip" with the woman, ending up at the end of the line. Each man and woman follow the same procedure twice around. However, each time* HUMDRUM *is in line to receive the juju cane, he is passed up, thus, he goes to the end of the line in order to try again. Having been passed up twice,* HUMDRUM *jumps into the middle of the "strip" and dances wildly by himself: the* COMMUNITY *stops to watch as the music trails off.*)

HUMDRUM (*awkwardly dancing alone*): C'mon, yawl. Wha'cha stoppin' for? Where's the music? Ain't yawl dancin' no more?

(*They stare suspiciously at* HUMDRUM.)

All I wanna do is join the crowd. (*No response.*) Well, why shouldn't I? (*Points at* MACDADDY) Why should he have all the fun, huh, tell me, why should he? (*No response*) What yawl got against me? I like stylin', flimflam, cakewalk too! (*No response*) He don't deserve to be here anyway . . . cause I did it! I killed your son. Hear that! Me, Humdrum, killed your Blood Son!

BLOOD LEADER (*the last to get the juju cane; ceremoniously*): Then we gotta dance for you for real!

(BLOOD LEADER *gestures toward* DRUM *with the juju cane, who initiates a fast rhythm with* MUSICIANS. *As the women back away into a tight group, clapping their hands, the men form a dancing circle with* HUMDRUM *in the center.* BLOOD LEADER *gestures with juju cane toward the* RED WOMAN *who becomes* DANCE; *she enters the circle with* HUMDRUM. *He now points toward one of the women in the chorus,* SONG, *who leads them into a jubilant rendering of "By-and-By." The gospel sound is infused with African percussive attitudes which informs the dancing rhythm of* DANCE *and* HUMDRUM, *while the men in the circle dance at a slower tempo, thereby insinuating a polyrhythmic quality in the total mode.*)

SONG:
Temptations hidden snares,
    often take us unaware.
And our hearts are made to bleed
    for each thoughtless word or deed.
And we wonder why the test
    when we try to do our best.
But we'll understand it better
    by-and-by.

BLOOD FOLK WOMEN (*rhythmic hand clapping*):
By and by
    oh when the mornin' comes
All the saints
    of God are gatherin' home
(And we will) tell the story
    how we've overcome
And we'll understand it better
    by-and-by.

(*The chorus is repeated several times as* SONG, DANCE, *and* DRUM *wear down* HUMDRUM. DANCE *drives* HUMDRUM *out of the circle and offstage, the singing women in pursuit, the men following, leaving the* BLOOD SON *to dance jubilantly at center stage where he receives a handshake from* BLOOD LEADER *before exiting in the opposite direction.* MACDADDY *grabs* LEIONAH, *who is infused with the spirit, before she leaves with the other women and prepares to leave downstage while* BLOOD LEADER *solemnly listens upstage for the seven bells which signal the* BLOOD SON's *spirit at rest. The voices of the women can still be heard.*)

BLOOD LEADER (*returning the juju cane to* MACDADDY *following the sound of seven bells*): MacDaddy! If you want to find Wine, listen back . . . listen back, and you'll hear what's happenin' up . . . listen *up,* and you'll be able to take what's goin' down. Jes keep an eye on the Blood Son!

(BLOOD SON *exits quickly to catch up with the singing voices, leaving* MACDADDY *confused, at first, about which direction to exit. He follows* BLOOD SON.)

TERMINAL RHYTHM

South Carolina sea island. Lights up on MACDADDY *and* LEIONAH
*standing on bare platform/wagons upstage gazing at the awesome spectacle
of the ashen-gray environment that surrounds them—the plastic material
now suspended throughout the house—appearing as vines or old trees of
a dense swamp. It is quiet, with the exception of the percussive pulses of
the* MUSICIANS. *As* LEIONAH *sits on her suitcase to gaze with disbelief,*
MACDADDY *steps down from platform to inspect environment more closely.*
LEIONAH *alerts* MACDADDY *to the sudden appearance of an ashen-gray
figure that backs its way into the environment. It is* WINE.

MACDADDY (*curiously*): Wine! Is that you?

WINE (*wiping brow; backing toward platform*): Well, well, well, ain't that
swell. Young MacDaddy!

MACDADDY: Great MacDaddy, Wine, and don't you ever forget that!
Where in hell you been? I been lookin' all over creation for you.

WINE: You been here that long? Thought I knew everybody in Creation.
Don't see how I could have missed yuh here in Carolina.

MACDADDY: Jes got here!

WINE: Oh, I see. It must have been kinda sudden.

MACDADDY: Are you kiddin'? That was one helluva trip!

WINE: You mean to tell me, yawl come this far and ain't dead yet?

LEIONAH: A feather bed ain't much service to the young corn!

WINE (*easing down onto edge of platform*): Well, if yawl that snappy, don't
see how yawl gonna be able to stay 'round here. Got too much life
in yuh!

MACDADDY: Ain't plannin' on stayin', really.

WINE (*lounging attitude*): Don't yawl get me wrong, now. Love to see you
young people 'round. But yawl come back when yuh ready to settle
down. When you really ready for a rest. Ain't much else to do here but
rest, you know, stretch out the ole limbs, that's best. Ain't nothin' in
the world like it!

MACDADDY: It do look pretty dead around here. Well, anyway, since you
done got your rest, I'm ready to take you back to L.A.

WINE: Uh-uh, nothin' doin'!

MACDADDY: I don't wanna hear it, Wine. I come too far to find you.
Now you goin' home!

WINE: Already home! And I'm home to stay.

MACDADDY: Don't be talkin' crazy, Wine! You know, when you left me
strung-out in L.A. I was madder than a broke-dick dog! If I had

caught up with you one minute sooner, I would've stomped your ass in the ground!

WINE: Yeah, I guess there ain't much you can do to me now.

LEIONAH: You know, Mac, you should never sweep dirt out of a door at night, or you'll sweep yourself out of a home.

WINE: Well, great-green-corn, this 'ere is a wise lil woman you got. Pretty as a grape, too. You sho know how to pick 'em!

MACDADDY: I know it!!!

WINE: Uhm-umm-mmm! How you stumble up on somethin' like that?

MACDADDY: Lookin' for you! I never figured you to do me in, Wine. Embarrassin' me in front of all my friends. Why would you do that to me, the son of Big Mac, why?

WINE: Got tired of the Man!

MACDADDY: What man?

WINE: All the Mans in the world! They kinda rough Wine up a taste. What in the world was I gonna do, the law always chompin' on my head, the lawless takin' my bread. If it wasn't one, it was the other Man.

MACDADDY: Listen, all you had to do was pull-my-coat!

WINE: And it would have come off yo' back too! Look, not a week went by without my gettin' tested or arrested. One time, ole Wine was on the wagon, my own wagon, too. But the police wouldn't even give me time to change my mind, said they were takin' me in for questionin', wanna know how I got on this wagon! Now, they jes happen to have two white boys down there accused of stealin' a horse and a cow. So I figures, since they look like the Man, they must know how to read his hand, so I would follow through on whatever they do. The first case come up b'foe the judge was the white boy accused of stealin' a horse. Judge say, "Guilty or not guilty," and the boy say "not guilty," cause he owned that horse ever since it was a colt. Case dismissed! Judge then asked the boy accused of stealin the cow, "Guilty or not guilty," and he owned that cow ever since it was a calf. Case dismissed too! Then he come on out and accuse me of stealin' that wagon and I said "not guilty," cause I owned that wagon ever since it was a wheelbarrow. Sombitch gave me thirty days!

LEIONAH (*sympathetically*): The worst road to the courthouse is through the pig pen!

WINE: You ain't jes passin' water, daughter!

MACDADDY: Okay, okay, when we get back, I'll get it all cleaned up. I'll even forget you left if you come back for a little breath.

WINE: Ain't that much breath left in L.A. Naw, MacDaddy, ain't nothin' finer than to be in Carolina.

MACDADDY: Awright then, have it your way! Just give me the formula and we'll split.

WINE: What formula?

MACDADDY: For the palm wine you do!

WINE: Aw, shucks, that won't do you no good. Ain't nobody enjoyin' what comes natural no more. You couldn't sell a pint! The Man got somethin' new goin' 'round, the worse thing in the world you ever did see, causin' havoc, makin' people raggedy and hungry for days. I tried to tell you 'bout it 'foe I left, but I didn't have time. The Man had put somethin' on my mind!

MACDADDY: What you talkin' 'bout, Wine?

WINE: This other Man, he gimme a taste of this new thing goin' 'round. It turned my stomach so bad that the Green Runner came to me in my sleep.

MACDADDY (*irritated*): What Green Runner?

WINE: You know 'bout the Green Runner, don'cha? He always comes to yuh when things get rough. He's outta this world! He's the strongest brutha that ever pulled a river straight. I've seen him sit down and eat a barrel of flour, a side of meat, and a water bucket full of greens and syrup, all in one meal. Then he would swell up and tell the heebie-jeebies to turn four bruthas loose from their labors cause he would do their jobs. And that's how I got a lotta of my wine done. And it was him that come and pulled that monkey off my back when the Man had fouled up my stomach track!

LEIONAH: Don't cross your eyes at a blinkin' owl, Mac, or you'll miss the point!

MACDADDY: So, Wine is through!

(WINE *nods.*)

And you're stayin . . . !

(WINE *nods.*)

Well, I guess comin' after you sure wasn't worth the trip.

WINE (*as they prepare to leave*): Oh, I don't know, it might a been. Had a talk with the Green Runner the other day. He gimme his personal formula for gettin' anybody back on their feet. Shoot, I reckoned it would win you more friends than any lost without Wine.

MACDADDY: Well, I sure hate to go back empty-handed. So, if you've got the word, let me have it.

WINE: Uhmmm! Are you sure you can handle it?

MACDADDY: I can do anything in this world!

WINE: Oh yeah? . . . Then tell me somethin' one half scientific!

MACDADDY: Scientific? What kinda scientific?

WINE: You know, somethin' that you break-down and put-together . . . like yo' momma mighta taught you. Somethin' simple, so I can see if you can handle my recipe.

(LEIONAH *whispers in* MACDADDY'*s ear.*)

MACDADDY (*confidently replying*): Py-R-Squared!

WINE: Wrong! But you almost got it!

(MACDADDY *stares at* LEIONAH *disgustedly as* WINE *gets up.*)

Pie . . . are round, and corn bread . . . ar squared! (*Facing them as he begins to leave backward*) Now, yawl make the best of your long haul to L.A.!

MACDADDY (*confounded*): Wine, wait . . . say it again . . . about the corn bread . . . !

WINE (*backing off*): You got the word, now take it on back out there where yawl from and use it! Bye yawl! (*Exits*)

MACDADDY (*perplexed*): Pie are round . . . corn bread are squared . . . is that all we got to take home?

LEIONAH: If the ash is out before the oak, it will be a summer of fire and smoke!

(*Lights fade as they exit through the ashened environment. Transitional Beat. Lights come up on* CHORUS/COMMUNITY *posed, as they were in primal rhythm, in a still-freeze party/dance attitude with* SCAG PHOTOGRAPHER *downstage with his head under black cloth of camera, arm raised with flash preparing to take a picture.* MUSICIANS *are playing up-tempoed Charleston. A flash from* SCAG PHOTOGRAPHER *sends up a billow of smoke, and rather than an energetic Charleston dance, the* COMMUNITY/CHORUS *droops over listlessly and begins the "Junkie Crawl" with saddened expressions on their faces, and the music changing to the attitude.* MACDADDY *and* LEIONAH *enter through the door upstage right as* SCAG *comes out from under black cloth and observes them curiously. He is holding up a pan of corn bread, while she holds up a pan of pie.*)

MACDADDY: Hey now everybody, MacDaddy's back in town . . . and he's brought you somethin' square 'n round!

SCAG PHOTOGRAPHER: How did I miss yawl in this picture?

MACDADDY (*approaching* SCAG PHOTOGRAPHER *furiously and pointing juju cane*): Get outta my life! Get outta my life and stay out!

(SCAG PHOTOGRAPHER *moves away, but seeks out better vantage points on stage to focus in on audience, even arranging segments of the audience for the proper angle, going under and out of the black cloth repeatedly as he adjusts his lens.* MACDADDY *and* LEIONAH *make vain efforts to get the* CHORUS/COMMUNITY *to accept the pie and corn bread, but are unresponsive, the weight of the Jones being too heavy.)*

Corn bread . . . c'mon, get yo' corn bread . . . it's good to yuh! . . . c'mon yawl, I'm talkin' 'bout corn bread . . . !
LEIONAH (*repeatedly*): Get yo' piece-of-the-pie!

(MACDADDY, *as* LEIONAH *continues moving among the* CHORUS/ COMMUNITY, *disappointed and angered, moves downstage and holds the corn bread aloft in one hand, the juju cane aloft in the other, and begins an incantation toward the audience as if beseeching the appearance of a super-force, a great spirit.)*

MACDADDY:
Great Guggah Muggah!
    This is MacDaddy talkin'!
Son of the Big MacDaddy
    who is dead,
makin' me the greatest Daddy
    of all the MacDaddies
who can do anything in this world
    'cept feed my bruthas!

Great Guggah Muggah,
    if you be out there
    and care,
give me yo' ear!

We got trouble in this city,
    Great Guggah Muggah,
can't you show us a little pity?
    The bruthas are wastin' away.
Whatever happen to those good ole
    grits and gravy days?

C'mon, Guggah Muggah,
    show me a rainbow sign,
not just yo' tired behind!
    Don't get me wrong,
    Guggah Muggah,
    I ain't mad with you.

All I wanna see is
  what you gon' do!

Beat on yo' chest
  and make the wind blow!
Beat on yo' chest
  shake ground like a fandango!
Beat on yo' chest
  send thunderbolts through the clouds
like our man Shango!

(*The music becomes more intense, and the "Junkie Crawl" more desperate
as the* CHORUS/COMMUNITY *seems to disintegrate, the Jones coming
down hard as they experience agonized pains of withdrawal induced by*
MACDADDY's *incantation. The* SCAG PHOTOGRAPHER *goes about his
business gingerly, setting the audience up for a portrait.*)

Great Guggah Muggah!
  if you all that they say
  you be,
  you must be
  at least
  as bad as me!
So do somethin'
  pleeezzzzze!
Can't you see these Bloods
  be sufferin' from
  a cripplin' disease?

They in a rut!
  I know what I'd do,
  if I were you,
  I'd kick some butt!
If I were you
  and they refused to eat
  I'd make 'em eat doo-doo!
If I were you
  and they stopped producin' yo' image,
  I'd castrate them too!
If I were you,
  and they stopped celebratin' yo' spirit,
  I'd take away they dancin' shoes!

(It is a calamitous moment: the CHORUS/COMMUNITY *writhing on ground.)*

No I wouldn't,
   I take it all back,
   Guggah Muggah,
   I wouldn't do nothin' like that.

These are my bruthas and sistas
   and I love everyone of 'em.
I'm just tryin' to help us get back
   where we been.
'Memberin' when nigguhs were happy,
   quick as a whip
   and twice as snappy.
I got the corn bread,
   square out the ground;
my woman's got the pie,
   round as a world
   kissed by the sky.
And we thinkin' 'bout good times now,
   'em bad pots hummin' loud
Come 'n get it!
   candied-yams and dumplin'!
   'em black-eyed peas is somethin'!
Collard greens, chicken and rice,
   c'mon get yo' corn bread, children,
   the staff of life!

(The calamity having subsided, the CHORUS/COMMUNITY *having shaken the Jones, they slowly rise and join* LEIONAH, *who has already begun to sing/talk, in song.* MUSICIANS *make a slow transition in the tempo and attitude of music.* SCAG PHOTOGRAPHER, *his camera positioned upstage center, now, facing audience, takes note of the* CHORUS/COMMUNITY's *revitalization. He tries desperately to regroup them, but to no avail.* MACDADDY's *staunch presence forces him to back off and exit.)*

LEIONAH:
  We gonna rise up
    this mornin'
  We gonna stay up
    all day.

Ain't
  no more sleepin'
  our lives away.

We gonna rise up
  this mornin'
We gonna stay up
  all day.

We ain't payin' out
  no more dues
  today.

We gonna rise up
  this mornin'
We gonna stay up
  all day.

Ain't
  gonna let
  nobody stand
  in our way.

We gonna rise up
  this mornin'
We gonna stay up
  all day.

Brutha/sista
  gonna find
  their way home
  someday.

(*Every effort is made by the* CHORUS/COMMUNITY *to get the audience/community to join them in the celebration. At the high point in the singing, the* CHORUS/COMMUNITY, LEIONAH *pulling a satisfied* MACDADDY *off last, exit out the door upstage right, with* MACDADDY *closing the door. Everything dims out with the exception of the* SCAG PHOTOGRAPHER'*s camera which is focused on the audience: if the audience is still singing, the light/special on the camera gradually fades out; if not, the* MUSICIANS *stop playing and camera light/special remains focused on the audience until they decide to exit the house.*)

IN CONVERSATION : An Afterword

GUS EDWARDS & PAUL CARTER HARRISON

African Americans have had a long and enduring presence, both as subject and artist, in the American theater firmament. However, as early as nineteenth-century minstrelsy, through the turn of the century presentation of musicals on Broadway, on through the Rose McClendon Players in Harlem during the 1940s, African-American theater artists have struggled to establish and sustain the legitamacy of a black theater as a permanent institution.

Lorraine Hansberry's *Raisin in the Sun,* produced on Broadway at the end of the 1950s under the direction of Lloyd Richards, was clearly the most pivotal theatrical event to signal the dramaturgical validity of the African-American experience as a source of universal themes that had the potential for raising the collective consciousness of the nation, thus worthy of institutionalization. Over the next few years, Lloyd Richards and the play's male lead, Sidney Poitier, would be engaged in meetings with various groups of funding agencies that felt it was time to initiate a formal, black-theater institution that would address the social needs and cultural expression of African Americans. Despite the best of intentions, the meetings were mercifully suspended after years of equivocation over the definition and objectives of such an ethnically inspired theater.

In 1964, the Off-Broadway production of LeRoi Jones's (Amiri Baraka) *Dutchman* inspired the Black Arts Movement which revealed a far less ambivalent urgency to institutionalize black theater in Harlem with an unequivocal cultural stance that focused the specific social and political interests of African-American people nationally. On the coattails of the early demise of the Black Arts Movement's unrestrained radicalism came Ed Bullins and Robert MacBeth to establish the New Lafayette Theatre around experimental works/rituals that advanced a penchant for neorealism in its explorations of the black experience.

Also pursuing a ritualistic theater uptown was Barbara Ann Teer with her National Black Theatre. While both theaters were located in the heart of the black community, the National Black Theatre has sustained itself institutionally into the present because it had tapped into black church and African praise rituals for its aesthetic process. On the other hand, the New Lafayette was unable to secure the support of the community which often viewed its exercises as being creatively insular, if not otherwise, too esoteric, thereby leading the institution to a short life.

In the meantime, another theater endeavor was taking root downtown. A workshop for black actors, conducted by Robert Hooks who had achieved recent celebrity for his performance in *Dutchman,* evolved into the performance company for Douglas Turner Ward's two providential one-act plays, *Day of Absence* and *Happy Ending,* both works produced by Hooks in 1965 at the St. Marks Playhouse in East Greenwich Village. On the heels of the production's instant success, Ward wrote a trenchant article in the *New York Times* which characterized the American theater as being "for whites only." Impressed with the forthright posture of the article, the Ford Foundation invited Ward into their offices to discuss the issues. Clearly, Ward's vituperation was a general reflection of the social unrest consuming the nation during the 1960s, but specifically revealed black frustration with having only limited access to the mainstream of American theater.

Still, the officials at the Ford Foundation became even more greatly impressed when they discovered in the meeting that Douglas Turner Ward knew exactly what he wanted to do to remedy the limited exposure of blacks in the American theater. He wanted to build a theater institution for African Americans patterned on the ensemble style of the Berliner Ensemble. In order to achieve the goals of ensemble playing, he wanted a professional training program to investigate a specific style of work. Most importantly, the company would concentrate on the development of new, challenging plays that reflected the diversity of the African-American experience. The company would be identified as *Negro,* an appellation that was losing popularity at the time but still globally recognized, in order to focus attention on the cultural source of its ensemble style. The purposeful clarity of Ward's agenda encouraged the Ford Foundation to invite him to submit a proposal for a grant to support the endeavor. A generous gift was granted, and in 1967, the Negro Ensemble Company initiated the beginning of its twenty-five years of nurturing many of the most celebrated black actors and award winning playwrights under its institutional umbrella.

Some might ask, why so much urgency to create a theater with a specific ethnic orientation? Blacks have a long history of entertaining whites for the sake of profit, or simply approval. Theater, like folk tales, is more than a vehicle for entertainment in the cultural life of African Americans. In addition to mirthful gratification, it is an opportunity for closer, illuminating insights into the collective experience for the dual values of education and celebration. When theater reflects the concerns of the group, any group, be it African, Asian, or Native American, its members are able to contextualize their identity in the larger American experience. The focus of African-American soldiers during World War II in Charles

Fuller's *A Soldier's Play* informed an entire nation about the military restrictions on black troops who were anxious to defend the nation. Such reinspection of history was also apparent in the film *Glory* that revalued the role of blacks during the Civil War. Further, the presence of the NEC became a symbol of career opportunities for young blacks studying theater as a serious discipline option at universities. When NEC appeared on the campus of Howard University in 1968 with personnel such as Ester Rolles, Rosalynn Cash, Clarice Taylor, and Denise Nicholas, the vast talent pool of the drama department which included Debbie Allen and Phylicia Allen-Ayers (Rashad), Buddy Butler and Clinton Turner Davis, and Pearl Cleage, among others, was consumed with a sense of optimism about their potential to secure a living in a profession that was considered traditionally exclusionionary.

Despite the many protestations from radical black arts groups, the Negro Ensemble Company resided downtown at the St. Marks Playhouse in East Greenwich Village, and produced works that not only allowed blacks a renewed sense of identity, but also provided an opportunity for the mainstream whites to become newly acquainted with a wide breath of characters and social orientations that make up the black experience. The creative intimacy of actors, writers, and directors at NEC made it possible for the codification of black character from within the culture, as opposed to becoming witnesses to illegitimate stereotypes created outside the culture. In the process of clarifying the black experience, a new affirmation was achieved. For example, the stock characterization of a Boot Black is a man popping a rag over a shiny pair of shoes. On stage, when searching beyond the skin surface, we discover that the invisible aspects of Boot Black's interior life that drives him as a man. Revealed are the social conditions, the frustrated dreams, the thwarted expectations, the daunted love, or like Johnny Williams, the hardworking postal worker in Joseph Walker's *The River Niger*, who struggles to claim his life in a poem. Such is the excitement of the theater, its ability to redress, even reinvent the expectations of limited awareness of an audience. So, as we reveal ourselves to ourselves, we are also revealing ourselves to the rest of the world, making it possible for many Anglo Americans to have their truly first encounter with African Americans without the support of their biases.

In addition to character fullness, NEC has fostered the development of plays by black authors that have opened the window onto a particularity of insight into the human experience. Institutionally, it had created the possibilities for authenticity of experience, and an authority of language that had formerly been exploited in the white theater institutions for its folksiness or ignored as inappropriate, if not otherwise incomprehensible, as a vehicle of communication for white audiences. Vernacular narratives allow for a density of metaphor and signification peculiar to the specific context of African-American experience. The rhythms of the narratives reflect the cultural nuances of African-American language. It had been, for example, the social conditioning of a white director who, on the occasion of directing a mostly black production of Jean Genet's *Deathwatch*, failed to appreciate the coded humor of the black cast. The director had cast a white actor to play Snowball, a role traditionally played by a black actor, thus opted to change the character's name to Blackball so as to gain a joke out of the obvious contradiction. It had been recommended, to no avail, that the name Snowball be retained because it would have an even more subtle visual humor in the form of African-American *signifyin'* codes.

While universal themes of love and hate, death and redemption are common to the literature of humanity, they are framed by the specific conditions of a person's experience. NEC also made it a point to represent the intradiversity of black experience by producing plays from the urban South, urban North, Caribbean, and Africa. Each of these experiences can claim their own uniqueness, yet they have the capacity to resonate as common or universal experience when validated through a dramaturgical process that seeks truth rather than convenient access through stereotypes.

Prior to the institutionalization of the NEC, few black writers were able to escape the humiliating circumstance of tailoring the black experience to accommodate the point of view of white audiences. Writers pursuing crossover appeal invariably had to sacrifice authenticy of voice, and were always at the mercy of the audience's appreciation of such manipulation. A considerable amount of gifted voices appeared in the 1940s from writers such as Loften Mitchell, Alice Childress, Ossie Davis, and William Branch, but their achievement was created in isolation without an ethnospecific sense of purpose, thus was not sustained as important cultural options for the African-American community. With the presence of NEC, black writers no longer had to work in a vacuum, submitting plays to theaters that responded gratuitously, joining special professional societies, or pursuing the right people to know. A play left at the St. Marks Playhouse office of the NEC was guaranteed a reading and possibly, if not mainstage, some form of production. NEC was the light at the end of the tunnel toward authenticity.

Though NEC initiated its life as an "actors'" theater, spending the first year of its existence working on a representative ensemble style that would inseminate its first collective creation, Peter Weiss's *The Song of the Lusitanian Bogey*, it soon became clear that the company was evolving into a "writers'" theater. Recognizing that African-American writing had always been viewed as an appendage to the American mainstream, NEC writers such as Charles Fuller and the poet Larry Neal frequently joined Ward in discussions about the cultivation of an independent African-American theater literature that, much like ethnocentricity of Russian, Japanese, or Irish literature, focused the social priorities and aesthetic sensibilities of African Americans. Included here would also be the development of new women writers that articulated the special interests of women in the black experience.

Under the guidance of Ward, an accomplished actor/director/writer, NEC avoided becoming a singleminded, bombastic, political theater. Instead, writers were encouraged to bring their own "voices" to the company, thereby making it possible for a wide diversity of social and aesthetic possibilities to be investigated. As is apparent in this classics edition of the NEC repertory, the stylistic range of the plays include realism, absurdism, and ritual. Each have their own peculiar voice and sense of dramatic scale to articulate issues common to African Americans. While ritual devices are scaled large in *The Great MacDaddy* and *Dream on Monkey Mountain*, the ritual scale of the checker game played by the two old friends in the realistic style of *Ceremonies in Old Dark Men* may seem diminuative, yet is no less important as a device for dramatic tension and illumination. The collective experience, thus, was defined by the particularity of a writer's voice. If the voice was weak, yet showed potential strength, Ward would function as dramaturge and offer the analysis and manipulation of text that would help the author find his voice. Responding to the vicissitudes of actor/director/writer, he relentlessly pursued clarity of scenes between characters. Ward was most satisfied when he discovered playwrights who were not simply writing autobiographically. His interest was the development of an African-American theater literature that was not arrested by the limited voice of private indulgence. Those writers that revealed the collective consciousness through their particularity of experience had a chance to become, by his estimation, "career writers" with works that could sustain the test of time in the future.

Institutionally, NEC has presented readings, short play series, and a mainstage season of new plays for more than twenty-five years, thereby exposing to the world at least 150 plays, many of which have become the nucleus of a formidable African-American theater literature. It is safe to say that NEC has laid the foundation for an African-American theater literature which includes the vital contributions of career writers from other institutions such as Ron Milner and Ntozoke Shange (Woodie King's New Federal Theatre), Ed Bullins and Richard Wesley (New Lafayette Theatre), and the self-sustained genius of Adrienne Kennedy and August Wilson.

In addition to recognizing the valuable work accomplished by the NEC, this edition of the classics of the NEC repertory is also a record of literary achivement which future generations can build upon and sustain with a renewed literature from new voices waiting to come on stage from all segments and experiences of the black community.